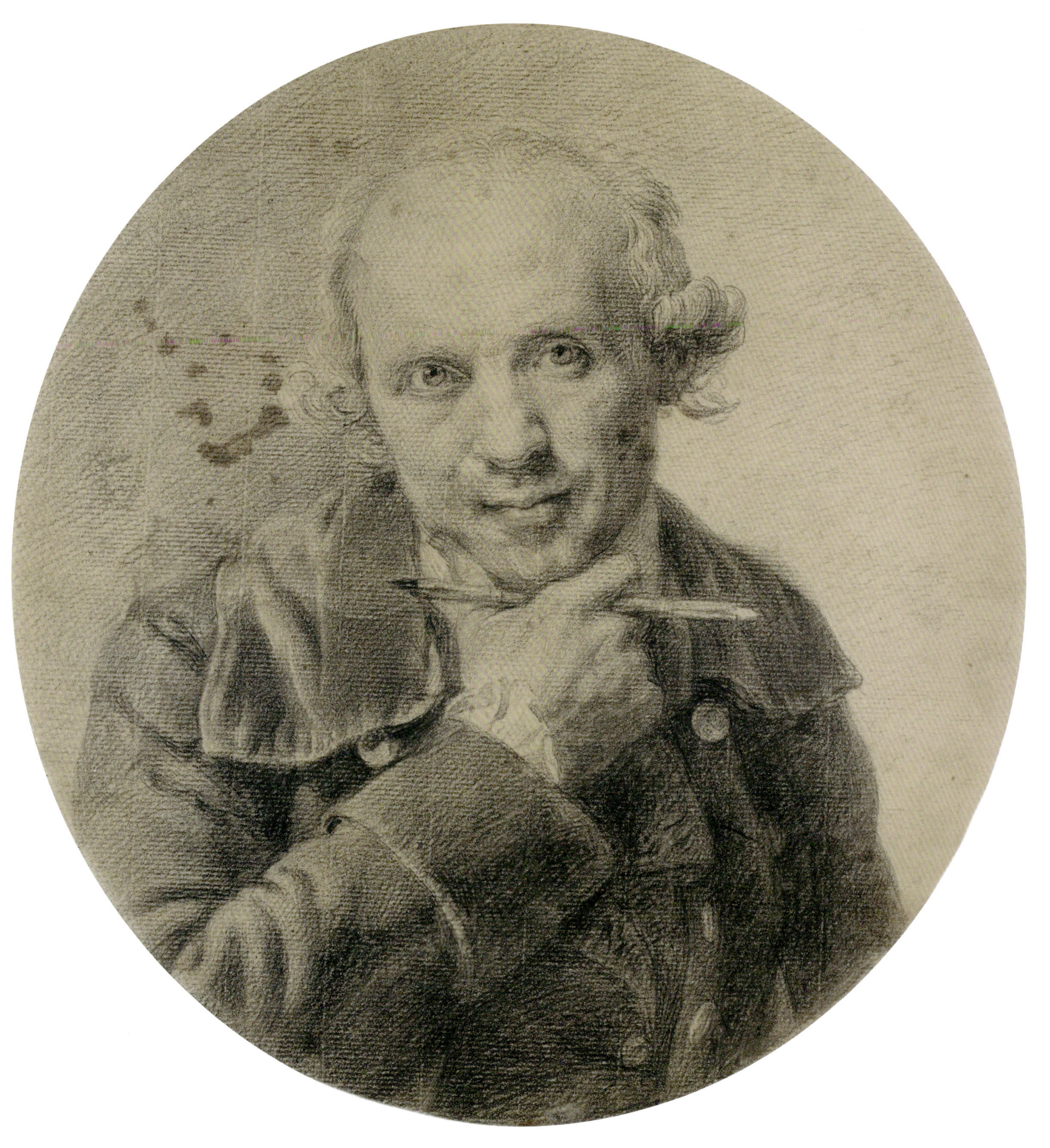

Johan Zoffany RA
Society Observed

Edited by Martin Postle

With contributions by
Clarissa Campbell Orr, Jessica David,
Gillian Forrester, Charles Greig, Maya Jasanoff,
Martin Postle, Kate Retford, Robin Simon
and MaryAnne Stevens

Yale Center for British Art, New Haven
Royal Academy of Arts, London
in association with
Yale University Press, New Haven and London

This publication accompanies the exhibition *Johan Zoffany RA: Society Observed*
Co-organized by the Yale Center for British Art, New Haven
and the Royal Academy of Arts, London
On view at the Yale Center for British Art from 27 October 2011 to 12 February 2012,
and at the Royal Academy of Arts from 10 March to 10 June 2012

Royal Academy of Arts 2009–2013 Season supported by 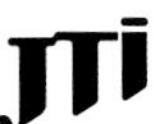

Library of Congress Cataloging-in-Publication Data

Zoffany, Johan, 1733-1810.
  Johan Zoffany RA : society observed / edited by Martin Postle ; with contributions by
Clarissa Campbell Orr ... (et al.).
     p. cm.
  Catalog accompanying an exhibition held at the Yale Center for British Art, New Haven,
Conn., Oct. 27-Feb. 12, 2012, and at the Royal Academy of Arts, London, Mar. 10-June 10,
2012.
  Includes bibliographical references and index.
  ISBN 978-0-300-17604-9 (alk. paper)
  1. Zoffany, Johan, 1733-1810--Exhibitions. 2. Zoffany, Johan, 1733-1810--Criticism and
interpretation. I. Postle, Martin. II. Orr, Clarissa Campbell. III. Yale Center for British Art. IV.
Royal Academy of Arts (Great Britain) V. Title.
  ND497.Z6A4 2011
  759.2--dc22
                    2011014513

A catalogue record for this book is available from the British Library.

Designed by Derek Birdsall RDI
Set in Monotype Bell by Shirley & Elsa Birdsall
Printed and bound in Italy by Conti Tipocolor SpA, Florence

Frontispiece:
*Self-Portrait c.*1775–6 (cat. 58)

Contents

Foreword

Of all the major artists working in eighteenth-century England, none explored with more imagination and wit the complexities of Georgian society and British imperial rule than Johan Zoffany. His body of work offers a unique perspective on key British institutions, including the art academy, the court, the theatre, the aristocratic and bourgeois family, and the British Empire. Yet although he achieved considerable success in England, Zoffany remained in many ways an outsider. In spite of his accomplishments he resisted complete integration into his adopted country, travelling for extended periods in Italy and India, and visiting Austria and his native Germany. Given the variety and virtuosity of his work, it is astonishing that there has not been a monographic exhibition devoted to Zoffany since 1977. The present collaboration between the Yale Center for British Art and the Royal Academy of Arts is therefore especially significant, not least because it celebrates the achievements of one of the earliest members of the latter institution.

New research undertaken by the curators, conservators, and contributors to the catalogue will bring new depth to our understanding of Zoffany and his career, and open areas for further scholarship and investigation, which his art richly deserves. The exhibition and accompanying publication build upon the research of previous scholars, including, notably, Ronald Paulson, William Pressly and Penelope Treadwell. A particularly important debt is owed to the painstaking studies undertaken over the past forty years by Mary Webster, who generously shared with the curators and catalogue authors her research and the manuscript of her monograph on Zoffany, which was published by Yale University Press earlier this year.

There are many individuals whom we would like to thank. We are especially grateful to Martin Postle, Assistant Director for Academic Activities at the Paul Mellon Centre for Studies in British Art, who curated the exhibition and edited the catalogue. We would like to express our gratitude to Gillian Forrester, the organizing curator at the Yale Center for British Art, where she is Curator of Prints and Drawings, and MaryAnne Stevens, organizing curator at the Royal Academy of Arts, where she is Director of Academic Affairs. For their roles in organizing the exhibition and its associated programs and events we also are grateful to the following members of staff and their respective teams, who are thanked more fully in the Acknowledgements: at the Yale Center for British Art, Timothy Goodhue, Registrar; and Eleanor Hughes, Associate Curator and Head of Exhibitions and Publications; and, at the Royal Academy of Arts, Clare Simpson, Exhibition Manager; Philippa Hemsley, Assistant Exhibition Manager; and Katia Pisvin, Curatorial Assistant. We owe a special debt of thanks to the staff of the Paul Mellon Centre for Studies in British Art, in particular Brian Allen, Ella Fleming and Maisoon Rehani.

We would like to thank Clarissa Campbell Orr, Jessica David, Charles Greig, Maya Jasanoff, Kate Retford and Robin Simon, along with Martin Postle, Gillian Forrester and MaryAnne Stevens, for their contributions to the publication in the form of essays and catalogue entries. Additionally, we would like to express our gratitude to David Moore Gwyn, Stephen Lloyd and John Stainton for their assistance in locating various works in private hands.

The Royal Academy of Arts wishes to acknowledge with gratitude the supporters of the London presentation: JTI, the 2009–2013 Season Supporter of exhibitions in the Sackler Wing of Galleries, and Cox & Kings.

Finally, we would like to express our immeasurable gratitude to the many private individuals and institutions who kindly have agreed to lend their works to London and New Haven. Most especially we thank Her Majesty Queen Elizabeth II, who has supported the exhibition through the loan of a number of major works from the Royal Collections Trust. We also are extremely grateful to the Government of India for graciously agreeing to the loans of two very important paintings from public collections in India, *Colonel Polier and his Friends* and *The Embassy of Hyder Beg Khan to Calcutta*. We would like in particular to thank Mr Jahwar Sircar, Secretary to the Government of India, Ministry of Culture; Mr Vijay Madan, Joint Secretary to the Government of India, Ministry of Culture; Professor Rajeev Lochan, Director, National Gallery of Modern Art, New Delhi; Professor C. Panda, Curator and Secretary, The Victoria Memorial Hall, Kolkata; and Mr Deepak Ashish Kaul, Director, Government of India, Ministry of Culture.

Amy Meyers
Director, Yale Center for British Art

Sir Nicholas Grimshaw CBE
President, Royal Academy of Arts

Acknowledgements

I would like to express my gratitude to all those individuals and institutions who have generously loaned works to the exhibition. I would also like to acknowledge the support I have received from staff at the Yale Center for British Art and the Royal Academy of Arts. In particular, I wish to thank Gillian Forrester, the organizing curator at the Yale Center and its Curator of Prints and Drawings, and MaryAnne Stevens, Director of Academic Affairs and organizing curator at the Royal Academy of Arts.

At the Yale Center for British Art, Amy Meyers, Director, has enthusiastically supported this project from the very beginning and has continued to provide exemplary leadership and guidance at every stage. I would also like to thank Eleanor Hughes, Associate Curator and Head of Exhibitions and Publications for her support and expertise in the planning and implementation of the exhibition and publication. Among staff at the Center I received invaluable curatorial consultation, support and logistical assistance from Cassandra Albinson, Associate Curator of Paintings and Sculpture; Abigail Armistead, Curatorial Assistant in the Department of Paintings and Sculpture; Mark Aronson, Chief Conservator of Paintings; Kaci Bayless, Communications Coordinator; Adrianna Bates, Curatorial Assistant, Department of Prints and Drawings; Diane Bowman, Senior Administrative Assistant; Craig Canfield, Publications Assistant; Jessica David, Postgraduate Associate in Paintings Conservation; Martina Droth, Head of Research and Curator of Sculpture; Amelia Ewan, Senior Administrative Assistant; Theresa Fairbanks-Harris, Chief Conservator, Works on Paper; Linda Friedlaender, Curator of Education; Tim Goodhue, Registrar; Imogen Hart, Assistant Curator, Department of Exhibitions and Publications; Richard F. Johnson, Installation Manager; Dong-Eun Kim, Associate Conservator, Works on Paper; Cyra Levenson, Associate Curator of Education; Amy McDonald, Senior

Manager of Communications and Marketing; Beth Miller, Associate Director for Advancement and External Affairs; John Monahan, Senior Curatorial Assistant, Department of Prints and Drawings; Corey Myers, Assistant Museum Registrar; Jane Nowosadko, Manager of Programs; Mary Regan-Yttre, Conservation Assistant; Julienne Richardson, Coordinator of Special Events and Advancement; Lyn Bell Rose, Senior Graphic Designer; David Thompson, Senior Curatorial Assistant, Department of Prints and Drawings; Angus Trumble, Senior Curator of Paintings and Sculpture; and Scott Wilcox, Chief Curator of Art Collections and Senior Curator of Prints and Drawings. I am also extremely grateful to Holly Shaffer, a PhD candidate in the History of Art at Yale University, who under the auspices of the Yale Center for British Art's Graduate Research Assistant program, and working under the mentorship of Gillian Forrester, has curated *Adapting the Eye: An Archive of British India, 1770-1830*, a complementary exhibition, selected primarily from the Center's collections, which will be on view at the Center in the autumn of 2011.

At the Royal Academy of Arts I wish to express my gratitude to Katia Pisvin, Curatorial Assistant (Exhibitions); Clare Simpson, Exhibitions Manager; Philippa Hemsley, Assistant Exhibitions Manager; Andrea Tarsia, Head of Exhibitions Management; Lorna Dryden, Summer Exhibition Manager; Nick Savage, Head of Collections and Library; Mark Pomeroy, Archivist; Helen Valentine, Curator (Paintings and Sculpture); Nick Tite, Head of Publishing Operations; and Peter Sawbridge, Managing Editor.

Throughout the preparation of the exhibition and publication I have received tremendous support from all my colleagues at the Paul Mellon Centre for Studies in British Art, and would like to thank in particular Brian Allen, Director of Studies, Ella Fleming, Emma Floyd, Maisoon Rehani and Mary Peskett Smith.

A number of scholars have made significant contributions to promoting a greater understanding of Zoffany's art and biography. First and foremost, I would like to thank Mary Webster, who has been generous in sharing her profound knowledge on the subject, as well as the research contained in her recently published monograph. I am also extremely grateful to Penelope Treadwell and William Pressly for their important contributions to the world of Zoffany scholarship, and for their support for the present project.

I am grateful for the intellectual and practical support, and information provided by Hugh Belsey, Philippe Bordes, Kate Brymer, Maureen Brymer, David Dashwood, Maldwin Drummond, Elizabeth Einberg, Deborah Gage, John Gayner, Richard Green, Craig Ashley Hanson, the Hon. Simon Howard, Douglas Hyland, Alex Kidson, Alastair Laing, Martine La Roche, Philip Littlejohn, Tom Lindsay, Helen McCormack, Amanda Paulley, Marcia Pointon, David Posnett, Lord Ronaldsay, Andrew Sanders, Rafael Valls, Jonathan Yarker and the Marquess of Zetland.

Major support in the form of assistance with collections and research materials has been provided by the staffs of institutions in the United Kingdom, the United States, Australia and India. I would like to express my gratitude in particular to Colin Harrison and Jevon Thistlewood at the Ashmolean Museum, University of Oxford; Jenny Bescoby, Antony Griffiths, Kim Sloan and Janice Reading at the Department of Prints and Drawings, British Museum; Marcus Risdell at the Garrick Club; Rupert Featherstone at the Hamilton Kerr Institute, University of Cambridge; Alexander Sturgis and Amina Wright at the Holburne Museum, Bath; Andrew Loukes

at Manchester Art Gallery; Larry Keith at the National Gallery, London; Oliver Fairclough at the National Museum of Wales; Mark Pomery and Helen Valentine at the Royal Academy of Arts; Sir Hugh Roberts and Desmond Shawe-Taylor at the Royal Collection; Emma Shepley at the Royal College of Physicians; Tabitha Barber, Tim Batchelor, Helen Brett and Rica Jones at Tate; Melanie Gardiner at Tullie House Museum and Art Gallery, Carlisle; Susan Bourne at the Towneley Hall Museum, Burnley; Clelia Alessandrini and Lucia Fornari Schianchi at the Galleria Nazionale, Parma; Martin Angerer at the Historisches Museum Stadt, Regensburg, Elisabeth Dühr at the Stadtmuseum Simeonstift, Trier; Eckart Köhne at the Rheinisches Landesmuseum, Trier; Mario Kramp at the Mittelrhein-Museum, Koblenz; Karl Schütz at the Kunsthistorischs Museum, Vienna; and Eric Zafran at the Wadsworth Athenaeum Museum of Art, Hartford, Connecticut.

For their help in identifying works and facilitating loans I would like to express my thanks to Toby Campbell, Deborah Gage, Emmeline Hallmark, Clementine Kerr, Stephen Lloyd, David Moore Gwyn, Guy Morrison, Francis Russell and John Stainton.

Special thanks are also due to the following, who, in addition to those acknowledged above, have assisted Gillian Forrester with the research and preparation of catalogue entries: Tim Barringer, Paul Mellon Professor, Department of the History of Art, Yale University; Zirwat Chowdhury, PhD candidate, Northwestern University; Edward Cooke, Charles F. Montgomery, Professor, Department of the History of Art, Yale University, Mr Elton d'Souza, Principal of La Martiniere College, Lucknow; Sylvia Waisbren Houghteling, PhD candidate, Department of the History of Art, Yale University;

Dipti Khera, PhD candidate, Department of History of Art, Columbia University; Lucy FitzGibbon; John McAleer, Curator of 18th-Century Imperial and Maritime History, National Maritime Museum, Greenwich; Morna O'Neill, Assistant Professor, Eighteenth- and Nineteenth-Century European Art, Wake Forest University; Ruby Palchoudhuri, Director of the Crafts Council of West Bengal; Katherine Prior; Kishwar Rizvi, Assistant Professor, Department of the History of Art, Yale University; Romita Ray Kapoor, Assistant Professor of Art History, Syracuse University; Tamara Sears, Assistant Professor, Department of the History of Art, Yale University; Holly Shaffer, Graduate Research Assistant and PhD candidate, Department of the History of Art, Yale University; Rebecca Szantyr, PhD candidate, Department of History of Art, Brown University; and Ian Warrell, Curator of Eighteenth- and Nineteenth-Century Collections, Tate Britain.

I owe a great debt of gratitude to the contributors to the publication which accompanies the exhibition for their scholarship, professional insights and collegiate support; Clarissa Campbell Orr, Jessica David, Gillian Forrester, Charles Greig, Maya Jasanoff, Kate Retford, Robin Simon and MaryAnne Stevens.

Derek Birdsall has designed a beautiful publication to accompany the exhibition. I am deeply grateful to him and to Elsa and Shirley Birdsall for their dedication and professionalism. I am also grateful to my copy-editor, Colin Grant, for his close attention to detail. Finally, I would like to thank Sally Salvesen and Catherine Bowe at Yale University Press for their editorial guidance and support in the production of this publication.

Martin Postle

Lenders

The Royal Collection, Her Majesty Queen Elizabeth II
Alice and Douglas Hyland
Amgueddfa Genedlaethol Cymru/National Museum of Wales
Ashmolean Museum, University of Oxford
The British Library, India Office Library & Records, London
The British Museum
Burnley Borough Council, Towneley Hall Art Gallery & Museums
Castle Howard Collection
The Dashwood Family
Trustees of the Firle Estate Settlement
Galleria Nazionale di Parma
The Garrick Club, London
Herbert Art Gallery & Museum, Coventry
The Holburne Museum, Bath
The J. Paul Getty Museum, Los Angeles
Kunsthistorisches Museum, Vienna
Manchester Art Gallery
Mittelrhein Museum, Koblenz
Musée des Beaux-Arts, Bordeaux
Museen der Stadt Regensburg
Museo Thyssen-Bornemisza, Madrid
National Gallery of Victoria, Melbourne
National Gallery, London
National Maritime Museum, Greenwich, London, Greenwich Hospital Collection
National Portrait Gallery, London
The National Portrait Gallery, London, and the Lloyd-Baker Trustees
Private collection
Rheinisches Landesmuseum, Trier
The Royal Academy of Arts, London
Royal College Physicians, London
Stadtmuseum Simeonstift Trier
Tate, London
Tullie House Museum & Art Gallery, Carlisle
Uffizi Gallery, Florence
Victoria Memorial Hall, Calcutta
Wadsworth Athenaeum Museum of Art, Hartford
White's Club, London
Yale Center for British Art, Hew Haven
The Zetland Collection

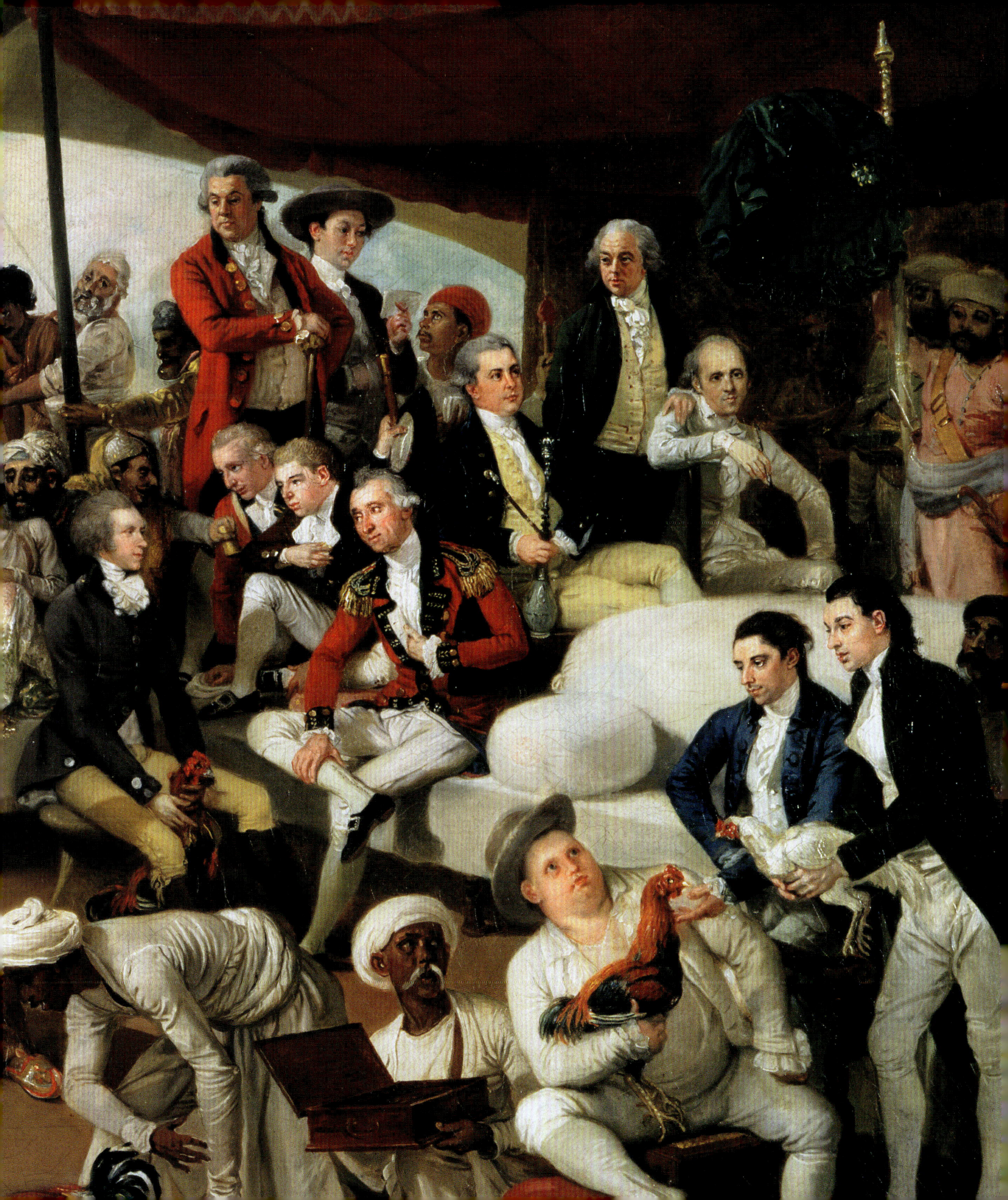

Martin Postle

Johan Zoffany: An Artist Abroad

Following an eight-month sea voyage from Calcutta, Johan Zoffany returned to London in the summer of 1789, enriched financially and culturally by his six years in India. Zoffany's arrival in England, the country that he had for thirty years called home, signalled an end to his travels. Aside from a brief visit to his native Germany in 1791, Zoffany did not venture again far beyond the capital or his riverside residence in Kew. However, he maintained a modest sense of adventure. In the summer of 1798 the sixty-five-year-old Zoffany went on an expedition to Norwood, south of London, in search of gypsies. He was accompanied by fellow artists Thomas Daniell and Daniell's nephew William, who, like Zoffany, had worked and travelled extensively in Bengal in the 1780s. In the forest at Norwood they questioned an old woman about the 'names of things', discovering forty words in the Romany language that were similar to those spoken by the natives of Bengal, twenty-six of which were precisely the same.[1] The gypsies of Norwood were an established tourist attraction, earning money through telling the fortunes of fashionable weekend visitors.[2] Zoffany made them the subject of at least one sketch.[3] He was also accused of taking a less than professional interest in 'a young Egyptian from Norwood, whom he believed to involve in her proportions the beauties of Pharaoh's daughter'.[4] Zoffany was notorious for his interest in beautiful young women, but his visit to Norwood with the Daniells had a more virtuous agenda. Their interest can be positioned within the context of the pioneering scientific investigations into the origin of the Romany language and race carried out during this period.[5]

This anecdote reminds us of Zoffany's own 'gypsy' wanderlust, as he pursued over forty years his various travels in Germany, Italy, England and India. It also highlights his intense powers of observation, and his enjoyment of colourful characters. For Zoffany facial expressions, mannerisms, personal eccentricities, social rituals and material possessions acted as important indices of behaviour and personal presentation. With painstaking detail, Zoffany portrayed ragged beggars, street vendors, artists and craftsmen, well-heeled connoisseurs, aristocrats cocooned in sumptuous interiors, exotic Indian princes, and British nabobs and courtiers draped in silks and satins.

Figure 1
Colonel Mordaunt's Cock Match
(cat. 86) detail

Paradoxically, Zoffany's penchant for detail has resulted in critics' neglect of the intellectual and satirical components of his art. His informative paintings are regarded as a rich visual resource for historical data. In the process, however, Zoffany himself has been reduced to a cipher, and the personal qualities and characteristics of the artist who formed such enticing images have often gone unheeded. In the assessment of Zoffany's achievement, his reputation, compared to other leading artists of the age – Joshua Reynolds, Thomas Gainsborough, William Hogarth, George Stubbs or Wright of Derby – has lagged far behind. There is also a biased perception of him as a 'foreign' artist, who was never fully integrated into the mainstream of the British School.

Zoffany died in 1810. He is interred with his wife, granddaughter and family nurse in the leafy churchyard of St Anne's, Kew (fig. 2), within a stone's throw of his Chiswick riverside residence, yards from the grave of the country's most 'English' artist, Gainsborough, and within spitting distance of Kew Palace, the country home of his greatest patron, King George III. In 1814 the Directors of the British Institution mounted a retrospective exhibition of three 'distinguished artists' of the burgeoning British School: Gainsborough, Hogarth and Richard Wilson. Zoffany was also included as an afterthought. The exhibition attracted considerable critical attention, and Zoffany's work was well received.[6] Even so, leading connoisseurs, including Sir Richard Payne Knight, had serious reservations and objected to Zoffany's inclusion on the grounds that he was not a 'British Painter'.[7] Despite the fact that Zoffany had been a member of the Royal Academy and had chosen England as his homeland, he was still an outsider, a transient German artist, and one who was also misidentified as an archetype of the 'wandering jew' trope. Zoffany did not feature in Allan Cunningham's *Lives of the Most Eminent British Painters* (published in 6 volumes from 1829 to 1833), the first popular biographical survey of the British School. Where Zoffany's name did crop up in dictionaries of British art, there was considerable misinformation about even the most basic facts.

In 1920 the first monograph devoted to Zoffany was published by Dr George Charles Williamson and Lady Victoria Manners. To emphasize Zoffany's British credentials, and his position in the academic mainstream, he was described in the book's title as 'John Zoffany, R.A'. And to set the record straight, Williamson noted how Zoffany's reputation had 'suffered woefully by reason of the many badly-drawn, badly composed and stiff little pictures which have frequently, without any reason, been assigned to him'.[8] However, this book muddied the waters, attributing to Zoffany a host of inferior works by other artists. Other obstacles to an understanding of Zoffany

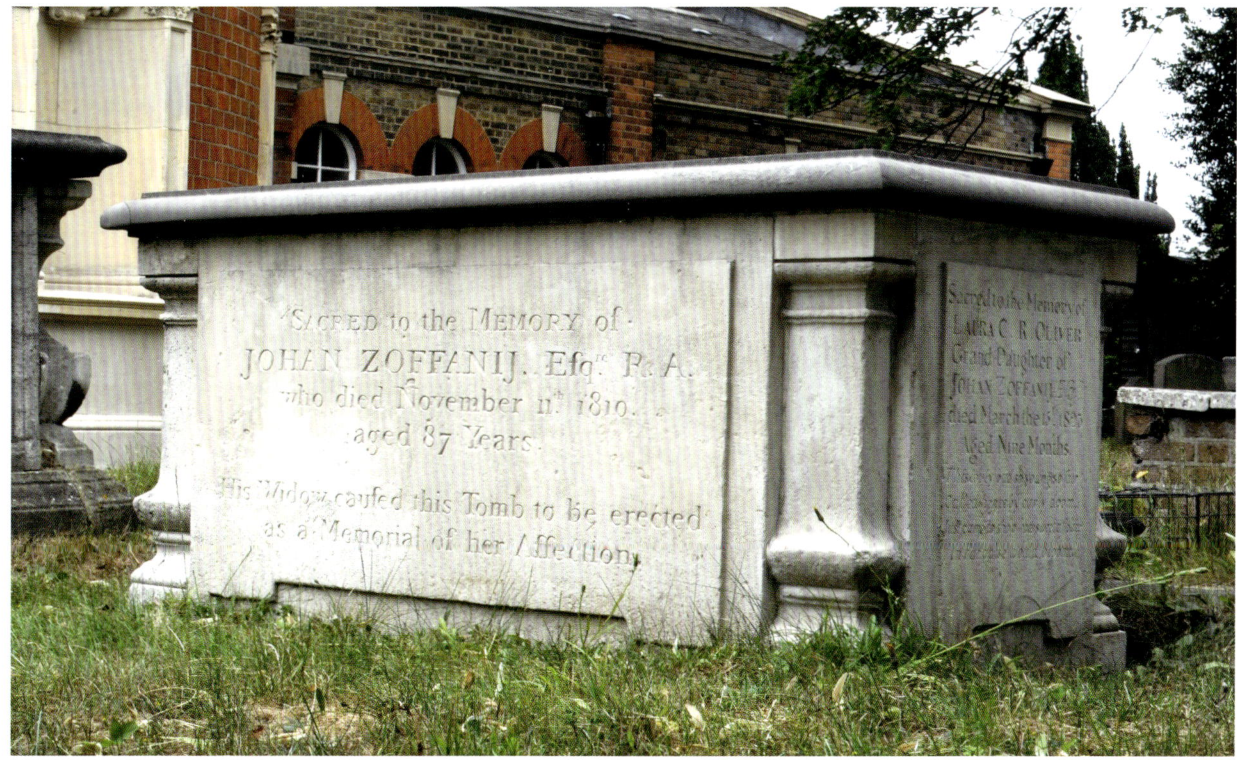

Figure 2
Zoffany's tombstone,
St Anne's Churchyard, Kew

were his lack of social cachet and the relative inaccessibility
of his works. The Royal Collection had an impressive number,
but there were few works in public collections. The National
Portrait Gallery purchased a supposed self-portrait (cat. 42) in
1875. Just over twenty years later, in 1896, the National Gallery
was given Zoffany's small oil sketch of Thomas Gainsborough
(fig. 3; subsequently transferred to the Tate Gallery) and
purchased the full-length portrait of Mrs Oswald (cat. 66) in
1938. Meanwhile, in 1929 the Tate Gallery received a portrait
of the clockmaker Stephen Rimbault (fig. 4). Appreciation of
Zoffany's art remained muted, a notable exception being
*Conversation Pieces: A Survey of English Domestic Portraits and
their Painters* by Sir Sacheverell Sitwell. Published in 1936,
the book devoted an entire chapter to Zoffany's contribution.

Yet, Sitwell conceded that he was 'a painter not of the first
order'. More disturbingly, Sitwell adopted the xenophobic
prejudices previously expressed by Payne Knight in asserting
that Zoffany was a foreigner and a Jew. The supposition was
central to Sitwell's interpretation of his art,[9] but he was
mistaken in this belief – an error that had been compounded
since the late eighteenth century.[10] To Sitwell Zoffany's
ethnicity was highly significant; ultimately, he concluded that
Zoffany was inferior to either Reynolds or Gainsborough,
who had 'a greater gift for painting and was an Englishman,
born and bred'.[11]

In 1953 Ellis Waterhouse identified Zoffany as an artist of
'real distinction'. Even so, his praise was qualified. According
to Waterhouse, Zoffany's art was already in decline by the

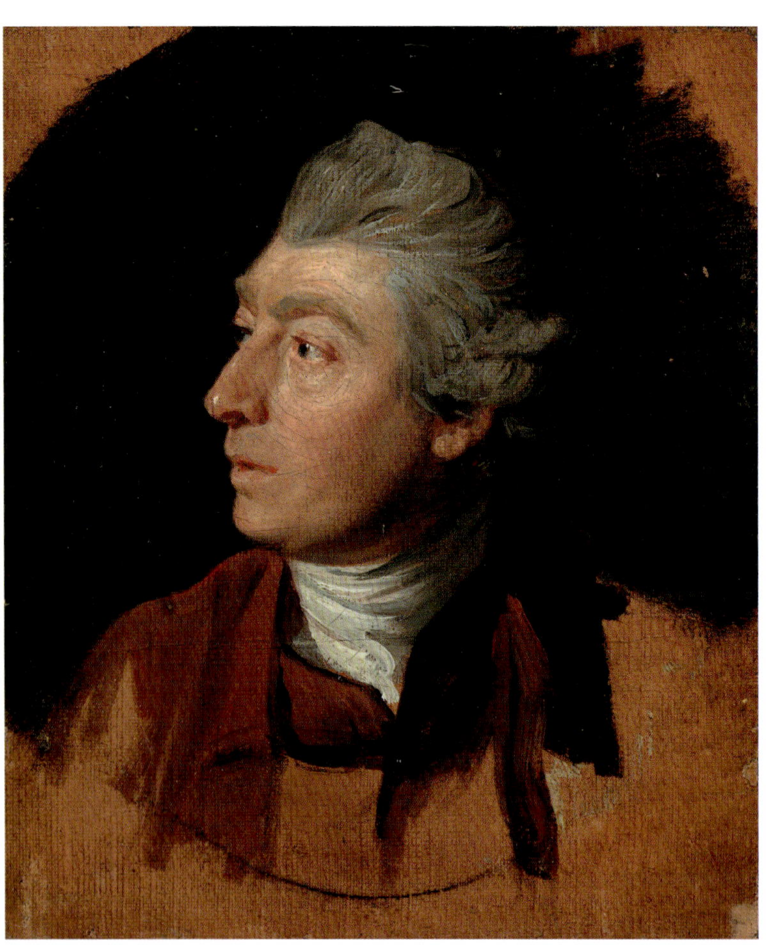

Figure 3 (cat. 45)
Thomas Gainsborough, 1771–2, oil on canvas, oval,
19.7 × 17.1 cm (7¾ × 6¾ in). Tate, London; presented
by the family of Richard J. Lane 1896

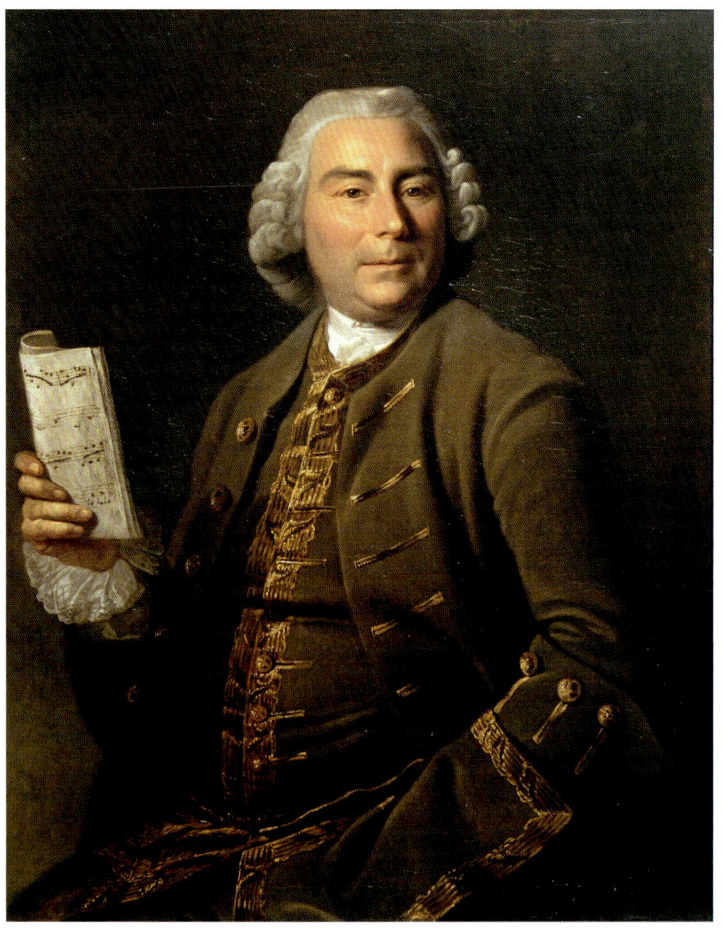

Figure 4
Stephen Rimbault, 1764, oil on canvas,
88.9 × 71.1 cm (35 × 28 in). Tate, London,
bequeathed by Mrs Aslett 1929

early 1770s, before he had painted arguably his greatest work, *The Tribuna of the Uffizi* (fig. 5). Zoffany, Waterhouse affirmed, was an 'intellectually lazy' artist. He admired the portrait of Queen Charlotte and her two eldest children (cat. 33) but cautioned that it was 'very far removed from anything which can be called "great art", in British painting before the age of Turner and Constable'.[12] In the 1760s Horace Walpole had compared Zoffany favourably to Hogarth, but for Waterhouse there was 'no real ground for comparison at all'. Yet, as Robin Simon demonstrates in this volume, similarities between Hogarth and Zoffany far outweigh differences.

Zoffany's art is often appreciated for its technical accomplishment and keen eye for detail. As with Hogarth, it is also distinguished by its incisive social commentary and irreverent brand of humour. It provides a sophisticated and often guileful commentary, which challenges the parameters of hierarchical structures, national boundaries and social mores. Zoffany, who was by turns amorous, irascible, capricious and extravagant, was, like Hogarth, temperamentally unsuited to follow the conventional career of the compliant 'society' painter. However, like Hogarth, Zoffany proved to be a consummate painter of society.

By the time he reached maturity, Zoffany had undergone a series of metamorphoses, in terms of his art, his cultural orientation and even his name. He was born in 1733 near Frankfurt. Baptized Johannes Josephus Zauffaly, he was the son of a Catholic cabinet maker, Anton Franz Zauffaly, who was then employed at the court of Prince Alexander Ferdinand von Thurn und Taxis. Zoffany spent his early years in the closeted environs of the court. During his teens he studied as a painter in Regensburg. Zoffany's first master, Martin Speer, had trained in Italy under the Baroque painter, Francesco Solimena, and it was natural that in 1750 Zoffany, at the age of seventeen, should have been encouraged to make his way to Rome. Zoffany chose to make his way on foot – a young pilgrim artist, sketching scenery as he journeyed along.[13] The years in Italy, which included visits to Naples and Venice as well as residence in Rome, transformed him into a cosmopolitan figure. In Rome life revolved initially around the studio of the influential painter Agostino Masucci, who, in addition to religious paintings in Rome's churches, received portrait commissions from British

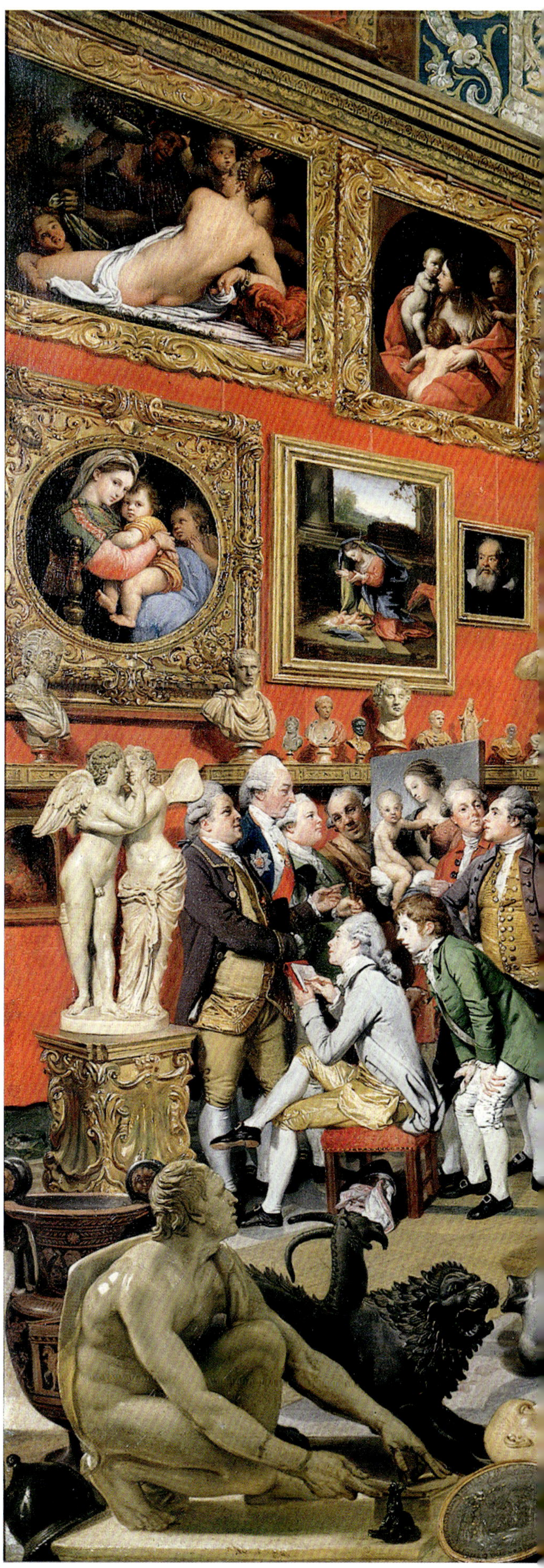

Figure 5 (cat. 53)
The Tribuna of the Uffizi, 1772–7, oil on canvas, 123.5 × 155 cm (48⅝ × 61 in). The Royal Collection, Her Majesty Queen Elizabeth II

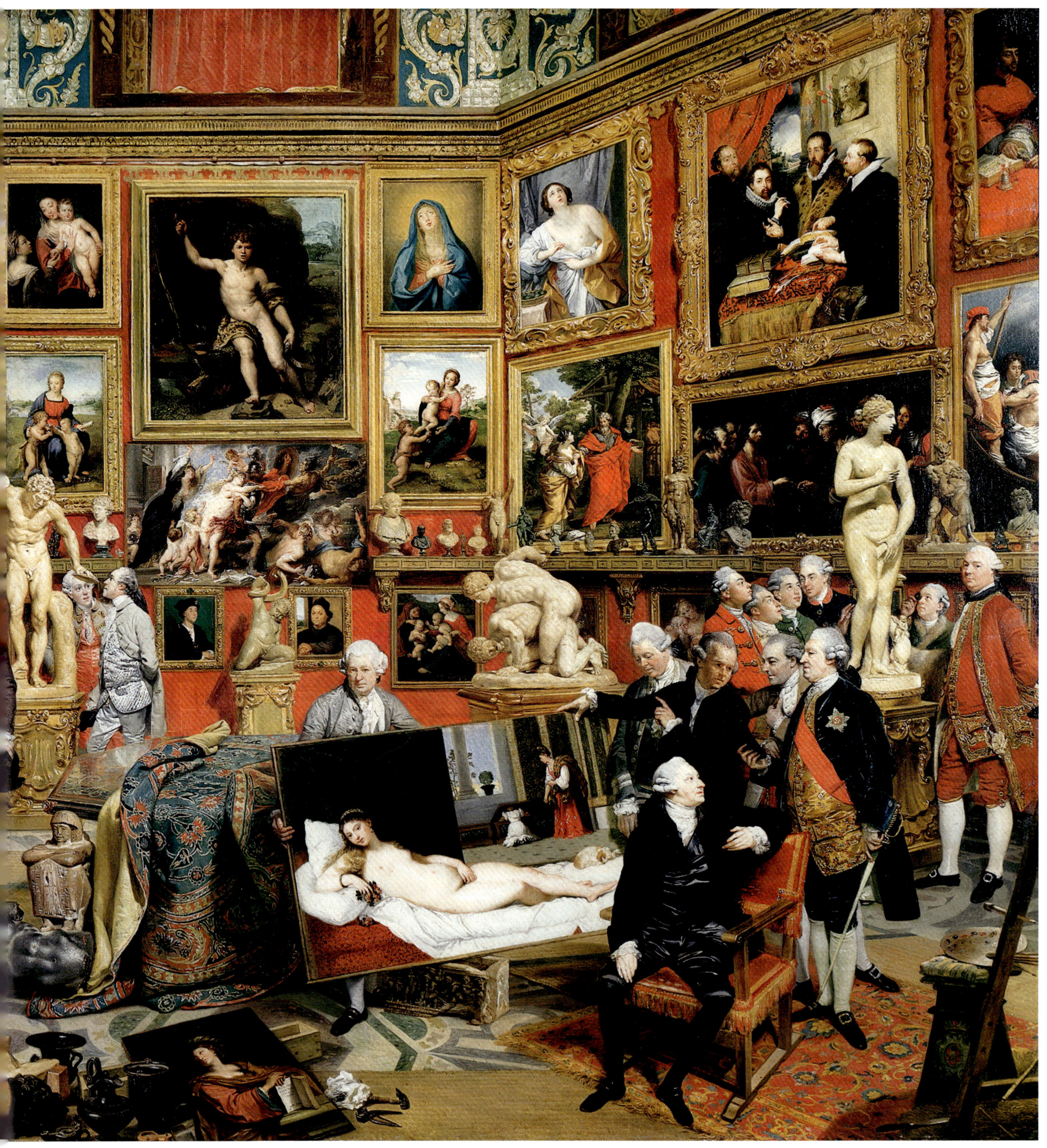

travellers and took on a number of pupils, including Pompeo Batoni, and the Scottish history painter Gavin Hamilton. Zoffany's Italian sojourn coincided with artists who were to be influential in shaping the canon of British art – Reynolds, Richard Wilson and the sculptor Joseph Wilton. There is no documented evidence that Zoffany associated with any of these artists in Rome, but his gregariousness and the compact size of the artistic community suggest that he must have rubbed shoulders with them. The importance of Rome as a nexus for contemporary artists from all over Europe meant that on his arrival in England he already had a visual lingua franca, even if he could not speak English.

In 1753 Zoffany travelled to Germany, at which time he probably painted the *Martyrdom of St Bartholomew* (fig. 6). Shortly afterwards he was back in Rome, where he began to study under his fellow German artist, Anton Raphael Mengs,
who was only five years Zoffany's senior. Zoffany had much more in common with Mengs, who had also grown up under his father's tutelage at the court of Frederick Augustus of Saxony. If Mengs was the model for Zoffany's *David with the Head of Goliath* (fig. 8), then their relationship may well have been particularly close. Mengs's establishment in Rome included a gallery of casts, where Zoffany in all probability made drawings (fig. 7). He would also have drawn from the living model at the Accademia di San Luca, where Mengs taught.[14] Zoffany was lanky, with a pockmarked face and a squint. He was also fiercely intelligent, confident, sociable and charming, especially to attractive young women. In Italy the artist we know as Zoffany began to spell his surname 'Zoffani'. Perhaps he chose Zoffani in order to avoid any potential confusion with the contemporary Roman bronze sculptor, Giacomo Zoffoli. Even so, on his return to Germany in 1757 he once again became 'Zauffalij' or 'Zauffaly'.

Figure 6 (cat. 2)
Martyrdom of St Bartholomew, 1753, oil on canvas,
104 × 81 cm (41 × 31⅞ in). Museen der Stadt Regensburg

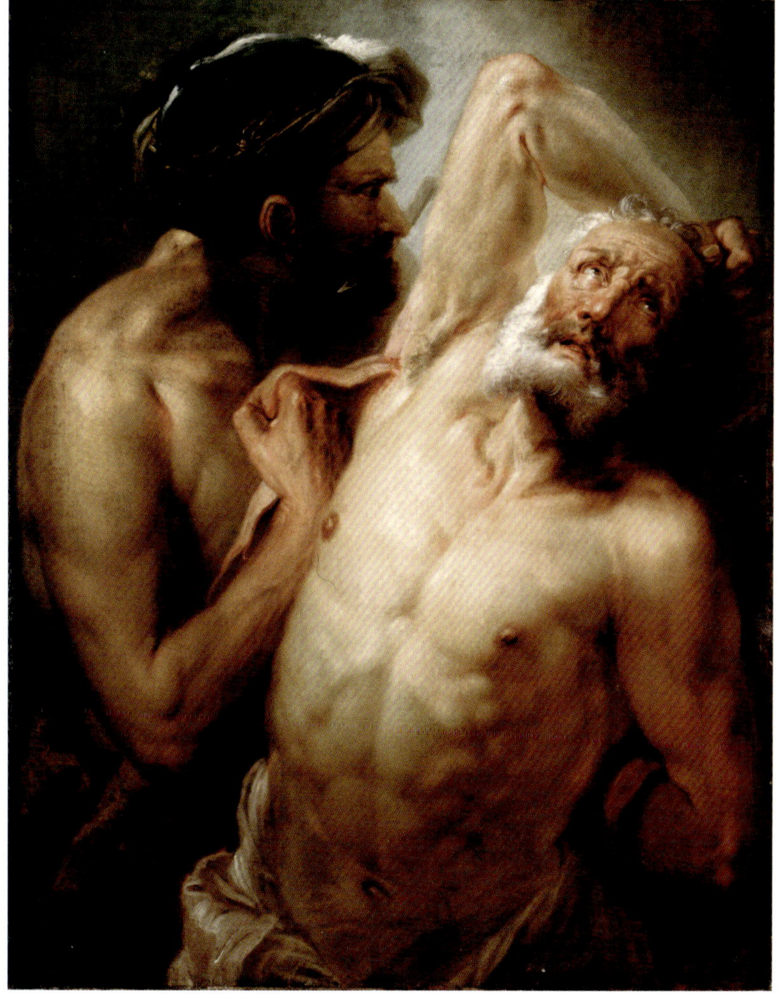

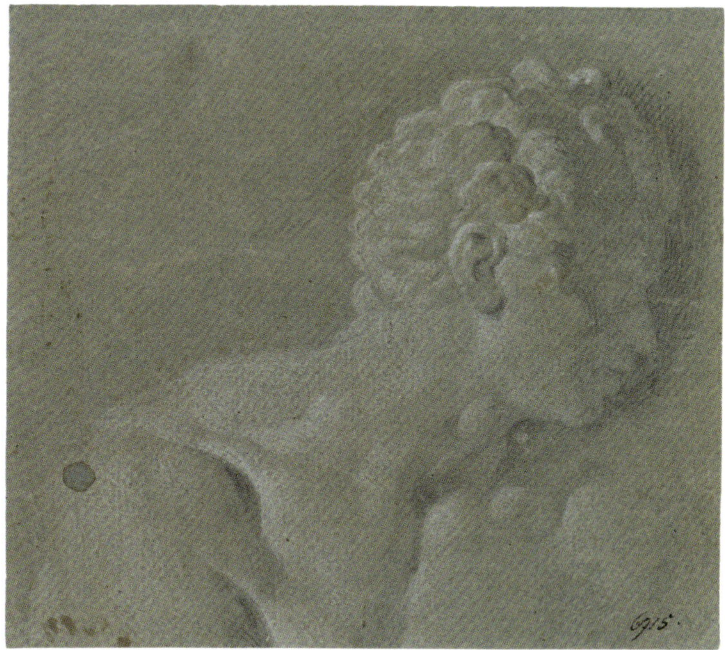

Figure 7
Study of a classical head, signed 'J. Zauffany', 1750's, 17 × 18.7 cm
(6⅝ × 7⅜ in), chalk on paper, Statliche Graphische Sammlung,
Munich Inv. -Nr. 13118 (alt: 6915)

Figure 8 (cat. 3)
David with the Head of Goliath, 1756, oil on canvas, 92.2 × 74.7 cm
(36¼ × 29⅜ in). National Gallery of Victoria, Melbourne; purchased
with assistance of the Isabella Mary Curnick Bequest and The Art
Foundation of Victoria, 1994 (ICI-1994)

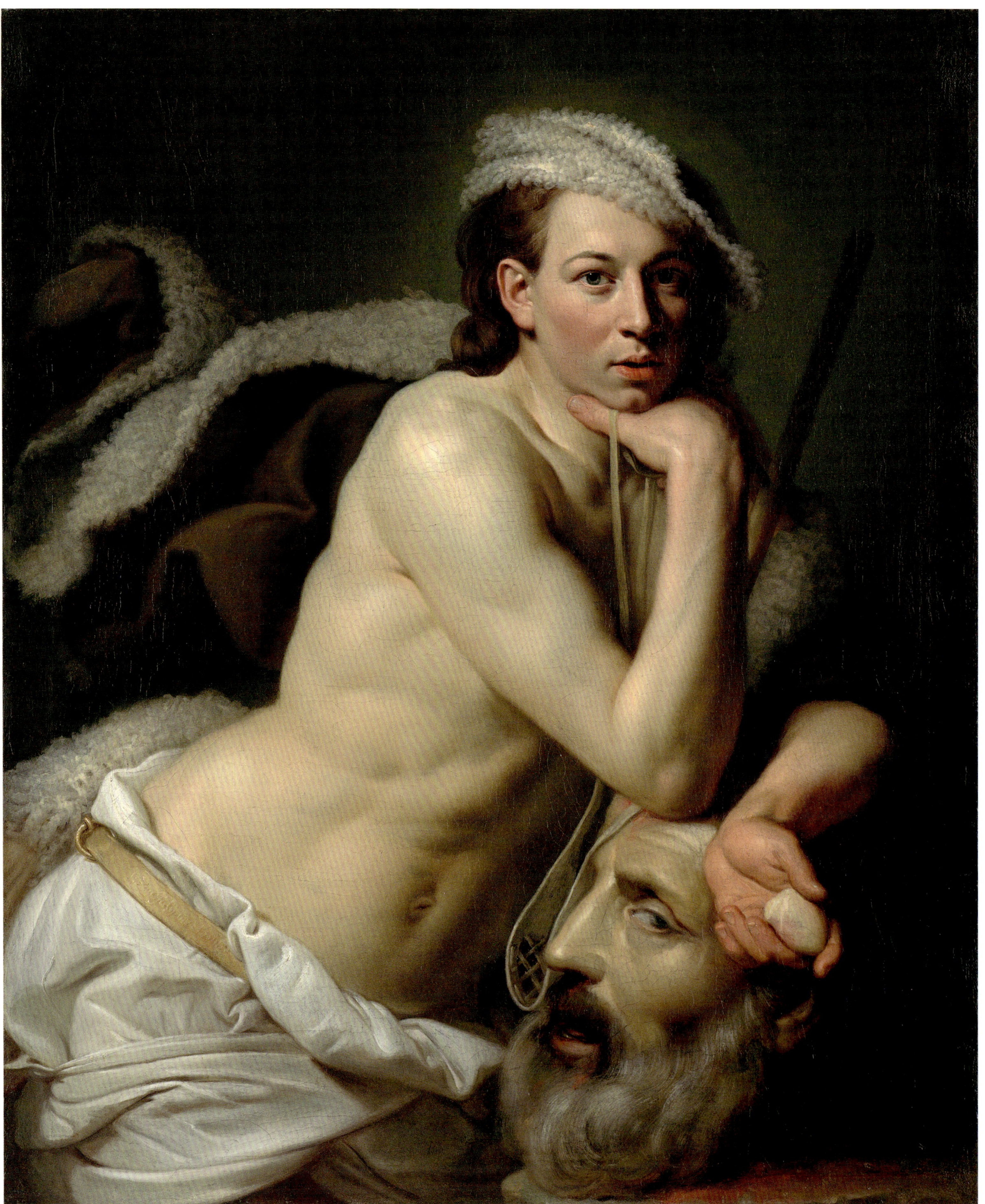

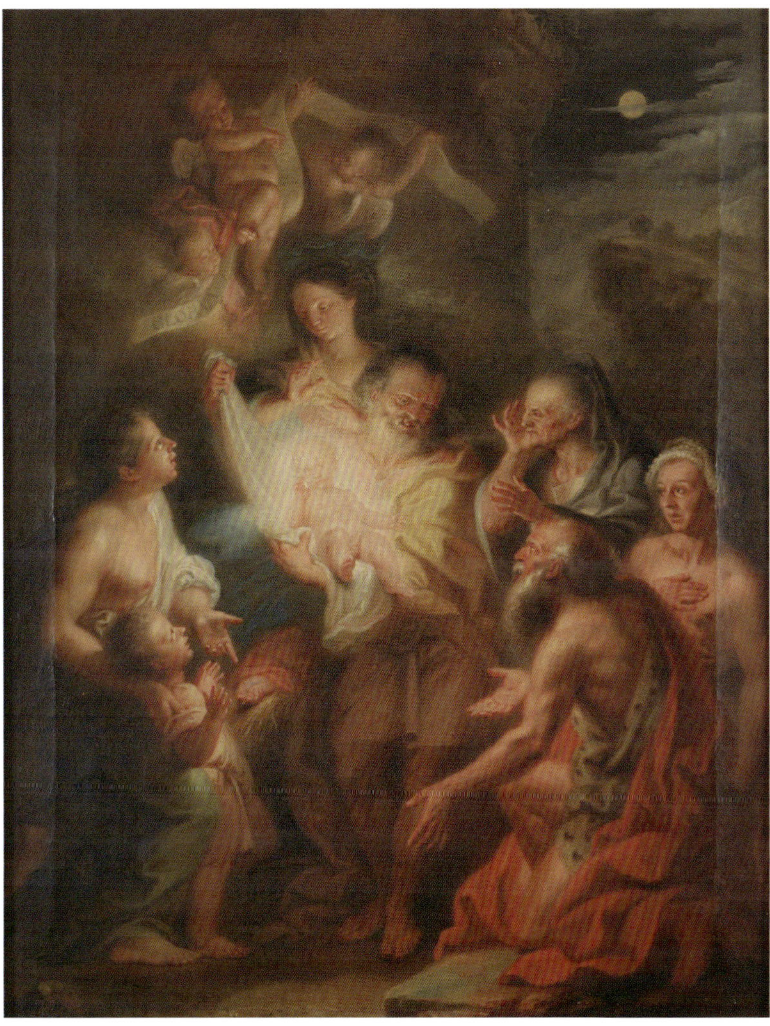

Figure 9
Adoration of the Shepherds, 1757, oil on canvas, 53 × 40 cm
(20⅞ × 15¾ in). Mainfränkisches Museum Würzburg, Germany

Figure 10 (cat. 8)
Susanna and the Elders, 1760, oil on canvas, 66.5 × 85.5 cm
(26⅛ × 33⅝ in). Rheinisches Landesmuseum, Trier

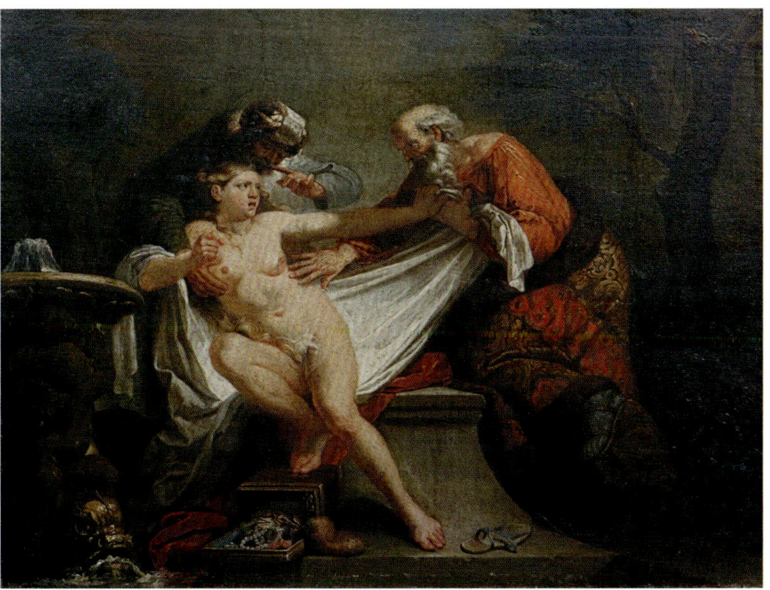

The homecoming was short-lived. Among the works Zoffany produced while in Regensburg was an *Adoration of the Shepherds* (fig. 9), influenced by Correggio's celebrated *La Notte* in the gallery at Dresden.[15] Shortly afterwards, Zoffany gained his first appointment as 'court and cabinet painter' to Johann Philipp, Graf von Walderdorff, the Prince-Archbishop and Elector of Trier. Included among the works he produced in Trier was probably *Susanna and the Elders* (fig. 10), which is dated to around 1760. Although he was kept busy, court culture in southern Germany must have presented a stultifying contrast to cosmopolitan Rome. In the summer of 1760, while apparently engaged on a series of murals at the palace in Trier, Zoffany resigned. He was replaced, or perhaps displaced, by the slightly older and more experienced painter Januarius Zick, who had himself just returned from Rome and the tutelage of Mengs.[16]

In the autumn of 1760 Johannes Zauffaly arrived in England, where he changed his name to Johan Zoffany (although it also appeared in print over the years as 'Zoffanij', 'Zoffani', 'Zaffani' and even 'Soffani').[17] Shortly afterwards he produced an allegorical painting, *Time Clipping the Wings of Love* (fig. 11), although he soon realized that there was little call for such work. Why, then, did Zoffany choose England rather than Italy, or France, which like his native Germany potentially offered far more scope for his abilities as a trained history and court painter? He would have been aware that it had welcomed artists from the Continent and that London, with its reputation for political and religious tolerance, offered opportunities for integration and assimilation. By the mid-eighteenth century London teemed with artists, engravers, book illustrators, sculptors, singers, dancers and musicians, who had trained or spent their early life abroad. Conversely, many of the indigenous individuals with whom Zoffany associated had spent time in Continental Europe. During his first period in London Zoffany became a confirmed Anglophile, attracted to and amused by English society.

Zoffany was accompanied to England by his German wife, Maria Juliana Antonetta Eiselein, whom he had married in haste less than a year earlier. The daughter of an innkeeper from Würzburg, Maria Juliana returned home shortly afterwards, although she continued to regard herself as his wife and to hound him for money. Zoffany was now to all intents and purposes a single man and set about forging a new artistic and personal identity. He was, nominally at least, a Roman Catholic, although completely secular in his outlook. Zoffany adapted quickly to his new life, thanks not merely to force of

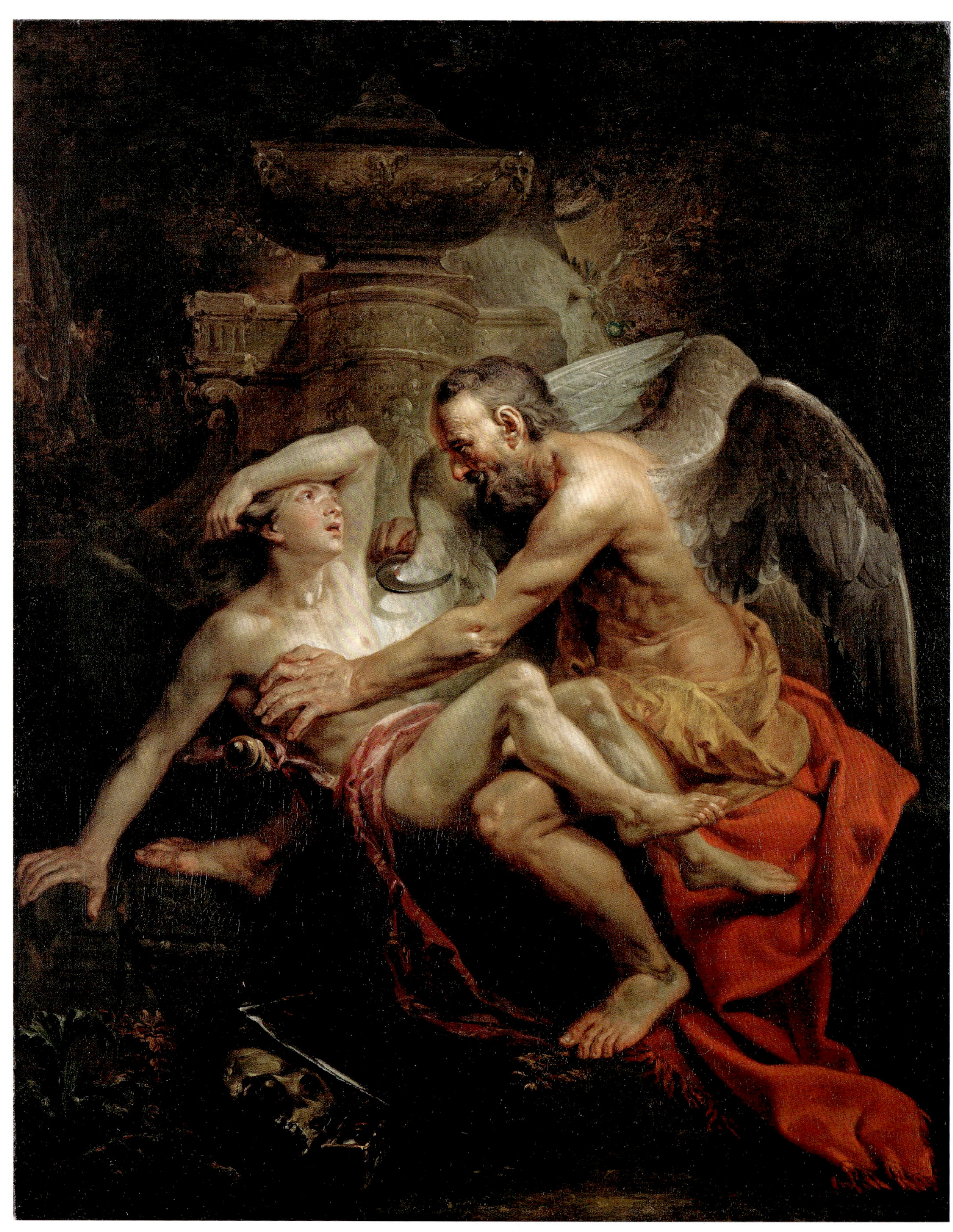

Figure 11 (cat. 9)
Time Clipping the Wings of Love, 1761, oil on canvas,
90.8 × 70.5 cm (35¾ × 27¾ in). Private collection

circumstance but to his willingness to embrace England as his home and its culture as his own. Zoffany spoke German and Italian. English, which he probably knew only slightly until the 1760s, remained his third language, and he evidently spoke it with a strong German accent.[18]

There was a thriving German community in London, and while he assimilated into his new environment, Zoffany remained conscious of his German identity. He continued to associate closely with German colleagues and patrons in the city and at court. One of his earliest London portraits was of the composer and music copyist, John Christopher Smith (fig. 12). Johann Christoph Schmidt, as he then was, had come to London as a child, his father then being employed by Handel as a copyist. At the time of Zoffany's portrait Smith was a respected figure in the capital's musical community, serving, on Handel's recommendation, as organist at the Foundling Hospital.

Figure 12
John Christopher Smith, 1761, oil on canvas,
88.9 × 67.9 cm (35 × 26¾ in). Gerald Coke Handel Collection,
Foundling Museum, London

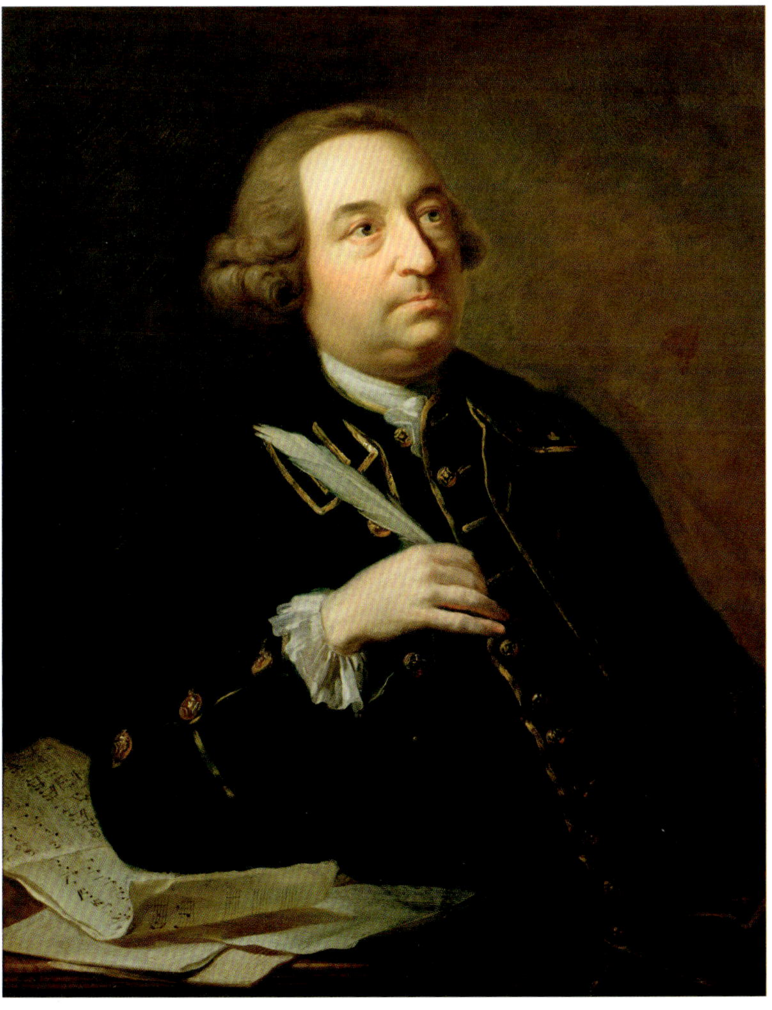

During the course of his London sojourn between April 1764 and July 1765 the German-born composer Leopold Mozart noted down the names of individuals he had met, including Zoffany and his neighbour in Lincoln's Inn, the cellist and composer Emanuel Siprutini. There is no evidence to suggest, however, that Zoffany painted portraits of Leopold Mozart or his gifted musical children, Wolfgang and Maria Anna ('Nannerl').[19] Aside from their racial ties, Mozart's note may have related as much to Zoffany's passion for music as to his art, since so many of Zoffany's friends in England had strong musical interests. Johann Christian Bach, who was also music master to the queen, was one of a number of Zoffany's German friends with court connections, and his own success in gaining the patronage of George III and Queen Charlotte by the mid-1760s was in no small part due to the common heritage and language he shared with a range of individuals. In later life Zoffany continued to maintain close ties with London's German community.

In 1793, having already been initiated into several Masonic Lodges, Zoffany was introduced by his friend Christoph Papendiek to the Pilgrim Lodge, London's only German-speaking Masonic Lodge, formed some years earlier by a group of German courtiers.[20] Papendiek, a member of the queen's chamber band, was married to Charlotte Albert, who was to become an intimate friend of Zoffany's second wife. Her memoirs provide an invaluable, if contentious, source of information about Zoffany's ménage in later life (see fig. 22).[21]

Zoffany's position may have allowed him greater social licence than his British peers. During the 1760s he undertook commissions for prominent aristocrats, including the Duke of Atholl, the Earl of Bute, and Lord Willoughby de Broke (see figs. 96, 100, 101, and cat. 72), but Zoffany's portrait career was not dependent on this aristocratic network. He attracted wealthy portrait clients, but often they represented 'new' as well as old money: members of the merchant class like the banker Andrew Drummond, the plantation owner Sir William Young, the army contractor Lawrence Dundas or the theatre impresario Thomas Rosoman (fig. 13). In contrast to Reynolds, Zoffany had limited artistic investment in Britain's armed forces or its political leaders – John Montagu, fourth Earl of Sandwich and First Lord of the Admiralty, being a notable exception. Sandwich was also an accomplished musician, devotee of the theatre, friend of Garrick and something of a hell-raiser.[22] Zoffany did, of course, paint members of the court, in Britain and Europe, and had a successful, if uneven, career as a court painter. But his friends and patrons included the scientist and

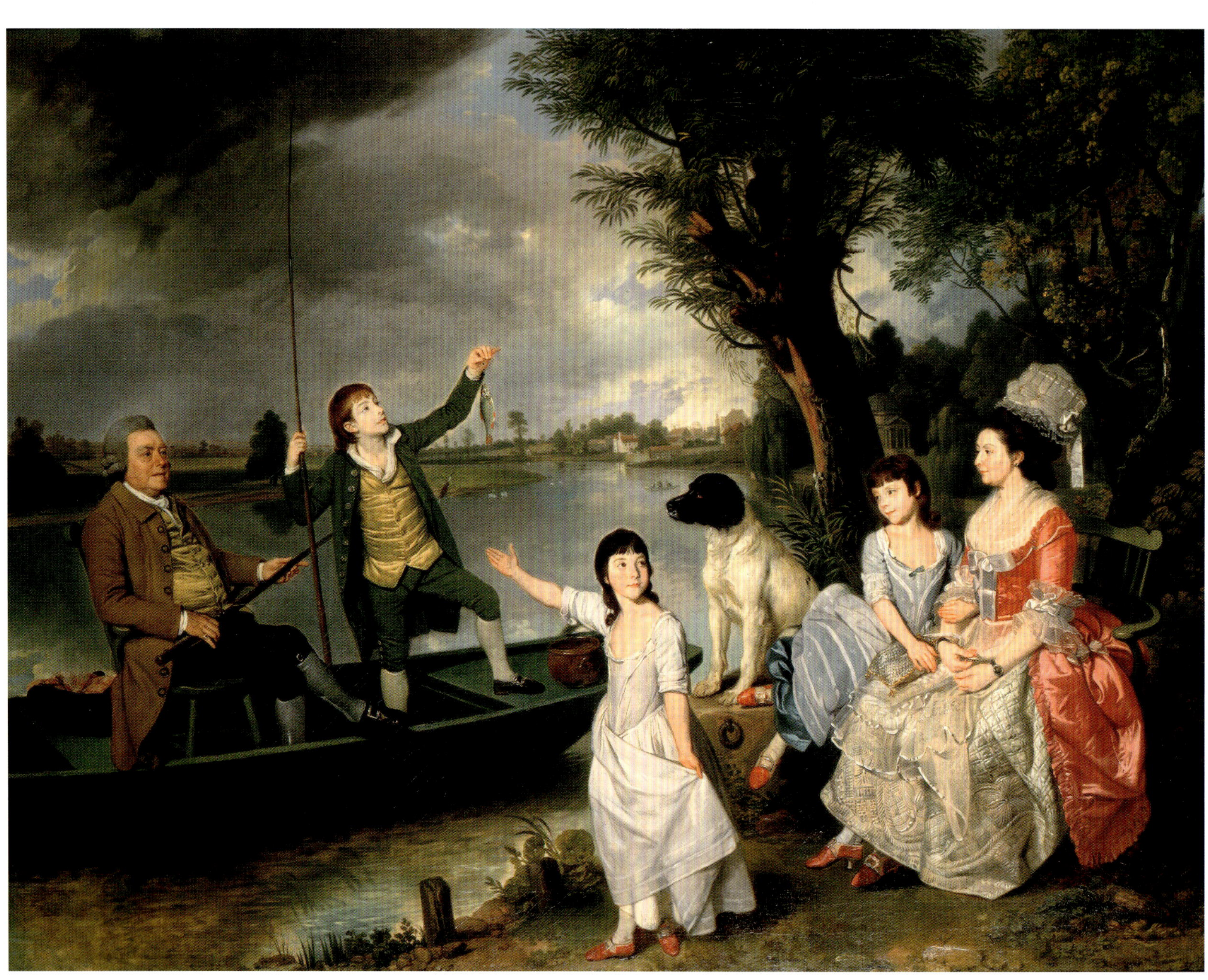

Figure 13
Thomas Rosoman and his Family, 1781,
oil on canvas, 101.6 × 127 cm (40 × 50 in).
Private collection

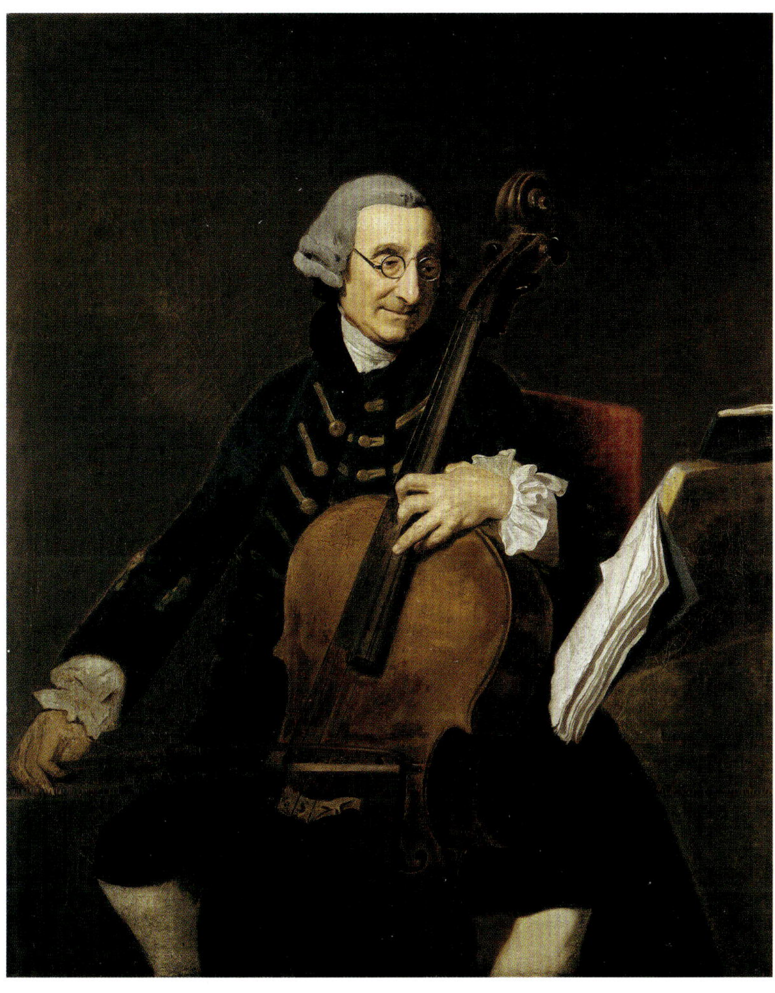

explorer Joseph Banks and the surgeons John Hunter and John Heaviside. Zoffany, who was evidently an accomplished instrumental performer, was deeply involved with the capital's musical community. As well as J.C. Bach, his friends included the cellist Giacobbe Cervetto (fig. 14), whose portrait Zoffany painted around 1770, and the celebrated oboe player Redmond Simpson, whose portrait he exhibited at the Royal Academy in 1782. Although that portrait is lost, Simpson may perhaps be the oboist in an accomplished, and hitherto unidentified, half-length portrait (fig. 15).

Among Zoffany's earliest patrons in London was the Huguenot clockmaker Stephen Rimbault, also an émigré, who employed him to paint vignettes on the faces of his musical clocks, and in 1764 Zoffany painted Rimbault's portrait. Rimbault recommended him to the portraitist Benjamin Wilson, for whom Zoffany worked in the early 1760s as a drapery painter. Although they had a stormy relationship, Wilson was the sort of multi-talented individual whom Zoffany admired instinctively, with interests far beyond professional portraiture. Wilson's experiments with electricity had gained him a fellowship of the Royal Society and the award of a gold medal in 1760. Wilson was also deeply involved in the stage, as a painter and theatre manager. And it was through him – albeit in acrimonious circumstances – that Zoffany met his most important theatrical patron, David Garrick.[23]

That Zoffany depended on London's cosmopolitan artistic community for support is attested by the actions of the French engraver Simon-François Ravenet (cat. 43), who rescued Zoffany from a brief lapse into dissipation and advised him to take up portraiture. From his studio in Covent Garden Zoffany enjoyed close relations with a number of artistic neighbours, including Richard Wilson and John Hamilton Mortimer. Zoffany must have been influenced by Richard Wilson, as he ventured into landscape painting through the riverscapes, gardens and parkland that feature prominently in his commissions for Garrick at Hampton and those including the Earl of Bute's estate, Luton Hoo.[24]

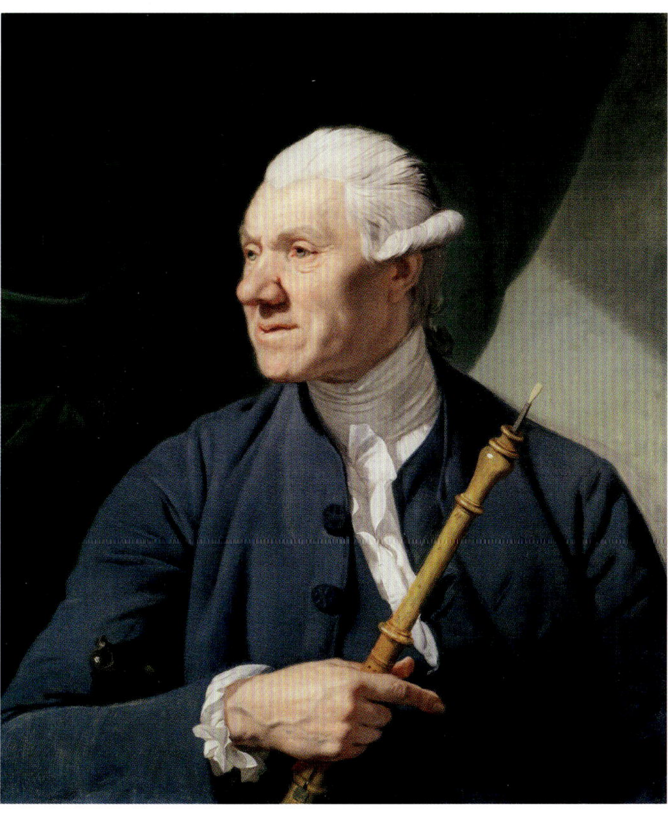

Figure 14
Giacobbe Cervetto, 1768–70, oil on canvas, 127 × 97.8 cm (50 × 38½ in). Private collection

Figure 15
The Oboe Player (? Redmond Simpson), *c.*1780–82, oil on canvas, 74.9 × 62.2 cm (29½ × 24½ in). Smith College of Art, Northampton, Massachusetts; gift of Mr and Mrs Allan D. Emil

Zoffany's two group portraits of his fellow artists, at the St Martin's Lane Academy in the early 1760s (fig. 16) and the Royal Academy in Old Somerset House (fig. 17), both emphasize the hermetic atmosphere of these homosocial institutions. Zoffany enjoyed cordial relations with his artistic peers, but he clearly had a temper and argued fiercely with a number of artists, including Mortimer, Francesco Zuccarelli and Allan Ramsay.[25] Reynolds, although he did not socialize a great deal with his fellow artists, was on good terms with Zoffany. He also appreciated Zoffany's art and in 1770 purchased his painting of Garrick with Burton and Palmer in *The Alchymist* (see cats. 21 and 22) for £100 at the annual exhibition, before agreeing to sell it to the Earl of Carlisle.[26]

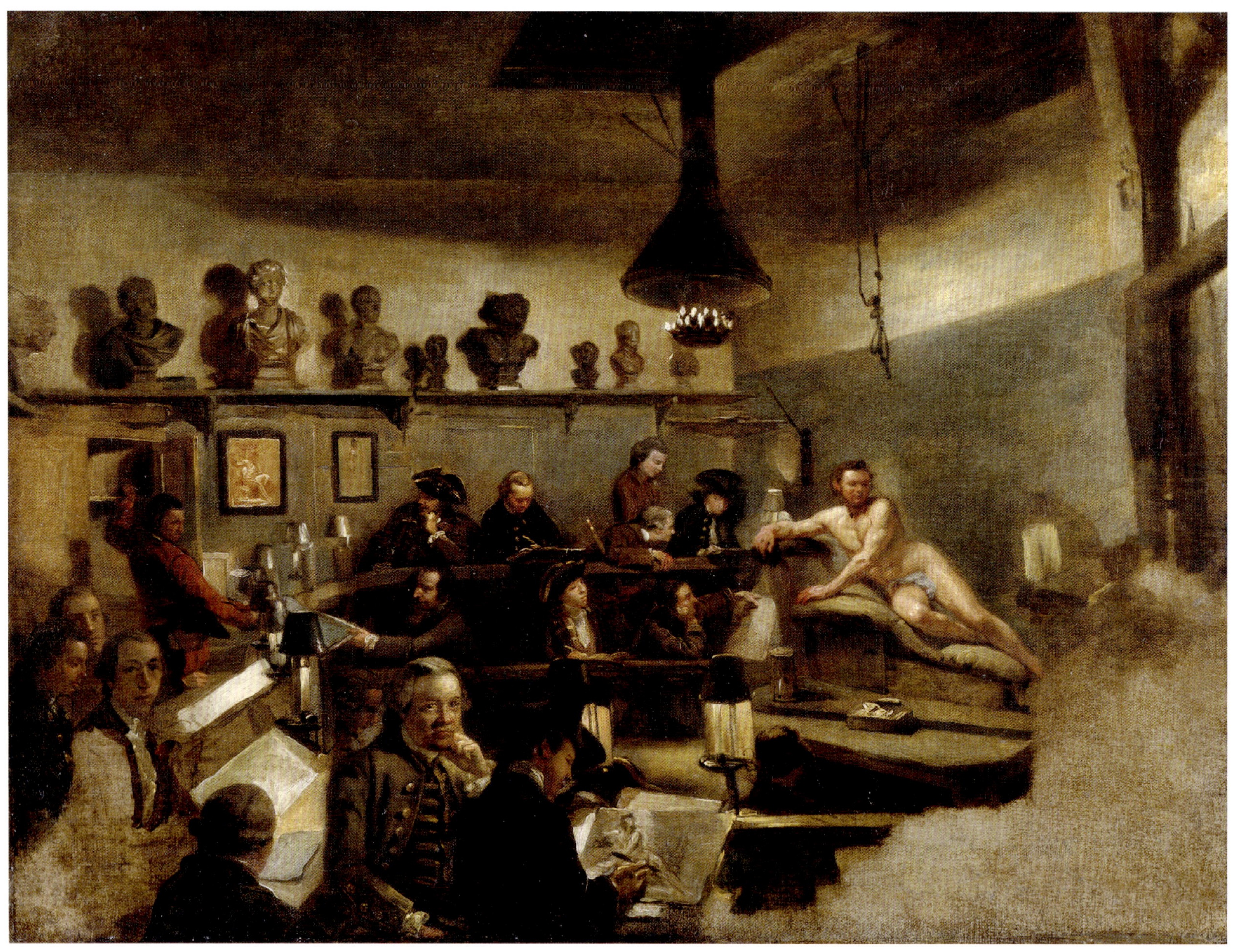

Figure 16 (cat. 41)
An Academy by Lamplight, A Life Class at St Martin's Lane Academy,
1761–2, oil on canvas, 50.5 × 66 cm (19⅞ × 26 in).
Royal Academy of Arts, London; given by William Smith, 1871

Figure 17 (cat. 44)
The Portraits of the Academicians
of the Royal Academy, 1771–2,
oil on canvas, 100.1 × 147.5 cm (39¾ × 58 in).
The Royal Collection,
Her Majesty Queen Elizabeth II

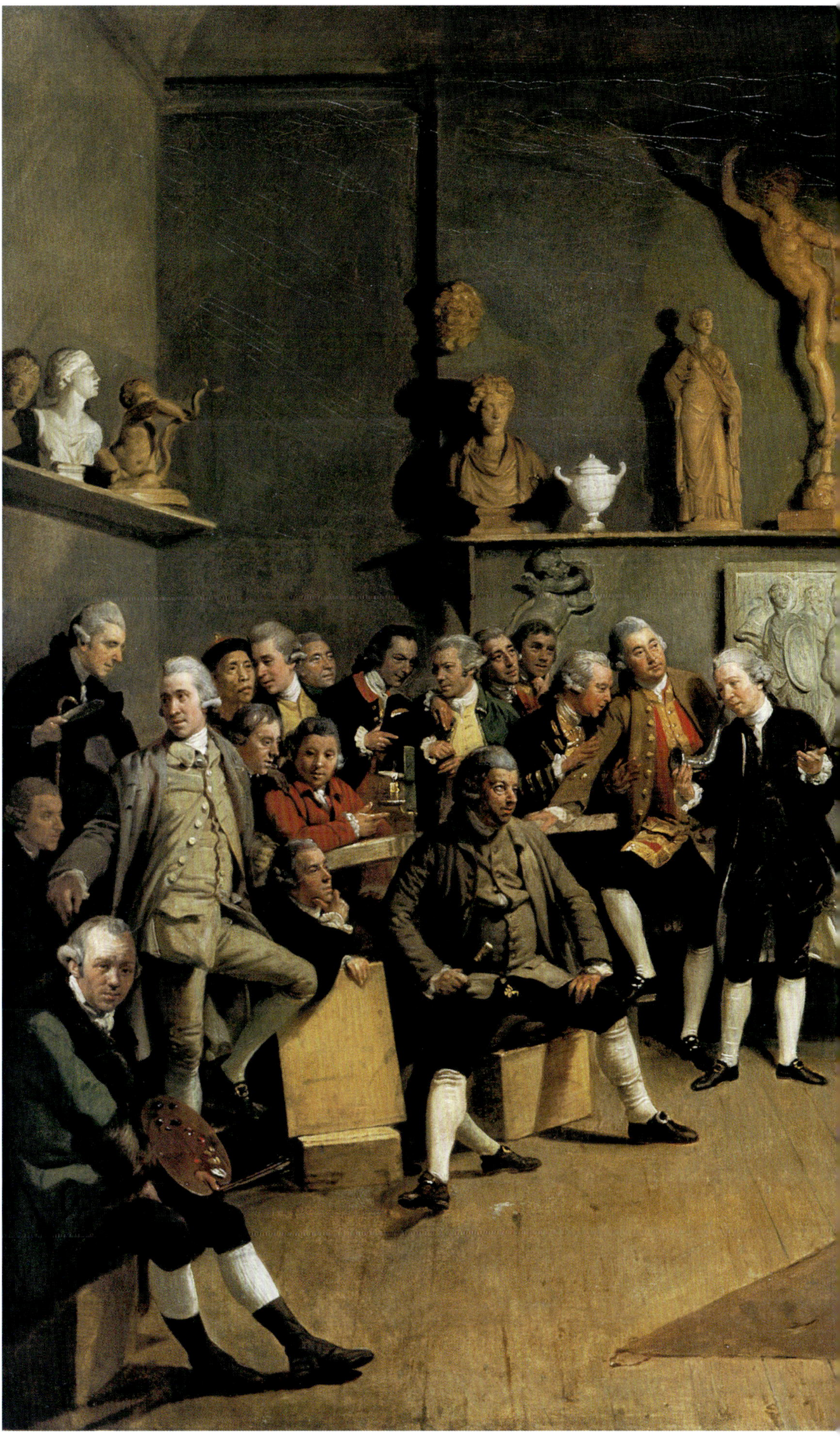

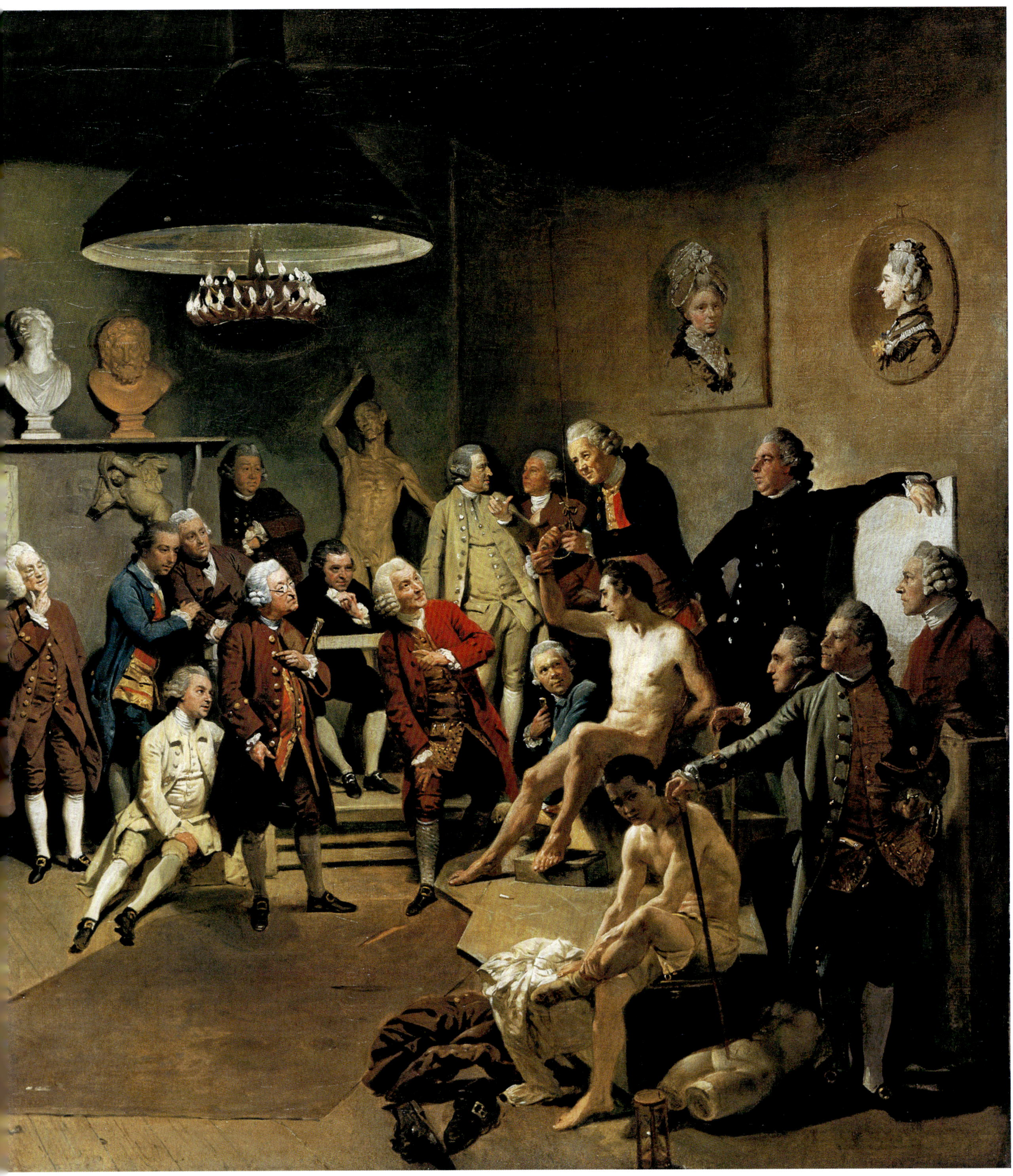

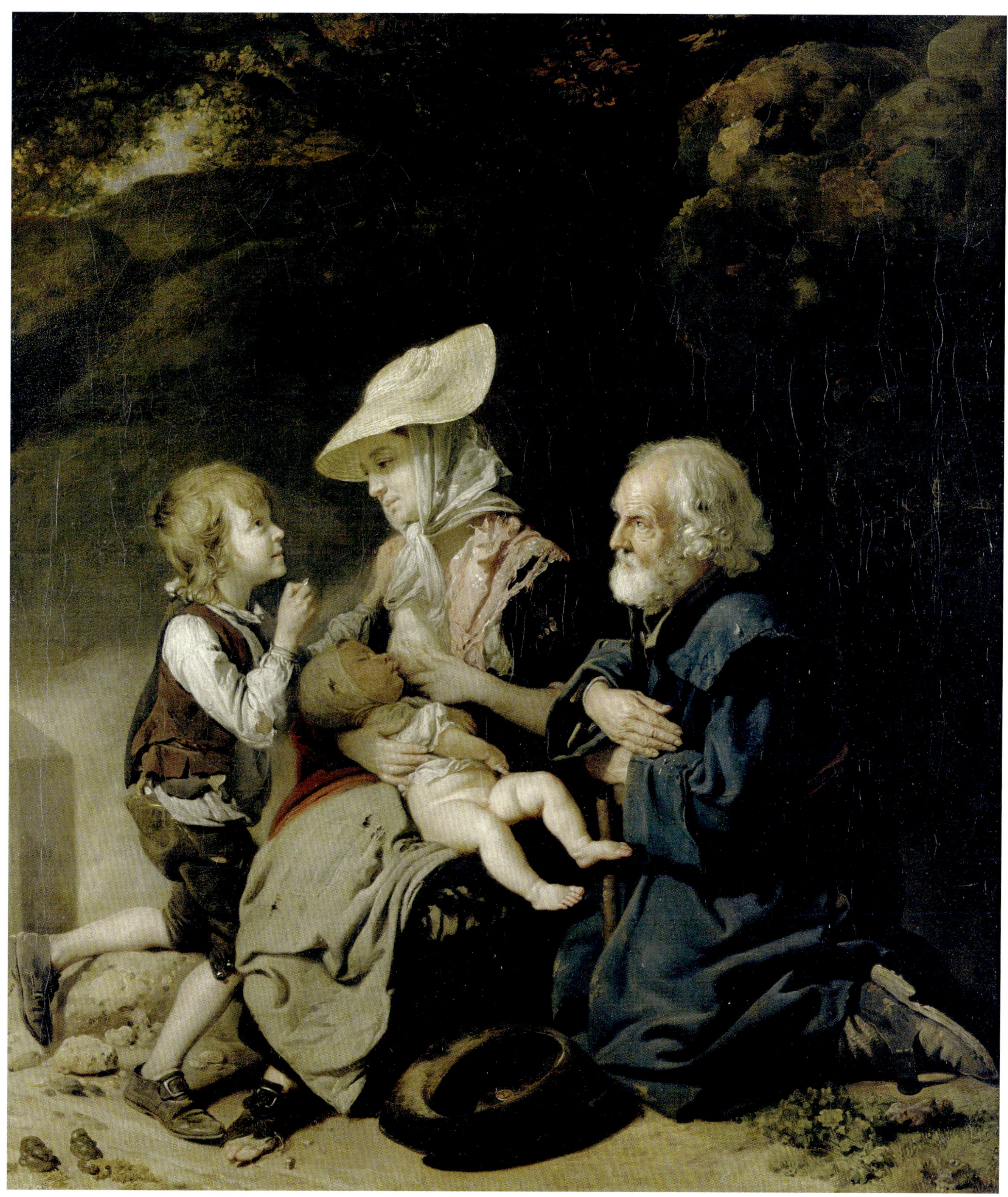

Figure 18 (cat. 50)
Beggars on the Road to Stanmore, *c.*1769–70, oil on canvas,
91.5 × 76 cm (36 × 29⅞ in). Private collection

Throughout the 1760s Zoffany was a regular exhibitor
at the Society of Artists, where Horace Walpole compared
his painting of Garrick in *The Farmer's Return* (see cat. 17)
favourably to Hogarth.[27] Zoffany also became involved in the
institutional affairs of the Society in October 1768, when he
was elected onto the committee of directors.[28] In 1769 he
exhibited no fewer than ten paintings, including *A Porter with a
Hare* (cat. 48), *Lord Willoughby de Broke and his Family* (cat. 72),
Hester Maria Thrale, 'Queeney' (cat. 68), and *The Bradshaw
Family* (fig. 19). Despite his evident strong affiliation to the
Society of Artists, Zoffany was compelled to resign when the
king personally recommended him as a member of the Royal
Academy. According to the Academician Joseph Farington:

> Those Artists who formed the Body of Academicians at the
> Institution of the Royal Academy were nominated by the King,
> but it was established that all future Vacancies should be filled
> by *Election*. To this, however, Mr Zoffany wd not submit;
> He would not place Himself at the option of the members of
> the Academy, therefore to obtain Him, it was proposed to the
> King to place him on a footing with the original members by
> nominating Him a Royal Academician.[29]

The Academicians must have been conscious of the quality of
his art and its public appeal. Since he would not submit to the
election process, nomination by the king was evidently a viable
alternative.

In 1771 Zoffany's exhibits at the Royal Academy included
an idiosyncratic half-length portrait of George III (see cat. 37),
and 'a beggar's family', better known today as *Beggars on the
Road to Stanmore* (fig. 18). Towards the end of that year he
was encouraged to join Joseph Banks on a second journey with
Captain James Cook to the South Seas. By the following March
Zoffany had contracted the terms of his employment with Banks
and was ready to depart. At this time he obtained patent letters
of 'denization'. This was a process, according to provisions set
out in the Act of 1708, 'for naturalizing of foreign Protestants',
passed in order to accommodate the influx of Huguenots into
the country. Zoffany was therefore effectively coming closer
to being regarded as a British subject. In January 1772 it was
reported in the press that

> Mr. Zoffani absolutely goes abroad with Mr. Banks, and
> is to have the profits of part of the work, and be paid in an
> extraordinary manner for what drawings he makes during
> the voyage. He set out for Bath last Wednesday morning to
> take his leave of some particular friends there, previous to
> his going on board.[30]

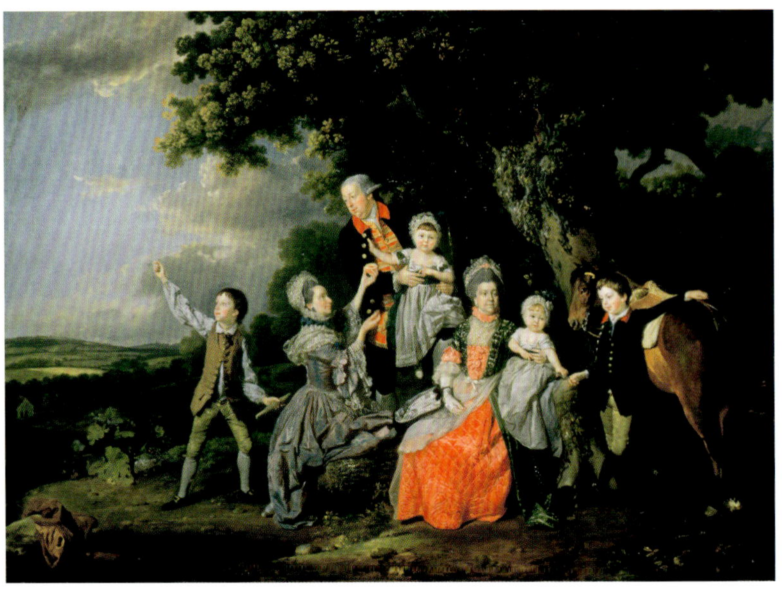

Figure 19
The Bradshaw Family, 1769, oil on canvas, 132.1 × 177.8 cm
(52 × 70 in). Tate, London; bequeathed by Ernest E. Cook
through the National Art Collections Fund, 1955

Figure 20 (cat. 48)
A Porter with a Hare, 1768–9, oil on canvas,
76.2 × 63 cm (30 × 24¾ in).
Herbert Art Gallery & Museum, Coventry

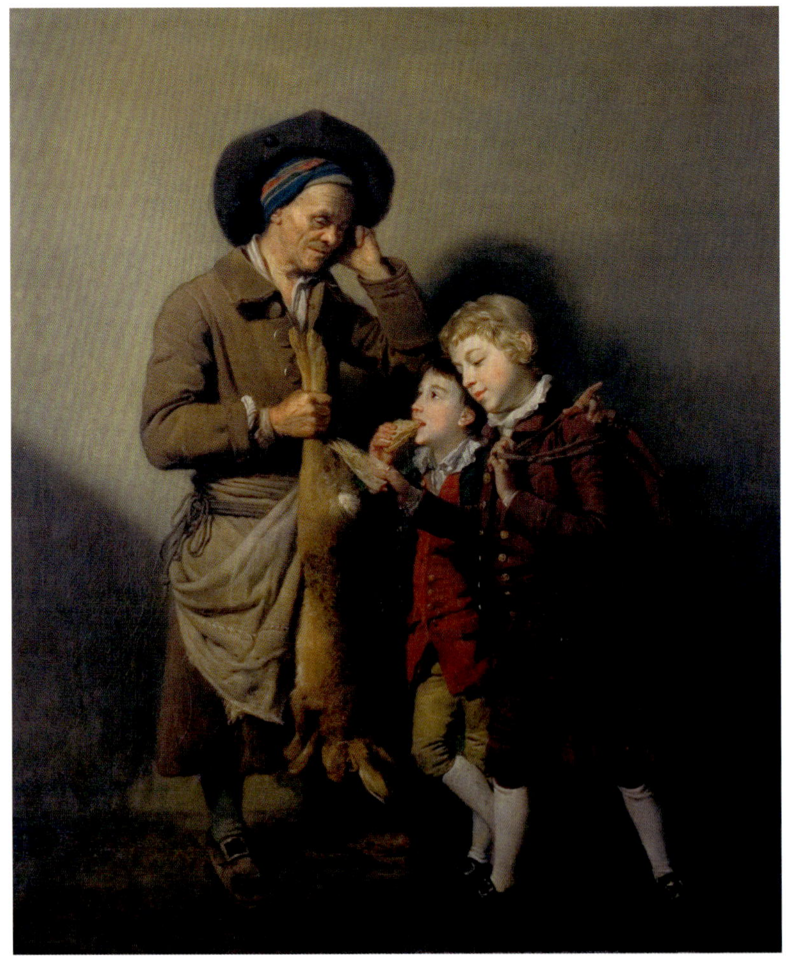

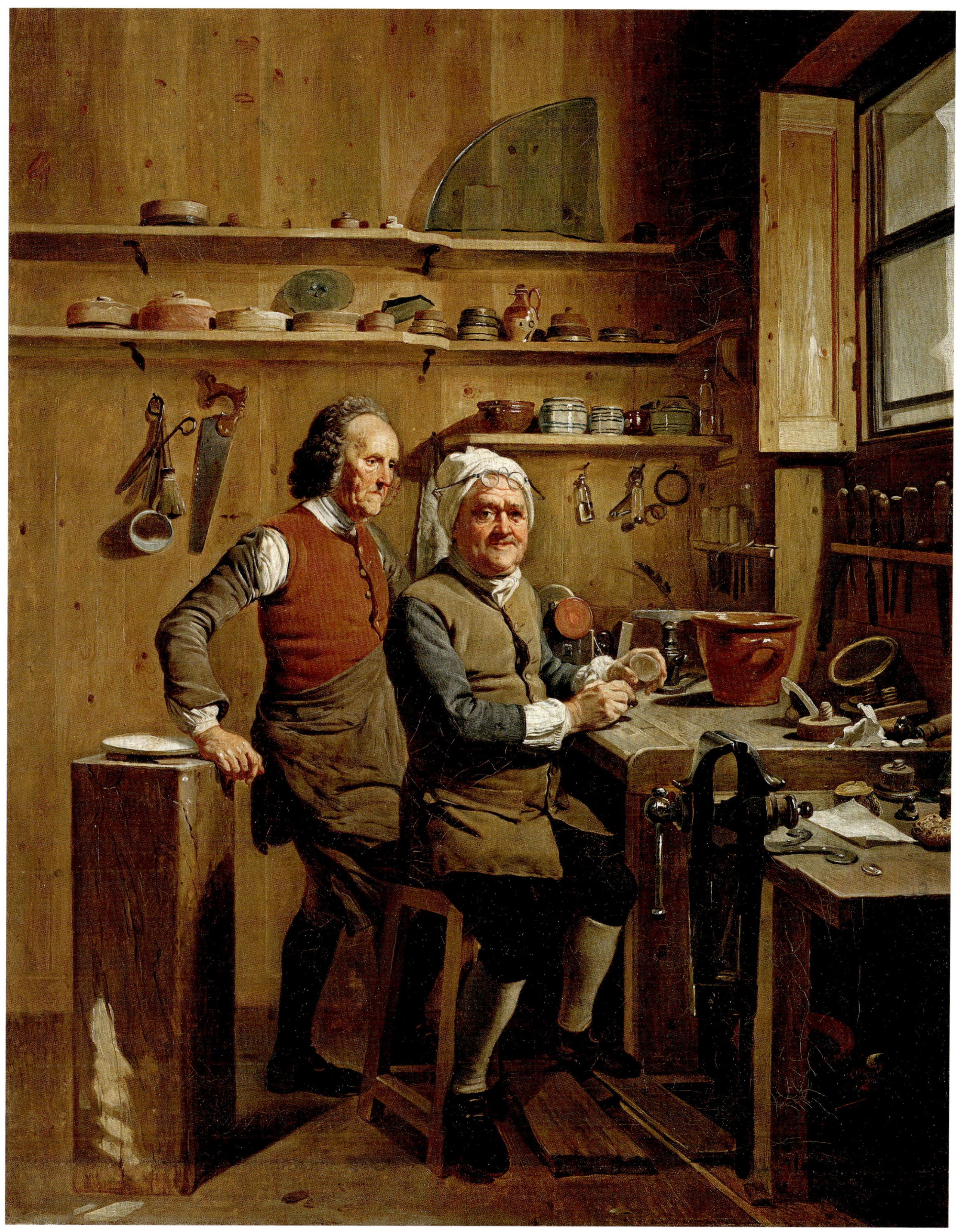

Among those friends in Bath was Gainsborough, who had given Zoffany several landscape drawings to take back with him to London and whose portrait, as MaryAnne Stevens notes (cat. 45), Zoffany probably painted during this visit.[31]

That spring Zoffany was enjoying life in London and clearly looking forward to his new adventure. Among the pictures he showed at the Royal Academy was *John Cuff and his Assistant* (fig. 21), which was apparently purchased at the exhibition by Lord Grosvenor, before passing into the collection of the King. In May he attended a masquerade at Mrs Cornelys', at Carlisle House, Soho, the capital's most fashionable 'celebrity' hotspot. Zoffany appeared in the guise of a Venetian sailor, while Joseph Banks was dressed as a gardener, with an orange seller on his arm, and the notorious brothel keeper Charlotte Hayes appeared as an abbess with several 'nuns'.[32] A few months later Zoffany sailed from England. He did not, however, head for the South Seas with Banks but to Italy, as Banks had been forced to abandon his plans. Zoffany, who had invested heavily in Banks's projected voyage, was saddled with significant debts.[33] Hoping to recoup his losses, he accepted Queen Charlotte's offer of a commission to paint the Tribuna of the Uffizi. Following his departure, the contents of Zoffany's country house were sold off by Christie's, who described him as 'John Zoffany Esq'.[34] The list of effects provides a tantalizing glimpse into Zoffany's domestic and social life. His musical interests are indicated by the presence of violins, guitars and a harpsichord, while his enjoyment of outdoor pursuits is evidenced by a 'fowling piece' (shotgun) and a pleasure boat. Even his horse was included in the sale. Expensive pocket watches, camera obscuras, thermometers and a four-foot telescope attest to his penchant for scientific instruments, while his love of lavish entertainment is indicated by his well-stocked wine cellar. Paintings were also on offer: views of Naples and the Ponte Salario, Rome; dogs by Jan Weenix; studies of lions and a cow by Rubens; two paintings of farriers' shops by Johann Heinrich Roos; as well as landscapes by Cornelis van Poelenburgh and Claude Joseph Vernet. Zoffany owned a small number of works by contemporary British artists: two sketches by the marine painter Charles

Figure 21 (cat. 51)
John Cuff and his Assistant, 1772, oil on canvas, 89.5 × 69.2 cm (35¼ × 27¼ in). The Royal Collection, Her Majesty Queen Elizabeth II

Figure 22 (cat. 78)
Mary Thomas (Mrs Zoffany), c.1781, oil on canvas, 75 × 61.5 cm (29½ × 24¼ in). Ashmolean Museum, University of Oxford

Brooking and a horse 'from the life' by Stubbs. No books were included in the sale, although there were architectural folios by William Chambers and James Paine, whom Zoffany knew personally.[35]

During the twelve years that Zoffany spent away from England between 1772 and his death in 1810 – in Italy, Austria and latterly India – his primary social affiliation was to Anglophone society. Yet, to others he remained a German artist. Arriving in Florence accompanied by his pregnant teenage mistress, Mary Thomas (fig. 22) – whom he passed off as his wife – Zoffany was described in glowing terms by the young Maria Hadfield as 'un Tedesco célèbre pittore della Regina d'Inghilterra' ('a celebrated German artist from the Queen of England').[36] Less flatteringly, the British envoy Sir Horace Mann referred to him as a 'one-eyed German'.[37] Zoffany's return to Italy, some fifteen years after his departure, had, however, altered the way in which he perceived his own cultural and national orientation. In January 1774 he wrote to Sir Joseph Banks: 'My works I hope will be finished by the latter end of March, when I shall immediately sett out on my return to Old England.'[38] The pressure of work compelled Zoffany to prolong his stay. He told his young friend and former pupil, George

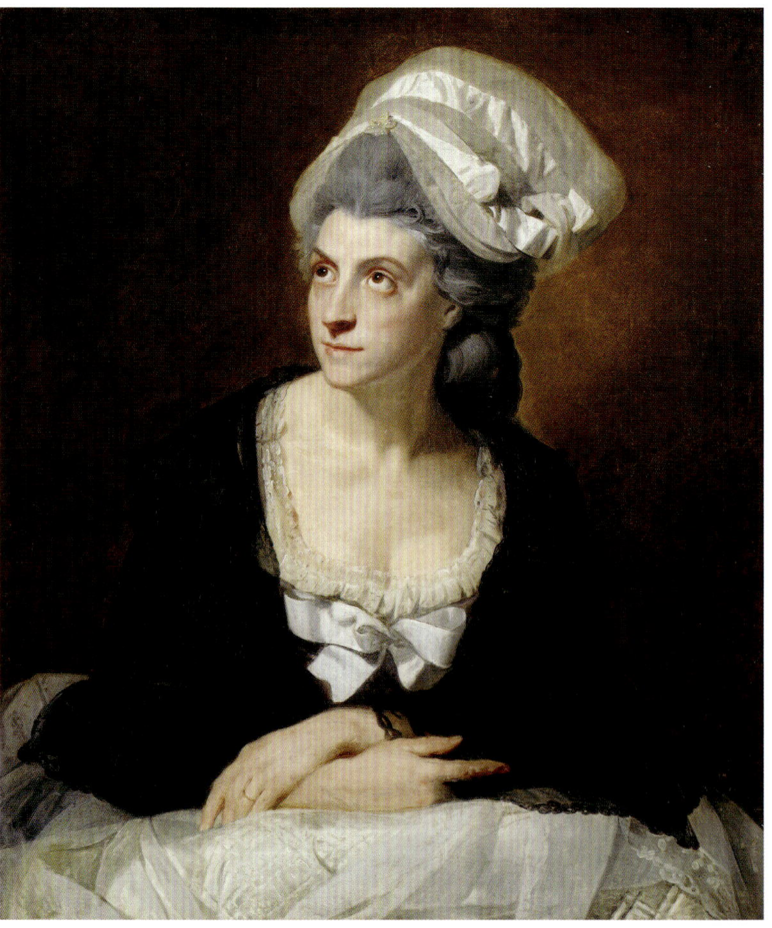

Huddesford, that the increase in work would hinder his ever seeing England again, 'if I was not perswadet dat der is no Contry Equel to it for Socieiati'.[39]

English society in Florence was more unbuttoned than that in either London or Rome, where Zoffany had resided during his previous Italian sojourn. At the heart of the English expatriate community in Florence were Sir Horace Mann and George Nassau, third Earl Cowper, who, through his intimate contact with the Grand Duke of Tuscany, was of vital importance to Zoffany. Basking in the reflected glory of his royal patron, Zoffany regarded himself as on equal social footing with the assorted *milordi*, dressing on state occasions in an elaborate pale pink court suit.[40] In December 1776, in recognition of the portraits he painted of her family, the Empress Maria Theresa made Zoffany a Baron of the Holy Roman Empire, presenting him with an elaborate coat of arms, which the *cavaliere* subsequently embroidered on the scarlet and gold livery of his servants at his Kew residence. In another accolade bestowed during his time in Italy, the engraver Giovanni Battista Piranesi dedicated a plate to Zoffany in his *Vasi, candelabri, cippi, sarcophagi, tripodi, Lucerne ed ornamenti antichi*. According to the flattering inscription Zoffany was not only 'Suo Carissimo Amico' but 'Pittore Celeberrimo de' nostri tempi'.[41]

One portrait, of Fra Giovanni Poggi (fig. 23), a lay-brother of the Servite order who worked in the service of the Grand Duke as a locksmith, was possibly made to bolster his artistic credentials. Fra Giovanni's finger, pointing towards his cranium, his secretive smile and even his clerical garb are reminiscent of another man of 'genius', Laurence Sterne, as portrayed by Reynolds in 1761 (fig. 179). Zoffany's portrait of Fra Giovanni, which he presented to the Accademia di Belle Arti, Florence, in 1773, was, like Reynolds's portrait of Sterne, a means of enhancing his own status while celebrating the talents of another. In August 1773 Zoffany was elected to

Figure 23
*Fra Giovanni Poggi, c.*1773,
oil on panel, 81 × 69 cm (31⅞ × 27⅛ in).
Uffizi Gallery, Florence

Figure 24
Self-Portrait, 1778,
oil on canvas, 72.5 × 58 cm (28½ × 22⅞ in).
Museo dell'Accademia Etrusca, Cortona

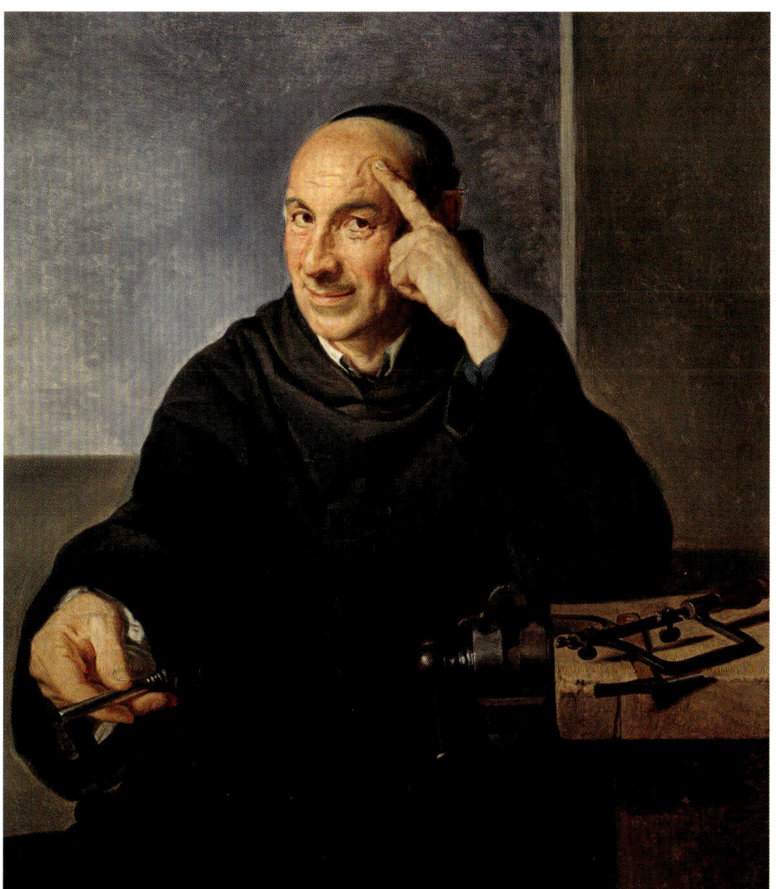

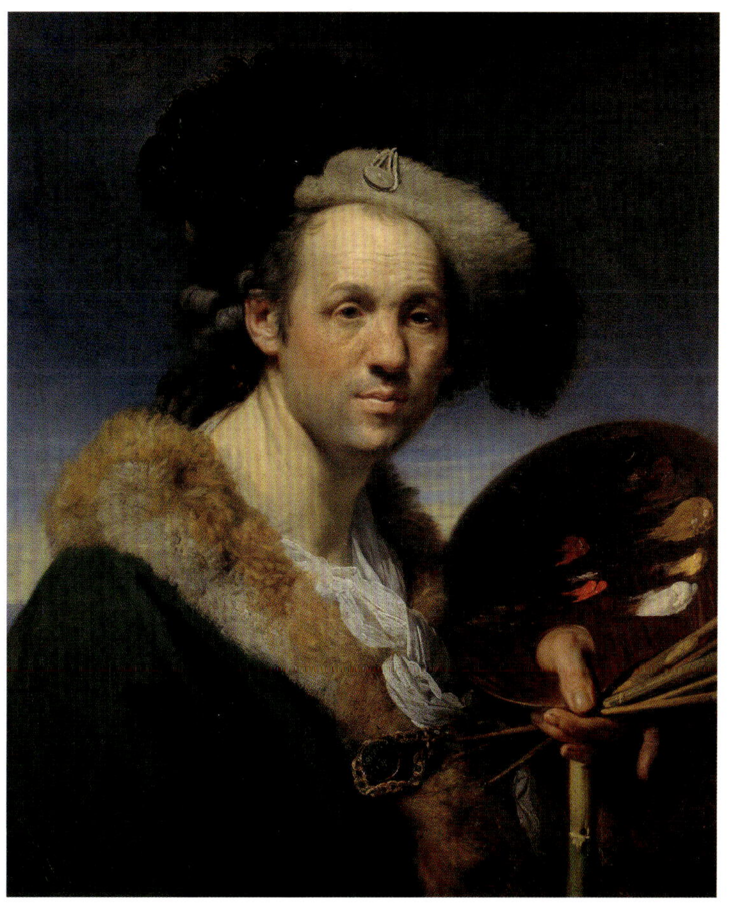

the Accademia in Florence. Membership of the academies in Bologna, Cortona and Parma followed. In Parma, in 1779, he painted a satirical portrait of himself donning a friar's habit (fig. 26), while the previous year, in recognition of his membership of the Cortona Academy, he presented an equally unconventional self-portrait (fig. 24). Mary Webster has observed that the plumed hat and gold knight's chain refer to Zoffany's ennobled status.[42] Yet there remains something faintly ridiculous about the portrait, Zoffany's fur-lined robe and antiquated headgear looking as if they have been plucked from a costume chest. James Northcote, who presented a respectful, profiled self-portrait in 1779, was critical of Zoffany's mercurial submission to the Cortona Academy. Perhaps he would not be pleased to know that his prim self-portrait today hangs next to Zoffany's supremely theatrical incarnation in the Museo dell'Accademia Etrusca.

In Florence the invitation to submit a self-portrait to the collection of the Uffizi conferred considerable kudos. In 1773

Mengs presented his self-portrait. Reynolds, who presented his the following year, may have been unaware that he had been proposed by Zoffany.[43] Was it for this reason that, when the self-portrait arrived at the Uffizi, Zoffany 'could not refrain from running to embrace the portrait of Reynolds'?[44] Northcote observed later that native Florentine painters were critical of Reynolds's self-portrait, stating that they were 'help'd on by Zoffany who tells them not only all its present defects but that it will soon fade and appear quite dreadful'.[45] While Northcote accused Zoffany of behaving maliciously towards Reynolds ('the greatest friend Zoffany found in England'), he was probably repeating what was no more than common knowledge regarding Reynolds's notoriously unstable picture surfaces. Zoffany did not present his own self-portrait (fig. 25) to the Uffizi until 1778. It was admired greatly and also copied, although, as with Reynolds's portrait, there were fears about its physical deterioration.[46]

Figure 25 (cat. 59)
Self-Portrait, 1778,
oil on panel, 87.5 × 77 cm (34½ × 30¼ in).
Uffizi Gallery, Florence

Figure 26 (cat. 60)
Self-Portrait with a Friar's Habit, 1779,
oil on panel, 43 × 39 cm (16⅞ × 15⅜ in).
Galleria Nazionale di Parma

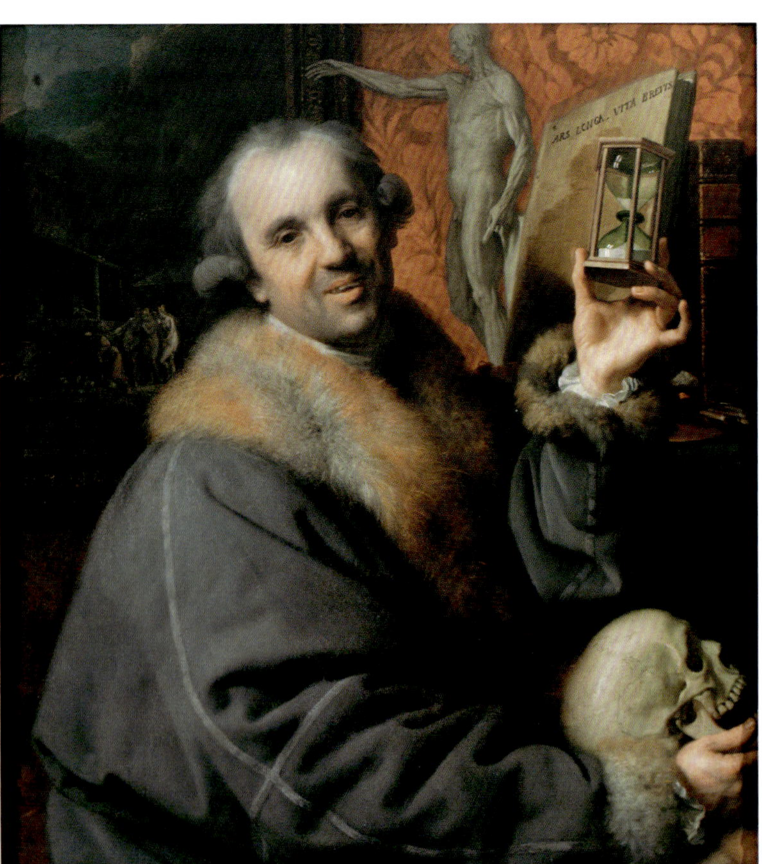

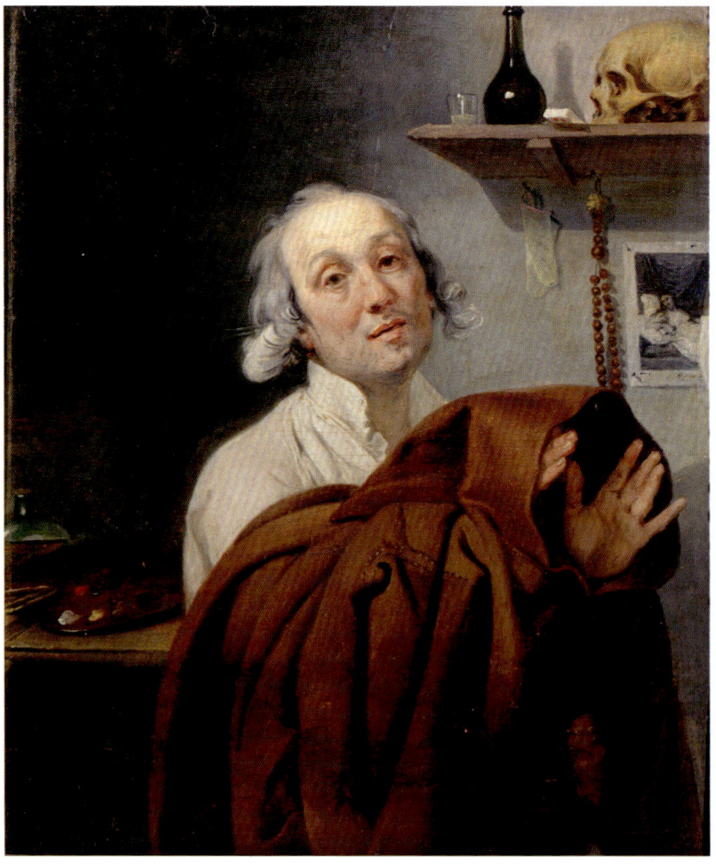

Zoffany's extended stay in Italy was determined principally by the commissions he received from Duke Pietro Leopoldo and other members of the imperial royal family, involving visits to Parma and Vienna. Collectively, these portraits were quite different from the kind of portraiture that Zoffany had evolved during his time in England. Now, he was expected to promote the dynastic personae of the extended family of the empress. An exception to the stiffness of the imperial commissions was the portrait of the four children of Duke Ferdinando and Archduchess Maria Amalia (see fig. 81). Here Zoffany punctured formality to produce a picture reminiscent of Hogarth's *Graham Children* (1742; National Gallery, London). In Italy Zoffany also produced two genre paintings (figs. 27, 29), both of which contained recognisable elements of Hogarthian satire and innuendo.

In the late spring of 1779 Zoffany returned to London with Mary Thomas, who was now to all intents and purposes his wife, and a daughter – his first child, a son, having died in a tragic accident in Florence aged only sixteen months.[47] Although he had endured intense grief at the loss of his son, the six and a half years that Zoffany spent in Italy changed his life for the better. As well as the payments he eventually received for *The Tribuna of the Uffizi*, Zoffany benefited financially through prestigious portrait commissions and a lucrative trade in selling old master paintings. They included Raphael's *Madonna and Child*, now in the National Gallery of Art, Washington DC.

On his return to London, Zoffany took a townhouse in fashionable Albemarle Street and a country residence on the banks of the Thames at Strand-on-the-Green, near the royal residence at Kew. Zoffany also contributed to the life of the Royal Academy, as a member of its council and as an exhibitor, displaying a fancy picture, *The Watercress Girl* (fig. 28), and *The Tribuna* at the inaugural annual exhibition at Somerset House in 1780. Although *The Tribuna* failed to please the king –

Figure 27 (cat. 57)
A Florentine Fruit Stall, c.1777, oil on canvas,
57.8 × 49.2 cm (22¾ × 19⅜ in). Tate, London; purchased 1955

Figure 28
The Watercress Girl, 1780, oil on canvas,
76.2 × 63.5 cm (30 × 25 in). Private collection

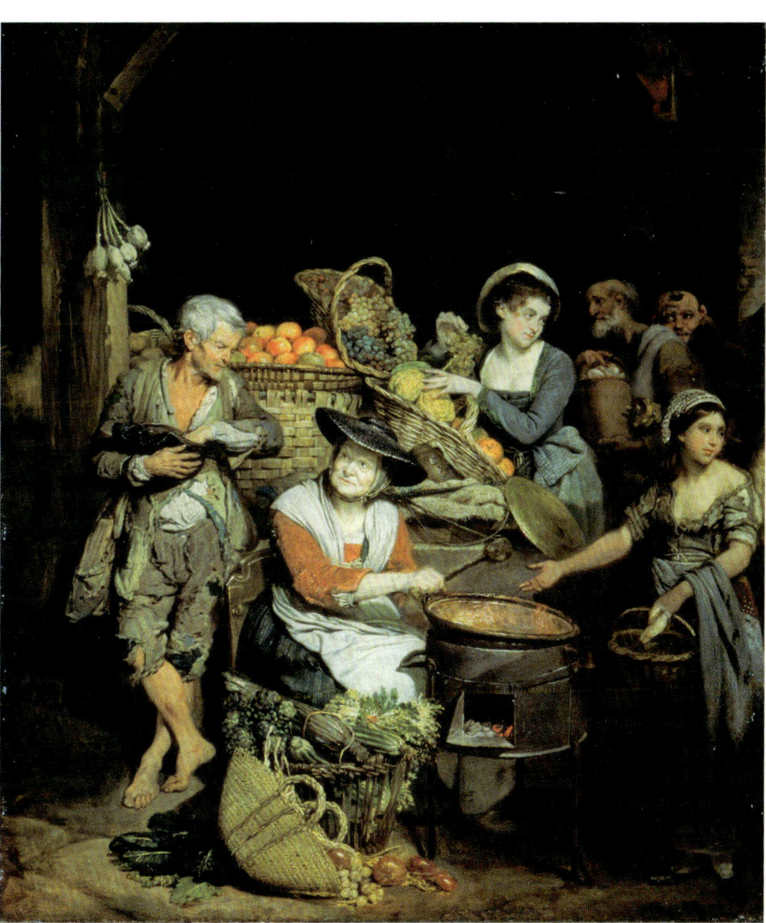

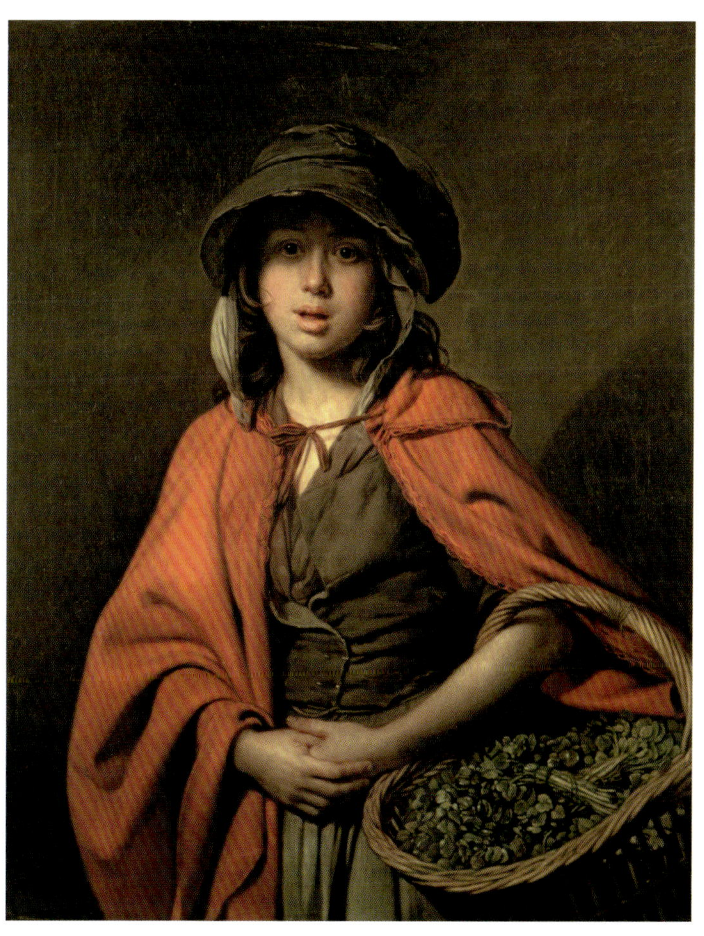

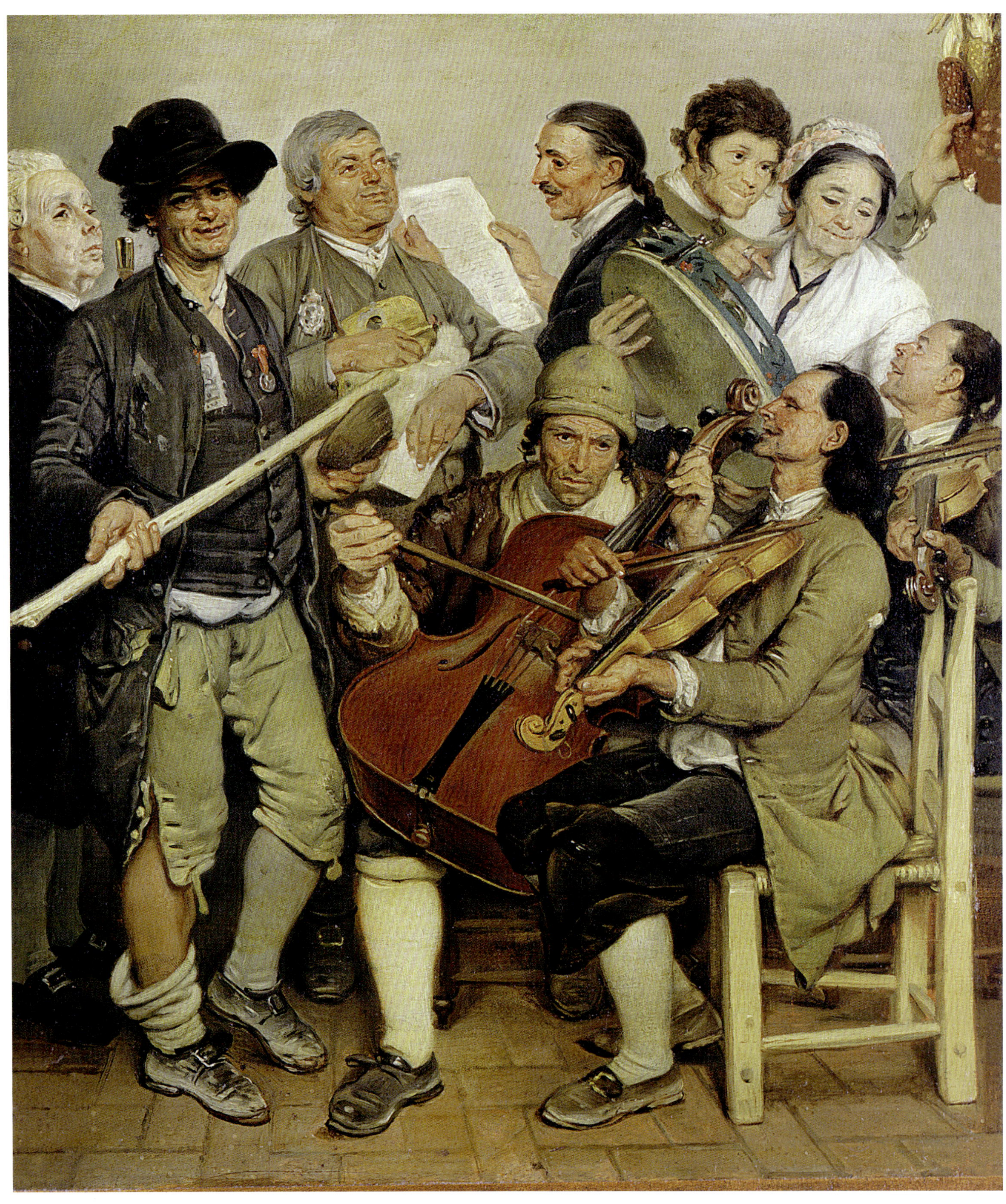

Figure 29 (cat. 62)
'La Scartocciata', the Festival of the Maize Harvest, 1778,
oil on panel, 43.5 × 38 cm (17⅛ × 15 in). Galleria Nazionale di Parma

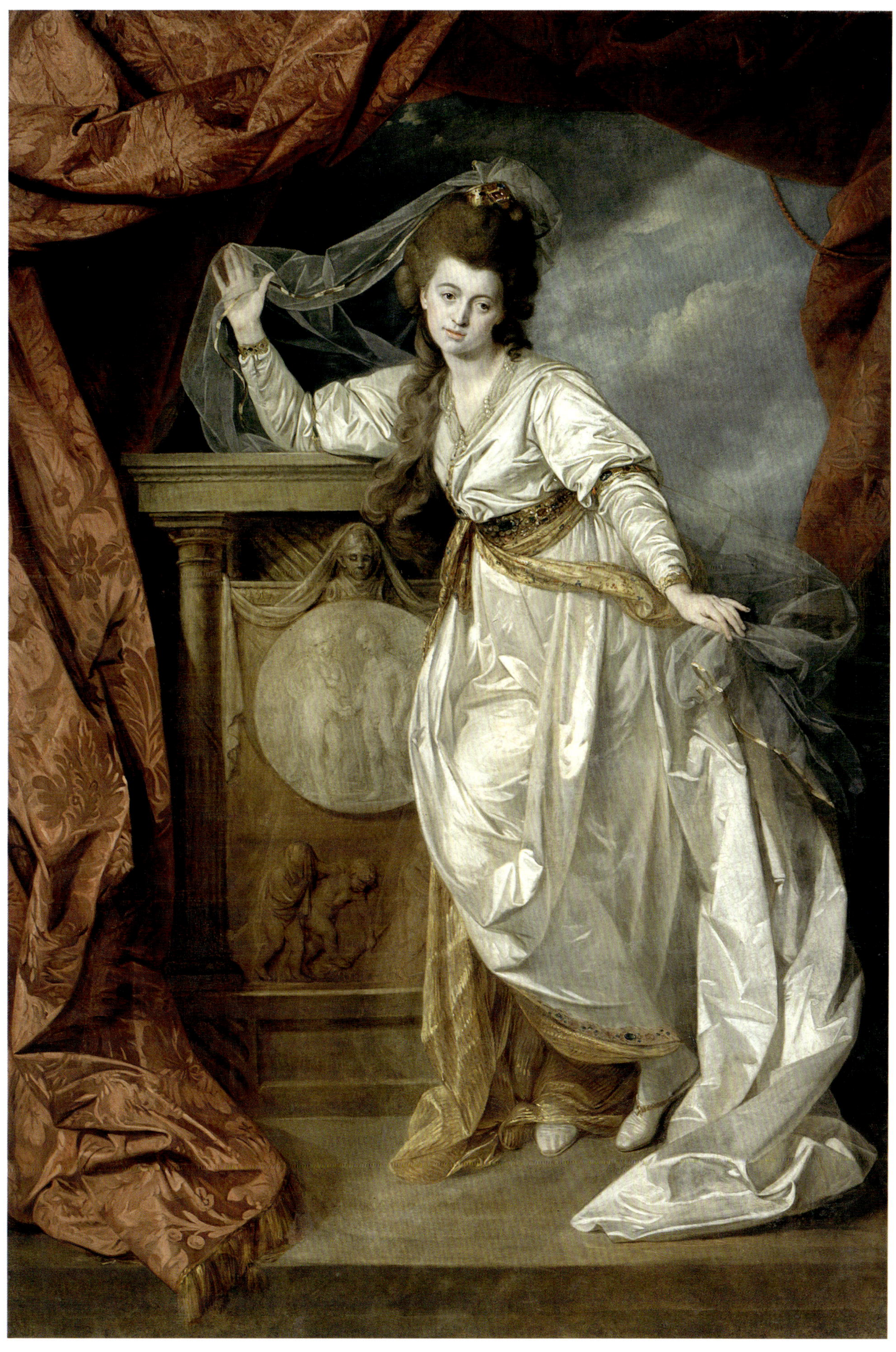

and was considered offensive to the sensibilities of the queen –
the effective termination of Zoffany's royal patronage meant
that he was no longer constrained by the demands of the court
and its etiquette.

His key patron David Garrick had died just before his
return, but Zoffany resumed close links with the stage through
the actors Tom King and Robert Baddeley, as well as forming
friendships with the celebrated Italian dancer and mistress
of the Duke of Dorset, Giovanna Baccelli, and the beautiful
young Shakespearean actress, Elizabeth Farren, whose
full-length portrait he painted in the role of Hermione
in *The Winter's Tale* (fig. 30).[48] Zoffany's social circle also
included musicians: his old friends Johann Christian Bach,
Carl Friedrich Abel and the Cervettos, father and son,
whom he featured in a large portrait together with himself
and his eldest daughter (fig. 31); each father is perhaps
portrayed in the act of passing on their particular gifts to
their progeny – a suggestion that may explain the otherwise
unaccountable phallic positioning of Zoffany's paintbrush
before his young daughter.

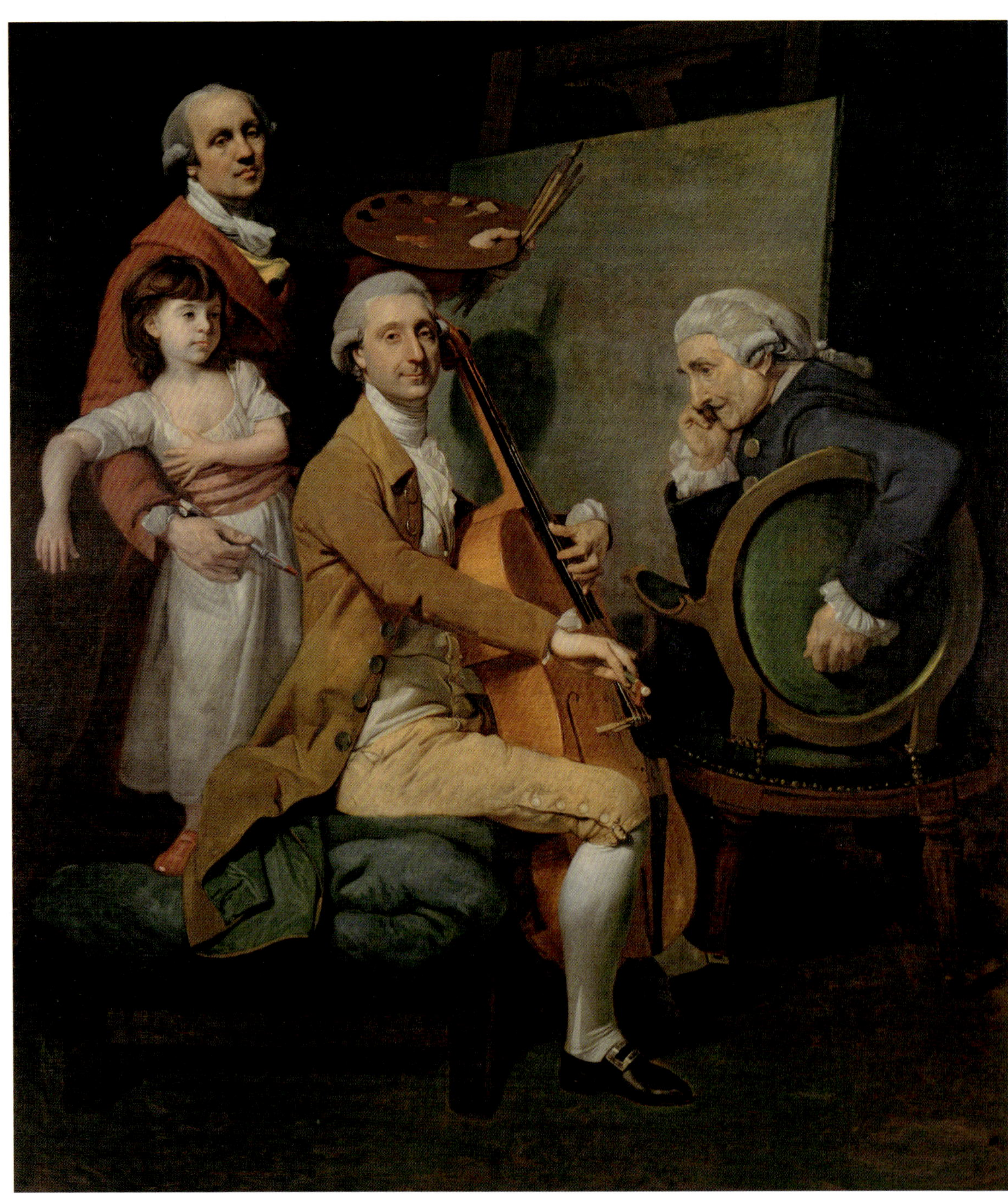

Figure 30
*Elizabeth Farren as Hermione in
'The Winter's Tale', c.1780,*
oil on canvas, 245 × 167 cm
(96½ × 65¾ in). National Gallery
of Victoria, Melbourne; Everard
Studley Miller Bequest, 1967
(1728–5)

Figure 31
*Self-Portrait with his Daughter
Maria Theresa, James Cervetto
and Giacobbe Cervetto, c.1780,*
oil on canvas, 193 × 164.5 cm
(76 × 64¾ in). Yale Center for
British Art, Paul Mellon
Collection

New friends at this time included the eminent French dental surgeon Charles Dumergue, whose portrait he painted (fig. 33), together with that of his daughter Sophia cradling a cat in her arms (fig. 32). Perhaps because he could afford to pick and choose, the majority of Zoffany's portraits, painted either speculatively or as commissions, were of people with whom he sympathized or had a close professional association, like the celebrated musical Sharp Family, the stockbroker John Maddison and the Shakespearean editor George Steevens, who had amassed the most complete collection of Hogarth's engravings and copper plates. Zoffany's most important associate was the collector and antiquarian Charles Townley, whom he had probably met in Florence. The painting of Townley's library in Park Street (fig. 34), which was to occupy Zoffany intermittently until the late 1790s, was made entirely of his own volition and articulates the values and interests he shared with Townley's liberal, enlightened circle.

Why exactly in the spring of 1783, at a time when he was clearly enjoying a fulfilled professional and social life in London, Zoffany decided to travel to India is uncertain. Money, always a motivation both in terms of getting and of spending, was clearly an issue. And, as his fellow Royal Academician, Paul Sandby, observed just prior to his departure, Zoffany 'anticipates to roll in gold dust'.[49] Zoffany did well financially in India. According to Elijah Impey, within a year or so of his arrival he had earned some £10,000 – 'a sheet anchor to help him to a comfortable enjoyment in old age' – while a report in the London press in January 1785 stated that Zoffany had already sent home £36,000, with a promise of a further £30,000 'as soon as he has finished the portraits that are bespoke'.[50] Zoffany may also have been induced to leave England by changes in the contemporary art market, where small-scale conversation pieces could suffer by comparison with the swaggering Grand Manner portraits of Reynolds, Gainsborough and Romney. Ultimately, however,

Figure 32
Sophia Dumergue, 1780–81,
oil on panel, 76 × 61.5 cm (29⅞ × 24¼ in).
Victoria Art Gallery, Bath and North East Somerset Council

Figure 33
Charles Dumergue, 1780–81,
oil on canvas, 76 × 64 cm (29⅞ × 25⅛ in).
Victoria Art Gallery, Bath and North East Somerset Council

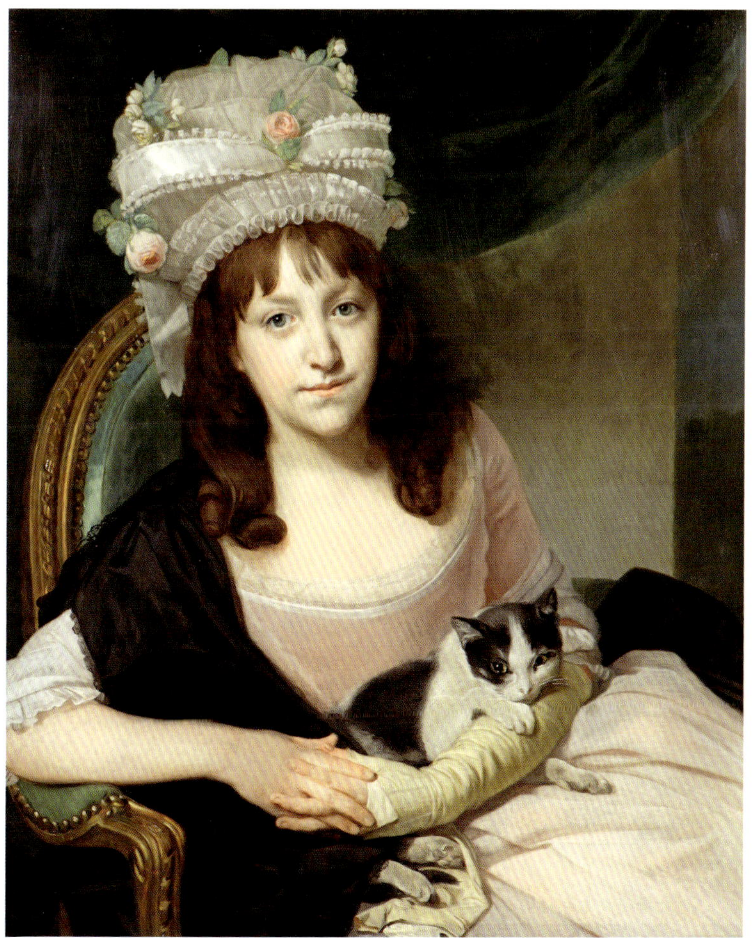

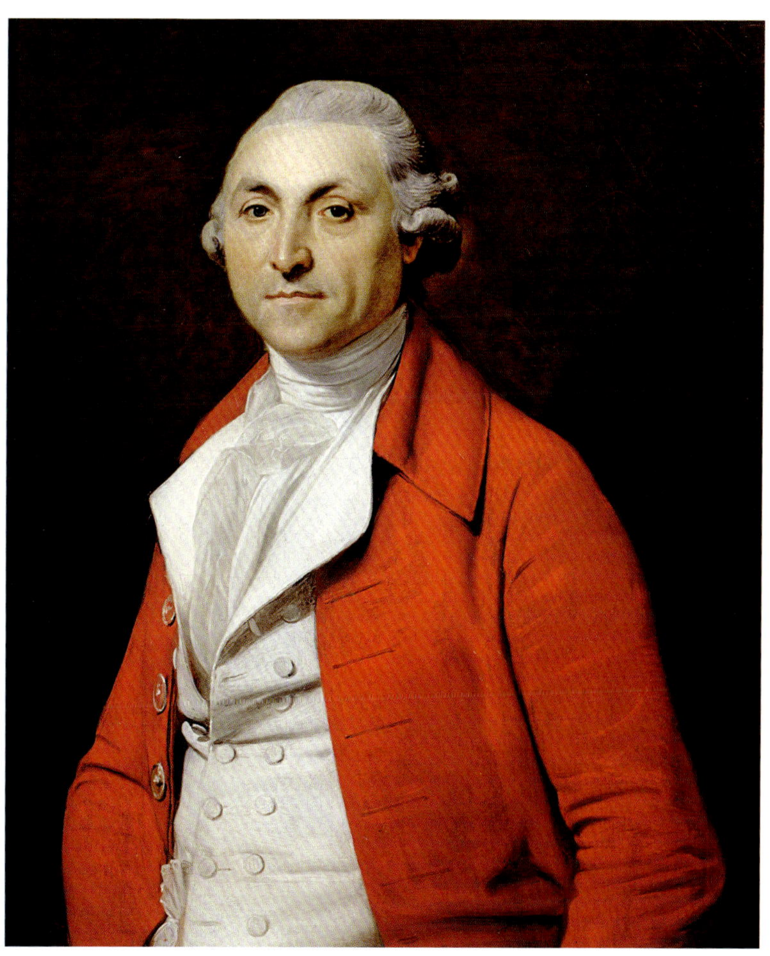

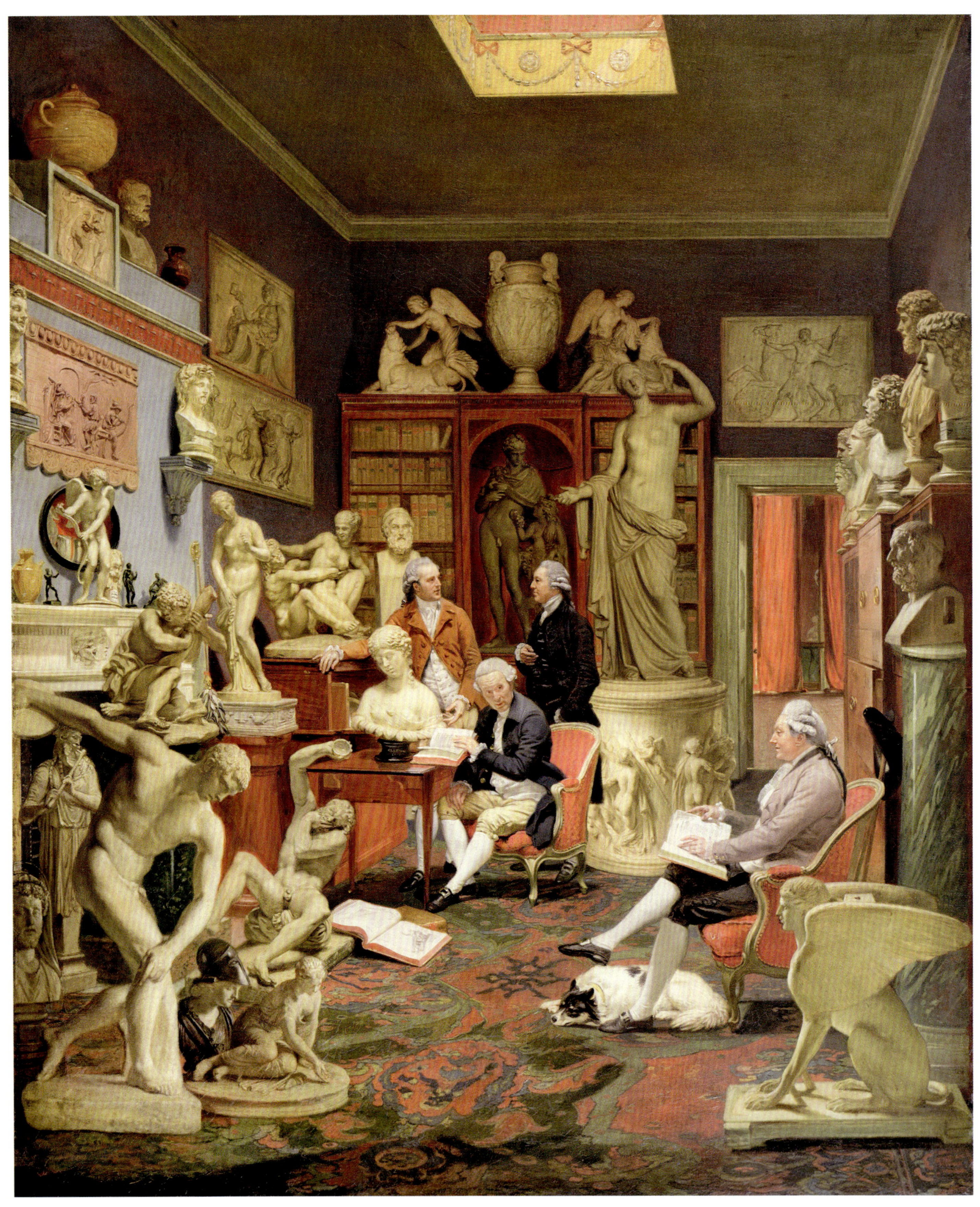

Figure 34 (cat. 63)
Charles Townley's Library, No. 7 Park Street, Westminster, 1781–83, 1792, 1798,
oil on canvas, 123.5 × 99.5 cm (48⅝ × 39⅛ in). Burnley Borough Council, Towneley Hall Art
Gallery & Museums, Purchased with the Assistance of the National Art Collections Fund, 1939

Zoffany's innate wanderlust may have been the deciding factor since, as a friend remarked, 'Zoffany, like Tristram Shandy, discovered always an unaccountable obliquity in the manner of setting up his Top'.[51] And on 8 March 1783, after bidding a fond farewell to friends and family, he embarked on his 'Shandean' passage to India.

Zoffany was given permission by the Directors of the East India Company to travel to India in the capacity of a portrait painter. Yet his interests, as expressed through the paintings and drawings he made there, were directed also towards India's landscape, its people, rituals and traditions. Zoffany's time in India is explored here by Maya Jasanoff and Charles Greig, but it is worth remarking the salient features of his six-year sojourn, as they relate to the trajectory and character of his career.

Figure 35
Major George Maule, 1783, oil on canvas,
61.5 × 47.5 cm (24⅕ × 18¾ in).
Private collection

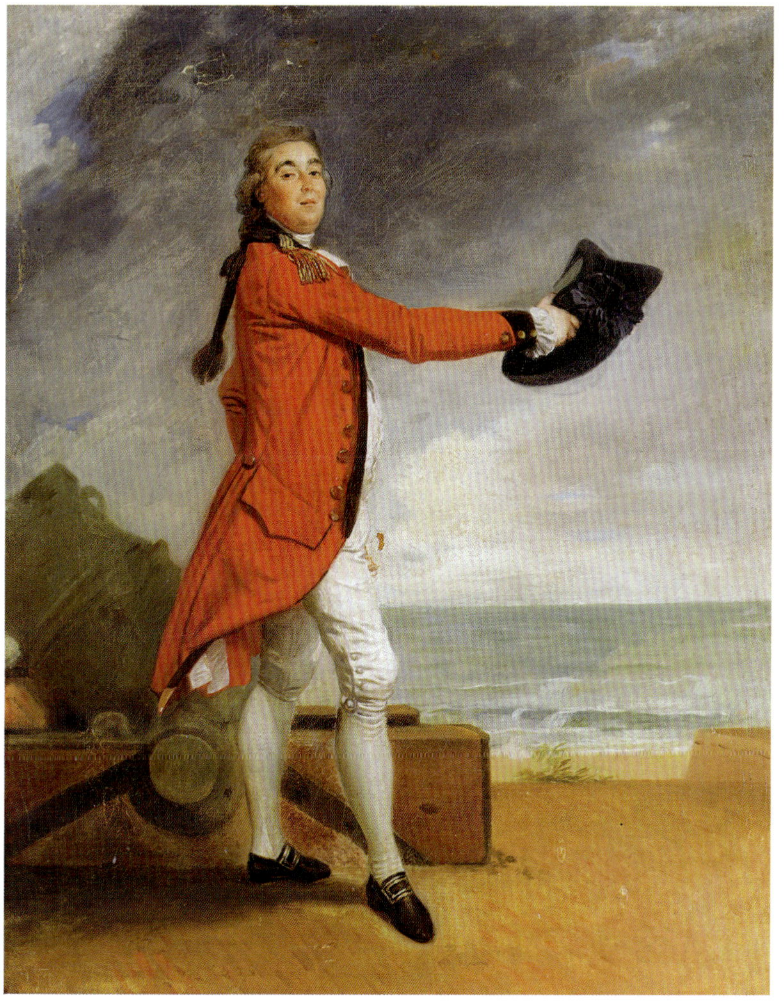

In order to succeed in India Zoffany needed to impress not only through his abilities as a painter but also by his status. The range of influential patrons he attracted – Warren Hastings, Elijah Impey, Claude Martin, Asaf-ud-Daula – indicates that he was adept at doing so. Shortly after arrival in Madras in July 1783, Zoffany demonstrated his credentials by painting the portraits of several officers in the East India Company. Among these was Major George Maule (fig. 35), at that time responsible for the city's naval battery. Modest in scale, the portrait nonetheless has all the hallmarks of Zoffany's witty and unconventional approach to such commissions. Although only the portrait of Maule appears to have survived, Zoffany evidently impressed at least one of his patrons, the Governor of Madras, George, Lord Macartney, whose portrait he also painted and who recommended him as 'without dispute the greatest Painter that ever visited India', as well as being an 'easy unaffected well informed agreeable man'.[52]

Zoffany was based principally in Calcutta and latterly in Lucknow. He was also on the move, undertaking travels that, as Charles Greig observes through his own recent expeditions (see pp. 141–65), must have involved a great deal of hardship and perseverance. As he journeyed, Zoffany made paintings and drawings of temples, mausoleums, rock formations, 'sati' scenes, tiger hunts, as well as character studies of Indian people – drawings that are now sadly lost, but impressed contemporaries.[53] Architecture, too, clearly fascinated him. In the early autumn of 1786 he journeyed from Lucknow to Agra and Delhi, where he visited two of the greatest examples of Mughal design, the Taj Mahal and the Jami Masjid mosque. He was captivated, apparently exclaiming, 'Where is the case to cover so many beauties? For this is too fine to be exposed to the impression of the air.' As Mary Webster observes, the fact that his appreciation was recounted in several versions suggests that Zoffany's comments had gained a certain celebrity and that his opinions on such matters were of interest.[54]

Zoffany's stimulus in absorbing the landscape and culture of India into his artistic endeavours was not just the country itself but the company he now kept, for as can be seen in several of his Indian portraits – notably *The Blair Family* (cat. 92) and *Colonel Polier and his Friends* (cat. 90) – the paintings by Zoffany that hang on their walls reflect a common interest, nurtured through conversation, collecting and scholarship. In 1784 the Asiatic Society of Bengal was founded by the Orientalist, Sir William Jones, with the intention of inquiring to the 'History, Civil and Natural, the Antiquities, Arts, Sciences, and Literature of Asia'. Members included Warren Hastings, Antoine Polier,

Claude Martin and Zoffany, who maintained an active interest even after he had returned to England. For men such as Martin and Polier, who had lived in India for nearly thirty years, the accumulation of wealth was accompanied by an immersion in Indian language, religion, history and mythology, as well as the adoption of native dress and taking on Indian mistresses. In Lucknow Zoffany lived in Martin's house, the Farhad Baksh, where he established a 'portrait chamber' and where many of the forty-seven recorded pictures and sketches he produced for Martin were made.[55] In many ways Martin and his circle resembled the esoteric coterie of Charles Townley. In 1784 Zoffany established links between Martin and Townley, resulting in the shipment to Martin by Townley of drawings, prints, bronzes, marbles, medals, coins, Wedgwood pottery and other collectables, and the cultivation of their common interest in the theories surrounding the relationship between classical and Indian mythology and their attendant sexual practices.[56]

In Lucknow Zoffany lived on the fringes of the sybaritic court of the nawab, Asaf-ud-Daula (fig. 36), and under the roof of Claude Martin. Given his own libidinous predisposition, it was inevitable that Zoffany should have taken an Indian mistress, with whom he had several children, including a son. Although Zoffany left his Indian family in the care of Claude Martin on his return to England, gossip surrounding his private life in India found its way home. In 1796 the satirical writer John Williams ('Anthony Pasquin') painted a picture of Zoffany as 'he fumigated gracefully with his *snake*, while the *hooker badaar* kept pace with his bearers. He had a band of Abissinian nymphs to dance before his ravished vision, while he drank a bumper to Venus and her dominion, in his *lumba piala*!'[57]

Whether or not Mary Thomas, already encumbered by rumours of a bigamous relationship, was aware of Zoffany's Indian family, she must have been struck by the indelible mark that India had left on him. He was a wealthy man but broken in health.[58] Indeed, just before his arrival in England, Zoffany's death had been reported in the British press (as it had been once before, shortly after his departure for Italy).[59] As significant as financial gains and physical hardships was the impact of Zoffany's Indian experience on his mind's eye. In Bengal Zoffany had witnessed a world remote from his Eurocentric consciousness. And as Zoffany gradually subsided into old age and infirmity, his memories of India – its extremes of wealth and poverty, licentiousness and abstinence, high culture and institutional corruption, ancient and modern culture – continued to haunt his imagination.

In March 1791 a London newspaper reported that Zoffany was working on a new picture that was

> a representation of the Nabob of Oude, his brother, and all his courtiers, at a Cock-fighting in India. It is copied from a sketch which the Artist took from Nature while he was in the East, and contains about an hundred figures, attending this Royal game, in their long and stately robes, each according to his rank. Every figure displays as much eagerness for the success of his favourite bird, as is exhibited in Hogarth's print of the Cock-pit.[60]

This report, which has not previously been noted, revives the speculation, first raised in the early nineteenth century, that the original of *Colonel Mordaunt's Cock Match* had been lost at sea on its way from India, and that the picture (cat. 86) painted for Warren Hastings was a replica made on Zoffany's return to London.[61] To be sure, this intriguing speculation clearly merits further investigation.

Figure 36 (cat. 82)
Asaf-ud-Daula, 1784,
black, red and white chalk on paper, 21.7 × 15.2 cm (8⅟₁₆ × 6 in)
The Royal Collection, Her Majesty Queen Elizabeth II

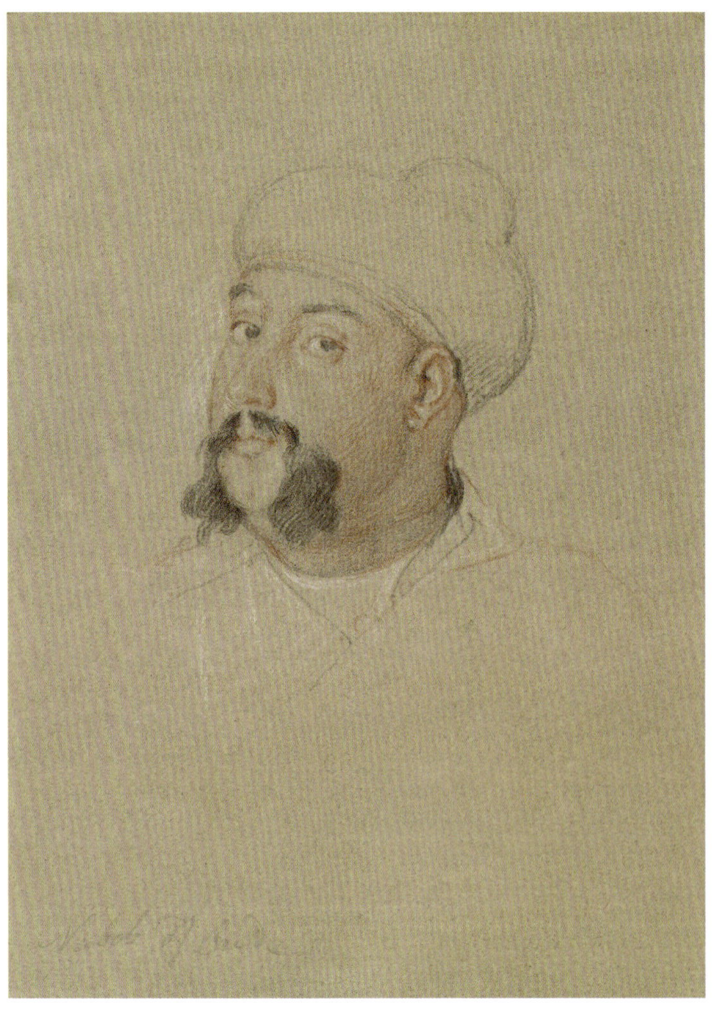

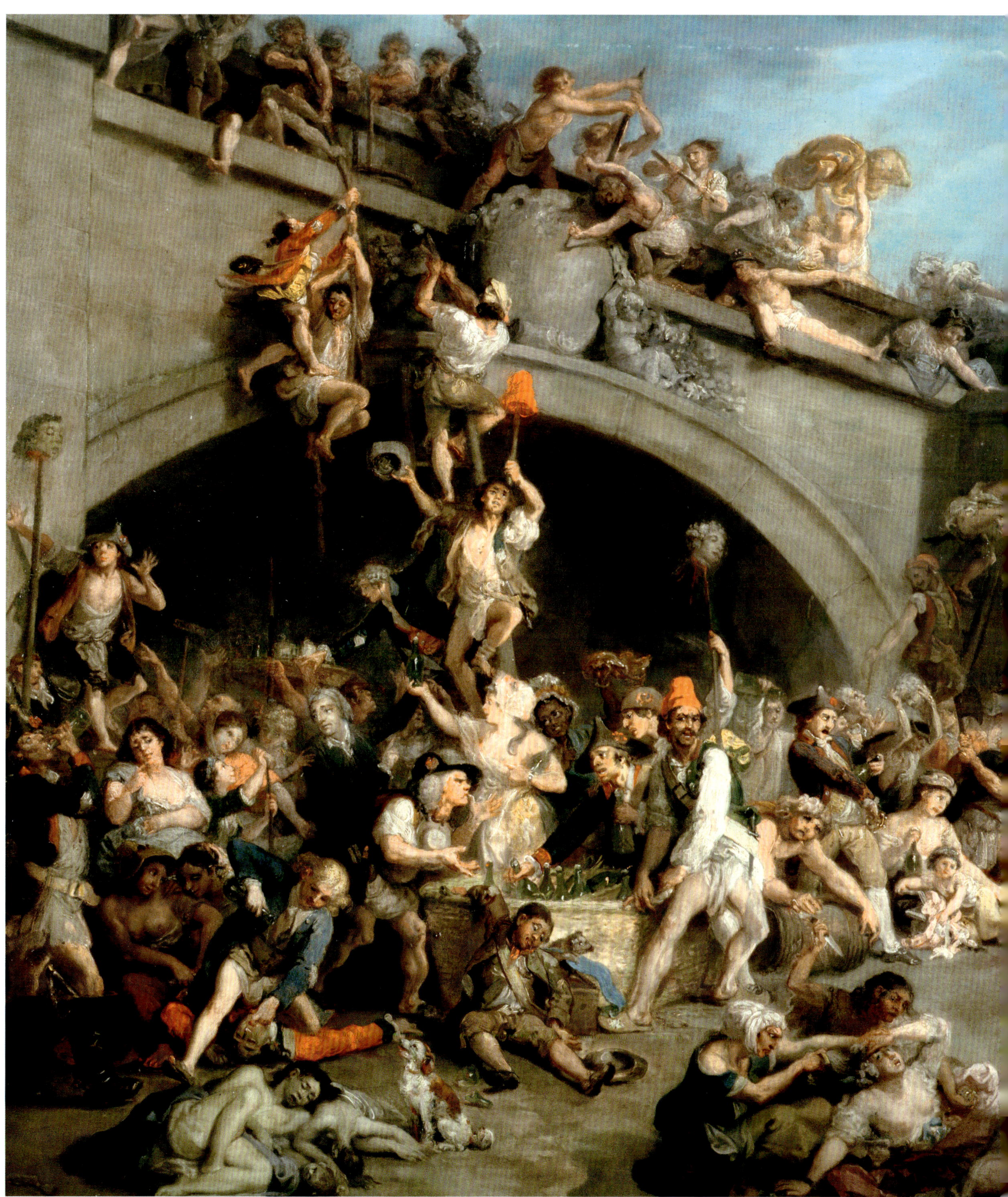

During the 1790s Zoffany also made a number of new compositions based on studies made in India, as well as episodes from modern Indian history. They included *The Sacrifice of a Hindoo Widow upon the Funeral Pyre of her Husband* (cat. 93), *Tiger Hunting in the East Indies* (cat. 103), *Hyderbeg on his Mission to Lord Cornwallis* (cat. 101) and the now lost 'Death of Gholam Cawdor by Elephants, containing a numerous assemblage of Figures', which apparently portrayed a bloodthirsty Afghan chief being trampled to death by elephants, following his plunder in 1788 of the imperial treasure chest in Delhi. All these works, which were painted of Zoffany's own volition – and remained in his studio – involved graphic scenes of violence.

Extreme violence, which had been a feature of Zoffany's early German history paintings, was also to be found in two disturbing paintings based on events during the Terror in Paris, in the aftermath of the French Revolution (fig. 37; cat. 104). It is not surprising that the critic Anthony Pasquin argued that *Plundering the King's Cellar at Paris* reflected the artist's own 'hunger of degradation' [*sic*], suggesting that Zoffany was himself culpable through revelling in the acts portrayed.[62] Politically conservative, Zoffany was horrified by stories of mob violence in Paris, tales that could only have strengthened his feelings of loyalty towards his own adopted country and his monarchist sympathies. Presumably, Zoffany's anglophilia, allied to an eye for the market, ensured that Richard Earlom's mezzotint of the scene (cat. 105) was available for public consumption by the time his original painting was exhibited at the Royal Academy. The imagery of Zoffany's picture is horrific; it also represents a pictorial tour de force. The compositional device of the arch with grappling figures would appear to be derived from Rubens's celebrated tapestry design of the *Battle of the Milvian Bridge* (1622; Kunsthistorisches Museum, Vienna), while the grotesque, dehumanizing characterization of the rabble below recalls Hogarth, who, as Ronald Paulson observed, appears to be the model for one of the characters in the foreground.[63] Zoffany's picture is also remarkable as the only contemporary work of art, beyond the sphere of caricature and popular print, to address this contentious subject.

Figure 37 (cat. 104)
Plundering the King's Cellar at Paris, 1794, oil on canvas, 103 × 126.5 cm (40½ × 49¾ in). Wadsworth Athenaeum Museum of Art, Hartford, Connecticut

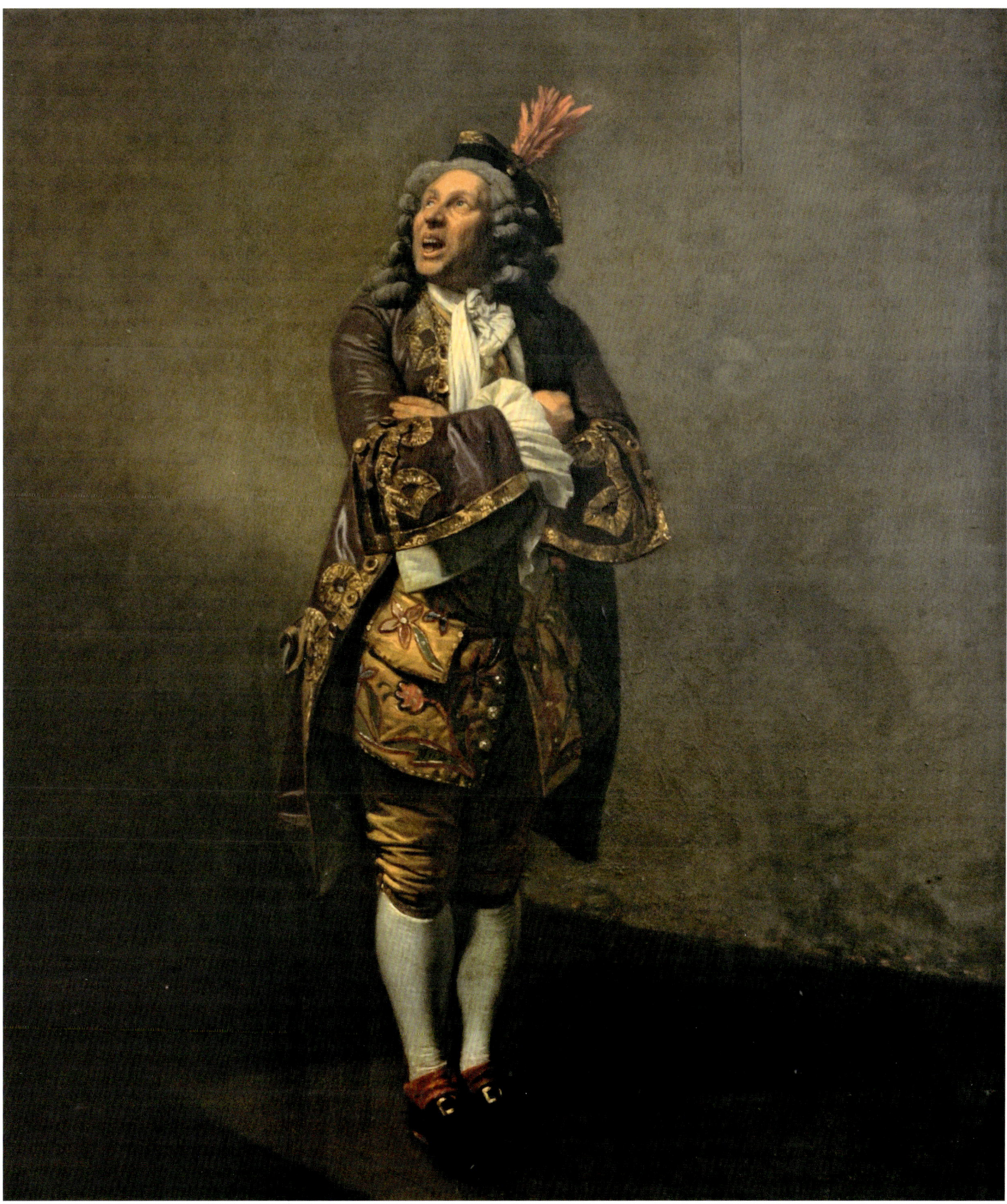

During the 1790s Zoffany once more savoured the prospect of royal patronage. The artist's granddaughter recalled how George III would invite him for an hour to ride in his carriage around Kew, 'to entertain him, and to tell him all about the paintings he was then carrying out and the persons who were sitting to him'.[64] In 1796 the king, who had enjoyed a performance of Frederick Reynolds's comedy *Speculation* early that year, commissioned Zoffany to make a painting of a scene from the play.[65] In the event he did not purchase the work. However, on 1 April 1796, encouraged by the prospect of further royal patronage, Zoffany approached Joseph Farington, who was on the hanging committee at the Royal Academy, requesting prominent places for the four pictures he intended to show at the annual exhibition and 'which He was to shew to the King before they were sent'.[66] The following day it was duly reported in the press that 'ZOFFANI, the respectable graphic veteran, will enrich the ensuing Exhibition with four pictures. One will be a representation of an Indian scene, another of a Lecture in the Royal Academy, and, we believe, two Dramatic Portraits'.[67] As Mary Webster has conjectured, the 'Lecture in the Royal Academy' may have been a replica or version of *Dr William Hunter Teaching Anatomy at the Royal Academy* (cat. 46), which Zoffany had painted in the early 1770s, but left unfinished on his departure for Italy.[68] The 'Indian scene' was *Hyderbeg on his Mission to Lord Cornwallis* (cat. 101), while the two 'Dramatic Portraits' were 'Mr Knight as the clown in the farce of the Ghost' and 'Mr Townsend as the beggar in the pantomime of Merry Sherwood'. Both these works appeared in the 1811 studio sale. The portrait of Thomas Knight also belongs to the Garrick Club, while the portrait of Edward Townsend is presumed to have been lost.[69] However, Townsend is identified here for the first time with a portrait of an unknown actor who is clearly depicted in the act of singing (fig. 38). 'The Beggar' written by John O'Keeffe for the pantomime *Merry Sherwood or Harlequin Forester* was, as Mary Webster notes, a favourite song in Townsend's repertoire.[70]

The year 1796 was the last in which Zoffany exhibited from a central London address – 7 Bennet Street, St James's – after which he worked from his rural retreat at Strand-on-the-Green (fig. 39).

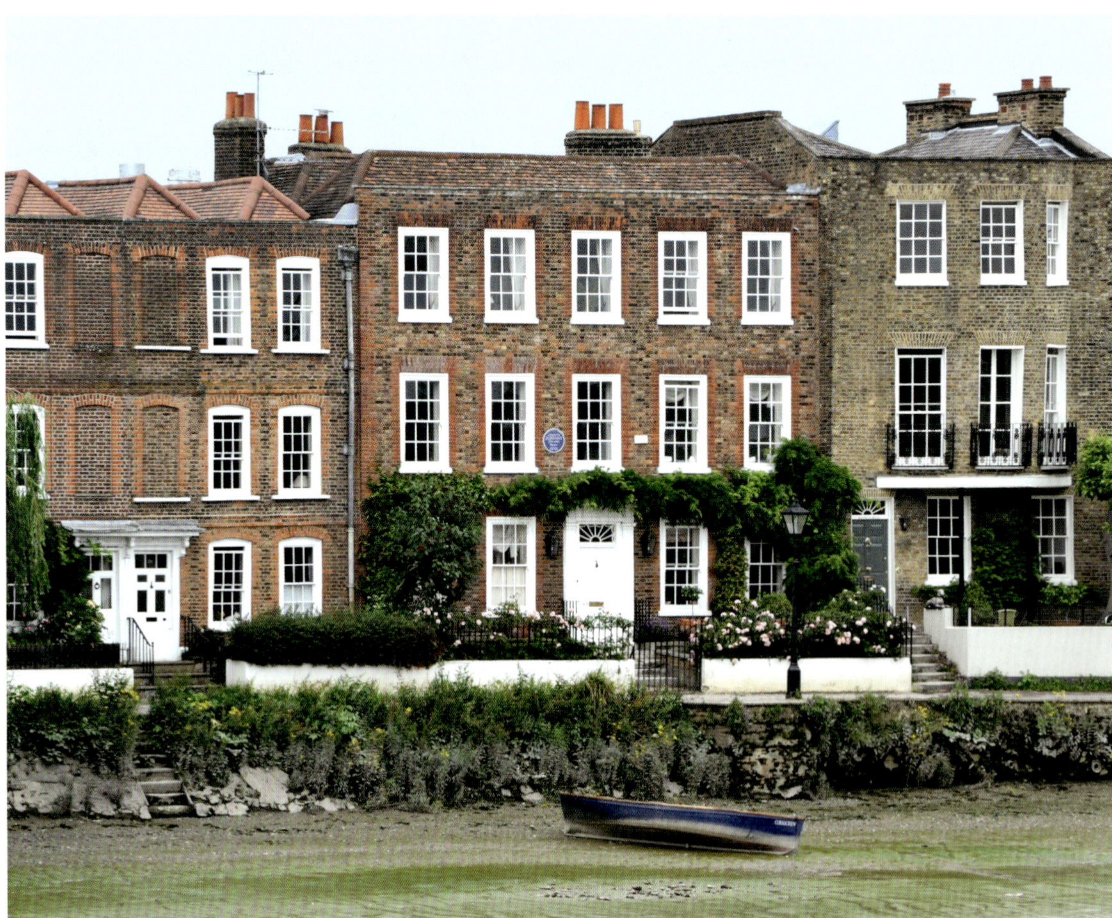

Figure 38
Edward Townsend Singing 'The Beggar',
1796, oil on panel,
76.2 × 63.5 cm (30 × 25 in)
Private collection, UK

Figure 39
Zoffany's house,
65 Strand-on-the-Green, Chiswick

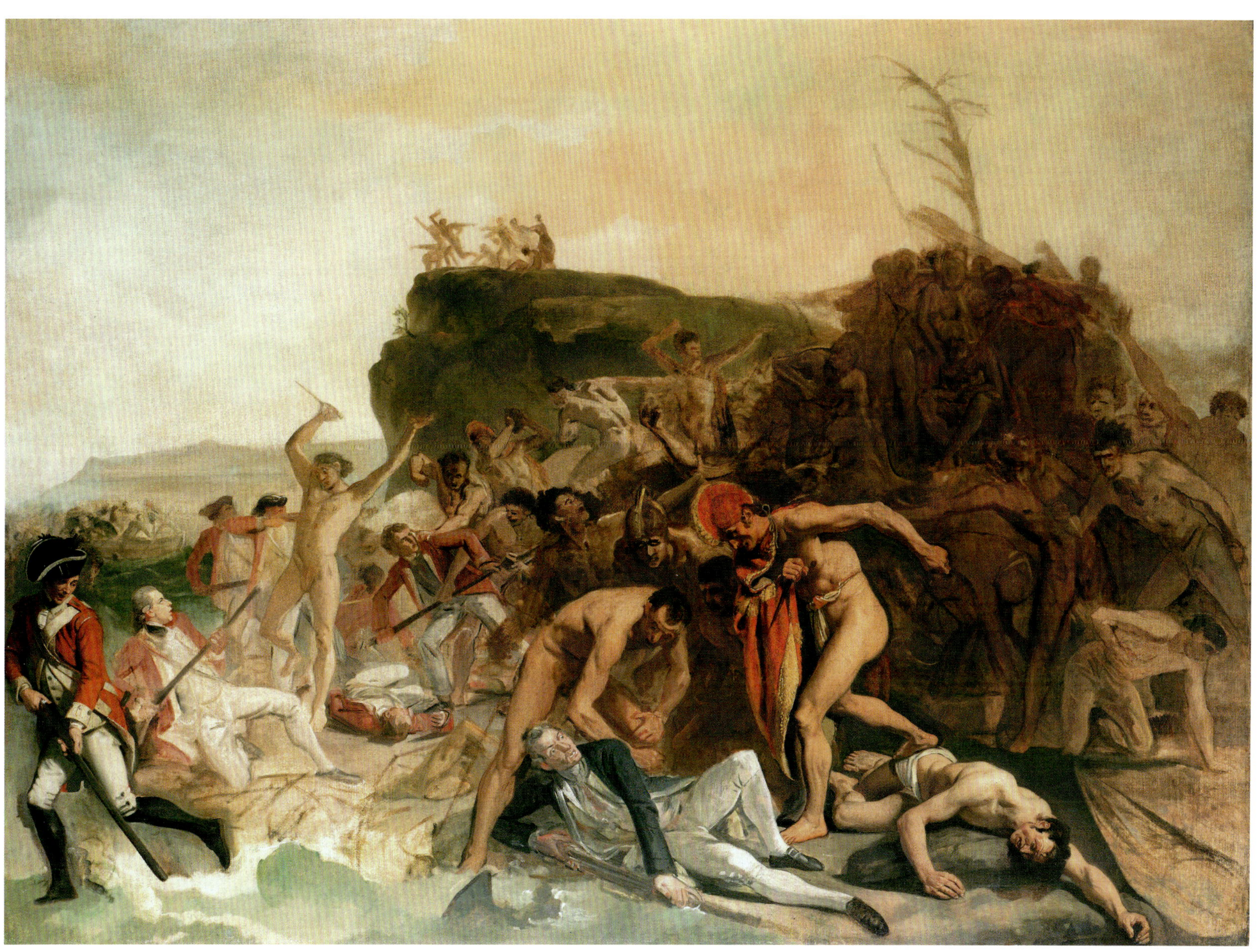

Figure 40 (cat. 107)
The Death of Captain Cook, *c.*1798, oil on canvas,
137.2 × 182.9 cm (54 × 72 in). National Maritime Museum,
Greenwich, London, Greenwich Hospital Collection

Figure 41 (cat. 111)
Self-Portrait with the Artist's Family, *c.*1802–3,
oil on canvas, 81.3 × 104.1 cm (32 × 41 in).
Private collection

In the late 1790s there is evidence of a significant diminution in the quality of Zoffany's work and an inability to complete projects, including his last major modern subject picture, *The Death of Captain Cook* (fig. 40). In 1798 Zoffany's exhibits at the Royal Academy included an unidentified portrait of 'A Professor of the Harp'. Circumstantial evidence suggests that the exhibit may have been a portrait of the German-born musician, John Erhardt Weippert.[71] Sadly, the portrait, which is untraced, provided for one critic 'incontrovertible proofs of the decay of abilities. M. Zoffani has fought a good fight; but Garrick retired from the stage in due season.'[72] Another critic, while giving 'honourable notice' to the sixty-five-year-old Zoffany and several other established artists, looked towards a younger generation and paid 'a proper tribute of praise … to the great abilities displayed by Mr. Turner, a young artist'.[73] At the beginning of 1798 it had been reported that 'Sir John Zoffani, though at a very advanced period of life, is again preparing to visit Bengal as an Artist, having obtained the Company's permission to proceed thither, for the express purpose of practicing in his profession as a Painter'.[74] By the summer he had abandoned any such plans. The remainder of his time was spent in his adopted homeland, tinkering with his pictures in his Thameside home, watching his daughters grow, marry and produce grandchildren (fig. 41). And, until he became infirm, he continued to socialize with friends and to take an active interest in the affairs of the Royal Academy.[75] He could look back on an extraordinary career spanning six decades – and still make the occasional excursion to Norwood in search of gypsies.

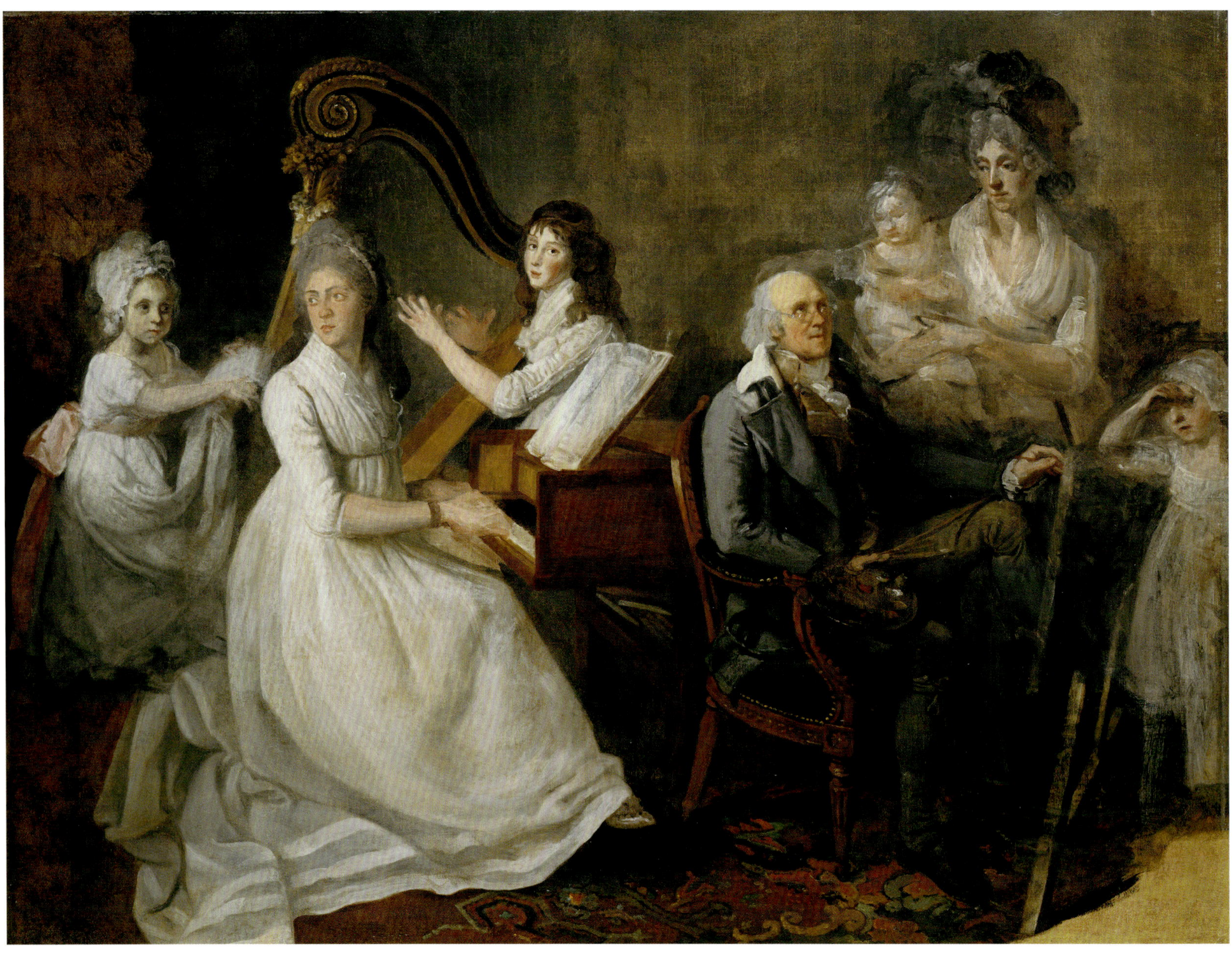

1. Farington 1978–84, vol. 3 (1979), 1051. The visit to Norwood, described to Farington by Thomas Daniell, was made on Wednesday 29 August 1798.
2. See Eric Otto Winstet, 'The Norwood Gypsies and their vocabulary', *Journal of the Gypsy Lore Society*, 1915, vol. 9, no. 3, 129–65.
3. 'The Gypsies at Norwood, and Diana and Calista', were among several unfinished sketches in Zoffany's posthumous studio sale, Robins 1811, no. 63 (9 May).
4. Pasquin n.d., 34.
5. For early investigations into the linguistic ties between the Romany and India, see Johann Christian Christoph Rüdiger, *Von der Sprache und Herkunft der Zigeuner aus Indien* (Leipzig, 1782); H.M.G. Grellman, *Dissertation on the Gypsies*, trans. Mathew Raper (London, 1787); William Marsden, 'Observations on the language of the people commonly called Gypsies. In a Letter to Sir Joseph Banks, Bart. P.R.S. From Mr. Marsden, F.S.A.', *Archaeologia*, 7, 1785.
6. William T. Whitley, *Art in England 1800–1820*, Cambridge, 1928, 226–8.
7. Farington 1978–84, vol. 13, 4495 (23 April 1814).
8. Manners & Williamson 1920, 151.
9. Sitwell 1936, 22–3.
10. See Treadwell 2009, 3–4.
11. Sitwell 1936, 43.
12. Ellis Waterhouse, *Painting in Britain, 1530–1790*, London, 1953, 219.
13. For Farington's biographical notes on Zoffany, see vols. 2 and 4 of Farington's MS notebooks on artists, the Royal Library, Windsor, published in Millar 1966, 37–9.
14. Zoffany's posthumous studio sale, 9 May 1811, nos. 17–25, included 57 'Studies and Academy Figures', at least some of which may well have been made in Rome.
15. Webster 1976, 31.
16. Webster 1976, 47.
17. A trawl through the online seventeenth- and eighteenth-century Burney Collection of newspapers at the British Library has revealed all these variations on the spelling of Zoffany's name.
18. See for example his letter to George Huddesford of 1775 in Webster 1976, 625.
19. It has been stated, incorrectly, that a picture of a young boy holding a bird's nest (Mozart Museum, Salzburg) is a portrait of Wolfgang Amadeus Mozart by Zoffany. See Treadwell 2009, 153–4 (repr.). It has also been asserted recently that the portrait of a girl called Anna Maria Mozart (*Portrait of a Young Girl at Chocolate*) was painted by Zoffany as a result of the visit by Leopold Mozart. See Daniel N. Leeson, *The Mozart Cache: The Discovery and Examination of a Previously Unknown Collection of Mozartiana*, Bloomington, Ind., 2008, 21–7. However, the portrait in question is clearly not by Zoffany. Also, a portrait, said to be Leopold Mozart by Zoffany, was exhibited at Fishel, Adler and Schwartz, New York, 1897, by the art dealer Julius D. Ichenhauser. See *New York Times*, 11 April 1897. For an image of what appears to be the portrait in question see http://www.corbisimages.com/Search#q=zoffany (accessed 14 Jan. 2011). The painting is not, however, by Zoffany.
20. On 19 December 1763 Zoffany joined the King's Arm Lodge, No. 28. On 21 February 1780 he joined the Thatched House Tavern (the Lodge of Nine Muses) and on 27 March 1793, the Pilgrim Lodge. See Webster 2011, 95, 385–6, 555; Treadwell 2009, 127–8.
21. See Papendiek 1887.
22. See Webster 2011, 97–8.
23. Webster 2011, 65–8.
24. See Treadwell 2009, 82, citing Manners & Williamson 1920, 13–14.
25. For Mortimer and Zuccarelli, see Angelo 1828–30, vol. 1, 139–40, 360–61; for Ramsay, see Whitley 1928, vol. 1, 202.
26. 'Sir Joshua agreed to give a hundred guineas for the picture; Lord Carlisle half an hour after offered Reynolds twenty to part with it, which the Knight generously refused, resigned his intended purchase to the lord, and the emolument to his brother artist. (He is a gentleman!)': Mary Moser to Henry Fuseli, 26 July 1770, in David H. Weinglass, *The Collected English Letters of Henry Fuseli*, New York and London, 1982, 11. *The London Chronicle* (1–3 May 1770), which also reported that Reynolds had given the money to Zoffany, went on to state: 'This picture is so much esteemed that we hear Lord Ossory would have given fifty guineas more for it.' Joseph Farington noted sometime later that Reynolds had donated a £20 profit on the deal to the Royal Academy Fund. See Farington's MS notes on Zoffany in Millar 1966, 38.
27. 'Good, like the actors and the whole better than Hogarth's.' See Webster 2011, 187.
28. See Hargraves 2005, 67; Treadwell 2009, 168.
29. Millar 1966, 38.
30. *The Middlesex Journal or Chronicle of Liberty*, 9–11 Jan. 1772.
31. Thomas Gainsborough to the Hon. Constantine Phipps, 13 Feb. 1772, in Hayes 2001, 94, letter 56.
32. *The General Evening Post*, 7–9 May 1772.
33. 'Mr Zoffani, the celebrated painter, has, we hear, engaged, under penalty of 500l. to go out with Dr. Solander, so that the news-paper reports of his intention in this respect are not by any means destitute of foundation', *General Evening Post*, 14–17 Dec. 1771. For conjecture over Zoffany's financial losses over the abandonment of the voyage, see Webster 2011, 271.
34. Zoffany had rented London Stile House in early 1764. See Treadwell 2009, 95 n.37, 219.

35. The auction catalogue is reproduced in Webster 2011, Appendix 7, 639–43.

36. Tino Gipponi, *Maria e Richard Cosway*, Lodi, 1998, 11.

37. Lewis 1937–83, vol. 24, 33, Horace Mann to Horace Walpole, 23 Aug. 1774.

38. Zoffany to Joseph Banks, 15 Jan. 1774, in Webster 2011, p. 299.

39. Webster 2011, 316.

40. Webster 2011, 303.

41. Webster 2011, 313.

42. Webster 2011, 353.

43. Webster 2011, 349.

44. Whitley 1928, vol. 1, 313–14.

45. James Northcote to his brother Samuel, 11 Sept. 1778: Northcote Papers, Royal Academy of Arts, NOR/44.

46. Treadwell 2009, 278.

47. 'Their eldest child was a boy, who died from an accident at sixteen months old. This calamity nearly lost poor Zoffany his life; indeed, he never thoroughly overcame it' (Papendiek 1887, vol. 1, 86).

48. Gainsborough exhibited his full-length portrait of Giovanna Bacelli (Tate) at the Royal Academy in 1782, while Thomas Lawrence's full-length portrait of Elizabeth Farren (Metropolitan Museum, New York) was exhibited there in 1790.

49. James Gandon and Thomas J. Mulvany, *The Life of James Gandon, Esq., with original notices of contemporary artists, and fragments of essays*, Dublin, 1846, 67.

50. George C. Williamson, *Life and Works of Ozias Humphry, R.A.*, London, 1918, 119; *Whitehall Evening Post*, 11–13 Jan. 1785.

51. Gavin Hamilton to Ozias Humphry, 15 Feb. 1789. Humphry Papers, Royal Academy of Arts, HU/IV/18.

52. Webster 2011, 454.

53. Webster 2011, 455.

54. Webster 2011, 526.

55. Webster 2011, 513, 515.

56. Webster 2011, 515.

57. Pasquin n.d., 34–5n, cited in Webster 1976, 529.

58. Horace Walpole noted on 18 August 1789: 'Zoffany, the painter, arrived a few days ago from India, in more wealth than health' (Horace Walpole, *Anecdotes of Painting in England* [1760–95], ed. F.W. Hilles and P. Daghlian, 5 vols., New Haven and London, 1937, vol. 5, 84). See also the *English Chronicle*, 10–12 Sept. 1789, which referred, in uncannily similar terms, to 'Zoffany the painter, who is lately returned from India with better fortune than health'.

59. 'Zoffani is dead in Asia', *St James's Chronicle or British Evening Post*, 2–5 May 1789. Curiously, a month earlier it had been reported in another newspaper: 'Zoffani, the ingenious artist, we are informed, is not dead, as reported, but in good health and circumstances in Calcutta', *Diary of Woodfall's Register*, 2 April 1789. Two decades earlier the *General Evening Post* (1–3 Dec. 1772) had reported 'DIED … Lately in Italy, Mr. Zoffanii, an eminent portrait painter'.

60. *Public Advertiser*, 11 March 1791.

61. The suggestion was first published by James Elmes, in *The Arts and Artists* (Elmes 1825, vol. 1, 12). See also Webster 2011, 505. For Elmes, see Tom Devonshire Jones, 'Annals of the Fine Arts. James Elmes (1782–1862), architect: from youthful editor to aged gospeller', *British Art Journal*, vol. x, no. 2, Winter 2009, 67–72.

62. A. Pasquin, *A Critical Guide to the Exhibition of the Royal Academy for 1796*. London, 1796, 20.

63. Ronald Paulson, *Representations of Revolution (1789–1820)*, New Haven and London, 1983, 151, 153 n. 70; see also Pressly 1999, 119, fig. 83.

64. Manners & Williamson 1920, 133.

65. Webster 2011, 583–5.

66. Farington 1978–84, vol. 2, 517, 1 April 1796.

67. *True Briton*, 2 April 1796.

68. Webster 2011, 586.

69. Penelope Treadwell identifies the work with the painting of a signwriter in Government House, Ottawa. However, the picture in question would appear not to be by Zoffany or a portrayal of Townsend. Treadwell 2009, 414 (repr.), 416.

70. Webster 2011, 585.

71. See Highfill *et al.*, vol. 15, 335–7. Mary Webster has suggested that the picture may have been *King David Playing the Harp*, which Zoffany presented to his parish church, St Nicholas, Chiswick, and which Webster dates to around 1795. See Webster 2011, 593. However, the description in the Royal Academy catalogue makes it seem more likely that it was a portrait of Weippert or possibly another prominent professional harpist of the period.

72. *Whitehall Evening Post*, 10–12 May 1798.

73. *London Chronicle*, 21–24 April 1798.

74. *Whitehall Evening Post*, 27–30 Jan. 1798.

75. On 14 March 1809 Joseph Farington reported at a dinner party: 'Miss Green told us Zoffany's faculties were gone. He is become Childish' (Farington 1978–84, vol. 9, 3421).

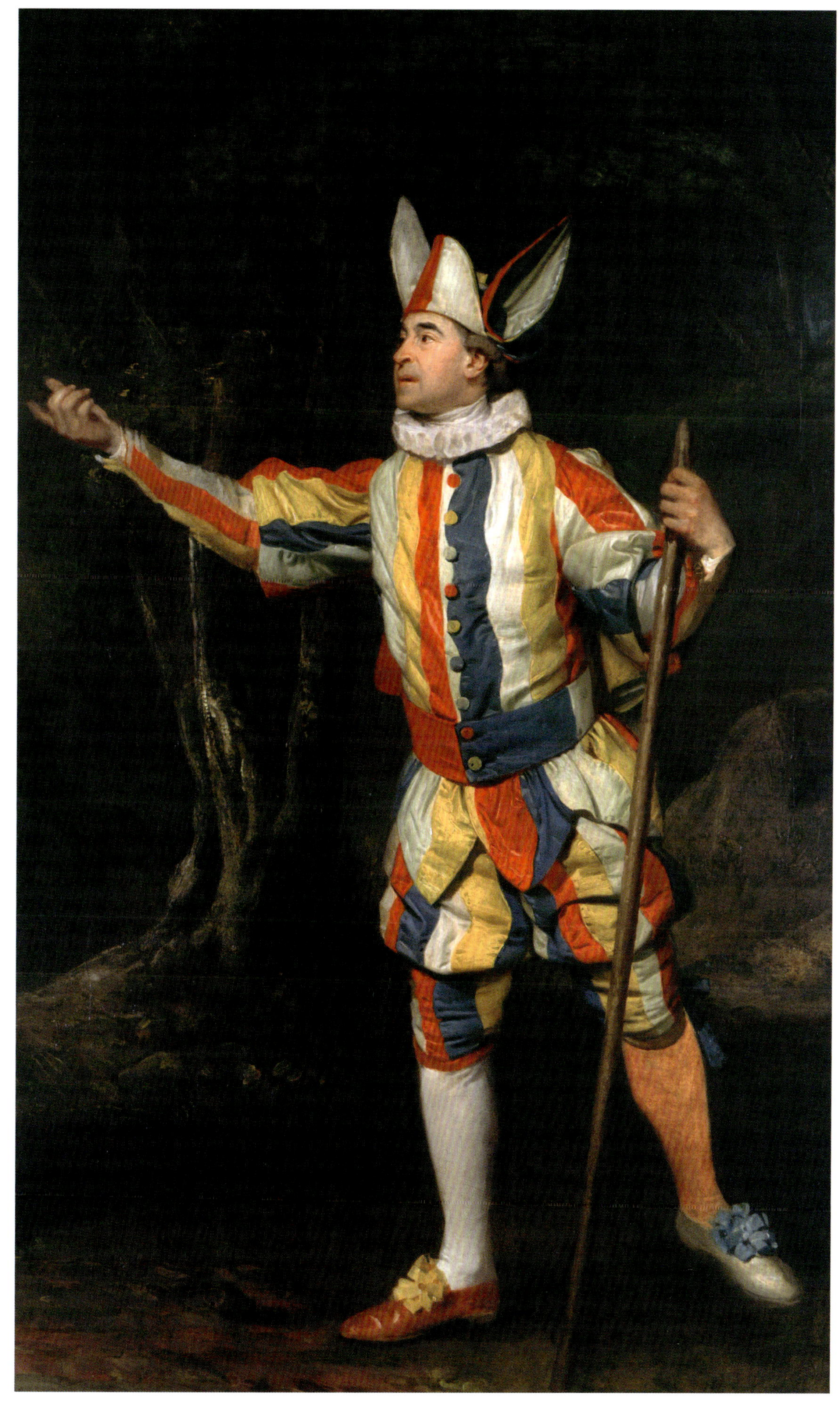

Robin Simon

'Strong impressions of their art': Zoffany & the Theatre

Zoffany's achievement as a painter of the theatre was unprecedented in its extent and variety. Study of the drama was recommended to painters by theorists of the Académie royale de peinture et de sculpture in Paris, but only as a preparation for 'history' paintings, where the retention of the recognizable likeness of any actor would have been a matter for censure. It was different in England, chiefly because of the pioneering works created by Zoffany's great predecessor William Hogarth, who was fundamental in establishing a native school that could rival the achievements of those in Europe. Hogarth made explicit his debt to the theatre, and for several early works created around 1730, including *Falstaff Examining his Recruits* (The Guinness Family) and his four paintings after *The Beggar's Opera* (example in Tate Britain), he made preparatory sketches direct from the stage. In these compositions Hogarth ensured that individual actors were recognizable and – a key point – that he was showing a precise moment in the action.

In Hogarth's masterpiece of 1745, *Garrick as Richard III* (fig. 43), he created a portrait of a famous actor in character that also bore a marked resemblance to academic history painting. The setting refers to the most celebrated French composition of the preceding century, Charles Le Brun's *Tent of Darius* (1661; Versailles), while Richard's pose echoes that of the main figure in a famous antique sculpture, the *Laocoön*. At the same time Garrick's likeness is unmistakable, and Hogarth himself sometimes referred to this painting as a 'portrait'.

Figure 42 (cat. 32)
Thomas King as Touchstone in 'As You Like It', 1780, oil on canvas, 91 × 55.5 cm (35⅜ × 21⅞ in). The Garrick Club, London

Figure 43
William Hogarth, *Garrick as Richard III*, *c.*1745, oil on canvas, 190.5 × 250.8 cm (75 × 98¾ in). National Museums Liverpool, Walker Art Gallery

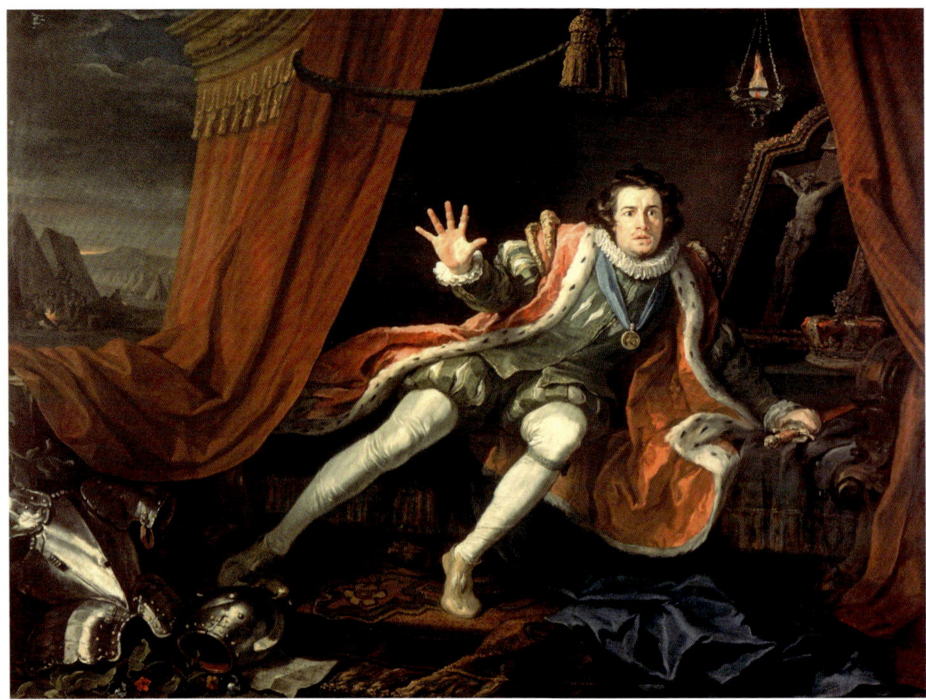

As an artist trained in Europe, Zoffany was familiar with the rules of history painting, and in adapting himself to painting the London stage, he retained a crucial element of academic practice: the axiom that any history painting should be based on a few words or lines in a chosen text, as Hogarth's paintings of the theatre had also been.[1] Zoffany's two versions of the pivotal scene in *Macbeth* reveal how he observed this rule: they differ from each other in a slight shift in the moment depicted, which can be traced to different phrases within the same few lines of dialogue (fig. 44). Zoffany's paintings borrow a kind of respectability from their reflection of this central tenet of academic practice, but at the same time they follow Hogarth's very British precedent of focusing on the particular likenesses of the actors portrayed. They are 'history' pictures of a kind, but they are also portraits.

The extent to which Zoffany's images are true to their stage setting or differ from it varies from one painting to the next. *David Garrick and Mrs Pritchard in Macbeth* (fig. 44), for example, does not exactly record the production as it appeared on stage. For one thing, the action is reversed from stage right to left. To take another instance, *Venice Preserv'd* (fig. 45), based on the play of the same name by Thomas Otway, shows a view of a Venetian church cupola and canal that is most unlikely to have been available as a backdrop. Indeed, we know that the scene in question (Act IV, Scene 2) took place in an interior: the directions specify 'The Senate-house' and call for the seating of at least eleven characters. There is no doubt, however, about the precise words illustrated in this painting, 'Oh! Mercy!', uttered at the moment when Belvedira sinks to her knees in supplication. *The Clandestine Marriage* (fig. 46) is set in a landscape of a kind and of a depth far removed from anything possible in the theatre, and suggests a Watteauesque scene of gallantry.

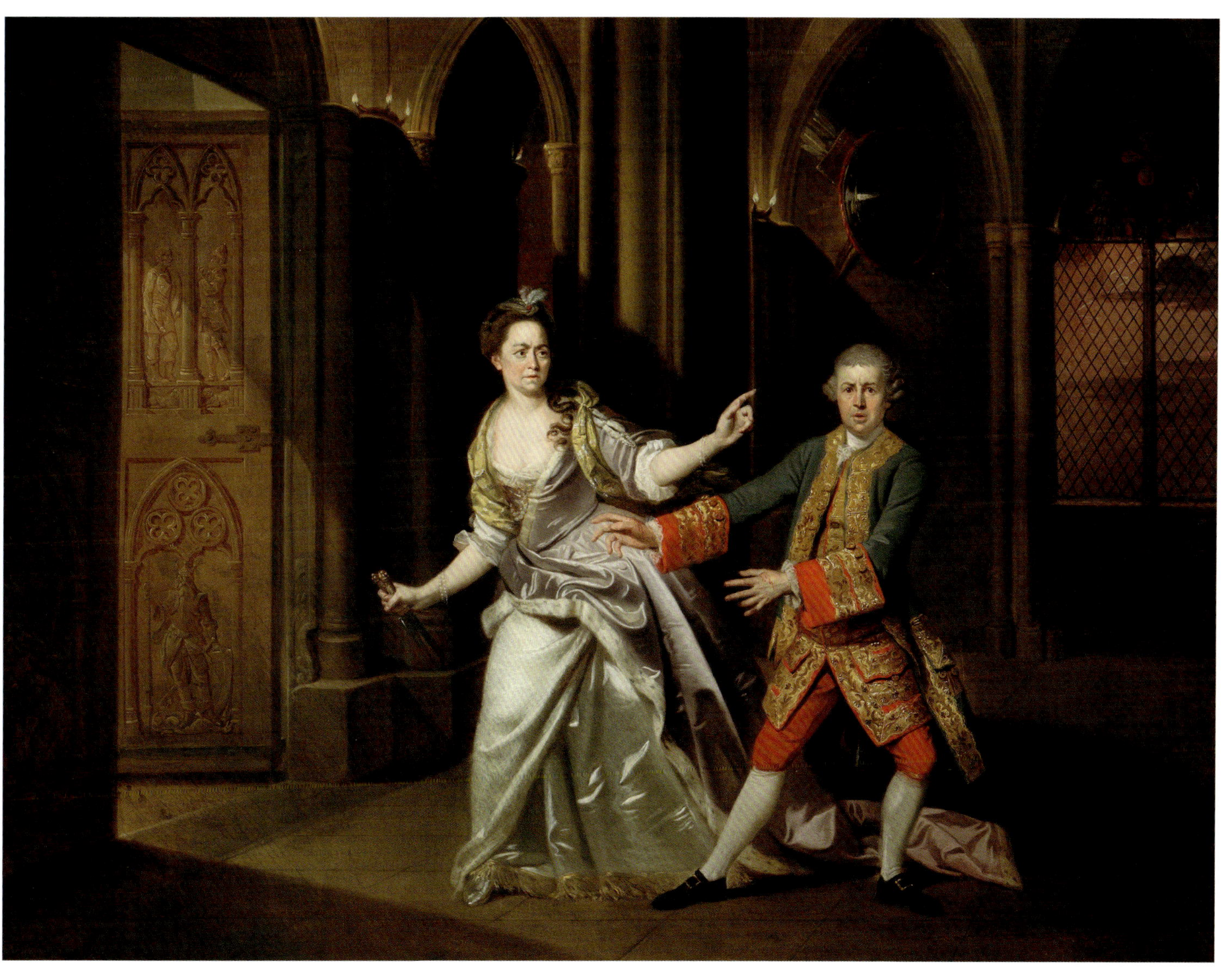

Figure 44 (cat. 28)
*David Garrick and Mrs Pritchard
in 'Macbeth'*, 1768, oil on canvas,
102 × 127.5 cm (40⅛ × 50¼ in).
The Garrick Club, London

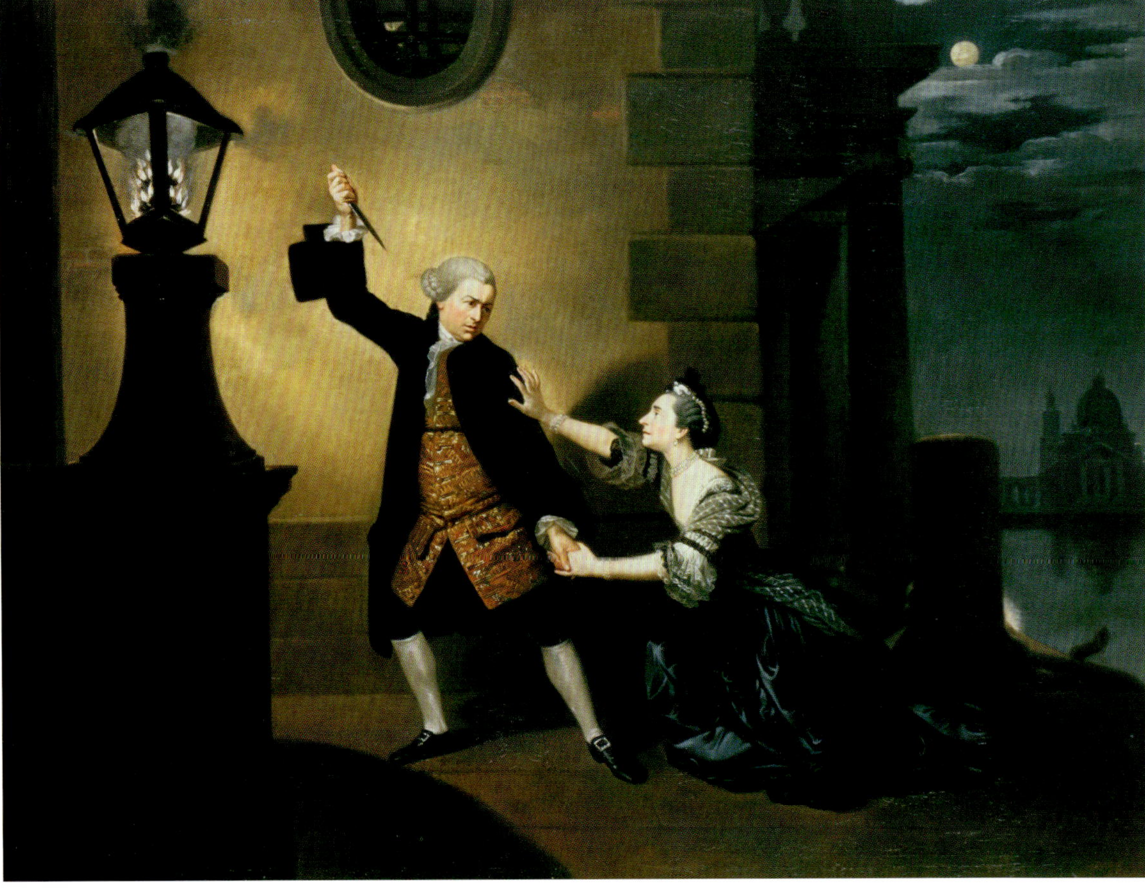

Figure 45 (cat. 19)
*David Garrick and Mrs Cibber
as Jaffier and Belvidera in 'Venice
Preserv'd'*, 1762, oil on canvas,
101.6 × 127 cm (40 × 50 in).
The Holburne Museum, Bath

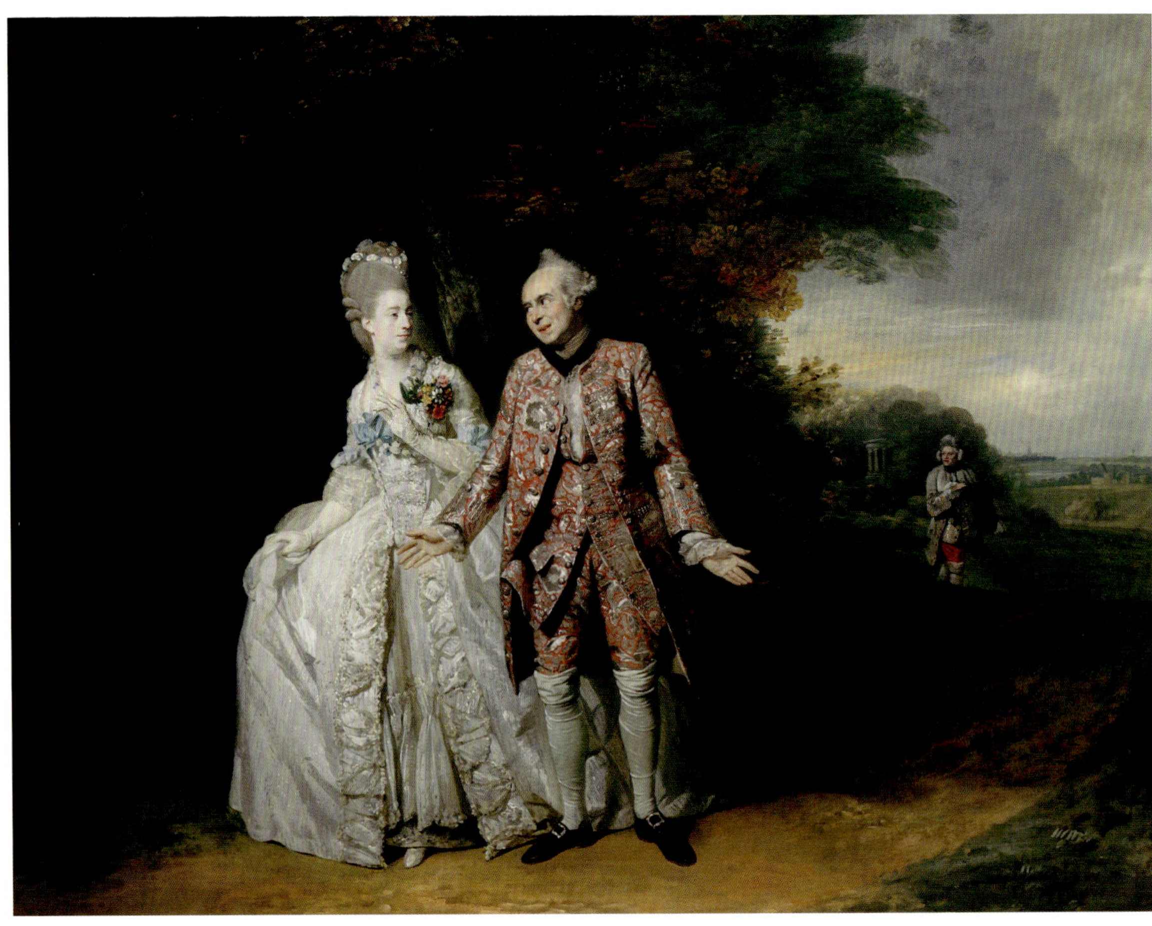

Figure 46 (cat. 31)
*Sophia Baddeley and Thomas King in
'The Clandestine Marriage'*, 1771,
oil on canvas,
94 × 125.5 cm (37 × 49⅜ in).
The Garrick Club, London

The drunken incident in *The Provok'd Wife* (fig. 47; see also cat. 20) is set in a recognizable corner of the Piazza in Covent Garden, something well beyond the resources of the scenery in Drury Lane. William Powell in *Cymbeline* (cat. 25) appears in a naturalistic landscape that seems almost to anticipate the studio sets of inter-war Hollywood, although its implausibility as a theatrical set mirrors the rich improbability of the action. The realistic impression conveyed by the interior of *The Alchemist* (fig. 47), on the other hand, is especially interesting because it is created by some of Zoffany's most brilliant passages of painting. If he did not actually add to established props in the complex still life at the left of the painting, his virtuoso depiction of them

and of the fall of light that describes them – which continues on into a lofty interior – convinces us, more than any theatrical effects could do, that we are looking into a 'real-life' room rather than a stage set.

The dramatic lighting effects of Zoffany's more spacious compositions, so often accompanied by an elaboration of the setting, achieve a sense of drama that, paradoxically, could only be aspired to on the stage and never so naturalistically accomplished as it could be in paint. In contrast with the generous space suggested in these paintings are such relatively cramped compositions as *The Mayor of Garret* (fig. 49), *The Devil upon Two Sticks* (fig. 50) and *Love in a Village* (fig. 51).

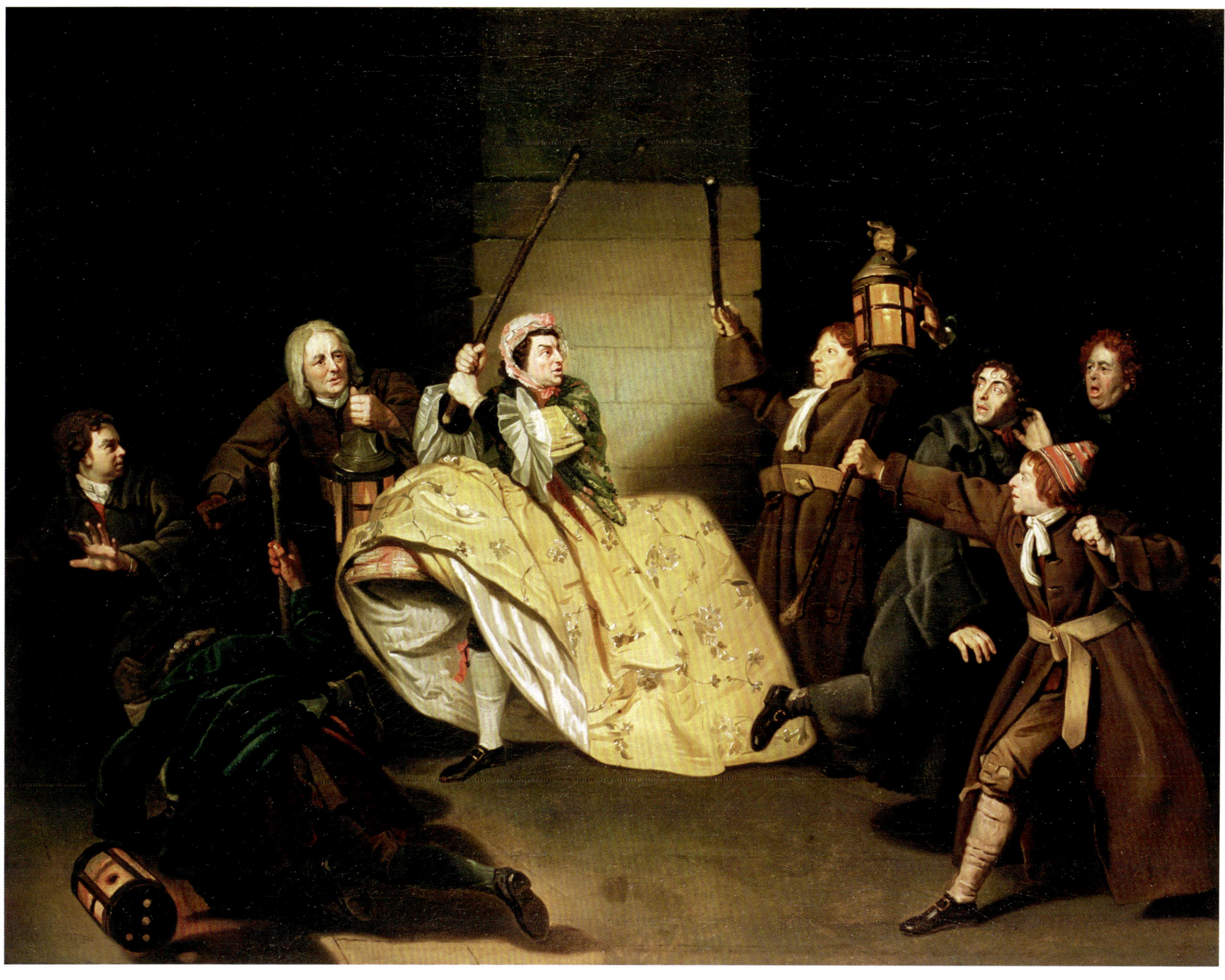

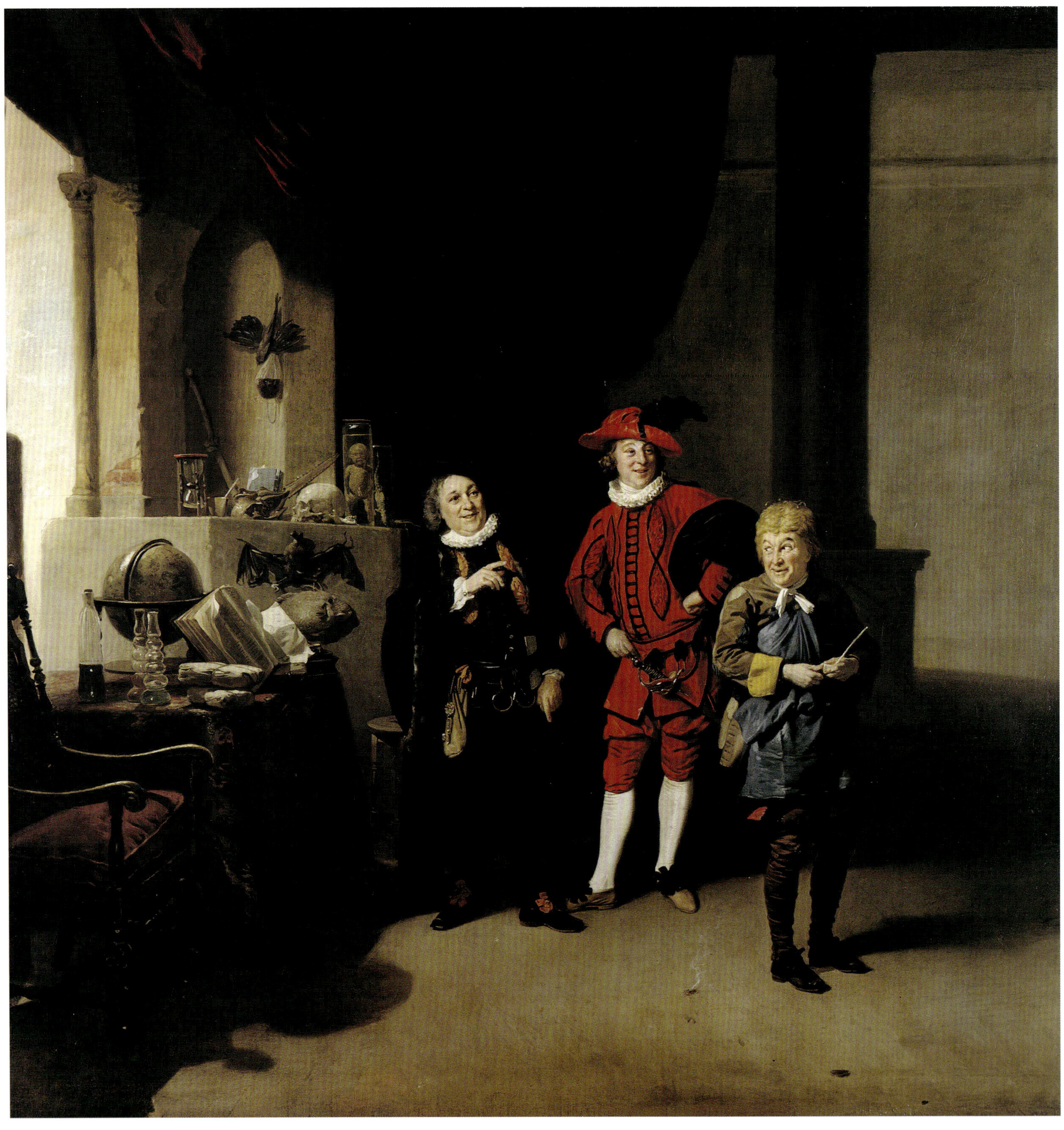

Figure 47
David Garrick as Sir John Brute in 'The Provok'd Wife',
1763, oil on canvas, 99 × 126 cm (39 × 49½ in).
Wolverhampton Art Gallery

Figure 48
David Garrick with Edmund Burton and John Palmer in the
'The Alchymist', 1770, oil on canvas, 104 × 99 cm (41 × 39 in).
Private collection

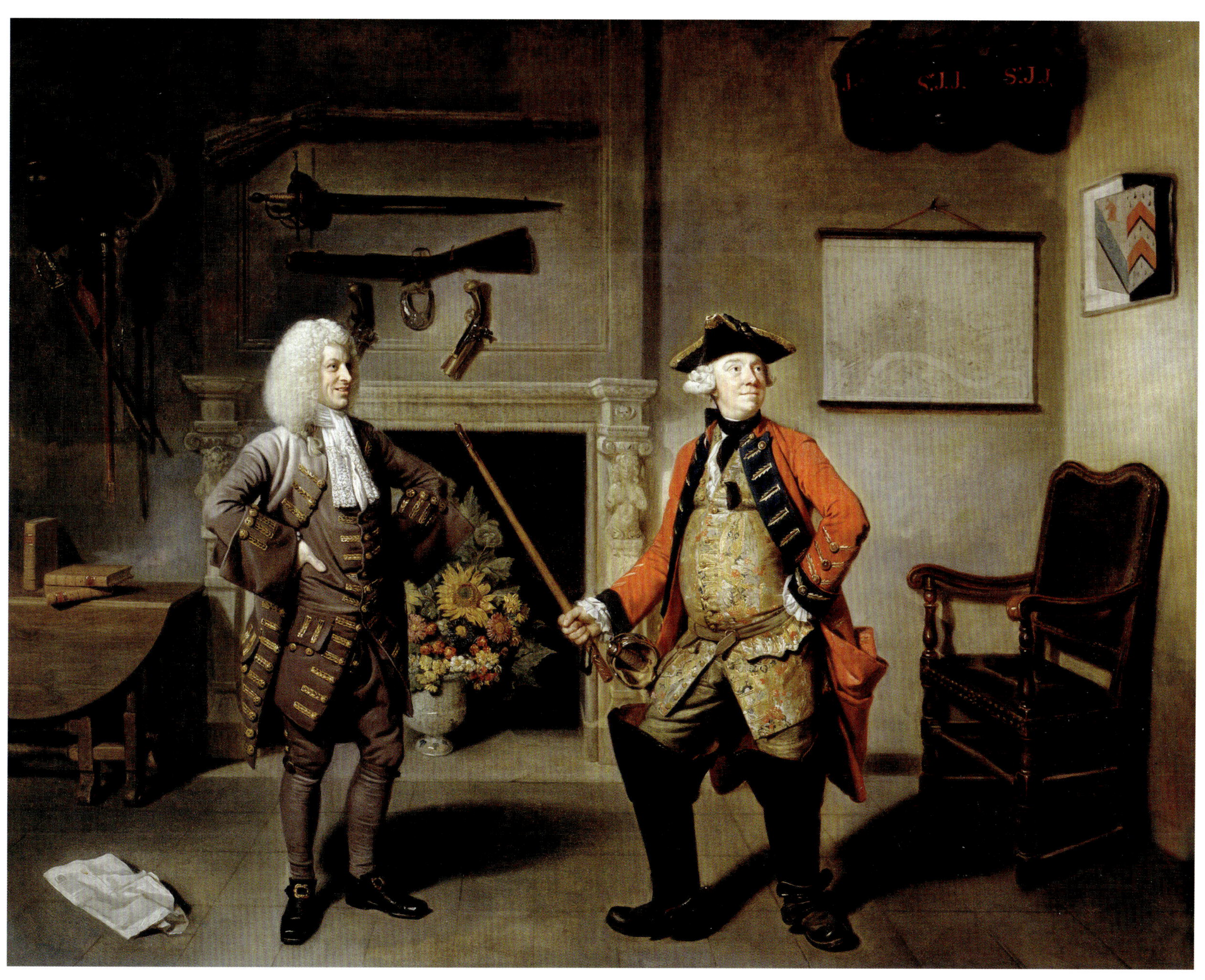

Figure 49 (cat. 23)
Samuel Foote as Major Sturgeon and Hayes as Sir Jacob Jollup in
'The Mayor of Garret', 1763–4,
oil on canvas, 101.6 × 127 cm (40 × 50 in).
Castle Howard Collection

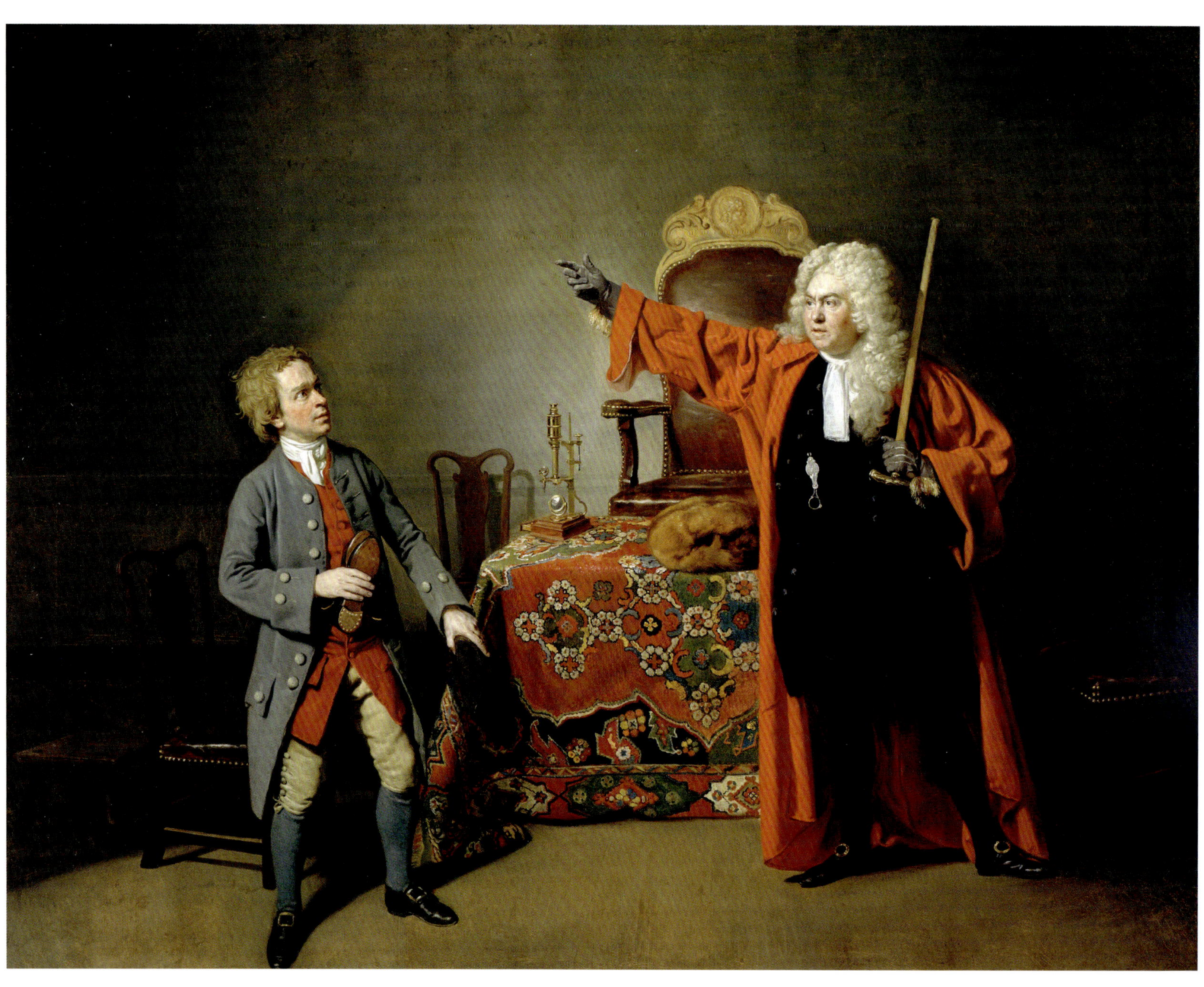

Figure 50
Samuel Foote as Dr Hellebore and Thomas Weston as Last in 'The Devil upon Two Sticks', 1768, oil on canvas, 101.6 × 128.3 cm (40 × 50½ in). Castle Howard Collection

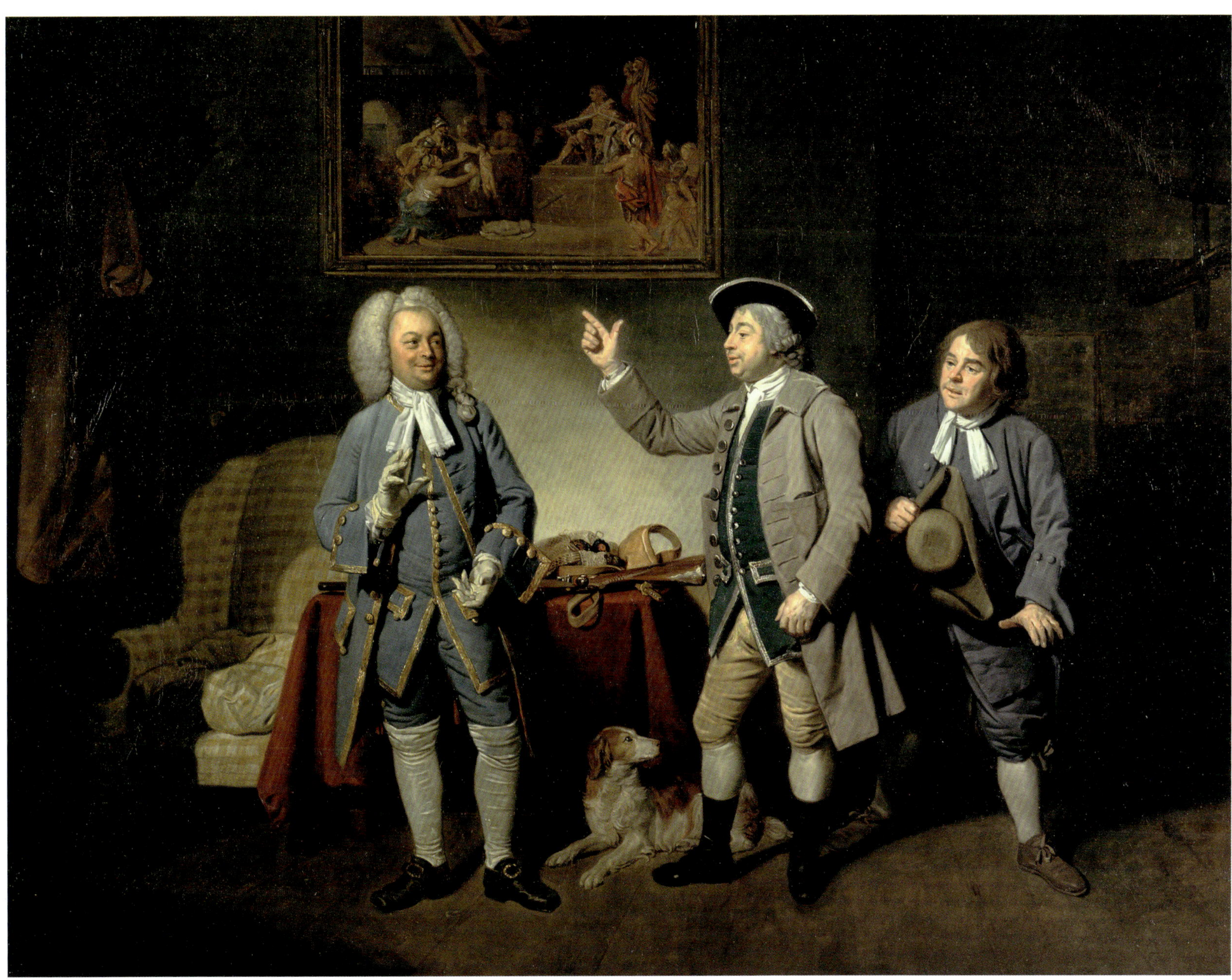

Figure 51 (cat. 26)
Edward Shuter, John Beard and John Dunstall
in Isaac Bickerstaffe's 'Love in a Village', 1767,
oil on canvas, 130.2 × 165.1 cm (51¼ × 65 in).
Yale Center for British Art, Paul Mellon Collection

Again, however, the lighting Zoffany deploys is never that of the contemporary theatre: these 'constrained' interior scenes are uniformly lit in a way that makes them eminently legible, but it was an effect achieved, as we know to have been the case, within a professional painting studio.[2] In each of them the space is too shallow accurately to reflect the stage on which the performance took place. Even the simplest scenery 'flat' is omitted in *The Devil upon Two Sticks*, where the props are set close against a plain backdrop. This is taken even further in *John Moody as Foigard in 'The Beaux Stratagem'* (fig. 52; see also cat. 30), where the actor is similarly set close against, and casts a shadow on, what can only be a studio curtain. Compared with, say, the wide-open spaces of *The Clandestine Marriage*, Zoffany's exaggeration in these compositions is entirely in the opposite direction. But there is method in his manipulation. Zoffany still suggests the theatre sufficiently for his overriding aim to remain unaffected, which was the presentation of convincing portraits of individual actors seen at their most characteristic moments. By artificially compressing the space in which they perform, Zoffany intensifies the sense of intimate contact with the actors that was an important aspect of the experience of the Georgian theatre: it was to be some time before the auditoriums were expanded in response to the much larger effects in which the Kembles excelled, in the generation that succeeded Garrick.

Zoffany's nuanced approach enabled him to create a distinctive effect: that of depicting the actors both in and out of character at the same time. This duality lies at the heart of his achievement; but it also reflects the contemporary practice of a number of leading comic actors who, in a tradition that survives in the British pantomime, would interact, sometimes even verbally, with the audience during performance. This is clearly seen in *The Mayor of Garret* where both actors are making the most of one of Samuel Foote's characteristic moments of high farce (see cat. 23). Indeed, the picture appears to record an incident of 'corpsing', as both actors struggle to regain their composure. This accords with Foote's particular theatrical strength, which was founded on his own personality and celebrity in the theatre that he ran, the Haymarket.[3]
The Devil upon Two Sticks, to take only the most famous such instance, featured a central character – played by Foote – who had lost a leg, was fitted with an artificial one, and who hobbled along with the aid of a golden cane, all of which was true of Foote (see cat. 24). Foote might also throw in an impression of a fellow actor, perhaps Garrick or Macklin, as a reminder of the uncanny mimicry that had made his reputation in the same theatre at the start of his career.

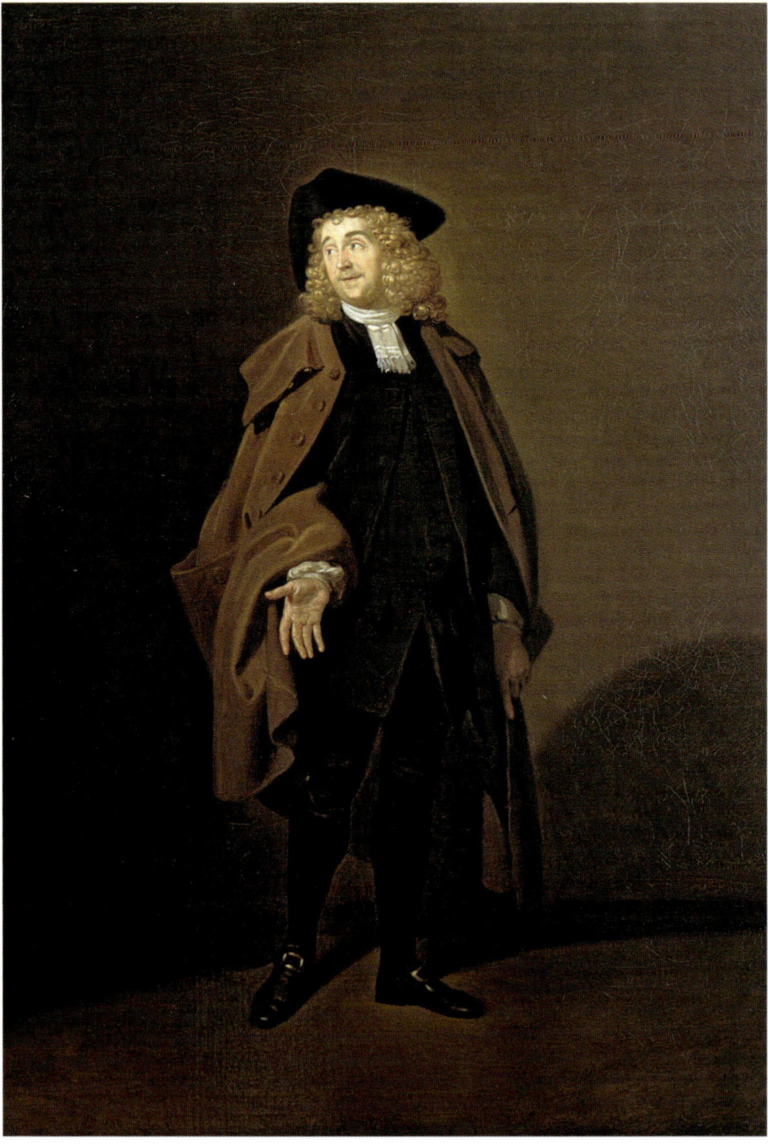

Figure 52
John Moody as Father Foigard in 'The Beaux Stratagem', 1763–4, oil on canvas, 88.2 × 60.3 cm (34¾ × 23¾ in). Private collection

Once his 'serious' career as actor-manager and playwright
was launched, Foote would also insert references to his previous
productions in any new play. Like an actor shifting in and out of
character, the audience momentarily emerges on such occasions
from its engagement with the drama, only swiftly to be drawn
back into it. It is a device famously employed by Mozart towards
the climax of *Don Giovanni*. Leporello hears a few notes (of
'Non più andrai') that recall the opera performed in the same
Prague theatre earlier that year (1787), *Le Nozze di Figaro*, and
announces: 'Questo poi la conosco pur troppo' ('I know this one
only too well').[4] It offers a frisson of pleasure that is as old as
the stage itself and was identified in the works of Shakespeare

Figure 53
Jeffery Dunstan as Dr Last in 'Dr Last in his Chariot', c.1782–3,
oil on canvas, 56 × 39 cm (22 × 15¼ in).
The Holburne Museum, Bath

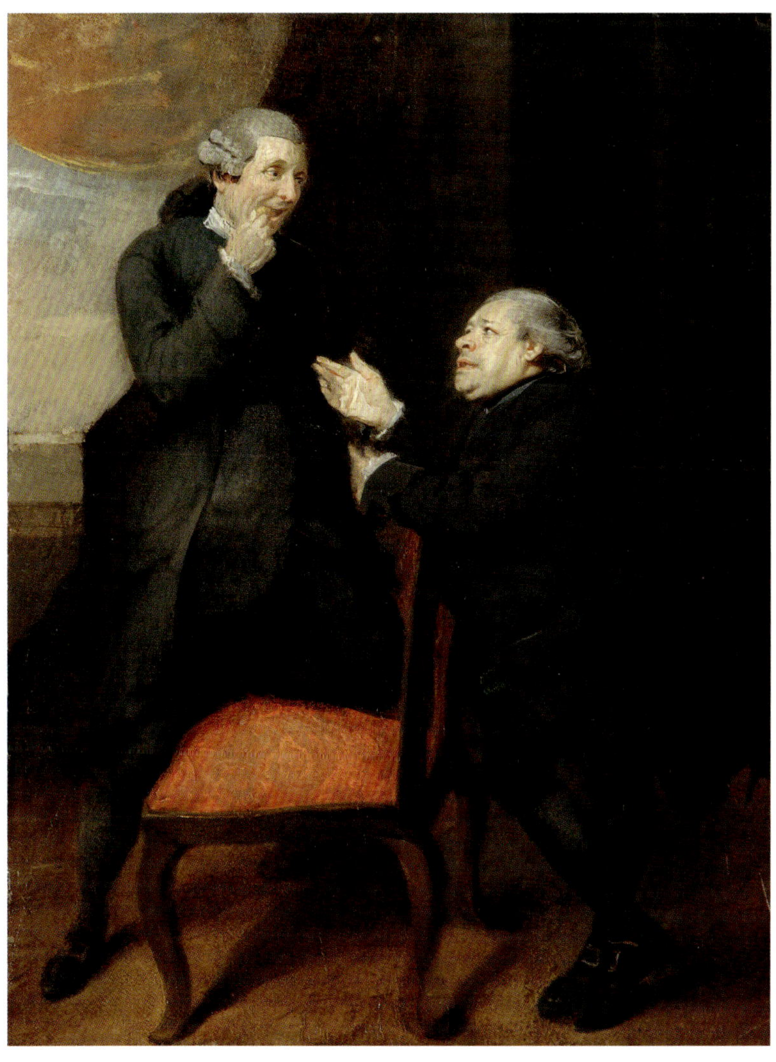

by Leslie Bethell. In *Twelfth Night* (Act III, Scene 4) Fabian
remarks: 'If this were played upon a stage now, I could condemn
it as improbable fiction.'[5]

And so it was that *The Devil upon Two Sticks*, with a plot
that revolved around topical problems at the Royal College of
Physicians, referred back to Foote's previous production, *The
Mayor of Garret*, a play that begins with allusions to the same
controversy at the Royal College, in the context of an exchange
between a dubious apothecary and a magistrate, Sir James Jollup
(the figure at the left of Zoffany's picture, fig. 49). Foote made
Jollup[6] re-appear in *The Devil upon Two Sticks* as an offstage
apothecary whom he recruits to man the fire engine, itself a
clear reference back to the fire buckets visible at the start of
the earlier play recorded by Zoffany: 'Let the engine be play'd
by old Jollup, from James-Street! Not one of the trade has a
better hand at handling a pipe … Bid old Jollup be ready to
unmask the engine at the word of command.' The practice in
the eighteenth century of exploiting celebrity went beyond the
example of Samuel Foote, although one of the most vivid
instances can be associated with a production in his theatre, in
the form of a painting newly attributed to Zoffany by Martin
Postle and Charles Greig (fig. 53).[7] This picture was formerly
in the Maugham Collection, where it was listed simply as
'Unknown subject by an unknown artist'.[8] It bears an
inscription on the stretcher giving the artist as Zoffany
(although this had long been discounted) and the information
'Foote and Weston in Dr Last'. As we shall see, although
incorrect, this is a suggestive record, because both these actors
appeared in the original production of *The Devil upon Two Sticks*
in which Foote played the Devil and Weston played the foolish
Dr Last. Spin-offs from that play provide a clue to the subject
of this picture.

Neither Foote nor Weston is portrayed in this painting.
The most striking thing to notice is that the actor on the right
is a dwarf, who can safely be identified as 'Sir' Jeffery Dunstan.[9]
He was four feet (1.2 metres) tall, with a large head and
deformed knock-kneed legs, and had been elected as 'Mayor
of Garratt' (see cat. 23 for the details of this event), at least by
1782. In doing so, he achieved extraordinary fame, which,
rather surprisingly, endured: he features prominently in many
political prints of the later 1780s and early 1790s.[10] Despite the
lack of any acting experience, on 30 December 1782 Dunstan
was cast in *The Examination of Dr Last before the College of
Physicians*, which formed a subsidiary entertainment at the
Haymarket Theatre (Foote had died in 1777) on the benefit
night of the well-known actor William ('Luke') Gardner.

The playbill survives, illustrated not by one of the many established actors in the company but by Dunstan (fig. 54), described as 'The present worthy Mayor of Garrat'. This 'afterpiece', as such entertainments were known, had been created out of the central episode in *The Devil upon Two Sticks*, in the original production of which Gardner had played Sir Thomas Maxwell. When it came to the big night, alas, Dunstan 'dried', as Charles Lamb recalled:

> In the flower of his popularity an attempt was made to bring him [Dunstan] out upon the stage (at which of the winter theatres I forget, but I well remember the anecdote) in the part of Doctor Last. The announcement drew a crowded house; but notwithstanding infinite tutoring … when the curtain drew up, the heart of Sir Jeffery failed and he faultered [sic] on, and made nothing of his part, till the hisses of the house at last in very kindness dismissed him from the boards.[11]

In fact, this painting does not show any identifiable episode from *The Devil upon Two Sticks*. Instead, it seems that Zoffany or, more probably, whoever commissioned him, 'cast' Dunstan as the risible Dr Last in a painting derived from yet another spin-off from *The Devil upon Two Sticks*. This was *Dr Last in his Chariot*, played on stage between 21 June and 31 September 1769, although not apparently published until 1794. It was essentially a translation by Isaac Bickerstaffe of Molière's *Le Malade Imaginaire*, with scenes added by Samuel Foote. In Zoffany's painting Dunstan as Dr Last holds a phial or glass, an incident that occurs in his encounter with the hypochondriac Ailwou'd in Act III (p. 61 in the text of 1794). The dark clothes worn by both characters can also be explained at this point. Dr Last has changed into them in order, as he thinks, to be married to Ailwou'd's daughter, in a plan devised to save Ailwou'd from paying any medical fees for the rest of his life. Meanwhile Ailwou'd is stated by Last to be wearing a lawyer's wig ('I presume by your wig, sir, you belong to the law'), which in turn would explain his sober appearance. This 'expert' identification was no doubt included because Dunstan in real life earned what he could as a hawker of old wigs. The following exchange then takes place, as Last offers Ailwou'd some 'medicine', which is the probable subject of this painting: '*Dr. Last.* Well, will you swallow this now? | *Ailwou'd.* Aye, come give it to me' (Act III, p. 63). The text is very careful to prepare the audience on several occasions for the imminent appearance of a dwarf playing Dr Last. These include such references as, 'He is but a little man I am told' (Act I, p. 13). Once this expectation has been established, and Dunstan has finally appeared on stage, his stature naturally becomes the theme of several comic moments, as when Dunstan/Last takes offence

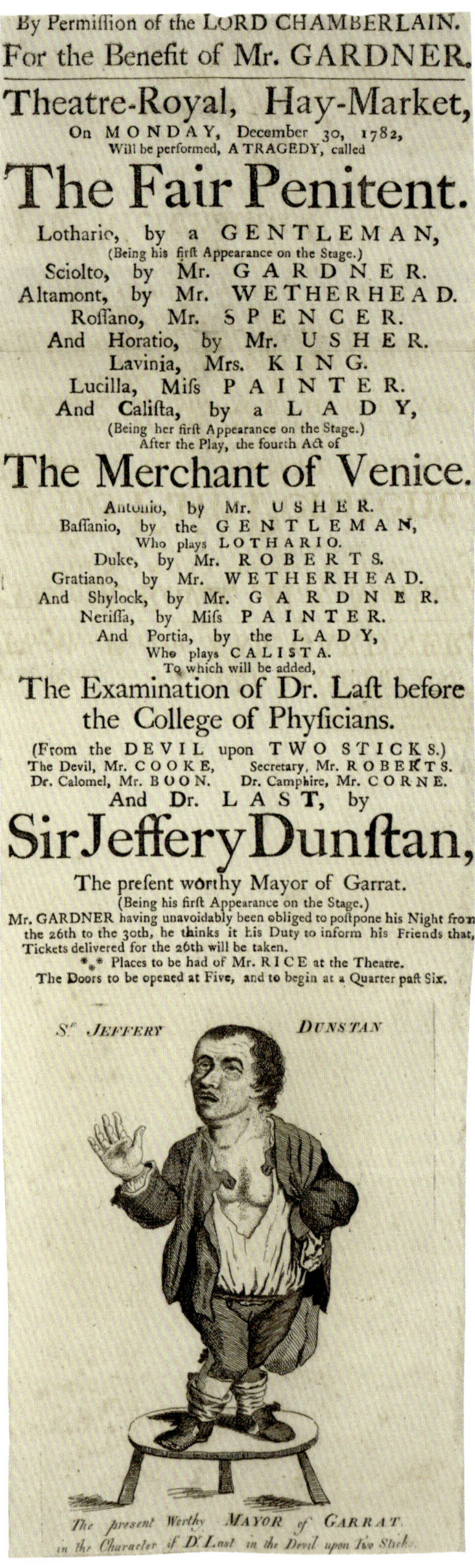

By Permiſſion of the LORD CHAMBERLAIN.
For the Benefit of Mr. GARDNER.

Theatre-Royal, Hay-Market,
On MONDAY, December 30, 1782,
Will be performed, A TRAGEDY, called

The Fair Penitent.

Lothario, by a GENTLEMAN,
(Being his firſt Appearance on the Stage.)
Sciolto, by Mr. GARDNER.
Altamont, by Mr. WETHERHEAD.
Roſſano, Mr. SPENCER.
And Horatio, by Mr. USHER.
Lavinia, Mrs. KING.
Lucilla, Miſs PAINTER.
And Caliſta, by a LADY,
(Being her firſt Appearance on the Stage.)
After the Play, the fourth Act of

The Merchant of Venice.

Antonio, by Mr. USHER.
Baſſanio, by the GENTLEMAN,
Who plays LOTHARIO.
Duke, by Mr. ROBERTS.
Gratiano, by Mr. WETHERHEAD.
And Shylock, by Mr. GARDNER.
Neriſſa, by Miſs PAINTER.
And Portia, by the LADY,
Who plays CALISTA.
To which will be added,

The Examination of Dr. Laſt before the College of Phyſicians.

(From the DEVIL upon TWO STICKS.)
The Devil, Mr. COOKE, Secretary, Mr. ROBERTS.
Dr. Calomel, Mr. BOON. Dr. Camphire, Mr. CORNE.
And Dr. LAST, by

Sir Jeffery Dunſtan,

The preſent worthy Mayor of Garrat.
(Being his firſt Appearance on the Stage.)
Mr. GARDNER having unavoidably been obliged to poſtpone his Night from the 26th to the 30th, he thinks it his Duty to inform his Friends that, Tickets delivered for the 26th will be taken.
. Places to be had of Mr. RICE at the Theatre.
The Doors to be opened at Five, and to begin at a Quarter paſt Six.

Figure 54
Playbill for the Theatre Royal, Haymarket, 30 December 1782, showing Sir Jeffery Dunstan as Dr Last in *The Examination of Dr Last before the College of Physicians*. By Permission of the Folger Shakespeare Library

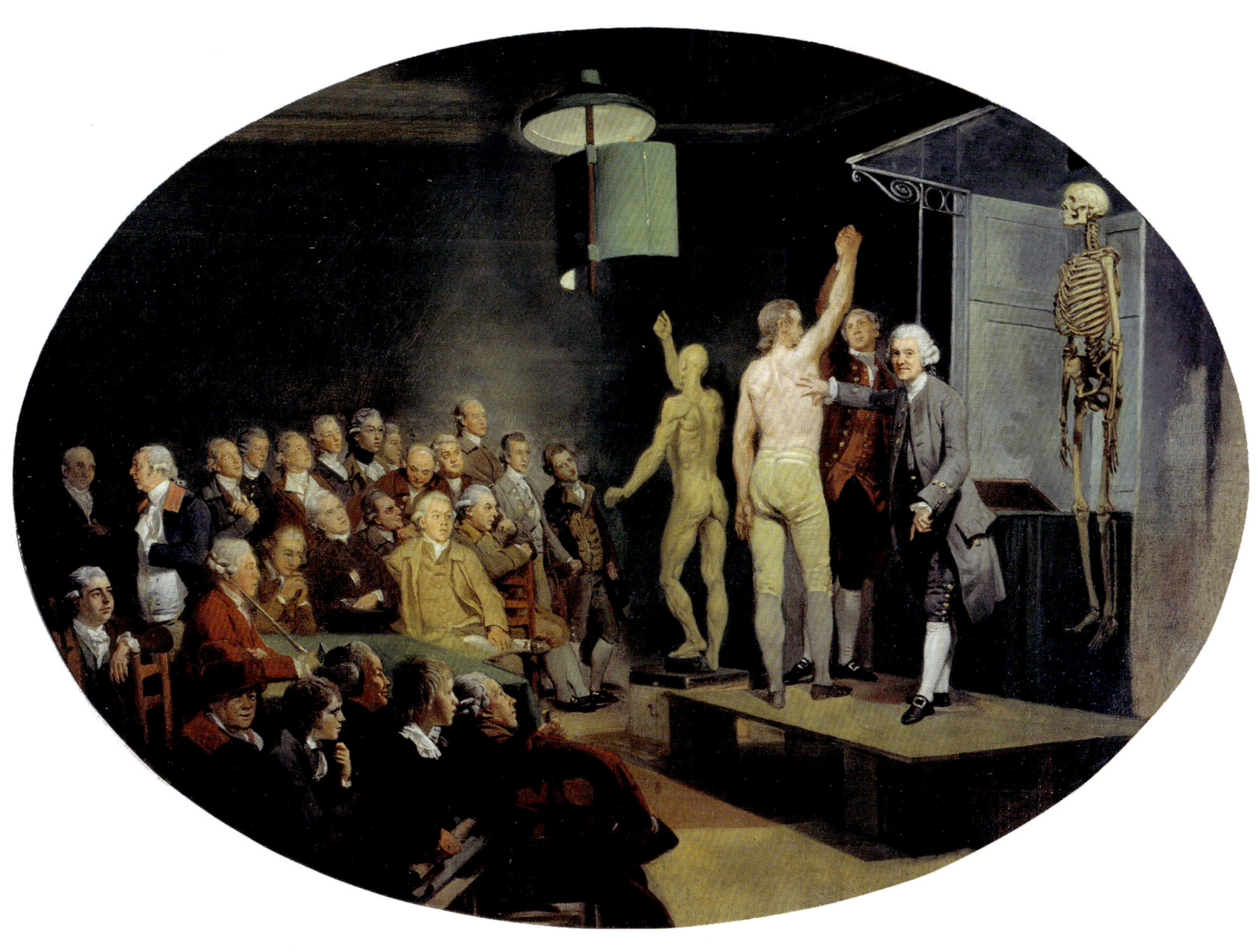

Figure 55 (cat. 46)
Dr William Hunter Teaching Anatomy at the Royal Academy, *c.*1770–72,
oil on canvas, oval, 77.5 × 103.5 cm (30½ × 40¾ in)
Royal College of Physicians, London

at being referred to in this way: '*Wag.* Who is your physician? | *Ailwou'd.* Dr. Last. | *Wag.* What! That little fellow? | *Dr. Last.* Little fellow! What do you mean by that?' (Act II, pp. 46–7).

All these unusual circumstances – the various inter-related plays by Foote, the casting of the distinctive celebrity dwarf, who was in real life the Mayor of Garratt, and the existence of this newly identified painting – may be explained by reference to the doctor (in real life) who owned versions by Zoffany of both *The Mayor of Garret* and *The Devil upon Two Sticks.* This was John Hunter, whose brother William was a Licentiate of the Royal College of Physicians and a central figure in the controversy surrounding the Royal College referred to in the opening scene of *The Mayor of Garret*, which also forms the culminating episode in *The Devil upon Two Sticks.* The painting of Dunstan as Dr Last is unfinished (it is also cut down), which could be explained by the fact that on 8 March 1783, shortly after Dunstan's appearance on stage on 30 December 1782, Zoffany departed for India. Not for the first time, he left incomplete canvases in his wake. Earlier works included *Dr William Hunter Teaching Anatomy at the Royal Academy* (fig. 55). The painting of Dunstan as Dr Last was presumably disposed of now by Zoffany, since on leaving for India he sold off all his unfinished portraits to a 'Mr Clark' of Princes Street.[12]

The Hunter brothers' interest in Dunstan as a medical specimen would have provided ample excuse for one of them to commission this particular composition from Zoffany. It would have gained added piquancy by featuring the actual Mayor of Garratt at a time when Zoffany's painting of the play of that name was already in John Hunter's possession. As a matter of fact, Dunstan's significance to the medical profession, and to anatomists such as the Hunter brothers in particular, is well attested. On his death in 1797 his corpse was only just rescued when in the very process of being snatched through the window by 'Resurrectionists' (body snatchers) for sale to an anatomist:

> No sooner had sir Jeffery ceased to breathe, than the resurrection men were on the alert to obtain his body. They had nearly succeeded prior to interment, by drawing him through the window of the room in which he lay. The surgeons of the day were eager to obtain a prize, but their hopes were disappointed by the late John Liptrap. Esq. who had the body removed to a place of safety.[13]

David Garrick (see fig. 56) had been the first person to employ Zoffany as a painter of theatrical scenes (see cats 17 and 18), in 1762. He was delighted to discover him because, with the precision that Zoffany could bring to theatrical paintings, Garrick's own marvellous performances could now be immortalized, which had become a crucial consideration. Garrick was not only the most celebrated actor of the age, he was also the biggest celebrity, whose fame might be extended through the exhibition of authentic paintings and, more importantly, the plentiful distribution of engravings taken from them.[14]

Garrick's celebrity was a reflection of the centrality of the theatre in British national life, a phenomenon that coincided with Zoffany's career. It was far and away the most important shared cultural experience in the capital. And, although there were several provincial theatres, for example in Norwich and Bristol, in which future stars such as Charles Macklin – and Garrick himself – might cut their teeth, British culture, and the theatre in particular, was essentially metropolitan. The fact that Garrick and his peers were in the habit of transporting

Figure 56 (cat. 15)
David Garrick, *c.*1766–7, oil on canvas,
47 × 35 cm (18½ × 13¾ in). The Garrick Club, London

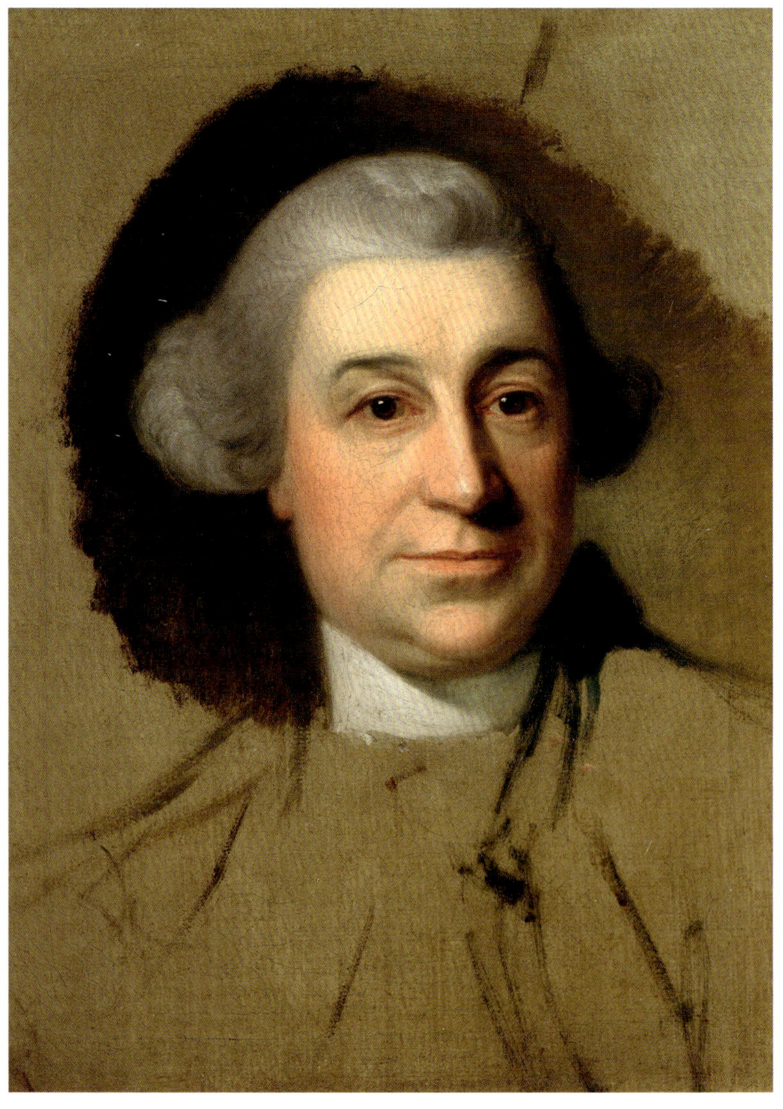

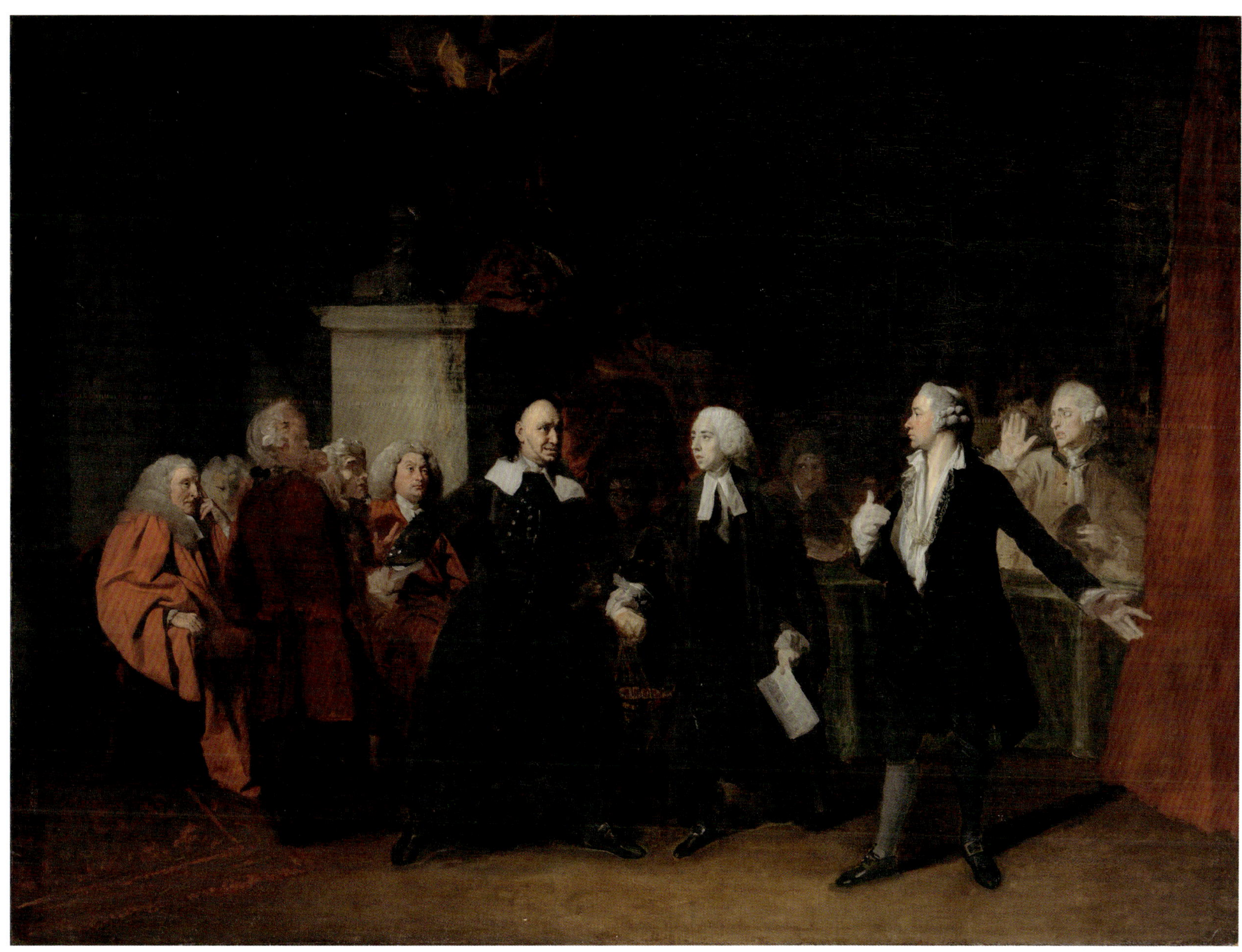

Figure 57 (cat. 29)
Charles Macklin as Shylock in 'The Merchant of Venice', c.1768,
oil on canvas, 116.2 × 151.1 cm (45¾ × 59½ in).
Tate, London; presented by the National Art Collections Fund 1951

their biggest hits for brief seasons to such other centres as Edinburgh and, especially, Dublin only emphasizes this fact.

The sheer quantity of drama staged in London was extraordinary. To take only the season 1761–2, during which Zoffany came onto the scene, no fewer than 533 theatrical performances were given in London, an average of more than ten a week. Most of these were at the two 'patent theatres', Covent Garden and Drury Lane, which enjoyed a monopoly imposed by the Licensing Act of 1737. The Act had been passed by the government of Sir Robert Walpole specifically to suppress the brilliant satirical political plays of Henry Fielding, who was forced to turn to writing novels (a change of career that altered the course of English literature). The very fact that the government felt impelled to control the activities of the theatres itself indicates their importance.

The two licences allowed under this new law were granted to the owners of the two royal patents awarded at the time of the Restoration of the monarchy (1660): the proprietors of Drury Lane and Covent Garden. The patent-holders were granted the right to perform spoken drama and 'the old plays', which included the works of Shakespeare. In Garrick's time an additional helping of glamour was lent to the glitz and glitter of London's theatres by the fact that, unlike most other European courts – and that of France in particular – the English royal family had no private theatre.[15] King George III and Queen Charlotte therefore, both of them keen on the drama, had to attend the public theatres in the centre of London, sometimes at a 'command performance'. Such special occasions as these, like a benefit night or a last performance to mark retirement, might be commemorated by a commission from Zoffany on the part of the producer or star performer (see *Love in a Village*, cat. 26; *Macbeth*, cat. 28).

An integral element in positioning the English drama at the centre of daily life was conspicuously absent from Europe, and from France in particular: a free press, which was accompanied by a high general level of literacy, as Continental visitors were amazed to observe. There were many, many more newspapers and journals in Britain than in any other country, and they were packed with critiques and gossip about the stage and its star performers: actors, dancers, composers, singers and producers. Best-sellers were also devoted to the subject. Charles Churchill's poetical – and decidedly critical – account of individual actors on the London stage, the *Rosciad*, was published in March 1761 and into its sixth edition by February 1762, when it had already sold 10,000 copies. It continued to appear in constantly updated form even after Churchill's death

in 1764, and the work was widely imitated. While he was alive, Churchill's mere presence in the pit (like that of Clive Barnes in New York in the 1970s and 1980s) could cause actors to panic and forget their lines.[16]

The operations of the theatres were on a scale to match the public fascination with them. Garrick was the owner, manager, director and star of Drury Lane where in 1761–2 he had a company of ninety-seven, sixty-six of them actors. At Covent Garden, John Beard (see cat. 27) at the same time had a record 114 performers, including 68 actors and 29 dancers. Such substantial companies imply the scale of the finances – and profits – involved, and when Beard sold on the Covent Garden patent in 1767 it was for the astonishing sum of £60,000 The purchaser of only a quarter share of this patent, William Powell, was so thrilled that he immediately bought a country house and commissioned paintings of himself by Zoffany and John Hamilton Mortimer (see cat. 25).

Although licensed performances were restricted to the 'season', which ran from September until the following June, the patent theatres possessed, in effect, a licence to print money. Theatrical impresarios such as Garrick, Powell, Beard and Foote could amass a fortune in barely more than one season. Foote cleared £2000 in 1768 alone, although he promptly gambled it all away. Charles Macklin, too (fig. 57), enjoyed great financial success, although, like his celebrated stage persona, Shylock, he was habitually involved in bitter legal wrangles. Garrick's recruiting of Zoffany coincided with his public affirmation not only as a celebrity but also as a man of serious financial substance. At this date the final touches were being applied to Garrick's country house at Hampton, which was set beside the Thames for easy river access to the city (see cat. 16). In a concatenation of celebrities the facade of the house and the Temple to Shakespeare were designed by Robert Adam; inside the temple was a sculpture by Louis François Roubiliac and a 'Shakespeare chair' designed by Hogarth; while the park was laid out by 'Capability' Brown.

When Zoffany was found to have left Benjamin Wilson in order to stay with Garrick and work for him in the summer of 1762, Garrick sent an emollient letter to Wilson (his neighbour at Hampton), almost (but not quite) apologizing for having lured Zoffany away, stating that Zoffany 'was warmly recommended to me by my Acquaintance'.[17] The artist 'acquaintance' Garrick knew best was Hogarth, who was also close to Wilson. According to Wilson's own account, he had been offered advice by Hogarth when he was learning to paint, and Hogarth had subsequently even suggested forming

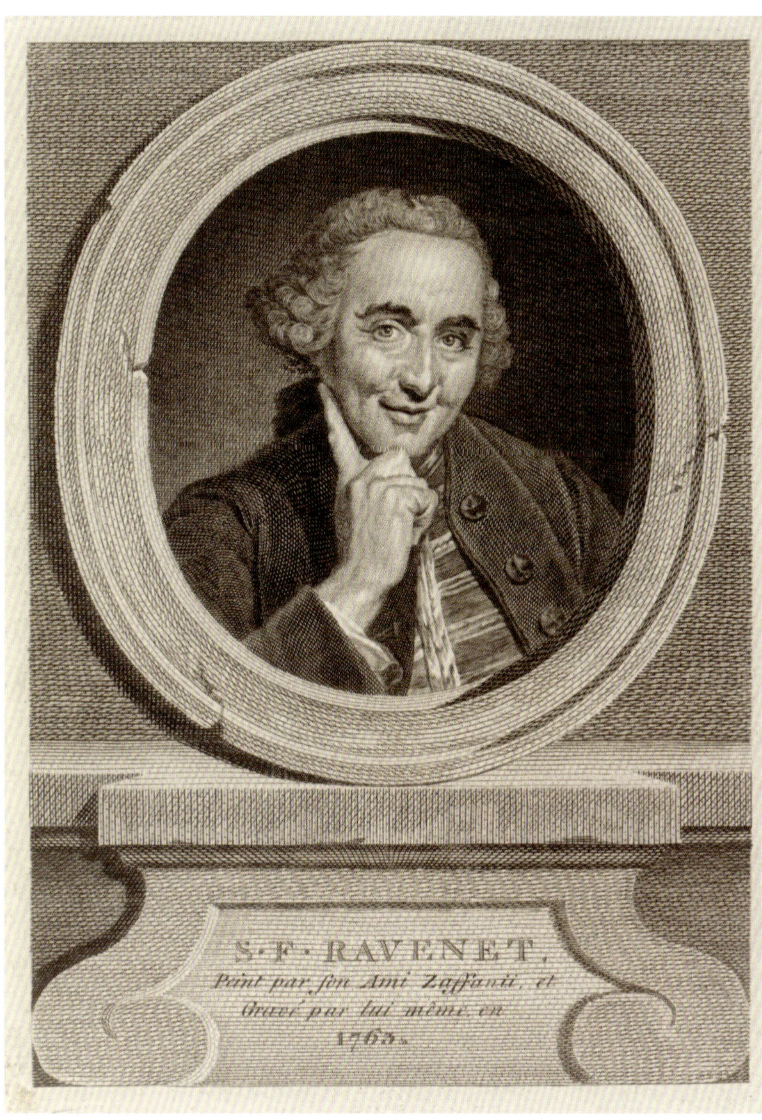

Figure 58
Simon-François Ravenet after Johan Zoffany,
Simon-François Ravenet, 1763,
line engraving, 18.5 × 12.5 cm (7¼ × 4⅞ in).
Victoria & Albert Museum, London

a portrait-painting partnership with him, to confront the growing dominance of Reynolds in that lucrative market.[18] In return Wilson had helped Hogarth with his *Analysis of Beauty* (1753).[19] Hogarth would therefore have come across Zoffany in Wilson's studio, and might have advised Garrick on his suitability.[20] There were other connections. One of Zoffany's first friends in London was an engraver for Hogarth, Simon-François Ravenet. In 1762 Zoffany painted Ravenet (cat. 43), who himself engraved the portrait, inscribing it 'Peint par son ami Zoffanii' (fig. 58). Ravenet had arrived in London in 1744/5 as a result of being co-opted by Hogarth to engrave plates 4 and 5 of *Marriage A-la-Mode*.[21]

Garrick's discovery of Zoffany transformed the artist's fortunes, but at the same time it also supplied the actor with the painter he had been looking for. Although he had painted *Garrick as Richard III*, Hogarth was far too busy to settle down into supplying even his very good friend with paintings of other performances. Benjamin Wilson had been commissioned by Garrick to portray him in *Romeo and Juliet* (the print of which, engraved by Ravenet, Wilson advertised as a companion to the engraving after Hogarth's *Garrick as Richard III*)[22] and also in *King Lear*, but this was *faute de mieux*. Although of interest as the record of two productions, neither of these pictures is a satisfactory work of art (figs. 59, 60). As Garrick remarked to Hogarth: 'Wilson is not an accurate Observer of things, not Ev'n of those which concern him most.'[23]

As Zoffany's *David with the Head of Goliath* demonstrates (cat. 3), Zoffany possessed a similar wit to Hogarth's, often embodied in visual/verbal interplay, such as the double meaning borne by the glans (also penis tip) that serves David as a sling-stone. Nonetheless, there is Zoffany before Hogarth, and there is Zoffany after Hogarth. Familiarity with Hogarth's art set Zoffany's genius free, transforming his compositions with a new complexity and allusiveness. Hogarth had developed a cross-referential manner of creating pictures, confessedly inspired by the stage, in which the meaning is mediated by visual details surrounding the main action. After his employment by Garrick, Zoffany began to develop a similar approach, seen at its most elaborate in such compositions as the Uffizi *Self-Portrait* (cat. 59) or *The Tribuna* (cat. 53). But just as important to the art of both artists was the extreme precision of facial and physical characterization that they were able to deploy, in which they have probably never been equalled. In his theatrical paintings Zoffany's ability to depict the exact direction of a glance or the reflection of a fleeting emotion was crucial to his success.

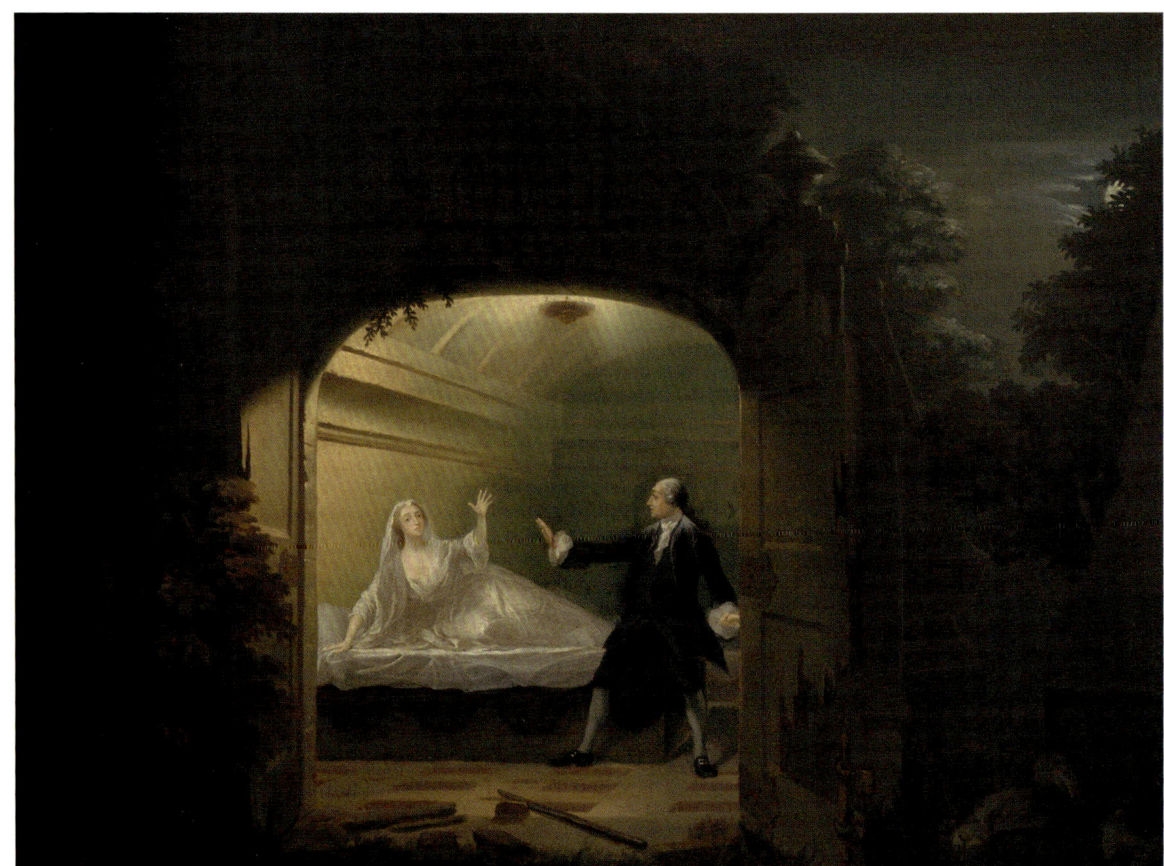

Figure 59
Benjamin Wilson, *David Garrick
and George Anne Bellamy in 'Romeo
and Juliet'*, 1753, oil on canvas,
138.7 × 184.2 cm (54⅝ × 72½ in).
Yale Center for British Art,
Paul Mellon Fund

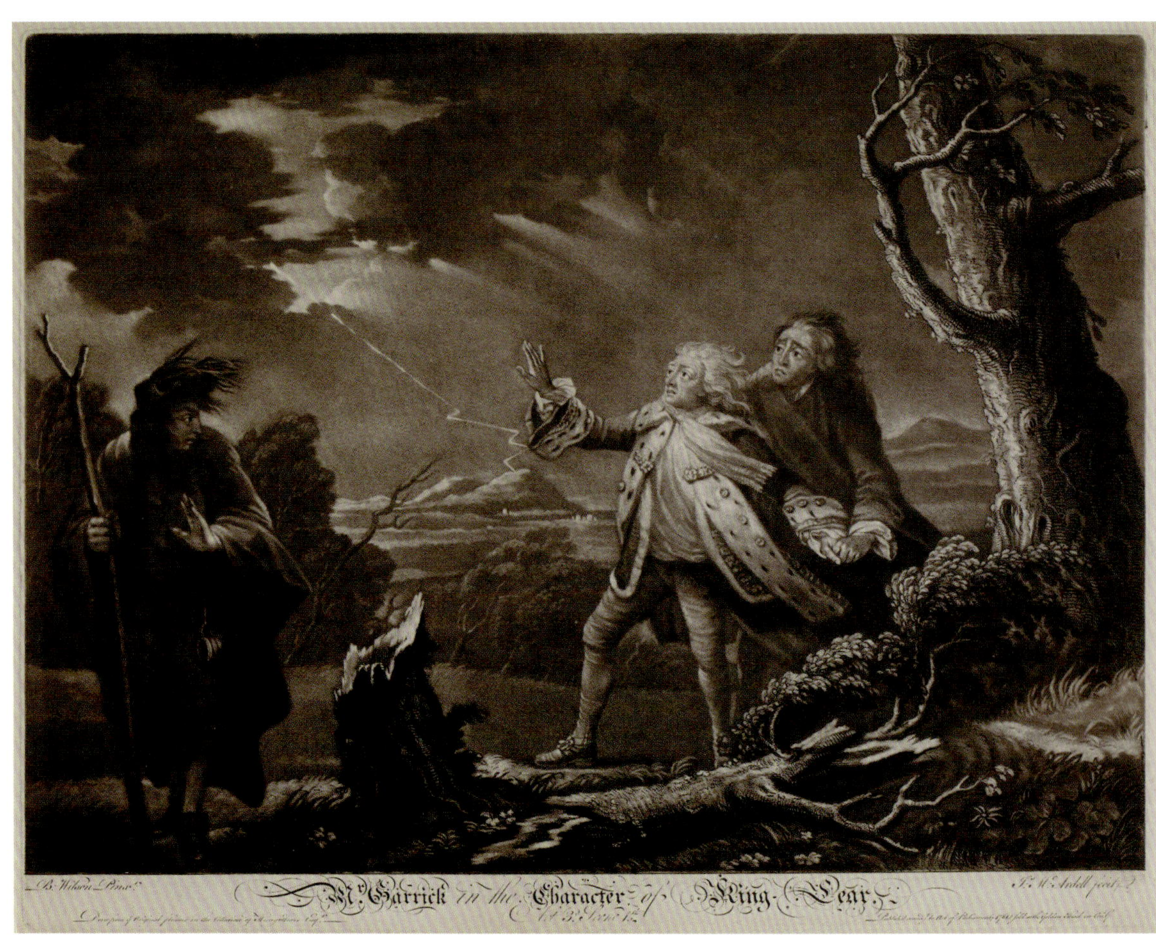

Figure 60
James McArdell after Benjamin
Wilson, *Mr Garrick in the Character
of King Lear*, 1761,
mezzotint engraving,
41.8 × 51.7 cm (16½ × 20⅜ in).
British Museum, Department of Prints
and Drawings, 1902, 1011. 3274

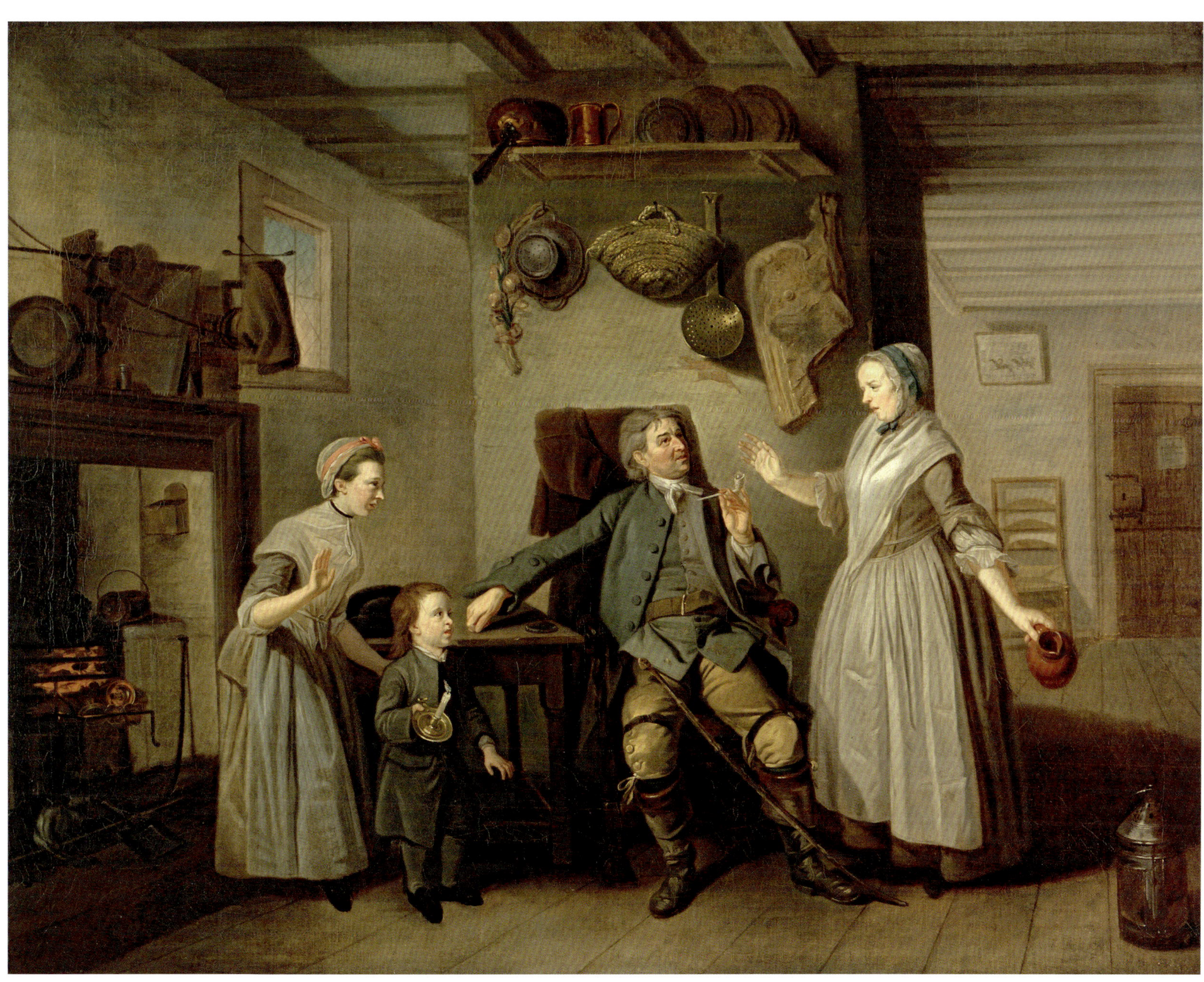

Figure 61 (cat. 17)
David Garrick and Mary Bradshaw in David Garrick's
*'The Farmer's Return', c.*1762,
oil on canvas, 101.6 × 127 cm (40 × 50 in).
Yale Center for British Art, Paul Mellon Collection

The art of both Hogarth and Zoffany is, then, peculiarly akin to that of the stage, with the all-important difference that theirs is an art of a more permanent kind. And it was precisely this that appealed to Garrick, whose awareness of the ephemeral nature of his achievement was feelingly stated in his prologue to *The Clandestine Marriage*:

O let me drop one tributary tear,
On poor Jack Falstaff's Grave, and Juliet's Bier!
'Tis in your hearts alone their Fame must live.
Still as the Scenes of Life will shift away,
The strong Impressions of their Art decay.

Zoffany's first venture into recording a theatrical performance was *The Farmer's Return* (fig. 61), a picture he showed at the Society of Artists exhibition of 17 May 1762. Since the first performance of this little play was on 20 March that year, and Garrick owned Zoffany's original painting (he hung it in his house as a pair with *Venice Preserv'd*, cat. 19), this marks the time of Zoffany's earliest employment by Garrick. And Hogarth was involved here, too. The publication of the play's text was justified, Garrick announced, only because of the imprimatur it had received in the form of a drawing Hogarth had made of it. This drawing, which Garrick had hanging in his house, has been lost, although it is known through an etching by James Basire (fig. 62). Zoffany's painting was evidently inspired by, although not quite identical to, Hogarth's sketch. In the 'Advertisement' printed at the front of *The Farmer's Return* Garrick explained:

The following Interlude was prepared for the Stage, merely with a View of assisting Mrs Pritchard at her Benefit; and the Desire of serving so good an Actress, is a better Excuse for its Defects, than the few Days in which it was written, and represented. Notwithstanding the favourable reception it has met with, the Author would not have printed it, had not his friend, Mr Hogarth, flattered him most agreeably, by thinking The Farmer and his Family not unworthy of a Sketch of his Pencil. To him therefore, this Trifle, which he has so much honoured, is inscribed, as a faint Testimony of the sincere Esteem which the writer bears him, both as a Man and as an Artist.

This was not the only time that Garrick stated his debt to Hogarth: he announced in the prologue to *The Clandestine Marriage* (cat. 31), produced in 1766, two years after Hogarth's death, that the play was inspired by *Marriage A-la-Mode*:

Poets and painters, who from nature draw
Their best and richest stores, have made this law:
That each should neighbourly assist his brother,
And steal with decency from one another.
Tonight, your matchless Hogarth gives the thought,
Which from his canvas to the stage is brought …
Each, as it suits him, takes a separate road,
Their one great object, Marriage-a-la-mode!
Where titles deign with cits [citizens] to have and hold,
And change rich blood for more substantial gold!
And honored trade from interest turns aside,
To hazard happiness for titled pride.

In the case of one of Garrick's most famous roles, that of Abel Drugger in *The Alchemist* (see cats. 21 and 22), the debt was the other way round: Hogarth could inspire Garrick, but Garrick's acting might equally suggest a character to Hogarth. We know this because of the rare survival of one of Zoffany's preliminary oil sketches made at a live performance in the

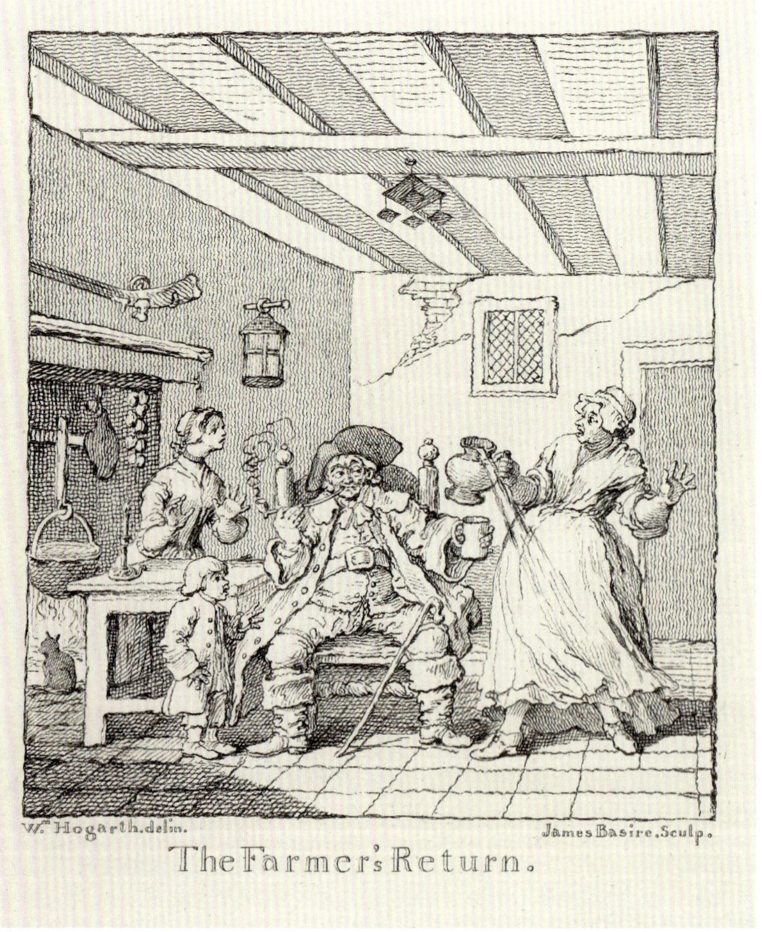

Figure 62
James Basire after William Hogarth, *The Farmer's Return*, 1762, etching, 25.1 × 21.4 cm (9⅞ × 8⅜ in). British Museum, Department of Prints and Drawings, 1868, 0822.1622

theatre, *Garrick as Abel Drugger* (fig. 63; if any other such sketches and drawings survived, they were perhaps burned for fear of cholera in 1832). When he adapted *The Alchemist* in 1743, Garrick brought Drugger's entrance forward to the beginning of Act I, Scene 1, in place of the original Act I, Scene 3, and this sketch shows Garrick at his first entrance (for the finished picture he chose a later scene).[24] In the left-hand figure we see Drugger, hat in hand, eyes averted, edging into the room; in the right-hand image he is pulling a crown out of his pocket for the pretended alchemist (Subtle), while getting into a muddle about what to with his hat. We should note the way in which Drugger's feet are parallel, one of the most powerful signifiers of lowly social status, as are his arms and hands, and also the way in which his knees sag with nervousness. Arms and hands ought, by the rules of contemporary deportment, to be pleasingly varied, disposed in differing directions, while the feet should be at right-angles to each other.[25] By a remarkable coincidence, the way in which the character was to be played (although at a different point again in the action) was recorded by Garrick himself:

[The actor's] toes must be inverted from the Heel, and by holding his Breath, he will unavoidably give himself a Tremor in the Knees, and if his Fingers, at the same Time, seem Convuls'd, it finishes the compleatest low Picture of grotesque Terror that can be imagined by a Dutch painter.

This appeared on 7 January 1744 in *An Essay on Acting: in which will be consider'd The Mimical Behaviour of a Certain fashionable faulty ACTOR … to which will be added, A short CRITICISM On His acting Macbeth*. At this date Hogarth was still finishing the series *Marriage A-la-Mode*, the last scene of which was painted at the end of the same year or even in 1745.[26] In that final scene we see a servant (fig. 64) in the pose adopted by Garrick for Abel Drugger, as recorded by Zoffany in his oil sketch. This resemblance would have prompted a comparison in the minds of contemporary viewers for a very good reason: that Hogarth's servant has been to an 'able drugger' in order to purchase the poison with which the Countess has just committed suicide.

The accuracy of Zoffany's record of Garrick both in the sketch and final canvas (see fig. 48) is confirmed by another passage in Garrick's essay, where he refers to Drugger's blue apron:

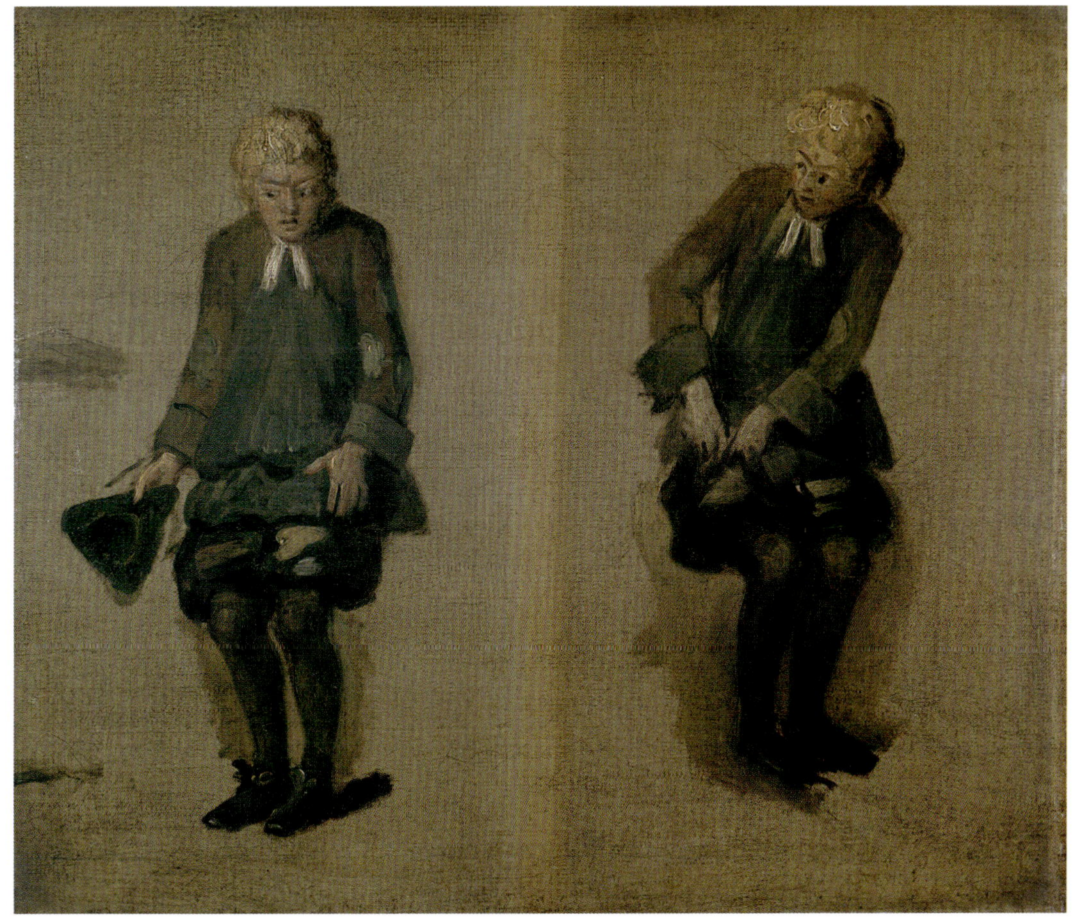

Figure 63
Studies of David Garrick as Abel Drugger in 'The Alchymist', 1769–70, oil on canvas, 33 × 38 cm (13 × 15 in).
Ashmolean Museum, University of Oxford

Figure 64
William Hogarth, *Marriage A-la-Mode: VI, The Lady's Death*, c.1743, oil on canvas, 69.9 × 90.8 cm (27½ × 35¾ in).
The National Gallery, London

Suppose the Murder of Duncan [in *Macbeth*] and the Breaking a Urinal [a famous piece of 'business' in *The Alchemist*] shall affect the Player in the same Manner and the only Difference is the blue Apron and lac'd Coat, shall we be chill'd at the Murder, and roar at the Tobacconist? Fie for Shame!

Zoffany's *David Garrick and Mrs Pritchard in Macbeth* (cat. 27) shows the 'lace coat' and also the main point of the essay: the potential problem of Garrick's diminutive stature. Garrick's curious publication was intended humorously to deflect any criticism from his forthcoming performance as Macbeth, a part hitherto associated in the public mind with the statuesque figure of the Irish actor James Quin. Revealingly, the argument of *An Essay on Acting …* is conceived by Garrick in terms of

how the play might be interpreted by a painter:

Valour and Ambition, the two grand Characteristicks of Macbeth, form in the Mind's Eye a Person of near six Feet High, corpulently Graceful, a round Visage, a large hazel Eye, aquiline Nose, prominent Chest, and a well calv'd Leg, rather inclin'd to that which is call'd an Irish Leg [all this is a description of Quin]; this, I say, would be the Painter's Choice, was he to give us the Macbeth of his Imagination; I mention this only to prove that Mr G———k is not form'd in the least, externally, no more than internally, for that Character, and tho' there are many figures in the World would become it very well, tho' not exactly co-incident with my Description, yet the nearer they approach to it, they will the better look Ambition, Heroism, and Murder.[27]

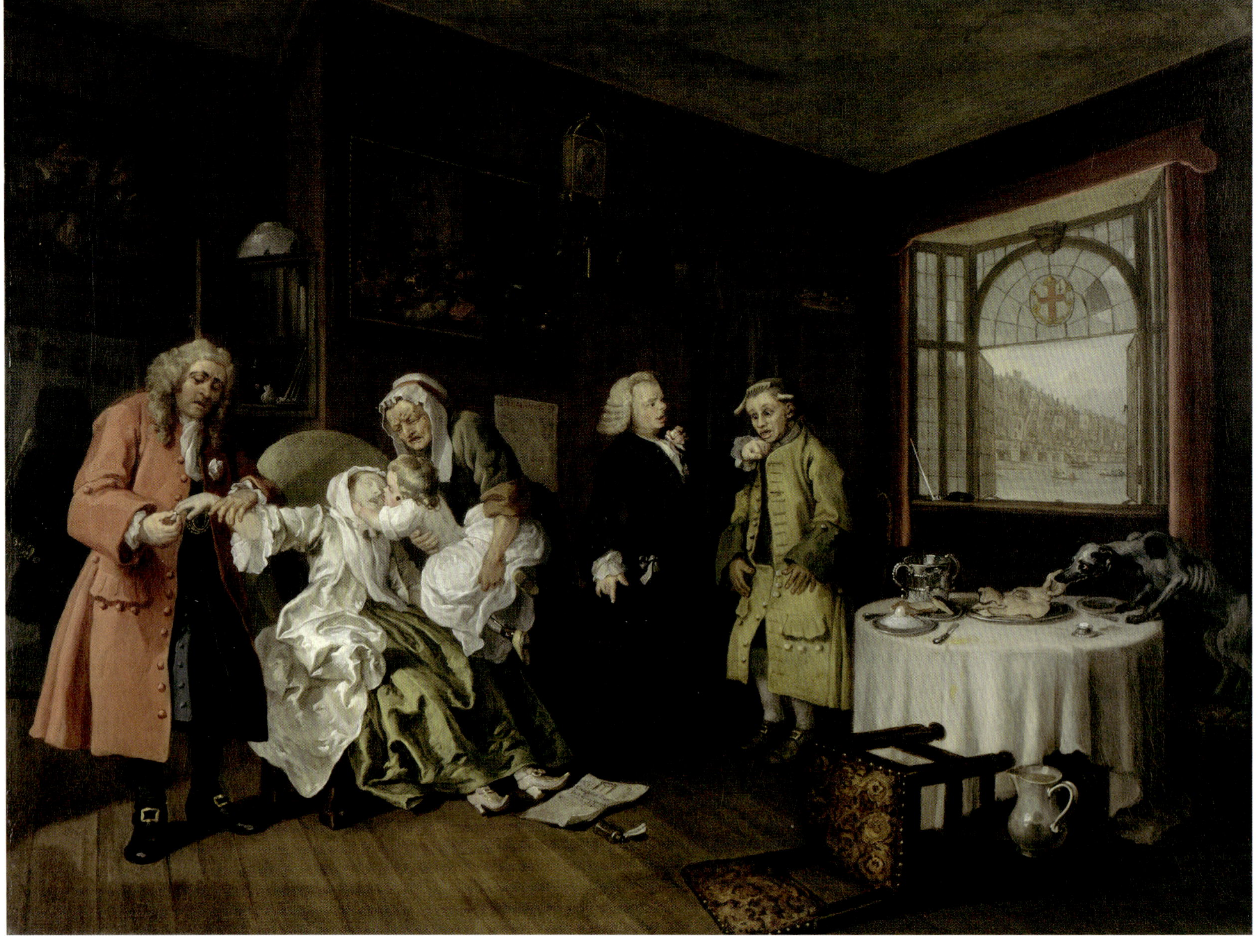

Hogarth's comparison of the relative proportions of Garrick and Quin (fig. 65) forms part of the same argument: that it is the correct proportion of the overall figure that counts, rather than mere height. And the humour of Garrick's *jeu d'esprit* is very Hogarthian. For example, Garrick is well aware of the incongruity not only of his physical size, but also of the playing of Macbeth in contemporary dress, which included the wearing of wigs. And so, Garrick humorously suggests, a key line of the banquet scene might be updated. The famous cry of Macbeth to Banquo's ghost, 'Shake not thy gory locks at me', would be more properly be played as: 'Never shake thy gory Wig at me'.[28]

Mrs Pritchard is shown in Zoffany's *Macbeth* (see fig. 44), with a degree of flattery. She merely looks tall in comparison with Garrick, whereas by now she was very overweight and showing her age. Garrick was fond of her, but described her unkindly in a letter at this time (8 February 1767) to his brother George. Garrick had just returned from his Grand Tour and was not looking forward to reviving his career by playing Oakly in *The Jealous Wife*, a part that he claimed to have entirely forgotten, when Pritchard would be playing opposite him as Mrs Oakly. He was not feeling well, and the prospect of facing Mrs Prichard could only make him feel worse: 'Sick– Sick– Sick– & Mrs P[ritchar]d will make me Sicker – great Bubbies, Noddling head, & no teeth– O Sick– Sick– Spew–.'[29]

In this respect therefore, as in so many others, Zoffany's paintings are as much a triumph of deception as the stage representations he immortalized with such an appearance of veracity.

Figure 65
William Hogarth, *The Proportions of Garrick and Quin*, 1746, pen with brown ink, over pencil, 22.6 × 18.5 cm (8⅞ × 7¼ in). The Royal Collection, Her Majesty Queen Elizabeth II

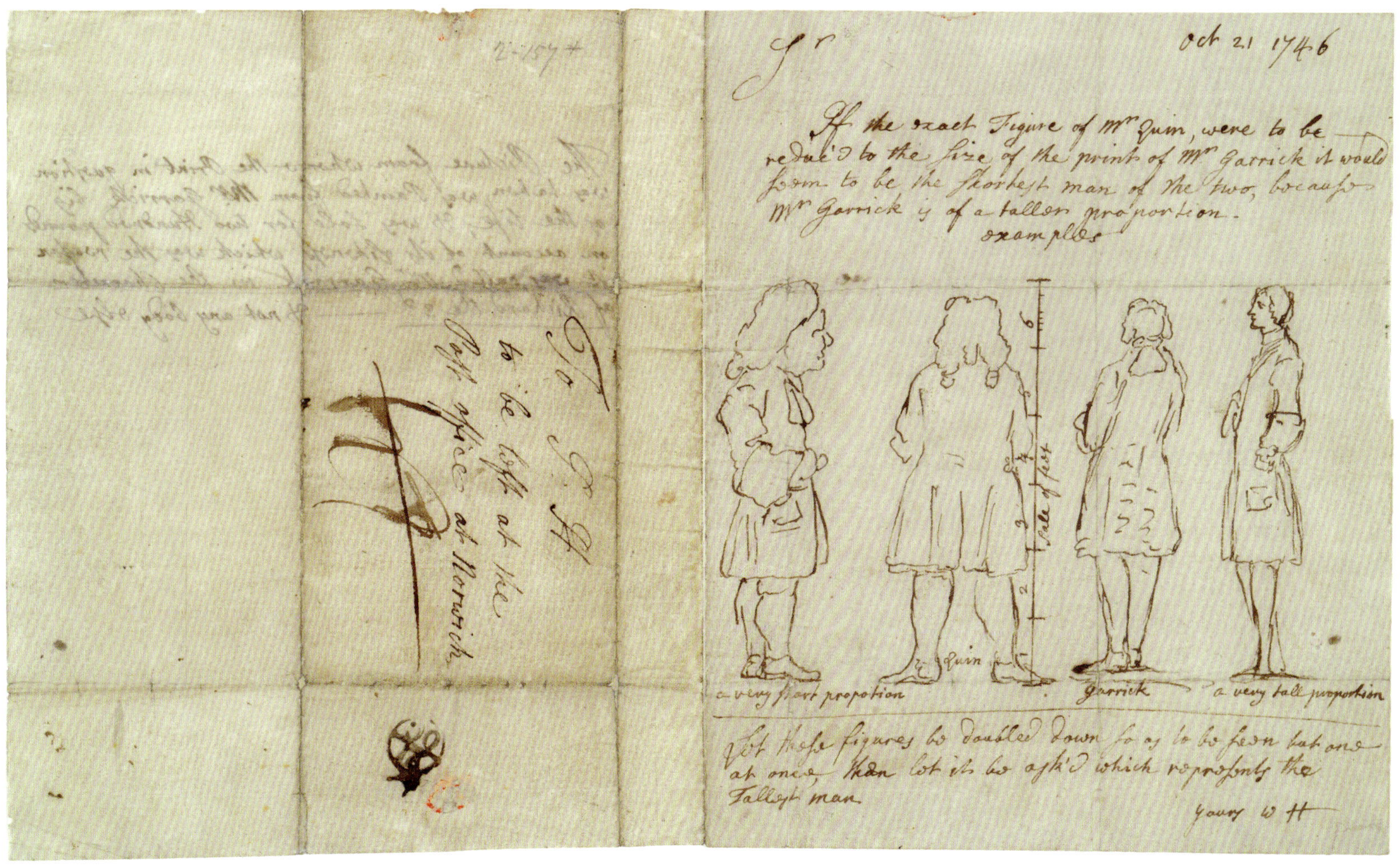

Notes

1. R. Simon 2007, esp. chaps. 4 ('Hogarth, Watteau and Voltaire') and 8 ('Art, Theatre and Old Masters in Britain and France').
2. See, for example, Angelo 1828–30, vol. 1, 147; Whitley 1928, vol. 2, 286.
3. For details, see cat. 24.
4. Mozart had famously improvised on the same aria at his benefit evening in the same city. The effect was telling for a different reason in Vienna, where the baritone singing Leporello had sung the first Figaro.
5. S.L. Bethell, *Shakespeare and the Popular Dramatic Tradition*, London, 1948. Bethell also drew comparisons with similar effects in the Marx Brothers' movies.
6. Jollup or 'jollop' was a substance used equally as a laxative or to ease a cough.
7. The phenomenon was the subject of Martin Postle's *Joshua Reynolds: The Creation of Celebrity*, exh. cat., Tate Britain and Palazzo dei Diamanti, Ferrara, 2005. Where the stage is concerned, present-day British pantomime retains the habit of exploiting current celebrity: the casting of the heavyweight boxer Frank Bruno as the Genie of the Lamp in *Aladdin* (1989) comes to mind.
8. Mander & Mitchenson 1980, cat. 83.
9. I am indebted to Marcus Risdell for first suggesting Dunstan.
10. BM Sat 5637, etc.: M. Dorothy George, *Catalogue of Political and Personal Satires in the British Museum*, vol. 6, London, 1938.
11. Hone 1837, vol. 2, n.p., '22 June'; on Dunstan, 'C.L.' (Charles Lamb), 'Reminiscences of Sir Jeffery Dunstan', addressed 'To the Editor of the Every-Day Book' (cols. 842–4).
12. Recorded by John Nichols, cited in Webster 2011, 407.
13. Hone 1837, vol. 2, col. 860.
14. Lennox-Boyd 1994.
15. More rarely, the drama might be wholly discouraged, as was the case at Queen Charlotte's home of Mecklenburg.
16. Thomas Davies apologized to Garrick for losing his way in *Cymbeline*, citing Churchill's presence as the cause, and it was said that his appearance in the *Rosciad* persuaded him to abandon the stage. He is best known for his *Life of Garrick* (1780) and *Dramatic Miscellanies* (1783–4).
17. Garrick 1963, vol. 1, no. 292 (at some point before 21 August 1762).
18. 'I told his majesty, that I had no master: for that I followed painting upon the advice of Mr. Hogarth and many of the principal artists, who used to visit me, whilst I lived at the Charterhouse. The King then enquired, what I did at the Charterhouse? I told him that I had a place there as a Clerk: and having a great deal of leisure, I studied painting. That Martin Folkes the President of the Royal Society, who was a particular friend of mine, recommended it to me to go over to Ireland, for a couple of years and paint there; that my first beginnings might not appear against me in this country.' (Andrew Graciano, ed., 'The Memoir of Benjamin Wilson, FRS (1721–1788): Painter and Electrical Scientist', *Walpole Society*, vol. 74, 2012.) My thanks to Andrew Graciano for permission to quote from his transcription.
19. R.B. Paulson, *Hogarth*, Cambridge, 1991–3, vol. 3, 62–4, for Wilson's connections with the *Analysis of Beauty*.
20 Wilson took part with Hogarth in a Rembrandt forgery joke on Thomas Hudson. R. Simon 2007, 140.
21. R. Simon 2007, 36. Ravenet was a pupil of Le Bas, the Parisian whom Hogarth had originally planned to have as one of his six engravers on the series.
22. 'The Size of the Print is the same with Mr. Hogarth's Garrick in Richard [III]' (*London Evening Post*, 27–9 March 1753).
23. Garrick 1963, vol. 1, 370, no. 299 (8 Jan. [1763?]).
24. It is essential to study the acting version published by John Bell, London, 1777, *As altered from Ben Jonson. Distinguishing also the Variations of the Theatre, as performed at the Theatre-Royal in Drury-Lane. Regulated by the Prompt-Book, By permission of the Managers, by Mr. Hopkins, Prompter* (reprinted in H.W. Pedicord and F.L. Bergmann, *The Plays of David Garrick*, vol. 5, 'Alterations of Others, 1742–1750', Carbondale and Edwardsville, 1982).
25. R. Simon 2007, 161ff.
26. R. Simon 2007, 42, 127ff.
27. David Garrick, *An Essay on Acting*, London, 1744, 13–15.
28. Garrick 1744, 20.
29. Garrick 1963, vol. 2, 445.

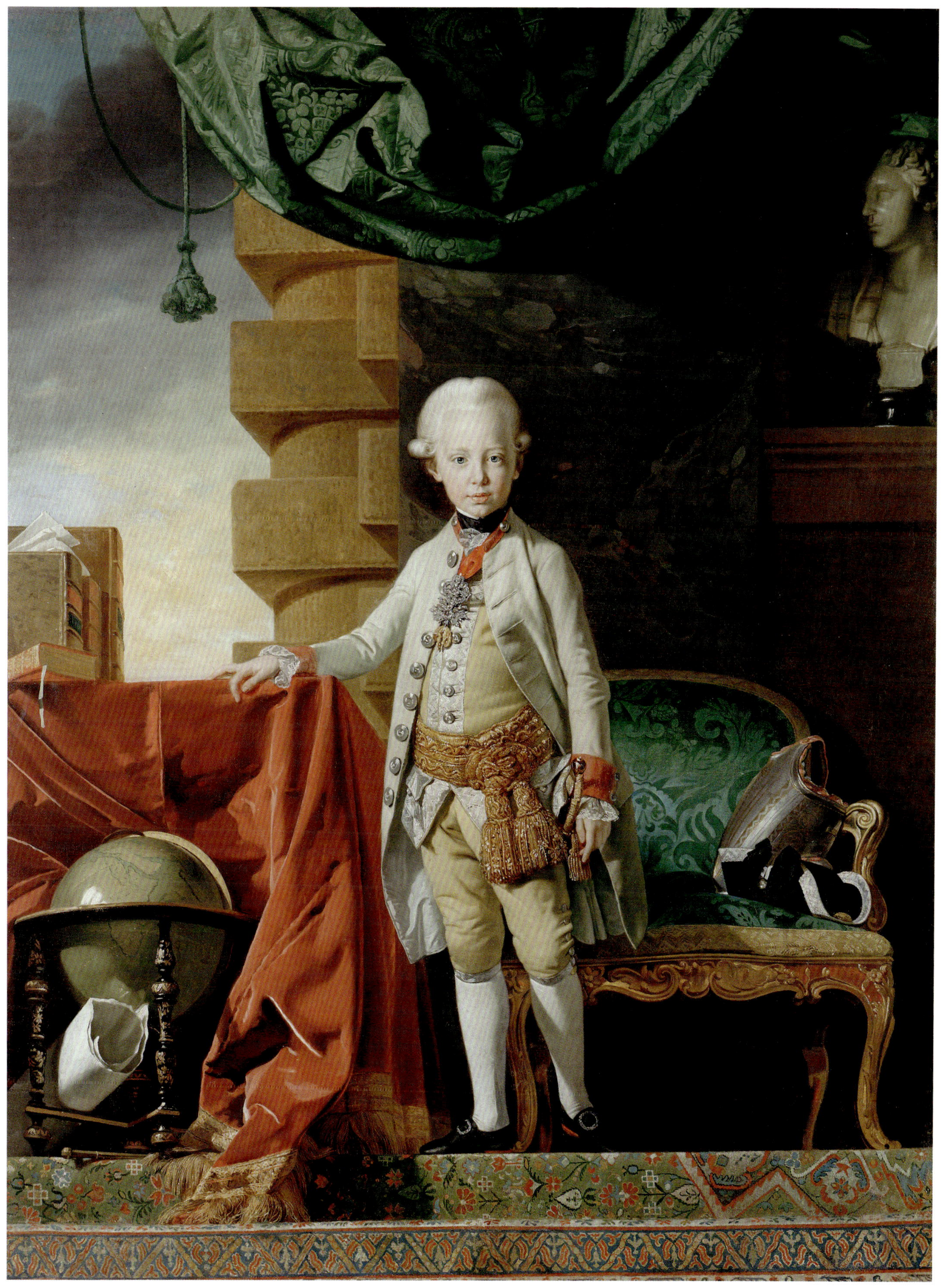

Clarissa Campbell Orr

Six Courts & Four Empires:
Zoffany as Courtier

Johan Zoffany's career is best known as that of a German-born painter in Britain who was closely associated with the court of George III and Queen Charlotte, the aristocrats and intellectuals who attended it, and the members of cultural institutions such as the Royal Academy whom he superbly depicted in his conversation pieces and portraits. Yet, exploring this court context opens a window not only on the life of the later Georgian court and fashionable society but also on the German dimension of the British court and the cosmopolitanism of some of its grandees and artists. Both restless and adaptable, Zoffany proved able to adjust to the dynamism of eighteenth-century Britain. But he also remained susceptible to the possibilities for advancement offered by the Habsburgs in Italy and Vienna.

This essay discusses the six European courts with which Zoffany was associated (Thurn und Taxis, Trier, London, Florence, Parma and Vienna) in the context of two of the three empires within which he operated: the British, German and Mughal empires. The fourth empire, the original Roman Empire, remained a dream and an ideal that haunted the imagination of cultured Europeans. They were fascinated by its monumental remains, educated by its literature, history and ethics, and perplexed by its decline and fall, which eighteenth historians like Montesquieu and Gibbon tried to explain. But Zoffany's career must first be situated in the context of that baffling historical entity, the Holy Roman Empire of the German nation. It could trace its origins to the first Roman Empire, which had adopted Christianity in the fourth century: hence the adjective 'Holy'. The empire that George III, Queen Charlotte and Zoffany knew had been consolidated in 1648 by the Treaty of Westphalia, closing thirty years of religious and constitutional civil war between its component parts. It was a paradoxical political entity, yet historians now consider it an effective federal structure, maintaining equilibrium within its diverse component parts by legal means until it was dissolved in 1806 by Napoleon.[1] Approximately 330 city states, knights and princes – both secular and ecclesiastical – claimed territorial sovereignty, including the right to determine what religious faiths would be tolerated. Yet at the same time they acknowledged the overlordship of an elected emperor, almost always a Habsburg. There were nine electoral princes: as well as the Archbishops of Cologne, Mainz and Trier, there were Electors of Bavaria, Saxony, the Palatinate (the southern Rhineland governed from Heidelberg), Brandenburg and Hanover, and the Kingdom of Bohemia (approximately, the modern Czech Republic). Hanover was the most recent to have acquired the coveted electoral status through the efforts of George III's great-great grandfather, so he and Queen Charlotte were Elector and Electress of Hanover, as well as British rulers.

Figure 66 (cat. 40)
Archduke Francis, 1775,
oil on canvas, 197 × 145 cm (77½ × 57⅛ in).
Kunsthistorisches Museum, Vienna

It was the ambition of German nobles to gain imperial, and not just local, titles, and this had been achieved by the patrons of Zoffany's father and grandfather, the Princes of Thurn und Taxis. They had acquired wealth and enormous influence by running the postal system throughout the empire from the sixteenth century. Their base after 1724 was Frankfurt-on-the-Main, the city where imperial coronations were held, so Zoffany's family would have seen the pomp of the coronation of Charles VII in 1742, when Zoffany was nine. German princes, whether they were secular or ecclesiastical, expressed their princely status in a Baroque manner: that is to say, they projected their position and importance through an essentially theatrical display of power, by means of processions, especially Catholic ones, magnificent temporary installations such as triumphal arches at coronations, dramatically striking architecture and room sets, jewels, sumptuous clothes, magnificent entertainments including operas and ballets, and a numerous entourage. Thus, Zoffany's father designed an elaborate triumphal arch for the third marriage of his patron, Prince Alexander Ferdinand (fig. 67).

Ecclesiastical princes were no exception. To be eligible for their high church office, the cathedral canons who chose them often needed sixteen or more quarterings of noble ancestry. They usually came from the highest princely families, and the rationale for the sumptuous decoration of rooms in episcopal palaces was partly that they needed suitable surroundings to entertain the emperor, should he travel through their domains en route to his coronation: hence the superb Kaisersaal in the bishopric of Würzburg, where Zoffany's first wife was brought up, with frescoes painted by Giovanni Battista Tiepolo and his two sons. Ruling archbishop-electors also felt entitled to summer palaces, such as the new quarters at the fortress-castle of Ehrenbreitstein in Koblenz, where the Trier electors resided (fig. 68). Here, and at Trier, Zoffany painted decorative schemes for his first patron, Johann Philipp, Graf von Walderdorff, including the exotic *Venus Marina* (fig. 69), and his only surviving still-life painting, of birds and game (fig. 70).[2] Throughout Catholic Europe the ceremonies associated with the daily, weekly and annual church calendar, as well as processions and traditions associated with saints' days, confraternities and monasteries, gave scope for a dramatic retelling of the Christian story, while painted and sculpted interiors were still being commissioned for religious buildings. Zoffany was trained to paint for this princely and ecclesiastical milieu.

As former entrepreneurs rather than soldiers and landed magnates, the Thurn und Taxis were an urban dynasty. When required to move to Regensburg, where the imperial Parliament met, to fulfil their duties as imperial commissioners, the Thurn und Taxis princes needed a more palatial building, resulting in increased work for Zoffany's family. His father was a valued court official and professional who ended his career with the title of chief architect. Zoffany, the future painter, was educated alongside the princely heir, Prince Karl Anselm, and so was inculcated with courtly manners as well as a classical education, but the difference in rank between the prince and Zoffany would always have been apparent.[3]

Northern European rulers like the Hanoverians were conscious that their courts were still catching up with creating cultural institutions and that their collections of art and antiquities might have been initiated a century after those of Italian dukes such as the Farnese in Parma. In seventeenth-century France Louis XIV had led from the top in creating Academies. But the British were sensitive to the idea that monarchs should be too dictatorial. Thus, when George III assisted a group of artists in forming the Royal Academy, of which Zoffany was an early, royal-nominated member, the king was accused by critics of 'tyranny'.[4] The British court's relation to the public realm and to commercialized culture was somewhat different from German courts, and George III and Queen Charlotte had to abide by British rules and customs. This affected the way that Zoffany could construct his career. The king and queen had official positions in their households for artists and architects, such as Painter in Ordinary or Master of the King's Works, but creating extra official positions for other artists would have stretched their civil list, which had been fixed in 1760 and was never renegotiated. Queen Charlotte had to meet the expenses of her growing family out of her never-modified allowance, which may explain later friction over Zoffany's extended Italian stay and expenses claims.[5]

The problem for ambitious painters like Zoffany was that 'cultural personnel' in court circles as well as in the wider marketplace had an ambiguous social status. Artists were on the whole ranked higher than musicians and actors. There was scope for upward mobility, especially if a male painter also had a good education and social confidence. Zoffany was quick to grasp that he needed to act and live like a gentleman in order to be accepted as one. George III's foundation of the Royal Academy raised the status of artists, and Reynolds and Lawrence would be given knighthoods, but there remained a subtle pecking order based partly on the status of the art being practised, as well as the sex of the artist, and also on the personal relationship of patron and artist.[6]

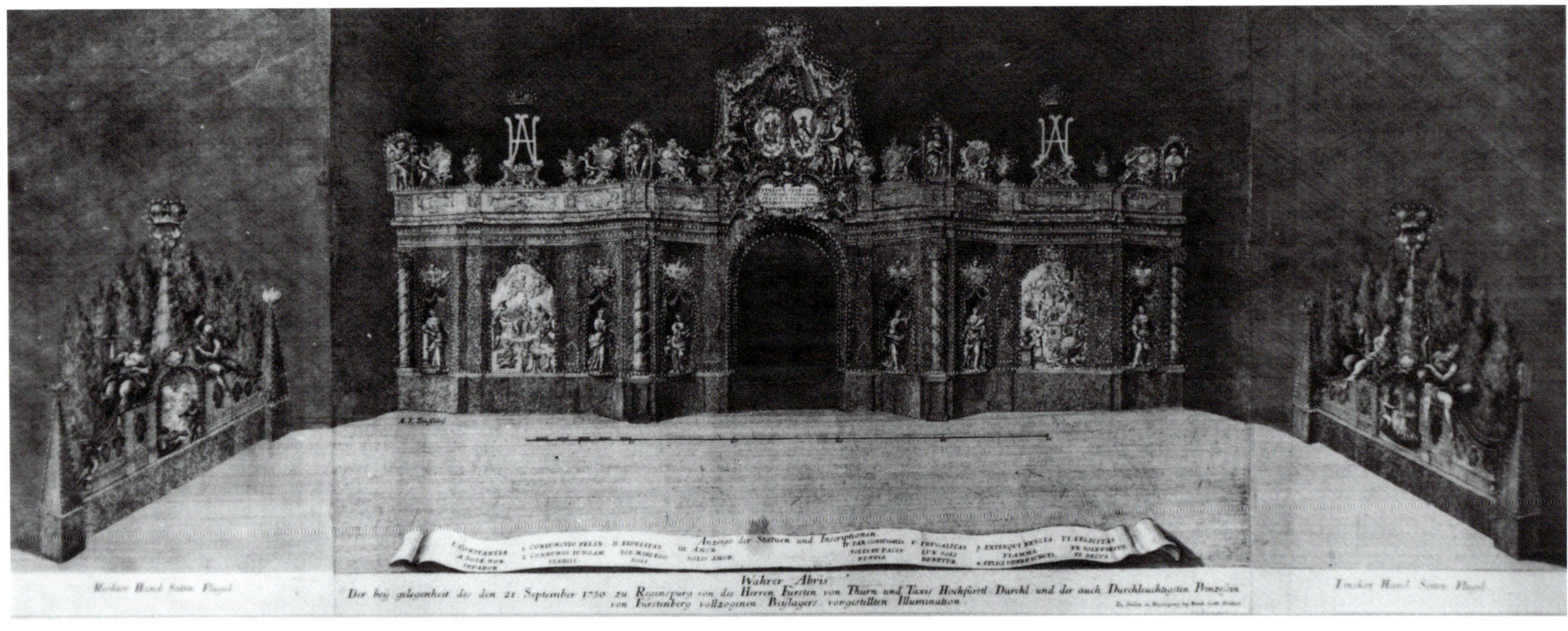

Figure 67
Bernhard Gottlieb Fridrich, after Anton
Franz Zauffaly, *Illuminated ceremonial arch
erected in the Emmeransplatz, Regensburg
for the wedding of Prince Alexander Ferdinand
and Princess Maria Henrietta von Fürstenberg-
Stühlingen, 21st September 1750*, 1750,
engraving, 28.5 × 16.5 cm (11¼ × 6½ in).
Thurn und Taxis Hofbibliothek /
Zentralarchiv, Regensburg

Figure 68
F. Hopkey, *Hermanstein* [Ehrenbreitstein],
a Strong Castle, Stands upon a High Rock,
1705, watercolour and ink on paper,
50 × 48 cm (19⅝ × 18⅞ in).
British Library (Maps K.Top.93.40.2)

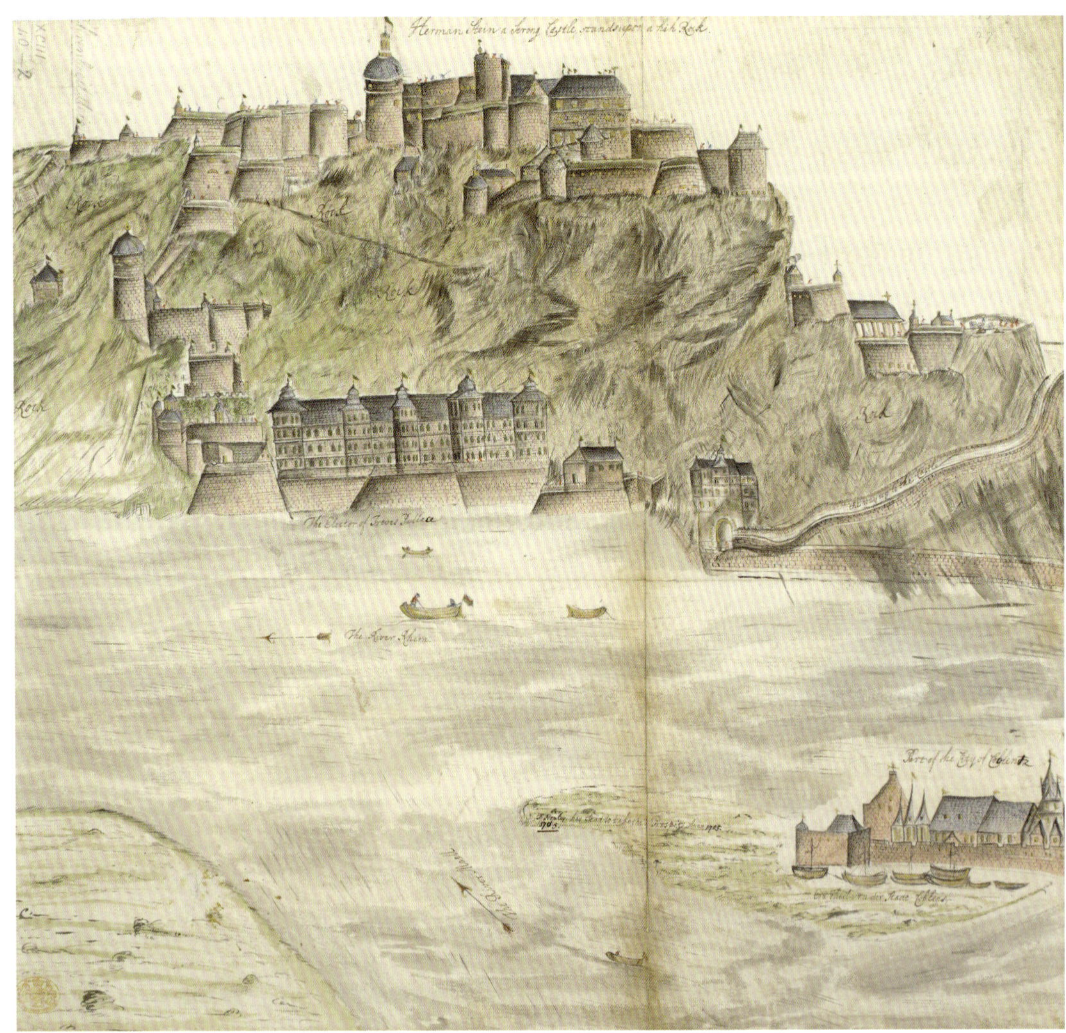

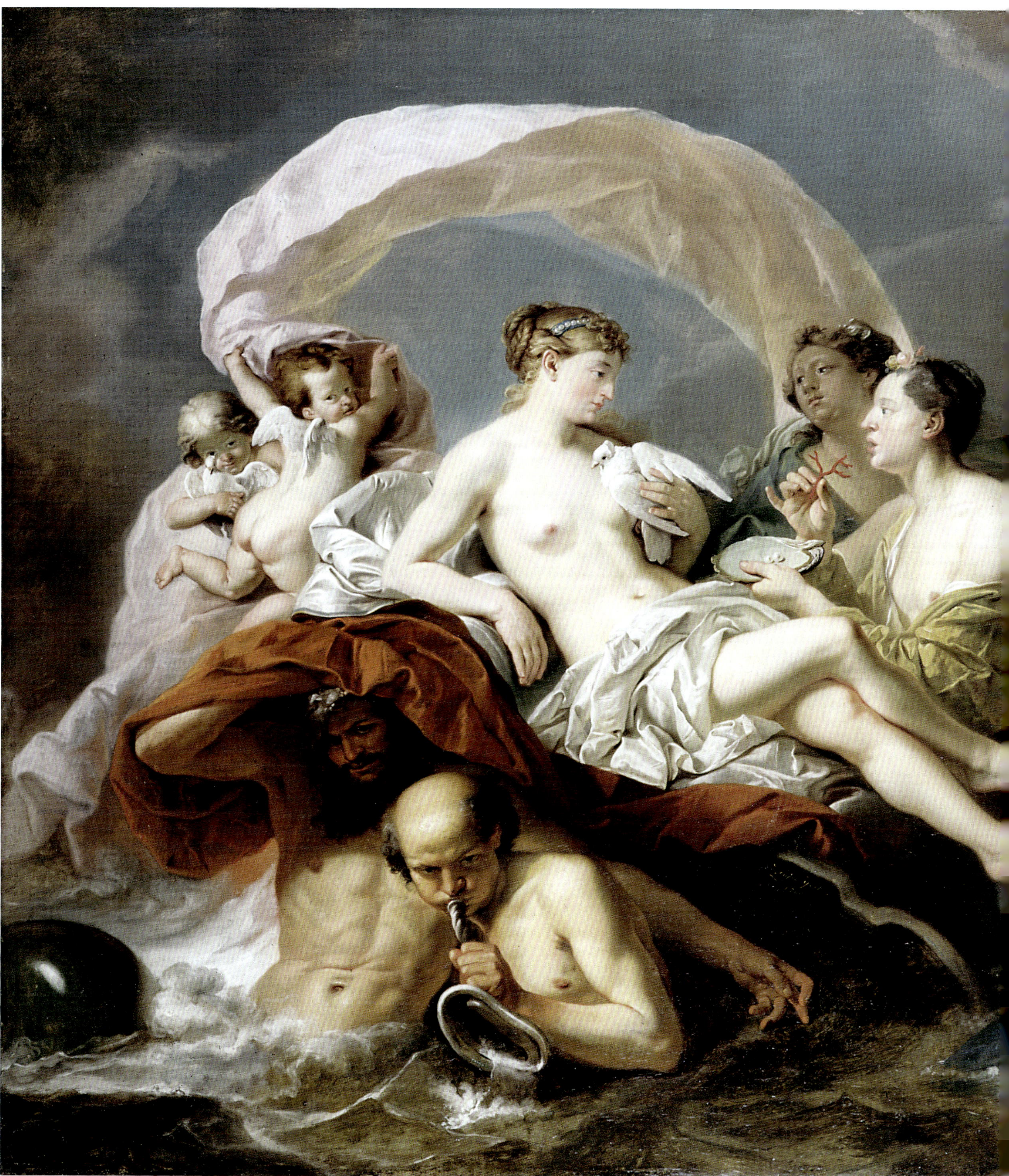

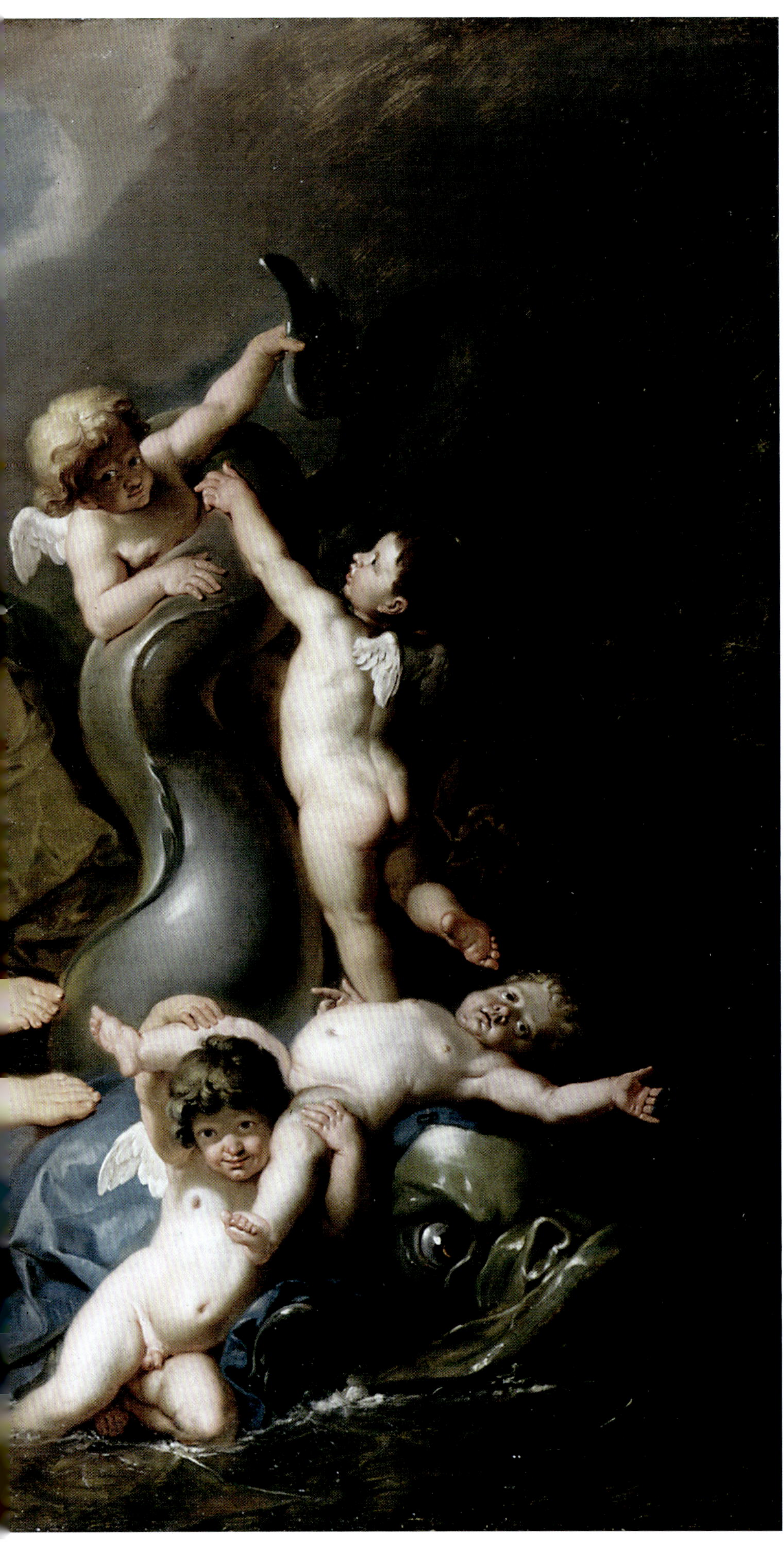

Figure 69 (cat. 7)
Venus Marina, 1760, oil on canvas,
125 × 171 cm (49¼ × 67⅜ in).
Musée des Beaux-Arts, Bordeaux

Another problem for Zoffany was his ambiguous marital status: separated but not divorced from his first wife, he was prevented from furthering his career by remarrying well. His contemporary Allan Ramsay, who also benefited from the Earl of Bute's patronage, eloped with his second wife Margaret Lindsay, the niece of the Earl of Mansfield, Lord Chief Justice, and the cousin of the diplomat and minister David Murray, seventh Viscount Stormont. Although her parents thoroughly disapproved, Ramsay was wealthy enough to support a genteel life, and his wife's connections helped confirm his status as a gentleman and intellectual. Zoffany however was sidetracked by his taste for pretty young women whose likely futures were in domestic service, the millinery trades or even prostitution. Though loyal after his fashion to his common-law wife, he was probably as dismayed as was the family friend Mrs Papendiek to find on his return from India that his daughters had not been inculcated with ladylike accomplishments so much as the arts of household management.[7]

When he arrived in England, Zoffany had struggled initially to find an entrée into polite society and affluent patrons who could commission works of art. But when he did so, it was through the passion for sociability that was a characteristic of British life, enjoyed by all from aristocrat to artisan, and was often reflected in clubs and societies. And his breakthrough was into circles that had ties as much to the queen as to the king. These included a group of friends who formed an informal club nicknamed 'The Common Room' and who had shared their Grand Tour. All of them sat for Zoffany: Lord Barrington, Minister at War; his brother-in-law Richard Price, an agricultural improver and father of the Picturesque theorist, Uvedale Price; Benjamin Stillingfleet, botanist, amateur composer and mathematician (fig. 71); and his cousin, the Norfolk landowner William Windham, to whom Stillingfleet acted as tutor.[8] The Norfolk Windhams were related to the Earls of Egremont, owners of Petworth House in Sussex. Charles Wyndham, second earl and an early minister of George III, was the husband of one of Queen Charlotte's Ladies of the Bedchamber, Lady Alicia, née Carpenter; she was also cousin by marriage to the Duchess of Northumberland, another Lady of the Bedchamber, who had family ties to the Earl of Bute, too. After Lady Egremont was widowed, she married in 1767 the Saxon ambassador, Count Hans Maurice Brühl, who had been taught at Leipzig by Queen Charlotte's favourite German moralist, C.F. Gellert, and shared the king's fascination with horology. Count Brühl thus illustrates the Saxon dimension to Charlotte's circle, which included the musicians Johann

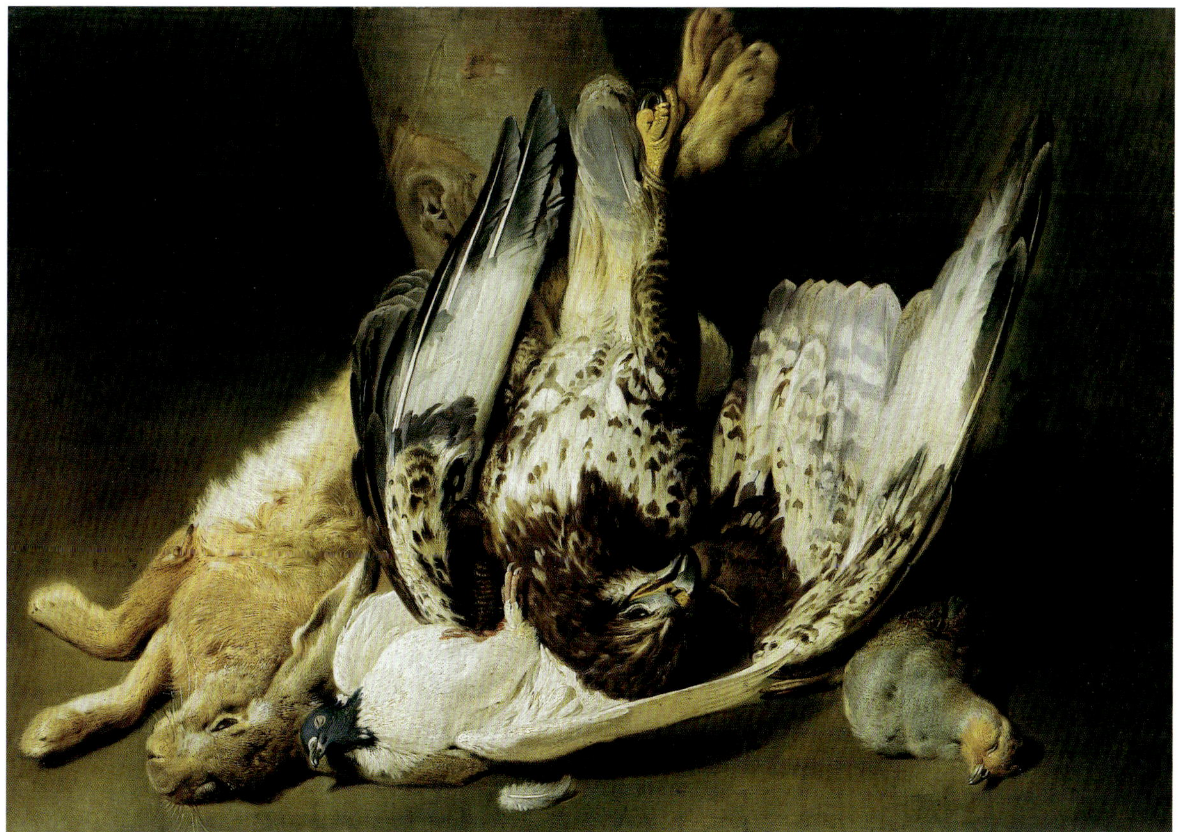

Figure 70 (cat. 6)
Still Life with Birds and Game,
1760, oil on canvas,
61 × 86 cm (24 × 33⅞ in).
Stadtmuseum Simeonstift
Trier (Inv. Nr. III.34)

Figure 71
Benjamin Stillingfleet, c.1761,
oil on canvas, 91.3 × 70.7 cm
(36 × 27⅞ in). National Portrait
Gallery, London; purchased
1999

Christian Bach, who taught her music, and Carl Friedrich
Abel, probably her favourite performer. Another member
of Stillingfleet's set was Handel's copyist and executor,
German-born John Christopher Smith (Johann Christoph
Schmidt), who also sat for Zoffany (see fig. 12).

As well as botany, music and agricultural improvement,
these gentlemen shared with George and Charlotte an
enthusiasm for education, and this linked Charlotte to the circle
attached to Mrs Montagu's assemblies, later to be known as the
Bluestockings. Stillingfleet was the eponymous Bluestocking,
from his habit of wearing blue woollen stockings to her
assemblies and not white silk ones. Lady Egremont and her
sister-in-law Mrs Grenville, also the wife of a minister, were
patrons of the cosmopolitan governess Mme LePrince de
Beaumont. A Frenchwoman from Rouen, she had first been a
protégé of Emperor Francis's mother in Lorraine and helped
educate his sister. LePrince de Beaumont wrote a conduct book
on princely education, which she dedicated to Francis and Maria
Theresa's eldest son Joseph, and when she came to London, she
educated several young noblewomen in court circles, including
two of Lady Egremont's daughters and the young Louisa
North, later Countess Willoughby de Broke (cat. 72), whose
brother was the Prime Minister Lord North (1770–78) and
whose father was Charlotte's treasurer. LePrince de Beaumont
was one of the pioneers of educational puzzles and her dissected
maps were used by Lady Charlotte Finch in the royal nursery.[9]

The Bluestockings in turn were linked to male and female
virtuosi such as the collector and scientific patron, Margaret,
second Duchess of Portland; the botanical artist and court
insider, Mrs Delany; Sir Joseph Banks, whom Zoffany so nearly
accompanied to Australia; and the botanist Daniel Solander.
The Scottish physician Dr William Hunter was the royal
gynaecologist as well as Zoffany's friend and fellow associate at
Jack's coffee house, where gentlemen met for regular discussion
of natural history. He also taught anatomy at the Royal
Academy (see cat. 46). Charlotte therefore had more in common
with Zoffany than their German birth and affection for dogs:
he fitted easily into the cultural intelligentsia in court circles.

Zoffany was thus able to befriend and benefit from the
patronage of various groups who contributed to Britain's
cultural life and also had ties to the royal court. He would paint
new money as much as old: bankers like the Drummonds or
Mrs Oswald; later the nabobs in India, whom the king rather
deplored, and Warren Hastings, whose German wife Marian
was a protégée of Queen Charlotte's first Keeper of the Robes,
Mrs Schwellenberg. Given these links, it is interesting that

Zoffany painted relatively few great magnates and courtier
families. However, Zoffany was fortunate in early attracting the
attention of John Stuart, third Earl of Bute, a significant patron
and collector.

As a politician Bute was probably the most unpopular man in
British political life in the reign of George III. His failures point
to the different way that political power was both exercised
and represented in Great Britain, compared with Continental
monarchies and principalities, and consequently the different
ways that an artist like Zoffany could represent the elite and
their world. Bute was effectively the royal favourite; when the
king made him Prime Minister in 1763, his position rested
solely on the monarch's support. But, since monarchs had to
function in partnership with Parliament, it was in practice
essential for them to have ministers who could command the
confidence of a larger grouping of peers, and to influence votes
in the House of Commons, where money bills were initiated.
The British court was one point in a three-way relationship,
which also included Parliament at Westminster and the
thriving commercial and journalistic life of London.

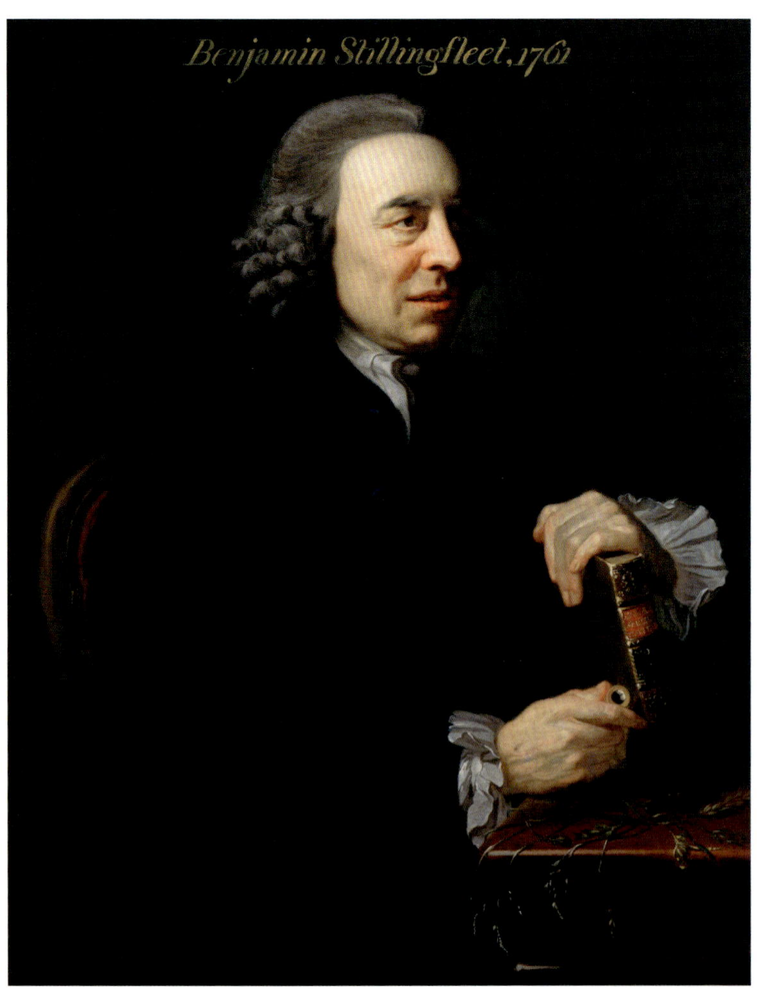

Bute attracted disapprobation partly because he was successful at court but not at Westminster, and he was paraded in effigy, and in a pun on his name, as a Jack-boot, alongside George's mother, the Dowager Princess Augusta of Wales, with whom he was erroneously supposed to be having an affair, symbolized by a petticoat. The opposition to Bute was orchestrated to a large degree by the rake and politician John Wilkes, whom Zoffany also painted, though this was after Wilkes had become much more of an establishment figure (fig. 72). Even normal elections were a kind of carnivalesque street theatre when everyday life was suspended for a while to hear speeches from the balconies of coaching inns, food and

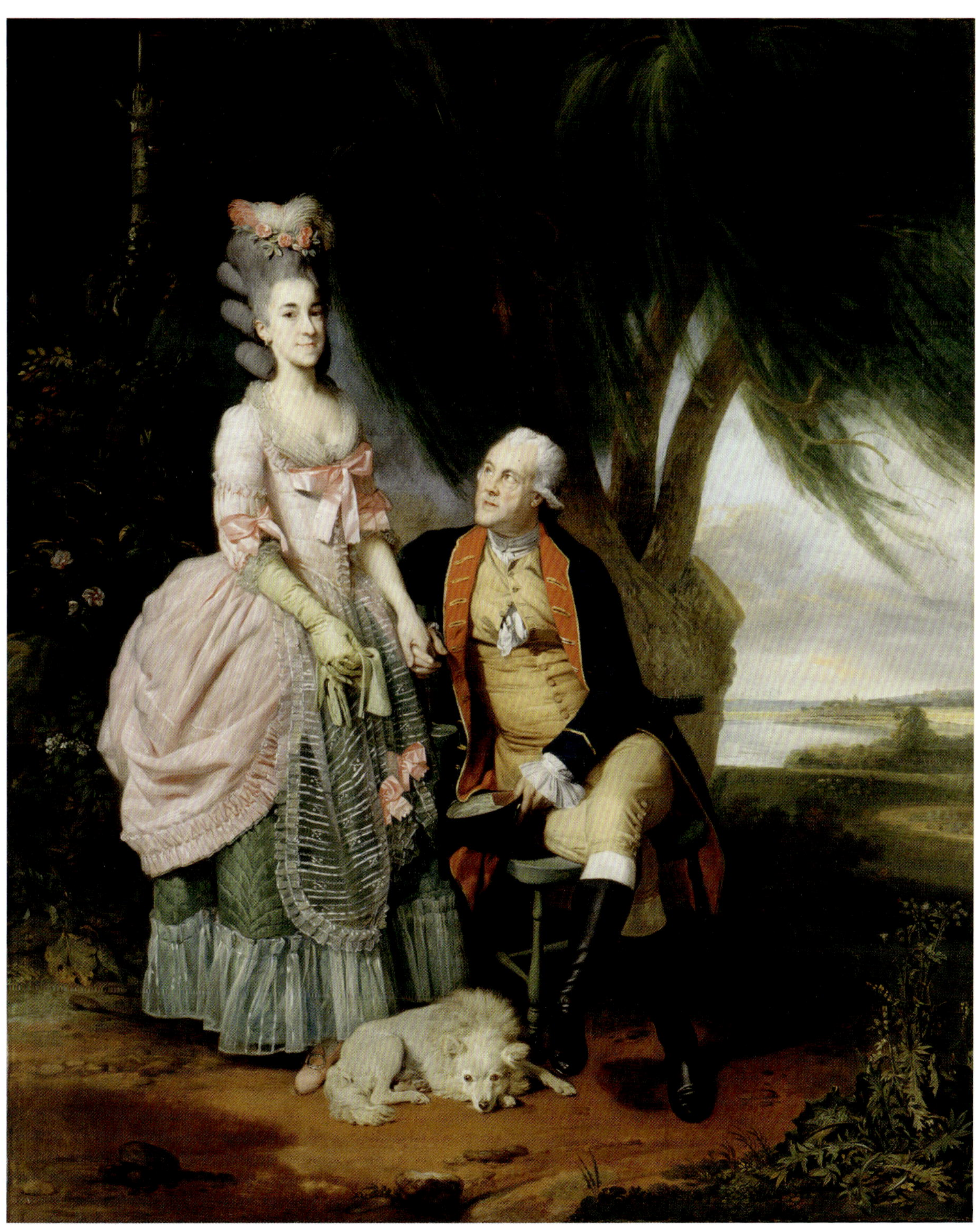

Figure 72 (cat. 76)
John Wilkes and his Daughter Mary (Polly), 1779,
oil on canvas, 126.4 × 100.3 cm (49¾ × 39½ in). National Portrait Gallery, London; purchased with help from the National Heritage Memorial Fund and The National Art Collections Fund, 1991

drink were liberally dispensed by rival candidates, and the
successful carried through the streets, to be followed by election
balls for the respectable hosted by mayors and councillors.[10]

Public life and parliamentary oratory were thus
performative and theatrical in a different way from the courts of
Italy and Germany and paralleled the immense popularity and
ubiquity of commercial dramatic entertainment in a golden age
of the English theatre. Through being commissioned to paint
David Garrick in both his private and professional life, Zoffany
had found a patron who in many respects was a pivotal figure in
George III's London. As a man of letters and former pupil of
Dr Johnson, Garrick pointed towards London literary life and
genteel circles. Johnson's club was linked to polite female circles
intersecting with the queen's entourage. Yet Garrick was also
the leading theatrical producer and actor in the entire nation.
Eighteenth-century popular and elite culture was expressive,
even rumbustious. Moreover, the royal court did not have, as
many European courts did, a separate and exclusive court
theatre. If George III and Queen Charlotte, keen theatre-lovers,
wanted to see a play, they went to the licensed theatres in
Covent Garden or the Haymarket.

Zoffany's sitters reflect the mix of public and private
patronage that characterized much of Britain's cultural and
scientific activity at the time. In their scientific interests the
king and queen were in many respects different only in degree,
not kind, from other landowners. The king absorbed himself
in agricultural improvement as well as astronomy, the queen
in literature, pedagogy, geology and botany. It is worth
speculating whether Zoffany's botanical study of a balsam on
a black background (fig. 73) was an attempt to imitate one of
Mrs Delany's flower collages (fig. 74), in which the royal family
took such an interest, helping to provide her with specimens
from Kew.[11] The Royal Society was not an institute through
which the state sponsored scientific research, for all its royal
title, but a club for amateur gentlemen. Thus when the
Lincolnshire gentleman Sir Joseph Banks learnt that the Royal
Society was contributing financially to an Admiralty-sponsored
voyage to southern Pacific to observe the Transit of Venus and
to map any undiscovered landmass, he was able to offer himself
as the expedition's chief botanist, who could travel and fit out
a cabin at his own expense. Zoffany had hoped to go along as
the artist recorder of the expedition, but Captain Cook vetoed
the inclusion of Banks and his over-numerous and over-
equipped entourage. The queen therefore suggested Zoffany
go to Florence instead to paint the Tribune room in the Uffizi
for her. What prompted this Italian commission?

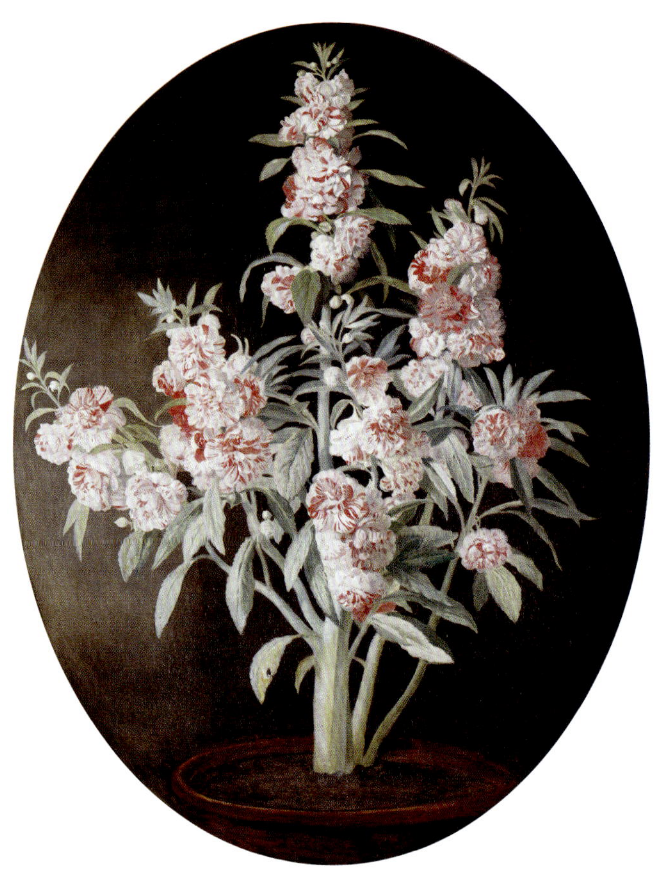

Figure 73
A Balsam, 1761–2, oil on canvas, 91.8 × 71.1 cm (36⅛ × 28 in).
The Royal Collection, Her Majesty Queen Elizabeth II

Figure 74
Mary Delany, *A Stem of Stock*, 1781, watercolour
and gouache on paper, cut and pasted onto
backing paper painted black, 25 × 17 cm (9⅞ × 6¾ in).
The Royal Collection, Her Majesty Queen Elizabeth II

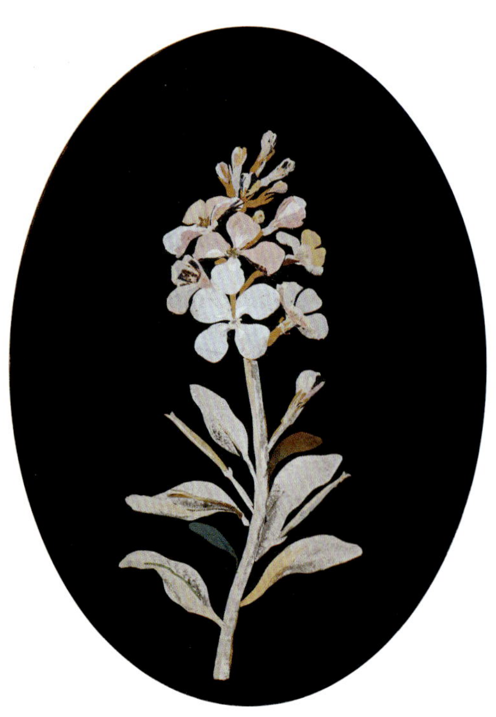

Neither George nor Charlotte had ever visited Italy: this put them at a considerable cultural disadvantage. As Dr Johnson said, a man who had never visited Italy was always conscious of some inferiority.[12] Most gentlemen completed their desultory education at Oxford and Cambridge with a Grand Tour that took in Rome, Florence, Naples and Venice when it reached Italy. The early Hanoverians had also been in thrall to Italy. George III's great-grandfather George I had regularly been to the Venetian carnival with his father and uncles, and George Frederic Handel had been his *Kapellmeister* in Hanover. The composer was already settled in London when George I came to the throne in 1714, ensuring the triumph of Italian opera in England. The Hanoverian summer palace at Herrenhausen had French gardens and Italianate Baroque decoration in its orangery, and there was a private court theatre in the Leine Palace, Hanover. Charlotte herself was from a small and poor north-eastern German principality, Mecklenburg-Strelitz, where the cultural standing of its thinly scattered nobility could be gauged by whether a visit had been made to Italy or to Vienna, the premier court of the Holy Roman Empire. It is understandable, then, that she would want a 'virtual' visit to one of the most famous artistic collections in Europe.

Italy also represented an intriguing, rather louche, alternative 'other' for British expatriates. Grand Tourists had their letters of introduction to princes and aristocrats, but for young men it was often also a place of sexual adventure and relaxed morals – and for some women, too: Lady Bute's mother, Lady Mary Wortley Montagu, came to Italy in 1739 ostensibly for her health but also to follow the object of her affections, the homosexual mathematician Francesco Algarotti. Despite romantic disappointment, she remained there until returning to England in 1760 to die.[13] Genteel poverty could also motivate residence in Italy. Also resident in 1739 was the young Lady Charlotte Fermor, later Lady Charlotte Finch, with her parents, the first Earl and Countess of Pomfret, and some of her older siblings. Lady Pomfret, a confidante of Lady Mary and also a retired Lady of the Bedchamber to the recently deceased Queen Caroline (George II's consort), spent several years in France and Italy to repair their finances. It was unusual for a young Englishwoman to have become acquainted with Florence like this, and her superior cultural credentials may have been a reason why Lady Charlotte was chosen by Queen Charlotte to be the royal governess.[14]

George III indicated to Zoffany that he should include young Grand Tourists in his *Tribuna* conversation piece, but those he portrayed came from the kind of high-minded titled families who provided courtiers, soldiers and statesmen, which George and Charlotte favoured. George Legge, Lord Lewisham, was heir to the pious second Earl of Dartmouth, who was a Methodist and later an anti-slavery campaigner. His eldest son was selected to be a Lord of the Bedchamber when the young Prince of Wales received his own household in 1784, George III clearly hoping he would be a good influence on his hedonistic but cultured son.[15] Viscount Lewisham later married a relative of Lady Charlotte Finch. Her own son George, the future ninth Earl of Winchilsea, was also included in the picture, as was Richard Edgecumbe, whose father, the first Earl of Edgecumbe, was a distinguished admiral and treasurer of George III's household.

A third type of English grandee abroad was George Nassau Clavering-Cowper, third Earl Cowper, who was a truly cosmopolitan aristocrat by virtue of his ancestry (fig. 75, cat. 54). His maternal grandfather was a second cousin of William of Orange, Stadholder of the Netherlands and after 1688 co-monarch with his wife Mary of Great Britain, and Cowper could also trace descent from James Butler, first Duke of Ormonde, who had followed the future Charles II into exile after the English civil war and at the Restoration been rewarded for his loyalty by the dukedom. The third Earl Cowper had elected to stay in Florence after arriving there during his Grand Tour and dallying with an Italian marchesa. The romance faded away, but his love affair with Tuscan life and Italian opera lasted and he was a principal adviser on musical matters to the Duke Pietro Leopoldo. When he inherited the title of Baron of the Holy Roman Empire from his maternal uncle, George III permitted him to use this title as well as his English one. But the king would have preferred him to live in Britain and perform his local and national duties as a resident peer, and refused Cowper's stream of requests that he be awarded one of the chivalric Orders, of the Garter or of the Bath, that he so craved.[16] In the ambition to rise higher in status, Cowper was not unusual – most peers wanted further advancement. Consequently, he deplored the fact that Zoffany dressed in pink coats in Florence, this colour being a prerogative in Britain of an earl, not a painter, however well educated.[17]

Figure 75 (cat. 54)
George Nassau, Third Earl Cowper, 1772–3, oil on canvas, 142.2 × 111 cm (56 × 43¾ in). Trustees of the Firle Estate Settlement

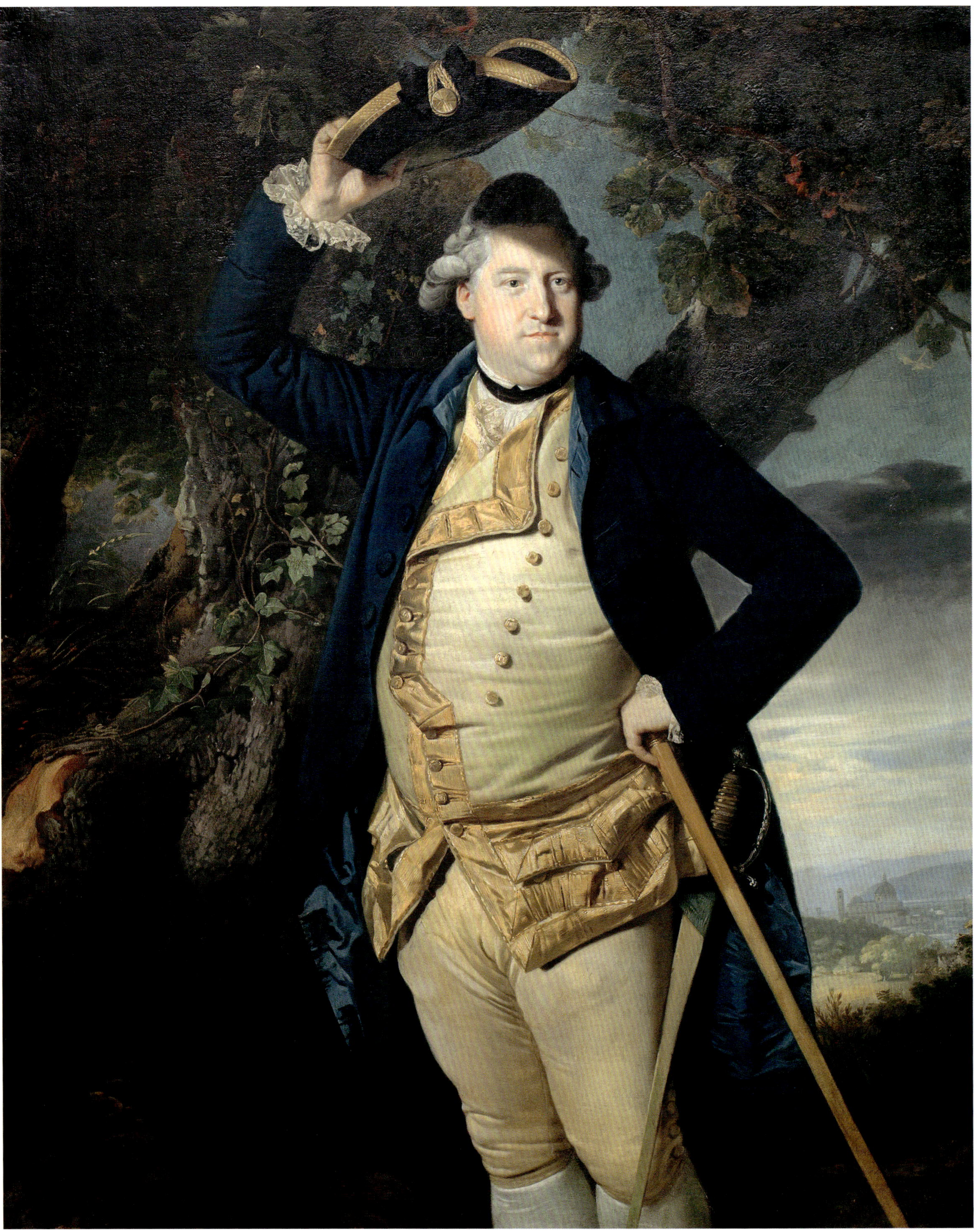

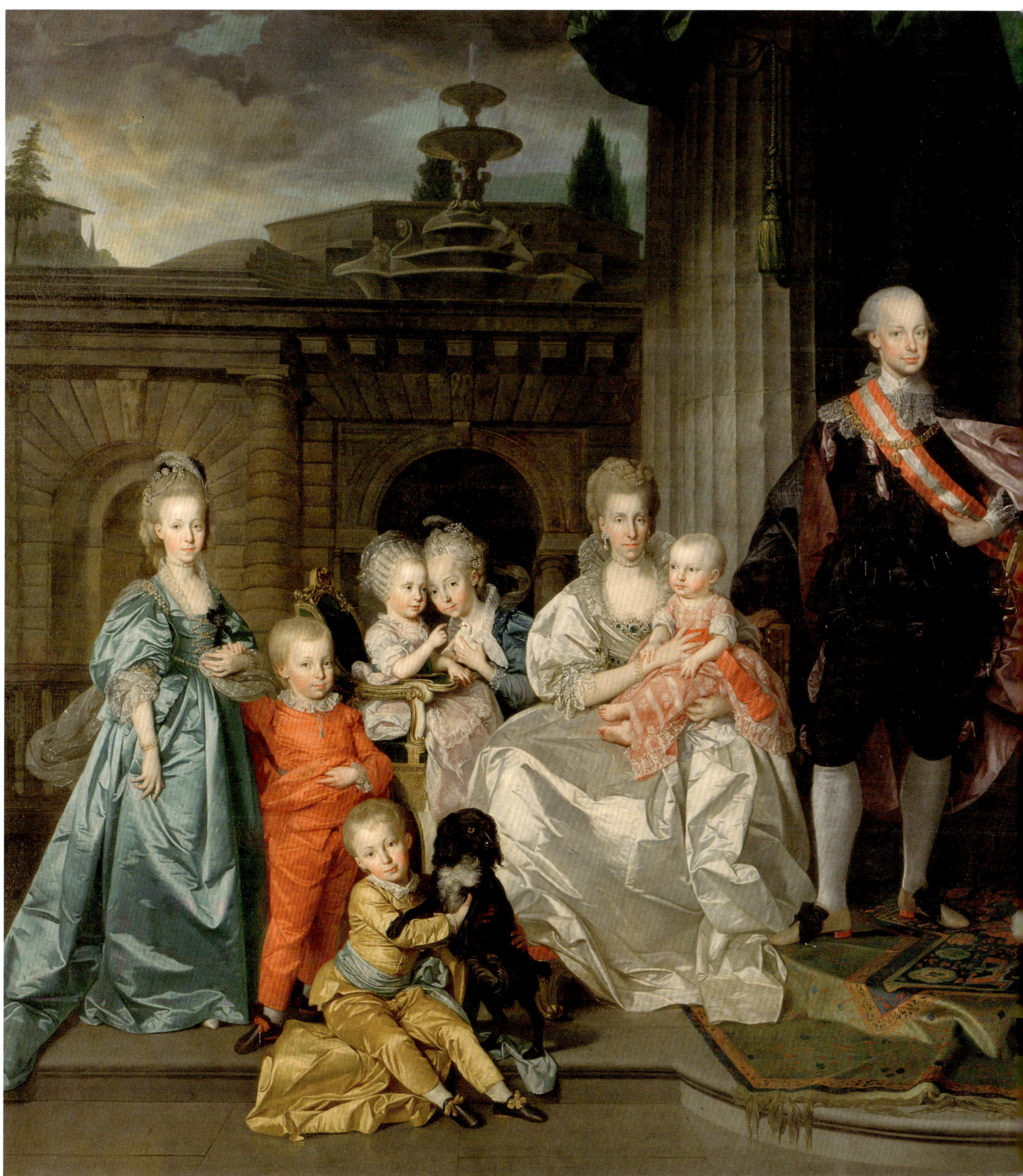

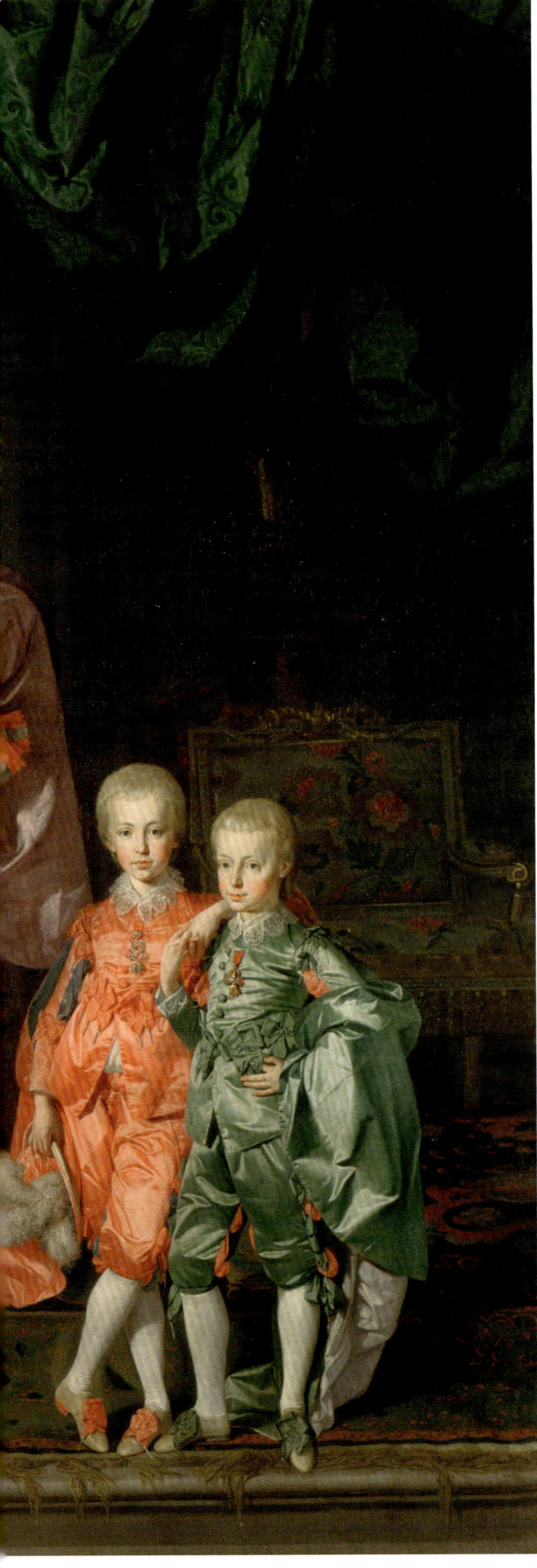

To understand Zoffany's time in Italy, it is also necessary
to review the role of princely courts in Italy and the ambitions
of the Habsburg dynasty there. Eighteenth-century Italy was
no more united politically than was Germany. Most of the
city states of the Renaissance era had become absorbed into
hereditary principalities or kingdoms, including the Duchy
of Milan, the Grand Duchy of Tuscany, and the Kingdom of
Naples and Sicily; the notable exceptions were the aristocratic
republics of Venice and Genoa. The peninsula was dominated
by the rival dynasties of the Bourbons and Habsburgs, each
of whom furthered hereditary rights over principalities by
insisting on historical claims, by creating 'secundogenitures',
or second lines for younger sons, by making useful dynastic
marriages and by international diplomacy.

At the start of the century the French Bourbons seemed in
the ascendant. Louis XIV's grandson Philip had become King
of Spain in 1713 and followed a traditional Spanish policy of
building influence in Italy. His second wife, Elisabeth Farnese,
a Princess of Parma, was especially keen to establish Italian
secundogenitures in Parma and Piacenza for her sons. Human
mortality disrupted this dynastic strategy. A series of deaths
meant that her son Charles became Duke of Parma, then Grand
Duke of Tuscany, then King Charles VII of Naples and Sicily,
then King of Spain. When Charles gave up his rights to
Tuscany, Francis of Lorraine had become its grand duke.[18]
His wife was the Habsburg heiress Maria Theresa, who was
ineligible to be elected as empress in her own right and could
only inherit the Austrian Habsburg family lands (including the
Kingdoms of Hungary and Bohemia). However, Francis Stephen
succeeded in getting elected as emperor in 1745, so he was
able to revive the Habsburg monopoly of the imperial crown.
Furthermore, what Maria Theresa lacked in terms of gender
eligibility she made up for both in her intelligent statecraft
and her maternal fecundity. She and her husband, who also acted
as co-regent of the Habsburgs' hereditary lands, had a total of
sixteen children, ten of whom survived to adulthood, five being
deployed in marriages to increase Habsburg influence in Italy.

The son and heir, Joseph, married the future Duke
Ferdinando of Bourbon-Parma's sister, Isabella, in 1760, but she
died of smallpox only three years afterwards. Her mother Louisa

Figure 76
*The Family of the Grand Duke Pietro
Leopoldo*, 1776, oil on canvas,
325 × 398 cm (128 × 156¾ in).
Kunsthistorisches Museum, Vienna

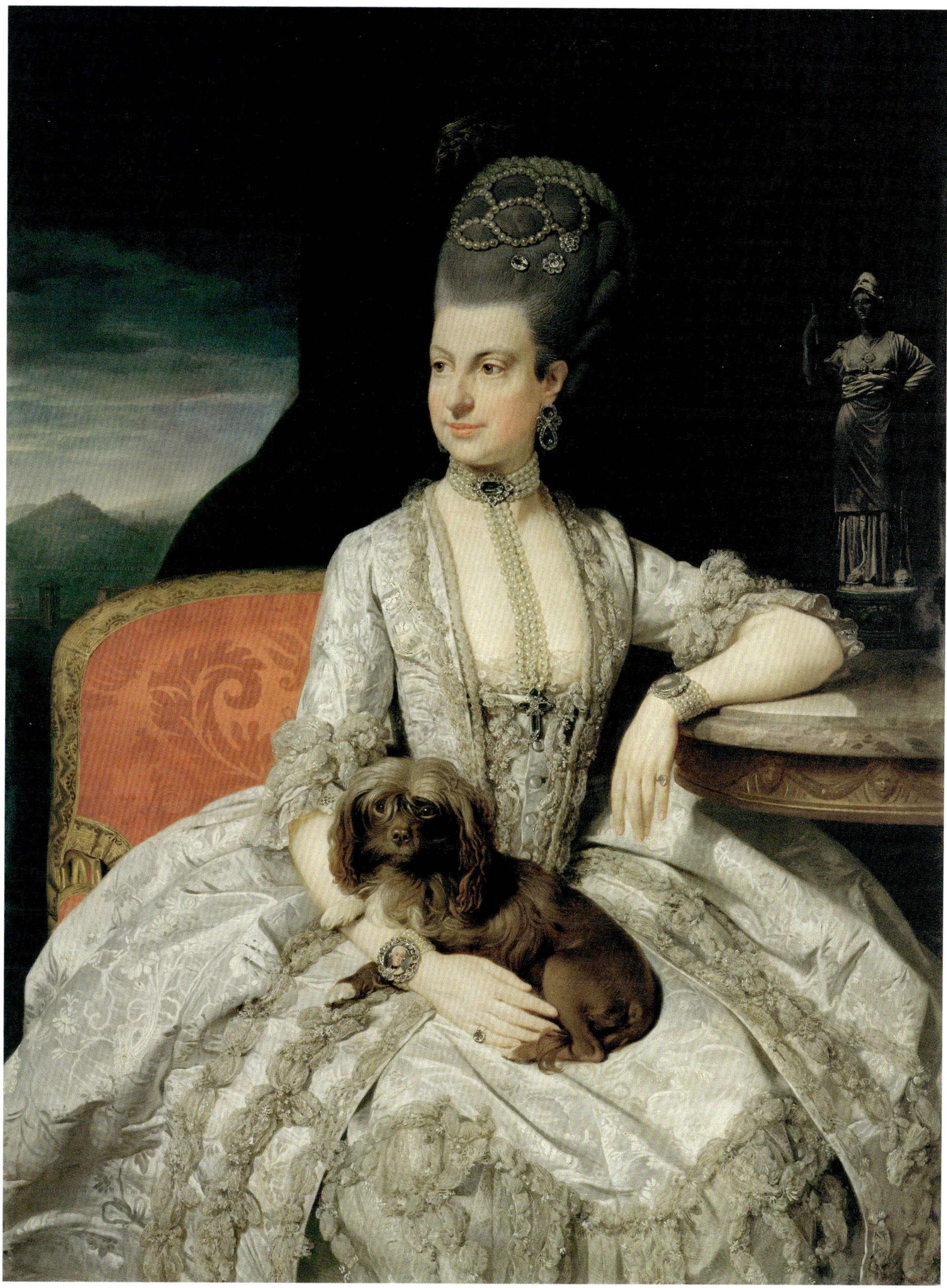

Figure 77
The Archduchess Maria Christina, 1776,
oil on canvas, 131 × 94 cm (51⅝ × 37 in).
Kunsthistorisches Museum, Vienna

was the eldest daughter of Louis XV of France, and the marriage signalled the new rapprochement of the French and Austrian monarchies after 1756.[19] Pietro Leopoldo, Francis and Maria Theresa's second surviving son, was designated as the heir to his father's Duchy of Tuscany and married a Spanish Bourbon princess, Maria Luisa, as part of Spain's recognition of his Tuscan title. Ferdinando, Pietro Leopoldo's brother, was due to inherit the Habsburg Duchy of Milan, acted as its governor when he came of age and married the sole heiress of the Duchy of Modena, inheriting that, too, when his father-in-law died. Maria Theresa's eldest daughter, Maria Christina (fig. 77), who sat to Zoffany during a visit to Florence in 1776, married her half-cousin, Prince Albert, Duke of Teschen. Maria Amalia, the third surviving daughter (fig. 78), was married to her brother-in-law Ferdinando, Duke of Bourbon-Parma (fig. 79), and Maria Carolina, the youngest but one daughter, was

given to the Bourbon King of Naples and Sicily, another Ferdinando.[20] The youngest daughter Maria Antonia became Marie Antoinette, Queen of France.

Emperor Francis had necessarily been an absentee duke, and the social life of English visitors had been enhanced by the hospitality of the British representative to the duchy, Horace Mann, who ensured they had news of each other and an entrée into Florentine society. However the court revived after 1765 with the energetic, micro-managing Duke Pietro Leopoldo. His rule coincided with the trend for rulers to be influenced by the ideals of the European Enlightenment. Broadly speaking, this meant that rulers tried to implement religious toleration, rationalize and modernize administrative and legal procedures, and encourage the natural sciences, although the movement was implemented differently in different contexts. In some cases, Tuscany included, rulers were inspired by the English model of

Figure 78
Zoffany? *Maria Amalia of Austria*, 1778–9,
oil on canvas, 104.4 × 87.6 cm (41⅛ × 34½ in).
Galleria Nazionale di Parma

Figure 79
After Zoffany, *Don Ferdinando di Borbone*, 1778,
oil on panel, 107 × 86 cm (42⅛ × 33⅞ in).
Galleria Nazionale di Parma

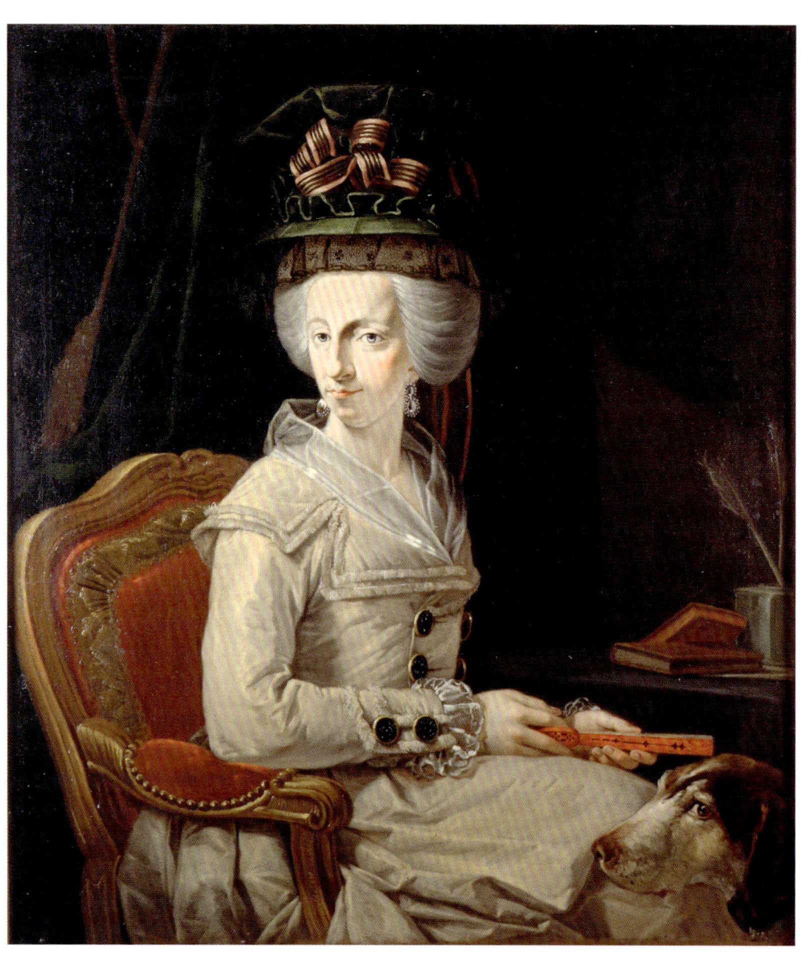

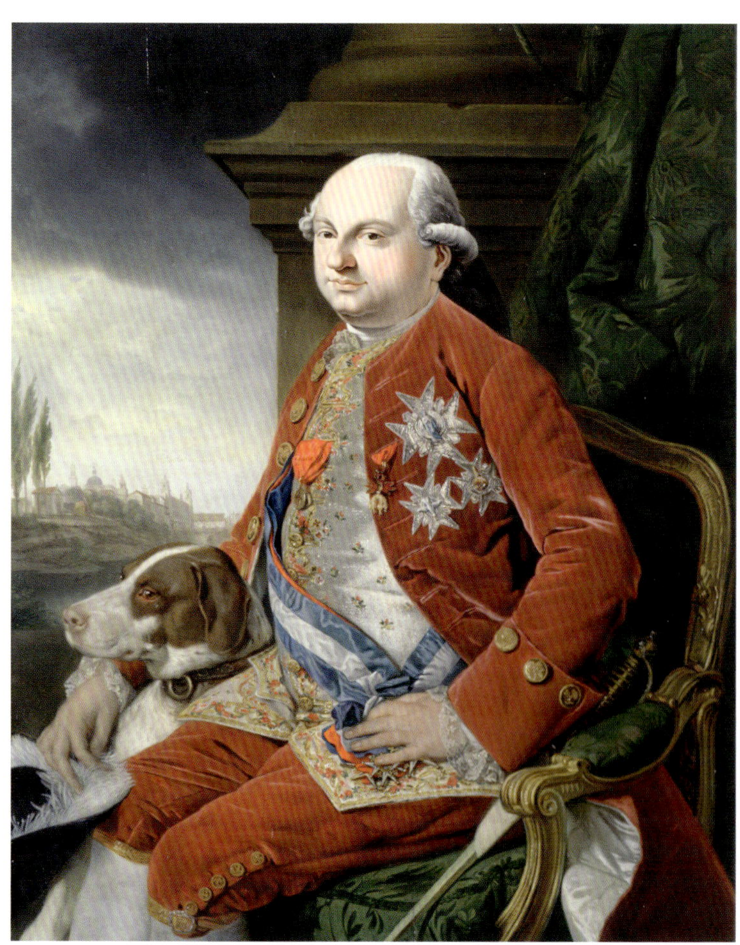

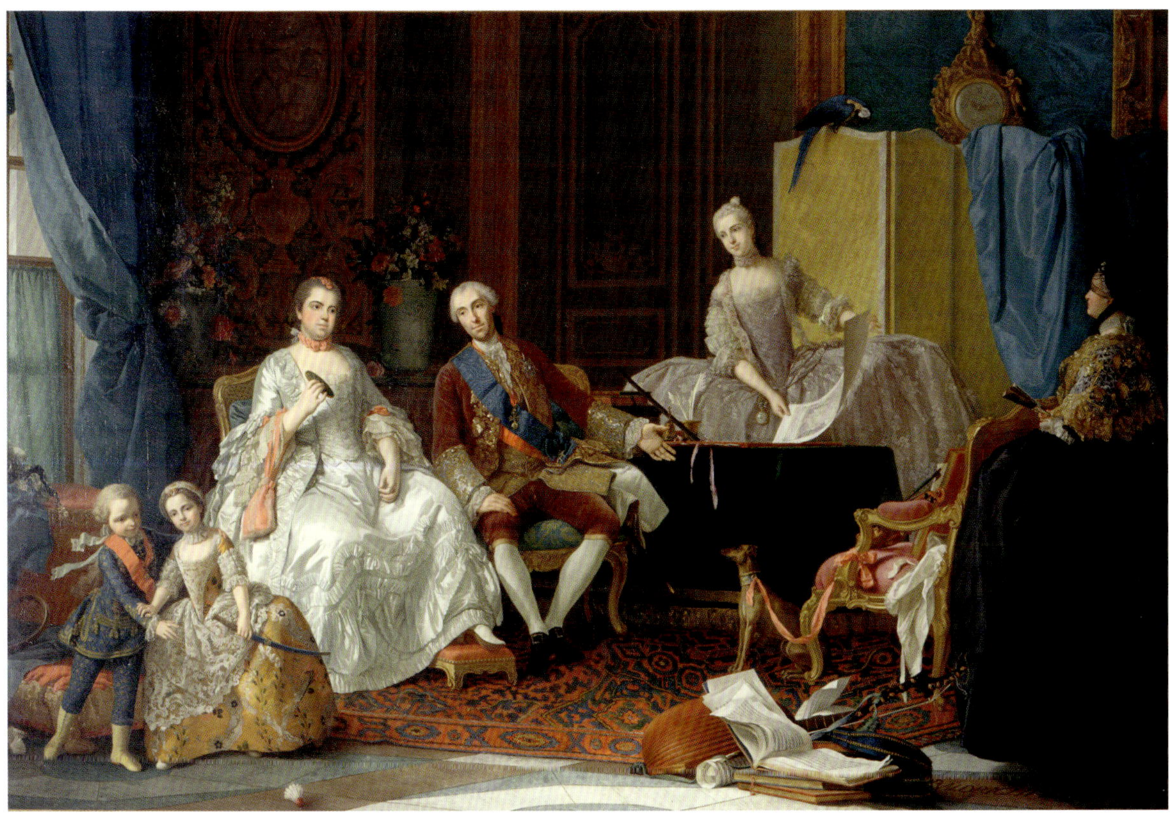

Figure 80
Giuseppe Baldrighi, *The Family of Philip Duke of Bourbon-Parma*, 1757–8, oil on canvas, 285 × 415 cm (112¼ × 163⅜ in). Galleria Nazionale di Parma

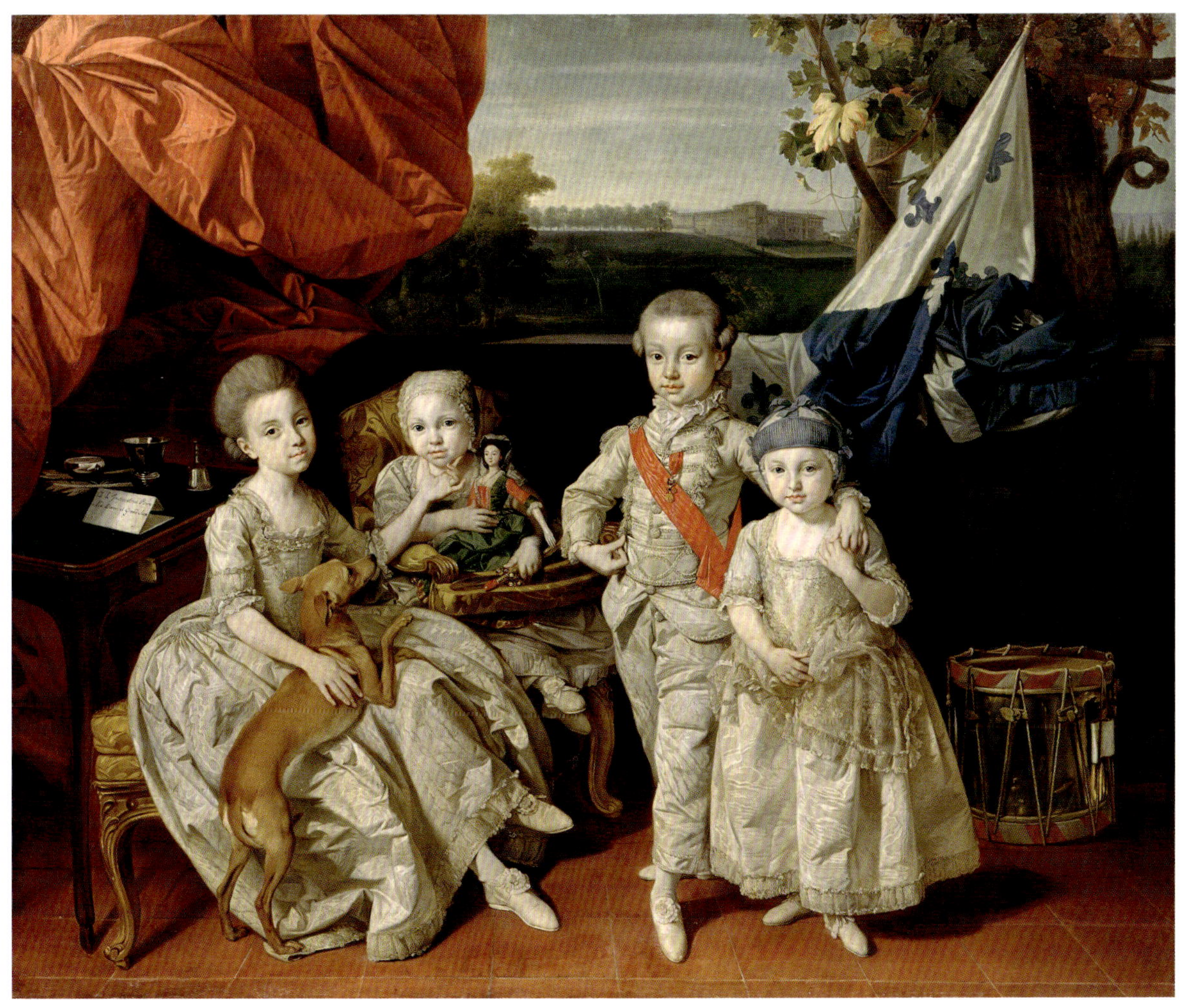

Figure 81
Four Grandchildren of Maria Theresa, 1778, oil on canvas, 159 × 184.5 cm (62⅝ × 72⅝ in). Kunsthistorisches Museum, Vienna

parliamentary monarchy, but more often they used their powers to humble powerful, privileged groups and institutions, such as the nobility, the Church, monastic orders, city councils and trade guilds, and introduce uniformity under princely law. Dynastic rulers began to justify their right to rule in terms of being the first servants of the state, rather than solely through divinely sanctioned hereditary rule.

Duke Pietro Leopoldo founded and revivified cultural institutions, and, like George III, he was interested in modern agriculture. Among many other projects, he reorganized the Academy of Sciences and the Uffizi, created a new literary institution, the Accademia Fiorentina, and reformed the city's libraries and archives. He also founded schools for the poor.[21] Education was indeed one of the main preoccupations of enlightened rulers and charitable patrons. New theories of knowledge, pioneered by John Locke, had emphasized that much secular knowledge was acquired, not innate. Individuals and societies could therefore be reformed by improving education; in Germany this was in tune with earlier ideas of rulers as paternalistic fathers of their people. This enthusiasm also embraced the education of royal and princely children, as seen in Baldrighi's portrait of Philip Duke of Parma and his family (fig. 80). There was nothing unusual about large dynastic families per se; what was new was the way in which their education often reflected new methods and fresh theories and observations about child development. The toys and games shown by Zoffany in his family portraits of the Duke and Duchess of Parma's children were part and parcel of this vogue (fig. 81).

An interest in education also blended in with more relaxed modes of royal and aristocratic domesticity. The Baroque style of rule had emphasized the prince being a constant player in a magnificent theatre of power. If the main justification of the enlightened ruler was to promote useful practices and the happiness of the people, then he could appear from time to time more informally among his people, while still maintaining the capacity for princely magnificence when occasion demanded it. He could have a less elaborate setting and routine for his private life, and yet at the same time be more accessible in this private style to his people. George III and Queen Charlotte and their children promenaded in the evenings along the terrace at Windsor Castle, where they could be approached informally, and Duke Pietro Leopoldo walked in the streets in Florence and encouraged visits to the Pitti Palace. Archduchess Maria Christina had in earlier years painted charming studies of Habsburg private life (fig. 82).

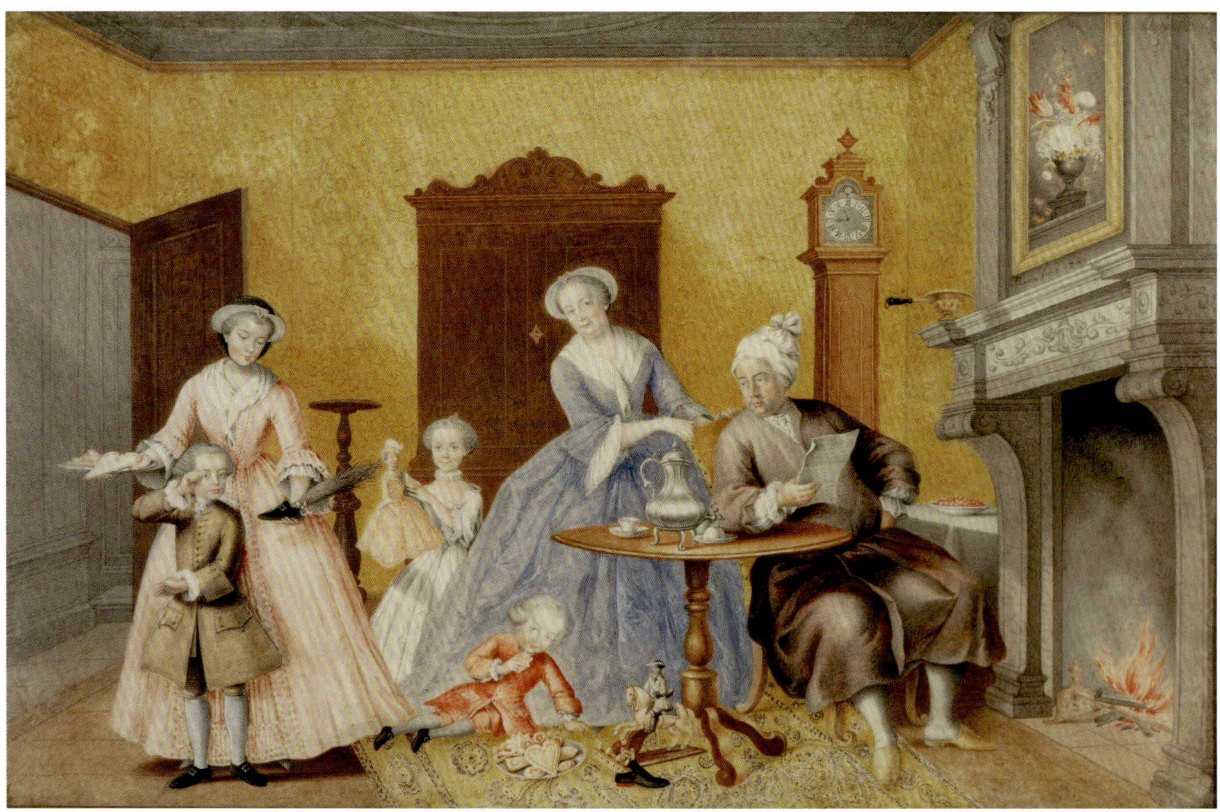

Figure 82
Archduchess Maria Christina,
*The Habsburg Family on
St Nicholas's Day*, 1762,
gouache on paper,
30 × 45 cm (11⅞ × 17¾ in).
Bundesmobilienverwaltung,
Vienna

The trend for simplicity on or off duty might also be a function of economy as well as taste: the Habsburgs in Vienna had less disposable income than many of their magnates, while for George III it was a principled matter of plain living and high thinking. An early riser, he lit his own fire before getting down to the business of the day.[22] Many princes were also soldiers and enjoyed wearing uniform on a regular basis, as Zoffany's magnificent portrait of Prince Ernest illustrates (fig. 83), while his picture of the king in general officer's uniform captures his modest and conscientious everyday mien to perfection (fig. 84).[23]

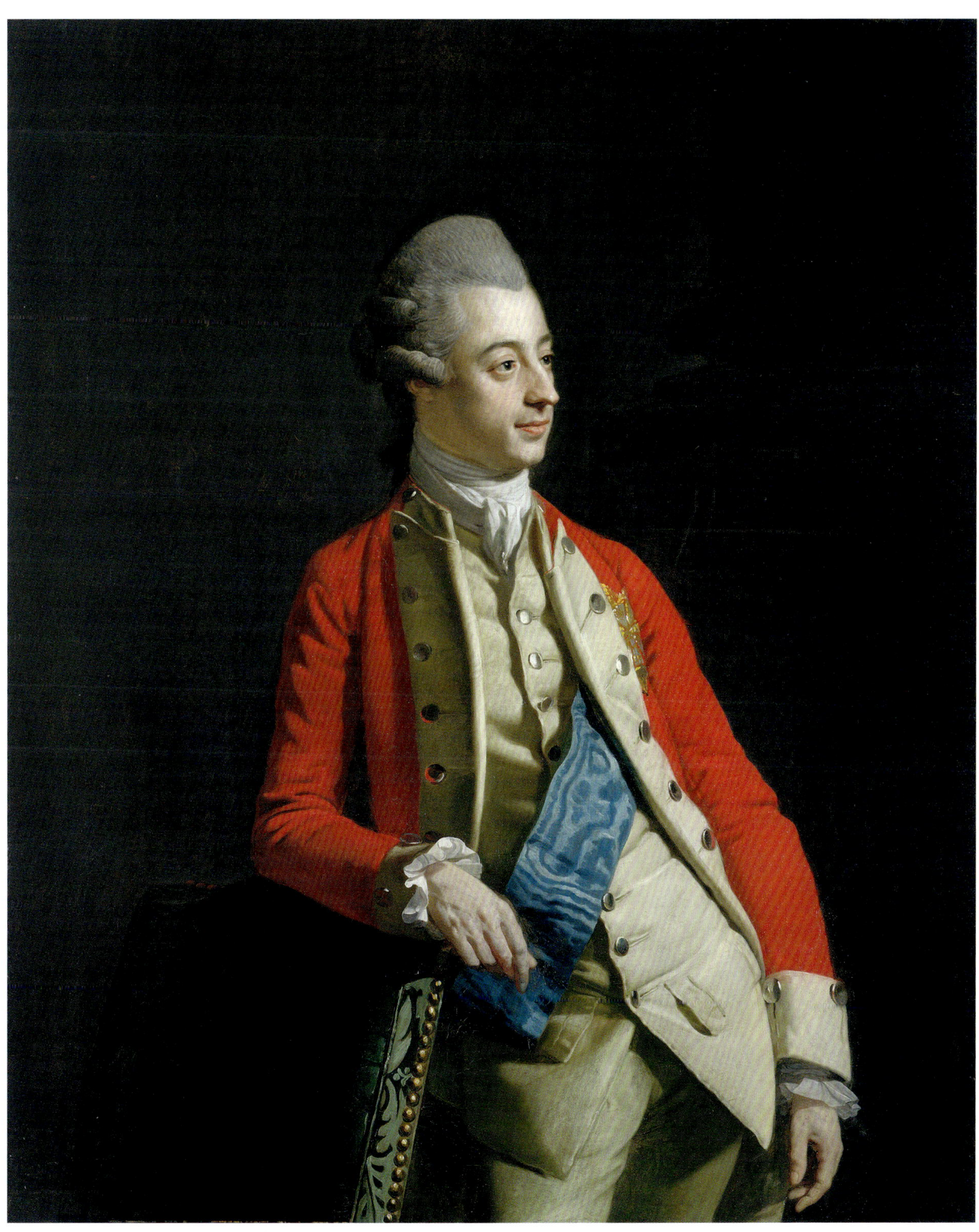

Figure 83
Prince Ernest Gottlob Albert of Mecklenburg-Strelitz, 1771–2, oil on canvas, 125.7 × 100.3 cm (49½ × 39½ in). The Royal Collection, Her Majesty Queen Elizabeth II

Figure 84 (cat. 37)
George III, 1771, oil on canvas, 161.9 × 138.5 cm (63¾ × 54½ in). The Zetland Collection

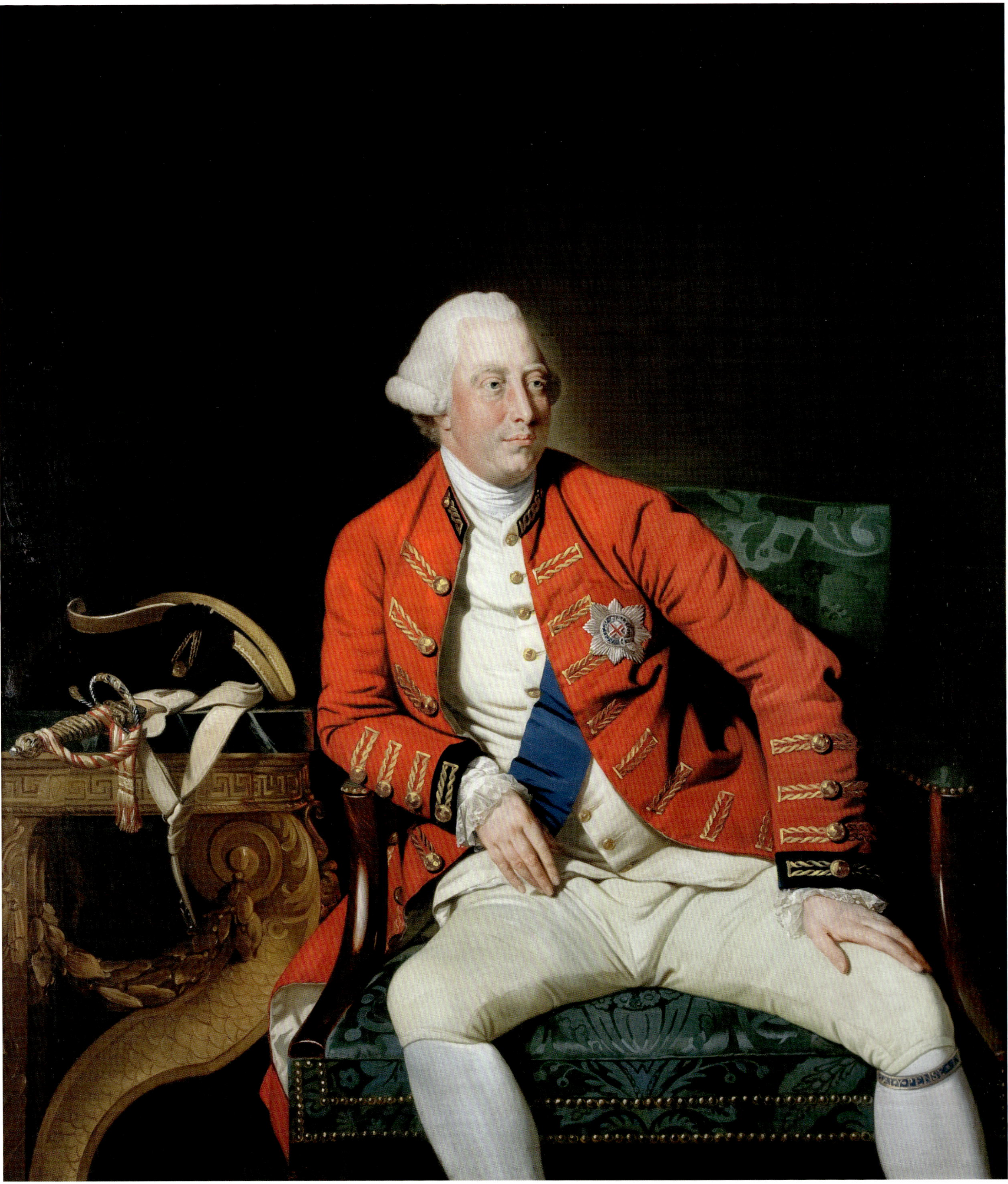

For religiously sincere princes and their consorts, such as George III, Queen Charlotte or Grand Duchess Maria Luisa of Tuscany, devotion to spouse and family was part of their Christian commitment. Men were always accorded more indulgence for sexual laxity. George III never had a mistress but Pietro Leopoldo's image of domesticity was belied by his frequent casual encounters and his longer-term affair with Lord Cowper's wife, née Hannah Gore (fig. 85). However, in his grand portrait of the Tuscan ducal family (see fig. 76) Zoffany has blended the conventions of the Austrian state portrait with British style. He has given the two eldest princes the Vandyke dress that was so popular in England and that he had deployed in his royal group portrait (fig. 86). In blending these pictorial conventions together, he perhaps suggests that the Habsburgs and the Hanoverians should be seen as part of the interconnected Continental dynasties and that Habsburgs could appropriately be painted in English style, as both families appreciated aspects of cultivated domesticity.

When Queen Charlotte commissioned Zoffany to go to Florence, it was easy for him to be drawn into the rest of the Habsburg family network and to go to Parma and Vienna. Additionally, the shortage of good painters meant that Maria Theresa was keen to commission such an able artist to paint some of her children, who lived and ruled in Italy.

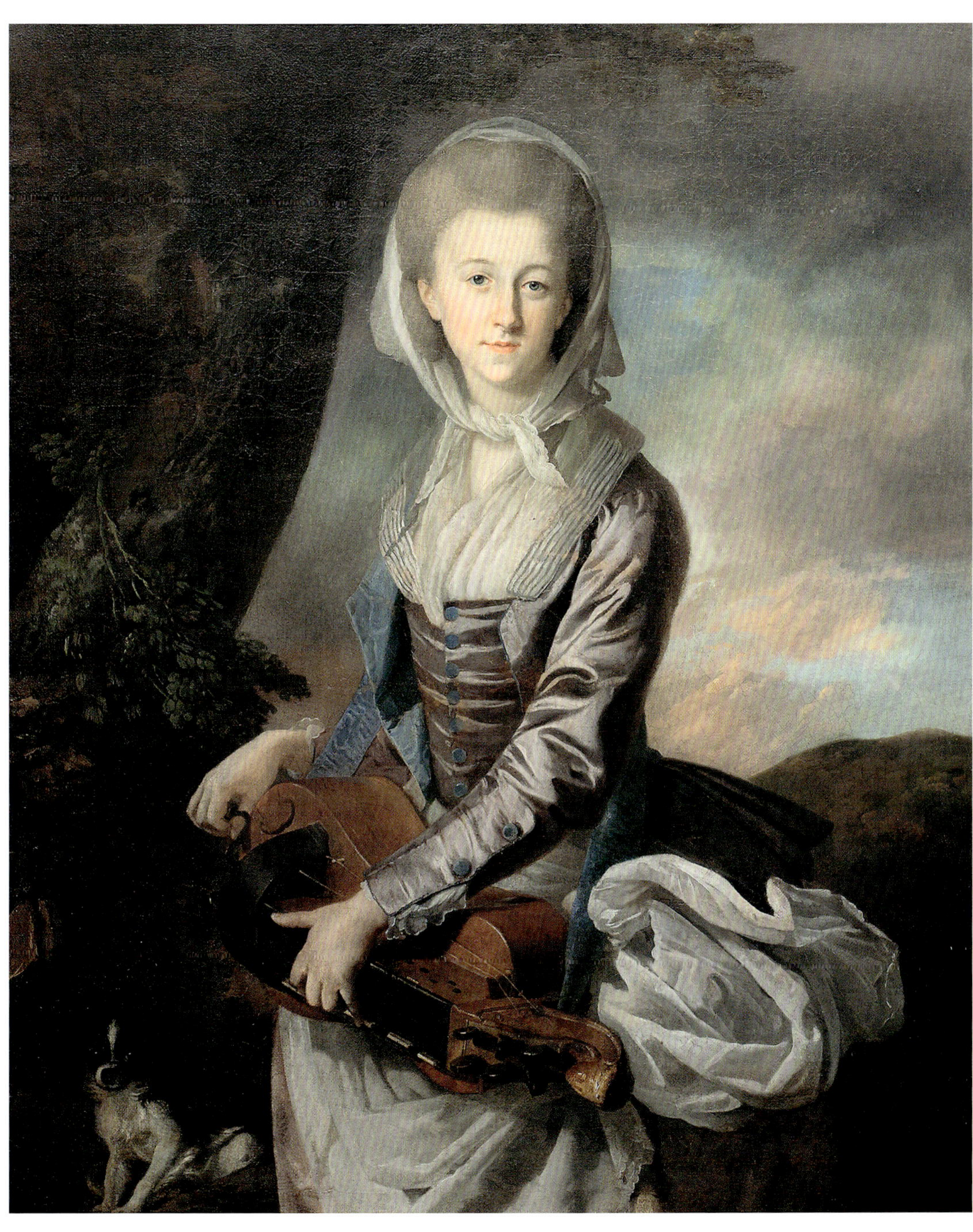

Figure 85 (cat. 55)
Miss Anne Gore as a Savoyarde, 1774,
oil on canvas, 121.9 × 97.8 cm (48 × 38½ in).
Trustees of the Firle Estate Setttlement

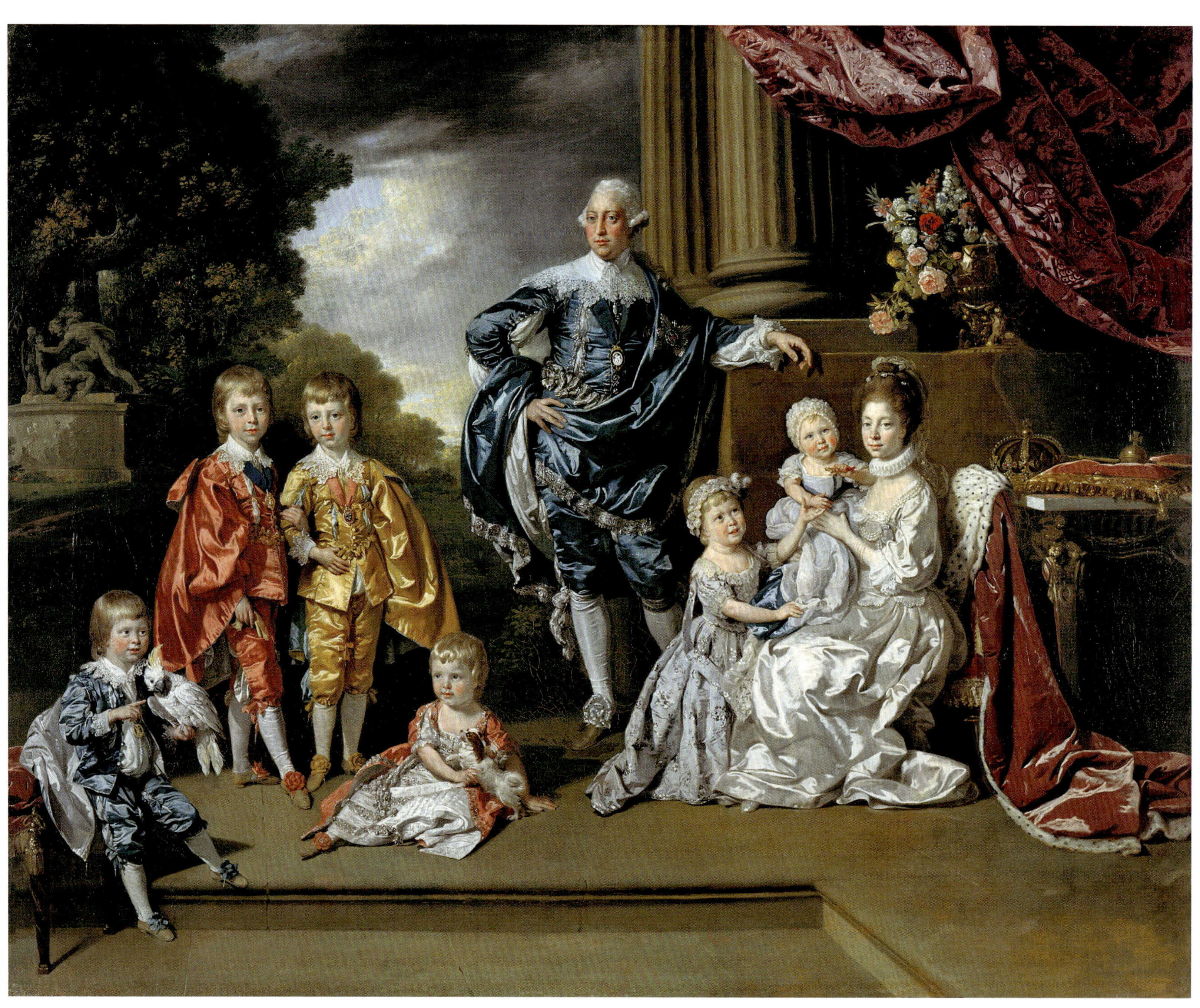

Figure 86 (cat. 34)
George III and Queen Charlotte with their Six Eldest Children,
1770, oil on canvas, 104.8 × 127.6 cm (41¼ × 50¼ in).
The Royal Collection, Her Majesty Queen Elizabeth II

He was clearly a much abler painter than Wenzel Werlin, whose stilted group portrait of the Tuscan grandchildren is naive in comparison (fig. 87). Even though Zoffany had just obtained residential status in Britain, it must have seemed the fulfilment of all his early training to paint for his former empress and then to receive an imperial barony from her. His re-encounter with a differently staged kind of religious and princely culture, and membership of Italian academies of art in Florence and then Parma, must have been irresistibly attractive, like rediscovering his lost youth.

Maria Theresa expected her daughters in Italy and France to represent the family interests of the Austrian Habsburgs and to influence policy (though avoiding overt meddling: a tricky balancing act).[24] Amalia, once Duchess of Parma, helped replace the pro-French first minister, Guillaume du Tillot, with a pro-Austrian one. In the portrait of her attributed to Zoffany (see fig. 78) Amalia looks out in the most startling way from the picture plane, almost as if the artist were trying to emphasize her foreignness, her lack of integration with previous dynastic connections and French influences, and her awkward relationship with her husband. Though dressed informally in a riding habit, her hat is as impressive as a crown, intimating her position as the power behind the throne: she insisted that decrees be issued in the joint name.[25] In an extraordinarily astute portrait this proud and unhappy woman is depicted as almost isolated from any surroundings. Similarly, and yet also in contrast, George III, the real and natural executive head of the British government, is, in Zoffany's portrait of him, isolated from much in the way of furnishing and accessories, but this

emphasizes his legitimate importance as king: he looks natural and does not stand out awkwardly from the neutral background (fig. 84). Charlotte is shown with a landscape view behind her, inclining towards her husband and adopting the natural female role as deferential consort (fig. 88). Duke Ferdinando, on the other hand (fig. 79), slumps a little in his chair, looking faintly apologetic, even sheepish; despite the convention of depicting his ducal landscape behind him, he does *not* look every inch a princely ruler[26]. He was five years his wife's junior and their marriage was not consummated for three months. To make up for their incompatibility, Amalia was said to have taken her pleasure among the grooms and footmen of the country residence.[27] Marriages for dynastic and political reasons took no account of the vagaries of sexual chemistry, and rumours of marital dissonance destabilized ruling families. Yet the duke continued with important cultural initiatives, including an annual competition held by the Academy of Art for just the kind of religious and historical paintings that Zoffany might have spent his lifetime producing, had he not chanced his fortunes in Britain when George III succeeded.

When Zoffany returned from India to Britain in 1789, he found Europe on the brink of unexampled and unforeseen change. Warren Hastings was already being impeached for misconduct in office in India, and some of the alleged impropriety was lapping at the feet of Queen Charlotte, as she was known to have received expensive presents of ivory furniture from him and his wife. There was also comment on the fact that the queen received Marian Hastings at court, despite her being a divorcée, and her extravagance was also mocked: she loved her jewelled clothes and let her kittens play in bowls filled with pearls.[28] However, unlike the French court, where at the same time Marie Antoinette was touched by a different scandal involving her alleged ambition to obtain a very valuable diamond necklace, the court at Windsor survived, and the British state emerged triumphantly from the wars against Revolutionary and Napoleonic France.

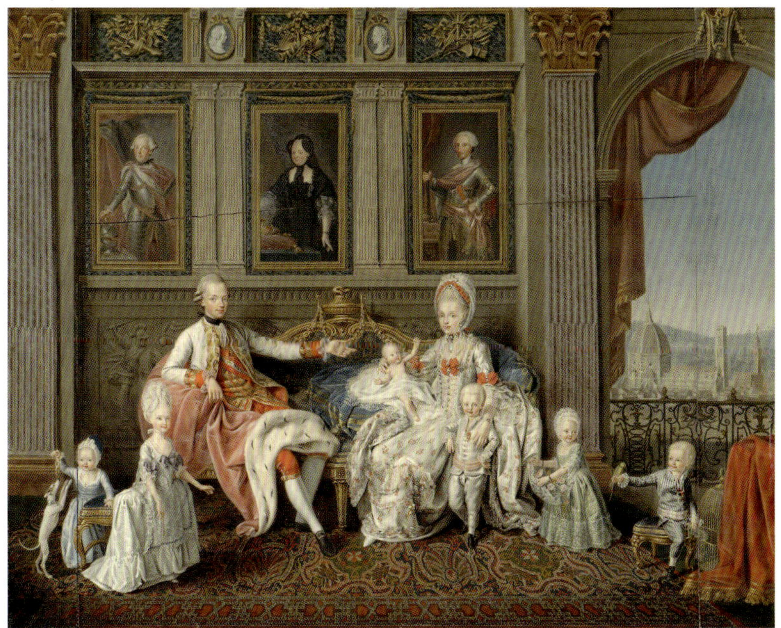

Figure 87
Wenzel Werlin, *Grand Duke Leopoldo and Six of his Oldest Children*, 1773, oil on panel, 67.5 × 81.5 cm (26⅝ × 32⅛ in). Kunsthistorisches Museum, Vienna

Figure 88 (cat. 38)
Queen Charlotte, 1771, oil on canvas, 163.8 × 137.5 cm (64½ × 54⅛ in). The Royal Collection, Her Majesty Queen Elizabeth II

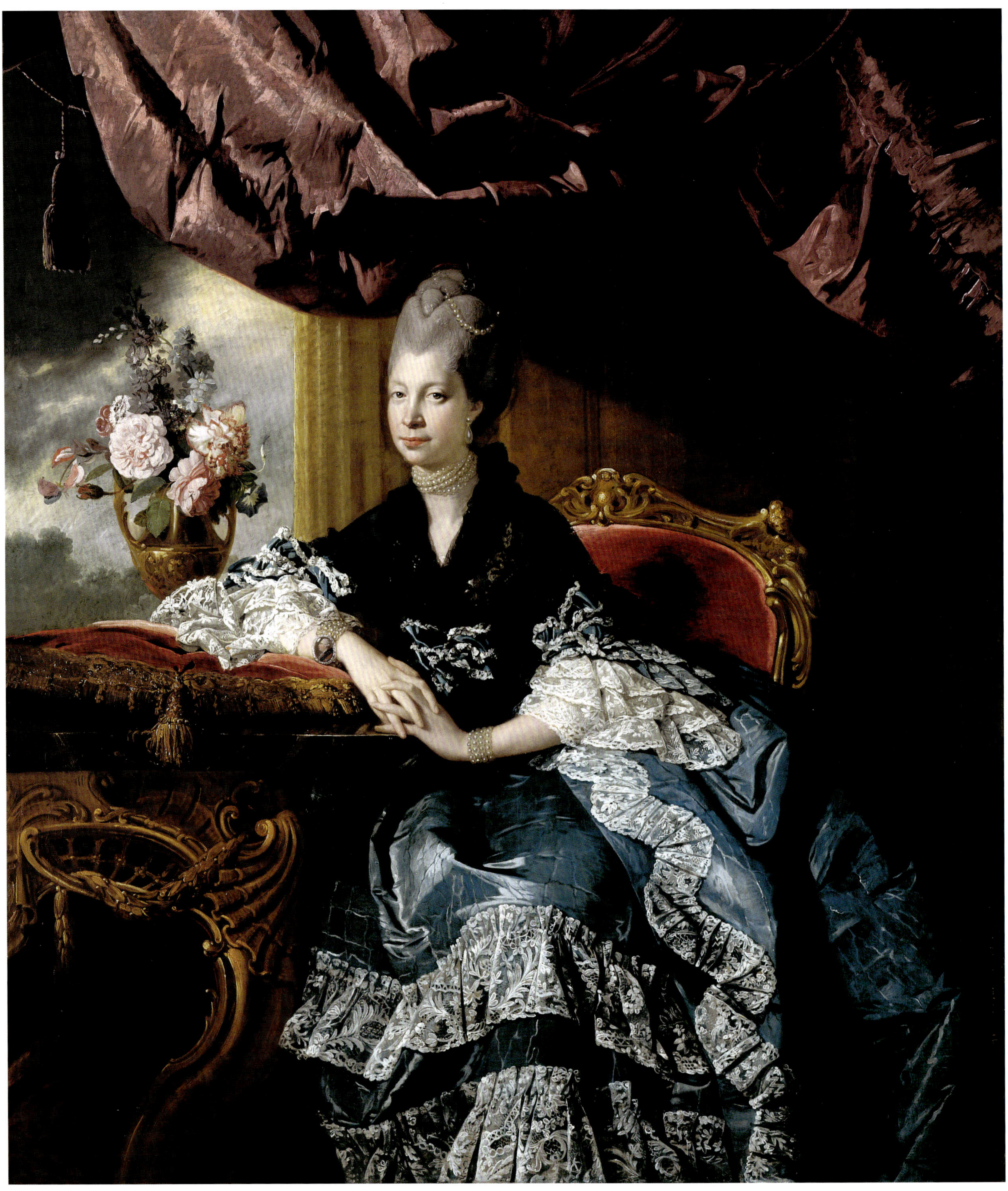

Zoffany's paintings of the attacks on the French king and queen and the bloodthirsty creation of a republic in 1792 (fig. 89) expressed his horror at the destruction of the courtly worlds in which his talent had been deployed. In his lifetime the Holy Roman Empire was dissolved and in 1804 the Austrian Habsburgs created their own empire as a riposte to Napoleon's self-proclamation as an Emperor of the French – a new Charlemagne crowned by the Pope. But courts and dynasties are adaptive institutions. In 1810, the year Zoffany died, Napoleon married as his second wife Maria-Louise, granddaughter of Pietro Leopoldo of Tuscany, signalling an alliance between an old and a new dynasty and empire.

When Napoleon was deposed, Maria-Louise was given her uncle's Duchy of Parma, which after her death reverted to the House of Bourbon-Parma, while the Habsburgs lasted as rulers in Vienna until 1919. The Thurn und Taxis acquired a new palace in 1812, the former Benedictine Abbey of St Emmeran. Its chatelaine was Queen Charlotte's niece Thérèse, daughter-in-law of Prince Karl Anselm, whose schooling Zoffany had shared. Though the second and third German empires have come and gone, the Thurn und Taxis splendours remain: on the official website the current Dowager Princess Gloria is photographed on a gold chair in front of baroque tapestries with a dog seated on her lap in a pose that Zoffany himself could have designed.[29]

Figure 89 (cat. 106)
A Scene in the Champ de Mars, Celebrating over the Bodies of the Swiss Soldiers on the 12th August 1792, with a Portrait of the Duke of Orleans, c.1794, oil on canvas, 92 × 125 cm (36¼ × 49¼ in). Museen der Stadt Regensburg

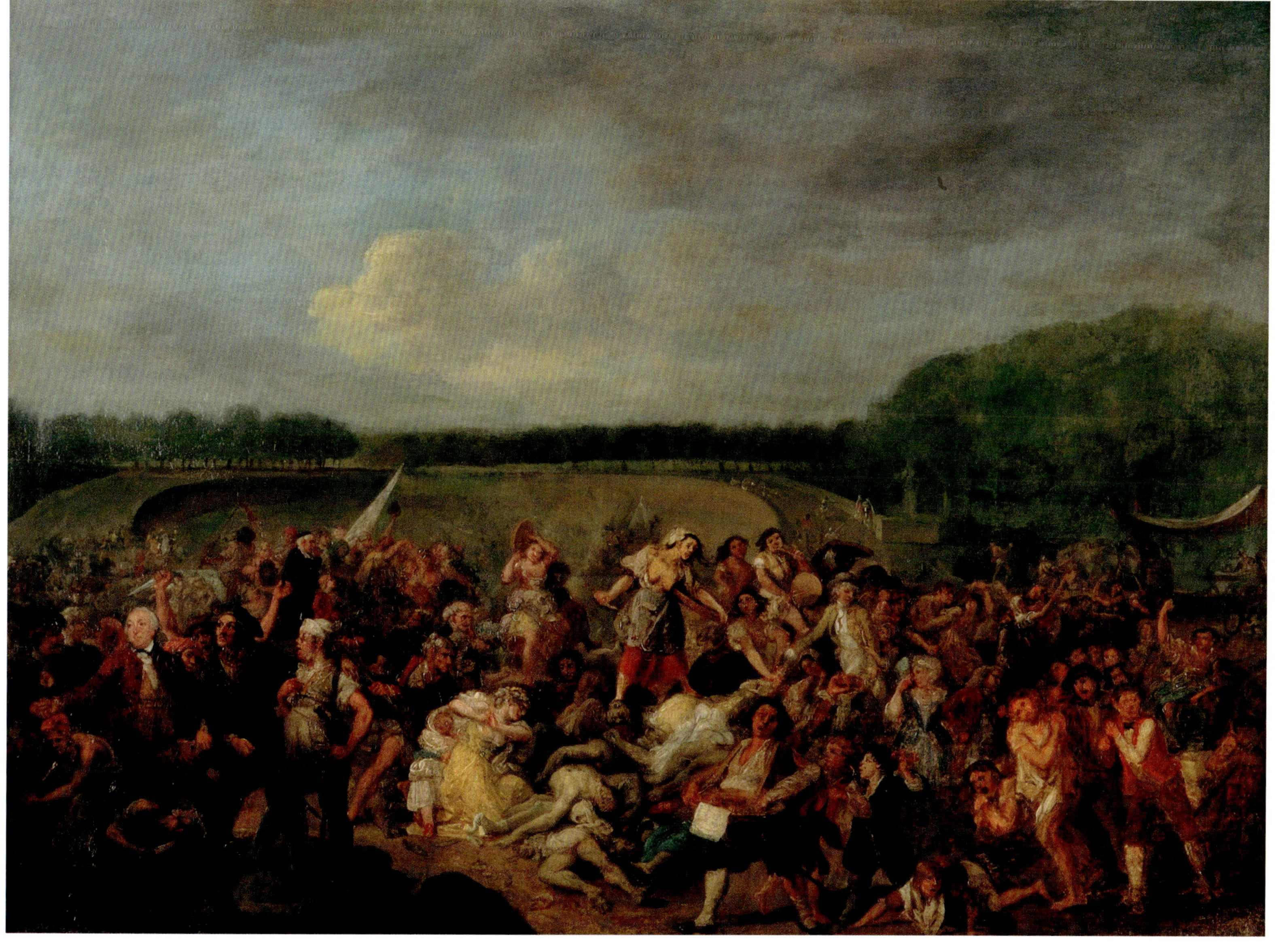

Notes

1. The Habsburgs turned their own dynastic lands into the Austro-Hungarian Empire in riposte to Napoleon's self-proclamation as Emperor of France in 1804. After 1806 the ecclesiastical states were secularized and their territories were grabbed by the principalities, some, like Saxony and Hanover, becoming kingdoms; after 1815 a new confederation of thirty-three states emerged. Peter Wilson, The Holy Roman Empire 1495–1806, Basingstoke, 1999; Alan Forrest and Peter H. Wilson, eds., The Bee and the Eagle: Napoleonic France and the End of the Holy Roman Empire, 1806, Basingstoke, 2009.

2. Walderdorff was the only one of his family, nobles in the Rhineland, to hold this position. Like many of the prince-bishops on the border between France and the empire, he was elected through French influence; Kings of France were guarantors of the empire's constitution after 1648.

3. Webster 2011, 12–15.

4. Hoock 2003, 144–9.

5. G.M. Ditchfield, George III: An Essay in Monarchy, Basingstoke, 2002; Olwen Hedley, Queen Charlotte, London, 1975.

6. Benjamin West was offered a knighthood but his Quaker principles prompted his refusal.

7. Treadwell 2009, 393.

8. Webster 2011, 68–73; R.W. Ketton-Cremer, Felbrigg: The Story of a House, London, 1962; Andrew W. Moore, Norfolk & the Grand Tour: Eighteenth-Century Travellers Abroad and their Souvenirs, exh. cat., Norwich Castle Museum, 1985, 40–48.

9. Clarissa Campbell Orr, 'Aristocratic Feminism, the Learned Governess, and the Republic of Letters', in Sarah Knott and Barbara Taylor, eds., Women, Gender and Enlightenment, Basingstoke, 2005, 306–25; Shefrin 2003.

10. Brewer 1976, 112–30; Joseph M. Levine, 'Why Neoclassicism? Politics and Culture in Eighteenth-Century England', The British Journal for Eighteenth-Century Studies, 25, (2002), 75–93.

11. Mark Laird and Alicia Weisberg-Roberts, eds., Mrs Delany and her Circle, New Haven and London, 2009.

12. James Boswell, The Life of Samuel Johnson, 2 vols., London, 1820, vol. 2, 496.

13. Isobel Grundy, Lady Mary Wortley Montagu, Oxford, 1999.

14. Shefrin 2003.

15. George Legge, second Earl of Dartmouth, was also the half-brother of Lord Frederick North, the Prime Minister, and Lady Louisa Willoughby de Broke, née North. He and Lord North had undertaken their own Grand Tour together.

16. ODNB George Nassau Clavering; Hibbert 1993, 208–25.

17. Webster 2011, 303.

18. On his marriage and as part of a complex series of diplomatic manoeuvres to preserve the European balance of power, Francis surrendered his Lorraine duchy on the border of France and the empire (to which it belonged) to Louis XV's new father-in-law, the deposed King of Poland, Stanislas Lesczynski.

19. Beales 1987–2009, vol. 1, 69–82; Sanger 1991.

20. Maria Carolina was obliged to marry the Neapolitan king because her older sister Maria Josepha, the intended bride, died of smallpox.

21. Hibbert 1993.

22. Hibbert 1999, 71.

23. Mansel 2005.

24. Beales 1987–2009, vol. 1, 194

25. Sanger 1991, 328.

26. The portrait illustrated at fig. 79 is evidently a copy of Zoffany's original painting, which is in a French private collection.

27. Treadwell 2009, 286. Maria Amalia had wanted to marry Charles II, Duke of Zweibrücken (a tiny territory strategically positioned on the Rhine). The family later inherited the Electorate of Bavaria, so this marriage would have made Maria Amalia into a significant German consort. Eventually, Ferdinando gained kudos by initially preserving Parma from Napoleonic annexation. Sanger 1991, 327–8.

28. P.J. Marshall, 'The Private Fortune of Marian Hastings', Bulletin of the Institute of Historical Research, vol. 37 (1964), 245–53; Marshall concludes that the size of her fortune was £107,725 and suggests that its sources would not be creditable, but she is known to have refused some bribes. Jeremy Bernstein, Dawning of the Raj: The Life and Trials of Warren Hastings, London, 2001.

29. http://www.thurnundtaxis.de/en/intro/ (accessed 12 July 2010). While this chapter was being written, the Constantinian Order of St George, a medieval knightly religious order that came under the control of the Dukes of Parma in the eighteenth century, celebrated a requiem mass on 28 August 2010 for the death of Carlos Hugo, Duke of Bourbon-Parma, secular head of the Order; the role has been inherited by his son Carlos. The mass took place in Parma at the church of Mary of the Steccata, the Order's religious headquarters and the necropolis of the Dukes of Bourbon-Parma.

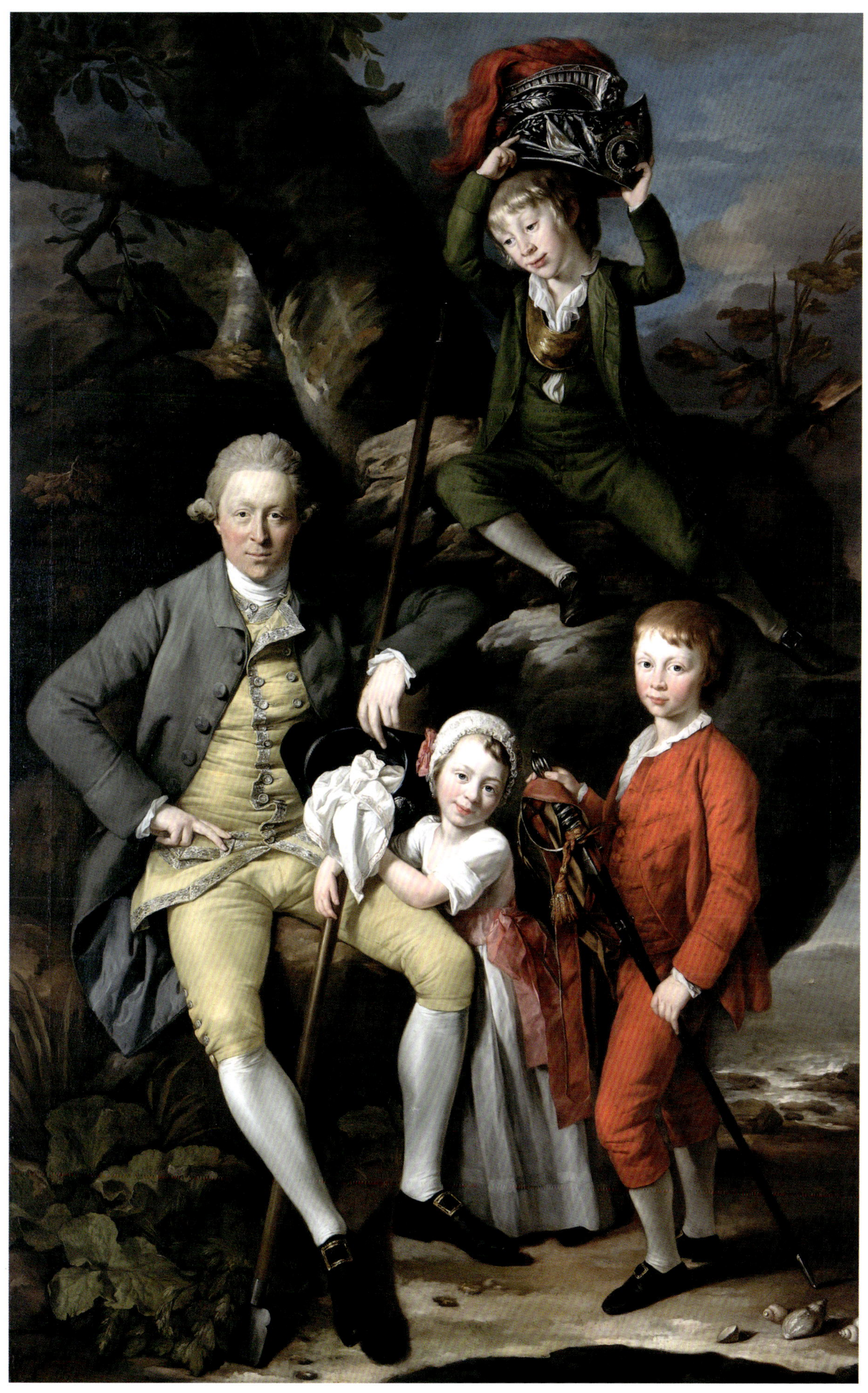

Kate Retford

'Peculiarly happy at taking Likenesses':
Zoffany & British Portraiture

Z——, a German, came to this country about twenty years since. Relying on his talents as an Historical Painter, but not having any friends, he soon found himself in that distress which many Foreigners with great talents have experienced in this country. He was advised by an eminent French engraver, Mons. Ravenet, to apply himself to Portrait-painting, as being the most beneficial, and the surest road to profit in England.[1]

So begins a biographical note on Johan Zoffany in Mauritius Lowe's pamphlet, *The Ear-Wig*, published anonymously in 1781. It was a truism in the eighteenth century that the sum of artistic aspiration among British patrons was to have their own likenesses – and those of their families and friends – captured for posterity on canvas. Those who hoped that the Royal Academy might promote history painting despaired at the predominance of portraiture in the annual exhibitions, and foreign commentators repeatedly remarked on the popularity of 'phiz mongering' in Britain. When William Hogarth came to review the recent history of portraiture in his *Autobiographical Notes* of 1763, he was scathing on what he perceived to be the result of this demand: a production line of mediocre likenesses produced by mediocre artists. Key to their unearned success were the 'Jour(n)ey men calld Back ground & Drapery painters', who enabled the portraitists 'to dispatch a great deal of business and if industrious get … more money in a week than ye greatest genious in any other branch of the art in 3 months'.[2] It was of course as one of these 'journey men' that Zoffany found himself working soon after arriving in London in 1760. His time in Benjamin Wilson's studio was clearly unhappy, and the way out, he must quickly have realized, was not by continuing to produce the kind of historical painting in which he had specialized on the Continent.[3] Rather, he needed to look to the fields in which Wilson practised: theatrical painting and portraiture.

According to *The Ear-Wig* account, Zoffany was encouraged by Simon-François Ravenet's advice to finish his half-length portrait of the engraver (cat. 43).[4] It is a lively, finely rendered and closely observed characterization, and it bespeaks a talent for capturing likeness for which Zoffany was to become known in England. In 1765 a critic in the *St James's Chronicle* wrote approvingly: 'Mr Zaffanij is peculiarly happy at taking Likenesses. Some may call this a mere Sign-Post Excellence, but surely a Portrait is not worth a Farthing without it.'[5]

Figure 90 (cat. 74)
Henry Knight of Tythegston with his Three Children, c.1770, oil on canvas, 240.5 × 149 cm (94⅝ × 58⅝ in). Amgueddfa Genedlaethol Cymru / National Museum of Wales

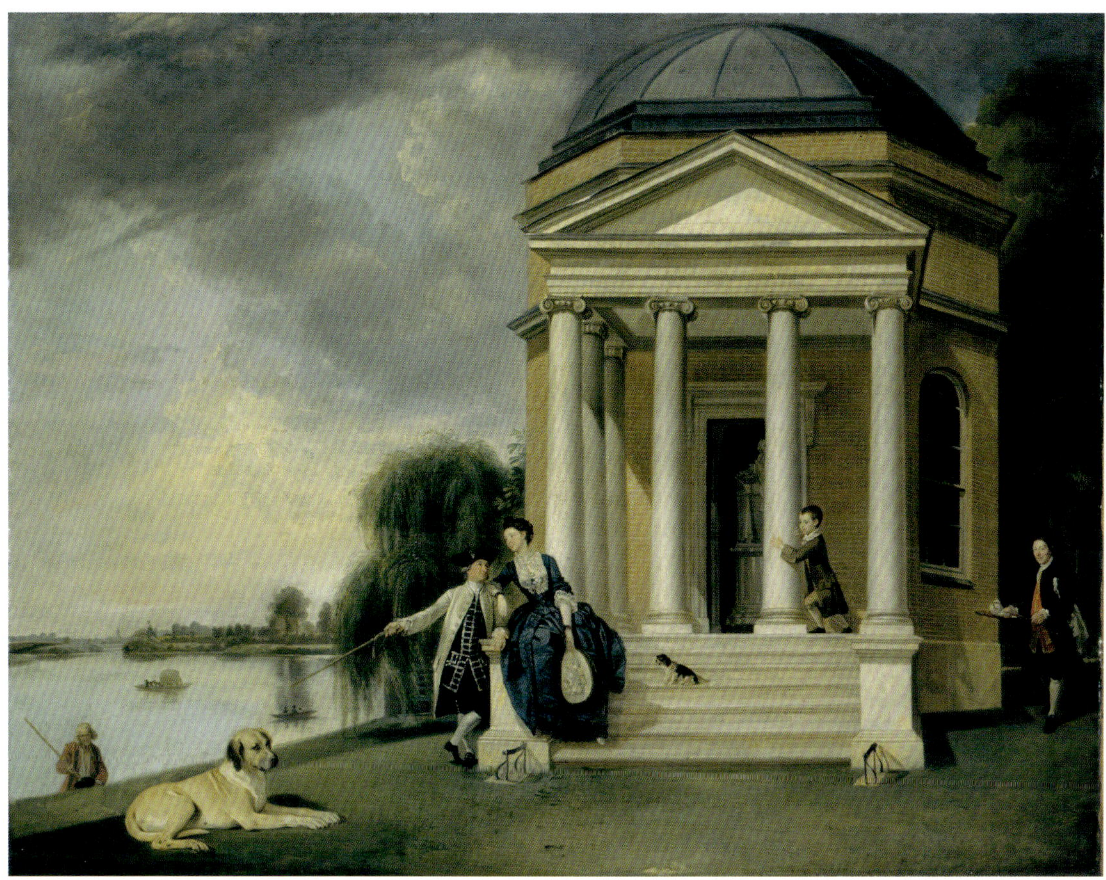

Figure 91
Mr and Mrs Garrick by the Shakespeare Temple at Hampton, *c.*1762, oil on canvas, 99.7 × 125 cm (39¼ × 49¼ in). Private collection

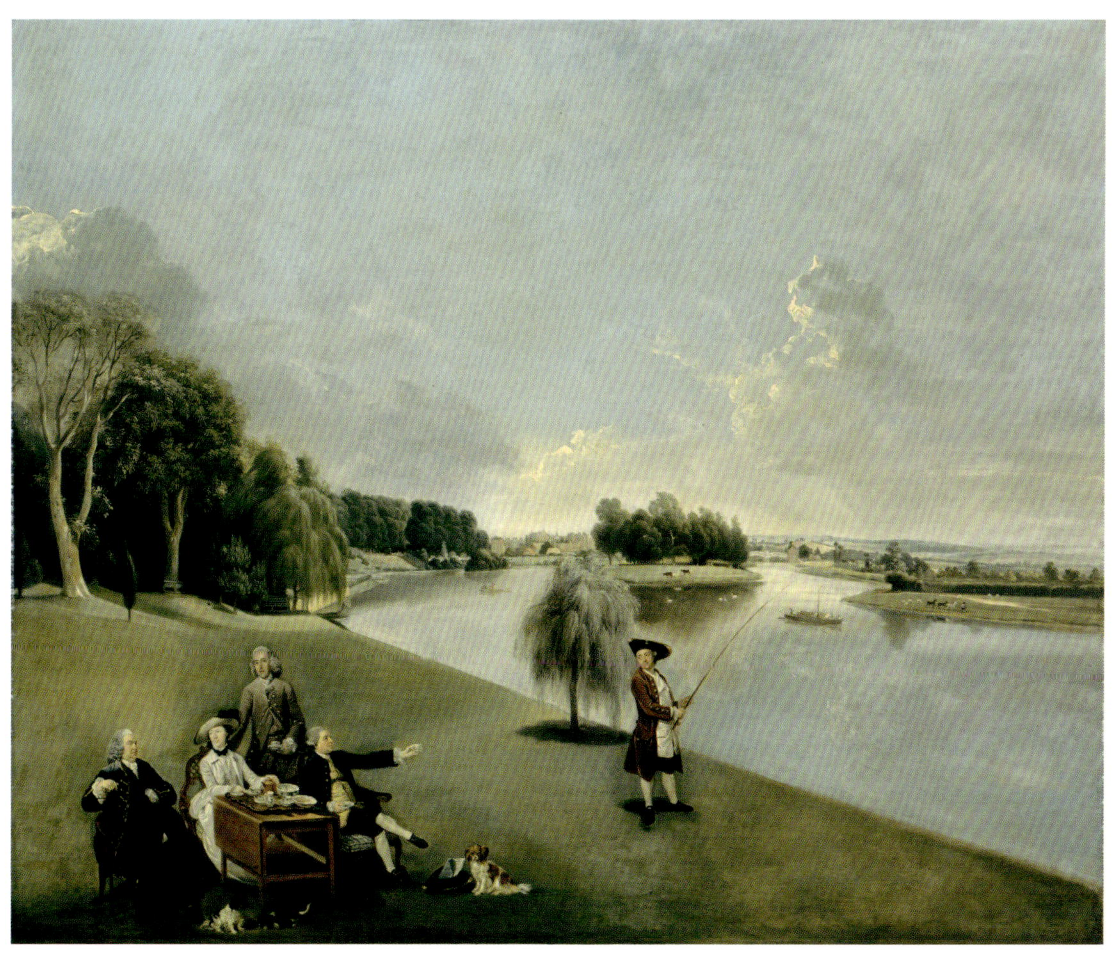

Figure 92
A View in Hampton Garden with Mr and Mrs Garrick Taking Tea, 1762, oil on canvas, 99.7 × 125 cm (39¼ × 49¼ in). Private collection

But it is the series of portraits that Zoffany executed around this time for the actor, playwright, theatre manager and impresario David Garrick, that indicate where the artist's greatest contribution to the field of British portraiture would lie. After Zoffany's success with *The Farmer's Return* (see cat. 17), Garrick invited the painter to spend the summer of 1762 at Hampton. While there, Zoffany produced two pairs of pendants, depicting Garrick, his family and his friends enjoying the grounds on the banks of the Thames.[6] This quartet of paintings was intended to identify David Garrick as a member of the genteel, polite, propertied ranks of society, as well as the leading light of the London theatre. These pictures also took Zoffany into the realm of small group portraiture, into the visual language and conventions of the 'conversation piece'.[7] While definitions of this term are distinctly fraught, the Hampton portraits can be securely located within the category, and not just thanks to employment of the phrase 'Conversation Piece' in two related letters.[8] The diminutive scale of the figures, the emphasis on setting, the attention to narrative and the interaction between the sitters, all exemplify the genre. Further, the way in which Zoffany pictures the landscape from various perspectives, effectively leading the viewer around the grounds at Hampton, is characteristic of a mode of portraiture that had strong links to the tradition of the 'Prospect'.[9] *Mr and Mrs Garrick by the Shakespeare Temple at Hampton* (fig. 91; see also

cat. 16) shows the couple posed on the steps of the pavilion which had been designed by Robert Adam in 1755, the adjacent Thames on the left of the canvas flowing in the direction of London. For the setting of the pendant, *A View in Hampton Garden with Mr and Mrs Garrick Taking Tea* (fig. 92), Zoffany turned his attention to look downriver, the Thames now on the viewer's right. The other two paintings are more modest in scale, but they are similarly geographically linked. On the left of Zoffany's image of Garrick's nieces, Arabella and Catherine (fig. 93), we see the entrance to the tunnel that the actor constructed to link Hampton house with its waterside lawns.[10] The other end of that tunnel can be viewed in the companion piece, which shows Garrick writing on the lawn in front of the house (fig. 94). The relationship of these images with the tradition of the Prospect is further strengthened by a focus on the maintenance, productive use and leisured enjoyment of the villa's grounds. We see Garrick and his wife entertaining in one painting, the couple enjoying the view over the river in another. In one version of *Mr and Mrs Garrick by the Shakespeare Temple at Hampton* (fig. 91) a small nephew weaves in and out of the colonnade of the pavilion, while his sisters play elsewhere in the gardens in another picture. The river both allows Garrick's brother George to enjoy fishing and provides a means of conveying David and Eva Maria to London. Servants bring tea, look after and sail the Garricks' boat, and roll their lawn.

Figure 93
Garrick's Nieces in the Garden at Hampton,
1762, oil on canvas, 65.4 × 77.5 cm (25¾ × 30½ in).
Private collection

Figure 94
A View of Hampton House and Garden and David Garrick Sitting on the Lawn Reading, 1762, oil on canvas, 61 × 73.6 cm (24 × 29 in).
Petworth House, Sussex

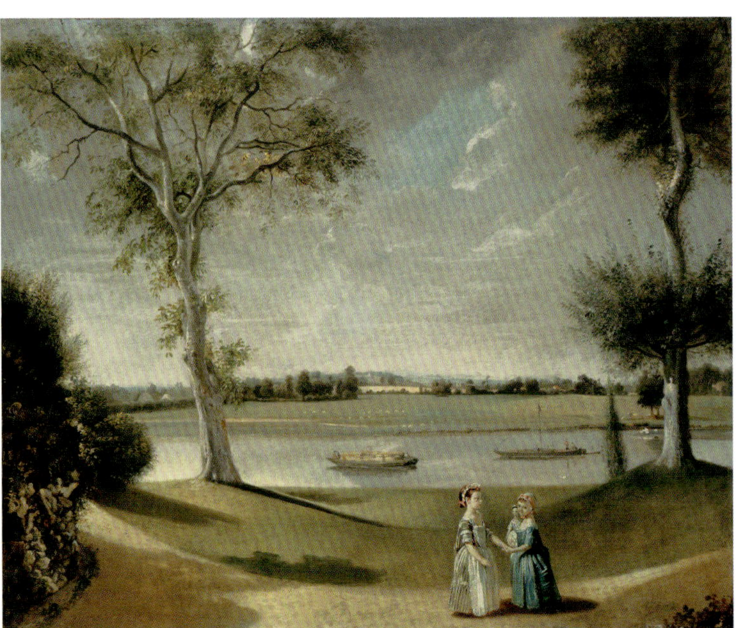

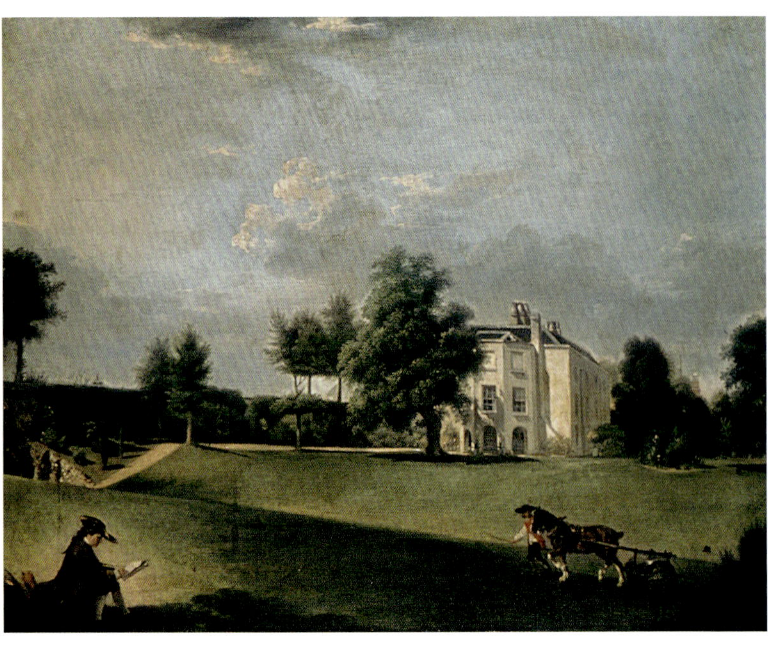

When Zoffany arrived in London the conversation piece was not faring well. Its real heyday had been in the 1730s, when the diminutive groups of Hogarth, Gawen Hamilton and Charles Philips had been in great demand.[11] Certainly, Arthur Devis, who had been consistently producing small, intricately detailed portraits since the early 1740s, was still attempting to plough this furrow (fig. 95).[12] However, his efforts were meeting with little success in a changed artistic milieu: one that favoured the full length over the small scale, the drama and impact of the grand manner over the details and intricacies of the conversation piece. Zoffany breathed new life into this ailing art form and did so with extraordinary success. Within two or three years of his work for Garrick, his small group portraits were being commissioned by the royal family. By that time he was able to charge considerable sums. Conversation pieces were typically priced per figure, and Zoffany's were no exception. For his portrait of John Murray, third Duke of Atholl and his family, painted in 1765–7, he asked 20 guineas for each of the nine sitters depicted, making an impressive total of 180 guineas (fig. 96).[13] As the most successful portraitist at this time in London, Joshua Reynolds, was asking 150 guineas for a life-size full length, the labour required to create such a highly detailed, group portrait was more than compensated.[14]

Zoffany's skill in evoking the material world of his patrons must have been a crucial element of his success. Raised in a German princely court, he had a deep, personal appreciation for the material trappings of wealth. He apparently offended Lord Cowper by wearing a pale pink, velvet coat more appropriate to an earl in Florence, and extravagantly indulged his expensive tastes on his return to England with a sailing boat staffed by

Figure 95
Arthur Devis, *William and Lucy Atherton*, c.1742–4,
oil on canvas, 92.1 × 127 cm (36¼ × 50 in).
National Museums Liverpool,
Walker Art Gallery

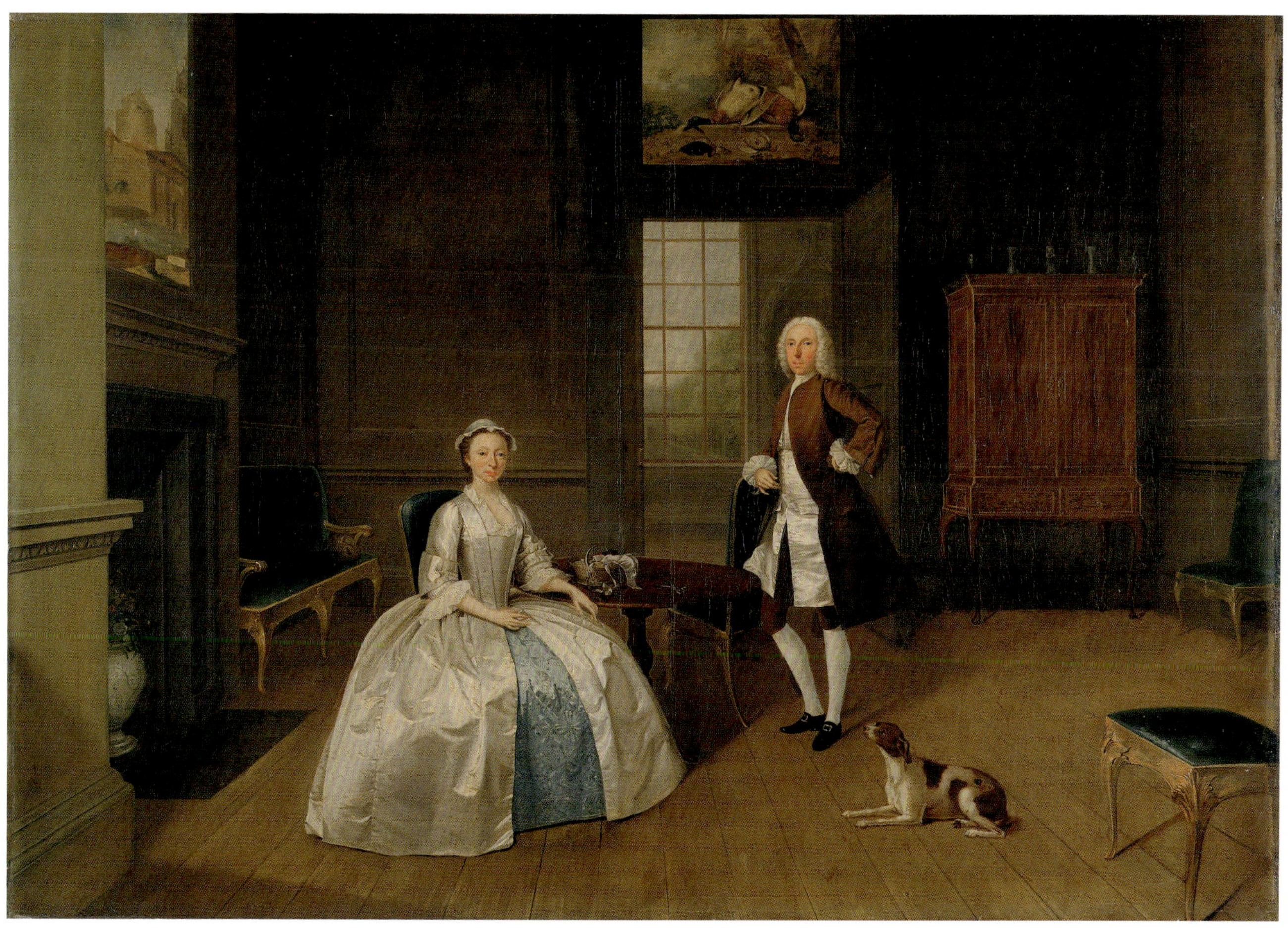

servants dressed in a livery of his heraldic colours.[15] And Zoffany's intricately meticulous style and the high finish of his paint surfaces, developed in the historical paintings that he had executed on the Continent, were beautifully suited to capturing the delights of luxury goods in paint. His manner derived both from the slick, smooth images of his master, Anton Raphael Mengs, and the attention to detail and exactitude exemplified by Dutch and Flemish artists. Indeed, it was surely the fact that Zoffany was so steeped in Netherlandish tradition – widely admired and imitated in eighteenth-century Germany – that commended him to important early patrons such as the Earl of Bute (cats 64, 65) and Sir Lawrence Dundas (cat. 71), whose collections favoured that school.[16] There is something of the *fijnschilder* (literally 'fine-painter') about the characteristic Zoffany conversation piece: an emphasis on sheer artistic

labour and care that renders the image of expensive, luxury objects an expensive, luxury object in its own right.[17] It is also Zoffany's prowess in commemorating the decorative arts of eighteenth-century England – his skill in evoking the textures, forms and detailing of fashionable consumer goods – more than his ability to detail his sitters' likenesses that has secured his enduring reputation. In 1930 Christopher Hussey exclaimed: 'How laboriously and lovingly he drew the teapots and chimney-pieces and pictures on the wall! … These things were as important to Zoffany as the people he was painting, and to us they are, perhaps, more important. He is the Jane Austen of English painting.'[18]

Earlier practitioners such as Hamilton and Devis had commonly recycled their painted interiors.[19] Zoffany was also necessarily involved in fabricating settings for portraits:

Figure 96
John, Third Duke of Atholl and his Family,
1765–7, oil on canvas,
93.5 × 158 cm (36¾ × 62 ¼ in).
Blair Castle, Perthshire

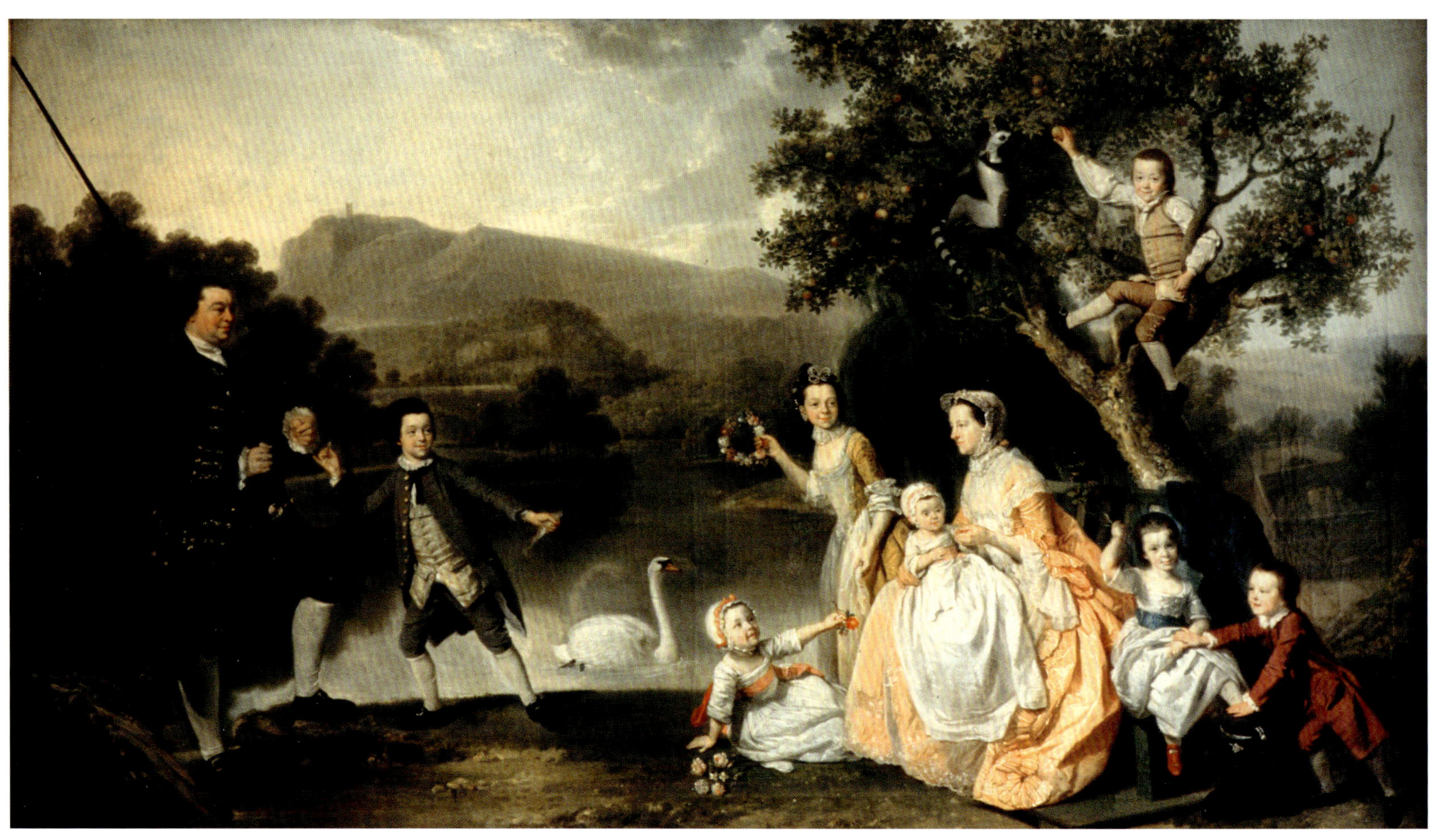

creating stage sets that conveyed decorum, taste and politeness; using and re-using props such as his sitter's chair.[20] However, there are a significant number of cases for which surviving evidence reveals a very different process at work. Some of the Zoffoli bronzes featured in the portrait of Lawrence Dundas and his grandson (fig. 97) are displayed on the chimneypiece beneath the picture at Aske Hall today, while the marine painting by Jan van de Capelle remained in the family's collection until acquired by the National Museum of Wales in 1994.[21] The longcase equation clock in Zoffany's portrait of Queen Charlotte and her two eldest sons is still, like the painting, in the Royal Collection (fig. 98). Such precision must be linked to the elevated level of patronage he enjoyed, particularly before his departure for Italy. Sir Lawrence Dundas or Queen Charlotte would be more than worth visiting at home, allowing the artist to make a proper record of their domestic milieu. They also owned the kind of expensive luxury goods, destined to become heirlooms, that were worth detailing. Such documentary specificity, however, was not incompatible with artistic licence. Even when the objects included were meticulously rendered recreations of the patrons' own possessions, they were often imaginatively relocated and regrouped to enable the painter to give the best representation of his sitters' wealth and taste possible. The type of veracity Zoffany offered provided the most complete record, rather than any kind of proto-photographic snapshot.

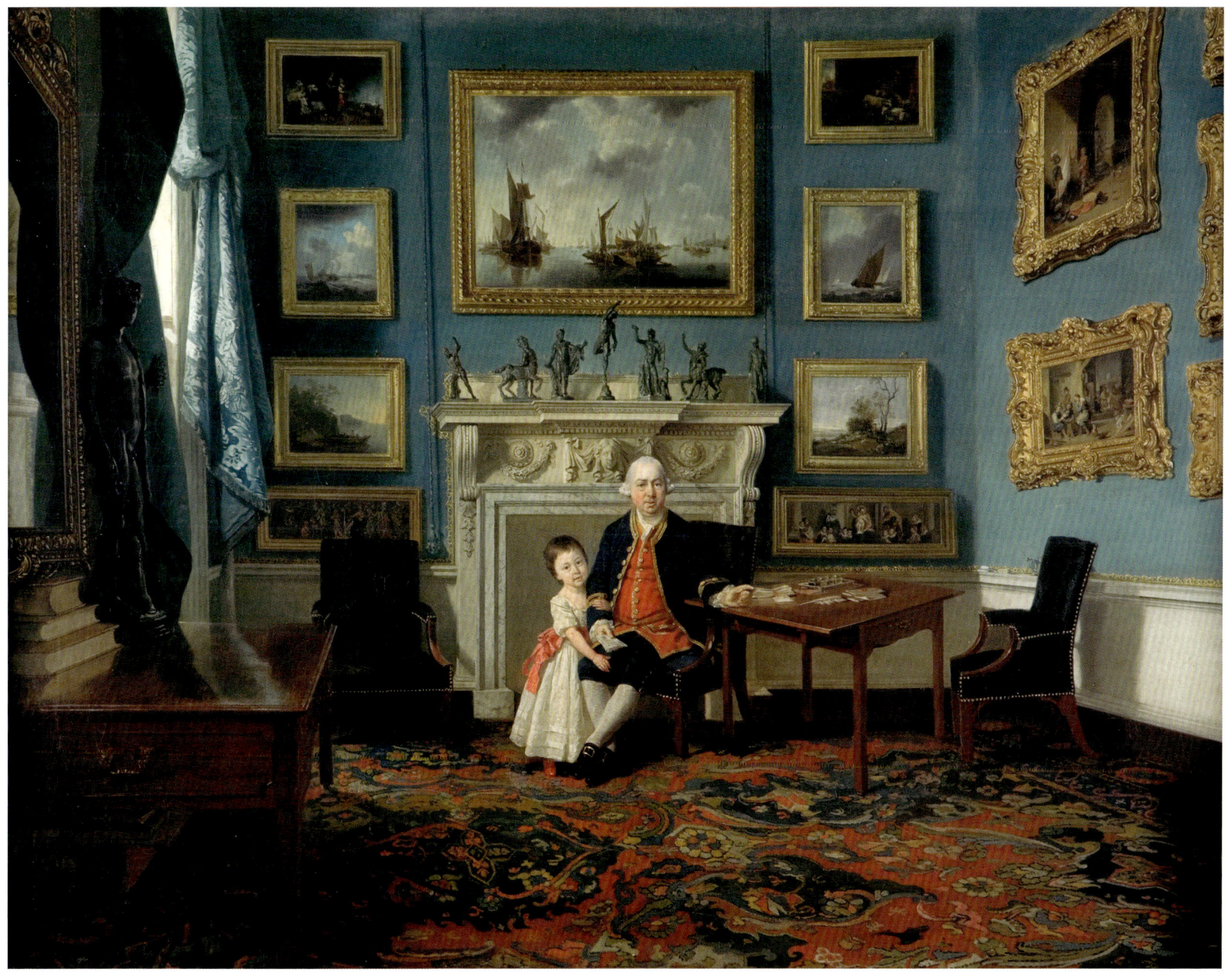

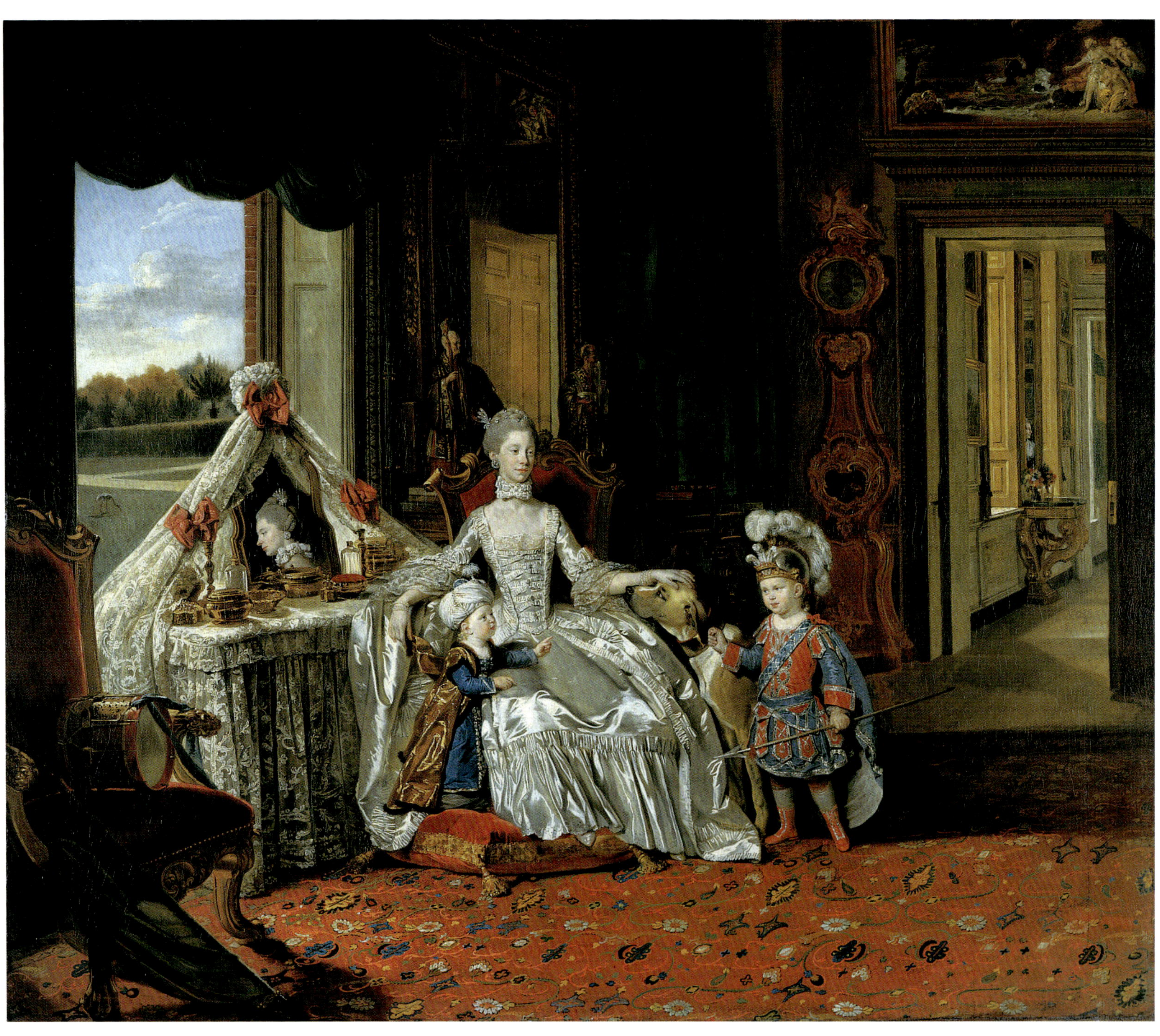

Figure 98 (cat. 33)
Queen Charlotte with her two Eldest Sons, 1764–5,
oil on canvas, 112.4 × 129.2 cm (44¼ × 50⅞ in).
The Royal Collection, Her Majesty Queen Elizabeth II

Figure 97 (cat. 71)
Sir Lawrence Dundas with his Grandson, 1769–70,
oil on canvas, 101.6 × 127 cm (40 × 50 in).
The Zetland Collection

In exterior scenes, such as the series for Garrick or Zoffany's portrait of the Murrays in the grounds of their seat at Dunkeld, we again find considerable accuracy of setting. However, while Zoffany's residence at Hampton in the summer of 1762 is well documented, it is equally certain that he did not set foot anywhere near Scotland in 1765–7. The Atholl portrait (fig. 96) was executed during family visits to London and, as a result, it has been speculated that the topographically detailed landscape must have been painted by another artist, perhaps Charles Stewart.[22] Certainly, such collaborative endeavour was commonplace in the execution of such images, which required facility in diverse fields. In 1783, around the time that Zoffany left for India, a large portrait of Henry and Mary Styleman (fig. 99) was shown at the Society of Artists' exhibition under the title: 'Portraits of Horses and Dogs in a Family Picture, the Figures by Mr. Zoffany, Landscape by Mr. [Joseph] Farrington [sic].' A review in the *St James's Chronicle* added the name of Sawrey Gilpin as the painter responsible for the horses, and gave qualified praise:

> It might be imagined that to unite the Skill of different Artists, each eminent in their respective Line, would be a certain Method to produce a capital Performance; but it does not always succeed; the different Ideas and Manner of each Master being discordant. To do Justice, however, to the Artists who have contributed to this Picture, the Remark must not be severely applied to them.[23]

However, as Mary Webster has observed, in the case of the Atholl portrait it is most likely that Zoffany was responsible for the landscape view, basing it on drawings provided by the duke.[24]

As the portraits of the Garricks at Hampton were hung in their London town house, so the scene of the Murrays at Dunkeld was shown at their other seat, Blair Castle.[25] But the landscape that envelops the family does more than provide a proprietorial record of one residence for display in their other. The grouping of the duchess and her younger children at the base of a leaning, mature tree is a familiar compositional device, to be found throughout Zoffany's oeuvre, from the pendants of the sons and daughters of the Earl of Bute, painted in the early 1760s (figs. 100, 101), through to *The Drummond Family* executed towards the end of the decade (cat. 69). Compositionally, this recurrent tree helped to stabilize and give height to the group of sitters, 'rooting' them in the landscape. Symbolically, it had overtones of the family tree, a significance underscored by the clear hierarchical arrangement of the figures. Zoffany's portrait of the Murrays is typical in emphasizing the close relationship between the eldest son and his father, arranging the other offspring in order of age and sex.[26] As the hearth, representing the heart of the home, the focal point for sociable gathering, was the key motif in the interior conversation piece, so the mature tree had a central role to play in its exterior counterpart, indicating the desirable permanence and stability of the elite family.[27]

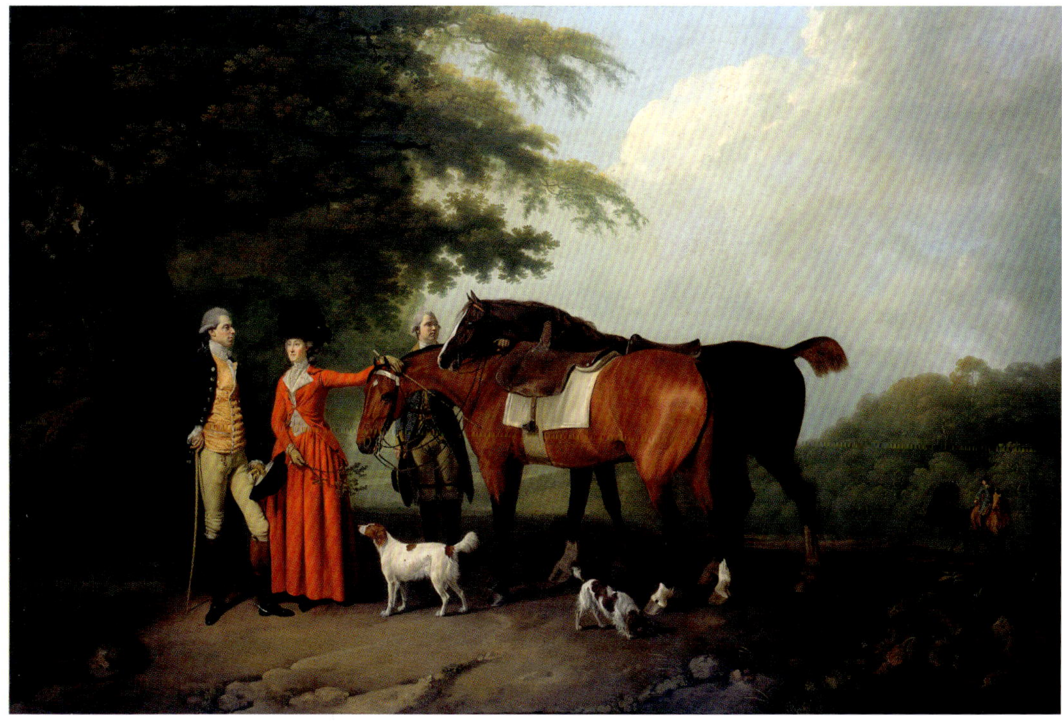

Figure 99
Johan Zoffany, Joseph Farington and Sawrey Gilpin, *Henry and Mary Styleman*, 1783, oil on canvas, 182.2 × 259 cm (71¾ × 102 in). Collection East Anglia Art Fund, Norwich Castle Museum and Art Gallery

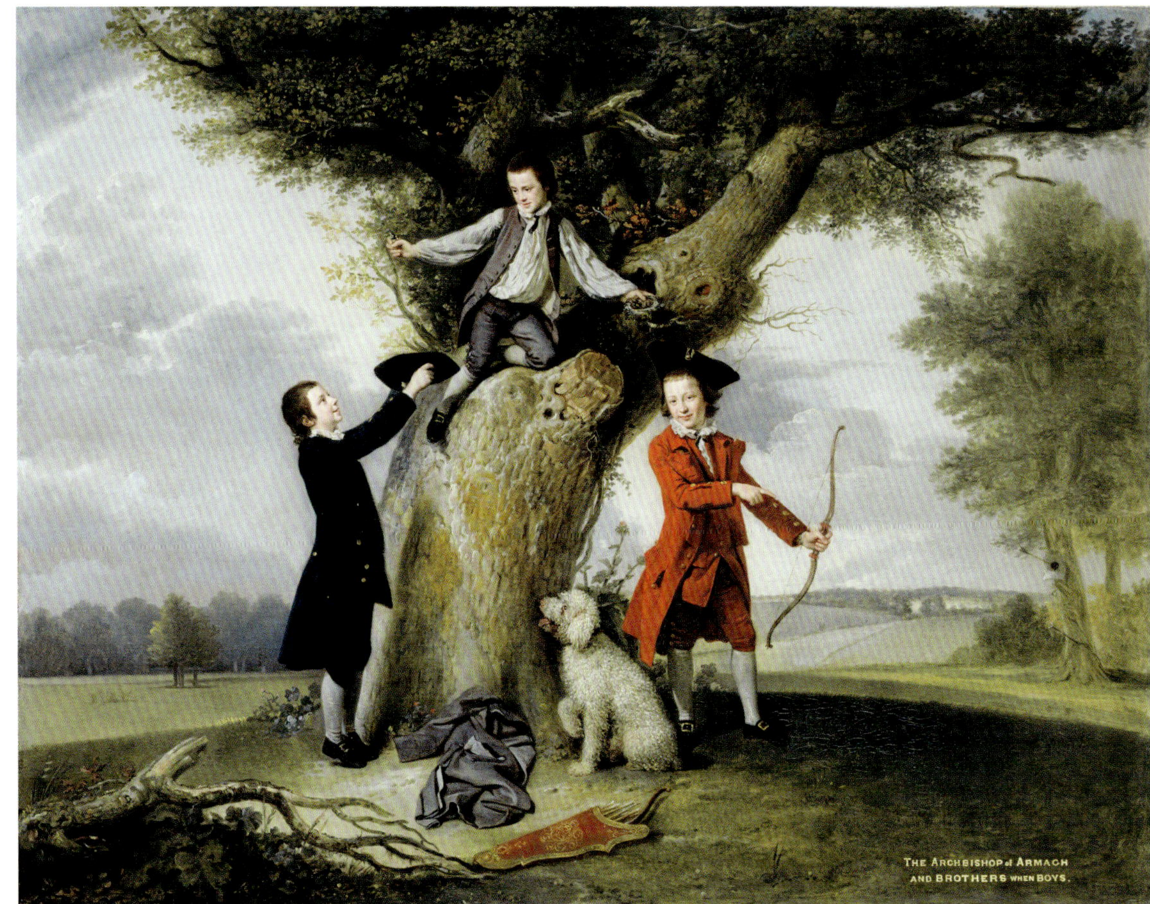

Figure 100 (cat. 64)
Three Sons of John, Third Earl of Bute, 1763–4, oil on canvas, 100.9 × 126 cm (39¾ × 49⅝ in). Tate, London; accepted by HM Government in lieu of tax with additional payment (General Funds) made with assistance from the National Lottery through the Heritage Lottery Fund, the National Art Collections Fund and Tate Members 2002

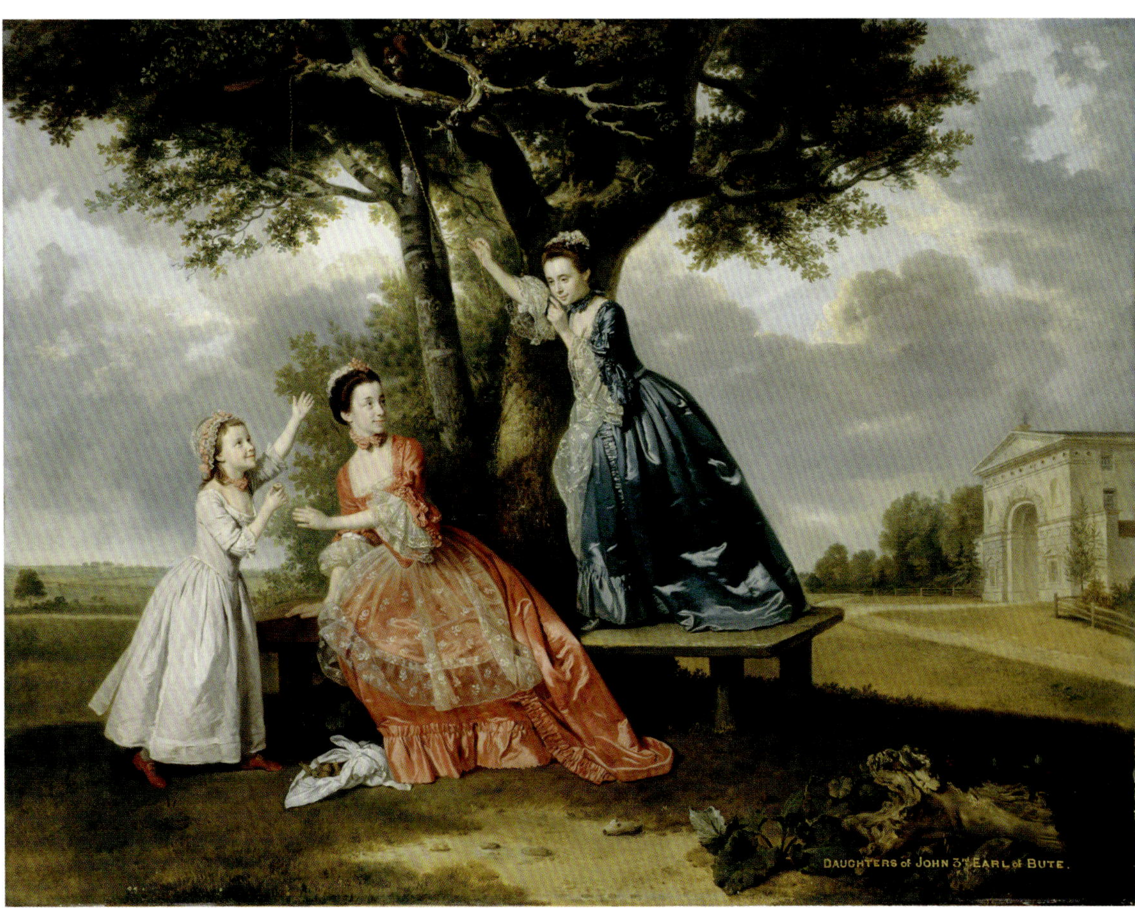

Figure 101 (cat. 65)
Three Daughters of John, Third Earl of Bute, 1763–4, oil on canvas, 101.2 × 126.5 cm (39⅞ × 49¾ in). Tate, London; accepted by HM Government in lieu of tax with additional payment (General Funds) made with assistance from the National Lottery through the Heritage Lottery Fund, the National Art Collections Fund and Tate Members 2002

A feature common to both Zoffany's interior and exterior group portraits is a pronounced element of humour, ranging from a touch of lively playfulness through to more uncomfortable and sometimes sexually loaded motifs. In the Atholl portrait James has ascended the tree in chase of a ring-tailed lemur.[28] The positioning of the Garricks' English mastiff in the foreground of their portrait accentuates his size, the dog's length equivalent to David Garrick's height. More complex and intriguing are the curious self-portraits that are scattered throughout these conversation pieces.[29] Zoffany's strangely isolated position and intense engagement with the viewer is difficult to fathom in groups such as *William Berry*

Introduced as the Heir to Raith (fig. 102). Equally striking are motifs such as the way in which Granville in *The Sharp Family* (fig. 103) holds his flageolets in his outstretched hand in such a way as to make the unmistakable sign of the cuckold's horns behind the head of his brother James.[30] Such idiosyncratic devices became more pronounced during and following Zoffany's stay in Italy. The developing mood indicated in his intensely introspective self-portraits (cats. 58, 59), exploring complex themes such as religion, death and desire, surely provides part of the reason. And, no doubt, the first-hand experience he gained of the Italian caricature tradition was crucial.[31]

Figure 102 (cat. 70)
William Berry Introduced as Heir to Raith, 1769, oil on canvas,
106 × 131.5 cm (41¾ × 51¾ in). Private collection

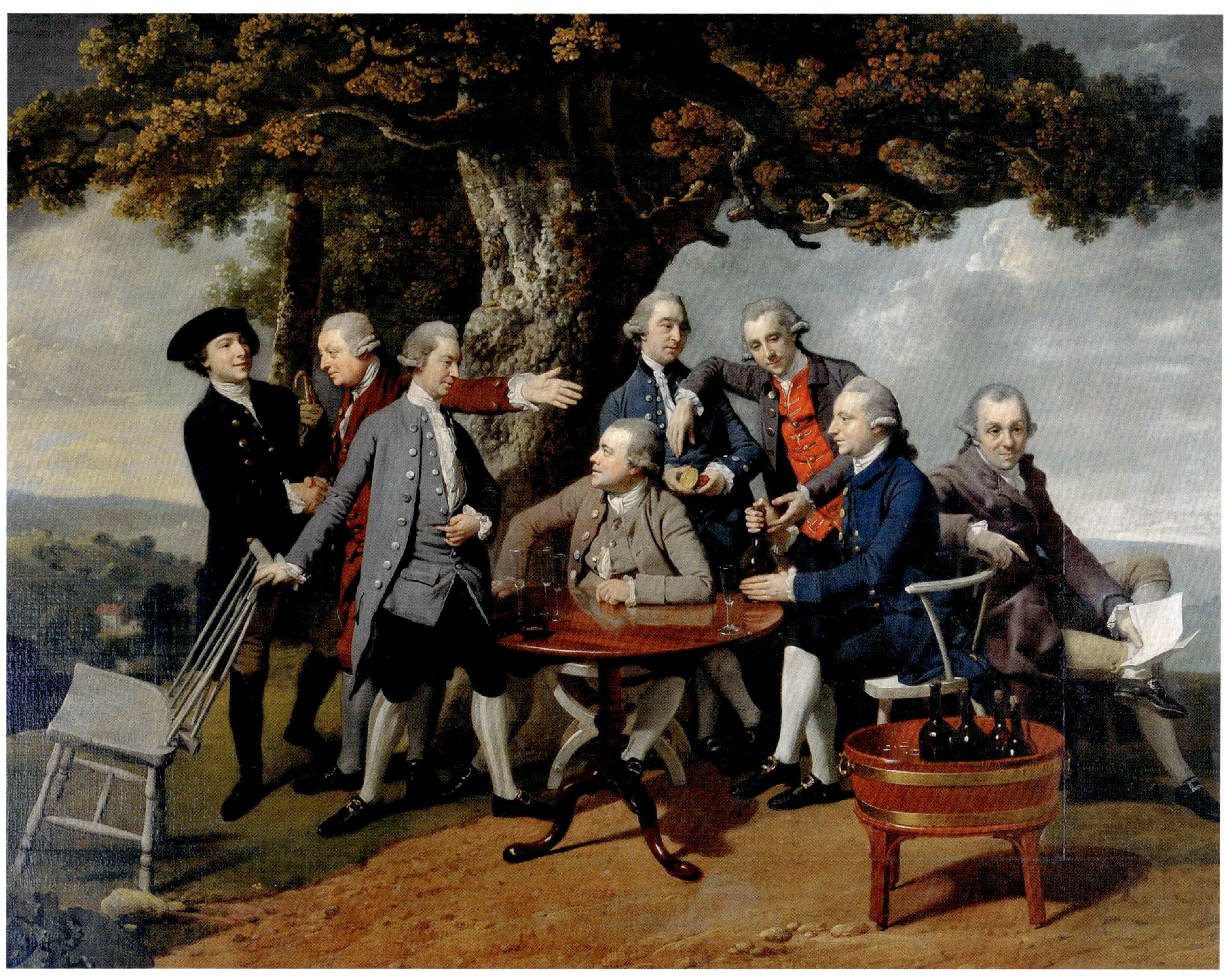

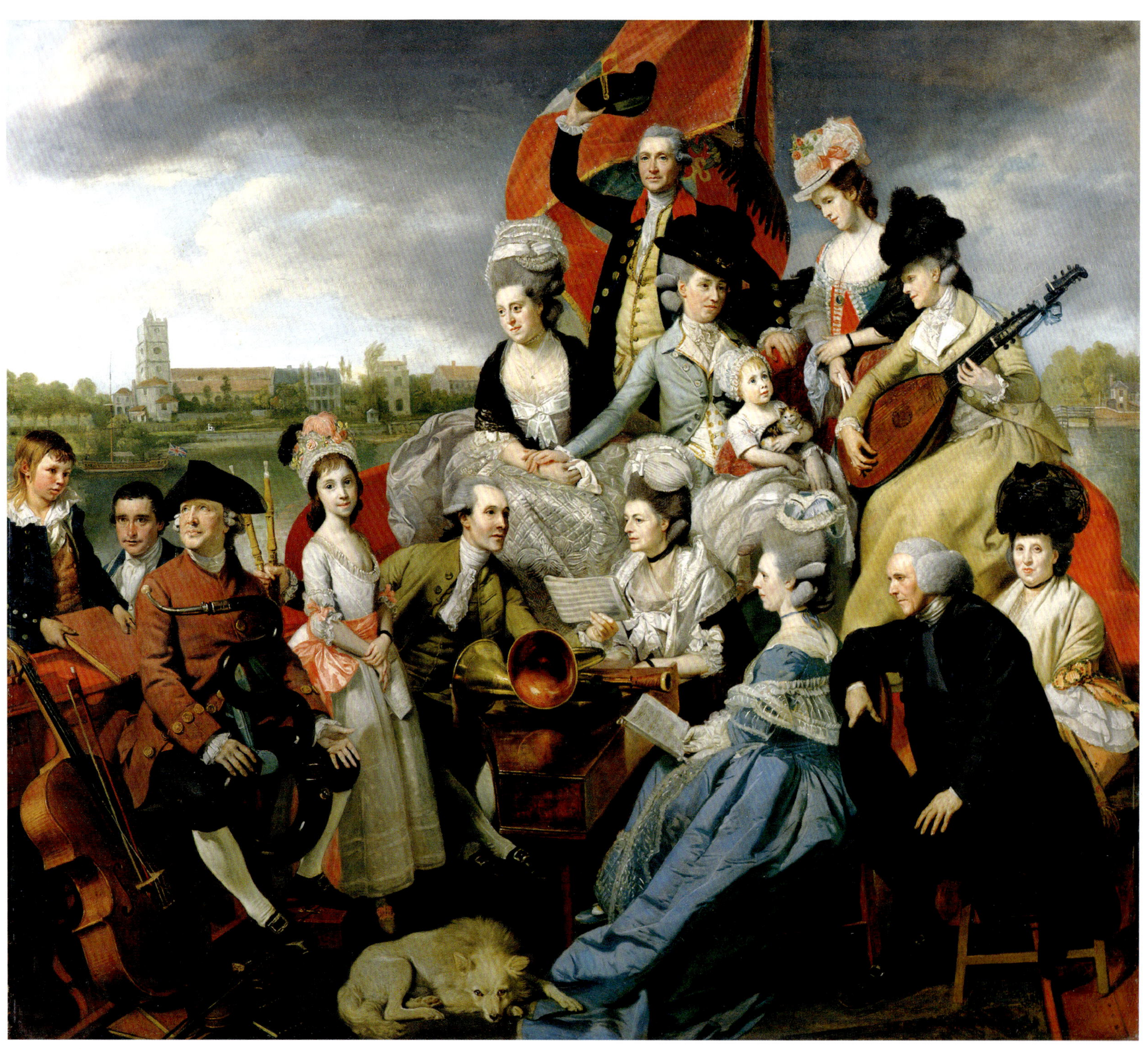

Figure 103 (cat. 77)
The Sharp Family, 1779–81, oil on canvas,
115.6 × 125.7 cm (45½ × 49½ in).
By courtesy of the National Portrait Gallery,
London, and the Lloyd-Baker Trustees

Humorous incident and subversive details were an
established element of the conversation piece tradition.
Such characteristics have often been observed in the work
of Hogarth, *The Jones Family* (fig. 104) providing a notable
example. The representations of Squire Robert, his siblings
and his widowed mother accord with the dictates of polite
portraiture. Yet, between the two groups of sitters a small,
ragged, barefoot boy appears to wrestle with a monkey. Harder
to pick out, but more startling, are the diminutive figures of
a copulating couple on a hayrick, located just below the
silhouetted shape of the Jones's family home, Fonmon Castle.[32]
Zoffany can in many ways be considered Hogarth's heir.[33]
His studio sale contained eleven lots of Hogarth engravings,
including 'Evening' from the *Four Times of the Day* series, in
which the clever juxtaposition of the cow and the harried, weary
dyer effectively bestows the horns of the cuckold, foreshadowing
Zoffany's *Sharp Family*.[34] Hogarth was not unique in including
humorous touches in his conversation pieces, although he did
push them further than any of his contemporaries. Minor
incidents are scattered throughout the oeuvre of other artists,
such as Hamilton and Philips, in the early eighteenth century:
small dogs purloining letters or tugging at the hems of ladies'
dresses; small girls pulling at tablecloths and thereby disrupting
card games.[35] Such motifs can, in part, like the intricately
detailed style associated with the conversation piece tradition,
be traced back to seventeenth-century Netherlandish art.
Indeed, Horace Walpole linked the two in discussing Zoffany's
Tribuna (cat. 53): 'His talent is representing natural humour;
I look upon him as a Dutch painter polished or civilised. He
finishes as highly, renders nature as justly …'.[36]

The appeal of these narrative devices probably relied on
'raillery': equivalent to a light-hearted banter that showed the
sitters' modest ability to laugh at themselves and that fitted the
relatively more informal and lively milieu of the conversation
piece tradition.[37] Zoffany's patrons no doubt enjoyed the wit
of his clever juxtapositions and narrative conceits, although,
on occasion, he surely must have been sailing rather close
to the wind. However, an evident contemporary delight in
play-acting and performance was also at stake. Zoffany was
one of a considerable number of artists, including Hogarth
and Benjamin Wilson, to produce both theatrical scenes and
portraits. In part, this must have been a pragmatic result of
the requirements of the two genres. If, like Zoffany, a painter
had a particular talent for arranging figures into groups, for

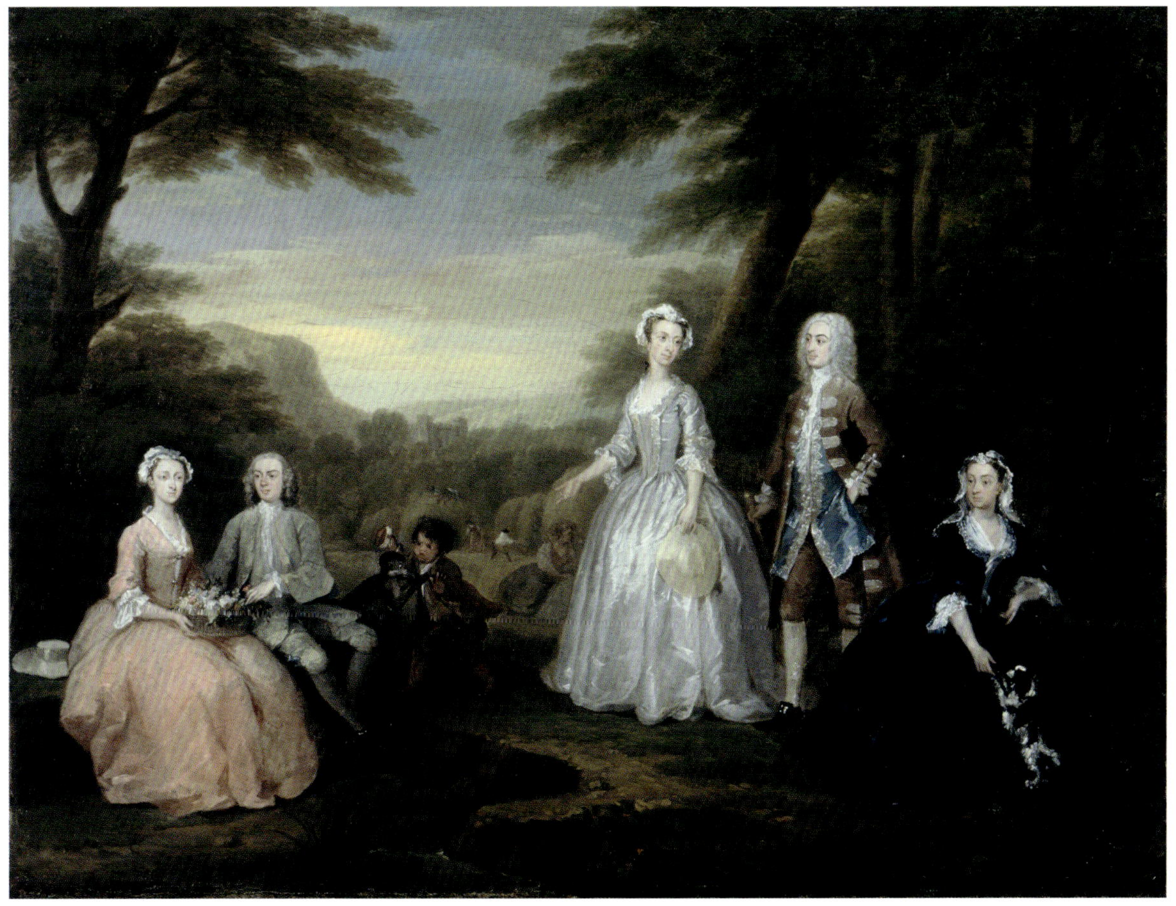

Figure 104
William Hogarth, *The Jones Family*,
c.1730, oil on canvas,
72 × 91.8 cm (28⅜ × 36⅛ in).
Amgueddfa Genedlaethol Cymru/
National Museum of Wales

inventing narrative devices to create interaction between those figures and for convincingly suggesting sociable exchange, then that talent invited attention to both theatrical work and portraiture. Inevitable slippage between the two is evident in this assessment of *Queen Charlotte with her Brothers* (fig. 105) in the *Middlesex Journal*:

In theatrical scenes and conversation-pieces, Mr. Zoffanij undoubtedly takes the lead; like a skilful dramatist, he gives all his actors a business which at the same time helps to set off the principal figure. In the conversation before us, the whole is well grouped, and the figures well animated and contrasted.[38]

Figure 105 (cat. 39)
Queen Charlotte with her Brothers Prince Charles and Prince Ernest of Mecklenburg-Strelitz and Three of her Children, 1771–2, oil on canvas, 105.1 × 127 cm (41⅜ × 50 in). The Royal Collection, Her Majesty Queen Elizabeth II

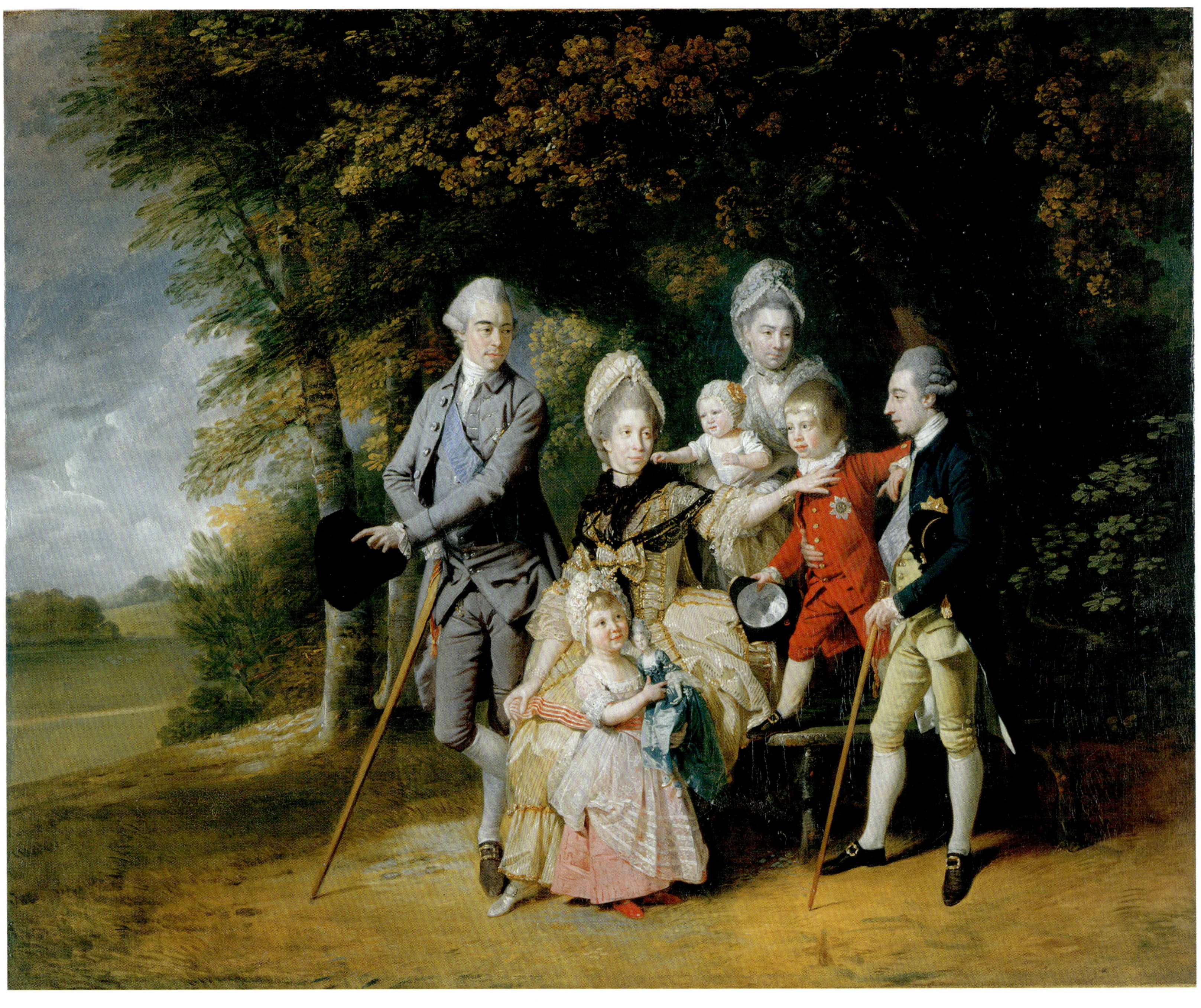

However, characteristic of the conversation piece as opposed to theatrical painting is a necessary tendency to create sub-groups, to break down a large gathering into two or three smaller clusters of figures. When the porcelain manufacturer Duesbury recreated Zoffany's portrait of George III, Charlotte and their children (fig. 106), it was quite straightforward to separate the family into three distinct units. Similarly, two portraits related to Zoffany's painting of the Young family (fig. 107) – likely to have been produced after rather than before the main picture – easily extract the children to the left and right of the painting to create satisfactory, smaller groups.[39]

That said, there is more to the close relationship between the conversation piece and the theatrical scene than mutual formal requirements. These narrative portraits convey a strong impression that the sitters are performing for the benefit of the viewer. The Young family certainly appear to be at home, enjoying various genteel, leisured pastimes on their estate. All are perfectly feasible and convincing activities for the elite family. But their activities are distinctly 'staged', the various signs of their wealth, taste and accomplishment displayed for the benefit of the viewer and posterity. And in this case the sense of a performance runs even deeper. Like other elite families in this period, the Youngs liked to dabble in private theatricals, writing to their friend David Garrick in 1758 to ask if he might loan them scenery and costumes ('Roman Shapes') for a production of *Julius Caesar*.[40] There is more than a hint of amateur dramatics about their portrait. Most of the women are dressed in outfits that blend the historical and the fashionable,

Figure 106 (cat. 36)
Duesbury & Co., *Set of three figures of the royal family*,
c.1773, porcelain, height 22 cm (8⅝ in).
The Royal Collection, Her Majesty Queen Elizabeth II

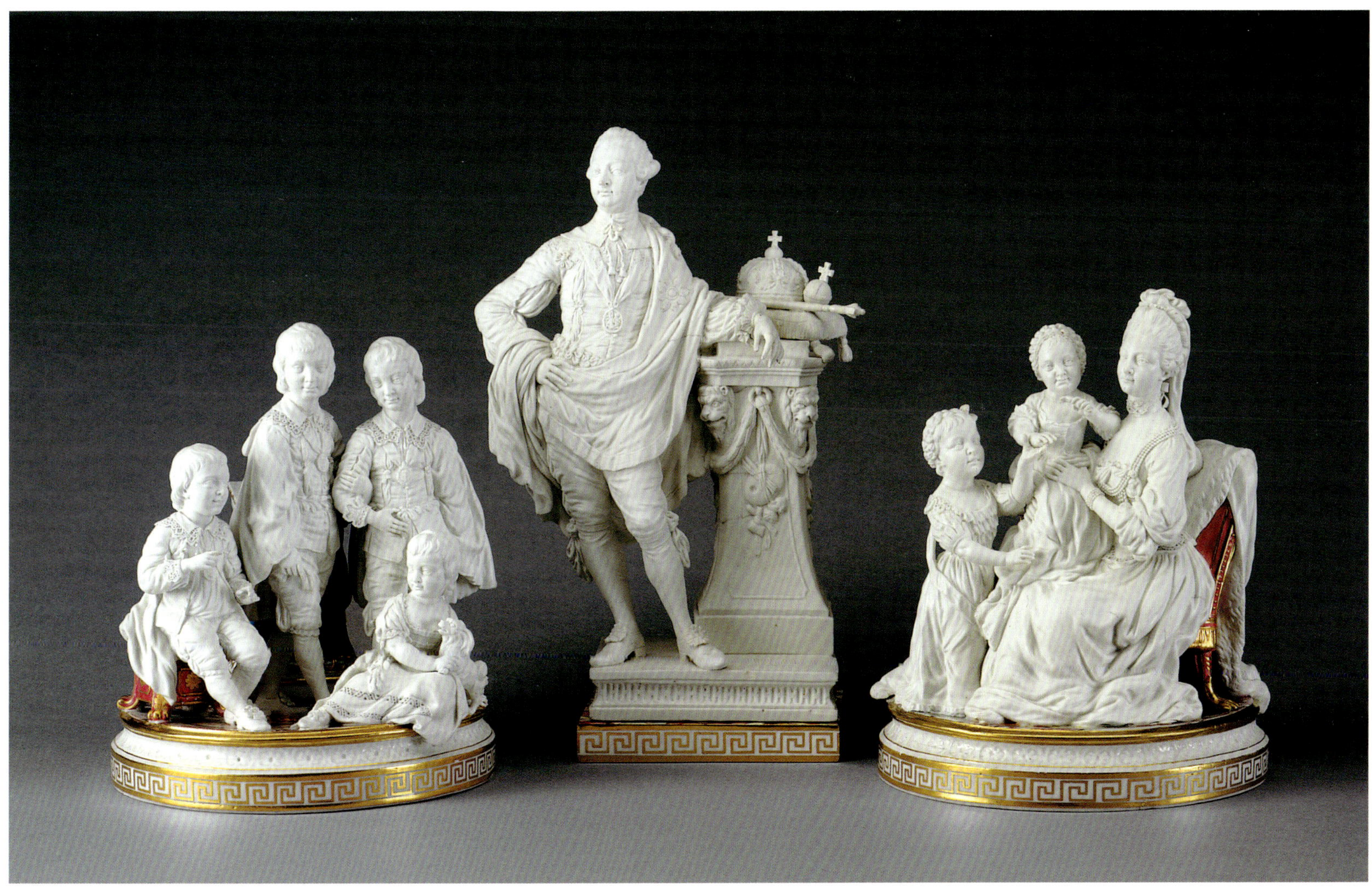

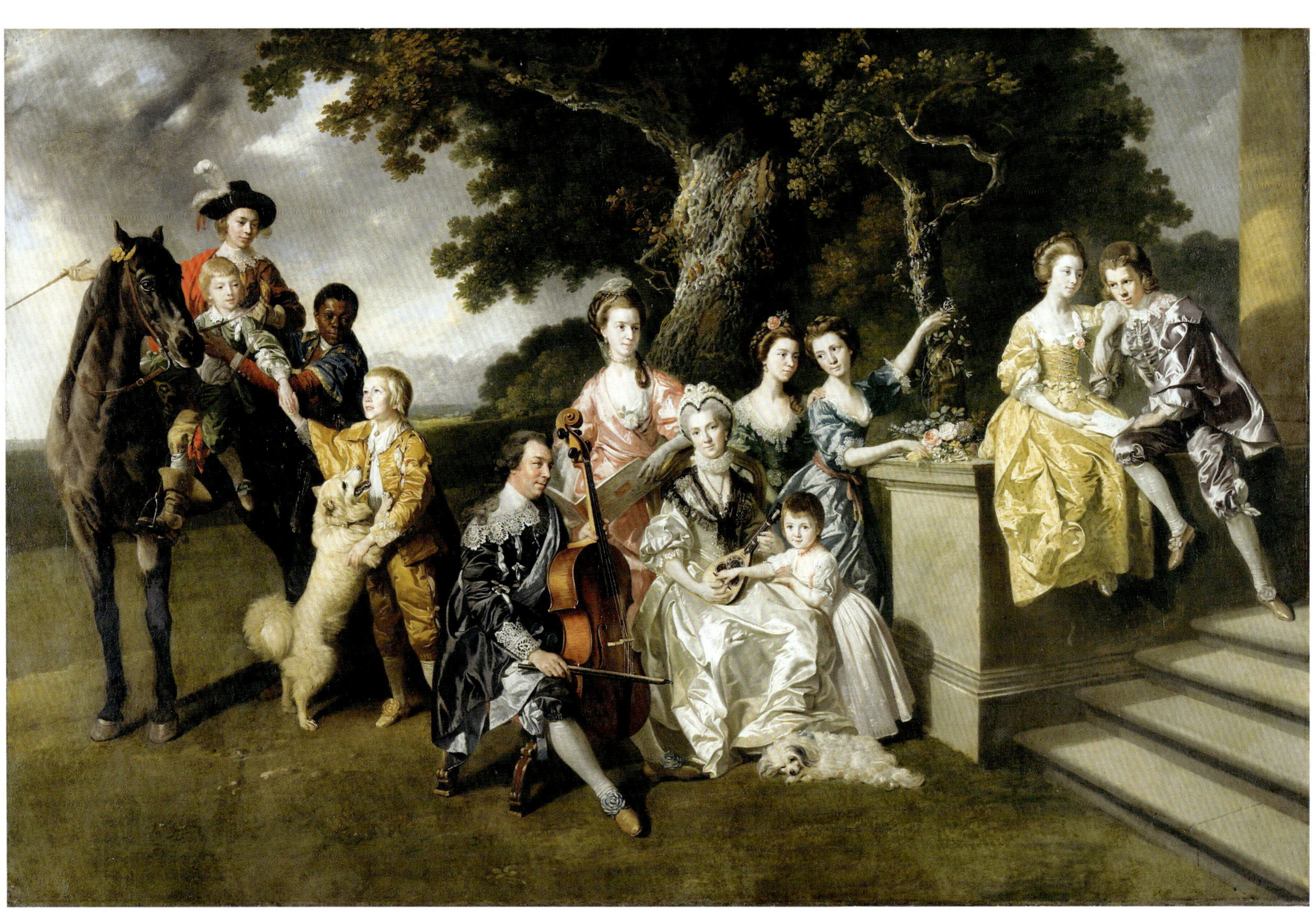

Figure 107
The Family of Sir William Young, 1767–8,
oil on canvas, 114.3 × 167.8 cm (45 × 66 in).
National Museums Liverpool, Walker Art Gallery

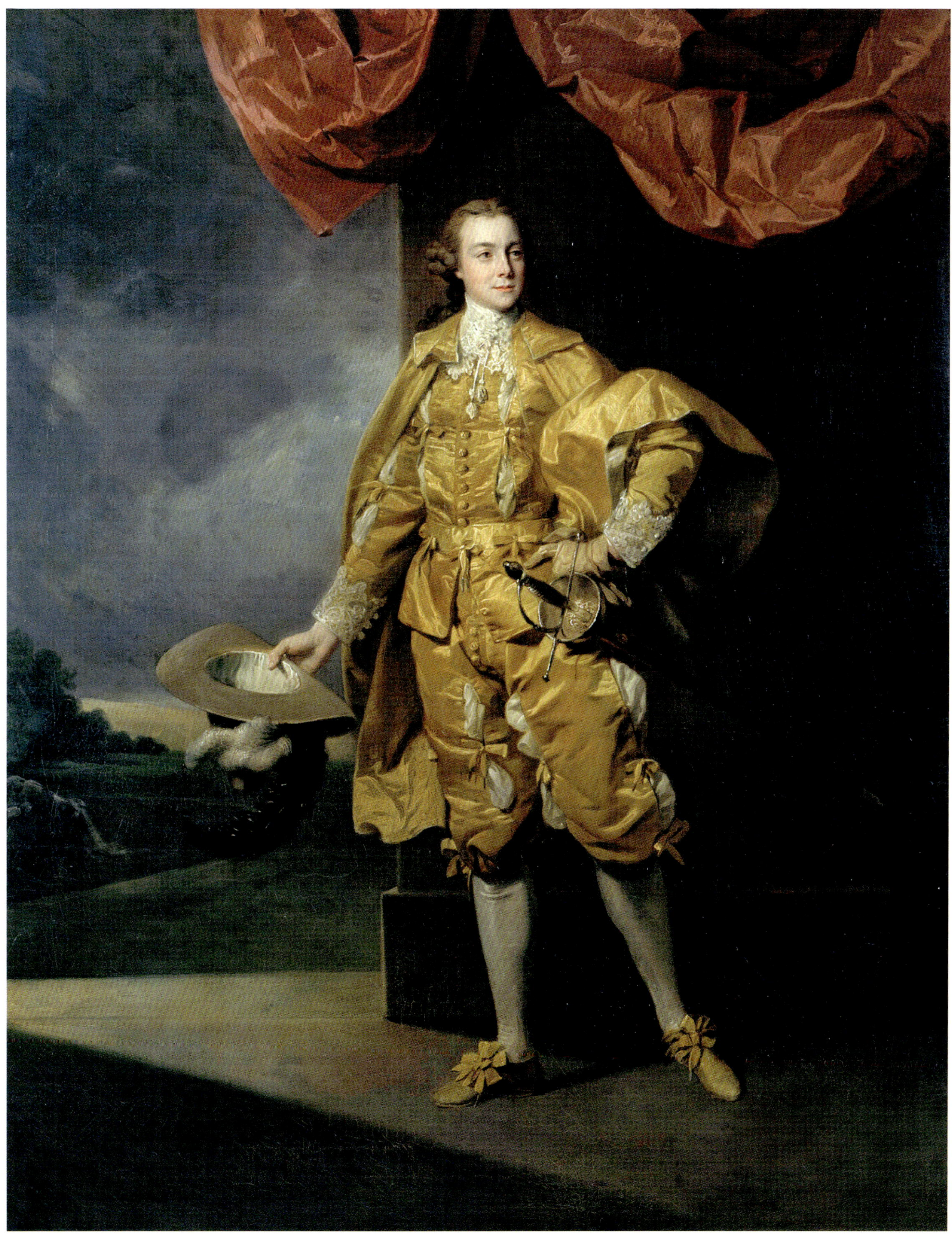

and the men wear so-called 'Vandyke costume'.[41] Such garb
was most commonly to be seen on the stage, as it was entirely
routine in this era for Shakespeare plays to be performed in
costume that approximated to early seventeenth-century
dress.[42]

The outfits worn by the Youngs reveal Zoffany tapping
into an important contemporary fashion in English portraiture.
Since at least the 1730s it had been modish to be depicted in
Vandyke dress, usually on a full-length canvas. The most
notable exponent of this trend was Thomas Gainsborough,
who garbed sitters in full Stuart costume as well as various
hybrids, mingling elements associated with the court of Charles
I with contemporary dress.[43] As Deborah Cherry and Jennifer
Harris have shown, the appeal of such outfits was myriad.
They tapped into a widespread nostalgia for the Caroline court,
promoted by writers such as David Hume.[44] Vandyke dress was
a popular outfit at masquerades.[45] And it was one answer to a
persistent problem of portraiture with which Van Dyck himself
had engaged: should portraitists show sitters in the height of
contemporary style, thereby attaining the greatest likeness
and flattering their fashionability, or should they dress them in
something with a more timeless air, helping the portrait to
outlive its moment of execution? The most common solution by
portraitists who favoured the latter option was broadly classical
dress, perhaps adorned with a touch of ermine to convey status
and perhaps tempered by a contemporary hairstyle. However,
the persistent popularity of Vandyke dress, and its prominence
in family portrait collections, allowed this temporally specific
style to attain a degree of timelessness of its own. Indeed, its
familiarity in the country house portrait gallery gave it an extra
appeal: it could help a contemporary addition to a collection
mingle comfortably with its predecessors.

Zoffany quickly engaged with the vogue for Van Dyckian
lace and ruffles after his arrival in England. His half-length
portrait of Sir Richard Neave is an early example, but his
slightly later depiction of John, Lord Mountstuart, is perhaps
the most remarkable (fig. 108). The sheen of the rumpled fabric,
the elaborate detailing of the trimmings and the vibrancy of
the colour rival Gainsborough's later, canonical exercise in
Van Dyckian portraiture: *Jonathan Buttall*, better known as

The Blue Boy (fig. 109).[46] However, Lord Mountstuart's figure is
on the same scale as the sitters in Zoffany's conversation pieces,
a swaggering but diminutive form, while Buttall is life size.
The two artists went head to head when Gainsborough's
portrait of Buttall was displayed at the Academy in 1770, the
same year as Zoffany showed his depiction of the royal family
in Vandyke dress (cat. 34). For George III and Charlotte the
broad appeal of this costume was sharpened by direct relevance.
Suggesting a seamless line of descent from the court of
Charles I and Henrietta Maria, it effectively smoothed over the
complexities of the Hanoverian succession and the Glorious
Revolution in its declaration of their royal lineage and heritage.

Figure 109
Thomas Gainsborough, *Jonathan Buttall: The Blue Boy*, *c*.1770,
oil on canvas, 179.4 × 123.8 cm (70⅝ × 48¾ in).
The Huntington Library, Art Collections, and Botanical
Gardens, San Marino, California

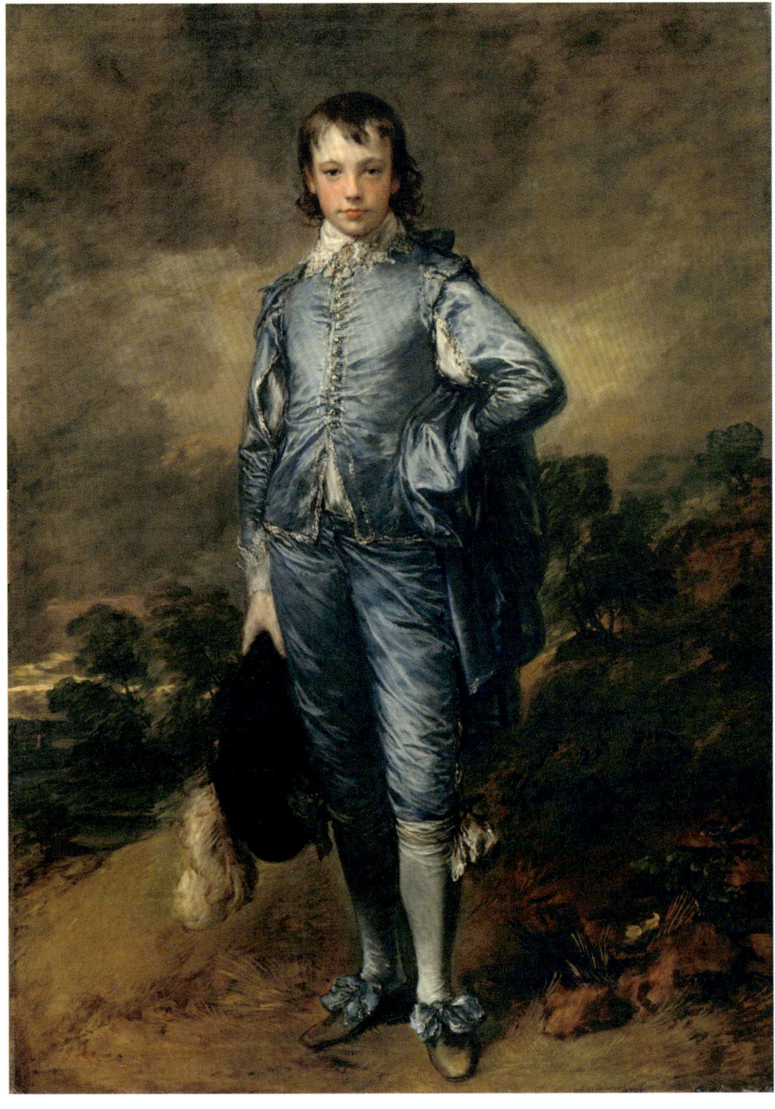

Figure 108
John, Lord Mountstuart in Masquerade Dress, 1765,
oil on canvas, 91.5 × 71 cm (36 × 28 in).
Private collection, UK

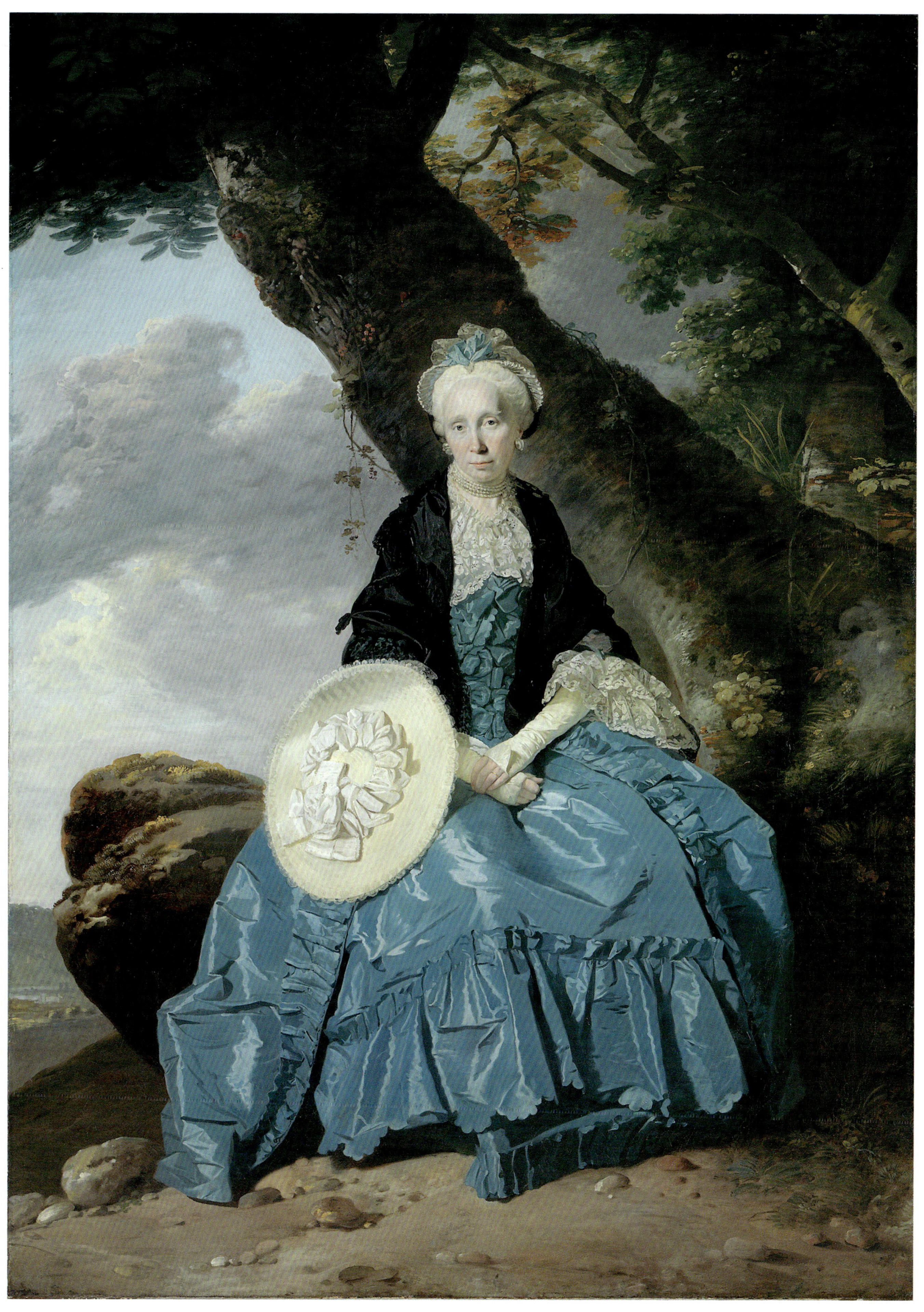

From the mid-1760s onwards Zoffany did venture into the
realm of the life-size full length, before producing many more
canvases in this format between his return from Italy and his
departure for India. He reused many of the elements of his
1770 depiction of the royal family, including the Vandyke dress,
in his 'large as the life' painting of *The Family of the Grand Duke
Pietro Leopoldo* (see fig. 76).[47] Zoffany's reputation in this branch
of portraiture was uncertain. In 1781 the *Public Advertiser*
commented on a male portrait on display at the Academy:
'In No. 223, *Zoffany* has succeeded better than he usually does
in portraits as *large as life*.'[48] This caustic remark is belied,
however, by the earlier triumph of *Mrs Oswald* (fig. 110). There
is an inexorable link between the detailed style in which Zoffany
specialized and the small-scale canvases he favoured, but here,
in the careful rendering of the blue drapery, white lace and
pearls, he successfully translates his painstaking idiom into the
larger-scale format favoured by Reynolds. Yet, it was with his
portrait of Mrs Wodhull (wife of the poet Michael Wodhull),
that Zoffany most clearly sought to emulate the President of the
Royal Academy (fig. 111). In this case the use of the full-length
format may well be explained by a story that the Wodhulls had
originally commissioned a half-length but had been so pleased
with the result as to request that the artist extend it.[49]

By 1770 Reynolds's position in the London art world was
pre-eminent. Foremost society portraitist of the day, he had
become first President of the Royal Academy on its foundation
in 1768 and its mouthpiece by virtue of his lectures on art
theory, collectively known as the *Discourses*. In the present
context it is highly significant that, in the course of these
lectures, Reynolds systematically downgraded precisely those
qualities that characterized the bulk of Zoffany's portrait
production. Zoffany's skill in creating lustrous and intensely
detailed representations of the material world fell foul of
Reynolds's dismissal of such artistic qualities as 'mechanical
dexterity', 'minuteness' and 'imitation'.[50] The third *Discourse*
(delivered in 1770), in particular, undermines Zoffany's
meticulous approach to portraiture.[51] First, Reynolds insisted,
the artist should always look to the generic, to that which united
mankind rather than to the particularities of the time and place
in which he found himself.[52] This left little space for Zoffany's
skill in rendering contemporary dress and the fashionable
tastes, possessions and pastimes of the British elite. Second,
the artist should not be seduced into trying to impress through
sheer technical expertise and illusionistic representation: only
the 'lower painter, like the florist or collector of shells' will
'exhibit the minute discriminations which distinguish one
object of the same species from another'. Looking beyond the
attractions of 'deceiving the eye', the 'painter of genius' will
rather turn his attention to the mind of the viewer, not wasting
'a moment upon … smaller objects, which only serve to catch
the sense, to divide the attention, and to counteract his great
design of speaking to the heart'.[53]

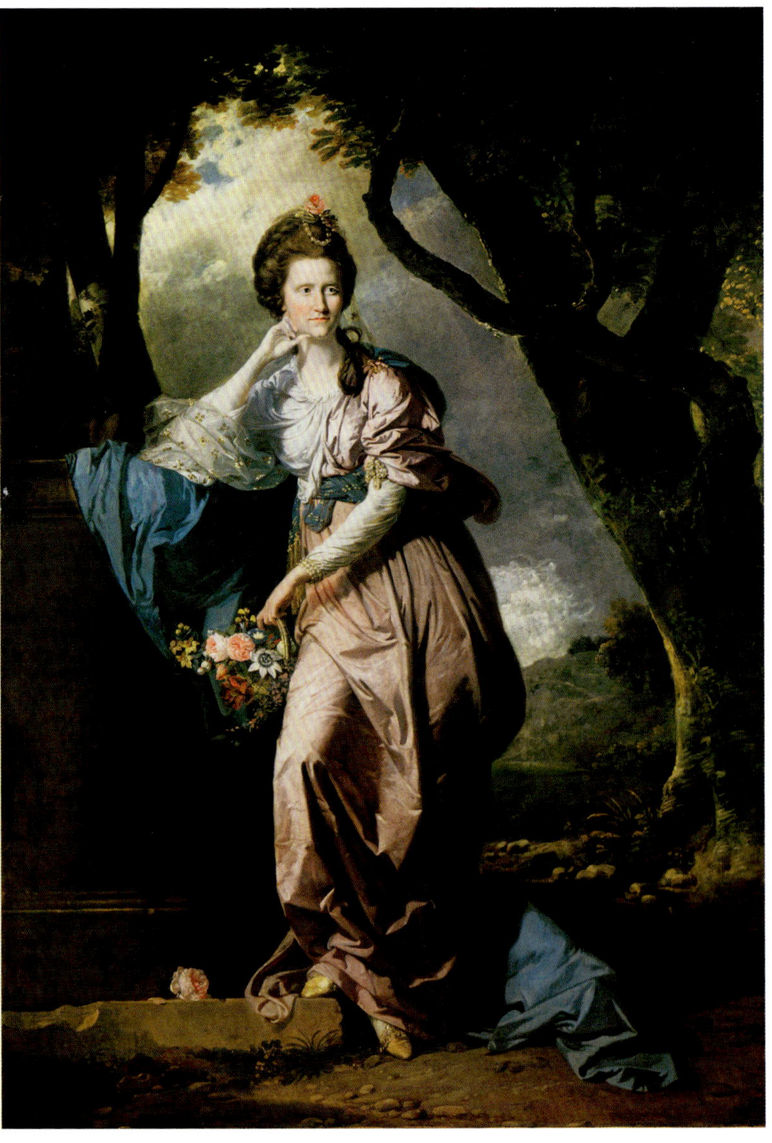

Figure 110 (cat. 66)
Mrs Oswald, 1763–5, oil on canvas,
226.5 × 158.8 cm (89⅛ × 62½ in).
National Gallery, London

Figure 111
Mrs Catherine Wodhull, c.1770,
oil on canvas, 243.8 × 165.1 cm (96 × 65 in).
Tate, London

Such edicts were well established within academic art theory and had been voiced in England earlier in the century by writers like the Earl of Shaftesbury.[54] Under the Royal Academy's aegis, however, they assumed a new dominance, and the place for alternatives was increasingly squeezed. In the field of portraiture the trend was towards the kind of grand manner practised by Reynolds, in which he attempted to embody his emphasis on the transcending of time and geography, and on the elevated and general above the technically skilled and precise. His portrait of the Duchess of Hamilton, shown at the first London art exhibition in 1760, the year of Zoffany's arrival, was something of a manifesto and a portent of things to come (fig. 112). The attempt to make this a picture with broader relevance than a mere detailing of the particular appearance of a particular sitter, evident in the loose, flowing dress and broadly rendered features, culminates in the artistic suggestion that this is also a history painting. Thanks to the relief, in which Paris bestows his apple on Venus in honour of her beauty, and the presence of two doves, which traditionally accompany that goddess, the Duchess is exalted to a domain well above that of the 'local' and 'temporary'.[55]

In his conversation pieces Zoffany catered to different concerns, to what Harry Mount has identified as 'the abiding taste of British consumers for highly detailed art works'.[56] Yet, it was now a very different environment from that experienced by conversation-piece artists in the earlier decades of the eighteenth century. As a consequence, careful mimetic transcription of material things could now engender the following comment: '[Zoffany's] merit consists in the truth of his representation, accompanied with great mechanical skill, but [he] never seems to attempt invention.'[57] However, he could, on occasion, work in the grand-manner tradition. Mrs Wodhull leans against a stone plinth in a woodland setting in much the same manner as the Duchess of Hamilton. Her costume is an equally impractical draped affair, and her proportions have been similarly distorted like those of late Renaissance sculpture, with a high waist and extended thighs. Zoffany also, at times, introduced elements of the grand manner into his conversation pieces. In portraits such as *The Reverend Randall Burroughes and his Son, Ellis* (fig. 113) or *The Gore Family with George, Third Earl Cowper* (cat. 56) Zoffany breaks with the traditions of the conversation piece in creating a liminal space, somewhere between interior and exterior.

Zoffany's adaptation of the conversation piece was also influenced by a new valorization of affectionate familial relations in mid-eighteenth-century England that had become the stuff

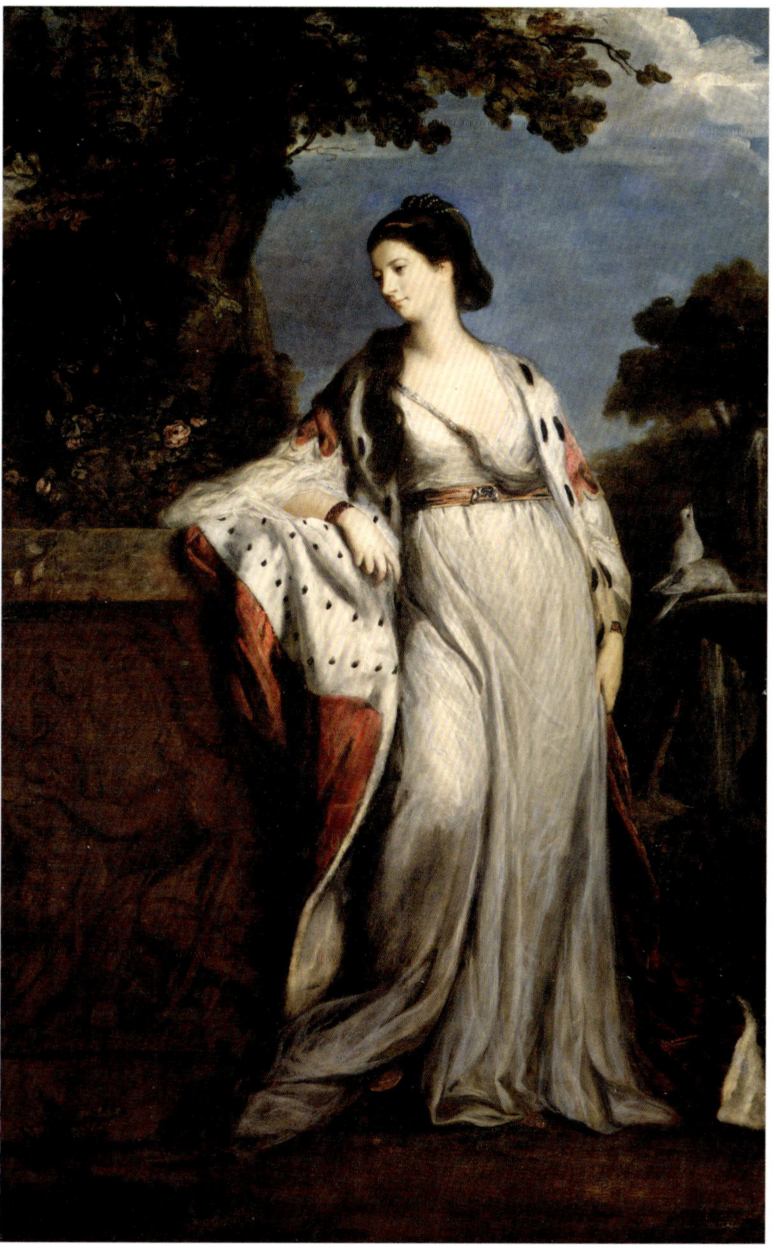

Figure 112
Joshua Reynolds, *Elizabeth Gunning, Duchess of Hamilton and Duchess of Argyll*, 1760, oil on canvas, 238.5 × 147.5 cm (93⅞ × 58⅛ in). National Museums Liverpool, Lady Lever Art Gallery

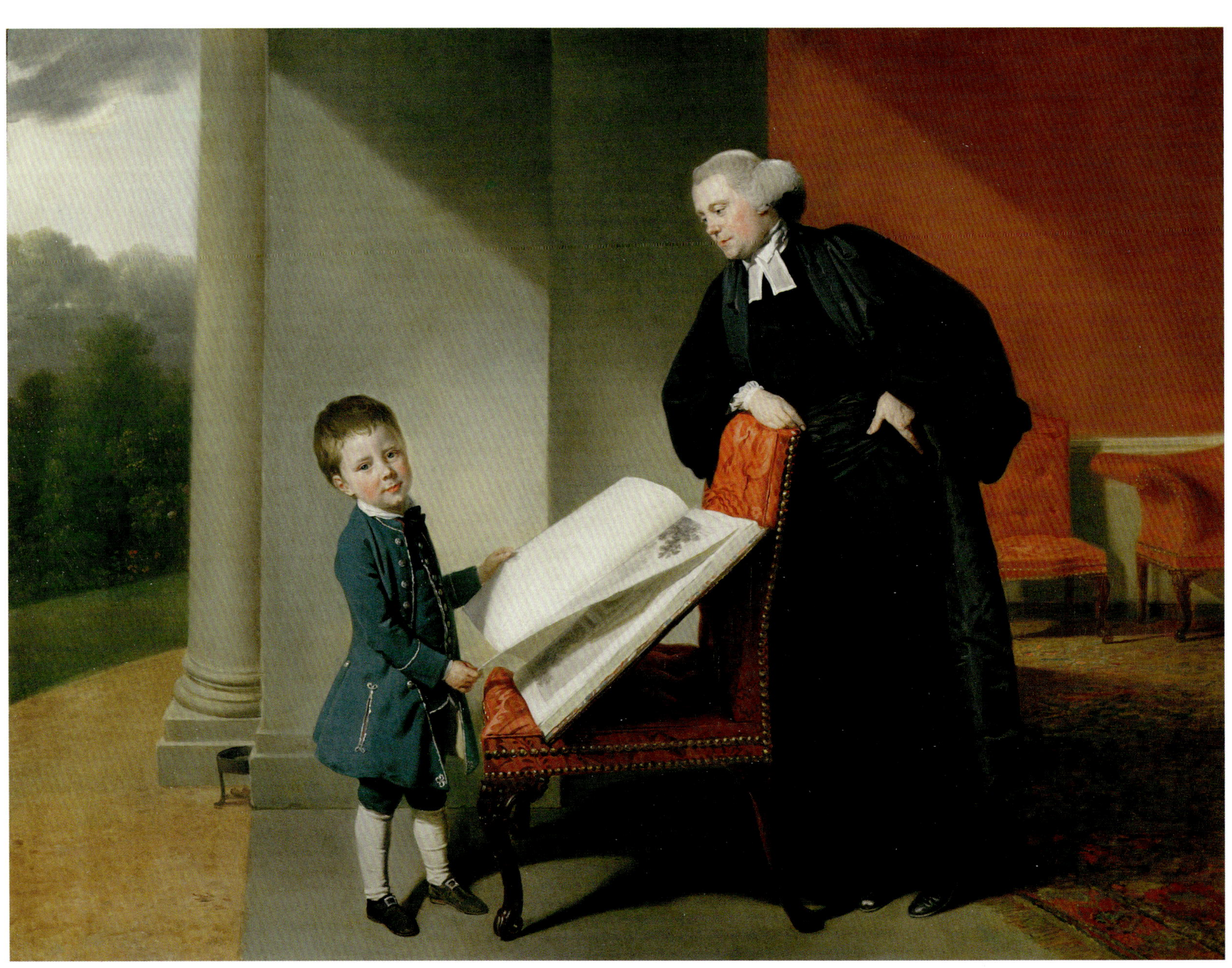

Figure 113
The Reverend Randall Burroughes and his Son Ellis, 1769,
oil on canvas, 71 × 89 cm (28 × 35 in).
Louvre, Paris

of sentimental literature.[58] Sir Lawrence Dundas may be a connoisseur, but he is also a tender grandfather to his namesake. Dundas does not seem too perturbed at being distracted from his paperwork by the little boy who tucks his hand through the crook of his arm. Neither does Lord Willoughby de Broke appear to be a terribly stern patriarch, despite the warning finger he raises to the small son who is about to steal a piece of toast from the breakfast table (cat. 72). Certainly, an emphasis on dynastic succession, on hierarchy, persists. As in the Atholl portrait, the eldest son is positioned in greatest proximity to his father, while the baby girl is supported by her mother. But the overwhelming impression is of an informal moment, a captured insight into affectionate family life. Zoffany could offer the clients for his portraits many things: an accurate likeness, a vivid evocation of their possessions, fashionable Vandyke dress if they wanted it, and historicizing grandeur in the manner of Reynolds if so desired. Yet, his skill at constructing narrative and arranging his figures also allowed him to unite families and friends in newly engaging, harmonious and witty groups.

Notes

1. Anon. 1781, iv.
2. William Hogarth, 'The Autobiographical Notes', in *The Analysis of Beauty with the Rejected Passages from the Manuscript Drafts and Autobiographical Notes*, ed. Joseph Burke, Oxford, 1955, 201–31: 202.
3. See Webster 2011, 62–6.
4. Anon. 1781, iv–v.
5. *St James's Chronicle*, 7 May 1765.
6. *A Catalogue of the Small, but Valuable Collection of … Pictures … of the Late David Garrick*, Christie's, 23 June 1823, lots 51 and 52.
7. For an introduction to the eighteenth-century conversation piece, see D'Oench 1980. The most recent text on the subject is Shawe-Taylor 2009.
8. Benjamin Wilson to David Garrick, quoted in Whitley 1928, vol. 2, 251; Garrick 1963, vol. 1, 363, David Garrick to Benjamin Wilson.
9. John Harris, *The Artist and the Country House: A History of Country House and Garden View Painting in Britain, 1540–1870*, London, 1979. Edward Haytley's pendant portraits of the Brockman family and friends at Beachborough Manor, painted in the 1740s and now in the National Gallery of Victoria, Melbourne, are also good examples.
10. Christie's, 9 June 2004, lot 4.
11. For contemporary comments on the conversation piece, see George Vertue, 'Notebooks', *Walpole Society*, vols. 18 (1929–30), 20 (1931–2), 22 (1933–4), 24 (1935–6), 26 (1937–8), 30 (1948–50).
12. D'Oench 1980, *passim*.
13. Blair Castle Archive, 5/139, 'Accounts for the year 1764 of John Duke of Atholl', and bundle 56A, receipt from Zoffany dated 16 Jan. 1767. Webster 2011, 148, notes that Zoffany charged the same price of 20 guineas per sitter for *The Children of the Fourth Duke of Devonshire*, *c.*1763–4.
14. See 'Reynolds's Prices' in David Mannings and Martin Postle, *Sir Joshua Reynolds: A Complete Catalogue of his Paintings*, 2 vols., New Haven and London, 2000, vol. 1, 21.
15. Treadwell 2009, 225–6, 320–21. See also the sale catalogue for the contents of Zoffany's house, Christie's, 17–18 Aug. 1772, reprinted in Webster 2011, Appendix 7, 639–43.
16. *A Catalogue of the Magnificent Collection of Pictures of the late Sir Lawrence Dundas, Bart …*, London, 1794. See Sutton 1967. For Bute, see Russell, 2004, chap. 12.
17. 'Fijnschilder' is a term commonly applied to seventeenth-century Netherlandish painters such as Gerrit Dou and Frans van Mieris who specialized in meticulous attention to detail and smooth surfaces.
18. Christopher Hussey, 'Conversation Pieces: Sir Philip Sassoon's Exhibition, March 4th–30th', *Country Life*, 15 Feb. 1930, 263–4.

19. Kate Retford, 'From the Interior to Interiority: The Conversation Piece in Georgian England', *Journal of Design History*, 20 (2007), 291–307.

20. The chair appears in *The Reverend Randall Burroughes and his Son, Ellis* (fig. 113) and *Mr and Mrs Dalton and their Niece, Mary Deheulle* (cat. 67). For another example, see Webster 2011, 100, fig. 97. Webster (2011, 148) goes further in proposing a considerable number of items, including those arrayed in Zoffany's portrait of the Willoughby de Broke family, to be depictions of the artist's own possessions. I would argue against this, however. See my entry for the Willoughby de Broke portrait (cat. 72) for a full discussion.

21. These were brought together in an exhibition of 1985; see Jackson-Stops 1985, cats 281–2, 284–6, 289.

22. John, Seventh Duke of Atholl, *Chronicles of the Atholl and Tullibardine Families*, 5 vols., Edinburgh, 1908, vol. 4, 17–19; Manners & Williamson 1920, 16.

23. *St James's Chronicle*, May 1783, Royal Academy Press Cuttings, vol. 1 (1769–93), f.120.

24. Webster 2011, 148.

25. Blair Castle archive, bundles 55 and 56A, inventories of 1777, 1794 and 1830.

26. Retford 2006, 129.

27. Unpublished paper by Matthew Craske, 'Conversations and Chimneypieces: the Eighteenth-Century English Conversation Portrait as a Conventionalised Representation of an Act of Hospitality'. I am most grateful to Dr Craske for allowing me to see an early draft of this work.

28. It is usually stated that this is a mis-representation of the family's pet racoon, named Tom. See, for example, Webster 2011, 148. However, as Martin Postle has noted, given the accurate depiction of the animal in question by Zoffany, such an error seems rather unlikely and may have more to do with family tradition than fact. The Murrays owned quite a menagerie of exotic animals and birds and could also have possessed a lemur.

29. See Pressly 1987.

30. For a fuller explication, see the entry to cat. 77.

31. For this period, see Paulson 1975, chap. 9; Pressly 1987.

32. For a recent account of this picture, see Mark Hallett and Christine Riding, *Hogarth*, London, 2006, p.102.

33. Paulson 1975, chap. 9.

34. Robins 1811, lots 3–13 (9 May): Webster 2011, 643.

35. See, for example, Gawen Hamilton, *The Porten Family* (*c.*1736; Museum of Fine Arts, Springfield, MA); Charles Philips, *The Finch Family* (*c.*1732; Yale Center for British Art); Charles Philips, *The Strong Family* (1732; Metropolitan Museum, New York).

36. Lewis 1937–83, vol. 24, 527, Horace Walpole to Horace Mann, 12 Nov. 1779.

37. D.H. Solkin, *Painting for Money: The Visual Arts and the Public Sphere in Eighteenth-Century England*, New Haven and London, 1993, 89–90.

38. *The Middlesex Journal*, 1 May 1773.

39. Webster 1977, 42; picture file, Walker Art Gallery, Liverpool. Martin Postle has proposed that Zoffany completed the secondary portrait of William and Mary, but left that of Brook, John and Harry unfinished on his departure for Italy to be completed by another hand.

40. Garrick 1963, vol. 1, 283–4, David Garrick to William Young, 3 Aug. 1758; 285–6, David Garrick to William Young, ?Aug. 1758. For private theatricals, see Sybil Rosenfeld, *Temples of Thespis: Some Private Theatres and Theatricals in England and Wales, 1700–1820*, London, 1978 (on p. 179 it is noted that there is no evidence that the performance of *Julius Caesar* actually took place); Gillian Russell, 'Private Theatricals', in Jane Moody and Daniel O'Quinn, eds., *The Cambridge Companion to British Theatre, 1730–1830*, Cambridge, 2007, chap. 13.

41. Ribeiro 1995, 210.

42. Diana de Marly, *Costume on the Stage, 1600–1940*, London, 1982, 52–4.

43. Deborah Cherry and Jennifer Harris, 'Eighteenth-Century Portraiture and the Seventeenth-Century Past: Gainsborough and van Dyck', *Art History*, 5 (1982), 287–309.

44. David Hume, *The History of Great Britain*, London, 1754–62.

45. For the relationship between Vandyke costume worn at masquerades and portraiture, see Ribeiro 1984, chap. 3.

46. It has recently been proposed that the sitter was not Jonathan Buttall but the artist's nephew, Gainsborough Dupont. See Susan Sloman, *Gainsborough in Bath*, New Haven and London, 2002, 78–80.

47. The choice of costume was apparently Zoffany's own. Farington 1978–84, vol. 3, 812, 31 March 1797

48. *Public Advertiser*, 4 May 1781.

49. Robin Gibson, *Paintings from the Collection of Dr. D.M. McDonald*, London, 1970, 78. Mezzotints by Richard Houston record both the half- and full-length versions. See Webster, 2011, 650.

50. For examples, see Reynolds 1997, 41, 58.

51. Although evidence exists to suggest that their relationship was, by and large, friendly. See, for example, Webster 2011, 109–10, 203, 210, 350, 408, 637.

52. Reynolds 1997, 48–9.

53. Reynolds 1997, 50.

54. Anthony Ashley Cooper, Earl of Shaftesbury, *Characteristicks of Men, Manners, Opinions, Times*, 3 vols., London, 1723, vol. 1, 142–3. See Harry Mount, 'Morality, microscopy and the moderns: the meaning of minuteness in Shaftesbury's theory of painting', *British Journal for Eighteenth-Century Studies*, 21 (1998), 125–41.

55. Reynolds 1997, 49. For this portrait, see particularly Desmond Shawe-Taylor, *The Georgians: Eighteenth-Century Portraiture and Society*, London, 1990, 147–52, and Robert W. Jones, '"Such Strange Unwonted Softness to Excuse": Judgement and Indulgence in Sir Joshua Reynolds's Portrait of Elizabeth Gunning, Duchess of Hamilton and Argyll', *Oxford Art Journal*, 8, 1 (1995), 29–43.

56. Harry Mount, 'Van Rymsdyk and the Nature-Menders: An Early Victim of the Two Cultures Divide', *British Journal for Eighteenth-Century Studies*, 29 (2006), 79–96, esp. 84.

57. *Morning Chronicle*, 9 May 1782.

58. Retford 2006, *passim.*

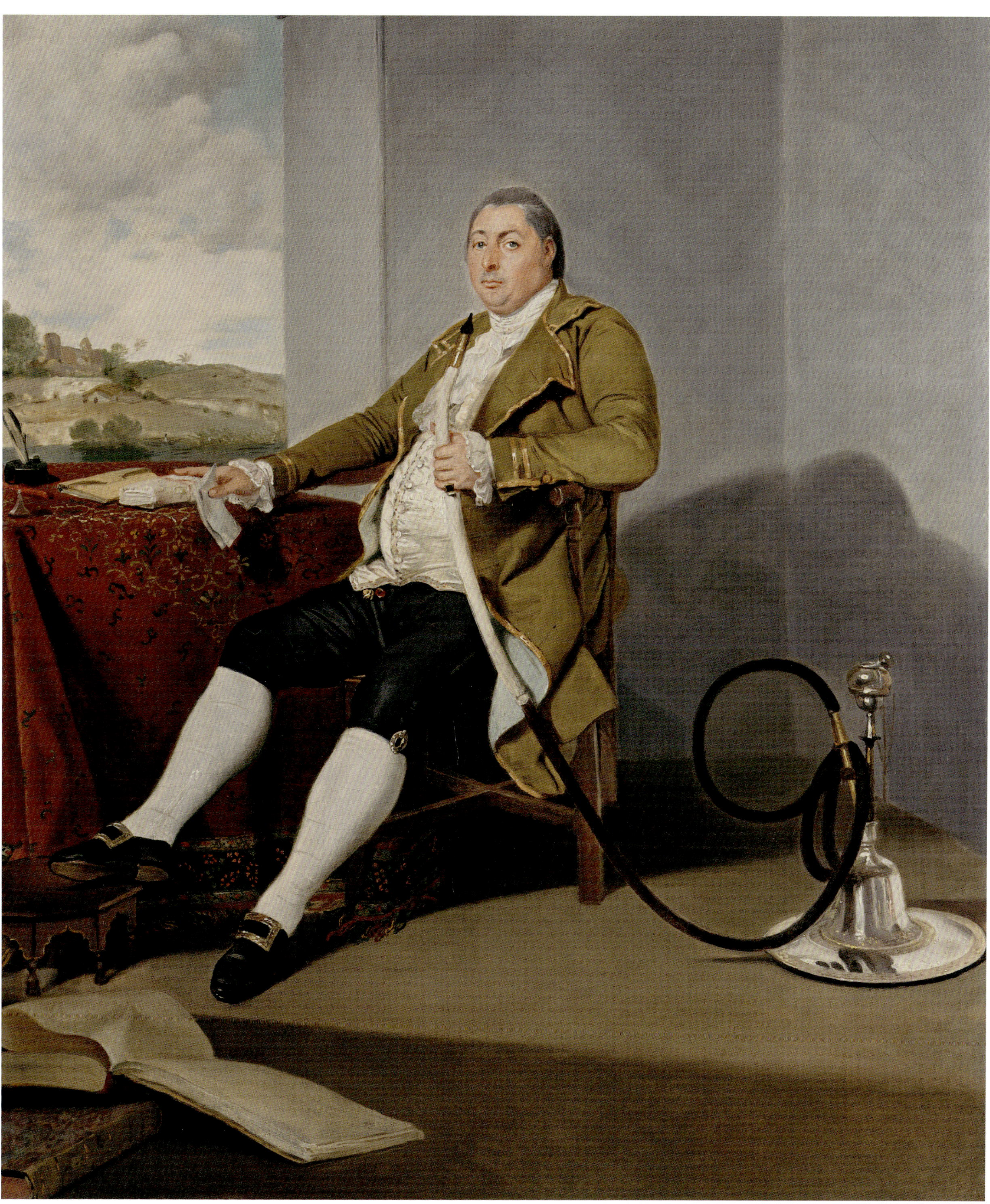

Maya Jasanoff

A Passage through India:
Zoffany in Calcutta & Lucknow

When Johan Zoffany launched his career in Britain in 1760, he arrived in a country busily engaged in global war and empire building. Victory in the Seven Years' War in 1763 added swathes of territory to the British Empire, including French Canada, a string of strategic posts in the Atlantic and Mediterranean, and, operatively for Zoffany's future, a growing stake in South Asia, where the East India Company asserted military supremacy in Bengal. Living and working at the centre of this expanding empire, Zoffany encountered Britain's global reach in numerous guises. His sitters included figures involved in British Atlantic affairs, ranging from the Jamaican heiress Mary Oswald (cat. 66) to the leading anti-slavery campaigner Granville Sharp (cat. 77) and the African-born Julius Soubise, a former slave and well-known London fop.[1] Another sitter, the collector Charles Townley (cat. 63), triggered Zoffany's curiosity in Egyptian and Indian antiquities, while Zoffany's patron Joseph Banks, the gentleman scientist who had sailed on Captain Cook's first voyage, linked Zoffany to the Pacific, even proposing in 1771 that Zoffany travel as an artist on Cook's second voyage. Though the project fell through (Zoffany's friend William Hodges made the journey instead), Zoffany eventually found his own way to venture beyond Europe. In 1783, as the end of the American Revolution restored peace to the British Empire, Zoffany left his family and set off nearly halfway around the world, to India.

What made him go? He said it was money ('he anticipates to roll in gold dust', reported fellow artist Paul Sandby), something he had special reason to seek in new places after the poor reception of *The Tribuna* by Queen Charlotte. Zoffany became one of several painters to follow the lead of Tilly Kettle, the first professional British artist to visit India, who enjoyed a warm and profitable reception there in the 1760s.[2] But times had changed since then, when Bengal had held out visions of fantastic wealth, personified by 'nabobs' like Robert Clive, who returned home 'all over estates and diamonds' (in Horace Walpole's memorable phrase), and lesser figures such as James Graham (fig. 114). The nabobs' excesses had already prompted the first parliamentary regulation of East India Company government; and the loss of the thirteen American colonies sharpened policy makers' focus on the parts of the empire that remained. The India Act of 1784 brought the Company under closer supervision, professionalizing British Indian administration and further curtailing the get-rich-quick opportunities of Clive's day.[3]

Figure 114 (cat. 89)
*James Graham of Rickerby and Barrock Lodge, c.*1784–6, oil on canvas, 90.8 × 66 cm (35¾ × 26 in). Tullie House Museum & Art Gallery, Carlisle

Service in India tended to attract ambitious strivers from slightly disadvantaged positions, including illegitimate sons and down-at-heel gentry who often hoped to repair or make a fortune. Zoffany, having lost royal favour and disgruntled by changing British tastes, shared something of the profile of the adventurous if marginalized Europeans who made the voyage east. But he was a painter, not a bureaucrat or soldier, and he remained well connected enough in London that hard times alone can only partly explain his choice. He must also have been attracted by the promise of inspiring new vistas, of new subjects to paint, examine and explore. This keen intellectual curiosity, Zoffany would discover, was another trait he had in common with the Europeans he met in India.

Zoffany reached the Subcontinent in July 1783 and spent the next four and a half years immersed in the north Indian cities of Calcutta and Lucknow. Each city exposed a different face of late Mughal India. Calcutta, the capital of Company-administered Bengal, showcased the increasing confidence of its small ruling population. Lucknow, the capital of the Mughal province of Awadh, witnessed a cultural renaissance against a backdrop of eroding indigenous authority. As Zoffany moved between Calcutta and Lucknow, he journeyed across a changing political, cultural and artistic landscape: from greater to lesser British control, and from lesser to greater Indian influence. If Zoffany's passage to India reflected generic expectations of wealth and novelty, his passage through India represented an ever-deepening engagement with local cultures and the Europeans absorbed in them.

Calcutta

After a brief stay in Madras, Zoffany arrived in Calcutta in September. This swampy delta settlement was fast evolving into a self-described city of palaces, a newly confident capital of British India. Popular aquatints produced in the 1780s by Thomas and William Daniell (figs. 115, 116) show broad avenues lined with gleaming public buildings, where carriages outpace palanquins, uniformed sepoys parade past loin-clothed bearers, and the symmetry of British planning tidily contains the implied disorder of native ways. City landmarks included the church of St John the Baptist, designed to resemble London's St Martin-in-the-Fields; shortly after its consecration in the spring of 1787, Zoffany painted an altarpiece of *The Last Supper* (fig. 126), which was installed on the communion table.[‡]

At first glance, European social life in Calcutta defied its local context with a squarely British commitment to hard drinking, heavy feasting and plenty of duels and scandals to keep the community abuzz. But around the edges Zoffany would quickly have detected the influence of local habits, such as hookah smoking and betel chewing, as well as the relatively common cohabitation of European men with Indian women.

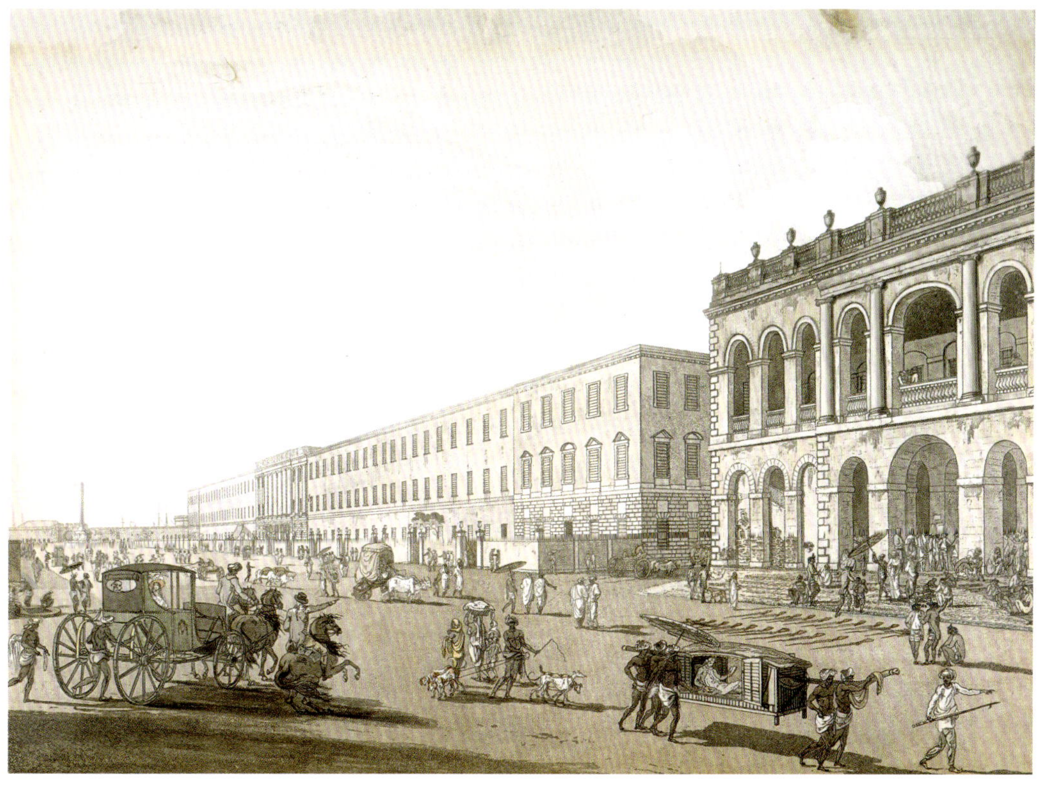

Figure 115
Thomas Daniell, *Old Court House and Writer's Building*, etching and aquatint, 40 × 52.7 cm, (15¾ × 20¾ in) from *Views of Calcutta*, 1786–8, no. 2. The British Library, London

He also saw an Anglo-Indian convergence in the founding in 1784 of Calcutta's proudest cultural ornament, the Asiatic Society of Bengal, intended to provide a forum for intellectually inclined Europeans to investigate Indian topics.[5]

The Governor General of Bengal, Warren Hastings, served as an apt figurehead for this burgeoning Anglo-Indian society, since he personified Orientalism in multiple senses. Hastings was an avid Orientalist in the classic use of the term, studying 'the Orient' by learning Urdu and Persian, collecting Asian manuscripts and actively patronizing various forms of scholarship and the arts. He commissioned translations of the *Bhagavad Gita* and indigenous legal codes; he established a madrasa and the first Bengali printing press; he funded expeditions to Tibet, Burma and Vietnam; and he paid for William Hodges to accompany him on up-country tours and make a visual record of Indian architecture and landscapes. Such activities would also make Hastings an Orientalist in the darker post-colonial sense defined by Edward Said, who considered such forms of knowledge gathering as handmaidens to the pursuit of imperial power. But to his eighteenth-century critics Hastings appeared Orientalized in a further if equally problematic way. He had become corrupted, as they saw it, by Indian money and modes of political intrigue. Accusations of extortion and oppression would lead ultimately to Hastings's resignation and his dramatic impeachment trial before

Parliament in 1788 spearheaded by Edmund Burke.[6]

Thanks to Zoffany's stature and the lack of serious competition, his diary quickly filled up with commissions. The miniaturist Ozias Humphry jealously attributed his success to the fact that 'the people here are ignorant of everything but likeness and smooth finishing'.[7] But Calcutta's European community had other reasons to flock to the painter. As a tiny cluster of five or six thousand in a swelling city of 200,000, they were obsessed by their physical and cultural vulnerability.[8] Zoffany would have seen the memorial pillar erected to the victims of the 1756 'Black Hole' incident, when about 150 of Calcutta's Europeans had been incarcerated in a hot, airless dungeon and several dozen had died. He probably also visited the South Park Street Cemetery, a thick mortuary forest of obelisks, pyramids and mausolea that seem by their sheer bulk to try to make up for premature deaths, far from home. Portraits and conversation pieces had heightened significance as memorials of a kind, too. They could be left behind as reminders for friends, when sitters returned to Europe. They could gloss over the lingering taint of nabobery by offering reassuring scenes of western lifestyles continuing in the east. And for those fortunate enough to retire in style, paintings could be powerful personal mementoes of an exotic phase of life.[9]

Two of Zoffany's earliest Calcutta commissions, paintings of Bengal Chief Justice Sir Elijah Impey, neatly capture these

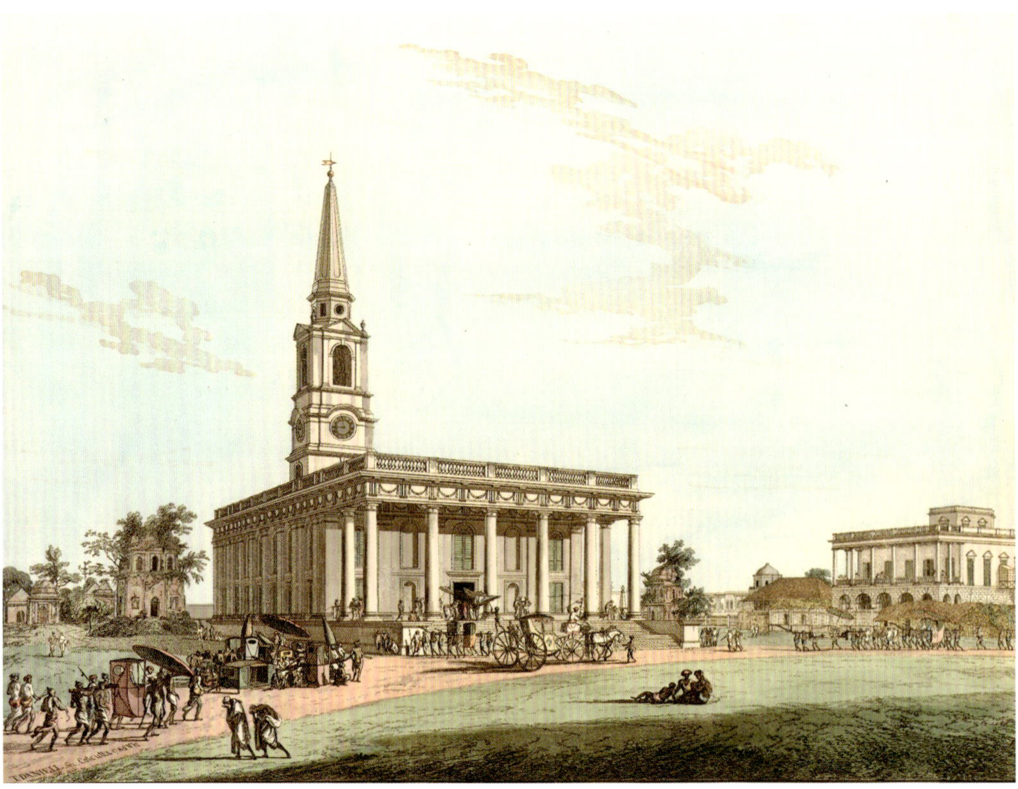

Figure 116
Thomas Daniell, *St John's Church*, 1788, hand-coloured aquatint, 40.2 × 52.5 cm (15⅞ × 20⅝ in). British Museum, Department of Prints and Drawings

preoccupations. The first was an official portrait of Impey, paid for by public subscription and meant to hang in Calcutta's new courthouse. Zoffany deploys his best skills as a theatre painter to portray Sir Elijah Impey in the role of chief justice (fig. 117). Fully costumed in wig, collar and robes, and surrounded by the props of his trade, Impey stands frozen in the throes of oratorical performance. The picture stresses Impey's professional attainment, rank and gravitas for an important reason: the chief justice had just been recalled to Britain for improperly accepting a second judgeship. When called on

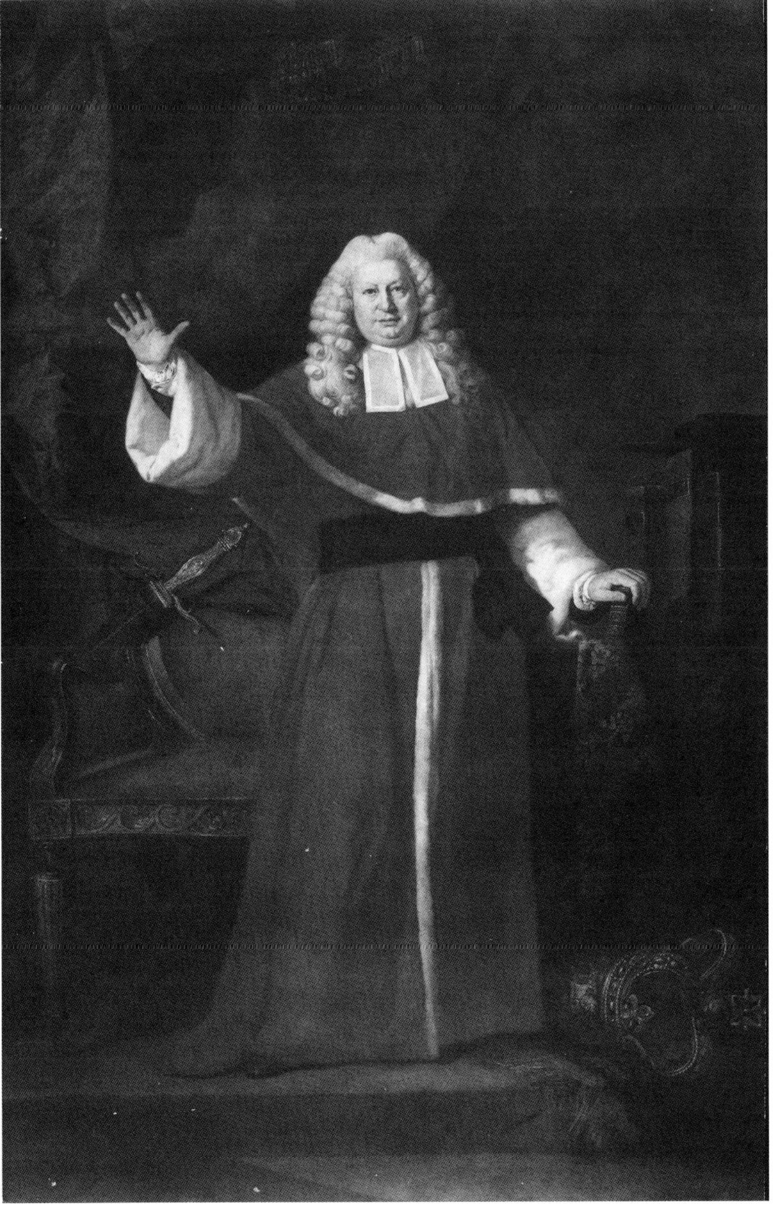

Figure 117
After Johan Zoffany, *Sir Elijah Impey*, 1783, platinotype, *c.*1900, photographer unknown, 52.4 × 32 cm (20⅝ × 12⅝ in).
The British Library, India Office Library & Records, London, P694

some years later to defend his conduct before Parliament, Impey cited the portrait (and its prominent place of display) as testament to his good character.[10]

Meanwhile, Zoffany painted a more personal record of Impey's Calcutta career. In keeping with the Orientalist tastes of the times, both Impey and his wife Mary actively collected and commissioned Indian art, including a splendid series of nearly two hundred natural history paintings. The Impeys were also very interested in Indian music, an enthusiasm at the centre of Zoffany's finely staged conversation piece of the Impeys at home (fig. 118).[11] The scene has a casual intimacy that belies its 'exotic' setting. Unlike in many of Zoffany's other Calcutta conversation pieces (such as his majestic treatment of the Auriol and Dashwood families), Indians are not merely ornaments on the margins, but actors integral to the scene – a role that anticipates his later Lucknow masterpiece *Colonel Mordaunt's Cock Match* (cat. 86).

Zoffany's most significant Calcutta patron, though, was Warren Hastings himself. Like many other clients, Hastings had sentimental commissions for Zoffany, including a portrait of his beloved wife Marian on the eve of her departure for Europe. The full-length canvas (fig. 119) pays graceful tribute to Marian's glamour and intelligence, while the naked caryatid on the side table takes a gentle jab at the somewhat scandalous circumstances of the Hastings's marriage, Marian having divorced her first husband to wed Hastings. Zoffany also painted the fond couple together at their garden house outside Calcutta (fig. 120). Although there is no mistaking the Asian setting, the picture fits squarely in the tradition of British country house portraiture and points to Hastings's personal ambition to earn enough money in India to buy back his ancestral estate in Gloucestershire.

But Hastings employed Zoffany for another, public purpose: to make art in the service of diplomacy. Eighteenth-century British imperial agents often circulated images of the king to cultivate alliances with indigenous rulers and inspire loyalty among distant imperial subjects. Hastings added a distinctive twist to this practice, by substituting images of himself for the king and soliciting pictures of Indian rulers in exchange.[12] What better a painter than Zoffany, formerly King George III's favourite, to produce such portraits for him? In early 1784 Hastings went to Lucknow on a diplomatic mission and sent for Zoffany to join him there. It was to be a transformative assignment. Hastings's summons introduced Zoffany to the Indian city that he would come to know best of all and that would most vividly inspire his work.

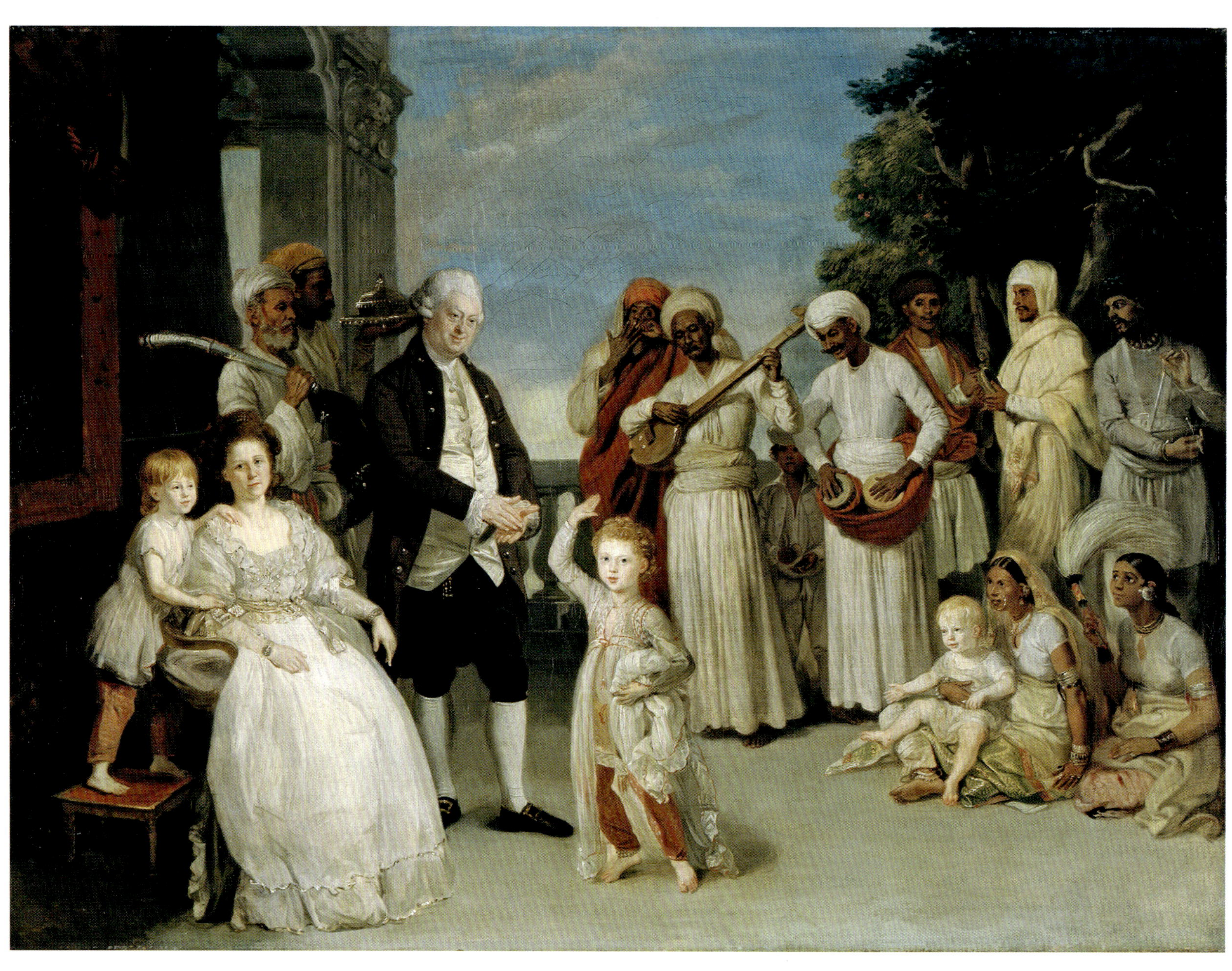

Figure 118 (cat. 81)
The Impey Family, 1783, oil on canvas,
91.5 × 122 cm (36 × 48 in).
Museo Thyssen–Bornemisza, Madrid

Lucknow

One thousand kilometres north-west of Calcutta, Lucknow presented a different face of India and a quite different relationship to British power. Compared to the Palladian facades of Calcutta, which was coming into its own as the capital of British India, Lucknow, established as capital of Awadh in 1775, was a fast-rising city of ribbed onion domes and minarets. One of the largest provinces of the Mughal Empire, Awadh had grown into a domain largely autonomous of Delhi and governed by its own hereditary dynasty. But during the reign of Asaf-ud-Daula, nawab from 1775 to 1797, Awadh fell increasingly prey to the East India Company's expansionist desires. Saddled with debts to the Company, the nawab was forced to cede large tracts of land, maintain a British resident in his court and employ British troops at his own expense.

Pressed between Mughal and British empires, Asaf-ud-Daula saw his political independence hemmed in, his finances strained, and his territory diminished. But there was one realm in which he managed to assert himself. With a lavish programme of building and cultural patronage, he set about developing Lucknow into a capital that would outclass imperial Delhi and striving Calcutta alike, to stand out as the cultural centre of north India. You would never know he was a debtor to see how much he spent, as critics were only too quick to point out. Over-consumption was inscribed in the folds of his obese body, fattened on Lucknow's celebrated cuisine. His stables held hundreds of elephants and thousands of horses, 'kept merely to look at', since he was considered too fat to ride. His palaces housed armies of servants to trim his moustache, snuff his candles, feed his pigeons and prepare his opium pipes. He lavished money on his art collection, while his 'building mania' was said to cost the state £100,000 a year. When Zoffany reached Lucknow in the summer of 1784, Asaf's greatest project would have been complete: the Bara Imambara, a shrine to the imams Hassan and Hussein.[13]

Yet what some labelled extravagance others called generosity. The Bara Imambara, most notably, supposedly doubled as a public works project designed to employ up to 40,000 hungry labourers at a time of famine. Artists and poets who had found patronage drying up in war-ravaged Delhi gratefully flocked to new consumers in Lucknow. And while critics deplored Lucknow's excess, champions lauded its refinement. In the city's bazaars you could find any rare spice, scent, gem or dye, and see the finest embroiderers, jewellers and calligraphers at work. Even ordinary pastimes – kite flying, animal fighting, pigeon racing – became sophisticated arts in Lucknow, while everyday Urdu speech, some claimed, reached such a pitch of perfection that common people spoke like poets.[14] Across the arts a distinctive 'Lucknow style' emerged, defined by hybridity.

Europeans, lured to Lucknow by well-paid jobs in the nawab's service, played a conspicuous part in the city's cosmopolitan culture. Contemporary observers often singled them out for scorn as imperial parasites who seemed to embody the corrupt relationship between the nawab and the British.

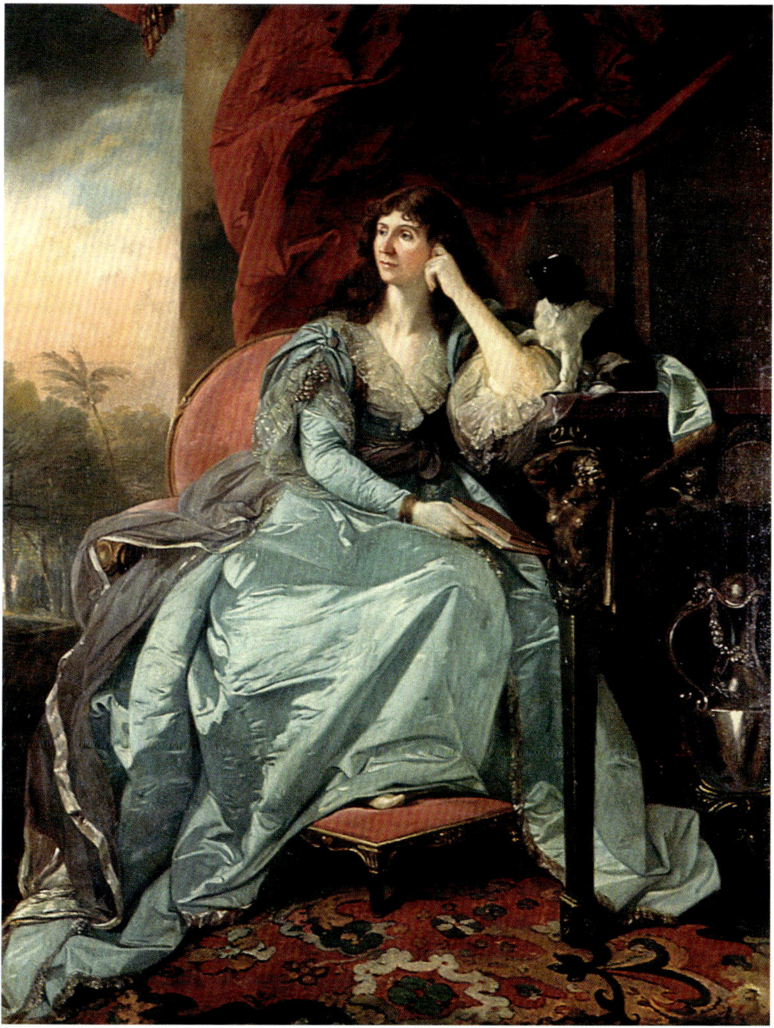

Figure 119
Marian Hastings, 1783–4, oil on canvas,
205.7 × 152 cm (81 × 59⅞ in).
Victoria Memorial Hall, Calcutta

Figure 120
Mr and Mrs Warren Hastings with an Ayah at Alipore, 1783,
oil on canvas, 90.5 × 120.3 cm (35⅝ × 47⅜ in).
Victoria Memorial Hall, Calcutta

Warren Hastings himself – who was to be impeached partly for his own supposed extortions in Lucknow – denounced Lucknow as 'the sink of Iniquity… [and] the school of Rapacity'. But as Zoffany quickly discovered, Lucknow's Europeans also attracted attention because they made their own visible contributions to urban life.[15]

At the forefront of this community were Antoine Polier and Claude Martin (see cat. 90), two soldiers, collectors and close friends who became Zoffany's companions and patrons in Lucknow. Both, like Zoffany, were Continental Europeans who had adoptive affiliations to Britain and had come to the city in search of better prospects. Swiss-born Polier had been a successful East India Company engineer until he ran up against a Company decree that no foreign soldier could rise above the rank of major. In 1773 he moved to Awadh instead, to work as an engineer for the nawabs. For fifteen years he strived to earn enough to retire comfortably to Europe, while developing a full life for himself in Awadh. He became an especially avid collector of Indian manuscripts, amassing an important library of at least 600 Sanskrit, Persian, and Arabic volumes. Such dedicated (and expensive) collecting must have been motivated by genuine personal passion; Polier seriously studied Indian languages, including Sanskrit with the pundit of the great Indologist Sir William Jones. Nor could it have hurt that Orientalism also helped Polier cement a place in prestigious social circles. He was elected a member of the Asiatic Society of Bengal and cannily presented manuscripts as gifts to important patrons such as Warren Hastings.

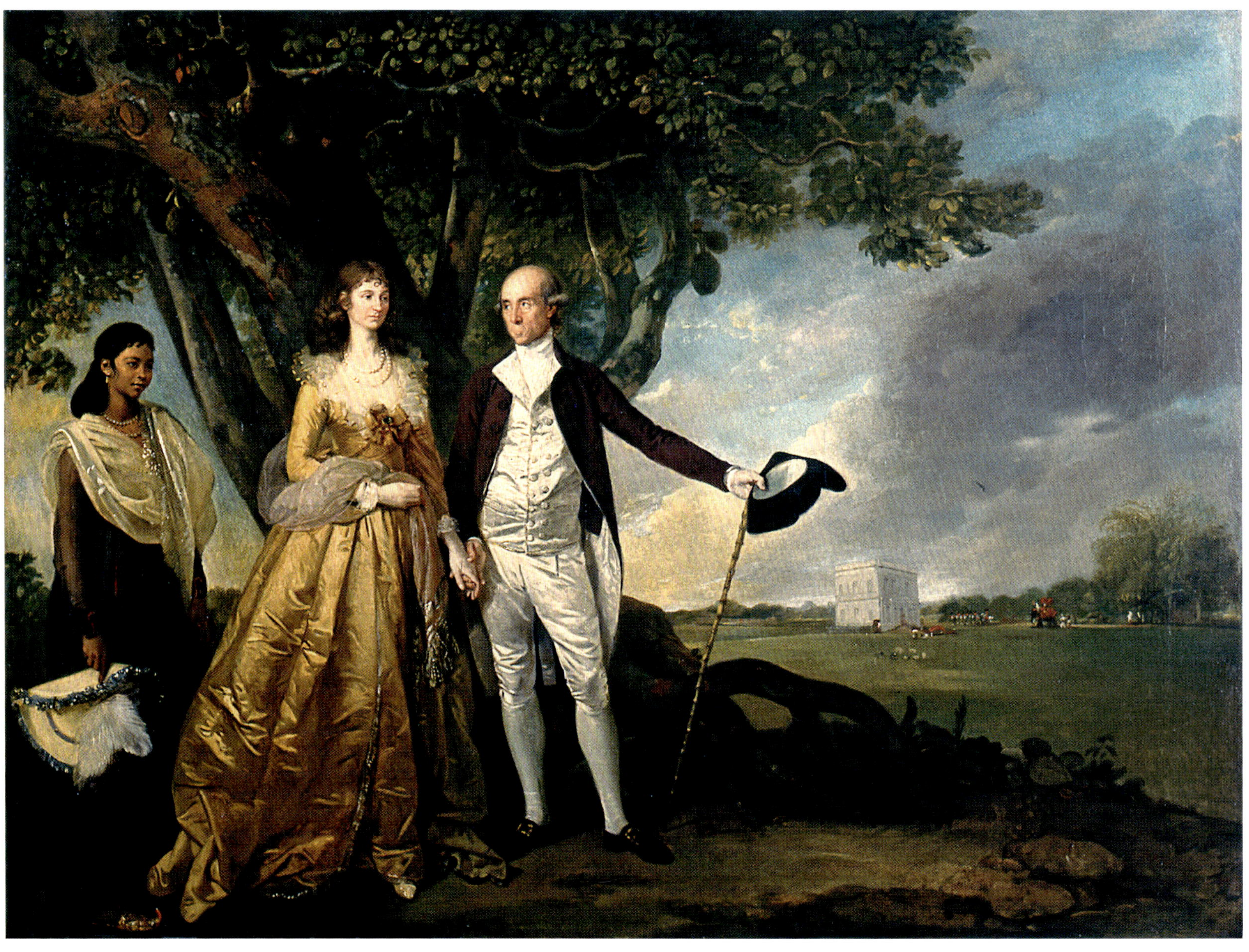

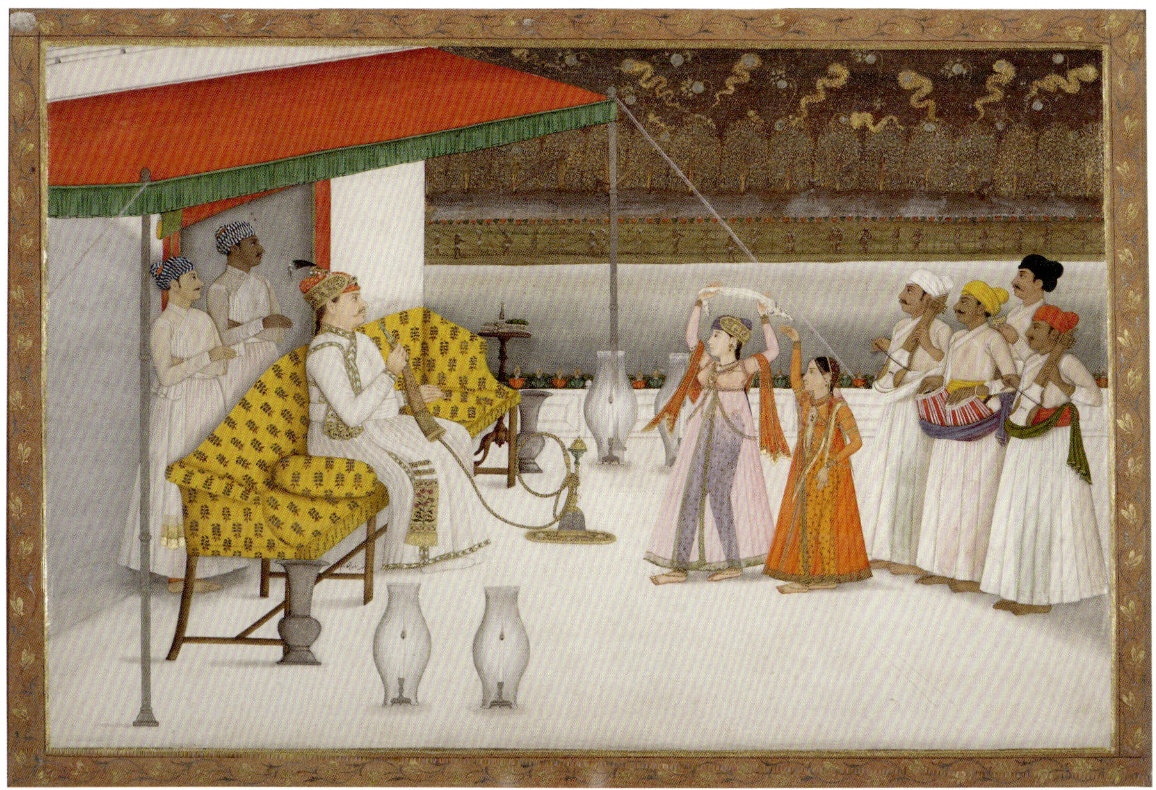

Figure 121
Mihr Chand, *Colonel Antoine-Louis Henri de Polier Watching 'Nautch' Girls*, *c.*1780, watercolour and gold on paper, 18.9 × 28.2 cm (7⅜ × 11⅛ in). Aga Khan Trust for Culture, Geneva

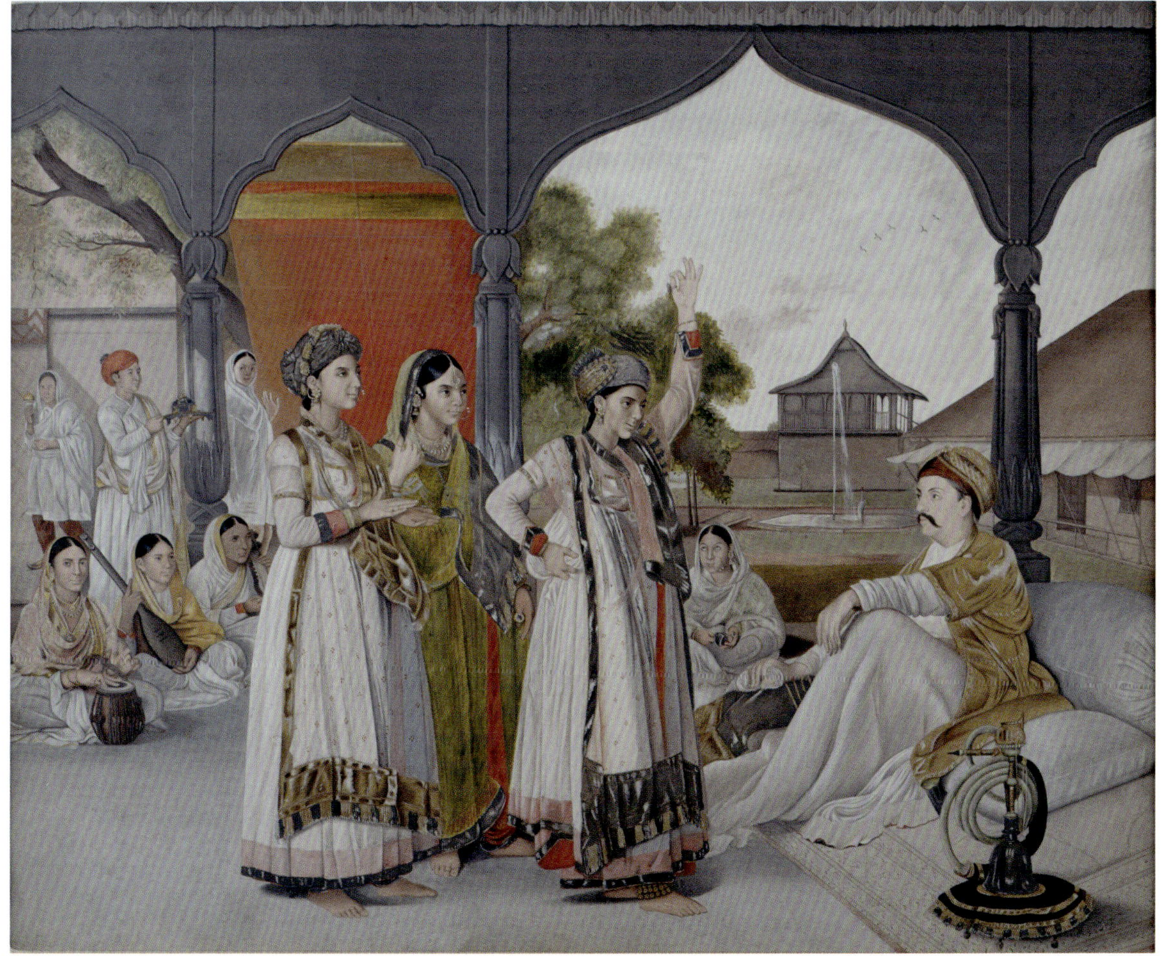

Figure 122
Unknown artist, possibly after Johan Zoffany, *Colonel Antoine-Louis Henri de Polier Watching 'Nautch' Girls*, *c.*1780, watercolour and gold on paper, 27 × 32.7 cm (10⅝ × 12⅞ in). Aga Khan Trust for Culture, Geneva

Yet Polier wasn't simply an Orientalist: he became
something of an Oriental too. His military services earned
him a title from the Mughal emperor, 'Arsalan-i Jang' (Lion
of Battle), and a *jagir*, or revenue-producing land grant.
In Lucknow Polier lived in the style of the Mughal nobleman
he was, with two Indian wives and three half-Indian children.[16]
Polier's correspondence in Persian, his household language,
gives an intimate look into the everyday life of such a
cross-cultural ménage. He instructed his agents to supply him
with everything from elephants and guns to chutney, pickles
and writing paper. On trips away from home he enjoined his
wives to be kind to one another and dispatched a stream of
sweets, gifts and paternal advice to his children.[17] His letters
also record his interest in collecting manuscripts and
commissioning art, activities that bespoke gentility in Mughal
India in much the way that collecting classical antiquities
signified status in Britain. Some of Polier's commissions to
Indian artists beautifully capture his 'Oriental' persona. One,
by the Lucknow miniaturist Mihr Chand (fig. 121), shows
Polier on his verandah dressed in a turban and crisp muslin
robes, nursing a hookah and watching a nautch. His face is
the plump, moustachioed profile of a north Indian nobleman.
Another portrays Polier in three-quarter view watching a
dance and reclining on cushions in a pavilion (fig. 122).
This, too, is by an Indian painter and may well be after a lost

painting by Zoffany.[18] Together the images strikingly illustrate
the aesthetic intermingling of east and west, so characteristic
of Lucknow at this time.

While Polier blended into the Lucknow elite, his friend
Claude Martin made a point of standing out. Originally from
Lyons, Martin had come to India in French service, defected
to the British in 1760 and moved to Lucknow in 1776 to
supervise the nawab's arsenal. Relentlessly entrepreneurial and
energetic, Martin promptly capitalized on the money-making
opportunities that surrounded him. He was at once a canny
financier, a *rentier* (landlord) drawing income from more than
a dozen properties in the area, and an export merchant
specializing in textile piece-goods and indigo. All this made
Martin quite possibly the richest European in India.[19]

Martin, like Polier, shared his house with Indian female
companions (often called *bibis*) and had an especially long and
close relationship with one woman called Boulone. Zoffany
immortalized Boulone in a rare surviving portrait of a *bibi*
(fig. 123), a tender canvas showing her fishing in a pond with
Martin's adopted son Zulfikar. But quite unlike Polier, who
self-consciously doubled as a Mughal nobleman, Martin
made it his goal to recreate the life of a British gentleman.
One way he did this was to design elaborate dwellings for
himself, just as his British patrician contemporaries invested
in stately homes. His townhouse in Lucknow, the Farhad Baksh,

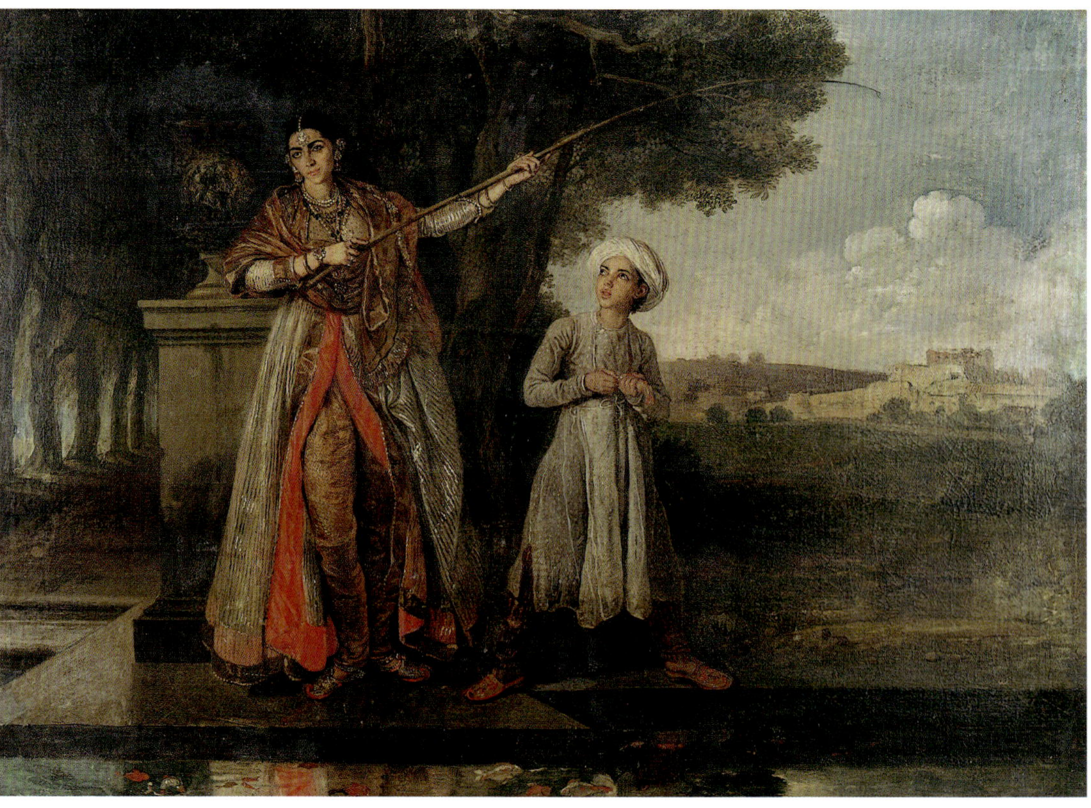

Figure 123
Boulone Fishing with Zulfikar Khan,
1786–7, oil on canvas,
61 × 76.2 cm (24 × 30 in).
La Martinière College, Lucknow

boasted an ingenious system of river water channelled in to cool the rooms. Martin devoted his later years to building a sprawling country pile, Constantia, bedecked with statues of sphinxes, mandarins and lions whose eyes glowed with lanterns. He filled his rooms with every European curiosity and contraption he could get his hands on: telescopes, steam engines, an oxygen pump and the makings of hot air balloons. He acquired prints and caricatures by the hundreds and developed what was surely the largest European library in India. His picture collection boasted at least seventy European oil paintings and as many more by Indian artists working in European style. In a period when the possessions of most Europeans in India might fill five or six pages of a probate inventory, the inventory of Martin's possessions at his death in 1800 ran to nearly eighty. Among them were forty-seven paintings and sketches by Zoffany.[20]

Zoffany had come to Lucknow expecting to keep busy with official commissions, and he did indeed paint several portraits of Asaf-ud-Daula and his ministers. But Lucknow pushed him in new and unexpected directions. In Polier, Martin and the city's other European residents Zoffany found not just clients but real friends, who valued his art as well as the whiff of European connoisseurship he brought to their circle. And he found much to like in them as well, for they were, after all, very similar to himself and many of his friends in London: cosmopolitan, intellectually curious and aesthetically sophisticated. So it was that after his initial stay of six months, Zoffany returned to Lucknow for sojourns amounting to two and a half years. He lived with Martin in the Farhad Baksh, and like his new friends he acquired an Indian mistress, with whom he fathered a son. Zoffany's Lucknow paintings provide the most vibrant extant record of this cosmopolitan capital. They also show how Lucknow influenced Zoffany in turn, as he took on Indian subjects and compositional styles, and carried his signature attention to movement to new dramatic heights.

Paintings, of course, are static things, but pairing Zoffany's dynamic images with a diary kept by one of his Lucknow acquaintances, Sophia Plowden, helps animate his world. Plowden and her husband Richard, a former member of Asaf-ud-Daula's bodyguard, had lived in Lucknow for several years, and in 1787, as they prepared to move back to Britain, they returned to Lucknow from Calcutta to collect an outstanding debt from the nawab. The young Englishwoman was warmly embraced by her old friends Martin and Polier and became a hit with Zoffany as well, who was so charmed by her two small sons that he 'declared he would like to paint

them both without any regard he was so taken with them'. She spent happy days visiting, gossiping, riding, dining and looking at art with her friends. Martin gave her 'a small picture of him self copied from one of Zofannys' as a keepsake. He also gave her a harpsichord, an especially welcome present, since music was Plowden's passion. In just the way that her male friends had applied themselves to Indian languages and literature, so Plowden had become a dedicated collector of 'Hindostannie airs', which she also learned to sing quite creditably herself. During her sojourn in Lucknow she met several times with the Kashmiri performer Shah Khanam, a leading nautch artist, to have songs transcribed, and in April 1788 Zoffany began a portrait of Khanam that Plowden hoped to keep.[21]

Plowden's activities provide an important reminder that Orientalism was not an exclusively male pursuit, and a nice counterpoint to Zoffany's most famous portrayal of European sociability in Lucknow, *Colonel Polier and his Friends* (fig. 124). It shows four friends relaxing one cool morning at Polier's house. On the right Claude Martin leans around John Wombwell, the Company paymaster, to point out a detail in a painting of the Farhad Baksh. At left Polier has been distracted from some of his Indian manuscripts (spread across the table beside him) by his gardener, who holds out a basket of produce for his inspection. Legs splayed, belly protruding from his uniform jacket, Polier surveys the fruit of his land with proprietorial care, every inch the lord of the manor, and a nabob from the neck up: with his fur hat and long drooping moustache, he uncannily resembles his employers, the nawabs. Tucked into the middle is Zoffany himself, winking at the viewer, mirrored by a scampering monkey. On the wall above him hangs a gallery of Indian scenes that demonstrate just how widely his repertoire has stretched since leaving Calcutta. All told, the painting pays tribute to wealth, leisure, companionship and erudition, the very qualities celebrated by Zoffany's British conversation pieces. Still, if these men have made their mark on Lucknow with their building, collecting and patronage, then Zoffany shows how Lucknow has marked them as well, with its objects, styles and aesthetic subjects.

Colonel Polier and his Friends remains a Eurocentric image, to be sure, but turning once more to the pages of the Plowden diary one gains a sense of how often Lucknow sociability drew together members of the European and Indian elite. At least once a week Plowden and her friends attended breakfasts, banquets and other entertainments with Lucknow's various notables. She also, more than once, 'went to a Cockfight at Col. Mordaunts the Nabob there and many of his Court'.[22] It was

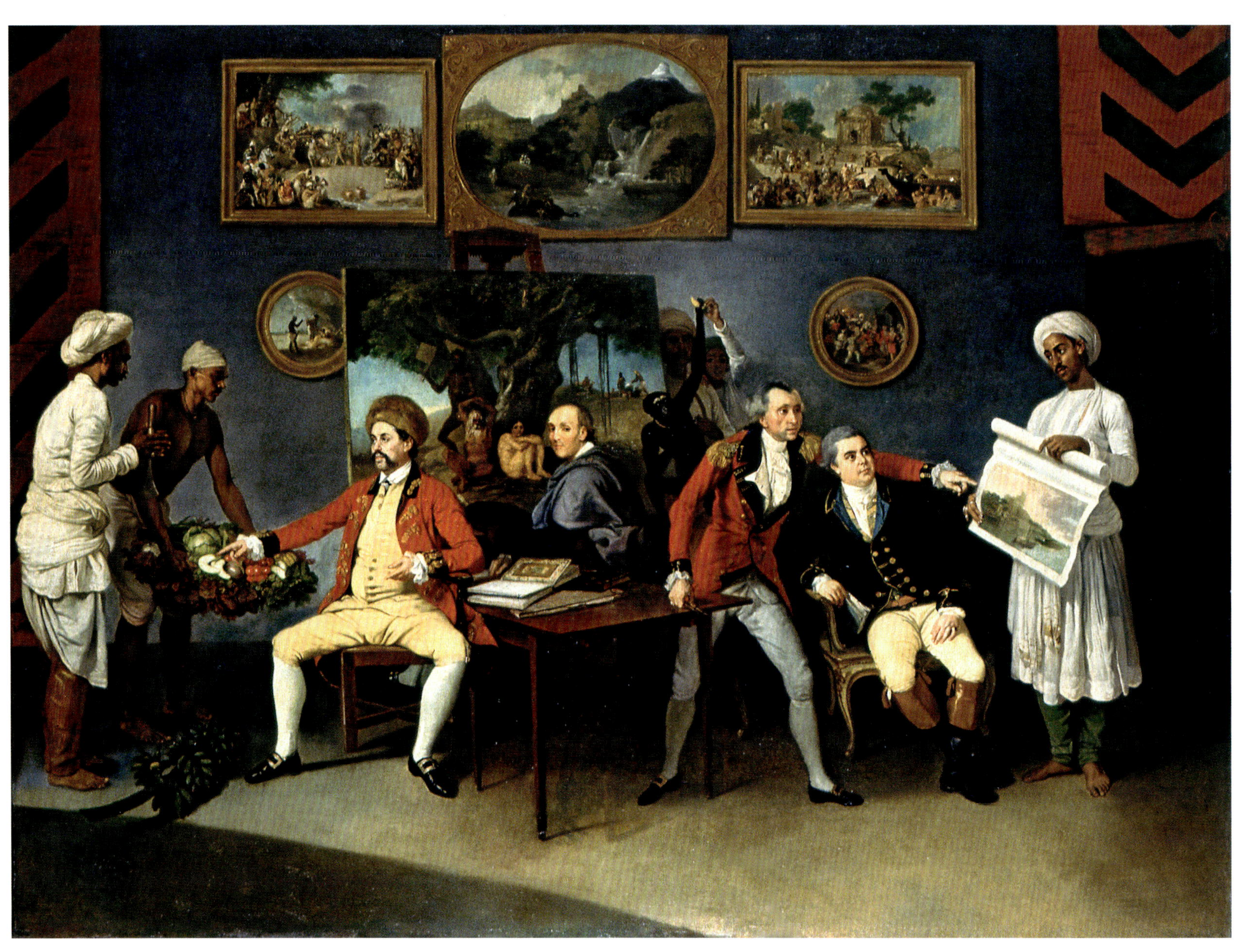

Figure 124 (cat. 90)
Colonel Polier and his Friends, 1786–7,
oil on canvas, 137 × 183.5 cm (53⅞ × 72¼ in).
Victoria Memorial Hall, Calcutta

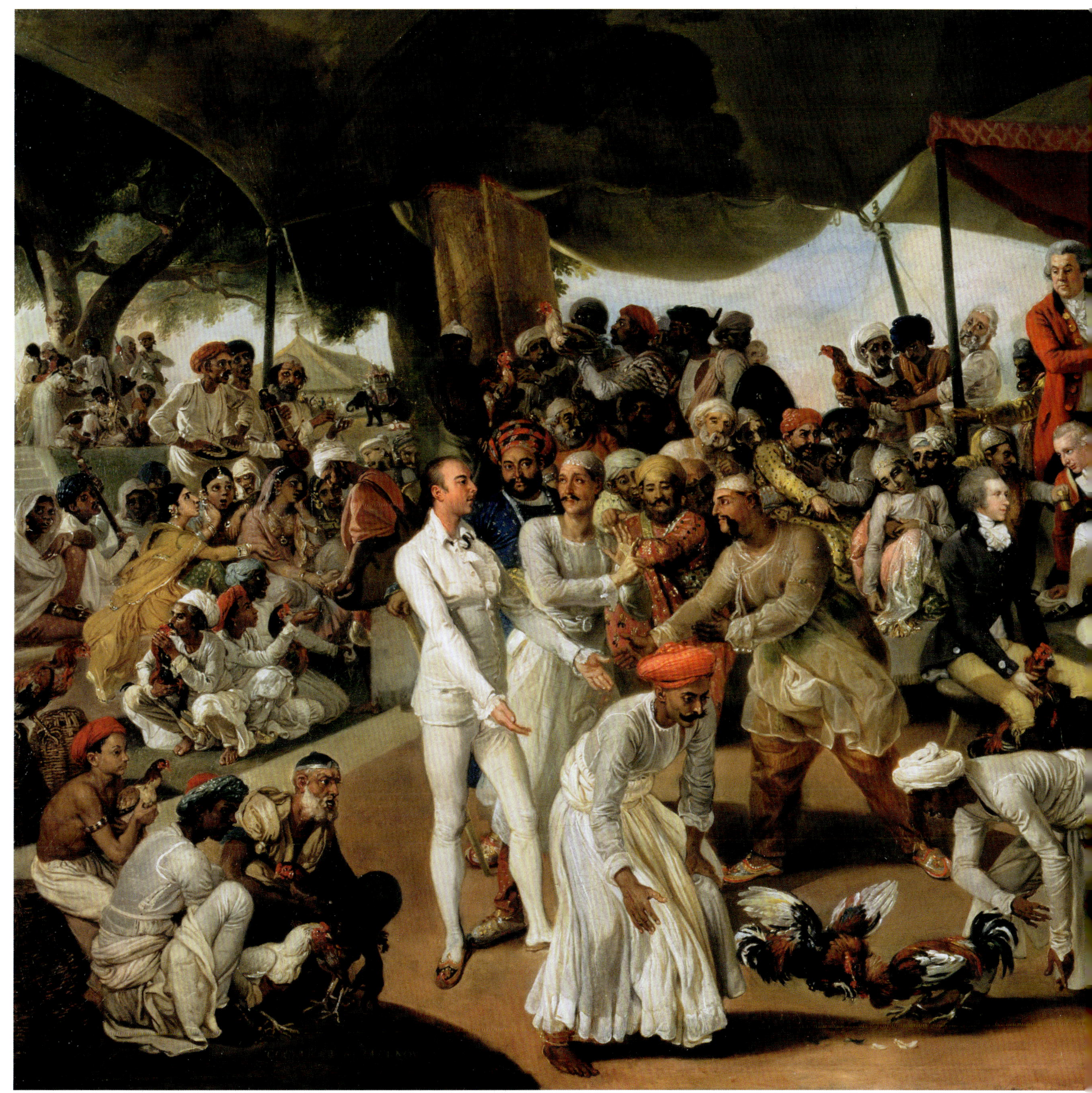

Figure 125 (cat. 86)
Colonel Mordaunt's Cock Match, *c.*1784–8, oil on canvas, 103.9 × 150 cm (40⅞ × 59 in).
Tate, London; purchased with assistance from the National Heritage Memorial Fund,
the National Art Collections Fund, the Friends of the Tate Gallery and a group of donors 1994

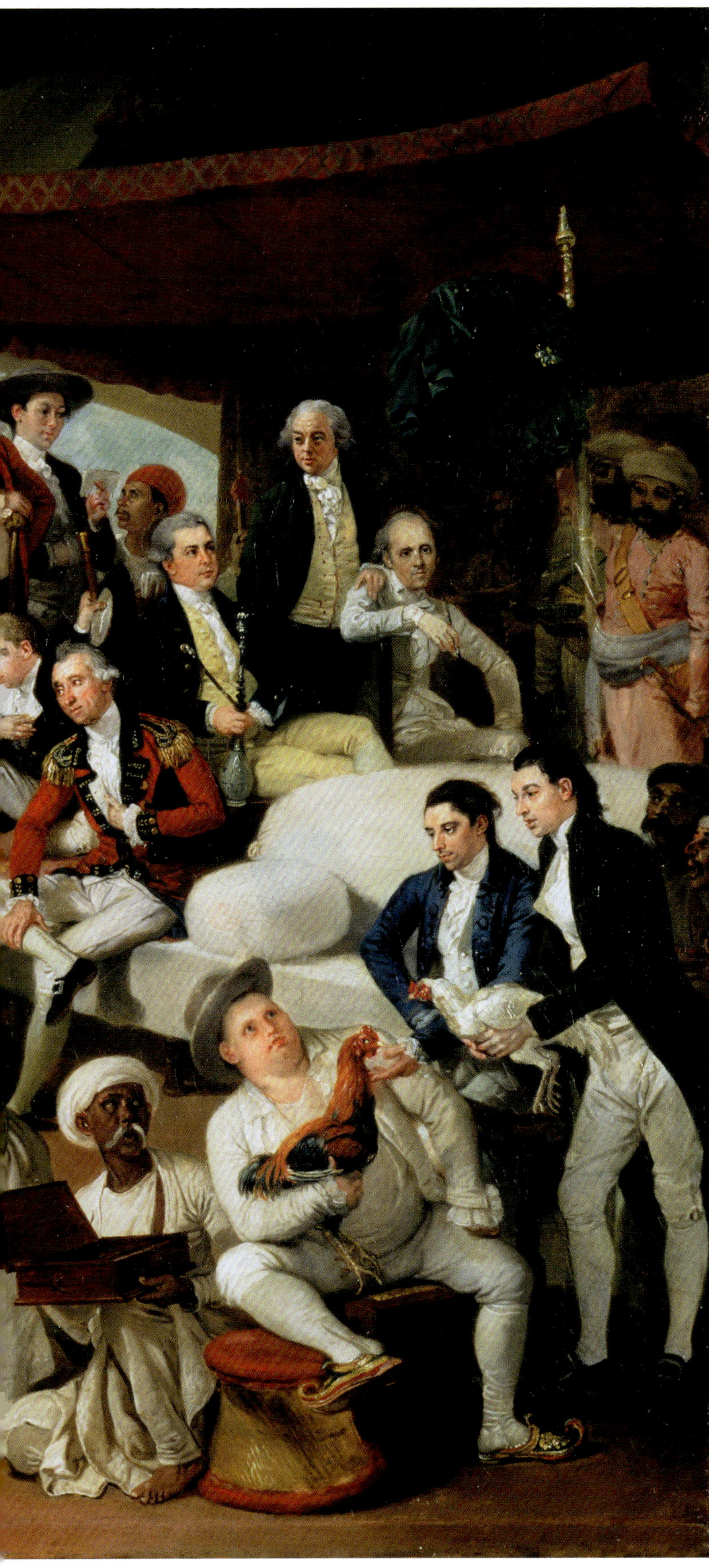

just such an occasion that inspired *Colonel Mordaunt's Cock Match* (fig. 125), Zoffany's triumphant celebration of Lucknow cosmopolitanism – and easily the liveliest illustration of early colonial India. The painting has sometimes been characterized as a conversation piece, but Zoffany himself saw it as a history painting, the highest genre of his day. It commemorates a real-life scene, is packed with real people and – this being Zoffany – is crammed full of inside jokes and observations.

Colonel John Mordaunt, the head of Asaf-ud-Daula's bodyguard, commands the centre of the piece, a strapping figure in pure white. It is an ironic colour choice, given that he was the illegitimate son of a British peer, as well as a conspicuous ne'er-do-well. Asaf-ud-Daula reaches out imploringly toward Mordaunt, in a supplicating pose that would remind those in the know of his political powerlessness and, more particularly, of his sexual impotence – for Asaf had failed to achieve the one thing all dynasts are expected to do, and sire an heir. Together the two men turn the picture into a big, crude joke: this is a cock match between the illegitimate and the impotent. The rest of the canvas teems with identifiable figures and small dramas. Here is Claude Martin on a sofa, hand tucked into his jacket. There is John Wombwell, holding a silver-trimmed hookah, sitting next to Zoffany's sometime rival Ozias Humphry, who claps a hand on Zoffany himself. A man clasps a limp doe-eyed boy, a British redcoat embraces an Indian woman, musicians perform, and a *bhisti* makes the rounds with his skin of water. Some stroke and preen their fighting cocks, while others rake in the bets.

If this is a history painting, then like most history, it presents at best a partial vision: there are no white women here, for instance, even though Sophia Plowden, for one, attended such events. Nevertheless, it offers a spirited glimpse into the hybrid community of late-eighteenth-century Lucknow, where what later observers saw as sheer exotica and excess looked to its participants like everyday reality. The painting also provides sharp insight into the impact of the voyage east on Zoffany's own *oeuvre*. Appropriately enough given its cross-cultural content, Zoffany began the project for Warren Hastings but made a second version for Asaf-ud-Daula (cat. 87). And though the painting may share compositional elements with Zoffany's earlier works, its style, like its substance, also invites a cross-cultural interpretation. In its microscopic detailing, its flattened perspective and its narrative density, *Colonel Mordaunt's Cock Match* is reminiscent of classic Mughal miniatures of just the kind Zoffany might have seen in Polier's collection. It is like *The Tribuna* 'gone native'. More than any other canvas, the painting illustrates the energizing effects of India on Zoffany's work. Judging by the sparkling quality of his Indian art, he seems to have found, metaphorically at least, the 'gold dust' he had gone in search of.

Legacies

Zoffany left Lucknow for the last time in late 1788 and sailed for England soon thereafter. What were the legacies of his Indian sojourn? According to Horace Walpole, he returned to London 'in more wealth than health', suggesting that his hopes for fortune had been met.[23] He came bearing aesthetic gains, too, in the form of bundles of sketches, new artistic directions and subjects that he continued to work on for years to come. He left traces on India in turn. Not least, he left his *bibi* and their son, who would be absorbed into Claude Martin's capacious household along with many other mixed-race children of departed European friends. He reciprocated Martin's generosity by helping him procure objects for his collection and by introducing him virtually to Charles Townley, giving him a valued place in an international web of connoisseurs.

Of course, Zoffany also left behind a number of his paintings, which resonated with fresh audiences. The fate of Zoffany's works in Calcutta and Lucknow reflected the evolution of these two capitals along the divergent trajectories Zoffany had seen. In Calcutta Zoffany's portrait of Impey still hangs in the Court House, and his altarpiece of *The Last Supper* (fig. 126) still graces St John's Church. *Colonel Polier and his Friends*, although it returned to England and stayed there until the late 1920s, is now displayed in the Victoria Memorial Hall, the finest gallery of British art in India. The survival of these works attests in part to the prominence Calcutta continued to enjoy as the capital of British India (a position it held until 1911) and, more recently, to the British architectural and institutional legacies embedded in the post-colonial cityscape.

In Lucknow, though, the cosmopolitan world Zoffany recorded quickly began to disintegrate under the pressure of British expansion. By 1800 all his major patrons were dead. Polier had retired to France, where he made the fatal mistake of buying a chateau at the height of the Reign of Terror. In 1795 he was murdered in its cellar by revolutionary bandits, hunting for the nabob's reputed stashes of wealth. Reeling from this distressing news, Claude Martin devoted himself with renewed energy to completing Constantia, which he envisioned to be as much a country house as 'my tomb or Monument'. He is buried in its vault.[24] Asaf-ud-Daula died in 1797, and his heirs proved less and less able to fend off East India Company advances. His version of *Colonel Mordaunt's Cock Match* was lost, presumed destroyed, along with most of the Zoffanys once owned by Martin. And in 1857 the city that had been characterized by hybridity would become one of the most bitterly contested sites in the Indian Mutiny-Rebellion. As if to punish Lucknow for its disobedience, British rulers tore down much of the nawabi capital and replaced it with easily policed avenues. You would be hard pressed to know, looking at the city they put up, what a cosmopolitan place this once had been. Fortunately, you can still turn to Zoffany's pictures and catch a glimpse of its golden age.

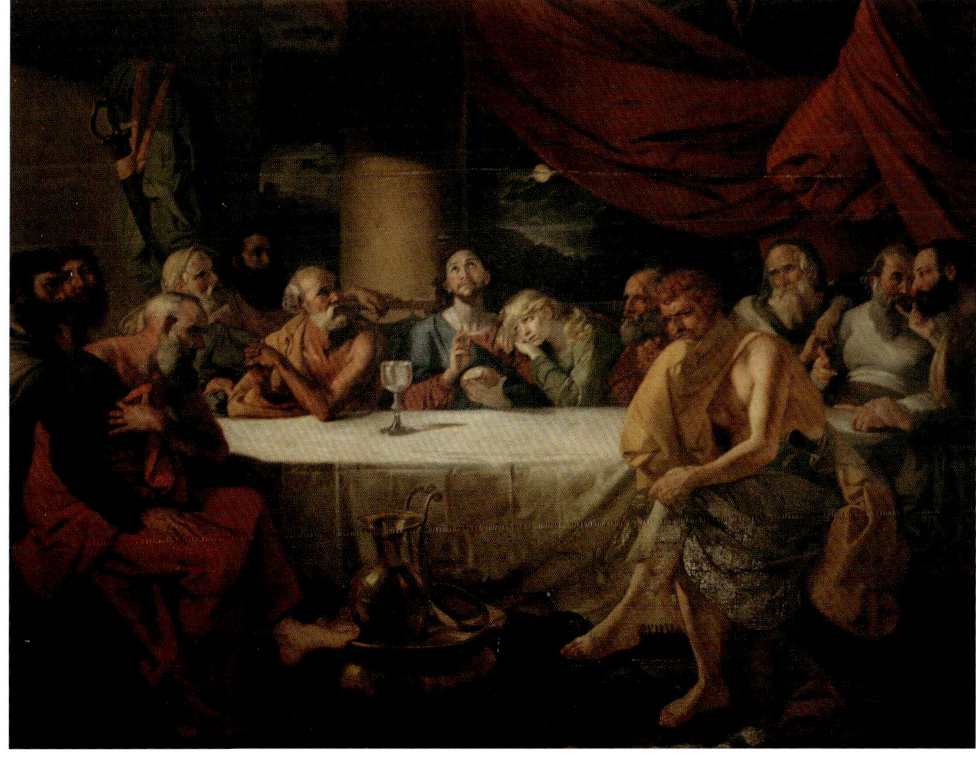

Figure 126
The Last Supper, 1787, oil on canvas,
246.3 × 299.5 cm (97 × 117⅞ in).
St John's Church, Calcutta

Notes

1. See Webster 2011, 104.

2. Quoted in Webster 2011, 448. Throughout this essay I have drawn biographical information on Zoffany from Webster 2011.

3. P.J. Marshall, *The Making and Unmaking of Empires: Britain, India, and America c.1750–83*, Oxford, 2005; C.A. Bayly, *Imperial Meridian: The British Empire and the World, 1780–1830*, London, 1989.

4. See Webster 2011, 533–6, fig. 402.

5. On British society in Calcutta, see among others Hickey 1913–25; Percival Spear, *The Nabobs: A Study of the Social Life of the English in Eighteenth-Century India*, London, 1963; O.P. Kejariwal, *The Asiatic Society of Bengal and the Discovery of India's Past, 1784–1838*, New Delhi, 1988.

6. P.J. Marshall, 'Warren Hastings as Scholar and Patron', in Anne Whiteman, J.S. Bromley and P.G.M. Dickson, eds., *Statesmen, Scholars, and Merchants: Essays in Eighteenth Century English History Presented to Dame Lucy Sutherland*, Oxford, 1973, 242–62; P.J. Marshall, *The Impeachment of Warren Hastings*, London, 1965; Nicholas Dirks, *The Scandal of Empire: India and the Creation of Imperial Britain*, Cambridge, Mass., 2006. Hodges published an account of his travels: *Travels in India, During the Years 1780, 1781, 1782, & 1783*, in 1793.

7. Quoted in Webster 2011, 461.

8. Robert Travers, 'Death and the Nabob', *Past & Present* 196 (Aug. 2007), 83–124. Mortality rates for elite civil servants in the 1780s had dropped below 50 per cent.

9. On portraiture in this period, see Archer 1979.

10. See Webster 2011, 464.

11. J.P. Losty, 'Impey, Mary, Lady Impey (1749–1818)', *ODNB* (http://www.oxforddnb.com/view/article/66 116, accessed 26 Dec. 2010).

12. Natasha Eaton, 'Between Mimesis and Alterity: Art, Gift, and Diplomacy in Colonial India, 1770–1800', *Comparative Studies in Society and History* 46 (2004), 816–40.

13. On Awadh under Asaf-ud-Daula, see Richard B. Barnett, *North India Between Empires: Awadh, the Mughals, and the British, 1720–1801*, Berkeley, 1980; Michael H. Fisher, *A Clash of Cultures: Awadh, the British, and the Mughals*, New Delhi, 1987.

14. Jasanoff 2005, 56–7.

15. Rosie Llewellyn-Jones, in Llewellyn-Jones 1985, traces this relationship through architecture. I have based my interpretation of Lucknow, and the profiles of Polier and Martin that follow, on Jasanoff 2005, chap. 2.

16. Durba Ghosh, *Sex and the Family in Colonial India: The Making of Empire*, Cambridge, 2006; William Dalrymple, *White Mughals: Love and Betrayal in Eighteenth-Century India*, London, 2002.

17. Alam & Alavi, 2001.

18. The painting was formerly considered to be a work in the style of Tilly Kettle, although it is now thought to be after a lost painting by Zoffany. I am grateful to Charles Greig for drawing this point to my attention.

19. Martin is the subject of an excellent biography by Rosie Llewellyn-Jones; see Llewellyn-Jones 1992.

20. 'Inventory of the Effects of the late Major General Claude Martin', British Library, Asia Pacific and Africa Collections: IOR/L/AG/34/27/24, Bengal Inventories, 1801, vol. 1.

21. Diary of Sophia Elizabeth Plowden, British Library, Asia Pacific and Africa Collections: MSS Eur F127/94, 22 Nov. 1787, 23 Jan. 1788, 3 March 1788, 21 April 1788, 26 April 1788, 29 April 1788. Ian Woodfield, 'The Hindostannie Air: English Attempts to Understand Indian Music in the Late Eighteenth Century', *Journal of the Royal Musical Association*, vol. 119, no. 2 (1994), 189–211; Nicholas Cook, 'Encountering the Other, Redefining the Self: Hindostannie Airs, Haydn's Folksong Settings and the "Common Practice" Style', in Martin Clayton and Bennett Zon, eds., *Music and Orientalism in the British Empire, 1780s–1940s: Portrayal of the East*, Aldershot, 2007, 13–38.

22. Plowden Diary, 8 June 1788.

23. Quoted in Webster 2011, 546.

24. On the ends of Polier and Martin, see Jasanoff 2005, chap. 3.

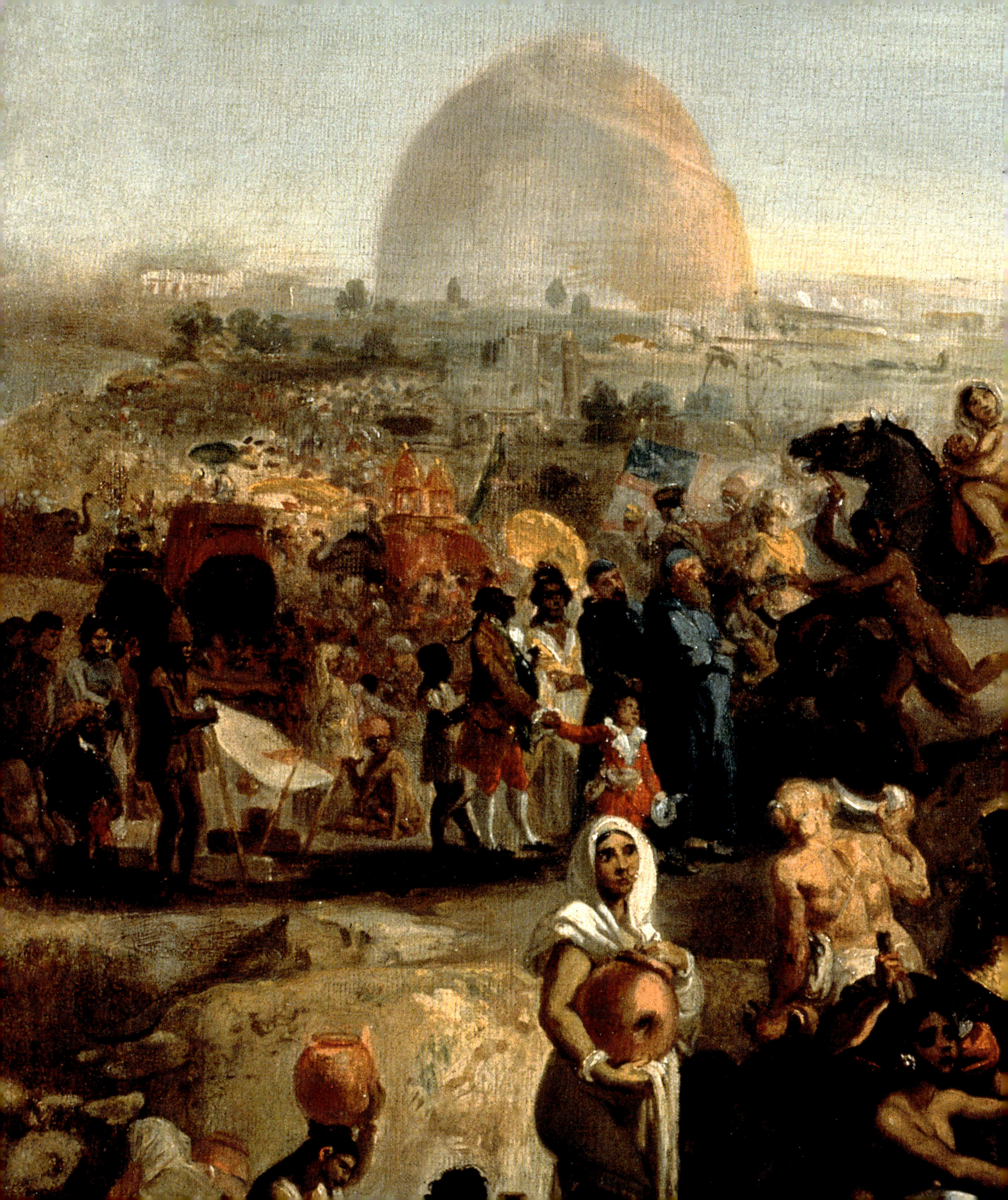

Charles Greig

In Zoffany's Footsteps: Journeys in Upper India, Past & Present

There were still three hours to go before dawn. I lay, sweating profusely, on a hard bed in a large but dingy room on the upper floor of the old Rest House in Rajmahal, Jharkhand (north of Calcutta). The temperature on my pocket thermometer registered over 80°F (27°C), even at 3 a.m., and any possibility of sleep had deserted me. Outside it was pitch dark, the silence of the night interrupted by the incessant buzz of mosquitoes, the scuttling of rats on the veranda below, and the distant hum of the ancient road that had carried travellers since Mughal times. It was early April and I was well into the first of two quests to follow the route of the various journeys that Johan Zoffany had made between Calcutta and Lucknow over a five-year period between 1784 and 1789. My journey had been tough, with shockingly bad roads, modest accommodation – only cold water and a bucket to wash in – and edible food difficult to find. Inevitably, my mind turned from my own discomforts to those that the artist must have encountered all those years before, and to considering how those long and difficult journeys would have changed him, influenced his work and left a lasting impression on his mind.[1]

In the late eighteenth century the journey between Calcutta and Lucknow marked the transition between two distinctly different worlds (fig. 127). Calcutta, despite its large Indian population, revolved around the European presence there. Life for most Europeans in the city mirrored life back in London with its rigid social structure and mores, its ostentatious displays of wealth, its masks, balls and theatre, and above all a narrowness of outlook that precluded any interest in Indians or Indian life. There were exceptions. Men like Sir William Jones and the Governor General, Warren Hastings (fig. 129), had a genuine and profound interest in Indian history, culture, religions, languages and art, but they were a small minority. William Hickey's vivid diary reveals a life of debauchery for many of the motley collection of individuals that made up society in the city – men drawn to India to make a fortune by any means possible and return to Britain before climate and disease ruined their health.[2] But for a man of spirit and adventure the atmosphere in the city must have been stifling.

Soon after his arrival in Calcutta in September 1783 Zoffany would have learnt of the world beyond the confines of the city from the landscape artist William Hodges. Hodges had travelled extensively in Upper India over a three-year period and made two visits to Lucknow. His descriptions of such journeys no doubt encouraged Zoffany to quit Calcutta when a suitable opportunity arose. For his first eight months in Calcutta he was preoccupied with completing numerous commissions from residents of the city to fulfil his chief objective of making as much money as possible in India for his retirement back in London.

Figure 127
Hyderbeg on his Mission to Lord Cornwallis, with a View of the Granary erected by Warren Hastings, Esq., at Patna
(cat. 101) detail

Figure 128
Thomas Rennell, *A Map of Bengal*,
published 1786, engraving,
70.5 × 145 cm (27¾ × 57⅛ in).
Private collection

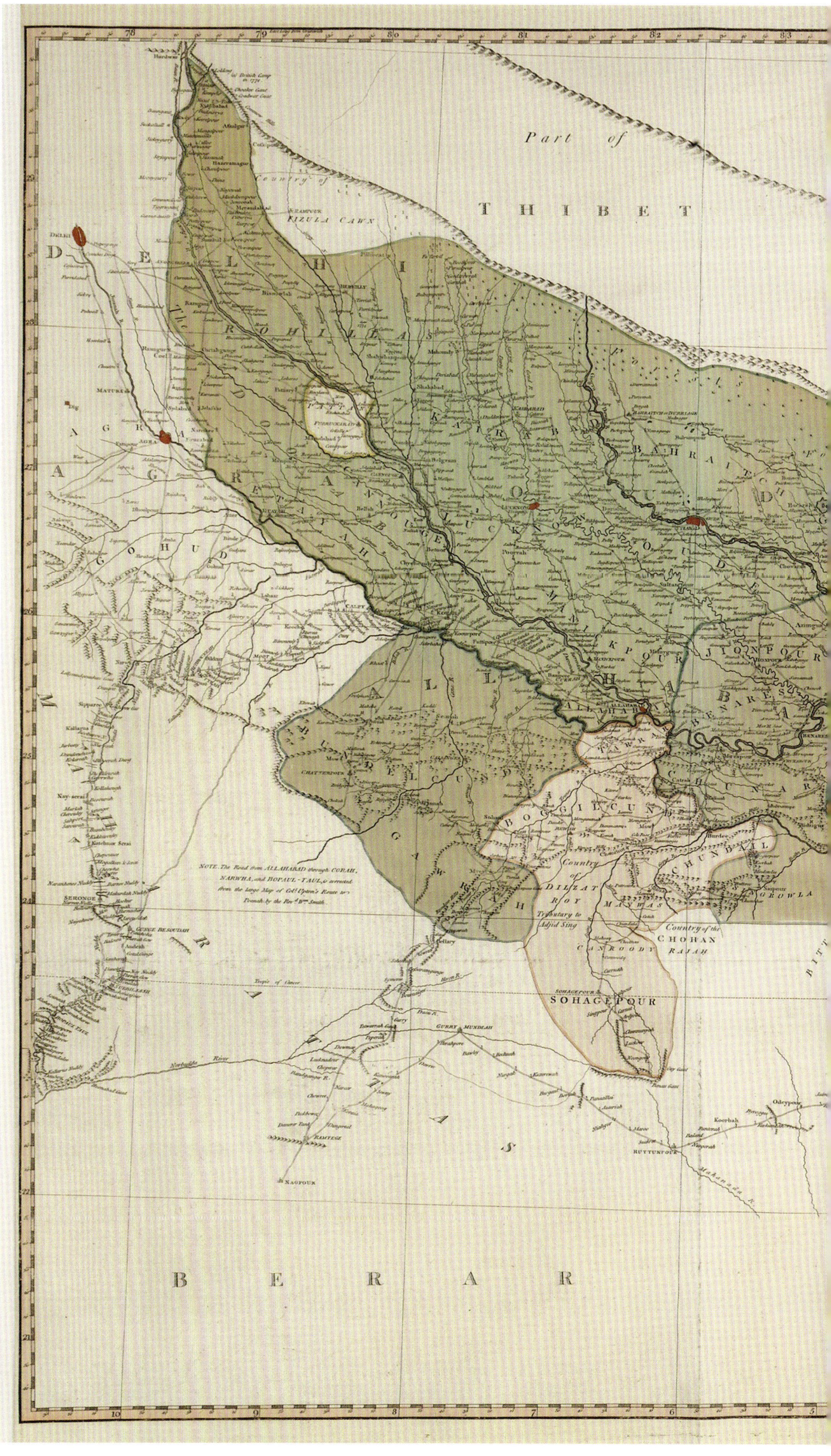

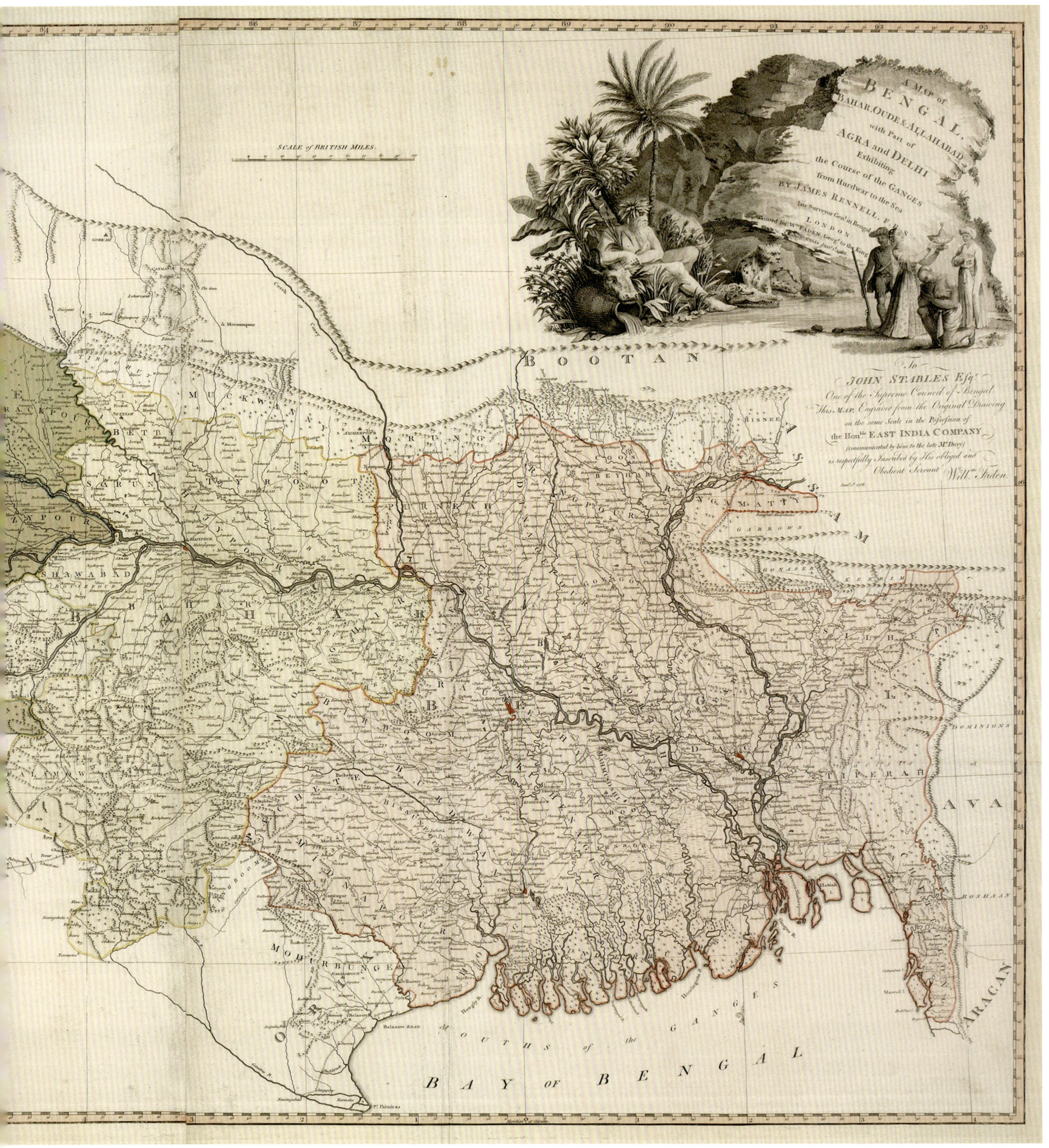
SCALE of BRITISH MILES.
A MAP of BENGAL, BAHAR, OUDE & ALLAHABAD, with Part of AGRA and DELHI
Exhibiting the Course of the GANGES from Hurdwar to the Sea
BY JAMES RENNELL, F.R.S. late Surveyor Genl in Bengal
LONDON. Printed for Wm FADEN, Geogr to the King, Charing Cross, Jany 1st 1786.
To JOHN STABLES Esqr One of the Supreme Council of Bengal
This MAP Engraved from the Original Drawing on the same Scale in the Possession of
the Honble EAST INDIA COMPANY
(communicated by him to the late Mr Ducy)
is respectfully Inscribed by His obliged and Obedient Servant Willm Faden.
Janl 1st 1786.
BOOTAN
MUCKWANNY
MORUNG
TIRROOT
SARUN
BAHAR
SHAWABAD
BIRBHOOM
BRAMPOOR
GARROWS
ASSAM
SILHET
TIPERAH
AVA
ROSHAAN
ARAGAN
MOUTHS of the GANGES
BAY OF BENGAL

An opportunity to escape the city arose with Hastings's visit to Lucknow to try to recover some of the vast debts due to the East India Company from the Nawab, Asaf-ud-Daula, and to curb the excessive and corrupt behaviour of some of the British residents there. Hastings departed with his entourage on 21 February 1784, travelling at the most pleasant time of year before the intense heat of the summer and with the winds from the Bay of Bengal carrying him swiftly upriver. Zoffany was obliged to remain behind in Calcutta to complete a number of commissions before departing alone at the beginning of May. Zoffany, of course, was no stranger to travel. He had made frequent excursions through western Europe and in 1772 he had been appointed by the Admiralty to accompany Joseph Banks on the second Cook circumnavigation of the world as the official artist of the voyage. His hopes of seeing the wider world were dashed when Banks withdrew from the expedition and Hodges was appointed as official artist in his place.[3] It must therefore have been a poignant moment for Zoffany when he at last departed Calcutta to travel in an exotic world so different from anything he had encountered before.

Figure 129 (cat. 80)
Warren Hastings, 1783–4, oil on canvas,
72.4 × 62.3 cm (28½ × 24½ in). Private collection, UK

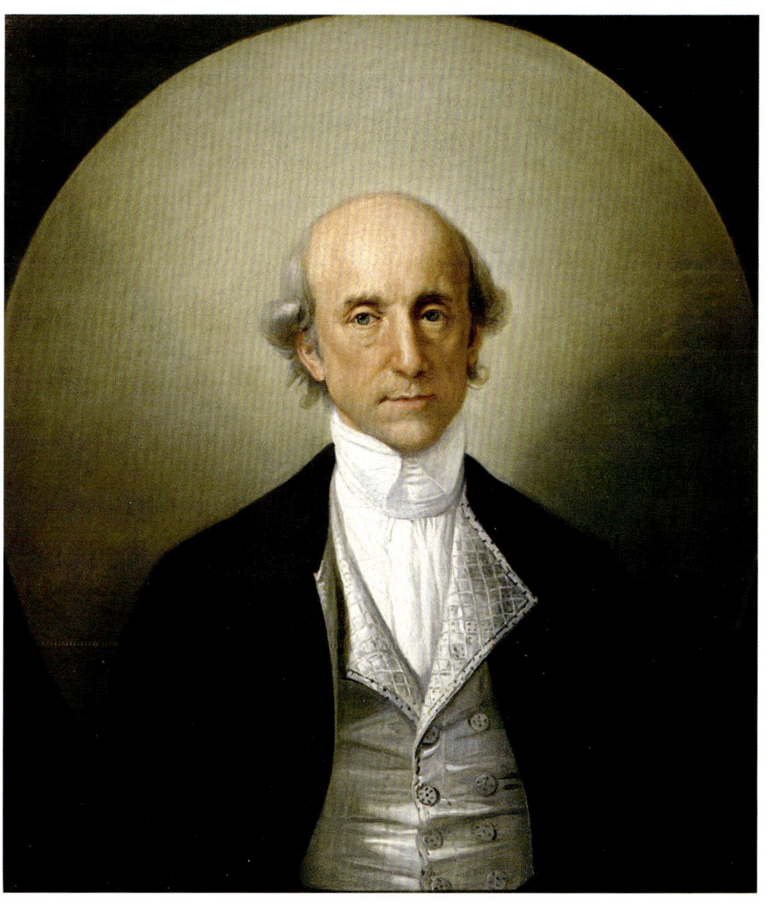

Other artists had made similar journeys in Upper India in the 1780s. Hodges, Ozias Humphry and the Daniells (Thomas and William) left detailed written accounts of their journeys, but not so, Zoffany. Indeed, almost the sole contemporary written reference to Zoffany's travels in India is in a letter from Sir William Jones in Bhagalpur in October 1784 to his legal amanuensis in Calcutta advising him not to travel up country 'since your ignorance of the country – language and manners, would expose you, as it did Mr Zoffany, to a thousand distresses on the way'.[4] This of course refers to Zoffany's first journey to Lucknow in May 1784. Eleven months later, when he departed Calcutta for Lucknow for the second time, Zoffany would no doubt have mastered something of the language and he would have been able to avoid at least some of the pitfalls that previously beset him. Inevitably, any reconstruction of these journeys is subject to a certain degree of surmise on my part and it is almost impossible to know on which journey he made excursions off the road to see a particular place. His route was that followed by almost all travellers of the time. Unless one journeyed in a large and well-protected party, it was extremely dangerous to take an alternative route across country. Dacoits were a constant threat at the time and even Europeans were not immune from the danger of 'Thugs'.[5]

The usual way of travelling up country from Calcutta was by river. Hastings would have been transported in his elegant and swift pinnace. Zoffany, on each journey, almost certainly embarked at the main ghat in Calcutta on a budgerow (*bajra*), which, though less lavish than a pinnace, provided a considerable degree of comfort with generous accommodation towards the fore. Venetian windows cooled the interior and a flat roof could be used as a promenade deck. It is likely that the budgerow would have been accompanied by two smaller boats, one for cooking, the other to carry horses for the artist's onward journey and for any servants that accompanied him. As European goods were largely unavailable outside Calcutta, Zoffany would have had to carry with him a large supply of artists' materials, such as colours, oil, canvases and stretchers, brushes, pencils and paper, together with any other necessities.

Ozias Humphry completed the journey to Lucknow in February 1786 in fifteen days, a remarkable feat for that time.[6] The intense heat and modest winds of April and May would have made Zoffany's progress north painfully slow and monotonous. He would have sailed up the Hooghly, a branch of the Ganges delta, passing the European settlements of Chandernagore, Chinsura, Hugli and Bandel, and on through the verdant flat Bengal plain with its rice fields and palm groves.

A month earlier he had made a brief excursion to Chinsura for a tiger hunt. It must have left a marked impression on the artist's mind as some ten or so years later, back home in London, Zoffany created a dramatic oil painting of such a scene (fig. 130) and this was engraved by Earlom and published in 1802. Four or five days after leaving Calcutta, Zoffany would have passed close to the battlefield of Plassey. On his first journey the Resident, Sir John Hadley D'Oyly, was living at Afzoulbang near Kazimbazar, not far beyond the battlefield of 1757. He was an old and loyal friend of Hastings, and Zoffany painted three-quarter-length portraits of both Sir John and his wife for Mrs Hastings.[7] These paintings have disappeared. Although it is possible that they were done in Calcutta on a visit by the D'Oylys to the city, it is much more likely that they sat for the artist when he broke his journey to stay in their house in May 1784. At this time Sir John probably accompanied Zoffany the short distance to Murshidabad, the former capital of Bengal. Here he would have had a first glimpse of a Shiite Muslim court, possibly visiting the young nawab in his European-style palace, wandering around the fine mosques and tombs and enjoying the delicious pulaos for which Murshidabad was famous. The nawab had been stripped of all power by the British some years before but maintained an elegant Muslim lifestyle that would have been something of a foretaste of what the artist would encounter in Lucknow.

Continuing up river, Zoffany would have passed Jungypore, a considerable town on the east bank of the river where the Company had a silk factory, reaching the small village of Sooty soon after. Here, during the dry months in the late eighteenth century, the Hooghly was so shallow that the river was impossible to navigate. On his first two journeys the artist would have been obliged to abandon his boat and proceed on horseback or on foot accompanied by a few servants with his baggage. A few miles beyond Sooty the Hooghly joins the main stream of the Ganges, which at this point resembles a sea. It would have been dangerous to continue upstream by another boat in April or May. The river is lower then than at other times of the year, but a budgerow with its flat bottom and lack of jib or side sails would have had difficulties against the violence of the stream and the numerous sandbanks and eddys that appear before the onset of the monsoon. On each journey Zoffany probably took the old Mughal road on the west bank of the river. The heat by midday would have been so fierce that, after riding for a few hours in the early morning, he would have been forced to seek shelter from the sun in a tent or a rest house if he could find one.

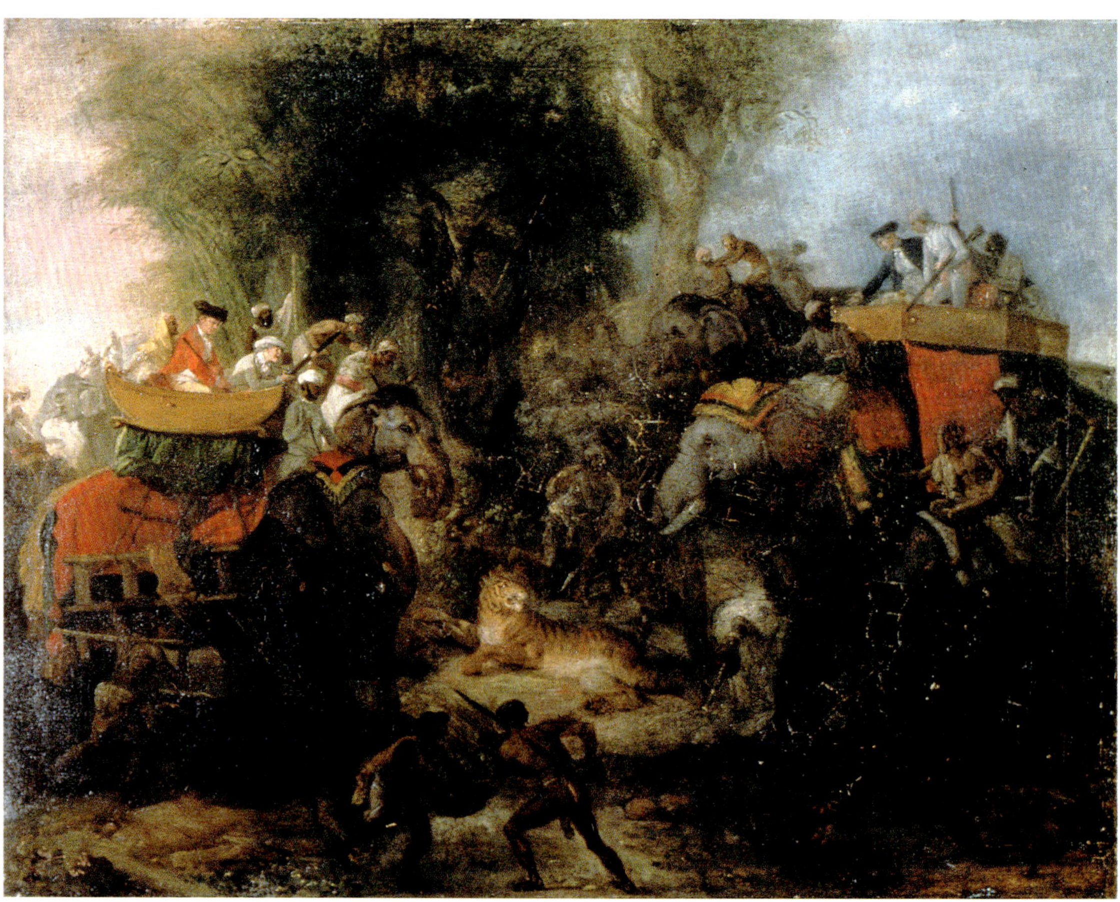

Figure 130
The Death of the Royal Tiger, c.1790,
oil on canvas,
102 × 127 cm (40⅛ × 50 in).
Victoria Memorial Hall, Calcutta

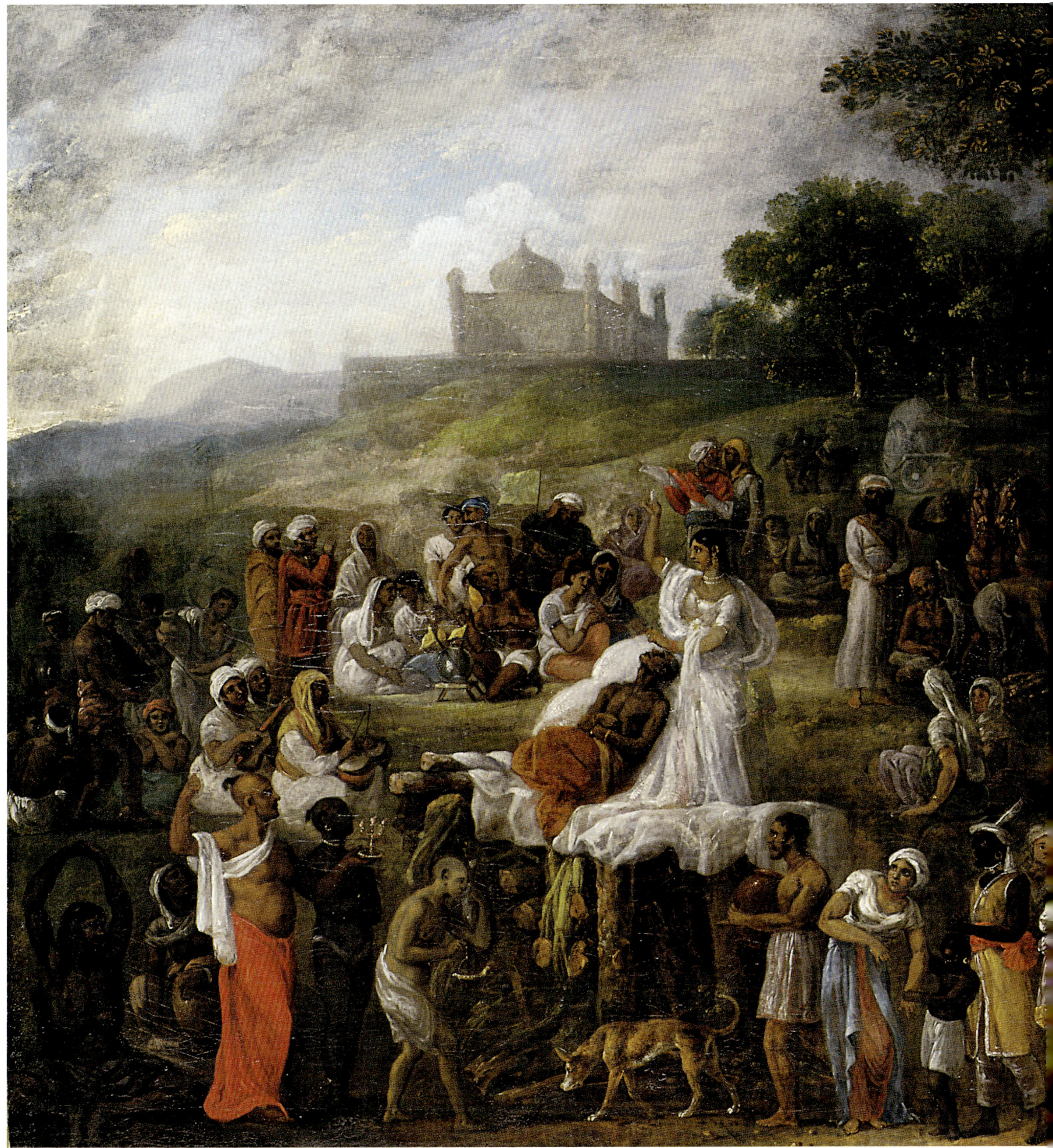

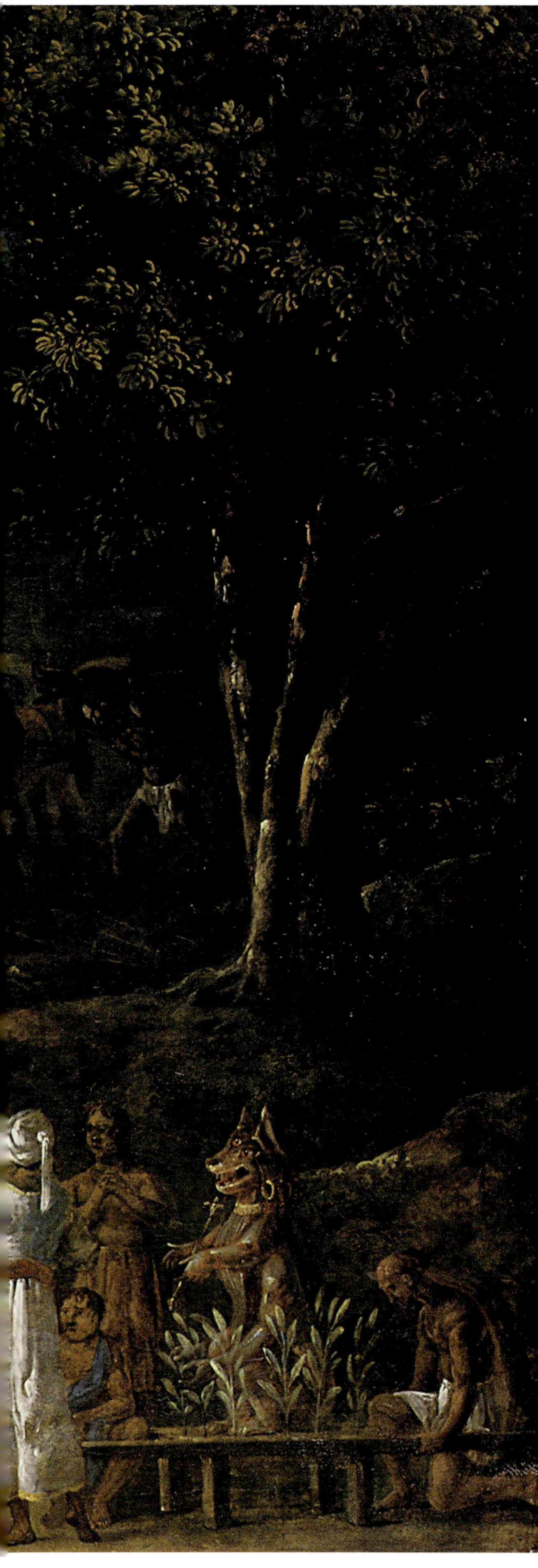

A couple of days from Sooty a traveller would have arrived at the old city of Rajmahal. Some historians believe that this is the site of the celebrated city of Palibothra, the great eastern metropolis in the time of Alexander. Man Singh, Akbar's famous Rajput general, chose Rajmahal as the capital of Bengal in 1592, but it was moved to Dacca fifteen years later. Shah Shuja returned the capital here again in 1639. By the 1780s his magnificent palace, the interior decorated with black and white marble removed from nearby Gour, was a ruin stretching some distance along the bank of the Ganges. I stayed in this ancient place on each of my journeys, and it was here that I found the first clues that Zoffany himself must have passed this way.

The Sangi Dalan (Hall of Stone) is now virtually the only surviving fragment of Shah Shuja's magnificent palace, but a few miles inland, tucked under a spur of the Rajmahal Hills, are the extensive ruins of the old Muslim city buried deep in jungle. On high ground there is a tomb, which resembles that found in Zoffany's late painting of a *sati* (fig. 131). Whether Zoffany actually witnessed a *sati* is uncertain, but given his fascination for the subject, he would certainly have rushed to see one if he had heard of such an occasion. On my visit I asked various villagers if widows ever committed *sati* in the district today. None denied that they happened.

Wandering through the district, one is immediately struck by the singular shape of the onion domes on some of the tombs and mosques that survive. Zoffany was never a topographical painter, but he must have sketched one or two, as he appears to have used them in the background of various portraits, in particular that of Robert Grant.[8]

A day's ride north of Rajmahal is possibly the most magnificent natural sight on the artist's long journey – the waterfall of Moti Jharna, or Fall of Pearls. It lies a few miles off the main road behind a high ridge. On my first journey a landslide had brought down a bridge over the stream that runs from the waterfall. Such was the heat that day that I never made it to the waterfall itself, but in November 2010, on my second journey, I was determined to see it at all costs. The bridge had been repaired and over a rough track one can drive to within half a mile of the falls. Nothing prepares one for the sight, such is the beauty and tranquillity of the place, the water falling like a torrent of crystals into the pool below. Behind the falls, in a

Figure 131 (cat. 93)
Sacrifice of a Hindoo Widow upon the Funeral Pyre of her Husband, c.1795, oil on canvas, 101.6 × 127 cm (40 × 50 in). Private collection

cave, are ancient Shivite images, and on that occasion only a few sadhus and a family were staying there. It cannot have been very different in Zoffany's day, although he would have needed a hill-man to guide him over the rough terrain and to alert him to the dangers of tigers, wild elephants and even rhinoceroses that abounded in the hills at that time. Zoffany, like me, would have been awed by the sublime scene of the waterfall descending from its high plateau and fascinated by the ascetics that frequented such places. In Zoffany's *Colonel Polier and his Friends* (cat. 90), hung high on the wall above the artist himself, is a painting of a waterfall (fig. 132) that closely resembles these falls of Moti Jharna, albeit with some artistic licence in the topography of the hills behind. In the foreground an elephant is being bathed by his mahout in the cool waters of the pool. When I visited the spot, the young boys of the family were splashing around, still enjoying the natural swimming pool today.

North of the falls the traveller is confronted with perhaps the most difficult part of the journey. Even today the road itself is little more than a rutted track. One passes through numerous small villages with their vivid blue painted houses, and yet it is difficult to find any sustenance other than an earthenware cup of tea and a few bananas. I survived on such fare and a little rice and dahl for three days while exploring the district on my second journey. Close to Sicri Gully itself, I slept in an ancient ruined caravanserai on a charpoy provided by villagers. I was joined by a young saffron-clad sadhu, who was making his way south before the onset of winter. I shared my simple supper with him and chatted long into the night about the mysteries of Hinduism and the life of a fakir in the fast-changing world of modern India. Zoffany was intrigued by these itinerant holy men and must have made numerous drawings of those he encountered on the road, since they appear so frequently in

Figure 132
Colonel Polier and his Friends (cat. 90) detail

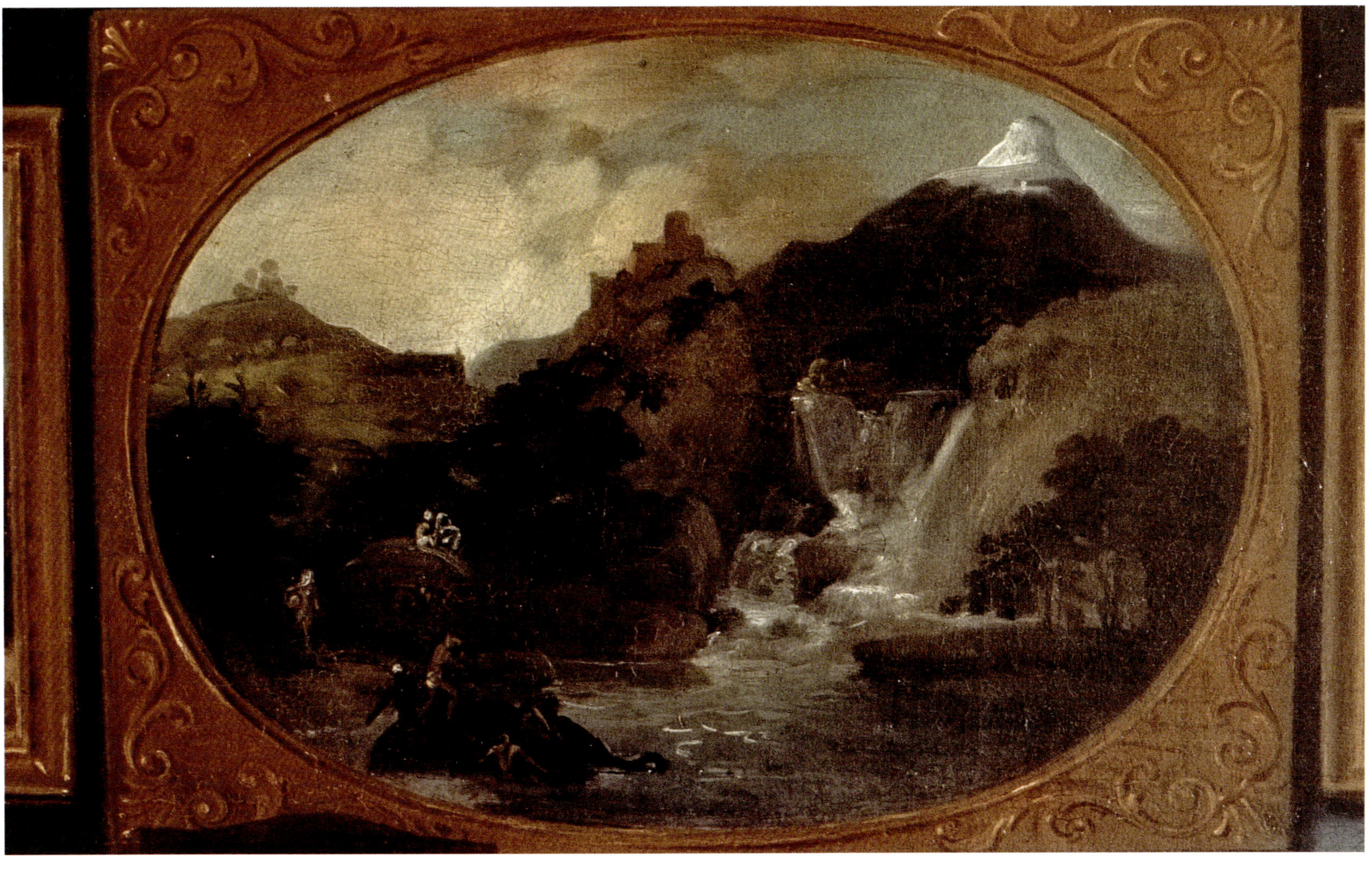

his paintings of Indian scenes. One of his surviving drawings
shows a fakir standing in a stream under an overhanging rock.[9]
No other drawings of fakirs appear to have survived, and a
painting of a fakir, recorded in Claude Martin's collection, is
similarly lost. Zoffany was not the only artist of the time to
have a fascination for these holy men. His chief rival as a
portrait painter in India at the time, Arthur William Devis,
made at least three paintings of byraggys (Hindu ascetics), the
most accomplished of which shows Rampersaud seated beneath
a banyan tree, his long hair reaching to the ground (fig. 133).
It may be compared to the painting on Zoffany's easel in *Colonel
Polier and his Friends*, which shows two similar figures (fig. 134).
Whether Zoffany's painting existed outside the context of the
Polier conversation piece remains a matter for conjecture.

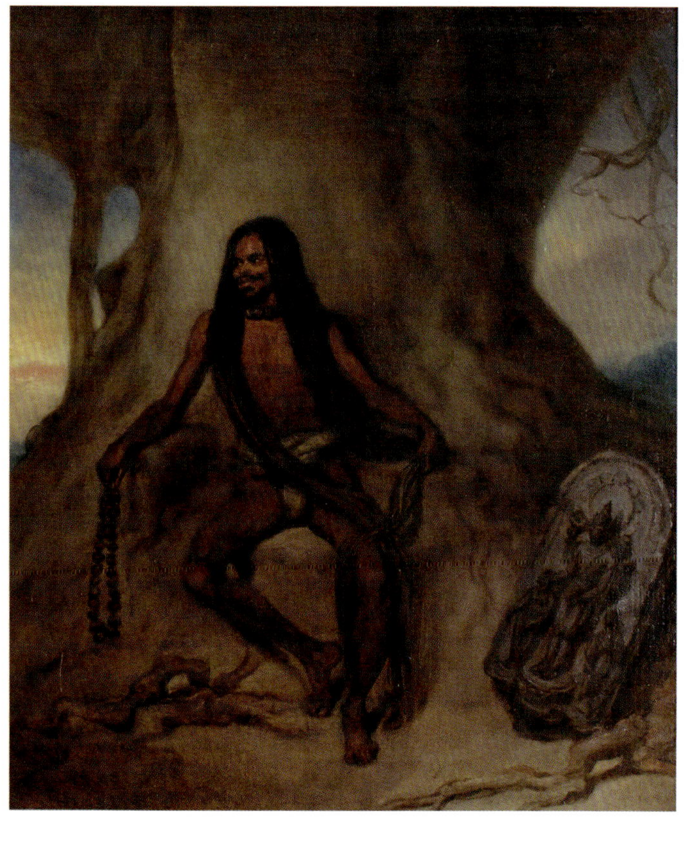

Figure 133
Arthur William Devis, *Rampersaud Seated beneath a Banyan Tree*,
*c.*1792, oil on canvas, 45.5 × 37 cm (17⅞ × 14⅝ in). Private collection

Figure 134
Colonel Polier and his Friends (cat. 90) detail

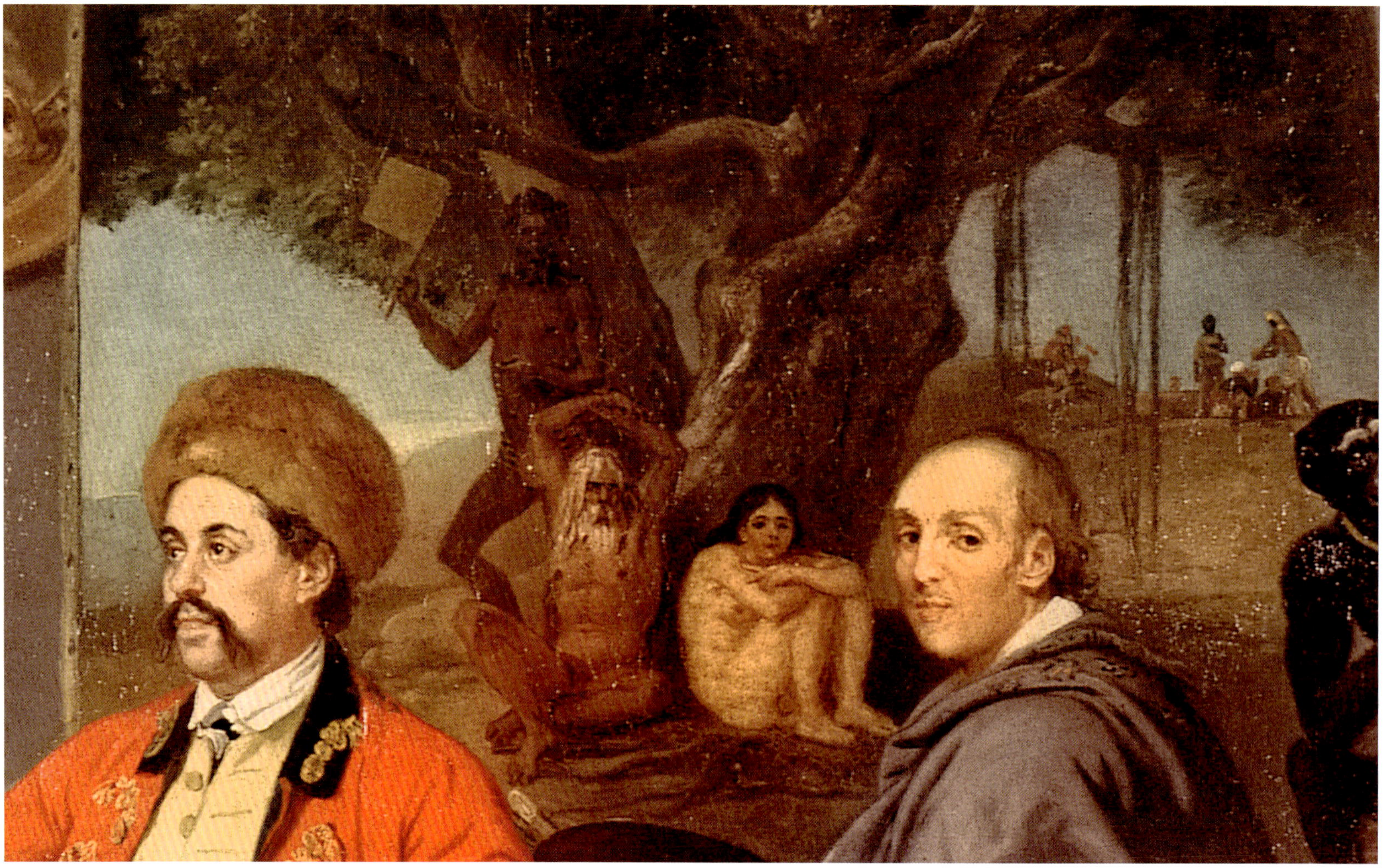

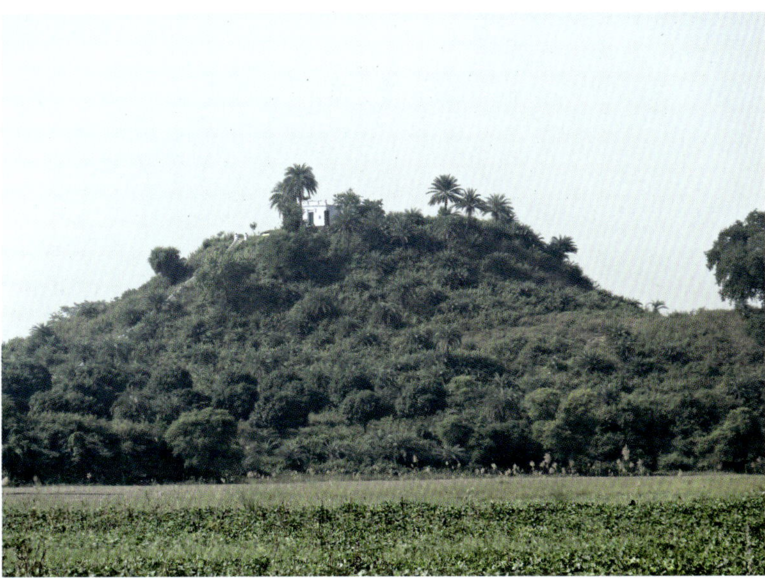

Figure 135
Hill with Muslim tomb at Sicri Gully, Bihar

Figure 136
Pala stone sculpture of Siva and Parvati at
Pathagata near Colgong, Bihar

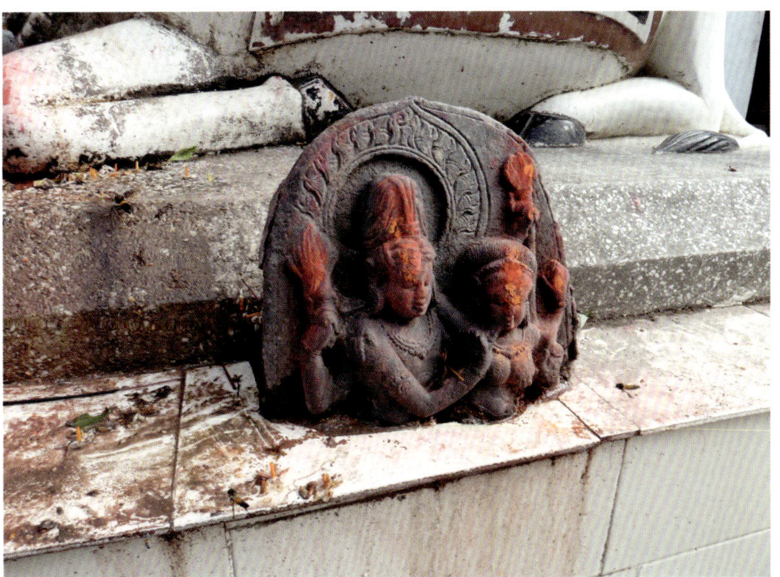

Sicri Gully pass marks the most northerly point of the
Rajmahal Hills and thereafter both the road and the river swing
sharply westwards. Below the pass and just above the ghats is a
small hill, on top of which there is an early tomb of a Muslim
saint (fig. 135). In Zoffany's time there was a small bungalow at
its base belonging to the British Resident in Bhagalpur. Zoffany
must presumably have stayed there and sketched the scene, since
in the Blair conversation piece the artist included a view of this
place in the centre of the wall behind Colonel and Mrs Blair
(fig. 137). The focus of this painting on the wall is not the
topography of the place so much as the scenes of Indian life
contained within the composition. In the foreground a family
clusters around a tent, while nearby a fisherman is trying to
pull his boat out of the fast-flowing river. Further back,
wandering along a track, are a group of travellers: a lady of
rank rides in a hackery cart drawn by white bullocks, preceded
by an elephant and followed by servants on horseback. A few
years later the bungalow in the picture was rebuilt and the
scene was painted by numerous other artists, including the
Daniells.[10] The bungalow disappeared long ago, but nearby
are the hulks of old budgerows rotting at the edge of the river,
and families still use the ghat to wash and swim in the river.

In the eighteenth century the pass at Sicri Gully marked the
border between Bengal and Bihar. From there the road proceeds
across the lush alluvial plain of the Ganges and through some
of the most productive land in India – the green rice fields
interspersed with mango groves that in May produce the
sweet-scented green mangos for which Bihar is so celebrated.
A day or two after crossing the pass Zoffany would have arrived at
Colgong. Here the famous but treacherous rocks in the middle of
the river were a constant threat to boats: Mrs Hastings had been
nearly shipwrecked there in 1782 (fig. 138).[11] Zoffany, probably
late in 1788, made a drawing of rocks remarkably similar to those
at Colgong,[12] but he would have been much more intrigued by
other sights in the area. A few miles to the north, at Pathagata,
is a little-known Shivite temple containing numerous ancient
carved stone stelae and sculptures some dating back to the Pala
period (AD 750–1174; fig. 136). Evidence of his interest in this is
implicit in a letter from Claude Martin to Charles Townley of
8 January 1789. He wrote: 'Zoffany (about to depart for Europe)
… will be able to give you a good description of the ancient
arts, religion, idols, etc of the Hindus and other of these parts.'[13]
At Pathagata today some of the sculptures are still worshipped,
while others remain hidden in undergrowth on the hill above.
Nearby is the ancient ruined Buddhist University at Vicramshila
and on Colgong Hill itself a cave contains further images.

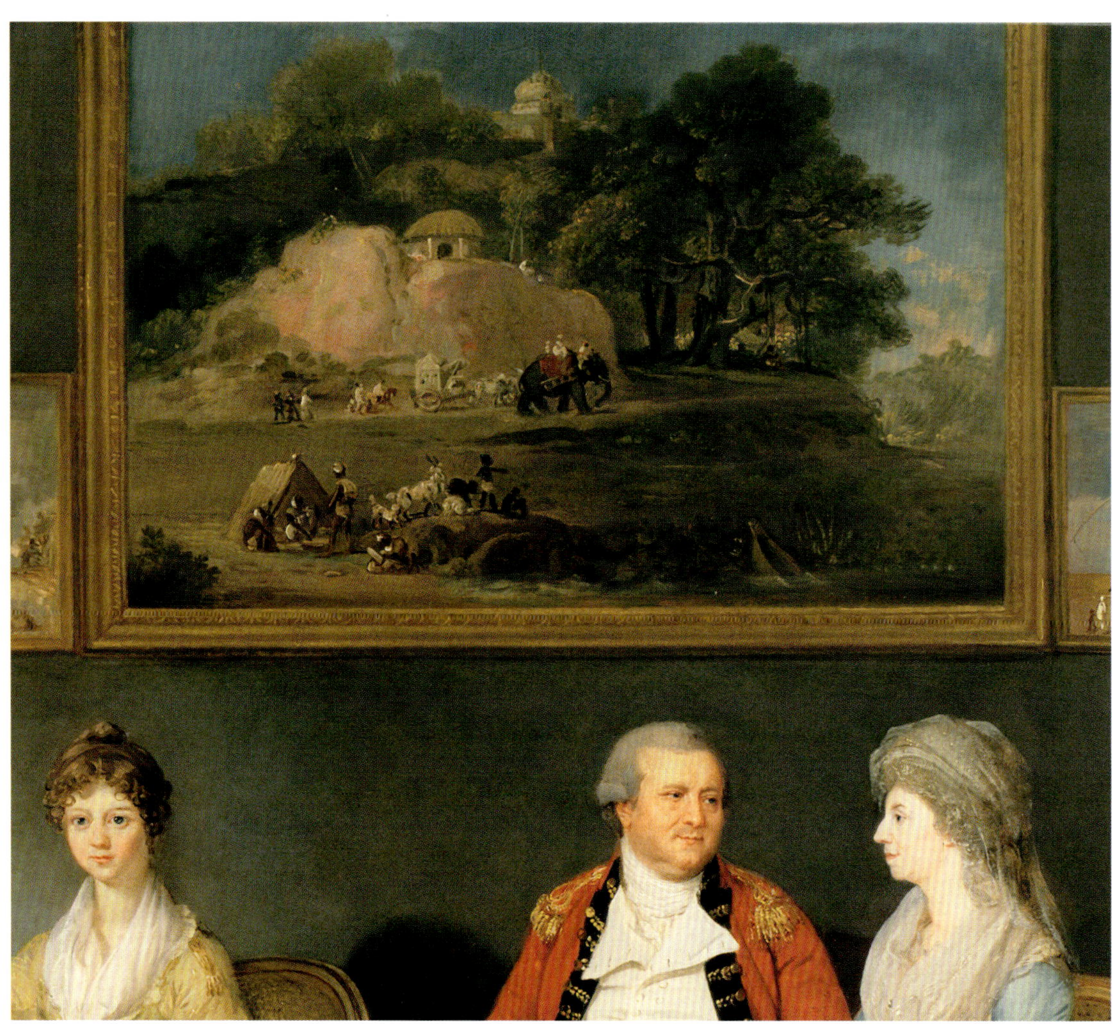

Figure 137
The Blair Family (cat. 92) detail

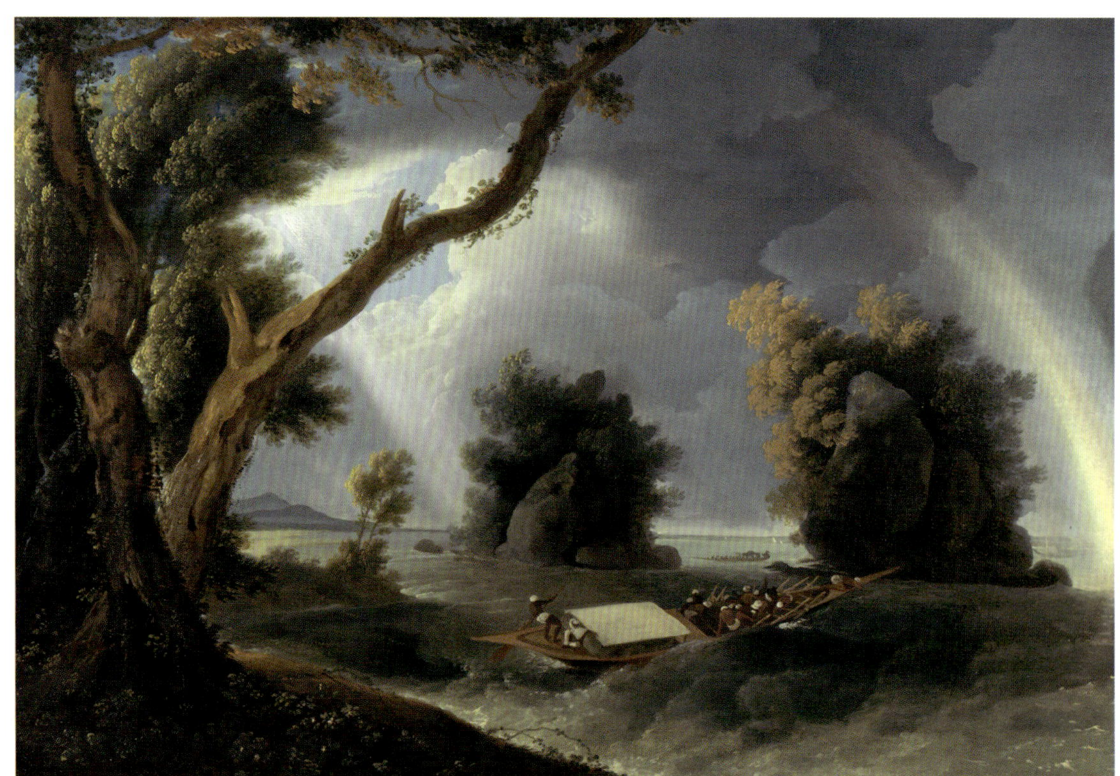

Figure 138
William Hodges, *Storm on the Ganges,
with Mrs Hastings near the Colgong Rocks,
c.*1790, oil on canvas,
127 × 182.9 cm (50 × 72 in).
Yale Center for British Art,
Paul Mellon Collection

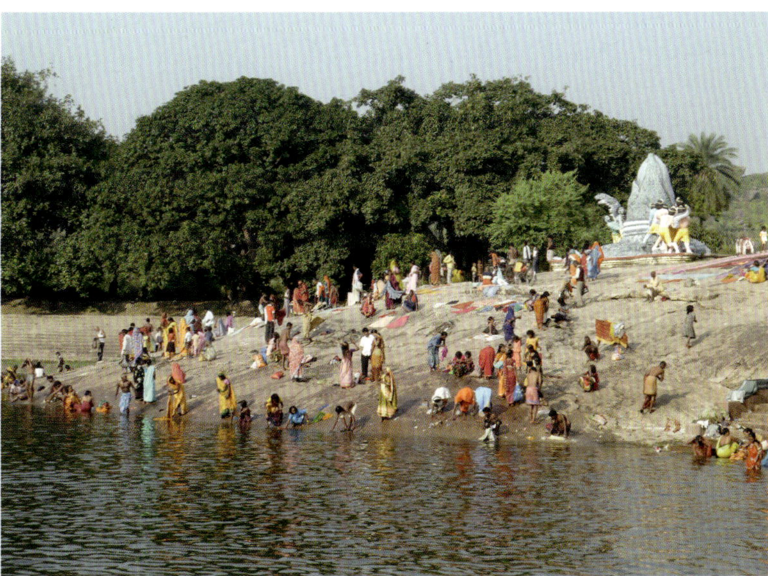

Figure 139
Pilgrims bathing at the Ghats at Hill Munder,
near Bhagalpur, Bihar

Figure 140
Gola at Patna, Bihar, constructed in 1786

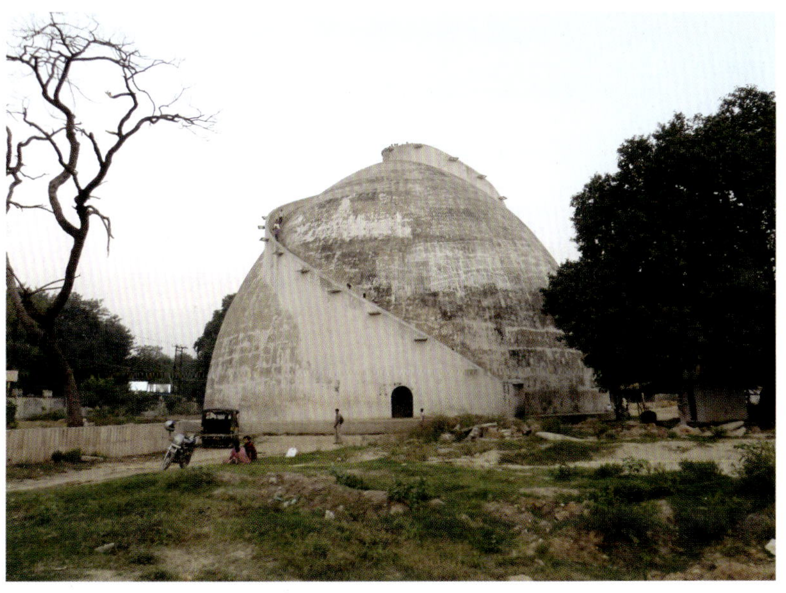

About 10 miles (16 km) beyond Colgong one reaches Bhagalpur (fig. 139). Here the Collector,[14] Augustus Cleveland, had built a fine white painted house (Tila Kothi) in the Palladian style on a commanding site on the edge of the town. It still stands today.[15] Cleveland had died shortly before Zoffany passed through the town in 1784, but on subsequent journeys he is likely to have stayed with the clever amateur artist Samuel Davis, who was appointed Assistant Collector of the district in February 1785. He lived in another pillared house on the estate. Davis possessed genuine antiquarian interests. He later wrote papers on Hindu astrology and the Indian cycle of Jupiter and he would have been able to provide Zoffany with much information on Hinduism in that part of India.[16]

The road runs for about 100 miles (160 km) from Bhagalpur to Patna. It passes the temple rock in the river at Sultangunge and the old Muslim town of Monghyr with its fine fortress that had been built by Danyal, the son of the King of Bengal, Sultan Shah Hussain, in about 1500. In the centre of the fort on a rocky hill known as Karnachaura is a large house built by General Goddard and it would have been here that a traveller such as Zoffany would have stayed. There are signs of ancient Hindu buildings on the hill and numerous carved stones and sculptured friezes are embedded in the walls of the fort itself. Nearby, just north of the road, are the hot springs at Sitacund. Here the water is so pure that travellers usually stopped to replenish their supplies for the onward journey. Today the springs are contained within a temple complex and the water that bubbles up from the earth is so hot that it is too warm to bathe in.

Patna, the modern capital of Bihar state, has an ancient history. It stands on the site of Pataliputra, Ashoka's capital, from where he ruled an empire (*c.*269–232 BC) that included almost the whole of the Indian peninsula, Kashmir, Afghanistan, Baluchistan and the valley of Nepal. The British presence in Patna dates back to 1620, when the first English merchants arrived from Agra. By 1657 a factory for saltpetre had been established in the district of Bankipore. Patna finally passed into British hands with the defeat of Mir Kasim at Buxar in 1764. At Bankipore on the western edge of the city of Patna Warren Hastings commissioned the building of the famous beehive-shaped granary known as the Golghar or Gola as a precaution against famine. It was completed in 1786 and still stands today having withstood two great earthquakes without appreciable damage (fig. 140). In Zoffany's late painting, *Hyderbeg on his Mission to Lord Cornwallis, with a View of the Granary erected by Warren Hastings, Esq., at Patna* (fig. 141), the Gola is prominent in the left of the composition (fig. 127).

Painted back in England in the early 1790s, *Hyderbeg on his Mission to Lord Cornwallis* reveals much about the legacy of Zoffany's journeys and what interested him about them. Yet the embassy of Haider Beg (Hyderbeg) itself is not central to the painting: he is indistinctly rendered, shaded by an umbrella and seated on an elephant disappearing into the distance towards Patna and the Gola. Rather, the focus is on the magnificent train of elephants, travellers of every description, armed soldiers, merchants and their families, local women, fakirs and a Muslim mullah. In the foreground the leading elephant, suddenly enraged by his mahout, has violently grabbed him in his trunk and other figures are slithering off his back. Close behind, in a howdah on the back of a female

elephant, Captain Kennaway (appointed by Cornwallis to accompany Haider Beg), is trying to give orders to his mahout to avoid a similar fate. Beside him Zoffany rides on a bay horse accompanied by a running servant. This scene of the great road is the real subject of the painting. It was of course not an actual scene that Zoffany witnessed – even the jagged hill on the right is merely a compositional device to balance the disappearing train and the Gola on the left. More significantly,

Figure 141 (cat. 101)
*Hyderbeg on his Mission to Lord Cornwallis, with a View of the Granary erected by Warren Hastings, Esq., at Patna, c.*1795–6, oil on canvas, 101.6 × 127 cm (40 × 50 in). Victoria Memorial Hall, Calcutta

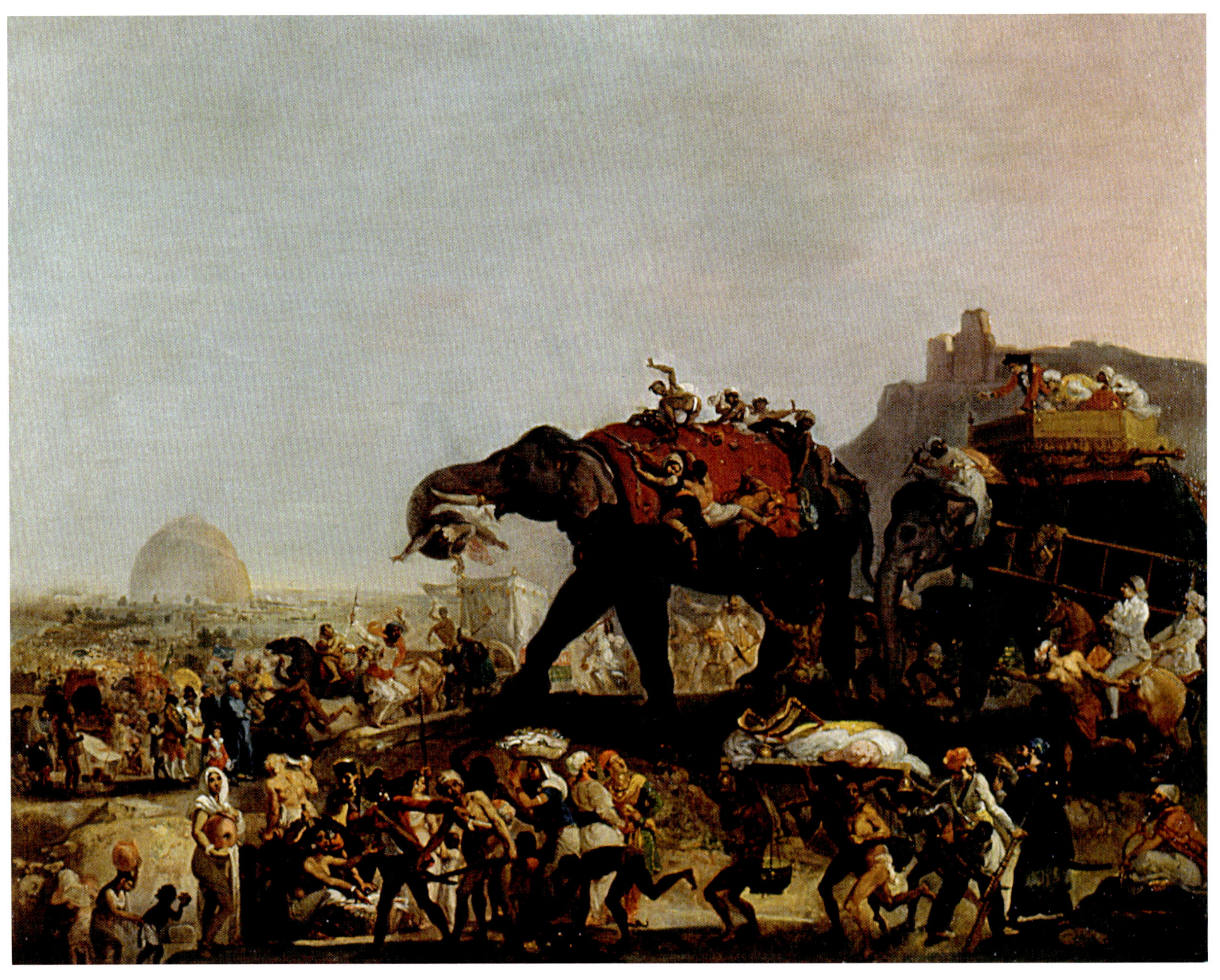

it is a synthesis of the artist's memories of his travels and the people he encountered in his path, their emotions evident on their faces and in their exaggerated gestures. Presumably, the painting was worked up from dozens of now lost drawings and sketches that he had made of the many characters that intrigued him on his journeys. There are other further undertones: a fascination for scenes of violence and the artist's observations on the disorderly way a great body of people progressed in northern India, whether it was a company of soldiers with their camp followers or a prince with his party of attendants. At the time Zoffany was creating the painting, Hastings was being impeached in London, and scurrilous rumours were being made about his venality. The Gola is, therefore, an implicit symbol of Zoffany's support for his former patron, who was eventually acquitted on all charges. No other artist of the period even attempted to paint anything comparable. In many of his views Hodges included interesting figures that he had seen on the road, but they never approached the extraordinary range of personalities and characters who appear in this dramatic and lively painting.

The route to Lucknow continues west beside the Ganges. At Buxar, the site of the decisive battle between the armies of Sir Hector Munro and Mir Kasim in 1764, one crosses the river for the first time by ferry and travels on the north bank for a few miles to Ghazipur. Before the battle the river here marked the

border with Awadh (Oudh), but by the 1780s the British had encroached into the nawab's dominions and the district of Ghazipur came under British jurisdiction. Since Mughal times it had been famous for its production of attar of roses, a luxury of great importance in an age when the stench of everyday life must have been at times nauseating.[17] Later, this trade would have been of considerable interest to Zoffany, since his friend and patron in Lucknow, Claude Martin, derived so much revenue from the production of attar on his estate at Najafgarh. The Company had an opium factory in Ghazipur. Here each year's harvest was gathered before being sent down river for export to China from Calcutta. It was the export of opium, after all, that transformed the finances of the East India Company in the latter part of the eighteenth century and brought about the return to Bengal of the vast quantities of silver that had been drained out of India in the early part of the century to fund imports (luxuries like tea, porcelain and silk) from China. Indirectly, it was the trade in opium that often enabled those who had made their fortunes in India, including Zoffany, to return those fortunes to England through Bills of Exchange for the China trade.

Zoffany passed through the town of Ghazipur for the last time on his journey down river in late November 1788. On that occasion he made a drawing of a Hindu being brought to die at the river's edge (fig. 142). It was at a time when the theme of

Figure 142 (cat. 98)
A Hindu Brought to the Ganges to Die at Ghazipur, 1788,
black, red and white chalk on blue paper,
27 × 34.6 cm (10⅝ × 13⅝ in).
Yale Center for British Art, Paul Mellon Collection

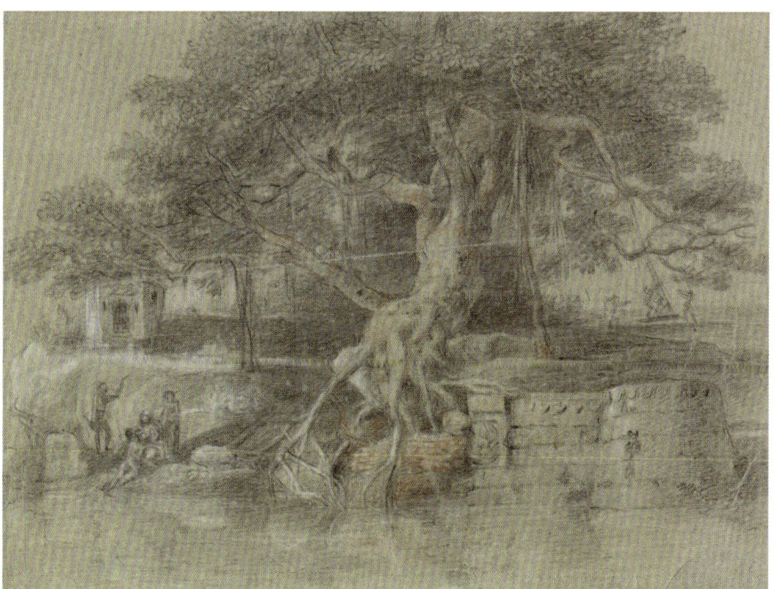

Figure 143
A Public Washing Place below a Temple at Currah, 1788,
black, red and white chalks, 27.3 × 35 cm (10¾ × 13¾ in).
Location unknown; by courtesy of the Witt Library,
The Courtauld Institute of Art, London

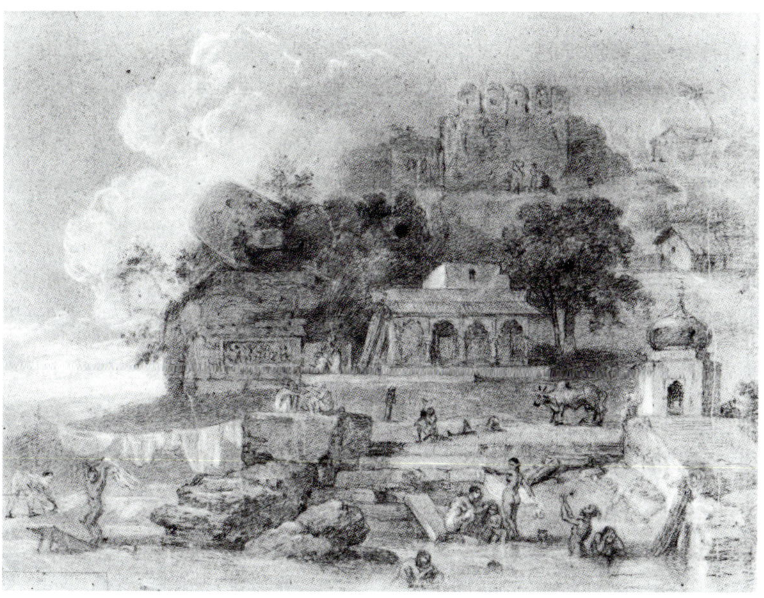

death seemed uppermost in his mind: perhaps, with his health failing, he feared that his own death was not too far away. Close to where he made the drawing is the Hindu burning ghat for the town that survives to this day. A little further along the riverbank are the ruined Chahal Situn (old palace) and numerous masonry ghats teeming with activity. There is no surviving drawing by Zoffany of the ghats here, but earlier on that final journey he made two drawings of similar ghats at Kara (Currah; fig. 143), the site of an old Muslim provincial capital.[18] Today Kara is difficult to find. It lies a couple of miles north of the Allahabad to Kanpur highway. An unmarked single track road leads to a sleepy little town on the south bank of the Ganges. The once impressive ghats have largely collapsed into the river but a small section survives and is recognizable in the sketch to the right of Zoffany's easel in the Polier conversation

piece (fig. 144). Many of Kara's ancient buildings were robbed of their stone and bricks and carried off for the construction of the city of Lucknow.

After Ghazipur the direct road to Lucknow leads away from the Ganges and follows its tributary river, the Gumti, to the city. Crossing into the nawab's territory and moving away from British-held territory and influence, the journey would have become ever more difficult for Zoffany. Faced not only with difficulties of communication, he would have had to be alert to the dangers from robbers on the road. Hodges described in his *Travels in India* how, on the journey down the Gumti from Lucknow, close to the village (now substantial town) of Sultanpoor, he was threatened by a famous marauder, Rah Singh, and he would almost certainly have been robbed but for the alertness of his sepoys.[19] Today things are somewhat

Figure 144
Colonel Polier and his Friends (cat. 90) detail

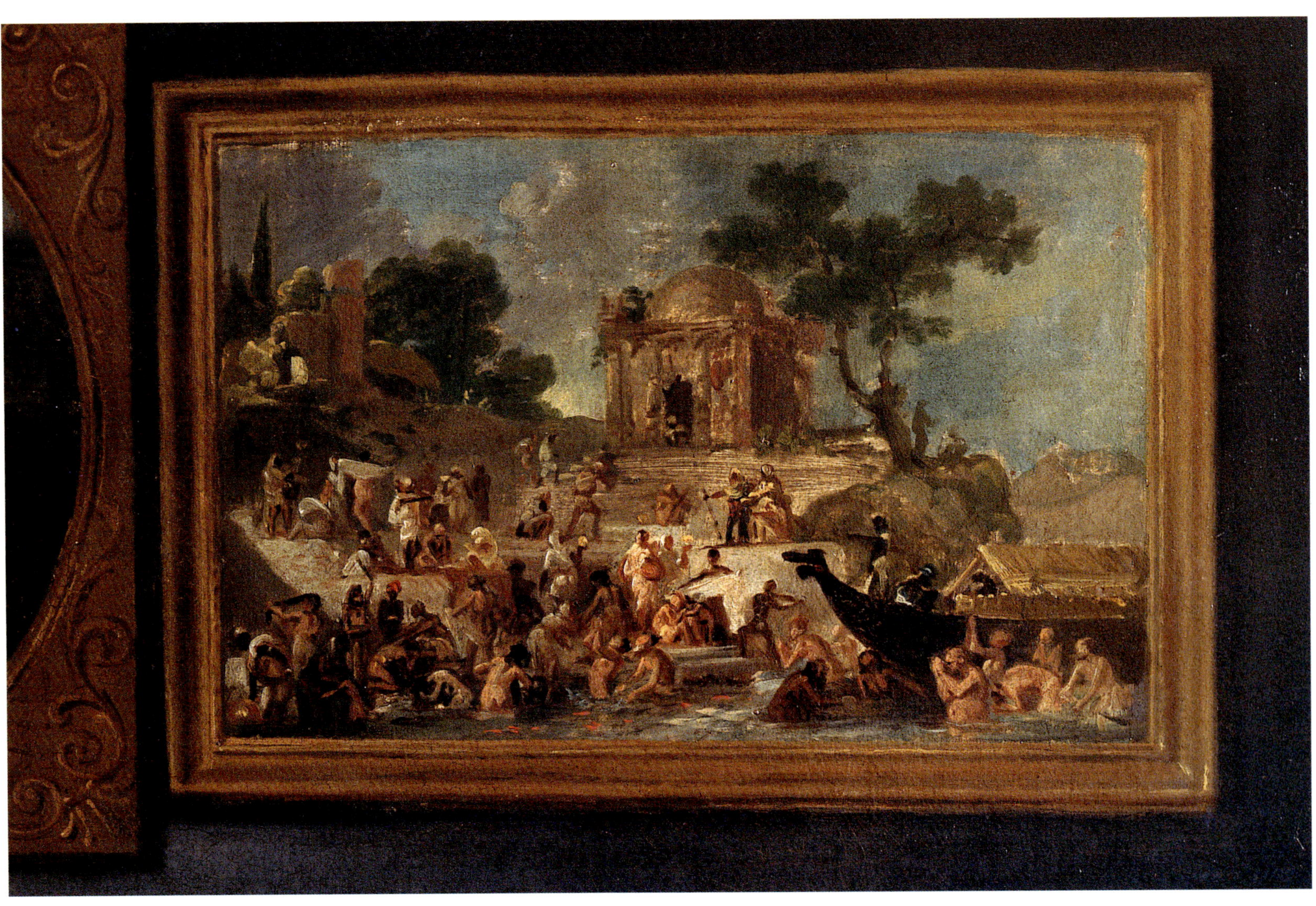

different. When I retraced this part of the journey, it was much the easiest part, for not only are the roads in an excellent state of repair and relatively safe, but here in Uttar Pradesh one can stop at almost any roadside *dharba* (eating house) and enjoy freshly prepared and delicious vegetarian food sitting cross-legged on a charpoy – so different from my experience in Jharkand.

The country through which Zoffany travelled in Awadh was, and is to this day, mostly agricultural. But a little short of halfway from Ghazipur to Lucknow one passes through Jaunpur, the former capital of a significant Muslim kingdom that flourished between 1397 and 1476 under the Sharqi dynasty, before it fell to Sikander Lodi. He destroyed many of the fine secular buildings, but Firuz Shah's fort, the later Mughal bridge and the mosques survive and are of considerable distinction. As Zoffany was usually in a hurry to reach Lucknow, he probably did not linger long to appreciate these architectural gems and no drawings by him done in the vicinity are known. But he would have been aware of the marked contrast between the severe austerity of the early Muslim architecture of the mosques at Jaunpore and the flamboyance of what he would see in Lucknow a few days later.

Zoffany arrived for the first time in Lucknow on 3 June 1784. Nothing he had seen before could have prepared him for Asaf-ud-Daula's city. Shortly after the death of Shuja-ud-Daula in 1775, his eldest son Asaf (fig. 145), the new nawab and hereditary vizier of the Mughal Empire, moved the capital of the province of Awadh from Faizabad to Lucknow and set about creating a city to exceed in magnificence any in India at the time. Awadh was the richest province in India, and nominally at least, its huge revenue was at the disposal of the nawab. In reality, following the defeat of the Muslim armies at Buxar in 1764, Shuja-ud-Daula had been obliged to accept a significant detachment of Company troops in Awadh at his expense and nine years later a permanent British Resident at his court. Despite these onerous expenses and further subsidies levied by the British, the new nawab spared little expense in building his Muslim capital. Central to this extravagant venture was extending an old fort, the Macchi Bhavan, to create a splendid palace arranged in a series of courtyards, gardens, a zenana and a durbar hall for visitors. Nearby stood the imposing Punj Mahal Gate and beyond – a little way down the hill – he built the Bara Imambara for the celebration of Muharram (Muslim sacred month). It was started in 1784 to provide employment following the catastrophic famine of that year and was finished well before Zoffany's final departure from the city.

After passing through two gateways, a traveller can only be awed by the vast scale of the Bara Imambara, the cavernous and richly decorated interior and its labyrinth above. Originally, it was fitted with huge gilt mirrors, chandeliers and lustres. No less imposing is Asaf-ud-Daula's mosque adjacent to it. Outside the gates, spanning the main road, is one of the marvels of the city, the Rumi Darwaza – an architectural fantasy. This splendour was extended to every other aspect of life in the court. His stables were filled with richly caparisoned elephants and horses, his carriages and palanquins were upholstered in cloth of gold and brocades, and his gilded and painted peacock pleasure boats plied the river. He attracted from imperial Delhi the finest painters like Mihr Chand, calligraphers, poets, musicians and dancers of the Kathak school. Cuisine was developed into an art form, clothes were created from the most sumptuous materials and Urdu was refined into a poetic language. One of Asaf-ud-Daula's chief preoccupations and pleasures involved animal and bird combats – elephants, buffalos, tigers, rams, partridges and cocks fought down by the river at Gow Gautee and in private gardens nearby. Less well known was the development of the arts of combat between young men – Lakri with sticks, Bank with knives, Barchha with spears, and Kushti, a form of wrestling. As a Muslim, he had a particular fondness for doves and pigeons, both of which were flown from the roof of his palace. The nawab was much criticized by Europeans at the time and since for his indolence, habitual extravagance, fondness for low life and addiction to opium. Yet, in some ways perhaps, the positives far outweighed the negatives, and his legacy is still evident today in the grand surviving buildings, his scattered collections, Lucknow cuisine, the refinement of speech and the chaste Urdu still spoken in the old city.

After the rigours of his long journey Zoffany must have felt that he had arrived in an enchanted place and he quickly fell for Lucknow's charms. He remained in the city for seven months, enjoying the delights. He returned again in May 1785 and remained there, with the exception of a brief excursion to Agra, and possibly Delhi, with his friend John Wombwell, until November 1785.[20] He was back for the last time in the autumn of 1787 and only departed in November 1788, having stayed there a total of two and a half years.

Figure 145 (cat. 83)
Asaf-ud-Daula, Nawab Wazir of Awadh, 1784,
oil on canvas, 129.5 × 105.5 cm (51 × 41½ in).
The British Library, India Office Library & Records, London

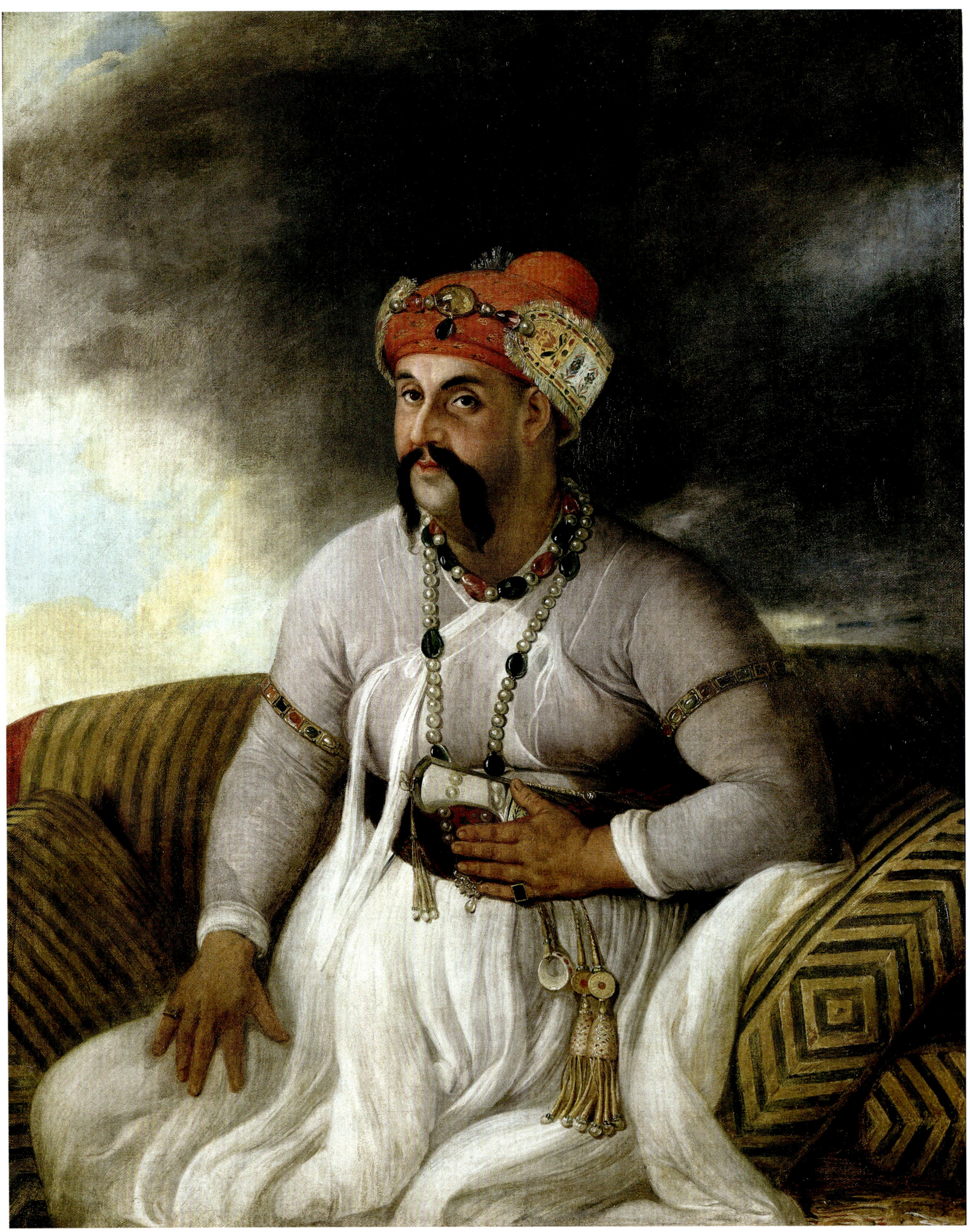

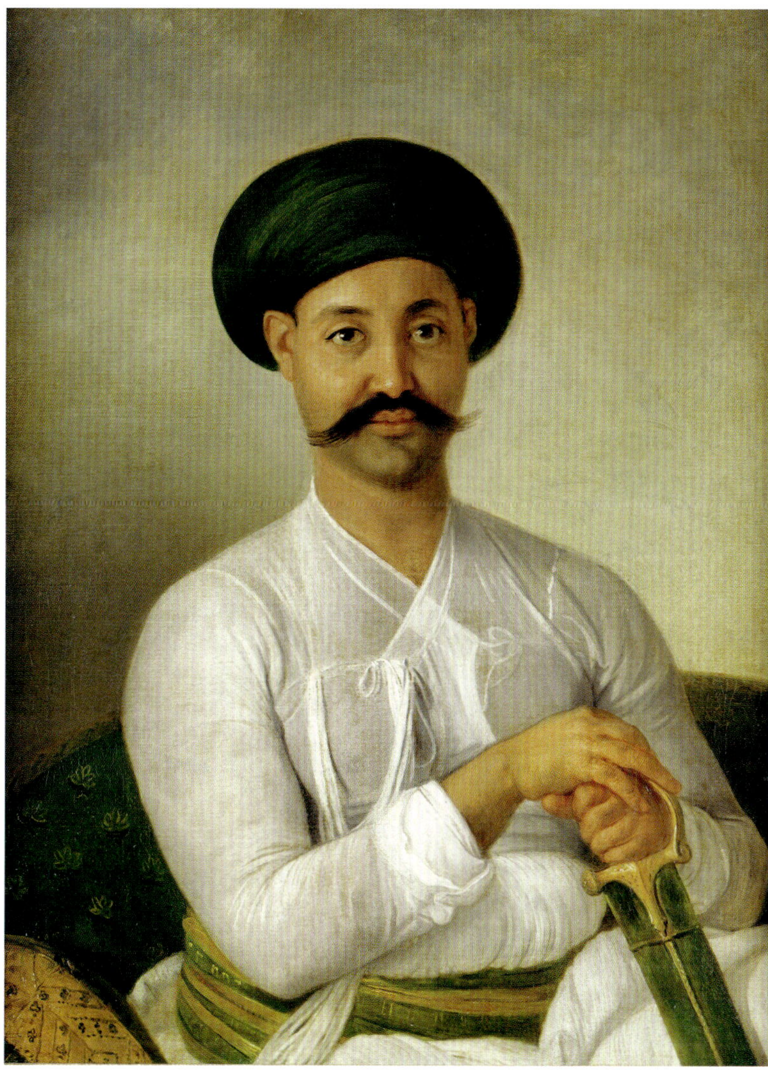

Figure 146 (cat. 85)
Prince Jawan Bakht (Jahandar Shah), 1784,
oil on canvas, 91.5 × 66.1 cm (36 × 26 in).
Private collection

Given the wealth of the province and the extravagance of the nawab, it is hardly surprising that Lucknow attracted Europeans of every description, there to make a quick fortune and to escape the confines of life in Calcutta. Zoffany was no exception. He hoped that the nawab and his courtiers would be generous benefactors. But he was to be sorely disappointed. The nawab's expenditure and mania for collecting resulted in him being hugely indebted and Zoffany is said to have never received a rupee from the nawab for his work. But other commissions came his way. Zoffany, as a foreigner, was always on the margin of English society, and in Lucknow, with its fusion of Muslim culture and an increasing British presence, he found himself at ease with others of a similar background. He soon made friends with two remarkable Frenchmen, Antoine Polier, the nawab's engineer, and Claude Martin. The latter had arrived in the city in 1777 to develop the nawab's arsenal, but he quickly turned his attention to building a great fortune through land, cultivation and moneylending. He had other formidable qualities as an engineer, cartographer, amateur architect, mathematician and avid collector. Zoffany was soon attracted to this man of the Enlightenment in India. Martin became his principal patron in the city, commissioning not only portraits but also landscapes, views of his properties and even a study of a fakir. Zoffany's sensitive portrait of Martin's elegant and beautiful *bibi* Boulone fishing in a tank (see fig. 123), accompanied by Martin's adopted son Zulfikar Khan, is evidence of just how far his journey to Lucknow had changed him and his art.[21] The formal portraits of members of the upper echelons of society in Calcutta have given way to a highly intimate study, which rejoices in the youth of his sitters, the gorgeous clothes and the rolling landscape of Awadh.

In Lucknow, for a brief period in the closing years of the eighteenth century, Indians and Europeans could meet on equal and friendly terms, something almost impossible in Calcutta. Zoffany himself found a mistress, or *bibi*, with whom he had a long desired son (even though propriety compelled him to leave him in the care of his mother on his departure). Interracial sociability is evident in another rare painting from Zoffany's first visit to the city (fig. 147). It shows Prince Jawan Bakht (fig. 146), heir to the Mughal emperor, on a *musnud* (cushion throne) surrounded by the nawab, Hastings, other Europeans and Indian courtiers, all seated on the ground in a moonlit setting. It is only a slight sketch but the emotional intimacy of the participants is overwhelming.

Zoffany was a frequent guest at Martin's town house, Farhat Baksh, which still stands close to the Chatar Manzil.

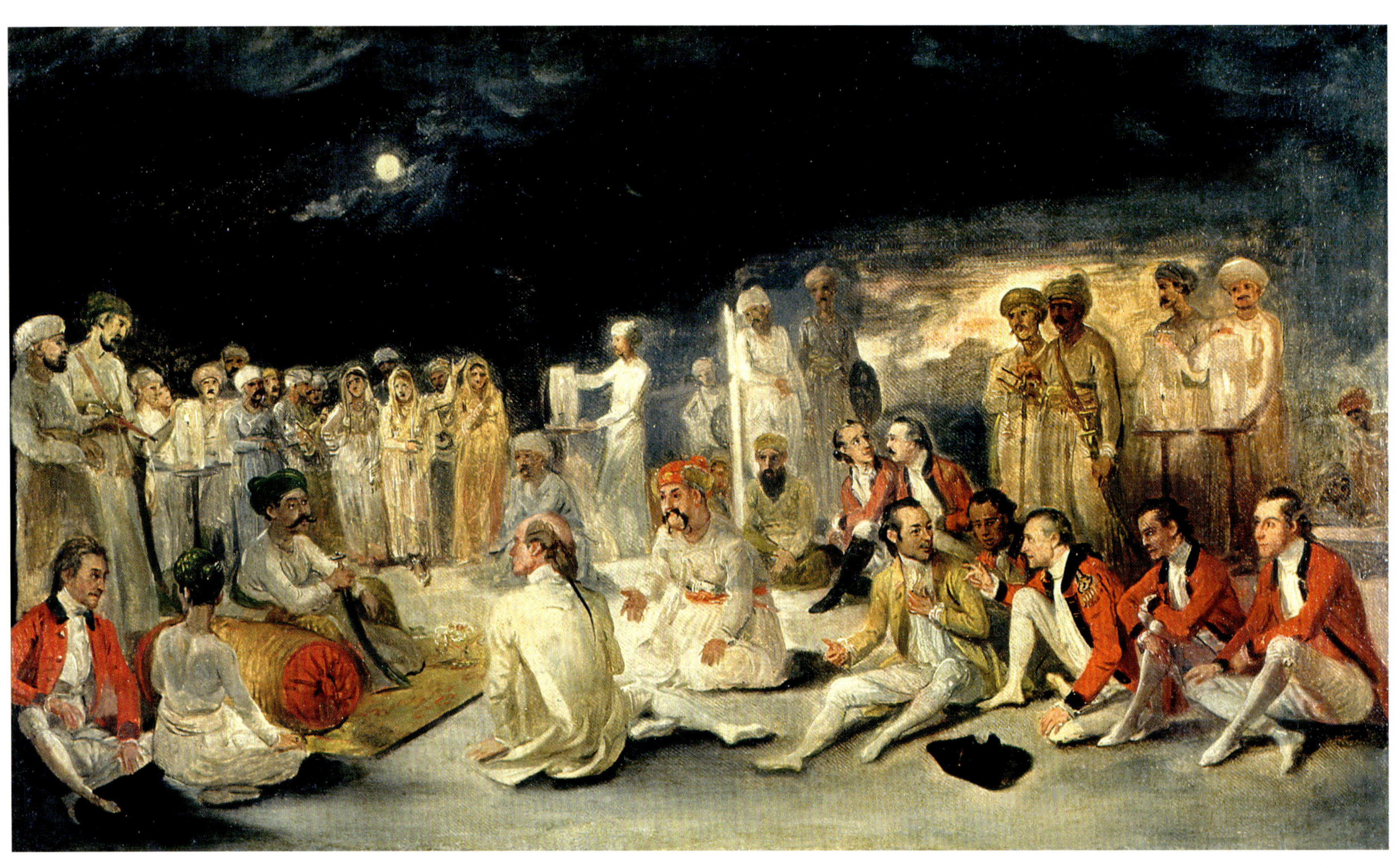

Figure 147
Warren Hastings Meeting Prince Jawan Bakht, the Son of Shah Alam,
1784, oil on canvas, 60 × 110.5 cm (23⅝ × 43½ in).
Victoria Memorial Hall, Calcutta

He evidently made at least two views of the house in 1784, which are now known only through engravings, both entitled *View of a House Built by Col. Claude Martin at Lucknow, Bengal* (figs. 149, 150).[22] Though previously attributed to William Hodges, the original compositions would appear to be by Zoffany. Accompanying descriptions of the engravings state that they were 'made from drawings taken on the spot in the year 1784'. Zoffany was the only European artist in Lucknow that year, and there is no evidence that Hodges, who had departed India in November 1783, ever painted or drew Martin's house.[23] There are further clues supporting the attribution of the views to Zoffany. In the more distant view of the house (fig. 149) the boat on the left-hand side contains a number of figures who appear in Zoffany's moonlight landscape, *Nagaphon Ghut* (cat. 95). In the same

painting some figures on the shore resemble those in the now destroyed landscape, which was probably a view done at or near Najafgarh.

Zoffany also painted an oil sketch of Martin's house. This is shown being held up by a servant on the right-hand side of the Polier conversation piece (fig. 148), and this view, on an unrolled canvas, is almost identical to plate 1 (fig. 150) in *The European Magazine*. The sketch has been the subject of much debate in the past. Mildred Archer suggested that the servant was holding a watercolour by Martin himself (she misread the compass held in his hand for paint brushes).[24] Others have presumed it to be a watercolour by Hodges. The squared landscape and stiffness of the roll support the opinion that this sketch was done in oils on canvas, and many such, by Zoffany, were included in Martin's inventory made after his death.

Figure 148
Colonel Polier and his Friends (cat. 90) detail

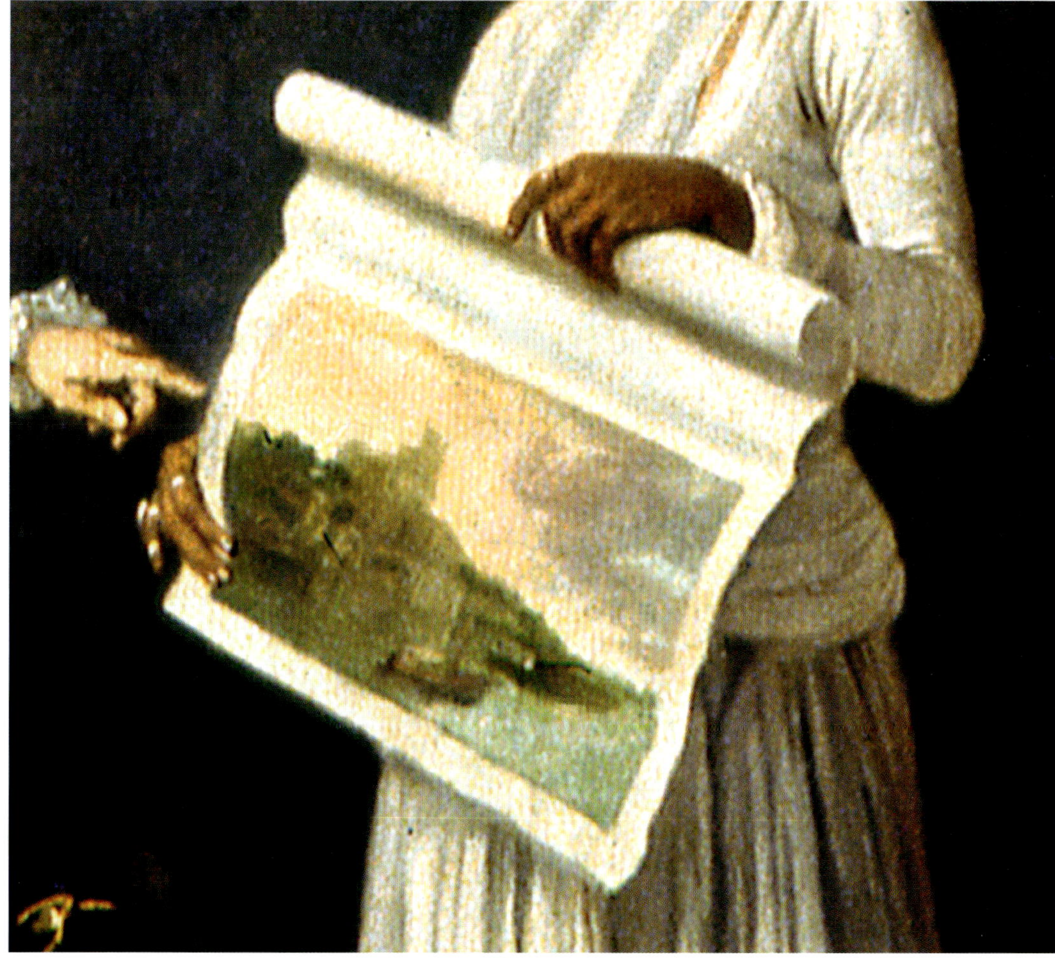

Figure 149
Thomas Morris after Johan Zoffany, *View of a House Built by Col. Claude Martin at Lucknow, Bengal, Plate 2*, 1790, engraving, 12.7 × 21.5 cm (5 × 8½ in), from *The European Magazine, and London Review*, vol. 18 (1 April 1790). Courtesy the Beinecke Rare Book and Manuscript Library, Yale University

Figure 150
Thomas Morris after Johan Zoffany, *View of a House Built by Col. Claude Martin at Lucknow, Bengal, Plate 1*, 1790, engraving, 12.7 × 21.5 cm (5 × 8½ in), from *The European Magazine, and London Review*, vol. 17 (1 March 1790). Courtesy the Beinecke Rare Book and Manuscript Library, Yale University

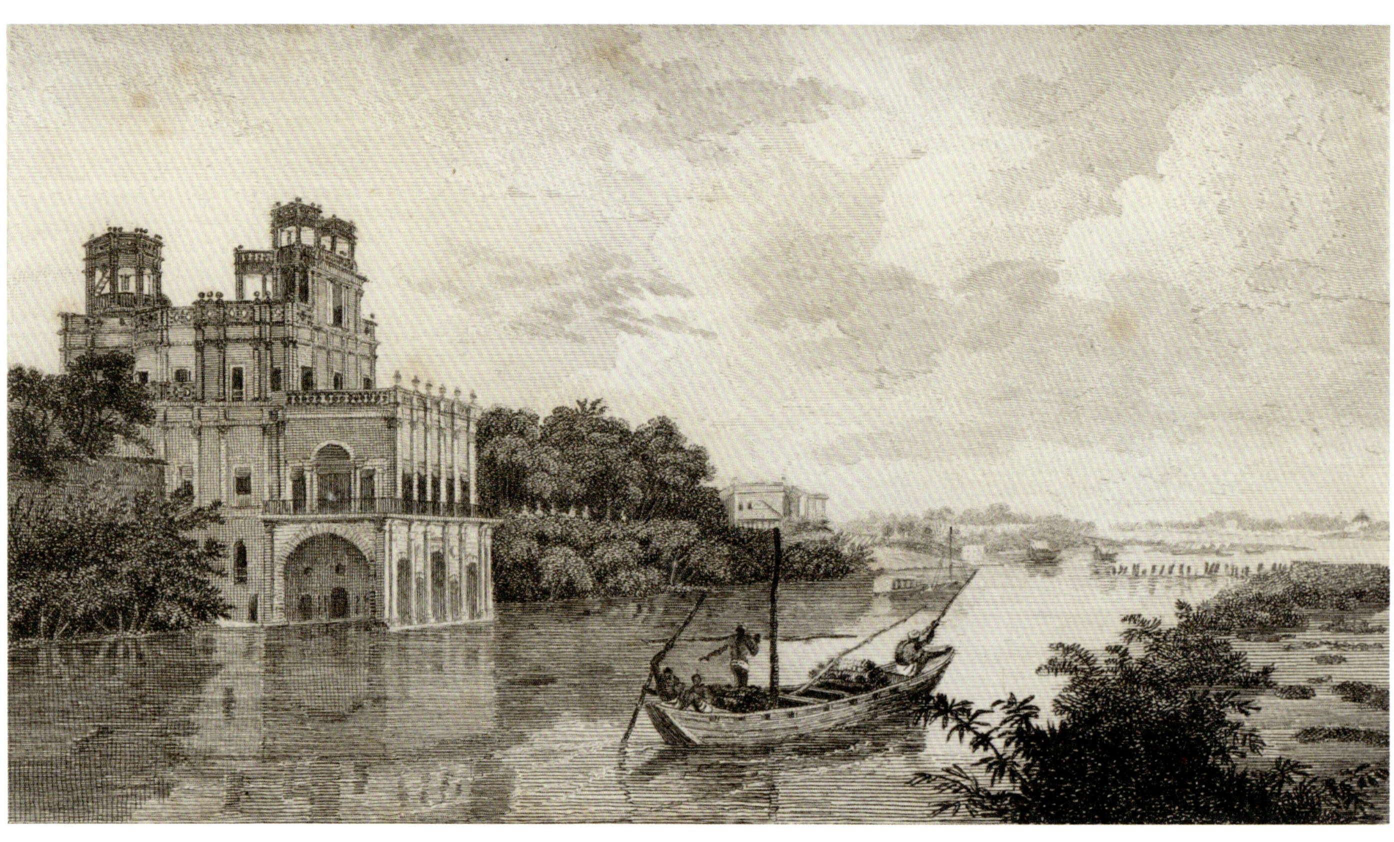

VIEW of a HOUSE built by COL. CLAUDE. MARTIN. at LUCKNOW.

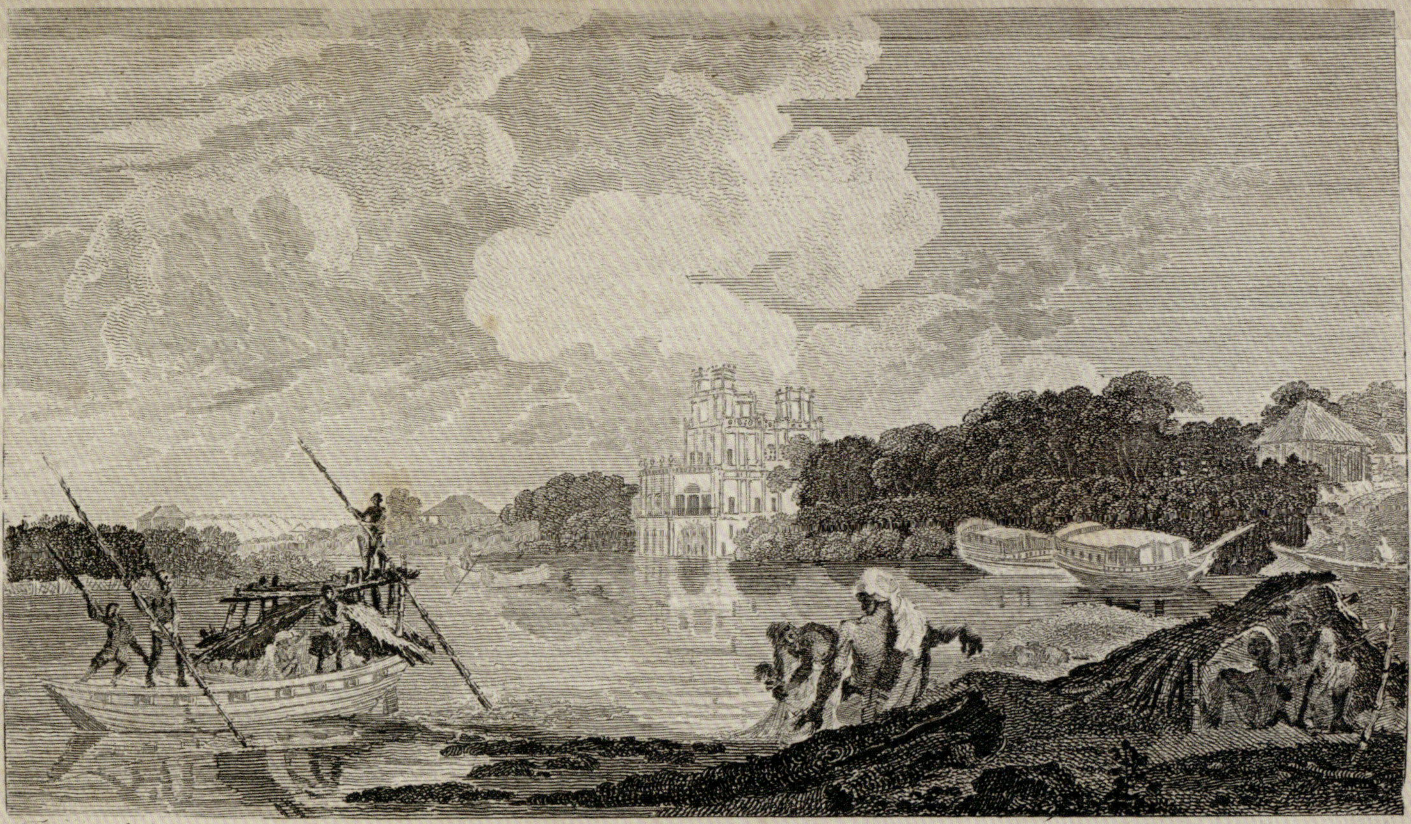

Plate. 2.

Pub.d April 1.1790 as the Act directs by I. Sewell Cornhill.

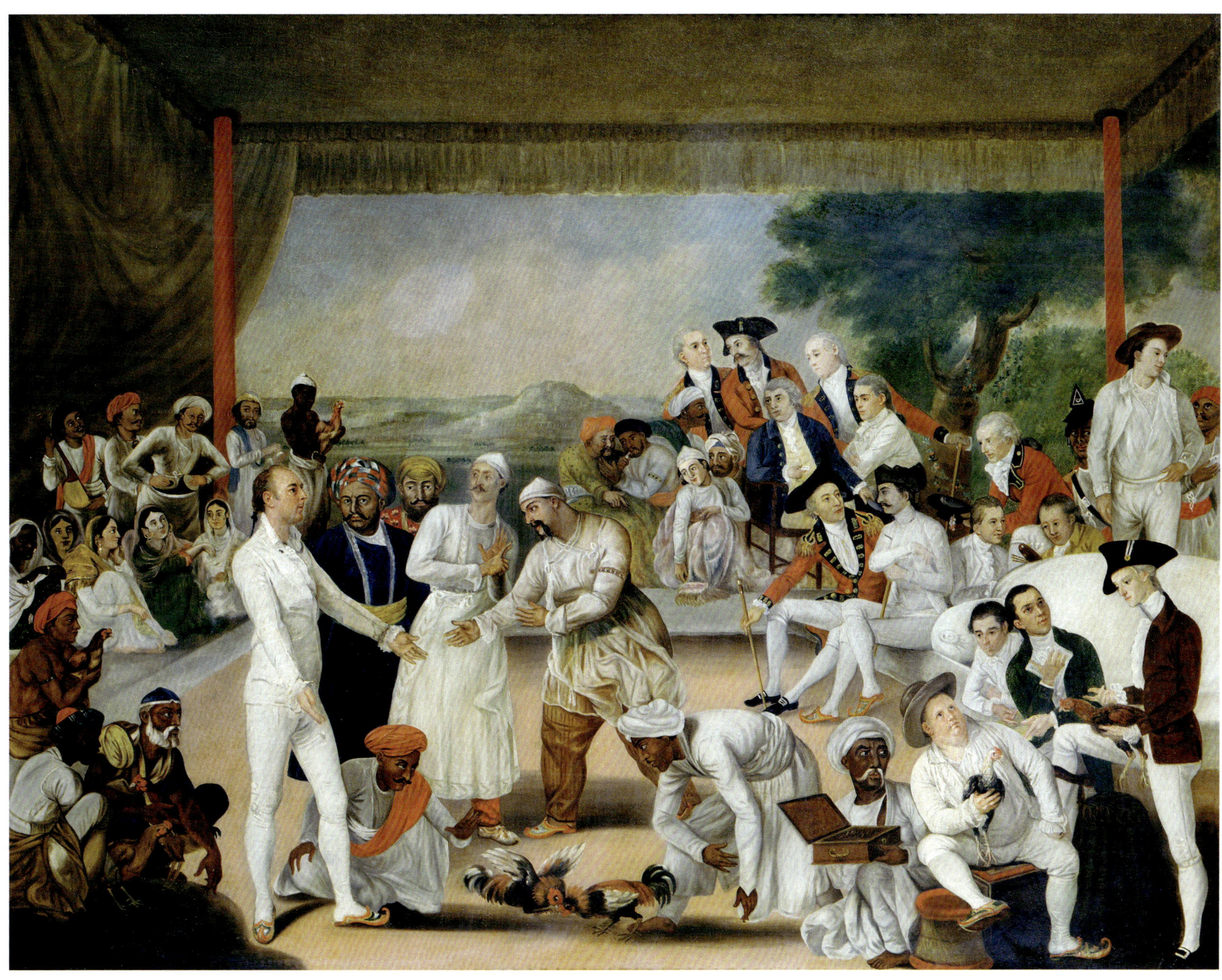

Figure 151 (cat. 87)
Johan Zoffany and a Lucknow artist, *Colonel Mordaunt's Cock Match*,
1786–*c*.1790, oil on canvas, 119.1 × 86.6 cm (46⅞ × 34⅛ in).
White's Club, London

Figure 152
Interior of the Kakori Kothi – the cockpit built at
Khayaligunj in Lucknow by Claude Martin, *c*.1785.

Farhat Baksh is now incorporated into the Central Drug Research Institute, and on a visit to Lucknow in 2009 I was refused permission to see the interior. It was a deep disappointment but a day later I had a most unexpected surprise at another of Martin's properties. Zoffany's painting, *Colonel Mordaunt's Cock Match*, done for Hastings is arguably the masterpiece of eighteenth-century Anglo-Indian painting.

The Nawab, impressed by Hastings's painting, commissioned another version for himself. At the time of Zoffany's final departure from Lucknow in 1788 it was still substantially unfinished as no payment had been forthcoming. The Nawab therefore employed an Indian artist to finish the painting, and this version survives at White's Club, London (fig. 151).

No other painting captures so vividly the dazzling brilliance of life in Lucknow at that period and the close cross-cultural relationships that made the city so vibrant and unique. I had heard that Martin's own cockpit, the Kakori Kothi, survived in the old district of Khayaligunj near the Kaiserbagh. I set out, accompanied by an old friend, the historian Rosie Llewellyn-Jones, and the photographer Antonio Martinelli. The distinguished Muslim family that now owns the property generously agreed to let us see the cockpit itself, which is flanked at either end by their living quarters. A rusty key was found and the panelled teak door opened to reveal a treasure beyond all expectation. The circular room is supported by fluted columns and lit by skylights close to the roof (fig. 152). All the original decoration and colour schemes were intact including intricate moulded plasterwork, the green painted ceiling, the yellow walls and the moulded chimneypiece (even Lucknow gets cold in the winter). For a moment one was transported back to the 1780s, imagining the room resounding to the clamour of Martin and his friends, Indians and Europeans of every description, just as Zoffany portrayed such a scene. It stands today as a testament to Martin's impeccable taste, and an eerie evocation of his friendship with Zoffany.

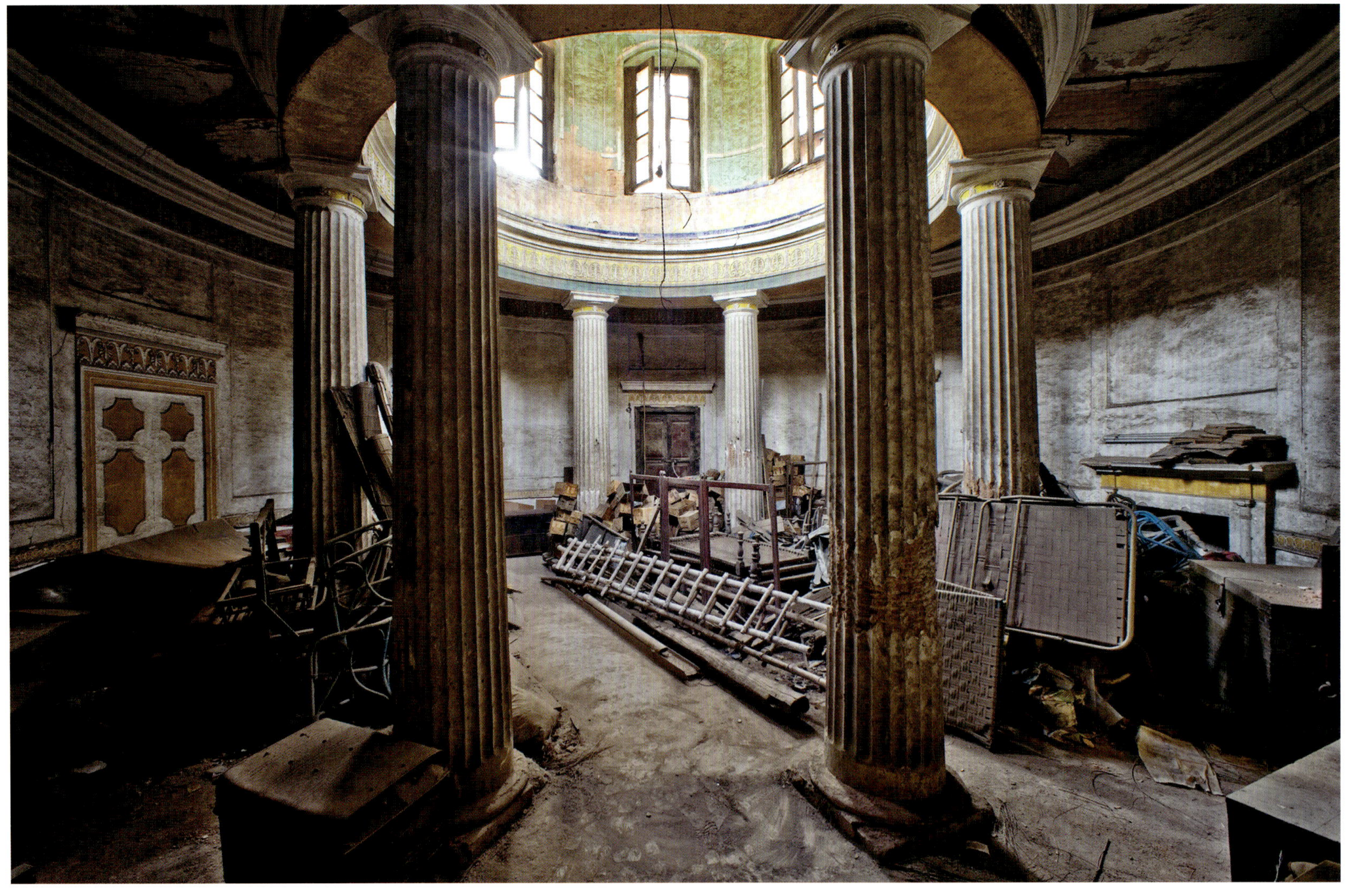

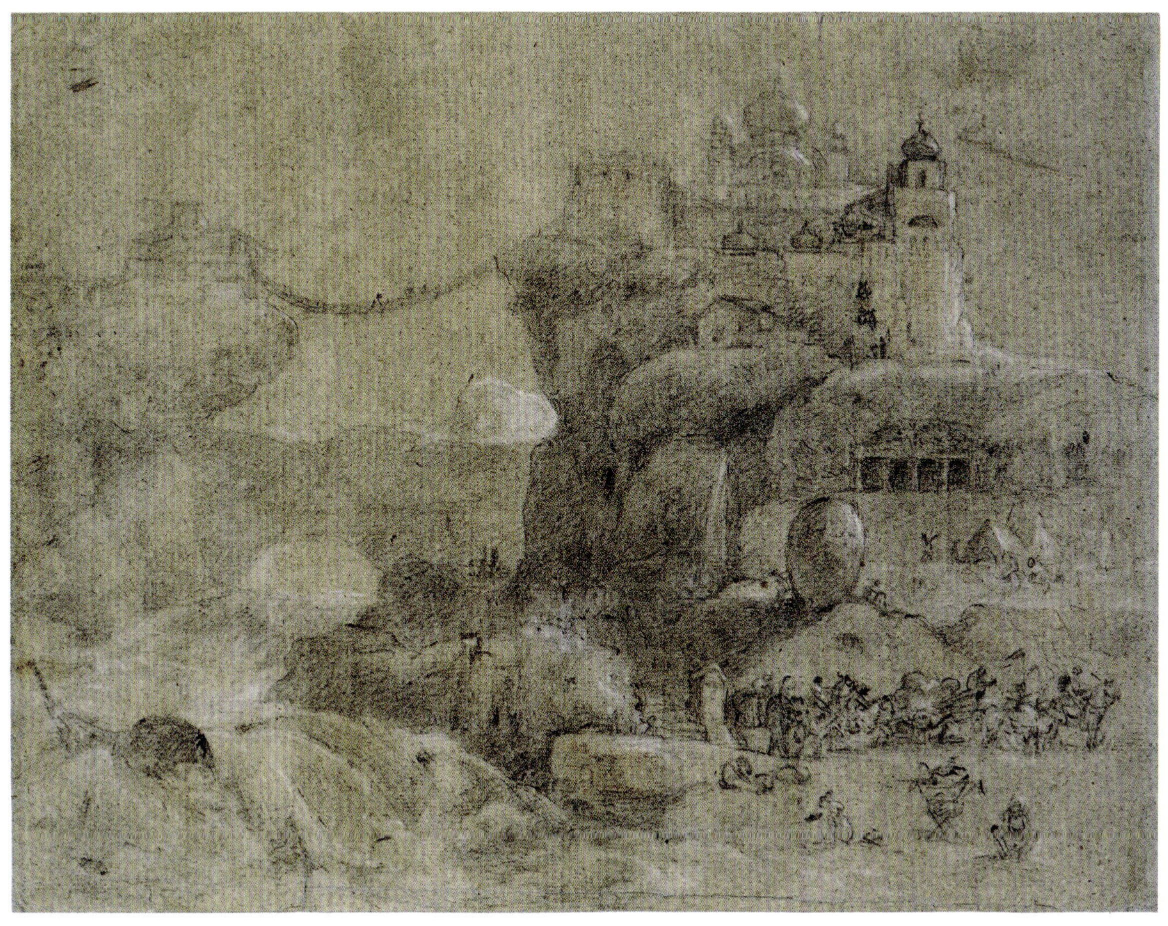

Figure 153 (cat. 99)
Rocky Landscape with Waterfall and Temples, Eastern India, 1788, red, black and white chalk on faded blue paper, 27.1 × 34.1 cm (10⅝ × 13⅜ in). British Museum, Department of Prints and Drawings, 1955, 0416.9

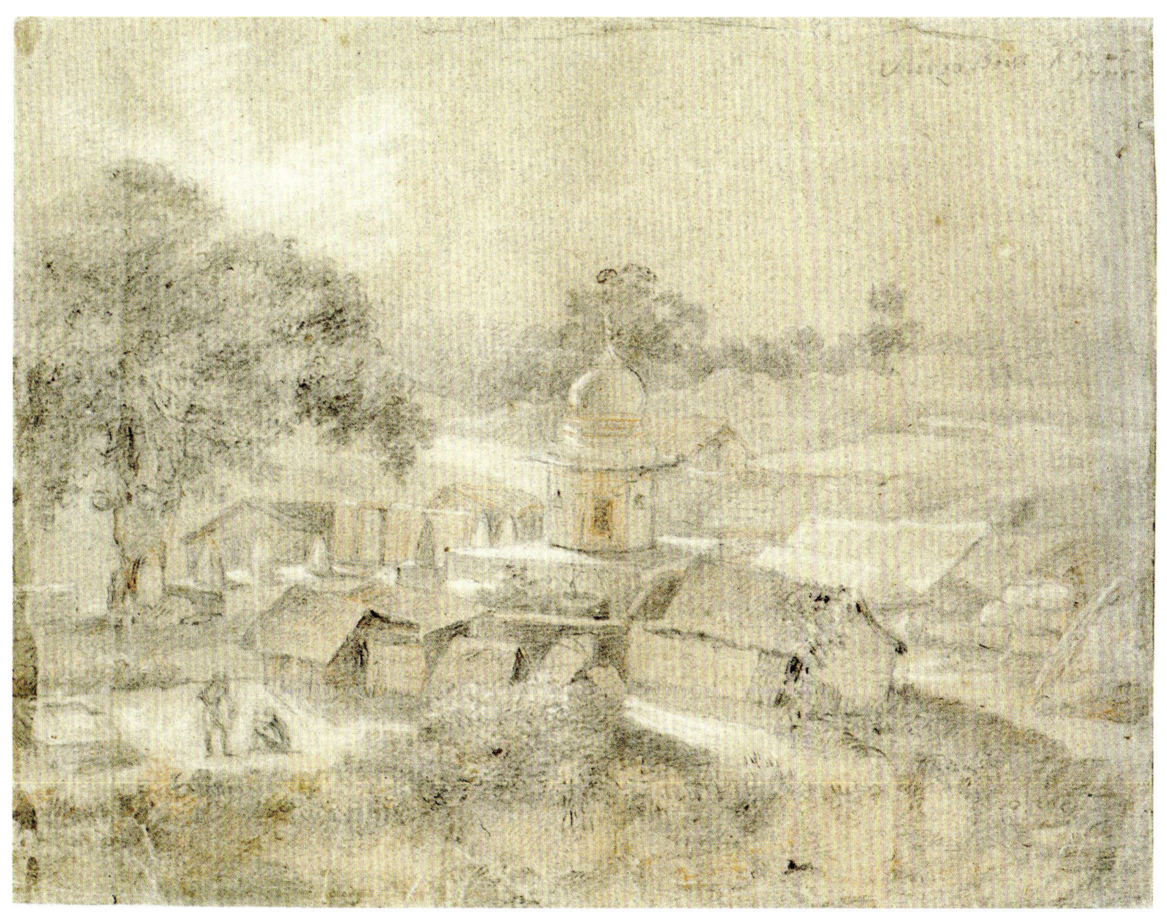

Figure 154 (cat. 97)
A Group of Buildings Surrounding a Suttee Memorial at Mirzapore, India, 1788, red, black and white chalk on blue/grey paper, 28 × 35.3 cm (11 × 13⅞ in). British Museum, Department of Prints and Drawings, 1955, 0416.7

Martin's friendship enabled Zoffany to see something of life outside the city. He must have made several excursions to Martin's estate at Najafgarh near Cawnpore (Kanpur). Among Martin's letters is one dated 13 April 1788 to his servant Sahib Ram Pandit, with an intriguing reference to a plan of the trees at Nakapur (one of the villages that comprised the Najafgarh estate) made by Zoffany on cloth. In another, written a few days earlier to other servants, Mian Jawahar and Ram Prasad, Martin requests ten bearers each for his and Zoffany's palanquins for the return to Lucknow. They were accompanied on that occasion by Martin's son Zulfikar Khan. On Zoffany's last journey back to Calcutta in late November and early December 1788 he travelled through Najafgarh, probably saying his final farewells to his *bibi* and his own son. The pain of separation and ill health must have made his trip down river deeply depressing. His series of drawings made on this final journey, some inscribed and dated, are intimate personal studies, done for himself to remind him of 'Indian' India (figs. 153, 154). At Mirzapore he made two drawings of *sati* stones, which have long since disappeared, but the ghats there today are much as they would have been in his time (fig. 155). Other drawings reflect his delight in elephants and horses, ancient trees, and Hindus bathing in the river. Many drawings are lost, but those that survive provide a tantalizing glimpse into his private world. And Zoffany's travels did not only have a profound influence on his work in India: one only needs to compare the slightly stiff, formal full-length portraits made in the mid-1780s in Calcutta with the later lively, vibrant, richly coloured portraits of General Norman MacLeod (fig. 156) and his wife Sarah, to see that they coloured the rest of his life. In the 1790s, while he was still able, Zoffany continued to paint exotic scenes, works that are filled with the people and incidents he had encountered on the road and by the river in an India he had left behind and to which he hoped one day to return.[25]

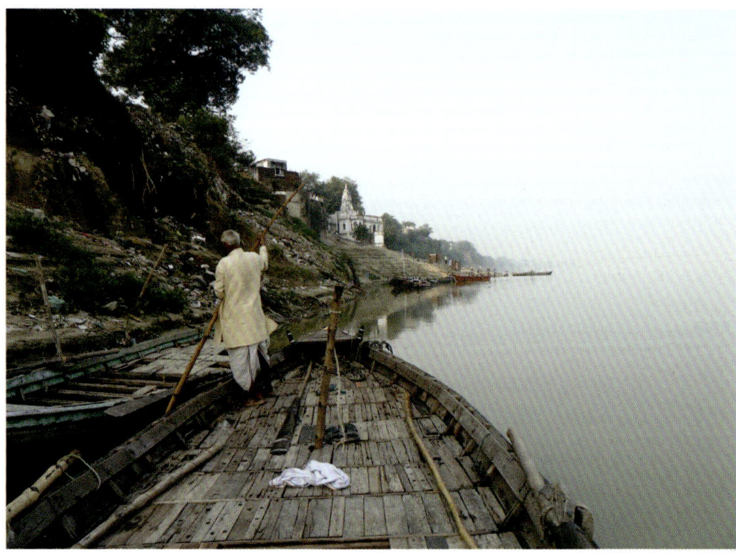

Figure 155
Ghats at Mirzapore, Uttar Pradesh

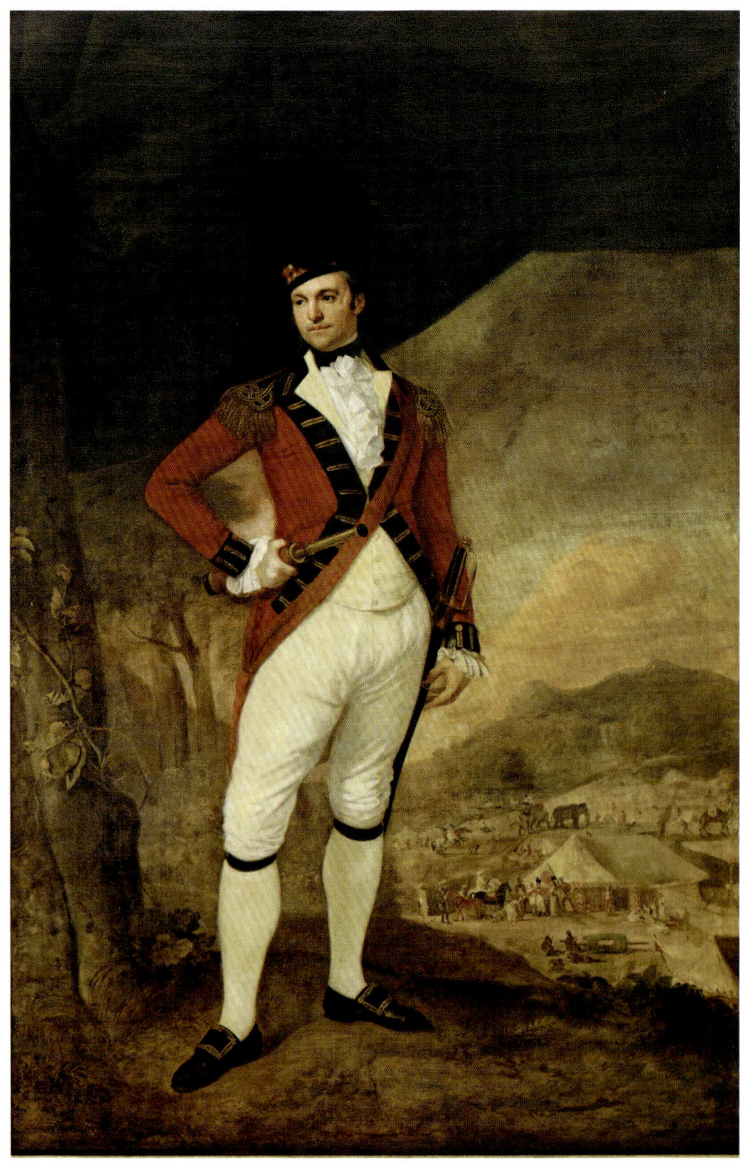

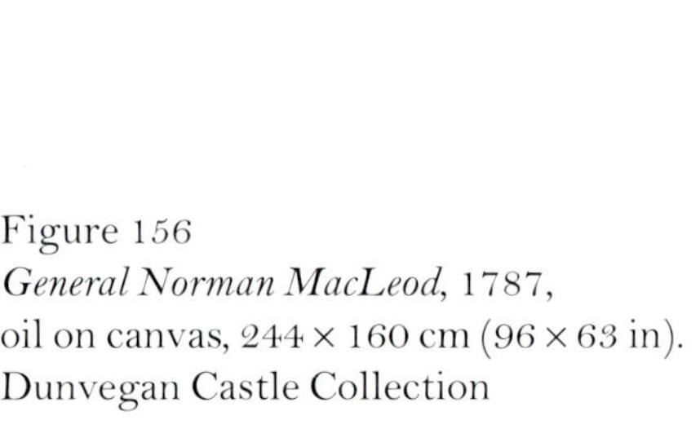

Figure 156
General Norman MacLeod, 1787,
oil on canvas, 244 × 160 cm (96 × 63 in).
Dunvegan Castle Collection

Notes

1. I travelled in Zoffany's footsteps in March and April 2008, travelling from Lucknow by way of Najafgarh, following the road close to the river all the way to Calcutta. On my second journey, in November 2010, I took the shorter route following more precisely the journey I have described.
2. See Hickey 1913–25, *passim*.
3. Webster 2011, 269–71.
4. Garland Cannon, ed., *The Letters of Sir William Jones*, 2 vols., Oxford, 1970, vol. 2, 655, letter 393 dated 1 Oct. 1784.
5. See Mike Dash, *Thug: The True Story of India's Murderous Cult*, London, 2005.
6. Humphry diary, Osborn Collection, Yale University Library, f. 26.
7. Zoffany invoice to Hastings, Hastings Papers (Private Accounts), British Library, Add. MS 29,229, f. 154, 21 Feb. 1785.
8. See Webster 2011, 539, pl. 405.
9. See Webster 2011, 519, pl. 387.
10. See, for example, Thomas Daniell, *Oriental Scenery*, 6 vols., London, 1795–1815, vol. 4, pl. 9.
11. See Geoff Quilley and John Bonehill, eds., *William Hodges, 1744–1797: The Art of Exploration*, New Haven and London 2004, 185–6, no. 70.
12. See Webster 2011, 547, fig. 415.
13. Llewellyn-Jones 2003, 171, letter 143.
14. The term 'Collector' derives from the Mughal system of land revenue adopted by the British. An administrator in a district was responsible for 'collecting' the land revenue from the zamindars (Indian feudal landholders) under his jurisdiction.
15. The Tila Kothi was painted by both William Hodges and Thomas Daniell. See Stuebe 1979, no. 433, fig. 263; Maurice Shellim, *Oil Paintings of India and the East by Thomas Daniell 1749–1840 and William Daniell 1769–1837*, London, 1979, no. TD 15, col. pl. II, Hill House at Bhagalpur.
16. Samuel Davis travelled out to India in 1780 in the ship in which Hodges also sailed. He joined the Madras Infantry and in 1783 was appointed by Hastings to accompany Captain Samuel Turner on his historic mission to Tibet. Davis was not permitted to enter the country and remained in Bhutan for six months, where he made some evocative watercolours of the scenery. On his return he was appointed to a writership in the Bengal Civil Establishment. From February 1785 to April 1792 he was Assistant to the Collector Registrar to the Court of Adawlat, Bhagalpur, and thereafter held a number of increasingly senior positions in Benares and in the 24 Parganas. He was an accomplished amateur painter in watercolours, having been trained by Hodges on-board ship. Many of his works survive in the Victoria Memorial, Calcutta.
17. Attar (perfume) is the oil and distillates of strongly scented flowers traditionally absorbed in sandalwood oil. Attar of roses (Gulab-attar), made from rose petals, was the favourite of the Mughal courts.
18. See also Webster 2011, 541, pl. 407.
19. Hodges 1793, 145/6.
20. For the journey with Wombwell, see Webster 2011, 526–8.
21. Webster 2011, 529–30.
22. 'An Account of Colonel Martin's Villa near Lucknow in the East Indies', *The European Magazine and London Review*, XVII, Feb. 1790, 86–7 (pl. 1); Aug. 1790, XVIII, opp. 88 (pl. 2).
23. For the attribution of the compositions to Hodges, see Stuebe 1979, 247, cats. 323, 324, figs. 207, 208. Stuebe, while noting that the inscription on the engravings, gives the date as 1784, suggesting that they were made by Hodges in May or June 1783, while he was staying at Martin's house. She also suggests that the articles in the *European Magazine* may have been written by Hodges. See also Giles Tillotson, *The Artificial Empire: The Indian Landscapes of William Hodges*, Richmond upon Thames, 2000, 119–20, fig. 45.
24. See Archer 1979, 156.
25. In early 1798 Zoffany gained permission from the East India Company to travel to India, arranging his passage in the late autumn. However, he abandoned the journey. See Webster 2011, 563.

Jessica David

Zoffany's Painting Technique:
The Drummond Family in focus

Beyond the dry details of financial transactions found in bank accounts and the occasional anecdote concerning his studio practice, there are relatively few contemporary insights into Zoffany's attitude towards the London art market, his interactions with portrait sitters and, most fundamentally, how he painted. Self-portraits indicate how he set his palette, and the inventory of his studio contents provides clues to Zoffany's working process, enumerating dozens of compositional oil sketches and over 180 works on paper, including life drawings, figure studies, animals, buildings and landscapes.[1] The few drawings and sketches that survive attest to his trained and discerning eye. The physical evidence provided by Zoffany's paintings themselves is more substantive. Through close examination of these works we can learn more about Zoffany's preference for particular canvas types, his methods of preparation, his preferred pigments and the idiosyncratic assembly of his compositions. This essay aims to provide a summary of what recent technical examination and conservation of Zoffany's works have revealed about his painting technique. It owes a particular debt to research conducted at Tate Britain, the Royal Collection, the Walker Art Gallery, Liverpool, and the Hamilton Kerr Institute, Cambridge.[2] The essay centres upon a case study of *The Drummond Family* (fig. 157), which has been conserved at the Yale Center for British Art over the past two years. Here, more than in any other of Zoffany's paintings yet examined, beneath the seemingly serene and polished surface lies an altogether more complex and intriguing account of his technique.

Certain aspects of Zoffany's painting technique are readily revealed on close inspection: the apparent ease with which a likeness is captured in confident strokes of pearly transparent flesh tones, animated by flashes of pure vermilion pigment to eyes, nostrils and mouths. Other facets of his painting practice are not immediately visible to the naked eye: the obsessive re-working and dramatic compositional changes made late in the painting process that reveal the laborious underpinnings of seemingly effortless execution.

With few exceptions, Zoffany used standard size, medium weight, plain-weave linen canvases, appropriate for the level of detail that his subjects required.[3] More interesting are the rare occasions on which Zoffany deviated from his prescribed canvas choice. In, for example, *The Tribuna of the Uffizi* (cat. 53) and *The Gore Family with George, Third Earl Cowper* (cat. 56), both completed in Florence, the canvases are distinctly coarser than the other canvases examined, the Gore family canvas being akin to burlap or sacking. Here, far from wishing to exploit the texture of his canvas, Zoffany made every effort to conceal and smooth over the canvas support with multiple oil ground layers.[4]

The majority of Zoffany's canvases are close to standard three-quarter, kit-cat and half-length sizes.[5] In some cases, however, Zoffany produced custom-made canvases for site-specific works, as in his group portrait of John, third Duke of Atholl and his family, 1765–77 (see fig. 96), which was designed as an overmantel for Blair Castle.[6] At other times Zoffany altered and adapted canvases as compositions evolved. The portrait of Mrs Wodhull, c.1770 (see fig. 111), for example, appears originally to have been a half-length portrait, but was extended into a full length, apparently at the request of the clients.[7] *William Berry Introduced as Heir to Raith*, 1769 (cat. 70), is comprised of five canvas pieces, Zoffany having added four strips of canvas around the original composition, one of which contains a self-portrait that was clearly conceived as an afterthought.

In a large proportion of Zoffany's works that have been subject to technical investigation there are two distinct layers of a lead white oil preparation separated by a thin application of adhesive, probably an animal-skin glue. This suggests that Zoffany, as was the norm, habitually purchased pre-prepared stretched canvases from a supplier who either used this specific recipe or was instructed to do so.[8] As with his choice of canvas preparations, Zoffany's selection of pigments is remarkably consistent, and cross-sections taken from a number of works demonstrate similar paint structures. His palette is typical of the mid-eighteenth century and comprises most of the available colours including natural ultramarine and Prussian blue, copper green (verdigris), lead-tin yellow, Naples yellow, yellow and red lakes, iron oxide pigments (ochres), red lead, vermilion, Vandyke brown, ivory black and lead white.[9]

In many of his self-portraits, notably that completed for the Art Academy of Cortona (see fig. 24), Zoffany prominently displays the contents of his palette, at once following a convention of self-portraiture and signifying his status as a

Figure 157 (cat. 69)
The Drummond Family, c.1769, oil on canvas, 104.1 × 160 cm (41 × 63 in). Yale Center for British Art, Paul Mellon Collection. Work shown after treatment.

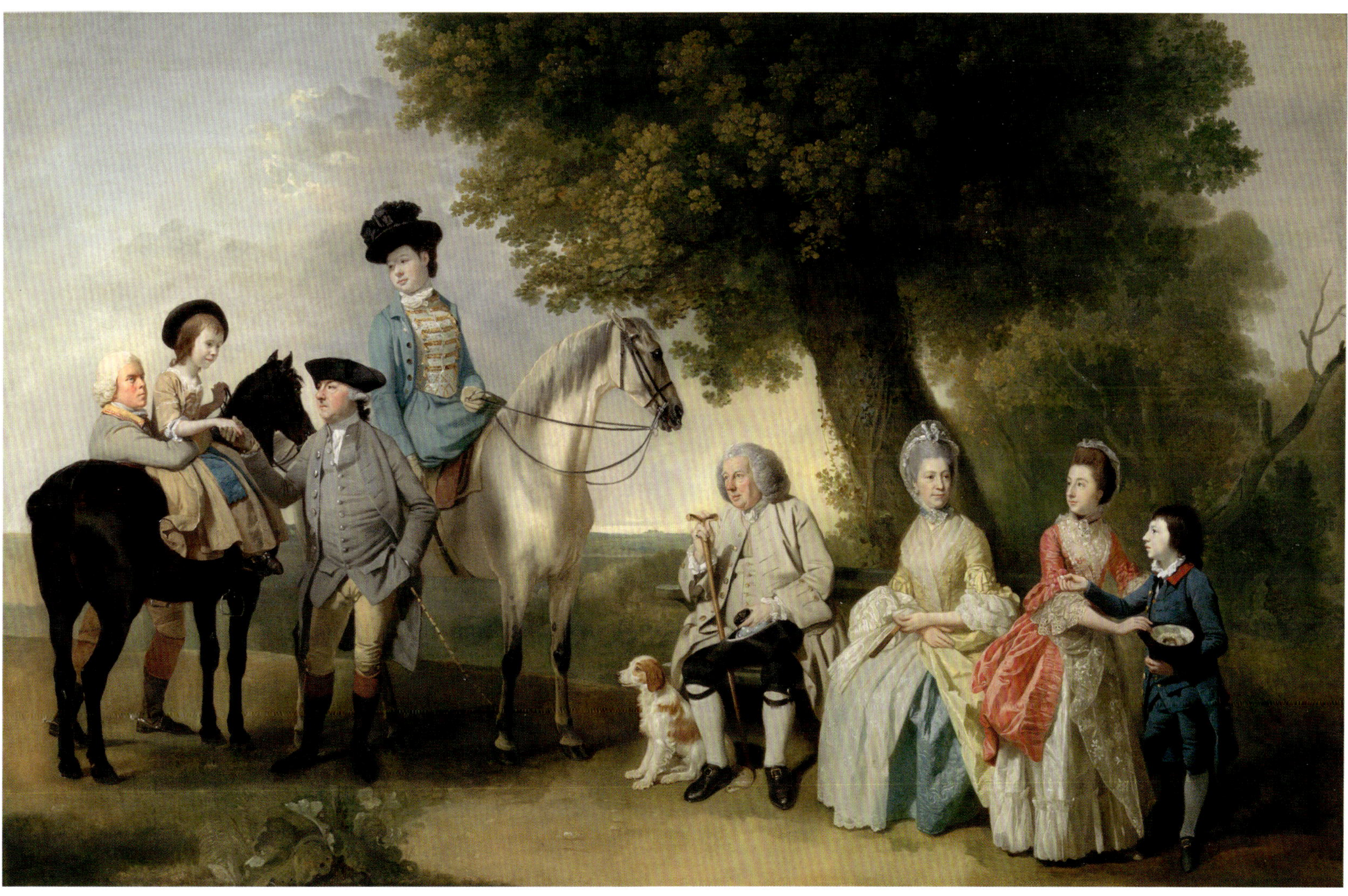

portrait painter. All of the palettes represented in his self-portraits are similarly laid out, beginning at the upper right with lead or flake white, light and dark yellow ochre, dark brown earth or raw umber, a red lake, a deep blue, probably Prussian blue, and black, below which are smaller piles of vermilion and a red earth colour.[10] This selection and arrangement of paints is both appropriate to the first stage of portrait painting and consistent with the pigments identified within Zoffany's paintings.

Fine, transparent brown lines rendered in oil have been observed in several of Zoffany's paintings, loosely following his subjects' contours as a preliminary sketch. *Charles Macklin as Shylock* (cat. 29) and *Queen Charlotte with her Brothers* (cat. 39) possess relatively bold and discreet brown outlines, while in other paintings the outline contours are extremely thin and were apparently integrated into upper paint layers while still wet.[11] Zoffany typically began a composition by laying in the background and leaving the locations of the figures in reserve. Thus, whether drawings on paper or loose chalk sketches on canvas assisted the process, the figures' positions were only loosely pre-determined from the outset. Even so, there is little evidence of underdrawing in Zoffany's portrait subjects on the prepared canvas, although lines associated with perspective and architectural forms have been observed in several paintings. *The Gore Family* (cat. 56), *The Tribuna* (cat. 53), and *Three Daughters of the John, Third Earl of Bute* (cat. 65), for example, contain sparse, black carbon-containing guidelines for elements that were more difficult to place in space.[12] In his *Self-Portrait with Daughter Maria Theresa, James Cervetto and Jacobbe Cervetto* (fig. 31) Zoffany stands before a canvas holding his palette and brushes in one hand and a porte-crayon in the other. Affixed in the porte-crayon are two pieces of chalk, red at one end and white at the other. No solid forms are visible on the depicted canvas but it is clear that painting has commenced. Soft gradations of blue interrupted by scumbled brushstrokes of white and pink denote the beginnings of a sky, but no trace can be seen of a red or white chalk sketch, as the drawing tool would suggest. The lack of underdrawing beneath Zoffany's figures suggests that they may have been sketched elsewhere, probably on paper. Similarities in the position and expressions of some of his recurring subjects, such as *Queen Charlotte with her Brothers* (cat. 39) and *George Nassau, Third Earl Cowper* (cat. 54), also support the probability of reused life sketches.

In paintings where Zoffany did not complicate the paint layer structure with reworking, he painted flesh tones and costumes in no more than three paint layers on top of the

preparatory white or off-white ground. He blocked in clothing with a thin toning or 'dead colour', typically an opaque mid-tone that was worked up wet-in-wet simultaneously with the flesh tones and background. This is evidenced by the intermingling of layers along the figures' contours where adjacent paint layers overlap and blend. Flesh tones were applied thinly over the light ground colour, which was invariably integrated as a mid-tone or highlight as necessary. Unblended licks of pearly highlights lend vitality to the figures' expressions, and the use of pure vermilion for the deeper shadows of the face is a technique reminiscent of both Rubens and Zoffany's former tutor, Anton Raphael Mengs (fig. 157a). Even so, despite the *sprezzatura* with which Zoffany laid paint to canvas, the proliferation of abandoned forms concealed just beneath the paint layer

Figure 157a
Macro-photo detail (10× magnification) of Charlotte Drummond in *The Drummond Family* (cat. 69) illustrating the dabs of vibrant red paint on her eyes, nose and mouth.

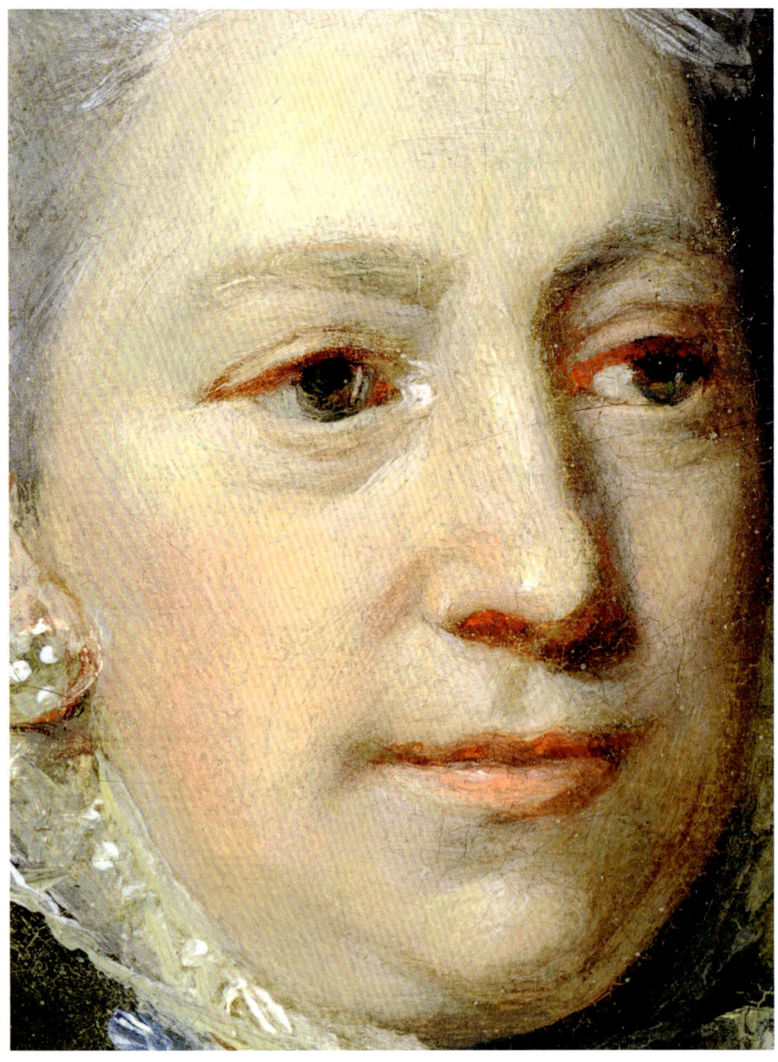

suggests a more complex process. Most changes relate to the position of figures and probably developed over the course of multiple portrait sittings.[13] *Mr and Mrs Dalton and their Niece Mary Deheulle*, 1765–8 (cat. 67), for example, underwent much upheaval before the figures were finally installed in their present positions. X-ray images (see fig. 190) reveal additional portraits of both Mr and Mrs Dalton hovering above the table, as well as significant changes to the layout and decor of the room.

The addition and deletion of figures from Zoffany's *Tribuna*, commented on wryly by contemporaries such as Horace Mann, have been confirmed by x-ray and infra-red documentation.[14] Indeed, Zoffany's reluctance to commit a likeness to canvas did not even preclude his own portrait. Technical studies of *The Tribuna* (cat. 53) and the *Academicians of the Royal Academy* (cat. 44) by conservators at the Royal Collection have shown that in both cases Zoffany added his self-portrait at a fairly late stage, on top of already completed paint passages. The constraints of aesthetics or politics may have caused him to hesitate before selecting his own position in the composition, although in the case of the *Academicians* his academic status ensured his inclusion, albeit slightly removed from his peers and directing his gaze towards the viewer. This ambivalence is equally evident in the unfinished *Self-Portrait with the Artist's Family* (cat. 111). Even this intimate, informal family portrait is a repository of disembodied and rubbed-out forms, as Zoffany's own foot appears to crash through the canvas on the easel before him.

To some extent Zoffany's extensively reworked canvases are as representative of his painting process as his less altered compositions, revealing his inclination to improvise and modify, his disregard of studio time, and not to mention the strains imposed on the patience of his patrons. In terms of time and materials, *The Drummond Family* (fig. 157) is, however, entirely on another level: a family portrait literally cut into pieces by the artist in order to achieve its successful completion. The story of its turbulent and time-consuming production touches on many of the technical issues discussed above as well as presenting some new ones. Recent conservation treatment of *The Drummond Family* at the Yale Center for British Art has provided an opportunity to undertake a close study of the painting's execution and condition history. Analytical methods including x-ray and infra-red photography, examination of paint cross-sections and pigment identification were used to establish how the painting compares technically to other works in Zoffany's oeuvre. While the materials and handling evident in *The Drummond Family* share many similarities with other works by Zoffany, certain aspects of its conception stand out as highly individual and unsystematic. Radical changes have occurred across the painting to the canvas support and the paint layers. The layering of paint in these reworked areas is complex, indicating multiple revisions, as is the rationale behind Zoffany's alteration to the family group.

The Drummond Family is a quintessential eighteenth-century dynastic family conversation piece. It encompasses octogenarian

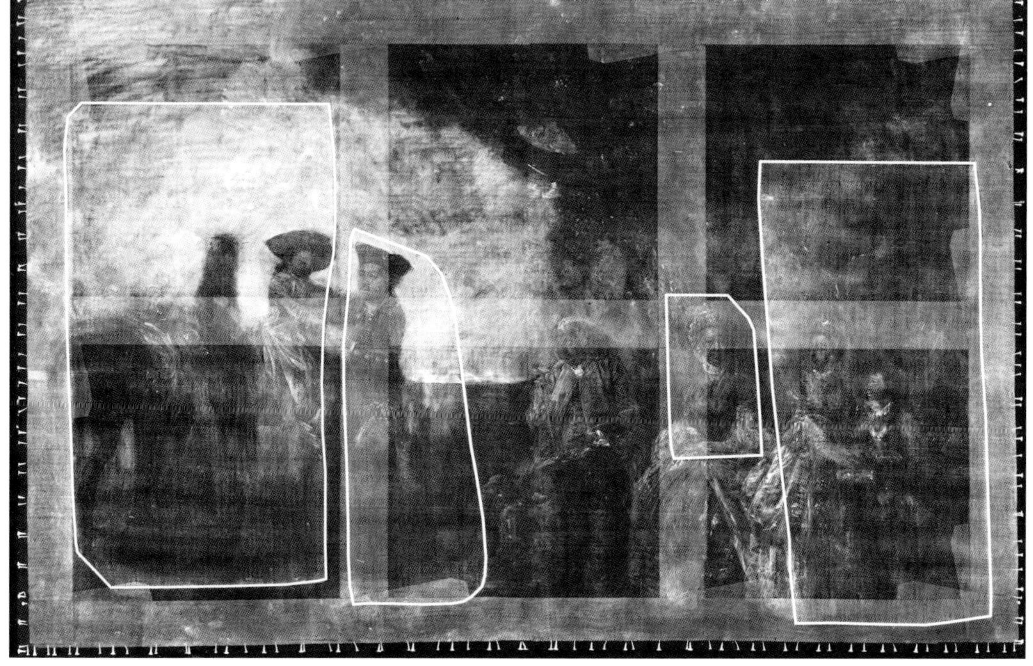

Figure 158
Overall X-ray image of *The Drummond Family* (cat. 69). White lines indicate the positions and shapes of the four canvas inserts.

Figure 159
X-ray detail of the left side of *The Drummond Family* (cat. 69) revealing the overpainted, earlier versions of the two John Drummonds. Visible along the left edge of the furthest left canvas insert is an independent pattern of 'cusping', the scallop shape that develops along the edges of a canvas when it is first stretched. That canvas piece evidently came from the very left edge of the previous composition.

and infant child, patriarch and groom, each positioned with personal effects that subtly allude to subtexts of family history. Three generations of Drummonds are depicted beneath a large oak in the grounds of Stanmore, the family's estate in Middlesex: a view of Harrow is visible in the distance. From left to right, a groom in Drummond livery assists the younger son John off his horse; John holds the hand of his father John Drummond senior, who stands with his back towards his elder daughter Jane. Andrew Drummond, founder of Drummonds Bank of Charing Cross, is seated beside his daughter-in-law Charlotte (*née* Beauclerk), next to whom stand Charlotte and John's younger daughter, also named Charlotte, and their elder son George.

To the naked eye the painting surface appears relatively undisturbed, yet the presence of four canvas inserts prompts questions about why the picture underwent such major reconstruction (fig. 158). Infra-red and x-ray imaging reveal that the seemingly arbitrary cuts around the front legs of the grey horse relate to a figure that lies beneath the upper paint layer, indicating that much of the composition was painted after the canvas had been cut and reassembled (figs. 159 and 160). In other words, elements of a previous composition had been physically cut out and rearranged into new positions and then completely obscured with paint, comprising in some passages no fewer than eight distinct paint layers. The amount of painting that took place after the canvas's refashioning clearly confirms Zoffany as the originator of its patchwork construction. The actual evolution of the work was as follows: four sections cut from the original composition were placed like pieces of a puzzle into a new canvas that had windows made to receive them. This canvas was then glue-lined onto another piece of canvas for support. The canvas used to create the new background for the cut-out figures is similar but slightly finer in thread count than the original canvas. And, whereas the original canvas was prepared with Zoffany's standard double lead white ground, the canvas added to the background bears a single white ground containing sparse pigment particles. This detail suggests that Zoffany may have sourced the second canvas hastily and perhaps prepared it in his own studio.

An obstacle to explaining the rationale of the construction of *The Drummond Family*, as set out here, is that the time saved by reusing four sections of canvas from a previously abandoned composition could hardly be worth the labour of reassembling the painting like a collage and then repainting the surrounding

Figure 160
Digital reconstruction of *The Drummond Family* (cat. 69) representing the positions of the canvas pieces cut from an earlier composition and placed into a newly prepared canvas. The canvas sections salvaged from the earlier painting are shown here in x-ray to illustrate what each piece contained before Zoffany began repainting.

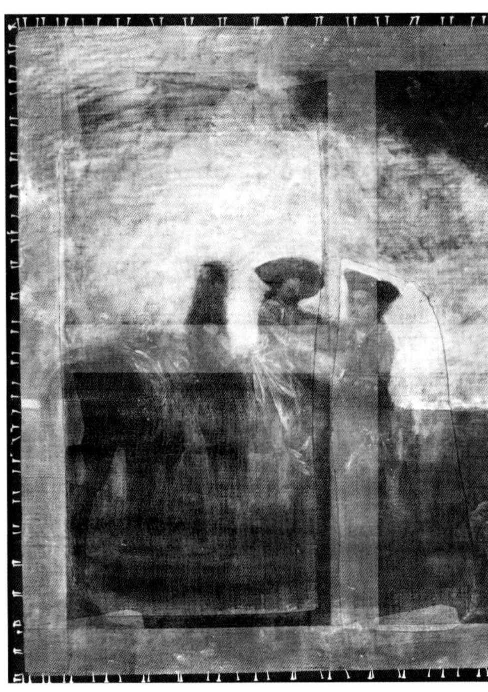

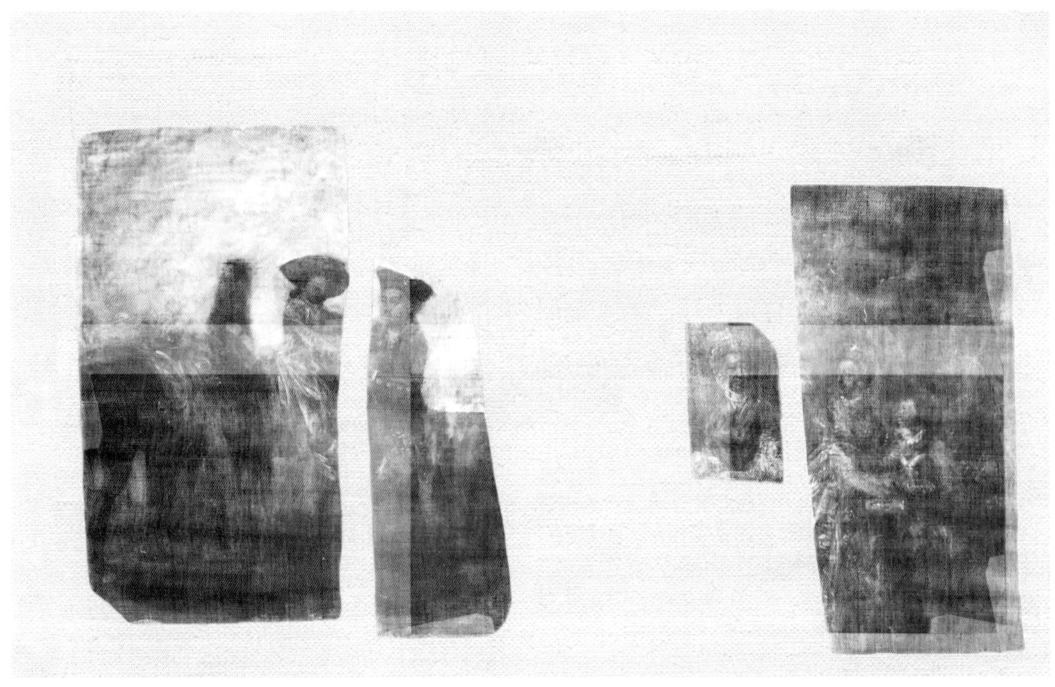

blank canvas. This is especially true if the salvaged elements were then obliterated by repainting. The portrait of Jane, for example, was certainly added after the reconstruction, as she is painted directly over the canvas insert containing the original portrait of her father (fig. 161). The portrait of young John Drummond on horseback, visible only in x-ray, was also overpainted. Both he and the groom were necessarily shifted to the left, along with John Drummond senior.

Zoffany's rearrangement of the left side of the painting was not easily realized. Aside from the two overpainted John Drummonds, senior and junior, there is an additional horse facing left and another figure in red, both overpainted. The now obscured figure in red was painted directly on top of the portrait of John Drummond senior that is visible in the x-ray. He does not reach up to young John Drummond but stands more passively, loosely gripping a cane. This is probably the second of three attempts Zoffany made at placing John Drummond senior in the composition.[15] Zoffany's predicament becomes somewhat clearer when one considers the central position of Andrew Drummond, who faces his much-repainted family members: if the group at the left had not been altered, then Andrew Drummond's gaze would have been level with the wrong side of young John's horse. The question remaining is why the figure of Andrew Drummond was not simply moved.

There is no extant documentation relating to this painting. The sequence of events surrounding the commission must therefore be divined from the work itself. It is dated to 1769, the year of Andrew Drummond's death, and it is highly relevant that he and his spaniel are the only subjects that were neither cut out nor reworked. Zoffany had established a professional relationship with the Drummonds from at least 1765, when he began banking with them.[16] Around that time he painted a full-length portrait of Andrew Drummond in which the latter appears in the same pose, holding his Malacca walking stick, snuff box and hat (fig. 162). This earlier portrait must have been the source for Andrew Drummond's likeness in *The Drummond Family*, and the fact that he died in 1769 would have been an additional reason to replicate it.

Whether or not Andrew Drummond was originally intended to be in the present painting, his posthumous inclusion is the most likely cause for its dramatic reworking. Zoffany may have hoped to avoid scheduling new sittings with the Drummonds by recycling portraits from the previous canvas, but his solution was obviously not a time-saver. An x-radiograph of George Drummond attests to this: beneath the paint layer is a considerably shorter, younger George, also holding a bird's nest (fig. 163). Two or three years may have elapsed between the family's first sittings with Zoffany and the painting's completion. For the older Drummonds this delay would not have made a sufficient impact on their appearance to justify repainting. For the children, however, and especially the young heir of Stanmore, a contemporary

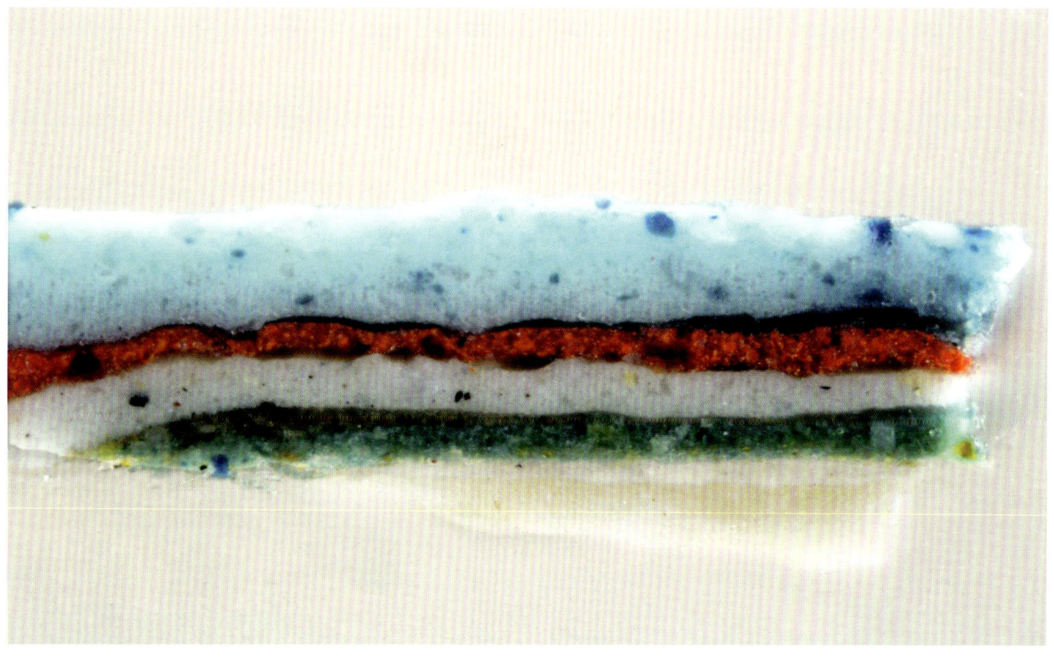

Figure 161
Cross-section from the skirts of Jane Diana in *The Drummond Family* (100x magnification). Five distinct paint layers are visible above the double white ground, beginning with two layers of green paint related to landscape, a relatively thick layer of white probably added to obliterate the landscape, followed by a layer of vibrant red from the coat of over-painted John Drummond senior and, finally, a thick layer of blue for Jane's skirt. The costly pigment, natural ultramarine blue, was found in both the lower-most paint layers of landscape and on Jane's blue riding habit, signifying how little the economy of materials influenced Zoffany's palette choice. Pigments were identified using scanning electron microscope/ energy dispersive x-ray analysis.

likeness would surely have been imperative. *The Drummond Family* is Zoffany's last-known painting commissioned by the Drummonds, although their banking relationship continued until the artist's death.[17] Since there is no evidence of the family's reaction to the portrait, their satisfaction with the final composition must be inferred by its presence in their collection until it was purchased by Paul Mellon in 1962.[18] Despite its complex technical history, the condition and overall appearance of *The Drummond Family* are impressive. The only indications of the picture's complex construction visible to the eye are the slight protrusion of the canvas seams and the faint shadows of overpainted figures and horses, which can be attributed to the natural ageing and increased transparency of the paint layers above them.

The study of Zoffany's painting practice based on technical examination and visual observation of his works has yielded evidence of a technically proficient, confident painter with a propensity for impatient and frequent reworking. The degree to which Zoffany manipulated his paintings to achieve an almost seamless product underscores his deep understanding of painting materials – their limitations as well as their potential – and contributes ultimately to our understanding of his success in the notoriously competitive market for portraiture in Georgian England.

Figure 162
Portrait of Andrew Drummond, 1765–6,
oil on canvas, 225 × 175 cm (88½ × 69 in).
The Royal Bank of Scotland

Figure 163
X-ray detail of George Drummond from
The Drummond Family (cat. 69) showing an
underlying, younger version of George.

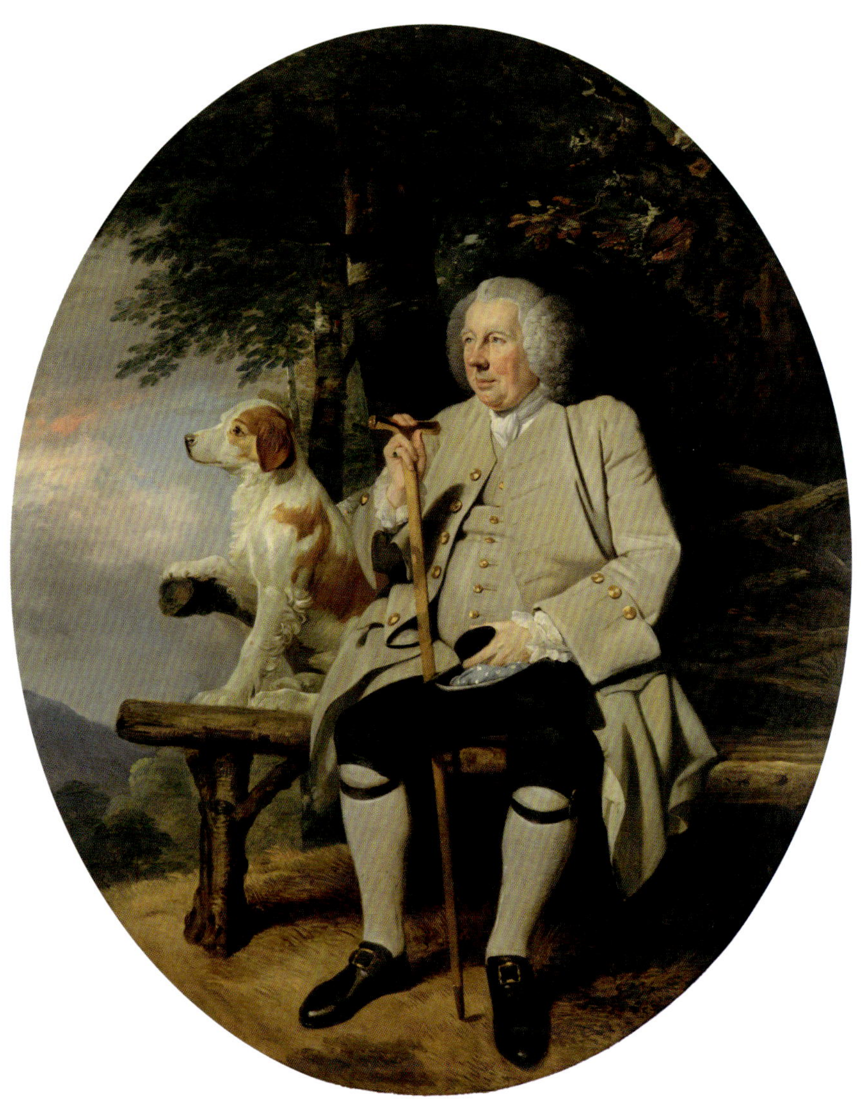

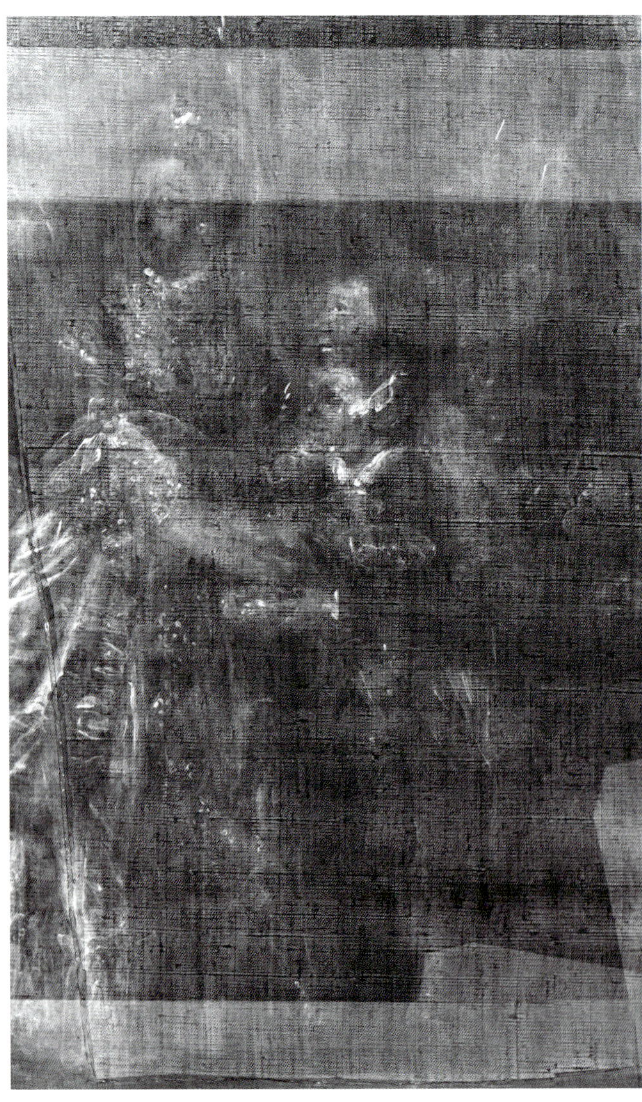

Notes

1. See Webster 2011, 643–4.

2. I am greatly indebted to the painting conservation departments at Tate Britain, London; the Royal Collection, Windsor; the Hamilton Kerr Institute, University of Cambridge; the Walker Art Gallery, Liverpool; and the Wadsworth Athenaeum Museum of Art, Hartford, Connecticut; and in particular to Rica Jones, Helen Brett, Rupert Featherstone, Lucia Scalisi, David Crombie and Tabitha Teuma for sharing their time, research and documentation.

3. Zoffany's canvases have a comparable thread count in the vicinity of 36 × 36 threads per square inch (or around 14 × 14 square cm). Specific thread counts and Zoffany's canvas weaves have been recorded in conservation documents at Tate Britain, the Yale Center for British Art and the Hamilton Kerr Institute. The canvas weights of other paintings, which were not available in records or for precise on-site calculation, were judged by visual comparison.

4. The canvas used for the Gore family was probably purchased in Italy. It was virtually trowelled over with several layers of ground in order to obscure its texture, the spatula marks being visible in x-ray. Based on x-ray and cross-section analysis, it is probable that Zoffany recycled a canvas that had some sort of painting on it for this commission. Another of the few documented examples of Zoffany recycling his canvases is the full-length portrait of Mrs Oswald of 1763–4 in the National Gallery, London (cat. 66). See Egerton 1998, 350–54.

5. These are: 30 × 25, 36 × 28 and 50 × 40 in/ 76.2 × 63.5, 91.4 × 71.1 and 127 × 101.6 cm, respectively.

6. It is unclear whether the canvas was prepared with ground layers before Zoffany received it. Manners and Williamson (1920, 16) imply that it was, based on their conviction that the painter Charles Stewart completed the landscape before passing the painting on to Zoffany.

7. See the unpublished examination report T.2217 (12 July 1978), Department of Painting Conservation, Tate; *The Tate Gallery 1976–8: Illustrated Catalogue of Acquisitions*, London, 1979, 38.

8. This layer structure has been observed in a number of Zoffany's works at Tate, including the portrait of Stephen Rimbault (fig. 4), *Charles Macklin as Shylock* (cat. 29), *The Bradshaw Family* (fig. 19) and *The Blair Family* (cat. 92). The same preparation has been found on *The Drummond Family* (cat. 69), *The Gore Family* (cat. 56) and *James Graham* (cat. 89). The layer of animal glue was identified using an acid fuchsin staining test

as well as microscopic examination of paint cross-sections with ultra violet light. The use of a double ground separated by a thin size layer is not unique to Zoffany. Hogarth employed a similar preparation, though the oil layers were usually tinted a light grey hue rather than white. See Rica Jones, 'The Artist's Training and Techniques', in Elizabeth Einberg and Rica Jones, *Manners & Morals: Hogarth and British Painting 1700–1760*, London, 1987, 24; and S. Hackney, R. Jones and J. Townsend, eds., *Paint and Purpose: A Study of Technique in British Art*, London, 1999, 48.

9. This list of pigments is based on the analysis of the following paintings: *The Drummond Family*; *The Gore Family*; *David Garrick and his Wife before the Monument to Shakespeare* (Yale Center for British Art); *Three Daughters of John, Third Earl of Bute*; *Stephen Rimbault*; *The Bradshaw Family*; *Charles Macklin as Shylock*; *Colonel Mordaunt's Cock Match*; and *The Blair Family* (Tate); and analysis undertaken at the Hamilton Kerr Institute on *The Woodley Family* (National Trust, Kingston Lacy). It is interesting to note that the materials used for Tate's version of the *Cock Match*, *The Blair Family* and *James Graham*, all of which were evidently completed in India, show no deviations from those completed in England or Italy. Relatively little medium analysis has been conducted on Zoffany's paintings, but analysis of the *Cock Match* confirms the medium as linseed oil (Tom Learner, Joyce H. Townsend and Rica Jones, unpublished analytical report T06856, Department of Painting Conservation, Tate, January 1995).

10. The palette held by Zoffany in his *Self-Portrait with Daughter Maria Theresa, James Cervetto and Jacobbe Cervetto* was examined using a handheld X-ray fluorescence spectrometer and stereo microscope at the Yale Center for British Art. The contents of his palettes in the Cortona portrait, *The Tribuna* and *The Academicians* were judged by visual comparison to the YCBA self-portrait and textual sources on eighteenth-century palette layout. See Thomas Bardwell, *The Practice of Painting and Perspective Made Easy …*, London, 1756, 7–15; F. Schmid, 'Some observations on Artists' Palettes', *Art Bulletin*, vol. 40, no. 4 (Dec. 1958), 334–6; and F. Schmid, 'The Painter's implements in Eighteenth Century Art', *Burlington Magazine*, vol. 108, no. 763 (Oct. 1966), 519–21.

11. As an unfinished canvas, *Charles Macklin as Shylock* offers great insight into the initial stages of Zoffany's painting process. An in-depth study of this painting is presently being conducted by Helen Brett of Tate.

12. On Zoffany's use of sketches, see also Webster 2011, 12, 22.

13. Zoffany's portraits could involve as many as nine sittings, as was the case with Matilda

Cleveland-Shore. The majority of portraits, aside from the royal family, took place in Zoffany's own studio. One recorded exception was Mrs Prowse, whom Zoffany visited at her home in Northamptonshire for her portrait in *The Sharp Family*. See Webster 2011, 392–3; John Kerslake, 'A Note on Zoffany's *Sharp Family*', *Burlington Magazine*, vol. 120, no. 908 (Nov. 1978), 752–4.

14. Lewis 1937–83, vol. 7, 519, Horace Mann to Horace Walpole, 28 Sept. 1773; vol. 8, 33–4, Horace Mann to Horace Walpole, 23 Aug. 1774; vol. 8, 539, Horace Mann to Horace Walpole, 10 Dec. 1779. X-radiography and infra-red documentation were generously shared by the Royal Collection. See also Millar 1966.

15. Significantly, this early configuration of figures and horses bears a close resemblance to the left portion of *The Family of Sir William Young*, *c*.1770 (fig. 107). I am grateful to Titus Kapher for drawing my attention to the *Young Family* portrait and to the Walker Art Gallery's department of painting conservation for sharing information on the painting.

16. On 21 November 1766 John Drummond paid £136 10s for a large portrait of his father, Andrew Drummond (Drummond's Bank records, Royal Bank of Scotland Archive). Zoffany certainly visited Stanmore, but it is unclear whether he did so before or after Andrew Drummond's death.

17. Drummond's bank records reveal the Zoffany maintained a modest balance, which fluctuated between £100 and £200 until his return from India to London in 1780, when the balance leaped from £109 37s to £3,747 10s. Following her husband's death, Mary Zoffany was granted final probate on 24 January 1811: Drummond's Bank records, Royal Bank of Scotland Archive. I am very grateful to Philip Winterbottom, Archives Manager, and his colleagues at the RBS archive for their assistance in viewing Zoffany's portrait of Andrew Drummond and in navigating the Drummond Bank records at the RBS archive, Edinburgh.

18. Another portrait of Andrew Drummond attributed to Zoffany, almost identical to that at Drummonds Bank with the exception of its rectangular format, remains with the family today. Interestingly, dozens of painting left the Drummond estate at Stanmore in a Christie & Manson sale of 1840, including several Lelys and Knellers. No Zoffany paintings were described in the sale. 'English portraits', *Gentleman's Magazine* (ed. John Mitford), August 1840, 179–80.

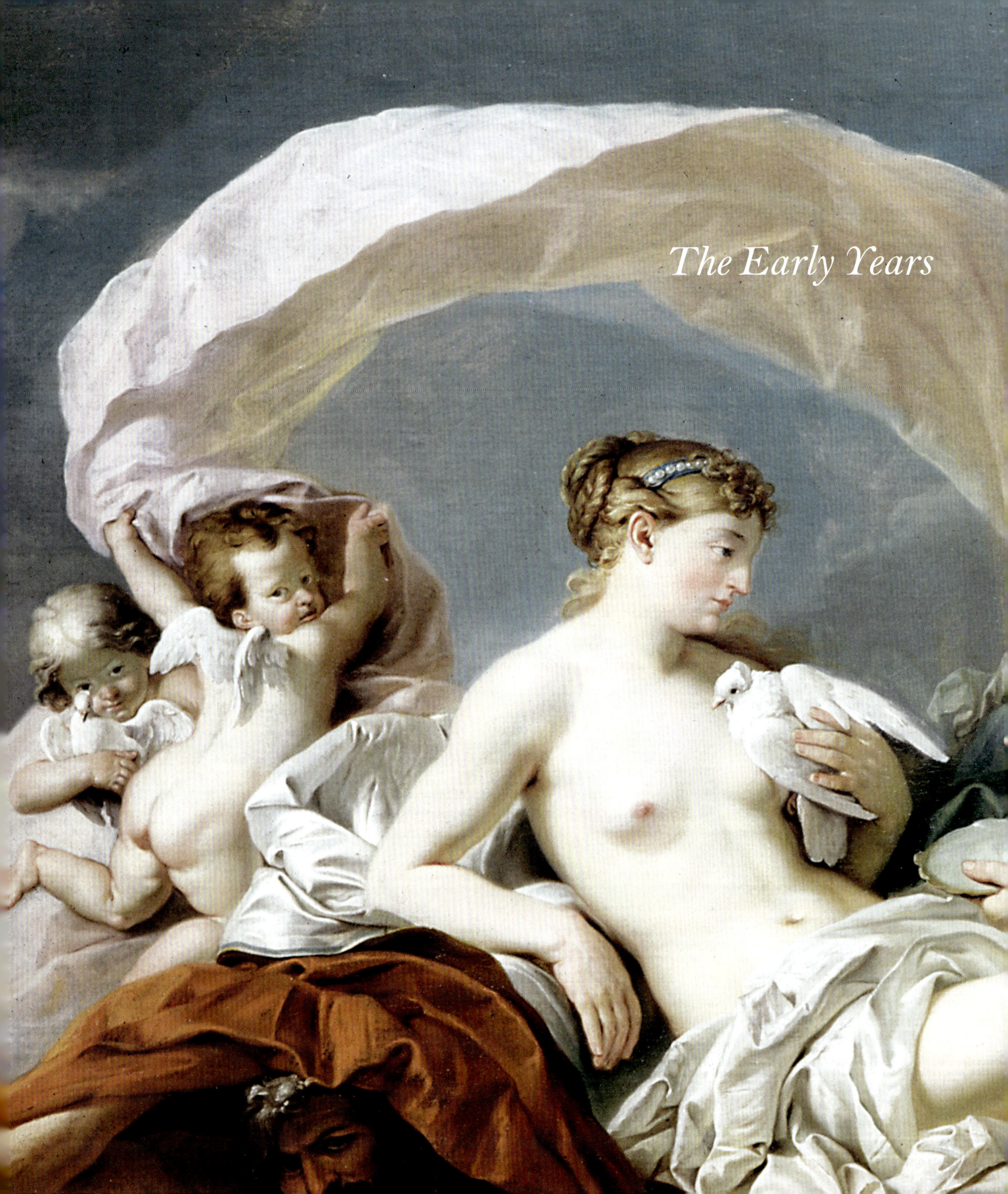
The Early Years

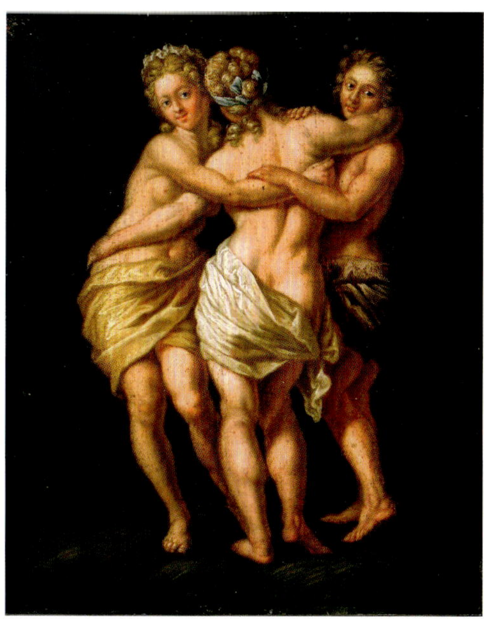

1

Three Graces
*c.*1749–50

Oil on panel, 25 × 19.8 cm (9⅞ × 7¾ in)
Inscribed in a later hand on the reverse: 'Zofani f.'
Museen der Stadt, Regensburg

Provenance: Dr Carl Reichardt, Neu-Ulm

Selected references: Webster 1976, 21, no.1; Treadwell
2009, 16–17; Webster 2011, 18–19

If, as has been suggested, this modest picture dates
from around 1749–50, it must count as Zoffany's
earliest-known work, made when he was in his mid-
to late teens.[1] At that time Zoffany had recently
moved with his family to Regensburg, where he
was placed under the tutelage of the history and
portrait painter Martin Speer, a friend of the
family. Speer was by that time an experienced
and well-travelled artist. Trained at the Vienna
Academy, Speer had visited Italy, France, England
and Bohemia, with further visits to Venice and
Naples, where he was influenced by Francesco
Solimena. The subject of the present picture, the
Three Graces, may have been suggested to Zoffany
by Speer as a kind of academic exercise, whereby
he could demonstrate his knowledge of figure
painting and anatomy. In choosing a subject related
since antiquity to sculpture, Zoffany may also have
been influenced by the Regensburg sculptor, Simon
Sorg, who along with Speer was closely associated
with the Zoffany family at the time.

In Greek mythology the Three Graces were
Aglaea (Splendour), Euphrosyne (Mirth), and
Thalia (Cheerfulness), traditionally identified
as daughters of Zeus and the Titan goddess,
Eurynome. Associated with festivals, the Graces
became objects of sacrifice and votive offering.
Since antiquity they have invariably been
represented nude or semi-naked in an act of
embrace, often with the central figure facing away
from the viewer and the flanking figures frontal
or side facing as in Zoffany's composition, a device
that in painting and sculpture allows the figure
to be viewed in the round. In painting the Graces,
Zoffany, as suggested by the two visible faces,
may have relied on the same model. However,
the pronounced musculature of the figures also
indicates that at this stage in his career Zoffany
may not have been working directly from the living
model but was inspired principally by secondary
sources, either paintings or prints, presumably
provided by Speer. Zoffany may, for instance, have
been influenced by established images of the female
figure, such as Raphael's celebrated *Galatea* from
the Villa Farnesina, Rome, whose pose is echoed
in the figure to the left. Even so, the tightly clasped
embrace that closely binds the three figures in
Zoffany's painting, and provides an added erotic
frisson, would appear to be his own invention.
The warm painting of the flesh tones and the crisp
handling of detail, notably in the coiffure and the
blue hair ribbon of the central figure, are also
characteristic of his own distinctive style as it
emerges at this early stage in his career.

MP

1. Webster 2011, 18.

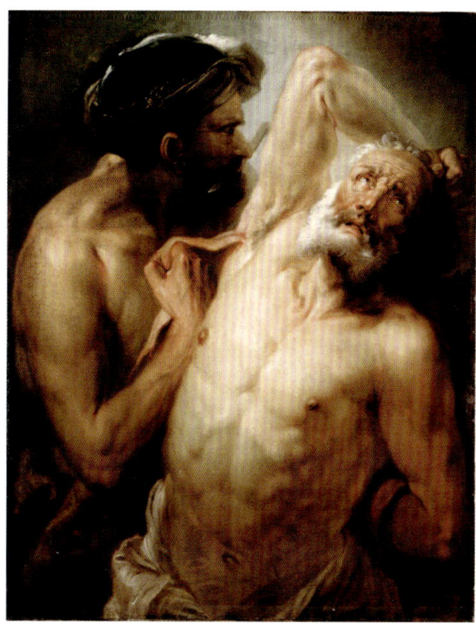

2

Martyrdom of St Bartholomew
1753

Oil on canvas, 104 × 81 cm (41 × 31⅞ in)
Signed and dated: 'Zauffaly inv. 175[?]'
Museen der Stadt, Regensburg

Provenance: Georg Schäfer; Altes Schloss Obbach,
Euerbach

Selected references: Webster 1976, 17; Treadwell
2009, 25–7, 114; Webster 2011, 19–20

By the mid-eighteenth century the martyrdom
of St Bartholomew was a well-established subject,
commemorating the gruesome death of the
eponymous saint, who, while spreading the gospel
in Armenia, was flayed alive before being crucified
upside down. This is Zoffany's first-known picture
as a mature artist, painted possibly in 1753, after he
had been studying in Rome for some three years.
It reveals both his strengths and weaknesses at this
early period. In 1750 Zoffany had commenced his
studies under Agostino Masucci. The present
picture is not, however, reminiscent of Masucci
but rather looks back to the traditions of
seventeenth-century Baroque art, where muscular
figures are depicted at close quarters in intense and
contorted poses, often involving extreme emotion,
physical pain and graphic violence. Zoffany's
picture may however have been painted in
Regensburg during a brief break from his Roman
studies. This is suggested by the existence of an
early copy in the Alte Kapelle, Regensburg
(inscribed on the reverse 'Zaufalli Pinxit 1753'), and
an early provenance that links it to the collection of
the Bishop of Worms, who from 1763 to 1768 was
Zoffany's patron. The subject may also have had a
particular significance for Zoffany, as he had been
baptized in the cathedral of St Bartholomew in
Frankfurt, and had also during his first sojourn in

Rome apparently lodged on the Isola Tiberina opposite the church of San Bartolommeo. The inventory of the books and pictures of Zoffany's mother, made after her death in 1779, lists a picture of the Martyrdom of St Bartholomew, although it is not known whether it was related to the present work.[1]

The comparative weakness of the figure of St Bartholomew's assailant is countered by the proficient handling of the saint's expressive countenance and muscular torso, which is modelled on the celebrated classical statue known as the *Barberini Faun* (fig. 164).[2] He may have also have adopted motifs from Mattia Preti's *Martyrdom of St Bartholomew*: the knife clasped between the teeth of the swarthy assailant and his clenched fist. Preti's picture was then in the celebrated Picture Gallery at Dresden. Although it is unlikely that Zoffany ever saw the original painting, in 1753, the probable date of Zoffany's painting, the German engraver Karl Ludwig Wust made a large print of Preti's picture as part of the first volume of the *Recueil d'estampes d'après les plus célèbres tableaux de la Galerie Royale de Dresden*, a work that would have been of intense interest to the young Zoffany.

MP

1. See Webster 2011, 19.
2. Penelope Treadwell has suggested that Zoffany was influenced by Pompeo Batoni's *Martyrdom of St Bartholomew* (Museo Nazionale di Villa Guinigi, Lucca), which he had painted for the church of San Ponziano, Lucca, in 1749. Treadwell notes that Zoffany could have seen the painting during his journey to Rome in 1750. However, while there are certain generic similarities between Batoni's and Zoffany's paintings of the subject, there is no evidence that Zoffany visited Lucca en route to Rome. For Batoni's *Martyrdom of St Bartholomew*, see Liliana Barroero and Fernando Mazzocca, *Pompeo Batoni 1708–1787. L'Europa delle Corti e il Grand Tour*, Lucca, 2008, 248–9, no. 30.

3

David with the Head of Goliath
1756

Oil on canvas, 92.2 × 74.7 cm (36¼ × 29⅜ in)
Inscribed in brown and yellow paint (diagonally): '1756 I: Zauffalÿ inv et pinx'
National Gallery of Victoria, Melbourne; purchased with assistance of the Isabella Mary Curnick Bequest and The Art Foundation of Victoria, 1994 (ICI-1994)

Provenance: Dessins et tableaux anciens (sale catalogue), Groupe Gersaint, Pavilion Joséphine, Strasbourg, 17 Nov. 1989, no. 265 (repr.), as by Anton Raphael Mengs; purchased by Richard L. Feigen and Co., New York, from whom purchased by the National Gallery of Victoria

Selected references: Pressly 1987, 88–101; Pressly 1995, 49–55; Watson 1995, 7–14; Ingamells 2004, 499; Treadwell 2009, 36–7, 44; Webster 2011, 28–9

This compelling image was completely unknown within Zoffany's oeuvre until it emerged at auction in the late 1980s. At the time it was attributed to Anton Raphael Mengs. However, during cleaning of the picture in New York, prior to its acquisition by the National Gallery of Victoria, Zoffany's signature and the date 1756 were discovered on the belt of David. Confirmation of Zoffany's authorship and its Roman provenance has led to further speculation on underlying pictorial references in the picture and its status as a possible allegorical self-portrait.

The subject of David with the head of Goliath (Samuel 17: 1–54) had been common in painting and sculpture since the Renaissance, featuring in celebrated works by Donatello, Giorgione and Caravaggio, and more recently by Bernini, Guido Reni and Guercino. Zoffany's composition may have been influenced quite specifically by a painting of David and Goliath attributed to the Flemish artist Michele Desubleo (fig. 165), which may have been in a Roman collection during the 1750s.[1]

According to William Pressly, the first scholar to write in depth about the present painting, the figure of David was a thinly veiled self-portrait of the twenty-three-year-old artist, in which Zoffany presented 'a highly personal restatement of a traditional theme that testifies to his maturing abilities'.[2] As Pressly observes, Zoffany's polished, classicizing composition is in the vein of the late Baroque, as exemplified by his master, Mengs, and Pompeo Batoni, who was also a dominant figure in Rome at the time. The heroic nudity and violent subject matter are also reminiscent of Zoffany's own earlier biblical subject, *Martyrdom*

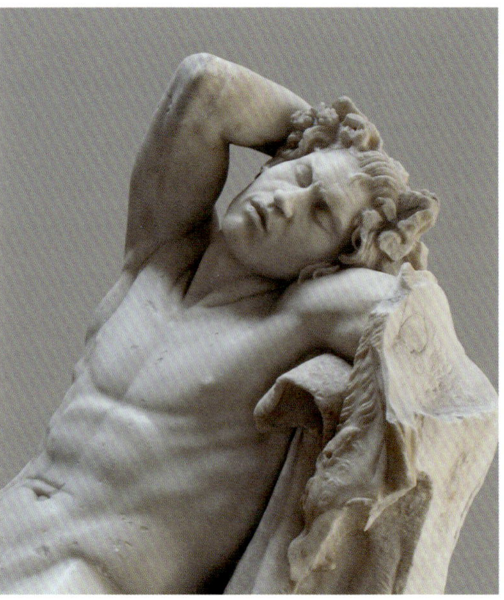

Figure 164
Barberini Faun, (detail),
c. 220 BC, marble, 215 cm (84½ in).
Glyptothek, Munich

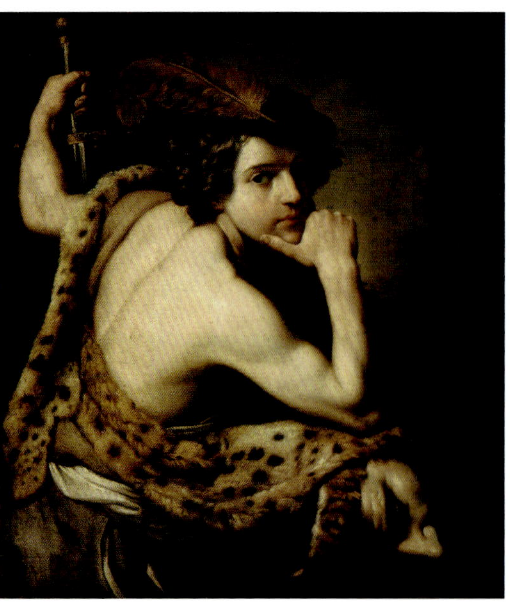

Figure 165
Michele Desubleo, *David with the Head of Goliath*, date unknown, oil on canvas, 98.5 × 84.4 cm (38¾ × 33¼ in). Museum of Fine Arts, Budapest

of St Bartholomew (cat. 2), of three years earlier. And, as Mary Webster observes, while it was painted in Italy, 'the folds of the drapery have a Germanic smoothness and neatness' that suggest the residual influence of Zoffany's early master, Martin Speer.[3]

The identification of the figure of David as a self-portrait, according to Pressly, may be bound up with Zoffany's artistic identity, as the white stone in David's hand 'doubles as artist's chalk and the staff as a mahl-stick'.[4] In the persona of David, Zoffany takes on the old order with his youthful virtuosity, while the homoerotic aspects of the painting, typified by the 'phallic' sling dangling close to Goliath's open mouth is characteristic of the artist's 'puckish', not to say obscene, wit. It has also been observed elsewhere that the stone in David's hand is, on closer inspection, the glans of a marble phallus from an antique statue, glans referring both to the glans penis and the lead or ceramic projectile used in a sling.[5] Certainly, the emphasis in the original Bible story on Goliath as the 'uncircumcised Philistine' makes reference to sexual as well as racial difference. Thus, the manner in which the severed head of Goliath rolls its eye in the direction of the stone glans may have a specific significance in Zoffany's idiosyncratic and punning iconography.

While certain aspects of Pressly's argument are persuasive, the identification of David as a self-portrait of Zoffany is questionable, since the likeness is not convincing, unless Zoffany was deliberately altering – even improving – his own physiognomy and changing his eye colour.[6] As Michael Watson has observed, a more convincing likeness, and one that also allows for an element of allegorical portraiture, is with Zoffany's master, Anton Raphael Mengs. In a self-portrait by Mengs aged about thirty, made during the late 1750s (Duke of Alba collection), Watson notes an 'uncanny' resemblance between Mengs's face and that of David. If an idealized Mengs was Zoffany's model, which is by no means certain, then David with the head of Goliath suggests a close relationship between master and pupil, and the meaning of the subject was not a self-congratulatory allusion to Zoffany's own prowess but a tribute to Mengs as the champion of a new wave of classicism.

MP

1. See also Webster 2011, 29, fig. 28, which illustrates a version of the composition at Haddo House, Aberdeenshire, National Trust for Scotland, as attributed to Domenichino. For Desubleo see Contini Alberto, *Michele Desubleo*, Soncino, 2001.
2. Pressly 1995, 49.
3. Webster 2011, 29.
4. Pressly 1995, 52.
5. Watson 1995, 10.
6. As Webster (2011, 29) points out, Zoffany's eyes were grey-brown rather than the grey-blue of David's.

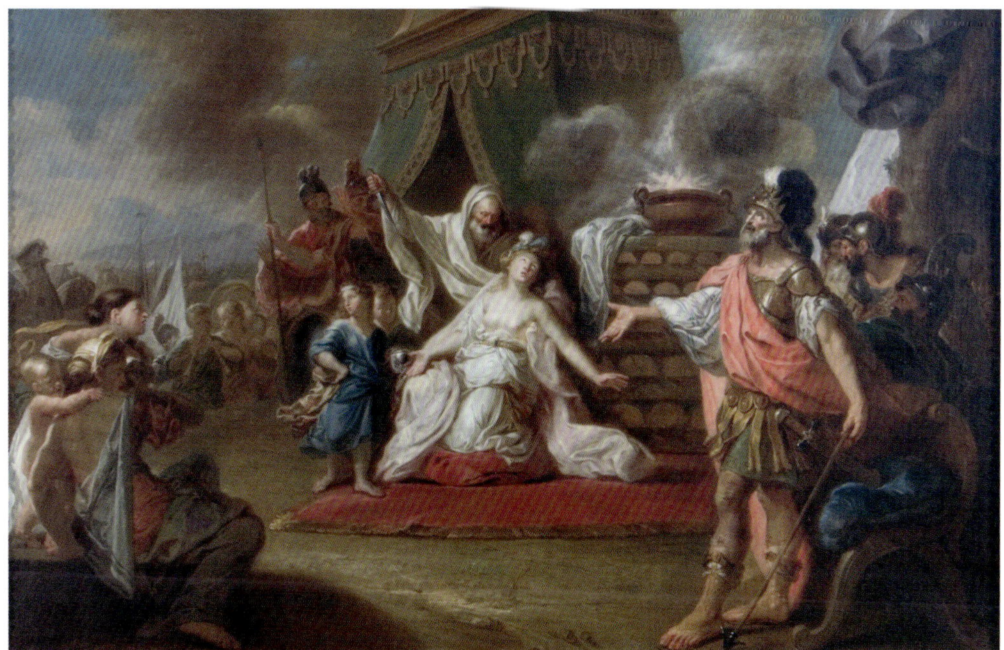

4

Sacrifice of Iphigenia
1758

Oil on canvas, 74 × 110.5 cm (29⅛ × 43½ in)
Signed and dated: 'Zauffi inv. | 1758'
Mittelrhein Museum, Koblenz

Provenance: Professor Dr Engelmann, Vienna, from whom purchased 1962

Selected exhibitions: Bregenz and Vienna 1968, no. 490; National Portrait Gallery 1977, no. 3; *Triumph und Tod des Helden: europäische Historienmalerei von Rubens bis Manet*, Kunsthaus, Zurich, Wallraf-Richartz-Museum, Cologne, Musée des Beaux-Arts, Lyons, 1987–8, no. 105; Munich 2003, no. 150

Selected references: Küster 2003, 204; Treadwell 2009, 40; Webster 2011, 35–7

Signed and dated 1758, this picture was probably made shortly after Zoffany's return from Italy, possibly for a patron in Regensburg. The story of the sacrifice of Iphigenia, popular within the canon of seventeenth- and eighteenth-century history painting, was the subject of the Greek Tragedy, *Iphigenia in Aulis*, by Euripedes, first performed in 405 BC. The episode was also known through its appearance in the epic poem, *De rerum natura* (*On the Nature of Things*), by Lucretius, in which it was used to denounce religious superstition. In the modern period it was also the subject of Racine's play, *Iphigénie*, first performed at the court of Louis XIV in 1674. Given his recent experiences in the cosmopolitan artistic community of Rome and his earlier exposure to German court culture, Zoffany would have been quite familiar with the narrative in its literary and visual expression.

According to the story told by Euripides and by Racine (with slight variations), the Greek fleet, commanded by Agamemnon, weighs anchor at Aulis, from where they are to set sail for Troy. Frustrated by Artemis, who has stilled the wind, Agamemnon is advised by the oracle to placate the goddess by sacrificing his daughter Iphigenia. He persuades his wife Clytemnestra to bring Iphigenia to Aulis under the pretence of marriage to Achilles, who attempts to prevent the slaughter. But Iphigenia offers herself as a patriotic sacrifice. In Zoffany's painting Iphigenia flings out her arms as the high priest, Calchas, prepares to wield the sacrificial knife. Agamemnon raises his eyes to the heavens as he attempts to propitiate Artemis, while to the left Clytemnestra sits in mourning with her young son Orestes.

The violent subject matter, tinged with eroticism, is characteristic of Zoffany's mythological subjects of the 1750s, such as his *Death of Lucretia* (Landesmuseum für Kunst und Kulturgeschichte, Munster), where the bare-breasted heroine – apparently the same model – is subjected to an even more gruesome ordeal.[1] The subject of *Sacrifice of Iphigenia*, by now common throughout Europe, reflects Zoffany's experience of the Baroque in Italy, particularly Venice, which he had visited on his return to Germany. It is also broadly reliant on the traditions of French academic history painting. Zoffany may, for example, have been influenced by Charles Le Brun, whose celebrated *Queens of Persia at the Feet of Alexander* (1661; Versailles) had been engraved by Jean Audran. A more specific influence was *The Anger of Achilles* (*c.*1711; Musée des Beaux-Arts, Tours) by Antoine Coypel.[2]

MP

1. See Webster 2011, 34.
2. Küster 2003, 204.

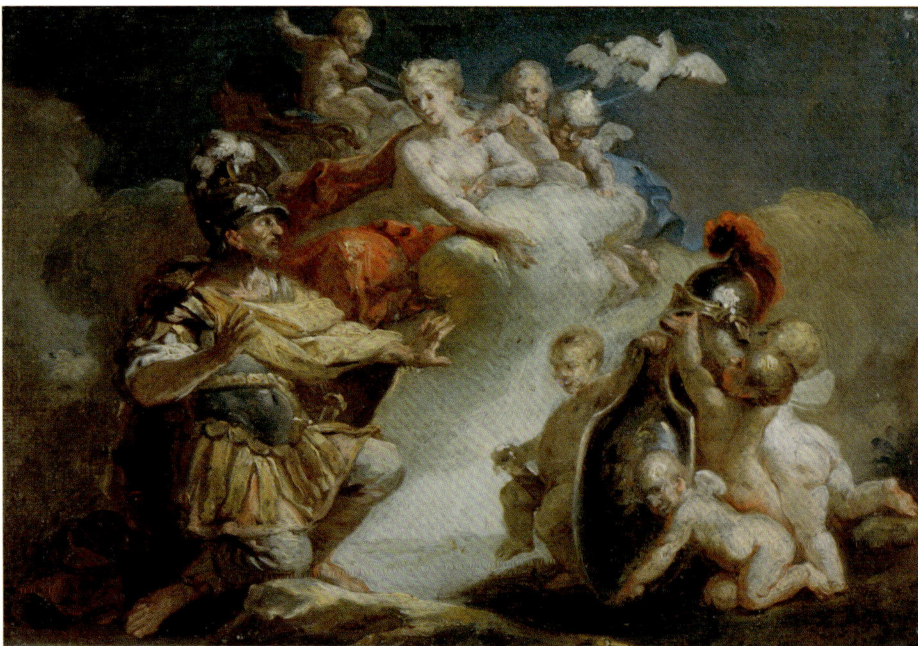

5

Aeneas Receiving Arms from his Mother Venus
1759

Oil on canvas, 27.6 × 37.8 cm (10⅞ × 14⅞ in)
Signed and dated: 'Zauffaly inv | 1759'
Manchester Art Gallery

Provenance: Purchased from Colnaghi, 1966

Selected exhibitions: Bregenz and Vienna 1968,
no. 491, pl. 120; National Portrait Gallery
1977, no. 4

Selected references: Webster 2011, 37–8

Only a small number of Zoffany's compositional
studies for decorative schemes are known,
including the present oil sketch, which reveals his
affiliation to the traditions of Baroque decorative
painting. Whether or not Zoffany ever produced
a finished composition relating to the present oil
sketch, or for whom it was painted, is uncertain.
However, it would appear likely that it relates to
his employment by Johann Philipp, Graf von
Walderdorff, Elector of Trier, at the court of
Ehrenbreitstein. There, Zoffany was commissioned
to paint the saloon and the chapel ceiling, while at
the Elector's palace at Trier, he decorated several
rooms in oils and in fresco, including the ceiling
of the electoral bedroom (*Homage to Athena as
Protectoress of the Fine Arts*) and ceilings in the
drawing room and audience chamber.[1] The angle
and foreshortening of the figures in this study
indicate that it was also intended for a ceiling.
Although all of Zoffany's decorative paintings
have since been destroyed, there is in the collection
of the Rheinisches Landesmuseum, Trier, a small
pastel painting by him of *Aeneas Saving his Father
Anchises from the Flames of Troy* of around 1759,
which indicates that Zoffany made at least one
other work relating to Virgil's *Aeneid* at this time.

The subject of Zoffany's study is taken from
Book Eight of the *Aeneid*, in which Venus descends
from the clouds to present her son Aeneas with
arms forged by her husband Vulcan in order to
allow him to defeat his enemy Turnus, leader of the
Italians, and found a new Troy at Rome. In the
present sketch Zoffany attends only to the general
outline of the narrative, although he emphasizes
the importance of the shield, supported by putti,
and the divine presence of Venus, who is seated on
clouds with several putti and two white doves that
draw her chariot. The subject of Venus bringing

arms to Aeneas was popular in seventeenth- and
eighteenth-century courtly mythological painting
cycles. Often depicted as part of a larger series, it
was preceded by Venus accepting the arms from
Vulcan and followed by the apotheosis of Aeneas,
the series being regarded as an allegory of
legitimate and triumphal kingship. Among the
more notable contemporaries of Zoffany who
illustrated one or more of the episodes were
Giovanni Battista Tiepolo, Pompeo Batoni and
François Boucher, whose composition Zoffany may
have known, as Mary Webster suggests, through
the engraving by Pierre François Courtois.[2]

MP

1. Webster 2011, 45–6.
2. Webster 2011, 38. For Courtois' engraving see James
   Fack, 'The Apotheosis of Aeneas: a Lost Royal
   Boucher rediscovered', *Burlington Magazine*, vol. 119,
   no. 897 (Dec. 1977), 887–93.

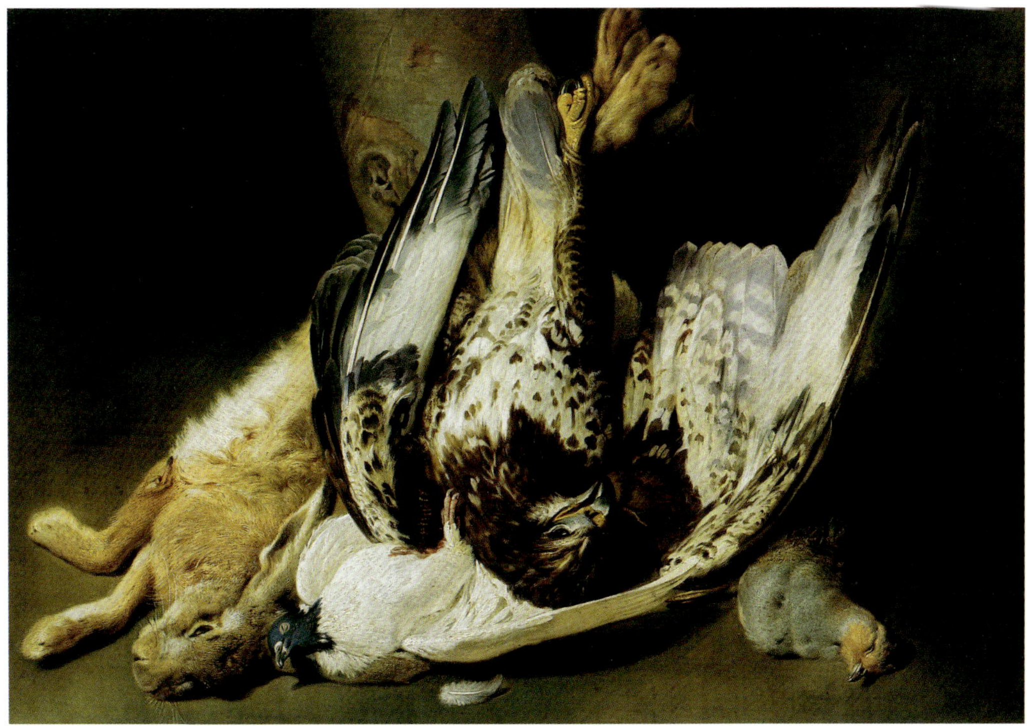

6

Still Life with Birds and Game
1760

Oil on canvas, 61 × 86 cm (24 × 33⅞ in)
Signed and dated: 'Zauffaly 1760'
Stadtmuseum Simeonstift Trier (Inv. Nr. III.34)

Provenance: Donated in 1830–31 to the city of Trier
by Johann Peter Job Hermes (1765–1833)

Selected references: Treadwell 2009, 38, 46, 48;
Webster 2011, 34

This is the only known still-life painting by Zoffany.
Signed and dated 1760, it was almost certainly
painted during the course of his work in Trier
at the Residenz of Johann Philipp, Graf von
Walderdorff, Archbishop Elector of Trier. Johann
Philipp, a man of considerable taste, lavished his
wealth on paintings and furnishing for his various
palaces. He also enjoyed hunting on his estates
and entertaining, suggesting perhaps that the
present picture was intended to furnish a dining
room, perhaps as a decorative over-door. Zoffany's
painting is a carefully orchestrated triangular
composition around the central form of a tree
trunk, from which is suspended the body of a
buzzard. To the left a hare lies diagonally across
the picture space, while the right-hand corner of
the triangle is formed by the grey partridge,
counterbalanced to the left by the pigeon. A single
white feather is placed artfully at the bottom centre,
drawing the eye towards the foreground. Zoffany's
sensitivity to the texture of fur and feather and
the carefully controlled colour reveal the formal
sophistication of what may otherwise be considered
an exercise in a minor genre.

While Zoffany's composition depended on close
scrutiny of the physical object before him, it is
influenced greatly by seventeenth-century Dutch
and Flemish still-life painters, in particular Jan
Weenix the Younger, whose work it most closely
resembles. Weenix made a number of sporting
still-life paintings for German patrons, including
Lothar Franz von Schönborn, Archbishop of
Mainz, at Schloss Weissenstein and Schloss
Gaibach, and Johann Wilhelm, Elector of the
Palatine, for whom he made twelve large, sporting,
still-life paintings for Schloss Bensberg. Zoffany's
debt to Weenix is apparent, for example, when
compared to the latter's _Dead Hare with Partridges_
(fig. 166), formerly in the collection of Baron
Schönborn. The comparison also reveals, despite
its more modest ambition, the sheer quality of
Zoffany's painting, which is able to hold its own
alongside the work of a recognized master in
the genre.

MP

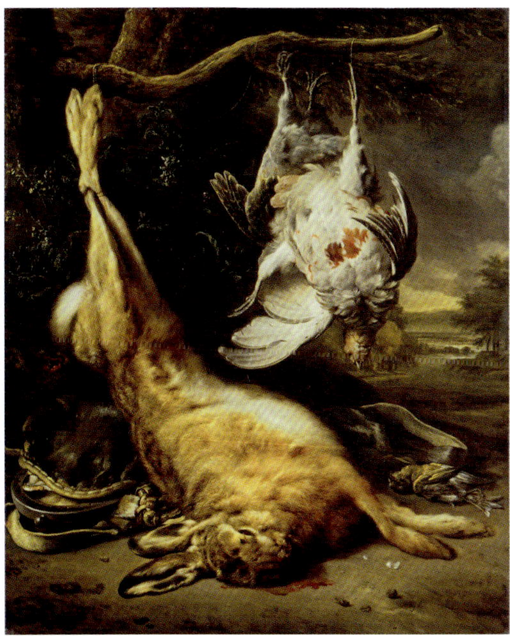

Figure 166
Jan Weenix the Younger,
Dead Hare with Partridges, 1702, oil on canvas,
87.3 × 70.5 cm (34⅜ × 27¾ in).
The Wallace Collection, London

7

Venus Marina

1760

Oil on canvas, 125 × 171 cm (49¼ × 67⅜ in)
Signed and dated: 'Zauffaly. inv. | 1760'
Musée des Beaux-Arts, Bordeaux

Provenance: Given by François-Lucie Doucet, 1805

Selected exhibitions: Les Chefs d'oeuvre des Musées de Bordeaux, Galerie des Beaux-Arts, Bordeaux, 1952–3, no. 57; *Peintures du 18e siècle au Musée des Beaux-Arts de Bordeaux,* Gallerie Cailleux, Paris, 1969–70; *Exposition des chefs-d'oeuvre du Musée des Beaux-Arts de Bordeaux,* Nagoya, Kamakura, Osaka and Fukuoka Art Museums, 1971–2, no. 37; National Portrait Gallery 1977, no. 6; *De Rubens, Delacroix à Corot,* Fukuoka, Hiroshima and Kanasawa Art Museums, and Sogo, Tokyo, 1983–4, no. 22; *Peinture d'histoire à sujets mythologiques,* Château Génicart, Lormot, 2000; *Le triomphe de l'Amour: Eros en guerre, une histoire amoureuse de l'humanité,* Hôtel de Sade, Avignon, 2004, no. 32

Selected references: P. Lacour, *Notice des tableaux et des figures exposés au Musée de la Ville de Bordeaux,* Bordeaux, 1821, no. 28 (as school of Charles-Joseph Natoire); P. Lacour, J. Delpit, *Catalogue des tableaux, statues … du Musée de Bordeaux,* Bordeaux, 1875, no. 516; E. Vallet, *Catalogue des tableaux, sculptures, gravures, dessins exposés dans les galleries du Musée de Bordeaux,* Bordeaux, 1881, no. 335; K. Nakayama, 'Nu féminin dans l'art', in *Mythologie: Venus,* vol. 1, Tokyo, 1980, no. 21; R. Rapetti, *Le Musée des Beaux-Arts de Bordeaux, Guide de collections,* Bordeaux, 1987, 41–2; Bergounioux & de Boysson 1990; M. Espagne, *Bordeaux-Baltique: la présence culturelle allemande à Bordeaux aux XVIIIe et XIXe siècles,* Paris, 1991; D. Dussol, *Art et bourgeoisie: la Société des Amis des Arts de Bordeaux (1851–1939),* Bordeaux, 1997, 25; F. Ribemont, 'A propos de quelques oeuvres allemandes du Musée des Beaux-Arts de Bordeaux', in *Présence de l'Allemagne à Bordeaux: du siècle de Montaigne à la veille de la Seconde Guerre mondiale,* Bordeaux, 1997, 304; Webster 2011, 41–3

Figure 167
*Amphitrite, c.*1760, pastel on paper, 44 × 58.5 cm (17⅜ × 23 in).
Museum der Bildenden Künste, Leipzig

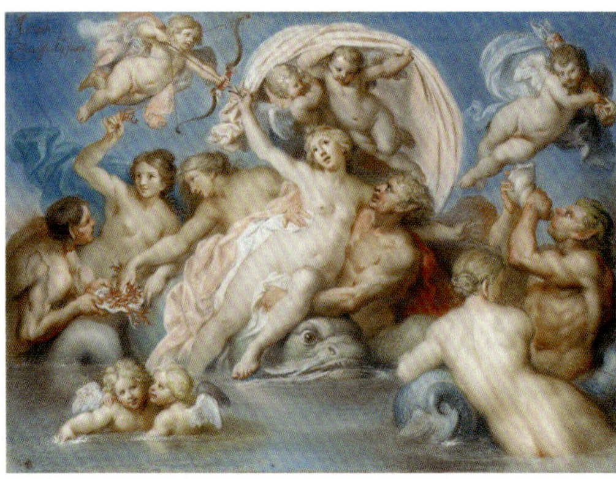

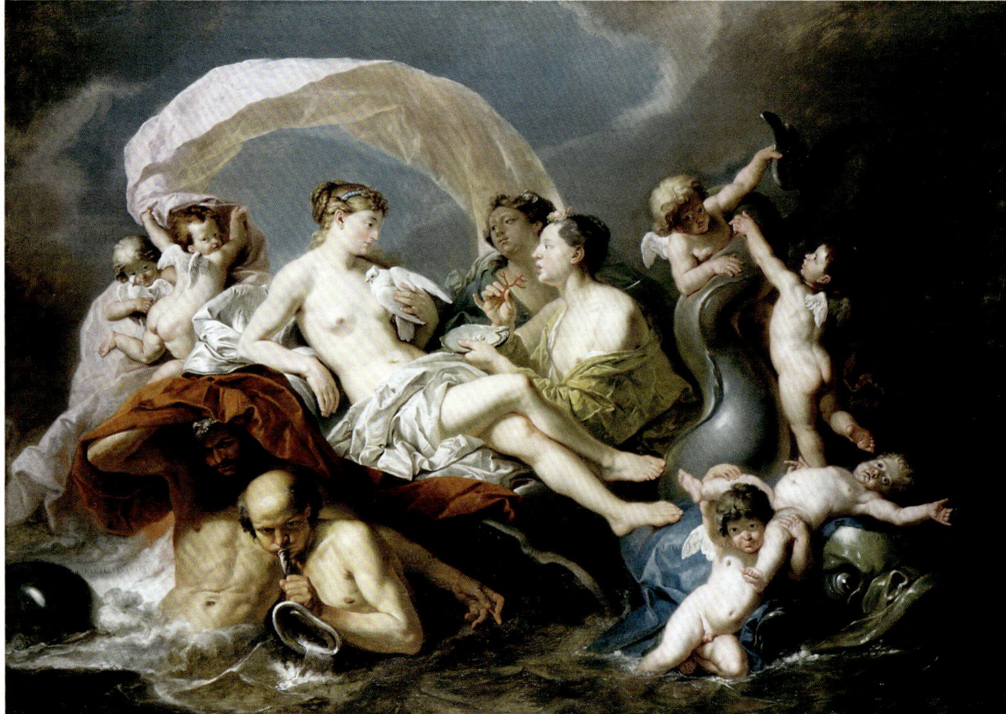

Venus Marina, or *The Triumph of Venus,* as it is also known, marks a watershed in Zoffany's early career, since it was among the last pictures he produced before leaving Germany to begin a new career in England. Circumstantial evidence suggests that it was one of several mythological paintings commissioned from Zoffany by Johann Philipp, Graf von Walderdorff, Archbishop Elector of Trier, as decoration for his palace in Trier, which was reconstructed between 1756 and 1761 by the architect Johannes Seiz.[1] Zoffany's employment is recorded in Seiz's account book. On 3 March 1760 it was agreed that Zoffany would decorate the prince's bedchamber, partly in fresco and partly in oil, for the sum of 333 Reichsthaler, 18 Albertsthaler. He was also employed to paint the ceiling of the audience chamber in fresco, with cartouches in oil, for the sum of 60 Carolin.[2]

Given the amorous subject matter of *Venus Marina* it may well have been intended for the archbishop's bedchamber. We cannot tell, however, since, following invasion by Revolutionary French troops in 1794 when the palace was used as a hospital and then as barracks, the oil paintings were evidently removed. *Venus Marina* was acquired by François-Lucie Doucet, who presented it to the gallery in Bordeaux in 1805. At the same time Doucet presented another painting by Zoffany to Bordeaux, the subject of which has been identified as Apollo and Coronis from Ovid's *Metamorphoses.* It is possible, as Mary Webster has suggested, that the two paintings, both painted for the palace at Trier (and of identical size), were conceived as pendants, the scene of jealous love in Apollo and Coronis contrasting with the joyful image of the goddess of love exhibited in *Venus Marina.*[3]

Venus reclines on a scallop shell, borne aloft by tritons. To her breast she presses a dove, the symbol of love and fertility, as an attendant sea nymph presents her with pearls and a branch of red coral, which like Venus herself are fruits of the sea. The image of 'Venus Anadyomene', Venus rising from the sea, was popular in Renaissance and Baroque art, and would have been well known to Zoffany, not least through his recent exposure to contemporary Roman Baroque painting. Stylistically, the hard-edged handling, particularly in the draperies, recalls his earlier training in Germany, under his former master in Regensburg, Martin Speer. In addition, aspects of the composition, notably the sea-monster, and the playful putti, recall an earlier pastel painting by Zoffany, *Amphitrite* (fig. 167), itself inspired by the frescoes of Annibale Carracci at the Palazzo Farnese, Rome. There are also strong parallels in the art of François Boucher, who painted the subject on a number of occasions. Yet, ultimately, rather than revealing an affiliation or debt to a particular artist or school, Zoffany's picture would appear to demonstrate the confluence of a number of styles. In this respect it anticipates his work in England, where he reveals a chameleon-like ability to absorb a variety of influences, adapting to prevailing trends and the requirements of patrons.

MP

1. For the reconstruction of the palace at Trier, see Eberhardt Zahn, 'Der Rokokoflugel des kurfurstlichen Palastes in Trier', *Trierer Zeitschrift fur Geschichte und Kunst des Trierer Landes und seiner Nachbargebiete,* no. 32 (1967), 341–82.
2. See Bergounioux & de Boysson 1990, 20; Webster 2011, 45, 647.
3. Webster 2011, 41.

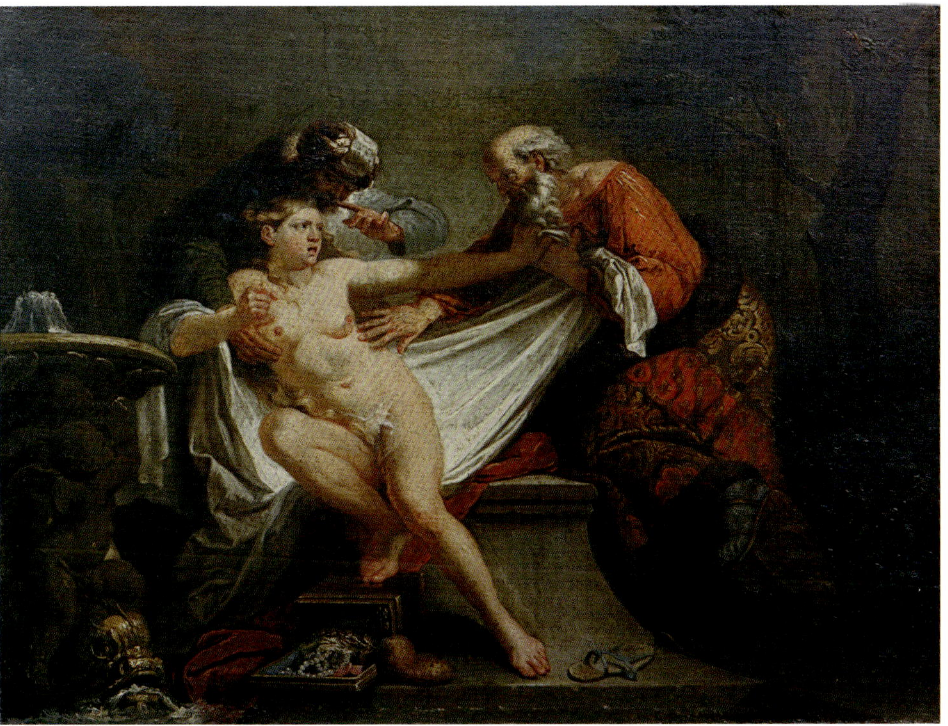

8

Susanna and the Elders
1760

Oil on canvas, 66.5 × 85.5 cm (26⅛ × 33⅝ in)
Rheinisches Landesmuseum, Trier

Provenance: Acquired at auction, Dr Fritz Nagel,
Stuttgart, 1991, Nr. 1907, fig. 152

*Selected exhibitions: Dienst und Herrschaft. Aspekte
adeligen Lebens am Beispiel der Familie Walderdorff,*
Bischöflichen Dom- und Diözesanmuseum Trier,
1998–9, no. 157

Selected references: A.L. Mayer, 'Ein Frühwerk
Zoffanys', *Der Cicerone*, no. 20 (1928), 235;
P. Seewaldt, *Neuerwerbungen der Mittelalterlichen
und Neuzeitlichen Abteilung des Rheinischen
Landesmuseums Trier*, Trier, 1991; *Trierer
Zeitschrift*, no. 56 (1993), 327; S. Faust, P. Seewaldt,
M. Weidner, *Erotische Kunstwerke im Rheinischen
Landesmuseum Trier. Funde und Ausgrabungen im
Bezirk*, Trier, 2007, 58–9, no. 37; Webster 2011, 35

The story of Susanna and the Elders first appeared
as one of the additions to the Greek version of the
Book of Daniel (chap. 13) and subsequently gained
canonical acceptance by the Roman Catholic
Church. In the story, Susanna, a beautiful and
devout woman, is married to Joakim. Two elderly
men, appointed as judges, are in the habit of visiting
Joakim and taking a walk in his garden, where they
begin to spy on Susanna. One day, finding Susanna
bathing alone, they attempt to blackmail her into
having sex, stating that if she does not they will
accuse her of taking a lover – having sent away
her handmaids for that reason. As the elders seize
Susanna, she raises the alarm, attracting the
attention of her servants, to whom the men tell
their tale. Susanna, on the recommendation of
the elders, will be forced to strip in public, and
condemned to death for her supposed adultery.
In the nick of time she is rescued by the young
Daniel, who exposes the elders' lies. According to
the Law of Moses, they are given the same
punishment as they sought to inflict.

While the probity of this particular biblical
story was questionable, *Susanna and the Elders*
proved to be among the most popular subjects
in western art from the sixteenth century
onwards, being painted by Tintoretto, Veronese,
Domenichino, Guido Reni, Guercino, Rembrandt
and Sebastiano Ricci, to name but a few. Its appeal
to male art patrons, as well as artists, is abundantly
clear.

In Zoffany's painting Susannah's right foot rests
upon her upturned jewel casket, symbolizing the
imminent threat to her virtue. He puts particular
emphasis on the menacing physical presence of

the elders, who, in addition to exposing Susanna's
nakedness by tugging at her draperies, touch her
body with bony fingers, the man behind reaching
forward to grope her breast. In this respect it
anticipates the unsettling sexual undertones found
in the close juxtaposition of the figures of Time
and Eros in *Time Clipping the Wings of Love* (cat. 9),
which Zoffany painted in England the following
year. The picture, which has been dated to 1760,
was perhaps among works like the *Triumph of
Venus* (cat. 7) that Zoffany made to decorate the
private apartments of Johann Philipp, Graf von
Walderdorff, Archbishop Elector, at his palace in
Trier. Towards the end of his career, in 1796,
Zoffany exhibited a painting entitled 'Susanna
and the two Elders' at the Royal Academy. That
picture, which is unlocated, is clearly a separate
work, but it may relate to a sketch of the same
subject that appeared in Zoffany's posthumous
studio sale in 1811.[1]

MP

1. Among the lots entitled 'UNFINISHED SKETCHES
   – by Mr. ZOFFANY' were 'Three sketches, Susannah
   and the Elders, Contemplation, and a Design of the
   Altar-piece of the Chapel at Brentford', Robins 1811,
   lot 58 (9 May).

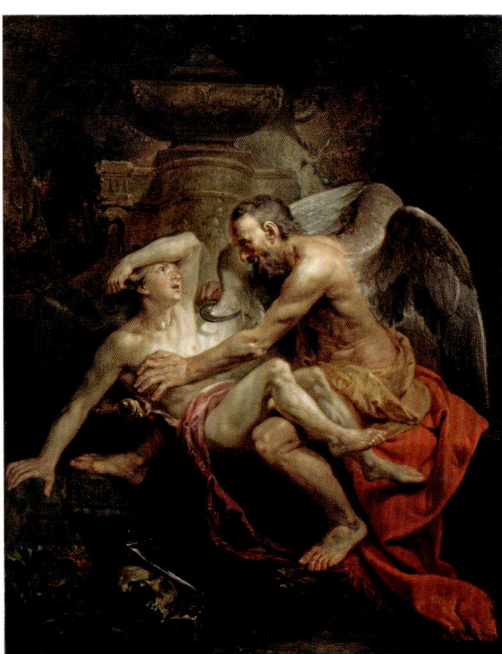

9

Time Clipping the Wings of Love
1761

Oil on canvas, 90.8 × 70.5 cm (35¾ × 27¾ in)
Signed and dated: 'Zoffany | inv. AE 1761'
Private collection

Provenance: Sold Langford's, London, 23 Feb. 1763
(45) for £4 14s 6d; John Birch by 1814; sold
Sotheby's New York, 28 Jan. 2010 (315)

Selected exhibitions: British Institution 1814, no. 131

Selected references: Webster 2011, 59–60

Recently discovered, its whereabouts unknown
since the early nineteenth century, *Time Clipping
the Wings of Love* forms a significant link between
Zoffany's formative years in Germany and Italy,
and the launch of his career in England, where the
present picture was made. The emblematic subject
of Chronos, the god of Time, clipping the wings of
Eros, the god of Love, was a popular allegory in
European art, alluding to the fading of passion
through the passage of time. While Zoffany would
have been aware of the subject prior to his arrival in
England, the immediate inspiration for Zoffany's
own composition appears to have been a painting
of *Time Clipping the Wings of Love* by Sir Anthony
Van Dyck, a version of which then belonged to
the Duke of Marlborough at Blenheim Palace.
However, it seems likely that Zoffany relied on the
mezzotint engraving after it by James McArdell
(fig. 168), which was shown at the first exhibition
of the Society of Artists in London in the spring
of 1760, as 'Time and Cupid: from Van-dyke'.
If Zoffany did not arrive in London in time to see
the print at the Society of Artist's exhibition, he
must have come across it shortly afterwards. It is
fascinating, therefore, to find Zoffany in the present
picture demonstrating his credentials as a history
painter, while at the same time demonstrating
by way of reference to Van Dyck, and indeed
McArdell, his affiliation to his new cultural and
artistic milieu.

In Van Dyck's work the figure of Eros, in
common with traditional representations of the
subject, is a chubby infant, the relationship between
the pair being reminiscent of a father with a
naughty child. Zoffany, by contrast, depicts Eros
as a youth, who despite his relatively muscular

form is disconcertingly androgynous in appearance,
adding an unsettling sexual element, wherein
Time's actions are akin to an act of rape: the
drapery around Eros's loins emphasizing his
vulnerability. Time, here, appears to force himself
on Eros, pressing down on his breast with an ugly,
gnarled hand, and, rather than pinioning his wing,
is intent on severing it completely from his body.
On the ground Time's scythe rests on a skull,
suggesting that the picture is not simply an allusion
to fading love but to the ravages of time and its
destructive power.

It is possible that Zoffany's studies for the naked
figure of Eros were made at the life class of the St
Martin's Lane Academy (see cat. 41). The reclining
pose is reminiscent, for example, of a similar figure
in a life drawing made at St Martin's Lane by
Francis Hayman (Royal Academy) for his painting,
The Good Samaritan (1752; Yale Center for British
Art).[1] *Time Clipping the Wings of Love* demonstrated
Zoffany's commitment to the principles of high art
in his new artistic environment. It did not, however,
prove commercially viable, and in the summer of
1762 Zoffany sold it at a public auction, alongside
works by other members of the Society of Artists,
George Lambert, Samuel Scott, Andrea Soldi and
Richard Wilson. The auction, which took place in
February 1763, proved a financial disaster for most
of the artists involved, including Zoffany who,
having estimated his picture at £13 15s 4¼ d, was
forced to accept a mere £4 14s 6d.[2] By this time,
however, Zoffany had already decided to relinquish
history painting, setting his sights instead on
earning a lucrative living through the manufacture
of agreeable conversation pieces and fashionable
theatrical portraits.

MP

1. See Brian Allen, *Francis Hayman*, New Haven and
   London, 1987, 57–8, cats. 47, 256; Ilaria Bignamini
   and Martin Postle, *The Artist's Model: Its Role in British
   Art from Lely to Etty*, exh. cat., Nottingham University
   Art Gallery and the Iveagh Bequest, Kenwood,
   London, 1991, 70–71, cat. 50.
2. Hargraves 2005, 39.

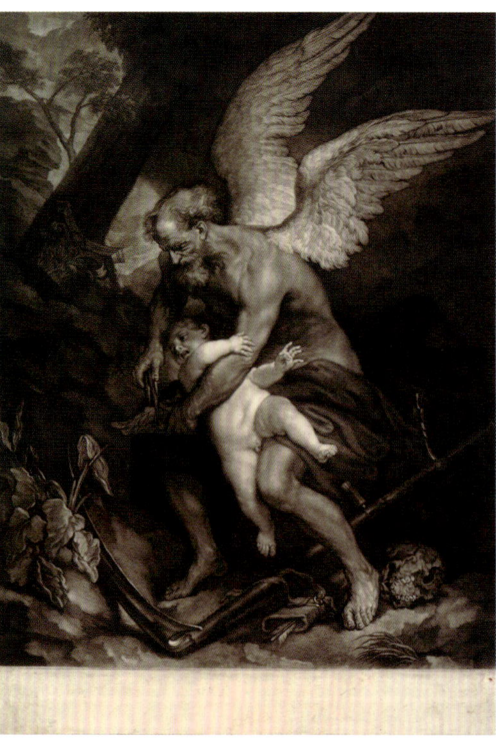

Figure 168
James McArdell after Sir Anthony Van Dyck,
Time Clipping the Wings of Love, 1742–65,
mezzotint engraving, 50.5 × 35 cm (19⅞ × 13¾ in).
British Museum, Department of Prints and Drawings
1875,0710.2759

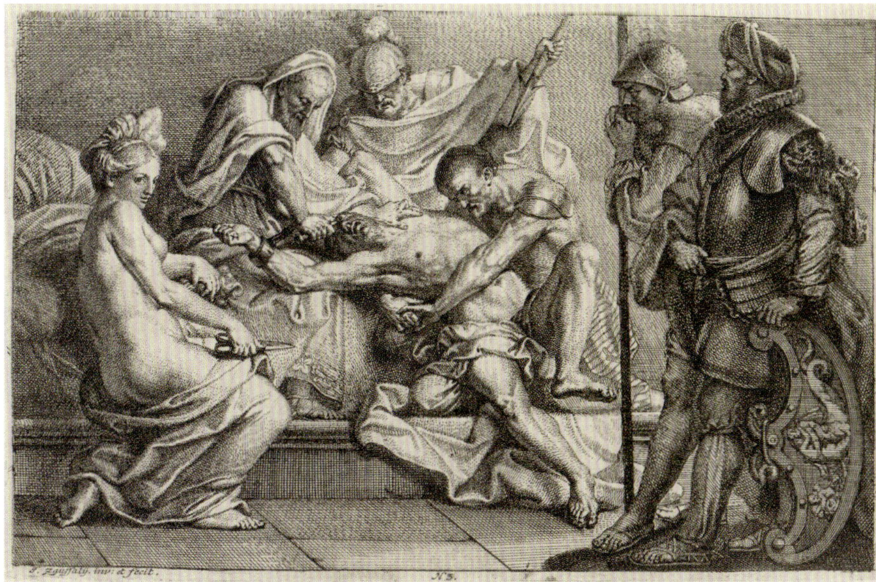

10

Samson Overcome by the Philistines
*c.*1758

Etching, 17.5 × 27 cm (6⅞ × 10⅝ in)
Inscribed lower left: 'J. Zauffalÿ. Inv: et fecit.';
and lower centre: 'N3'
Yale Center for British Art, Paul Mellon Fund

Selected references: Webster 1976, 86, no. 116;
Webster 2011, 25, 27

There are three recorded etchings by Zoffany, all
dating from the 1750s, the others being *The Death
of Lucretia* and *Brutus at the Death of Lucretia*.
However, only examples of the present etching are
known.[1] The print is undated, so a date of 1758
must remain speculative. Although Zoffany
probably learnt to etch before he left Germany,
possibly under the supervision of Martin Speer,
the composition also suggests the influence of
the Roman Baroque and of classical sculpture,
the struggling figure of Samson being modelled
partially on the statue of the *Barberini Faun*,
which Zoffany also referred to in *The Martyrdom
of St Bartholomew* (cat. 2).

The subject, taken from the Book of Judges
(16: 18–21), illustrates the seduction and betrayal
of the Israelite Samson by Delilah. In Zoffany's
etching Delilah holds the shears with which she
has cut off his hair, a motif found in many paintings
of the subject (even though in the Bible story
Samson's hair is cut off by one of the Philistines).
Under the watchful gaze of the Philistine chiefs
Samson is restrained while his eyes are gouged
out. The story, with its heady cocktail of seduction
and gratuitous violence, was widely illustrated in
Baroque paintings and prints, being depicted,
notably, by Guercino, Rubens and Rembrandt.

Characteristically, Zoffany has chosen the most
violent episode, recalling his oil paintings of the
1750s, including the *Martyrdom of St Bartholomew*
(cat. 2) and the *Death of Lucretia* (*c.* 1758;
Landesmuseum für Kunst und Kulturgeschichte,
Münster). Zoffany is also known to have painted
at this time *Samson at the Breast of Delilah as She
Delivers Him Bound to the Philistines*, commissioned
by one of his patrons in Regensburg, Baron von
Berberich, the Imperial Privy Councillor. At the
sale of his collection in 1784, this picture (now lost),
was described as a *chef d'oeuvre*.[2]

MP

1. Webster 2011, 25. See also F.J. Lipowsky, *Baierisches
   Kunstler-Lexikon*, 2 vols., Munich 1810, vol. 1, 188.
2. Webster 2011, 33–4.

11

Triumph of Venus
*c.*1760

Black and white chalk on paper, 28.4 × 45 cm
(11⅛ × 17¾ in)
British Museum, Department of Prints and
Drawings, 1920,1214.13

Provenance: Purchased from F.W. Barry, 1920

Selected references: Webster 2011, 46

The subject of the present drawing, which has not
hitherto been identified, would appear to relate to
the 'Triumph of Venus', in which the eponymous
goddess rises from the sea surrounded by a coterie
of cavorting nereids and tritons. The subject was
common in seventeenth- and eighteenth-century
decorative schemes, notably in Boucher's several
paintings, including the painting of 1740, now in
the Nationalmuseum, Stockholm, to which the
present sketch may be compared.

The drawing is very sketchy and represents only
a preliminary stage in the creative process, but
careful scrutiny reveals the general compositional
framework. The figures are grouped on a rocky
outcrop lapped by waves. At the upper left a seated
triton blows on a conch shell, a detail that provides
the first clue to the drawing's subject. The standing
female figure at the upper right, who points
imperiously, is presumably Venus (similar gestures
being found in other depictions of this subject).
Seated at her side is a rather excited triton, while
in the centre another seated triton turns back to
grasp a naked nereid. Below are several other
naked writhing figures, contributing to the erotic
atmosphere. At the lower left, a little difficult to
comprehend, is the open-jawed head of a large
dolphin, whose body stretches upwards towards
a (just visible) pointed tail. A similar motif is to be
found at the right-hand side of Zoffany's painting,

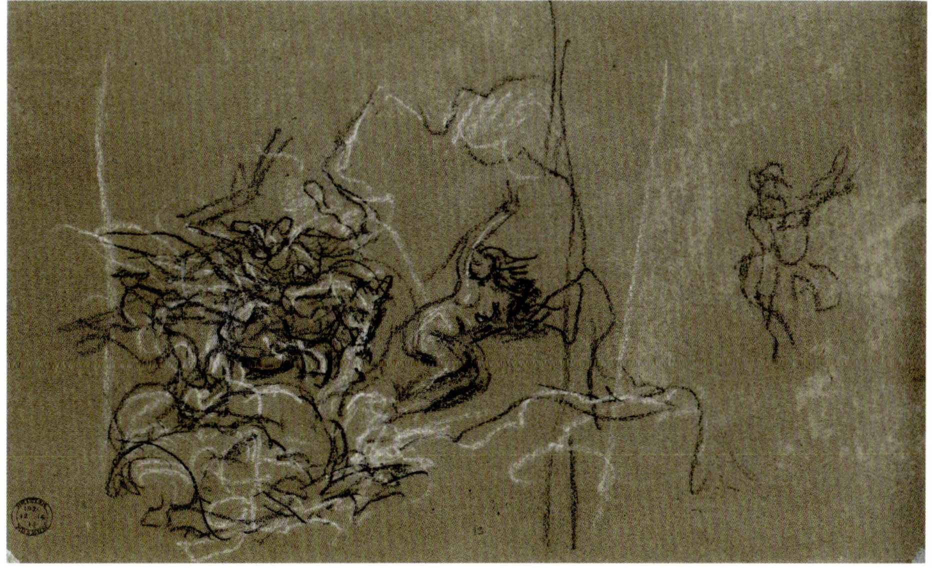

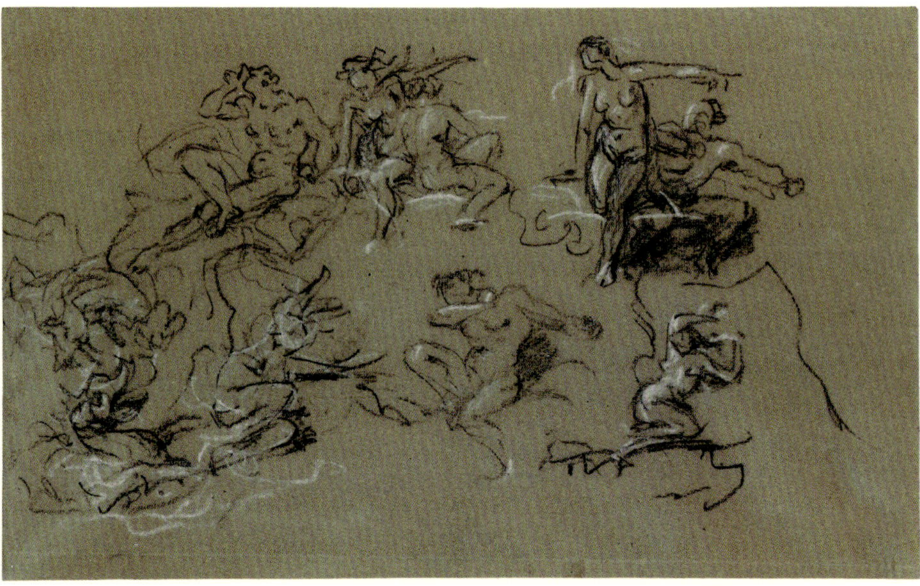

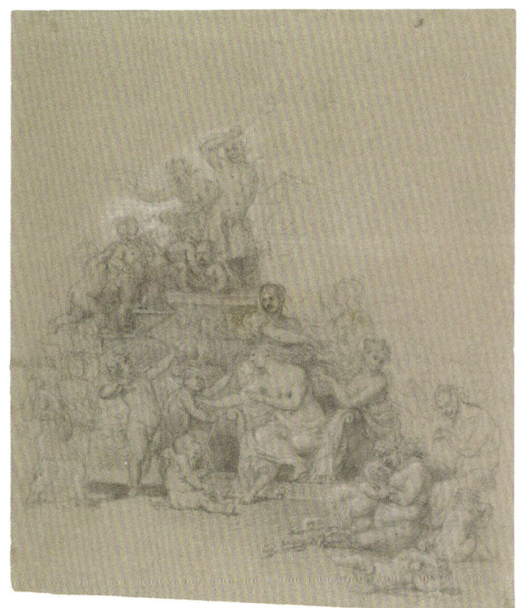

Venus Marina (cat. 7), where a group of putti clamber over a large dolphin. It is possible, therefore, that this drawing may have contributed to Zoffany's ideas for the painting. More likely, however, is that it is a separate composition for a ceiling decoration, similar to the *Allegory of Dawn* (cats. 13 and 14), relating possibly to the decorative schemes he projected for the electoral palace in Trier in 1760. In view of the subject of the present sketch, it may also relate in some way to Zoffany's drawing of a triton and nereid, now in the Royal Collection.[1]

During the preparation of this drawing for inclusion in the present exhibition a hitherto unknown drawing, also by Zoffany, was discovered on the reverse (fig. 169). At the centre the naked figure of Andromeda is chained to a rock, and to the left, Perseus, on his winged horse, Pegasus.

MP

1. See Oppé 1950, 106, no. 701; Webster 2011, 47, fig. 52.

Figure 169
Johan Zoffany, *Perseus and Andromeda*, *c.*1760, black and white chalk on paper, 28.4 × 45 cm (11⅛ × 17¾). British Museum, Department of Prints and Drawings, 1920,1214.13 (verso)

12

Sine Cerere et Libero Friget Venus

*c.*1759–60

Black and white chalk on brown-grey paper, 34.9 × 29 cm (13¾ × 11⅜ in)
The Royal Collection, Her Majesty Queen Elizabeth II

Provenance: Sir Frederick Gore Ouseley, 1919

Selected exhibitions: Royal Academy 1968–9, no. 658; National Portrait Gallery 1977, no. 120

Selected references: Oppé 1950, 106, no. 700, pl. 108; Webster 2011, 46

One of only a handful of known drawings relating to Zoffany's employment as a decorative painter in Germany in the late 1750s (see cats. 13 and 14), this compositional sketch may, like the others, have been made in the context of his employment in the service of Johann Philipp, Graf von Walderdorff, Elector of Trier, either for his palace at Ehrenbreitstein or, more likely, for his newly extended palace in Trier. The present drawing is among the most highly finished compositional sketches to have survived, suggesting possibly that it was translated into a finished painting, either in oils or fresco. However, since Zoffany's last remaining fresco at the palace in Trier was destroyed in the winter of 1947, one can only speculate.

A seated figure of Venus, with attendants, gestures towards a group of putti or Cupids, one of whom releases an arrow, while another holds a flaming torch. In the right foreground Bacchus nurtures a young satyr, a thyrsus (staff) lying by his cloven hooves. At the apex of the pyramidal composition a satyr stands on a decorated plinth, possibly holding an arrow aloft, while to the left more Cupids scramble up the stone staircase.

In the background are faint traces of a pedimented structure.

Although the specific iconography of the drawing has not hitherto been identified, it may be an illustration of the line from Act IV, Scene 6, of the classical comedy by Terence, *The Eunuch*: 'sine Cerere et Libero friget Venus', which can be translated as 'without Ceres and Bacchus Venus is cold'. Thus, in Zoffany's drawing Venus is attended by Ceres, the goddess of the harvest, and associated handmaidens, who hand over their bounty, while Bacchus ('Libero'), the god of wine, is seated below offering his own form of support. Terence's line, which was also quoted in Cicero's *On the Nature of the Gods*, was illustrated in Haecht's emblem book, *Mikrocosmos*, published in Antwerp in 1579 and was common in Dutch, Flemish and German paintings, drawings and engravings of the sixteenth and seventeenth century, where Venus is depicted in the company of Ceres, Bacchus and assorted Cupids, including some, as in Zoffany's drawing, with bows, arrows and flaming torches. The episode does not, however, appear to be found south of the Alps, and would therefore have been epoused by Zoffany's German patrons.

MP

13

Sketch for a Ceiling Decoration:
Allegory of the Dawn
*c.*1759

Black and white chalk on paper,
28 × 45.1 cm (11 × 17¾ in)
Inscribed with a series of numbers and on a
separate sheet of paper attached to the reverse
side of the mount: 'by Zofani'
British Museum, Department of Prints and
Drawings, 1920,1214.12

14

Sketch for a Ceiling Decoration:
Allegory of the Dawn
*c.*1759

Black and white chalk on paper,
28 × 44.8 cm (11 × 17⅝ in)
British Museum, Department of Prints and
Drawings, 1920,1214.11

Provenance: Sir Frederick Gore Ouseley, Tenbury
(1825–89); F.W. Barry, from whom purchased by
the Trustees of the British Museum

Selected references: Webster 1976, 86, nos 117, 118;
Webster 2011, 46, 48–9

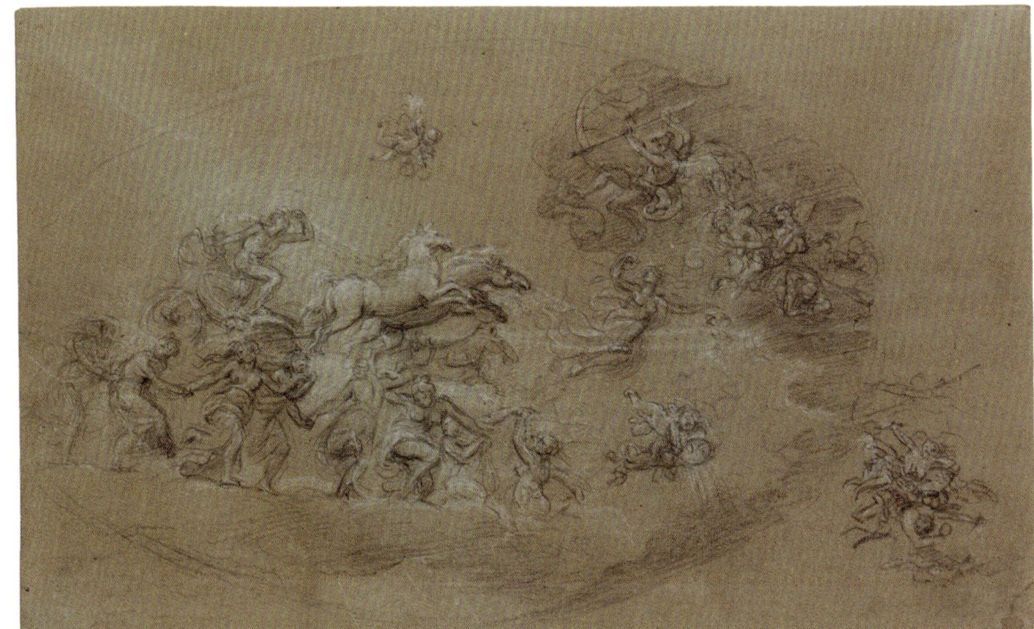

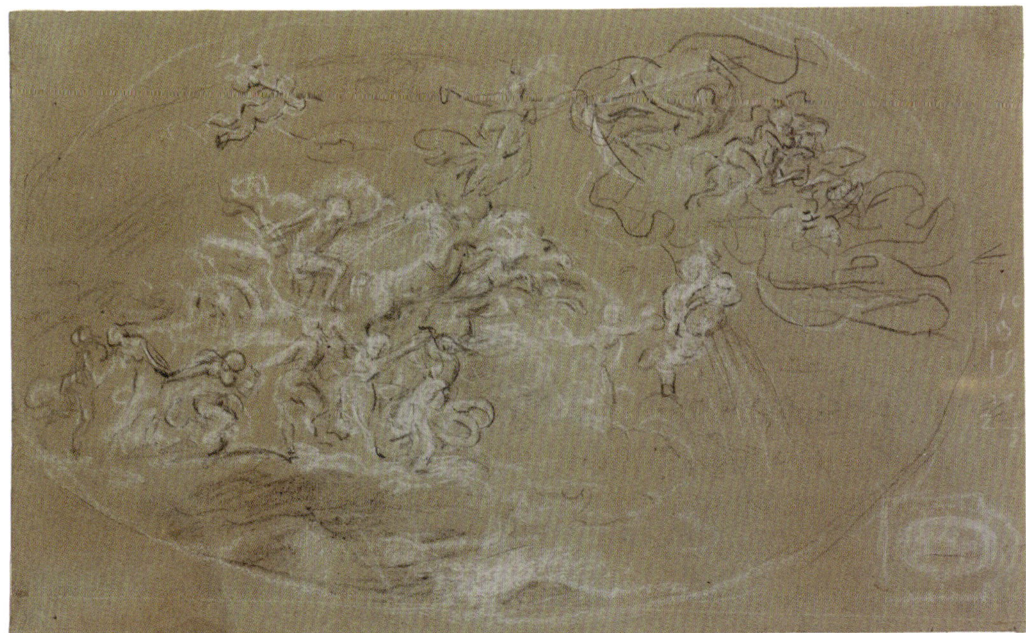

In March 1760 the architect Johannes Seiz, who
was in the course of designing a new wing at the
electoral palace in Trier, employed Zoffany to
decorate three chambers. The schedule specified
works in fresco and oil in the electoral bedroom,
a frescoed ceiling and cartouches in oil for the
drawing room, and the same for the audience
chamber. The bedroom, which survived intact until
1947, had a ceiling fresco depicting the homage of
Athena as Protectress of the Fine Arts, while the
cartouches contained allegorical figures of the
Arts and Sciences, including Painting, Drama,
Music, Philosophy, Sculpture and Astronomy.[1]
The decorative scheme for the other two rooms is
unknown. Zoffany was clearly an accomplished
decorative painter and it is unfortunate that a few
compositional sketches are the only surviving
evidence of this aspect of his career.

The two drawings shown here represent stages
in the evolution of a scheme for a decorative ceiling.
A third related drawing for the composition is in
the Royal Collection.[2] One (cat. 14) includes
measurements and a plan. Whether the drawings
relate to work carried out or projected for the
electoral palace at Trier or for the archbishop's
palace at Ehrenbreitstein cannot be established.
The subject matter is perhaps most suitable for a
bedroom. Although both compositions are quite
loosely sketched, it is possible to distinguish the
main protagonists, particularly in the more finished
drawing. To the centre left Apollo stands on his
chariot, before him Aurora, goddess of the Dawn,
who dispels the creatures of the Night, including
Time, who appear in the shadowed area to the
right. Below Apollo's chariot the Hours, goddesses
of the seasons, perform a ritualistic dance. The
composition is essentially Zoffany's own invention,
but he was certainly influenced by Guido Reni's
frescoed ceiling in the Casino dell'Aurora, in the
grounds of the Palazzo Pallavicini-Rospigliosi,
Rome.[3] Given that Zoffany had spent much of the
1750s in Rome, Reni's work must have been at
the forefront of his mind when devising his own
scheme. Whether Zoffany ever produced the final
composition for which these drawings were made is
unknown, since, only a few months after receiving
his commission for the palace in Trier, he left
Germany for England.

MP

1. Webster 2011, 45–6, fig. 46.
2. Oppé 1950, 105–6, no. 699.
3. See Webster 2011, 46.

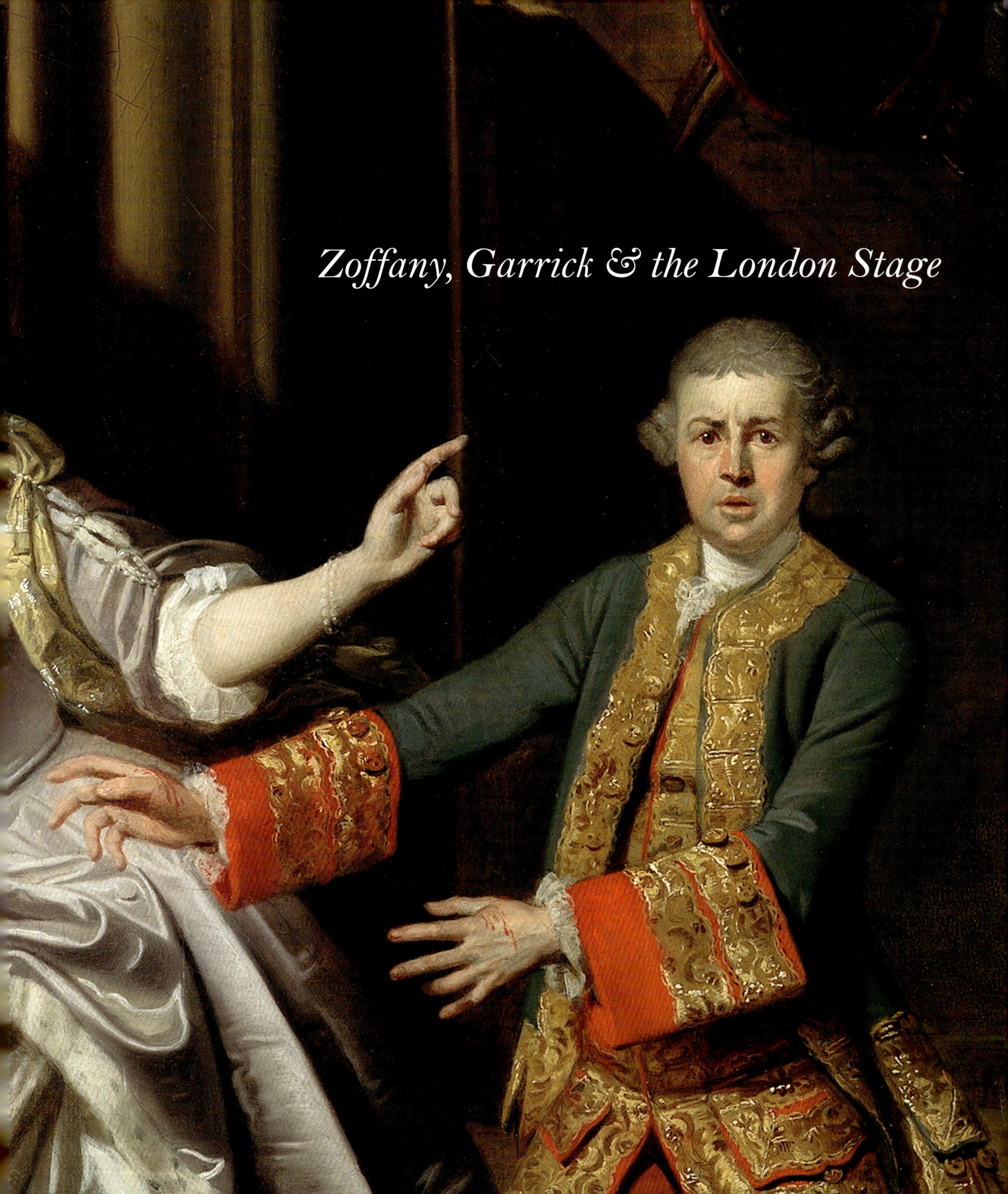

Zoffany, Garrick & the London Stage

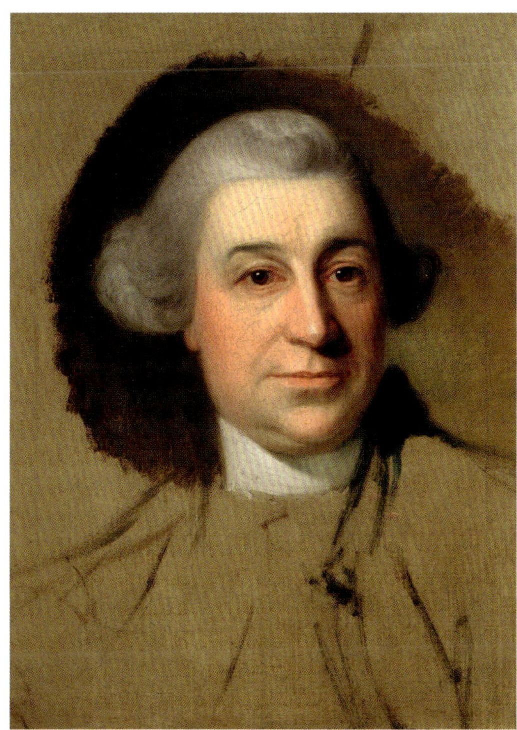

15

David Garrick

*c.*1766–7

Oil on canvas, 47 × 35 cm (18½ × 13¾ in)
The Garrick Club, London

Provenance: Robert Baddeley; 'Mrs Baddeley'
(Catherine Strickland); Billy Dunn; Roland
Stevenson; bt Mathews; sold to John Durrant;
his gift (?)

Selected exhibitions: Queen's Bazaar 1833, no. 123;
La vie Britannique à Paris (British Council),
Bibliothèque Nationale, Paris, 1948; Tate 1951,
no. 44; Hayward Gallery 1975, no. 89; *Every Look
Speaks: Portraits of David Garrick*, Holburne
Museum, Bath, 2003, no. 23

Selected references: Ashton *et al.* 1997, 138; Webster
2011, 91

Robert Baddeley, who owned this superb likeness,
played for many years under David Garrick at
Drury Lane, a theatre to which he remained
devoted, as he did to the memory of Garrick. He
was a member of 'The School of Garrick', a club
founded after Garrick's death, initially by those
who had been trained by him (other members were
John Moody and Tom King, cats. 30, 32). In his will
(in which this painting is referred to as 'Garrick's
head') Baddeley left money to the Drury Lane
Theatrical Fund, so that every Twelfth Night
(6 January) the company would have cake and a
glass of punch. The ritual of the Baddeley Cake has
continued to be celebrated since 1796. The Fund
had been started in 1766 by Garrick with Baddeley
as one of its directors.

The present painting has been cut down and was
originally intended for a larger composition that
was never completed. Baddeley's deep involvement
with Garrick and Drury Lane, and the fact that he
himself sat to Zoffany on more than one occasion,
would explain why, if not how, this fragment came
into his hands. We see him in the background of
The Clandestine Marriage (cat. 31), while his most
famous role, as Moses in *The School for Scandal*,
which he created at Drury Lane under Garrick's
successor Richard Sheridan in 1777, is the subject
of an especially fine single portrait by Zoffany of
about that date (private collection).[1] Judging
from the apparent age of Garrick in this portrait,
it must date from about 1766–7, as suggested by
comparison with Gainsborough's lost full-length
portrait of 1766, recorded in a mezzotint of 1769
by Valentine Green (fig. 170). By about 1770

Garrick had developed a fleshier, more rounded
face and a quite pronounced double chin. His face
appears to have aged rapidly over a decade, as his
features here are already rounder than they appear,
for example, in Zoffany's portrait of him in profile
of 1763 (Ashmolean Museum, Oxford).[2] No doubt
this was partly the result of his suffering from a
kidney stone, which was made all the worse since,
as his post mortem revealed, he had been born with
only one kidney. His oldest friend Dr Johnson gave
another explanation to Hester Thrale, shortly
before Garrick died in 1779:

> David … looks much older than he is; for his Face
> has had double the Business of any other man, –
> it is never at rest, – when he speaks one minute,
> he has quite a different Countenance to what he
> assumes the next; I don't believe he ever kept the
> same look for half an Hour together in the whole
> course of his Life.[3]

Because of the extraordinary mobility of his
features, Garrick was given to teasing portrait
painters to whom he sat, including his close friend
William Hogarth, and Gainsborough's obituary
(*Morning Chronicle*, August 1788) recorded the
same phenomenon:

> [Gainsborough] never found any portrait so
> difficult to hit as that of Mr Garrick, for when
> he was sketching in the eyebrows, and thought he
> had hit on their precise situation, and looked a
> second time at his model, he found the eyebrows
> lifted up to the middle of his forehead and when
> he a third time looked they were dropped like a
> curtain over the eyes.[4]

RS

1. The version of this painting in the Liverpool Museums
   appears to be a copy, probably after a mezzotint.
2. That image can in turn be compared with the fine
   profile drawing, of the same right-hand side, by James
   Keyse Sherwin of about 1774 (National Portrait
   Gallery, London, NPG 1187). See Holburne Museum
   2003, cats. 21, 41.
3. Peter Sabor and Lars E. Troide, eds., *Frances Burney
   Journals and Letters*, London, 2001, 94.
4. *Morning Chronicle*, Aug. 1788, quoted Holburne
   Museum 2003, 14.

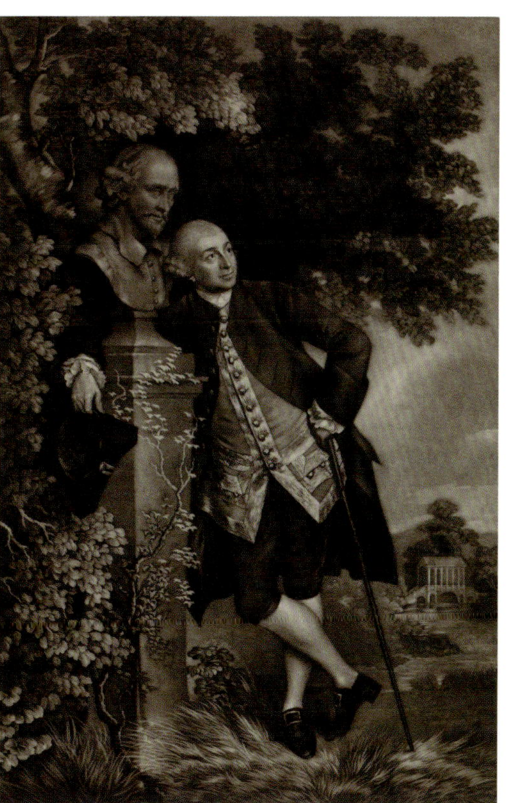

Figure 170
Valentine Green after Thomas Gainsborough,
David Garrick, 1769, mezzotint engraving,
61.7 × 38.8 cm (24⅜ × 15¼ in).
British Museum, Department of Prints and Drawings,
1870,0625.629

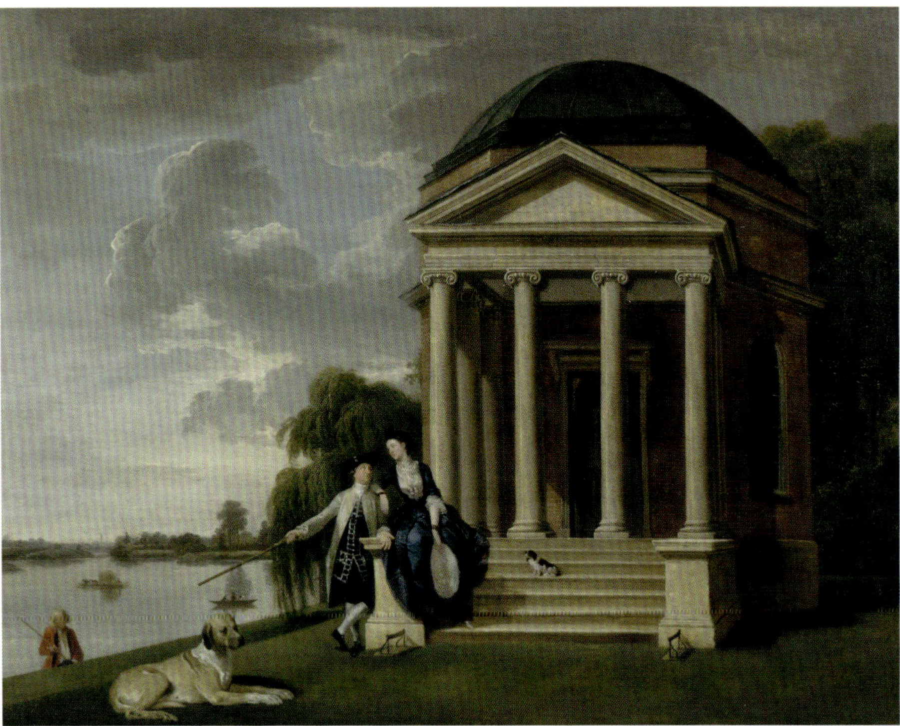

16

**Mr and Mrs Garrick by the Shakespeare Temple
at Hampton**

*c.*1762

Oil on canvas, 109.9 × 134.6 cm (43¼ × 53 in)
Yale Center for British Art, Paul Mellon Collection

Provenance: Frances, Lady Waldegrave, Strawberry
Hill, Twickenham; Harvey La Dew; Harvey La
Dew Topiary Garden Society; Paul Mellon

*Selected exhibitions: Exhibition of the Works by the Old
Masters*, Royal Academy of Arts, 1855, 1879, no. 34;
French and English Art Treasures of the 18th Century,
Parke-Bernet, New York, 1942

Selected references: Holburne Museum 2003, 49–51;
Treadwell 2009, 65–70; Webster 2011, 76–84

This painting is the second of two versions. The
one now in a British private collection (fig. 171)
was paid for by Garrick in a receipt of 23 April 1763
(Garrick Club), together with three other views of
the family in the garden of Garrick's country house
at Hampton, Surrey.[1] The Yale Center for British
Art's version differs in omitting the servant
approaching with a tray on the right and Garrick's
nephew on the steps of Shakespeare's Temple,
which itself is seen from a slightly different angle
(note the relative position of column and doorway).

Garrick bought his house at Hampton in 1754
and had a new facade designed by Robert Adam
the following year, when Adam also designed the
octagonal temple for the garden beside the Thames.
The grounds were designed by Capability Brown.
Clearly, only the very best would do for this
celebration of Garrick's extraordinary success
and prosperity. Inside the temple (and dimly
visible here) he placed a full-length marble statue
of Shakespeare (for which he paid £315 in 1757;
British Museum) by Hogarth's colleague Louis
François Roubiliac. Hogarth himself, one of
Garrick's closest friends, designed an elaborate
rococo chair for the interior, on which he painted
Garrick in a great double portrait (1757, Royal
Collection).

The painting asserts the centrality of
Shakespeare to Garrick's life and achievements, and
Garrick was to pursue his identification with the
Bard in the Shakespeare Jubilee that he devised for
Stratford on 6–7 September 1769. The high point
was Garrick's recitation of an ode to Shakespeare
that he had written, although the event was so
marred by rain that wags re-named the town
'Stratford-under-Avon'. He quickly staged an
all-singing, all-dancing Jubilee at Drury Lane with
a great 'Pageant' ('as it was intended for Stratford
upon-Avon') of Shakespeare characters and a
Prologue spoken by Tom King (cat. 32). Garrick
always appeared as Benedick in this entertainment,
which he staged no fewer than ninety-one times
between 14 October 1769 and the end of the season.

The composition, one of Zoffany's very first
works for Garrick, shows how swiftly he reinvented
himself as a master of the English conversation
piece. It was also one of his first exercises in
painting landscape, created during the summer
of 1762. Zoffany was staying at Garrick's house,
having broken from his employment under
Benjamin Wilson in circumstances that caused
some difficulty between Wilson and Garrick,
who were neighbours. By the time of the Jubilee,
Garrick and Wilson had long been reconciled and
Garrick obtained the commission for Wilson to
paint a portrait of Shakespeare for the Stratford
Town Hall.

The painting seems to be touched with the
melancholy of parting, as Garrick gestures to
the boatman drawing up on the river beside him.
Perhaps he is going back to town, leaving his
devoted wife behind in Hampton, as he prepares
for the new season, which began in September.
The omission of the boy and the servant in this
version was no doubt made because both were
personal to Garrick (Garrick's companions in the
private collection version can all be identified).
This painting (once asserted to have belonged to
Horace Walpole, although no evidence can be
traced) would have been created for a client more
interested in possessing, chiefly, a memorial of
England's greatest actor in a very English setting.
The Temple to Shakespeare, which dominates the
composition, appears as a grand memorial building
rather than a garden folly, and is almost as much
the subject of the picture as are the Garricks.

RS

1. Two of the others are, respectively, in the private
   collection and at Petworth, while the third, 'View in
   the Garden and two Miss Garrick's at Play, whole
   length', was in the collection of the late Mary, Lady
   Eccles, sold Christie's, 9 Jan. 2004 (4); see fig. 93.

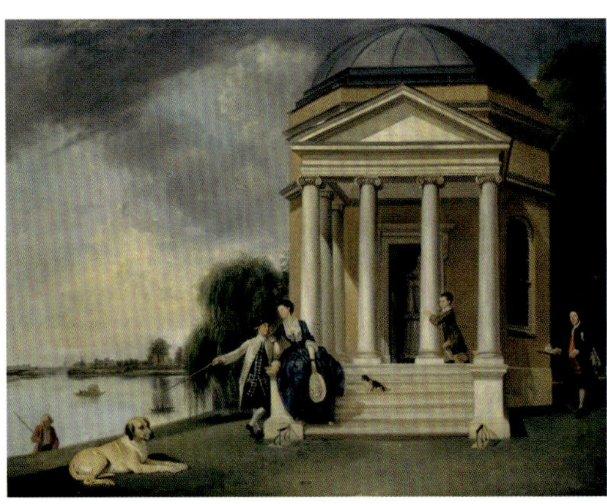

Figure 171
*Mr and Mrs Garrick by the Shakespeare Temple
at Hampton, c.*1762, oil on canvas,
99.7 × 125 cm (39¼ × 49¼ in). Private collection

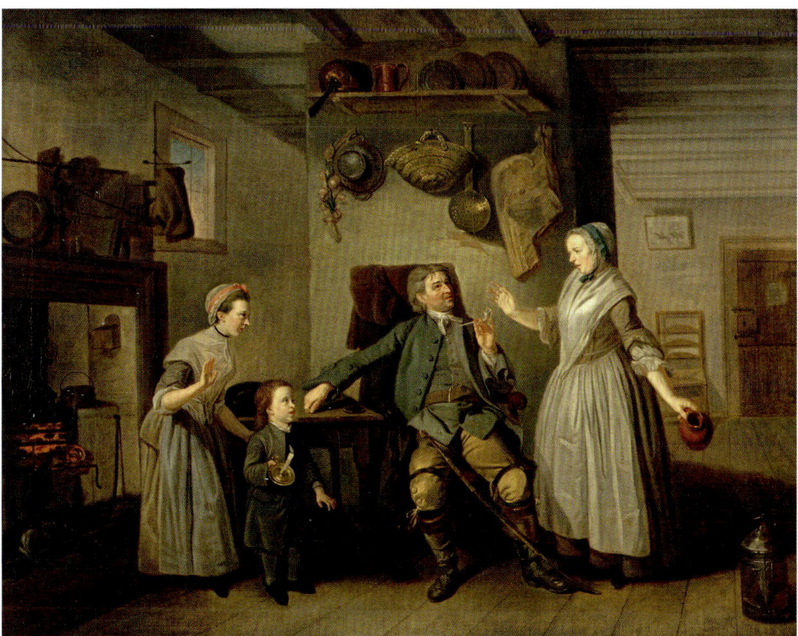 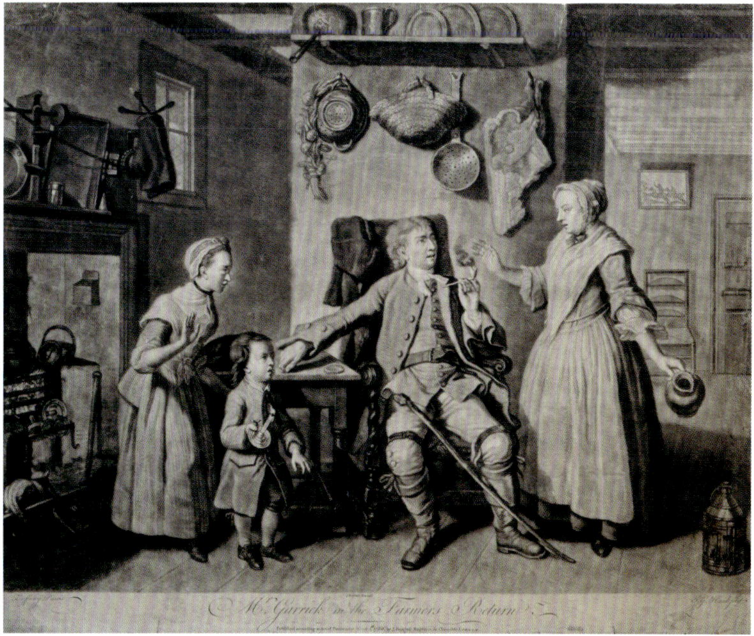

17

David Garrick and Mary Bradshaw in David Garrick's 'The Farmer's Return'
*c.*1762

Oil on canvas, 101.6 × 127 cm (40 × 50 in)
Yale Center for British Art, Paul Mellon Collection

Exhibited at the Yale Center for British Art only

18

Johann Gottfried Haid after Johan Zoffany, Mr Garrick in 'The Farmer's Return'
1766

Mezzotint engraving,
42.8 × 50.6 cm (16⅞ × 19⅞ in)
Inscribed: 'Zoffany Pinxit. | J. Boydell Excud: | JG Haid fecit. | Mr Garrick in the Farmers Return. | Published according to Act of Parliament March 1ˢᵗ 1766 by J. Boydell Engraver in Cheapside LONDON.'
Private collection

Exhibited at the Royal Academy of Arts only

Selected references: Dircks 1997, 289–312; Webster 2011, 75, 181, 184–7

The painting from which this print is taken was Zoffany's first theatrical composition, exhibited in the Society of Artists exhibition 17 May 1762 (no. 138). The publication of the play (also in 1762) was inspired by Hogarth having drawn this scene (see p. 69). Hogarth's drawing, which used to hang in the green drawing room of Garrick's house in the Adelphi, the Adam brothers' grand development overlooking the Thames in central London (now demolished), has been lost but is known from the etching by James Basire (see fig. 62). This short 'interlude', just ninety-four lines long, was written by Garrick as a benefit night for Mrs Pritchard – whose last performance was to be with Garrick in *Macbeth* a few years later (see cat. 28) – and first produced at Drury Lane on 20 March 1762.

The play revolves around the return of a farmer to his family in the country after a visit to London to see the Coronation of King George III and Queen Charlotte (which had taken place on 22 September 1761). There was a tradition on the London stage of showing a coronation in a coronation year, which Garrick had observed with a production of *Henry VIII*. This interlude was evidently a development from that and suited Mrs Pritchard's benefit, because she had been dressmaker to the queen for her wedding (on 8 September 1761) and coronation, the duties of which included advice on deportment.

It is always said that the pictures by Hogarth and Zoffany of *The Farmer's Return* show the same moment in the play. In fact, they show two different points in the farmer's report to his wife (played by Mary Bradshaw) and children, as he explains that he also went to see the phenomenon of the Cock Lane Ghost. This famous hoax was highly topical at the time of the play's performance, as it had only been uncovered as a fraud in February 1762, and was included by Hogarth in his reworking of *Credulity, Superstition and Fanaticism*, dated 15 March 1762, just five days before this play was performed.[1] Garrick's first draft of *The Farmer's Return* does not feature the ghost,[2] and so it was a very late addition, although one that created the climactic scene, which unfolds as follows (the spelling indicates a rustic accent): '*Farmer.* The top joke of all and what pleas'd me the moast | Some Wise ones and I sat up with a Ghoast …' At this point, the members of the family start back with horror, exclaiming: 'A Ghoast!' The farmer continues with the explanation of how the ghost communicates by knocking: 'With her nails and her knuckles she answer'd so noice! | For Yes she knocked Once and for No she knocked Twice.' Zoffany depicts these two lines precisely. Hogarth, however, chose the psychologically more acute moment when the farmer goes on to tease his wife by pretending that he asked the ghost whether his wife is true to him. The wife complacently replies that she supposes the ghost answers 'Yes'. At which point the farmer swears that it said 'No'. Her distress is clear, after which the farmer defuses the situation by saying: 'Come, prithee no Croying | The Ghoast, among Friends, was much giv'n to Loying.'

Together, the two pictures form a remarkable record of two closely sequential moments in the performance of a great actor. Hogarth's interior must be closer to the actual set, while Zoffany elaborated it, making the painting more of an interior genre scene than a record of the stage.

RS

1. R.B. Paulson, *Hogarth's Graphic Works*, 3rd ed., London, 1989, 177–8.
2. Dircks 1997, 291.

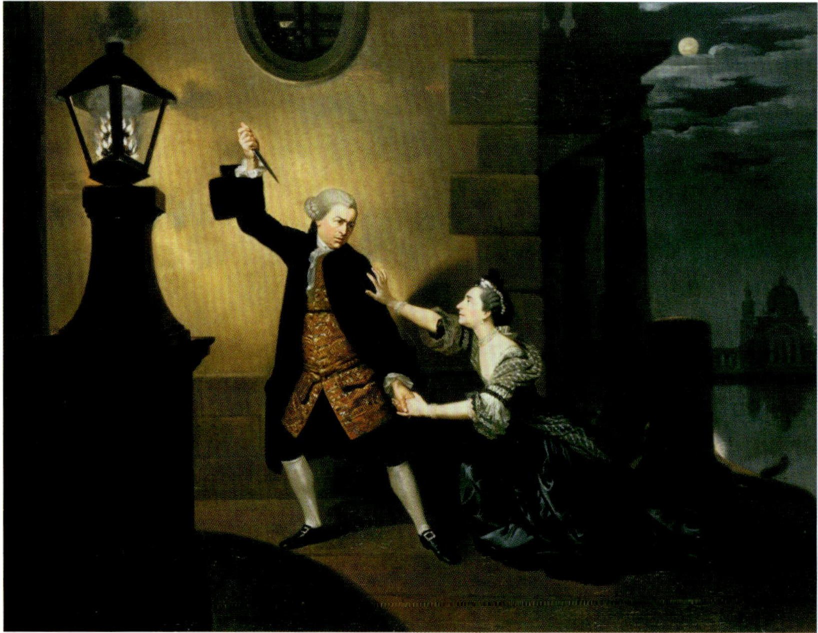

19

David Garrick and Mrs Cibber as Jaffier and Belvidera in 'Venice Preserv'd'
1762

Oil on canvas, 101.6 × 127 cm (40 × 50 in)
The Holburne Museum, Bath

Provenance: Henry Irving; Somerset Maugham; Trustees of the Shakespeare Memorial National Theatre Trust; transferred to the Holburne Museum, Bath, 2010

Selected exhibitions: Hayward Gallery 1975, no. 23

Selected references: Mander & Mitchenson 1955, 4–11; Mander & Mitchenson 1980, no. 3; Lennox-Boyd 1994, 55–7; Webster 2011, 183, 187–9

This is a version of one of Zoffany's earliest theatrical compositions for Garrick; the original painting (private collection) is mentioned with *The Farmer's Return* (see cats. 17, 18) on Zoffany's receipt of 23 April 1763 (Garrick Club). Garrick hung the two paintings together in the dining room of his house in the Adelphi where they served to show Garrick off in both humorous and tragic roles. Thomas Otway's *Venice Preserv'd, Or, A Plot Discover'd* (first performed in 1682) was considered to be the greatest tragedy after those of Shakespeare. The painting commemorates one of the great partnerships of the eighteenth-century stage, since it was recognized that Susannah Cibber's naturally passive character was ideally suited to playing against the emotionally charged acting of Garrick. They were 'formed by nature', Francis Gentleman considered, 'for the illustration of each other's talents'.[1]

The present picture is one of several versions (others Garrick Club and Fine Arts Museum, Budapest) recording the performance on either 20 October (a revival after a two-year gap) or 16 November 1762, Garrick and Cibber having first taken the leads together at Drury Lane on 8 February 1748. The original painting was already completed and could be viewed in Zoffany's studio by 11 January 1763.[2]

The plot is wrought to an almost impossibly high pitch in a tale of conspiracy against the Venetian state, double dealing, secret marriages, threatened rape, broken vows, betrayal of friendship and conflicts of loyalty. It offered Garrick the chance to portray countless transitions of mood, in which he was considered unequalled, as his character is flung this way and that by the twists of fate. Zoffany depicts the moment when the rather equivocal hero Jaffier, horrified at how he has been duped by the Venetian Senate into betraying his friend Pierre, who has been plotting the assassination of the Senators, blames his wife Belvedira for what has happened and makes to stab her. In a drawn-out climax to the scene (Act IV, Scene 2), during which Jaffier makes successive threats, Belvedira falls to her knees in the moment depicted here:

> *Jaffier.* I gave this dagger with thee, as in Trust,
> To be thy Portion, if I e'er proved false.
> On such Condition was my Truth believ'd:
> But now 'tis forfeited, and must be paid for.
> [*Offers to stab her again*]
> *Belvidera* [*kneeling*]. Oh! Mercy!

She then forces him to kiss her and he throws away the dagger. But tragedy is not to be averted, and in the end all the principal characters die. Jaffier stabs Pierre (to save him from a shameful death on the wheel) and then himself, while Belvedira expires at the sight of Jaffier's ghost.

Venice was a by-word for the all-powerful state and for treachery, assassination and betrayal. Zoffany has made the most of it with his dramatic use of lighting, the action played out beneath a flaring lamp. The convincing moonlit setting beside the Grand Canal, with a distant view of a characteristic church cupola, was his elaboration of the stage setting (which was an interior at this point).

RS

1. Francis Gentleman, *The Dramatic Censor*, 2 vols., London, 1770, vol. 1, 85–6.
2. And so the composition cannot be based (as is sometimes said) on their next performance, 13 March 1763; Lennox-Boyd 1994, 56.

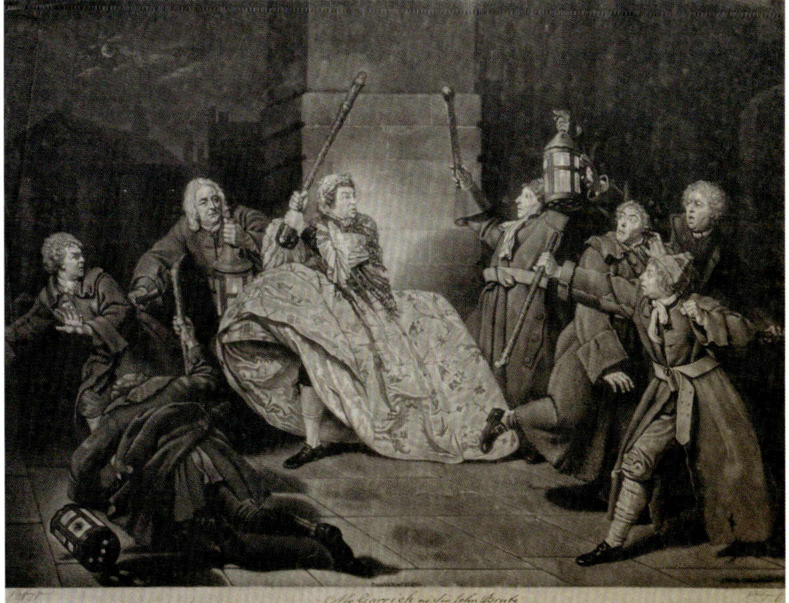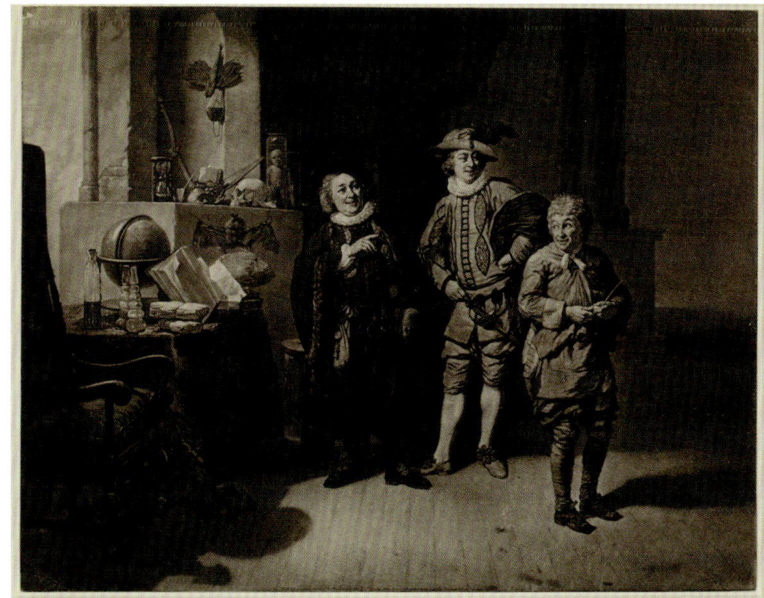

20

John Finlayson after Johan Zoffany, *David Garrick as Sir John Brute in Act IV, the Drunken Scene, in Vanbrugh's 'The Provok'd Wife'*
1768

Mezzotint engraving,
47.3 × 57.5 cm (18⅝ × 22⅝ in)
Inscribed: 'MR. GARRICK in the character of
S^R. JOHN BRUTE, M^r. Vaughan, M^r. Hallet,
M^r. Clough, M^r. Parsons, M^r. Watkins, &
M^r. Phillips, in the Characters of the Watchmen.
THE PROVOK' D WIFE. ACT IV, SCENE 1 …'
Private collection: exhibited Royal Academy
of Arts
Yale Center for British Art, Paul Mellon Collection:
exhibited Yale Center for British Art

Selected exhibitions: Society of Artists, 1769
(mezzotint), no. 266

Selected references: Mander & Mitchenson 1955,
46–53; Lennox-Boyd 1994, 37–8; Webster 2011,
183, 189–92

The action here was an eighteenth-century
variation of a scene (Act IV, Scene 2) in the play by
Sir John Vanbrugh of 1697.[1] Sir John Brute, who
fancies himself unhappily constrained by his recent
marriage, has been drinking with his friends Lord
Rake and Colonel Bully when he meets a tailor in
Covent Garden carrying a new gown for his wife
Lady Brute. The original play called for a parson's
outfit, but the change, perhaps initiated by Colley
Cibber, made for a more amusing incident 'in drag'.[2]
Sir John takes the dress and puts it on, whereupon
the (rather violent) revellers are interrupted by
the Watch. When asked to stop, Brute refuses
('May-hap not'), and when asked, 'And who are you,
Madam, that seems to be at the head of this noble
crew?' he replies (in further additional lines):

'Sirrah, I am Bonduca, Queen of the Welchmen;
and with a leek as long as my pedigree,[3] I will
destroy your Roman legions in an instant. Britons,
Strike home. [*Snatches a Watchman's staff, strikes
at the Watch, and falls down; his party drove off.*]'

Garrick played Brute no fewer than 105 times
and his success in the part ('his favourite') is
testimony to the charm that he was able to exert
over his audience.[4] He transformed the character
from James Quin's 'coarse drunk-sodden boor',
and made him more complex than Colley Cibber's
'soured and overbearing' character. Garrick created
an attractive 'gentleman debauchee', whom even
women found appealing, much of the charm arising
from the astonishing naturalism of Garrick's comic
'business'.[5]

Garrick played Brute at Drury Lane on 18 April
1763 and it has been asserted that the cast of the
Watch identifies the composition as having been
based on that evening's performance, although it
is not clear on what evidence; the assertion that
the performance of that evening was a revival is
incorrect.[6] In 1762 Garrick had played Brute in
February, March and April and did so again on
29 October 1762, followed by a performance on
12 January 1763. Garrick must have sat for the
painting before he left England on his Grand Tour
in September that year. He returned on 27 April
1765, when the painting was already on exhibition
at the Society of Artists (no. 167).

Henry Angelo recorded that the 'first studies
from Garrick, for the drunken scene in the *Provoked
Wife*' were painted in Zoffany's studio in the Piazza,
Covent Garden, but that the whole painting was not
finished until Zoffany had moved to Lincoln's Inn
Fields, which was towards the end of 1764. He also
tells us how the yellow dress was brought from the
theatre for Garrick to put on during the sitting.[7]

RS

1. The scene is numbered '1' on the print, although in
practice it was the second scene, since the act opens
in Lady Brute's bedchamber and then shifts to this
scene in Covent Garden; the text of 1777 'regulated
from the Prompt-Book' at Drury Lane (Bell's edition)
does not number the scenes.

2. The altered scene, sometimes said to have been
written by Vanbrugh, first appears in print in the
Dublin edition of 1743, 'in which is inserted, an
original scene, never before printed'. Cibber last
played Brute at Drury Lane on 23 January 1744
(Quin was still playing the part at Covent Garden
at this time). Garrick first played Sir John Brute on
16 November 1744.

3. The frequent satirical references to the length of a
Welsh pedigree partly arose from the custom of
establishing legitimacy in Wales through the recital
of several generations, each one prefaced by 'ap'
('son of'). In addition, there was an understandable
pride among the Welsh in having been established
as the original 'Britons' who had fought the Romans,
long before the arrival of the Anglo-Saxons, hence
the dragging in also of 'Bonduca' (Boudicca).

4. Lichtenberg 1938, 71.

5. Lichtenberg 1938, 71. For Garrick's playing, see
George Winchester Stone, Jr., and George M. Kahrl,
David Garrick: A Critical Biography, Carbondale, Ill.,
1979, 490ff.

6. Iain Mackintosh and Geoffrey Ashton, *The Georgian
Playhouse: Actors, Artists, Audiences and Architecture
1730–1830*, exh. cat., Hayward Gallery, London, 1975,
no. 27; Mander & Mitchenson 1980, no.6.

7. Angelo 1828–30, vol. 1, 147. The small-scale,
full-length study made on that occasion is now at the
Holburne Museum, Bath. When Garrick returned to
England, he took a dislike to the head, which Zoffany
repainted on an oval piece of canvas inserted into the
whole. He did the same with the finished, large-scale
painting exhibited at the Society of Artists (Lord
Normanby collection). Garrick then commissioned a
replica, painted on one coherent canvas, which he left
to his brother George (now Wolverhampton Art
Gallery; see fig. 47).

John Dixon after Johan Zoffany, *David Garrick as Abel Drugger in 'The Alchymist'*
1771

Mezzotint engraving,
47.8 × 60.1 cm (18¾ × 23⅝ in)
Inscribed: 'I Zoffany Pinxt. | Publishd according to Act of Parliament January the 12th 1771 by John Dixon in Kemps Row opposite Ranelagh Chelsea and Sold by A Dury in Dukes Court St Martins Lane Ca. Bowles in St. Pauls Church Yard and J. Boydel Cheapside | To Fredk Howard Earl of Carlisle Vict. Morpeth | This Plate is humbly Inscribed by his Lordships Obedt Servt, John Dixon | J Dixon Fecit'
British Museum, Department of Prints and Drawings (1902,1011.745)

Exhibited at the Royal Academy of Arts only

John Dixon after Johan Zoffany, *David Garrick as Abel Drugger in 'The Alchymist'*
1776

Mezzotint engraving, 39.4 × 27.9 cm (15½ × 11 in)
Inscribed: 'I. Dixon Fecit | J. Zoffany Pinxᵗ |
Publish'd as the Act directs March 18 1776 by
R. Sayer and J. Bennett'
Yale Center for British Art, Paul Mellon Collection

Exhibited at the Yale Center for British Art only

Selected references: Lennox-Boyd 1994, 60–62;
Webster 2011, 183, 206–10

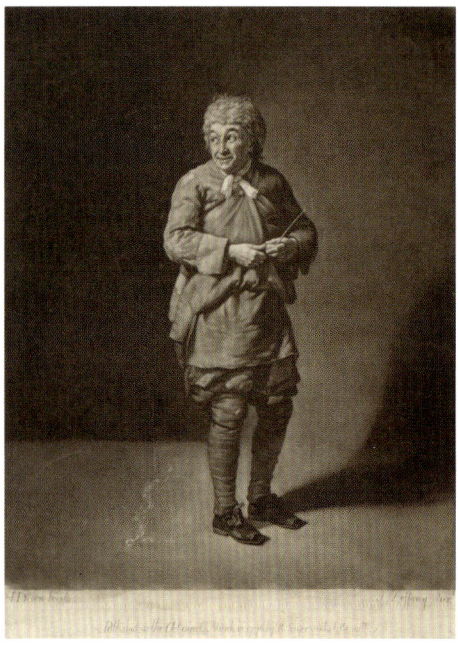

Both prints record Garrick's most astonishing comic performance, immortalized by Zoffany in a painting formerly in the Castle Howard collection (see fig. 48). In a part of barely thirty speaking lines Garrick stole every scene in which he appeared. The other actors are Edmund Burton[1] as Subtle, and John 'Plausible' Palmer as Face. Ben Jonson's play, *The Alchemist*, first performed in 1610, was adapted in the eighteenth century and Garrick first played the role of Abel Drugger in 1743, developing variations in eighty performances until 11 April 1776. If any doubts persist about Garrick's capacity fully to inhabit a character and perform it with extreme naturalism, Zoffany's composition refutes them, an impression confirmed by a host of admiring contemporary accounts.

There has been considerable confusion over which scene of *The Alchemist* is represented in this composition, because the stage business with which Garrick chiefly created the character is not usually recorded in the stage directions.[2] In Act II Drugger (at the right of the print) has arrived to ask advice of a conman, Subtle (left), who is masquerading as an alchemist, a confidence trick in which he is aided by a butler or housekeeper, Jeremy, in the persona of 'Captain' Face (centre), the action taking place in the town house of the absent Lovewit. The 'tobacco boy', Drugger, wants a shop sign for his new premises. Face suggests that they devise one on the basis of Drugger's astrological sign, but Subtle dismisses this idea as old-fashioned and suggests one spelled out in the form of rebuses, pictures that suggest words:

I will have his Name
Form'd in some mystic Character …
He shall have a Bell, that's Abel;
And by it standing one whose Name is Dee,
In a Rug Gown; there's D, and Rug, that's Drug:
And right anenst [against] him a Dog snarling Er;
There's Drugger, Abel Drugger.

There now followed a sequence invented by Garrick, with additional dialogue and business, as Drugger now exclaims, almost to himself: 'My name!' A contemporary recorded: 'Garrick makes him keep his joy to himself … So Garrick turns aside, hugging his delight to himself for a few moments, so that he actually gets those red rings round his eyes which often accompany great joy … when violently suppressed.'[3]

In the painting the redness of Drugger's face can be clearly seen. Although the present picture is a fine mezzotint, it is noticeable that it cannot quite match up to Zoffany's acute depiction of Garrick's expression. But the moment in the action is clear: Subtle is pointing to Drugger as he says, 'There's Drugger, Abel Drugger', while Face turns towards him in confirmation of the 'Doctor's' ingenuity. The subsequent action (Garrick's development of a hint in the text) is meanwhile suggested by the pipe of tobacco and smoking plug from it that has fallen on the floor. In Jonson's original play Drugger simply hands over a pipe of tobacco as a gift. In Garrick's version, however, Face catches sight of the pipe ('What's got there, Nab?'), which Drugger is partly trying to conceal, and then forces him to hand it over as a 'present' for the 'Doctor'.[4]

The print of Garrick alone (cat. 22), published on 18 March 1776, was evidently prepared by Dixon from the whole plate (the difference in dimensions indicates as much). It must have been swiftly produced in order to cash in on the news of Garrick's imminent retirement from the stage, which was announced on 7 March 1776, although negotiations over the sale of Garrick's patent at Drury Lane Theatre had begun in January. There followed a stampede for tickets for Garrick's farewell performances, which included Abel Drugger on 13 April.

RS

1. Not William Burton or John Burton as sometimes stated. John Burton (d. 1797) was Edmund Burton's son and 'worthy only in little parts', playing Kastrill in *The Alchemist* (1770 and 1777 editions).
2. The various editions of the play vary considerably in the dialogue, reflecting the variations that Garrick brought to different performances. The best guide is the edition published by John Bell in 1777, which was created from the promptbook of the Drury Lane prompter William Hopkins. Reprinted in H.W. Pedicord and F.L. Bergmann, *The Plays of David Garrick*, vol. 5, 'Alterations of Others, 1742–1750', Carbondale and Edwardsville, 1982.
3. Lichtenberg 1938, 3–4.
4. For the two sketches made by Zoffany of Garrick in this role (Ashmolean Museum, Oxford), often referred to as preparatory for this composition, see fig. 63.

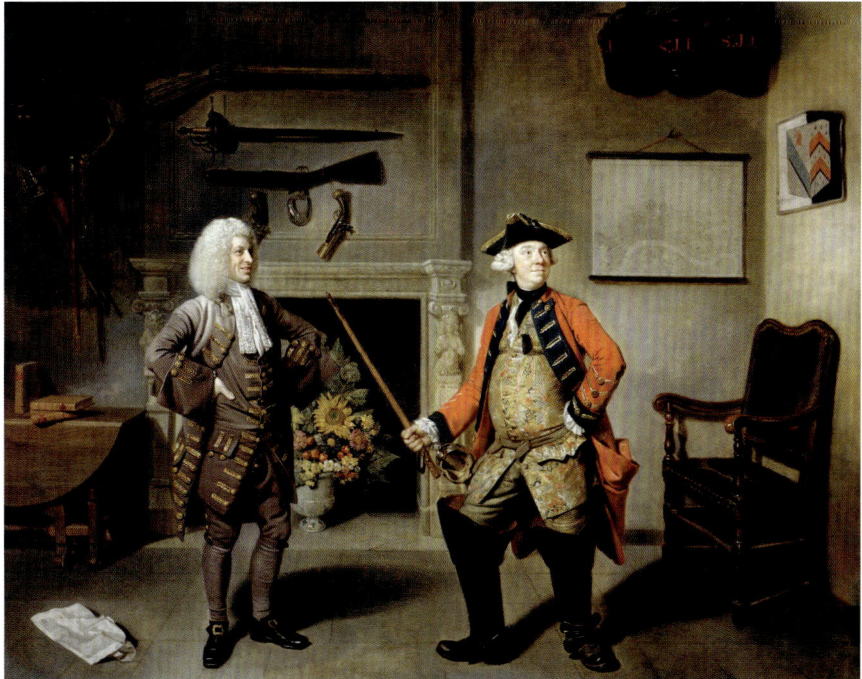

23

***Samuel Foote as Major Sturgeon and Hayes as
Sir Jacob Jollup in 'The Mayor of Garret'***
1763–4

Oil on canvas, 101.6 × 127 cm (40 × 50 in)
Castle Howard Collection

Provenance: Commissioned by Samuel Foote; his
sale, Christie's, 26 Jan. 1778 (13), bt Whitefoorde;
George Colman sale, Christie's, 4 Aug. 1795 (97);
bt Woolmer, sale Christie's 7 May 1796 (106);
bt Bryan for the Earl of Carlisle

Selected exhibitions: Society of Artists, 1764, no. 140;
Hayward Gallery 1975, no. 24; National Portrait
Gallery 1977, no. 23

Selected references: Lennox-Boyd 1994, 33–4;
Webster 2011, 181, 182, 193–5

Engraving: Mezzotint by Johann Gottfried Haid,
1765, for John Boydell

The picture illustrates Act I, Scene 1 (p. 7), of the
play by Samuel Foote, *The Mayor of Garret*, first
produced on 20 June 1763. Foote's accounts record
a payment for the picture of £42 to Zoffany on 25
October 1763, which accords with the 20 guineas
per whole-length figure that Zoffany was charging
at this time. The painting hung in the dining room
at Foote's town house in Suffolk Street, off Charing
Cross, while *The Devil upon Two Sticks* (see cat. 24)
was in the drawing room.[1] The action takes place
during the mock election of a 'mayor' in the tiny
hamlet of Garratt in Surrey,[2] an old tradition that
became increasingly popular in the latter part of
the eighteenth century.[3] There had been an election
in the year the play appeared, but the tradition's
popularity had reached new heights on the previous

occasion, 20 May 1761, when it was attended by
Foote, together with Garrick and John Wilkes.

Foote plays the part of Sturgeon (stage left),
a fishmonger who has been made a major in the
militia. The scene turns on his hopeless attempts to
live up to what he perceives as his new military and
gentlemanly status. Sir Jacob Jollup, a magistrate
(originally played by 'Hayes', whose first name is
not recorded but who is shown here[4]), is himself
rather touchy about his new knighthood and tells
Sturgeon he wishes that he had been present a
moment sooner, as he has just had a visit from an
impudent 'pill-monger' (Lint), to which Sturgeon,
looking off stage left in the direction of the
departed Lint, cries out: 'Insolent companion!
Had I been here, I would have mittimus'd the rascal
at once.'[5] This martial explosion is deflated by the
fact that, instead of drawing his sword which,
unfortunately, he is wearing on the wrong side,
Sturgeon is brandishing his cane. Jollup, in allusion
to this fact, replies: 'No, no, he wanted the Major
more than the magistrate; a few smart strokes from
your cane would have fully answer'd the purpose.'
It is clear that Zoffany depicts the two men holding
their poses, milking the applause: we see the actors
in and out of character at the same time. This was
a distinctive aspect of Foote's acting, as he made
a point in his productions of exploiting his own
celebrity.[6]

The action continues with Jollup teasing
the fishmonger about his training in the militia.
Sturgeon's ludicrously outsized boots draw
attention to his clumsy attempt to adopt the correct
deportment of a gentleman, with 'turned out toes',[7]
the feet at right angles to each other (we note that
Jollup adopts the correct position):

Jollup. Was it not rather late in life for you, to enter
upon the profession of arms?
Major. A little aukward in the beginning, Sir Jacob:
The great difficulty they had was, to get me to turn
out my toes; but use, use reconciles all them kind
of things.

When about to transfer his play to Drury Lane,
Foote appears to have taken advantage of Garrick's
recent departure on his Grand Tour (15 September
1763) by employing Zoffany.

RS

1. Francis Russell, 'Samuel Foote's villa and a neglected
   view painter', *Burlington Magazine*, vol. 126, no. 980
   (Aug. 1984), 500–503, esp. 500.
2. 'Garret' is the spelling on the published edition of the
   play in 1764, but 'Garratt' is used in later editions.
3. Hone 1837, vol. 2, cols 819–65 (22 June); Robert
   Chambers, ed., *The Book of Days: A Miscellany of
   Popular Antiquities …*, 2 vols., London and Edinburgh,
   1869; Edward Walford, *Old and New London*, 6 vols.,
   1878, vol. 6, 479–89.
4. 'Hayes', whose initial was probably 'F.', played the part
   in the original production and was identified correctly
   as being portrayed in this painting in the Foote sale,
   1778. The identification of the actor in this painting
   as Robert Baddeley (who is listed in the first published
   edition of this play) is incorrect. Hayes took the part
   again in 1764. For Hayes, see Highfill *et al.* 1973–93,
   vol. 7, 205–6.
5. 'Mittimus': a writ for sending to prison.
6. A real-life 'Mayor of Garret', 'Sir' Jeffery Dunstan,
   was put on stage at the Haymarket as a celebrity to
   play Dr Last in 1782 in an excerpt from Foote's
   The Devil upon Two Sticks: see pp. 61 and 63.
7. R. Simon 2007, 161ff.; and see cat. 62.

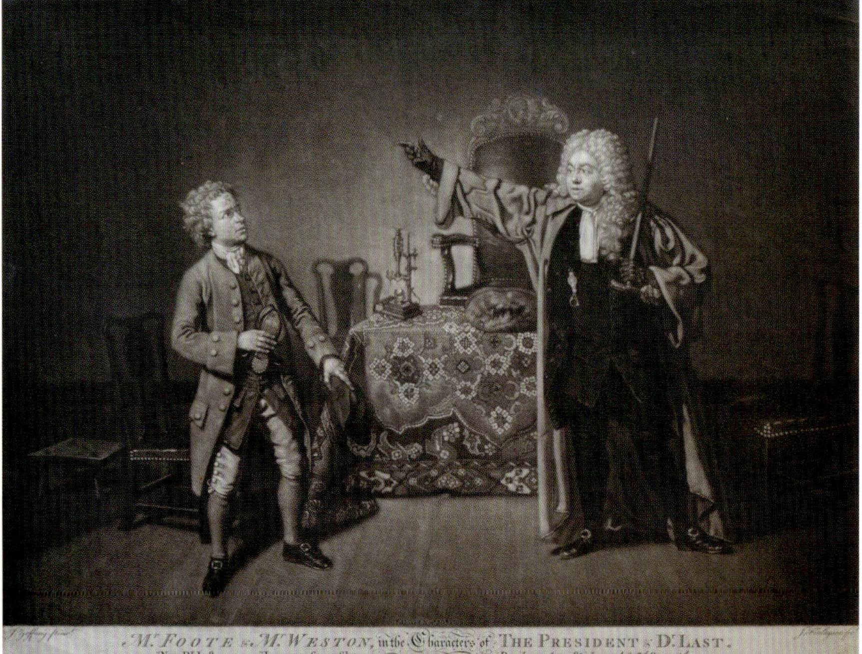

24

John Finlayson after Johan Zoffany, *Mr Foote and Mr Weston in the Characters of the President and Dr Last in 'The Devil upon Two Sticks'*
1769

Mezzotint engraving, 46 × 56.8 cm (18⅛ × 22⅜ in)
Inscribed (private collection impression): 'J Zoffany pinx.t Published Nov.r 30th 1769 J. Finlayson fec.t | M.r FOOTE & M.r WESTON, in the Characters of THE PRESIDENT & D.r LAST. | "Now D.r Last —" I am come for my Shoes. Devil on two Sticks, Act 3.d Scene 2.d | Sold by M. Zoffany in Lincoln's Inn Fields, M. Finlayson, & M.r Parker at N.o 82 in Cornhill.'
Private collection: exhibited Royal Academy of Arts
Yale Center for British Art, Paul Mellon Collection: exhibited Yale Center for British Art

Selected exhibitions: Society of Artists, 1769 (painting), no. 214; Society of Artists, 1770 (mezzotint), no. 204

Selected references: Mander & Mitchenson 1955, 38–45; Lennox-Boyd 1994, 65–6; Phyllis T. Dircks, 'Foote, Samuel', *ODNB*, http://www.oxforddnb.com/view/article/9808 (accessed 21 June 2011); Black 2007, cat. 92; Webster 2011, 181, 182, 195–7

Like *The Mayor of Garret* (cat. 23), *The Devil upon Two Sticks* was characteristic of Samuel Foote's writing and playing for the stage. His theatre, the Little Theatre, Haymarket, was not initially one of the two licensed by royal patent (Drury Lane and Covent Garden), but Foote then lost a leg in an accident when thrown by a horse belonging to the Duke of York in February 1766 and was subsequently granted a limited patent, allowing

him to perform plays for the summer season every year, which enabled Foote to advertise as the 'Theatre Royal' and 'His Majesty's Company of Comedians'. Foote had a specially carved wooden leg for use on stage, mounted with a silk stocking and gold-buckled shoe, and walked with the aid of a golden crutch: both are seen here.

The Devil upon Two Sticks, first performed 30 May 1768, earned Foote a fortune, £2,000 in 1768 alone. Far from hiding his disability, Foote exploited it, in the character of a devil who at his first appearance announces: 'I got lame on this leg and obtained the nick-name of the Devil Upon Sticks' (Act I). Act II leads straight into a highly topical satire on the Royal College of Physicians in London, which was being torn apart by demonstrations against restrictive practices. The great anatomist William Hunter had actually taken part in the notorious storming of the building by Licentiates in September 1767. Hunter owned a mezzotint of Zoffany's composition, while his brother John (a particular friend of Zoffany) was subsequently in possession of a version of the oil painting.[1]

The Devil assumes the guise of the President of the College, Dr Hellebore (Act II, 1778 edition, 54ff.), whose presidential chair can be seen centre stage behind the table, as he organizes his fellow-physicians against the coming attack of the Licentiates. Meanwhile, he proceeds to the examination of a cobbler, Emmanuel Last, an ignorant rustic, who prefers to pay in London for a licence to practise than for a 'diplummy' from Scotland. To make the most of his visit, Last is at the same time bringing a pair of shoes for a neighbour's son in Cheapside. Last is duly admitted as a Licentiate of the College, but the following

lecture is interrupted by the storming of the College. A characteristic scene of farce ensues, with rapid dialogue amid entrances and exits through different doors, in which Foote was an important pioneer. In the midst of the brouhaha, the President is surprised, and momentarily lost for words, by the re-appearance of Last, who has merely re-entered to collect his shoes. This was one of the most famous moments of the actor playing Last, Thomas Weston (1737–76), who was a master of comic characterization and timing.[2] And the relevant lines and scene were printed on a later state of the mezzotint: '[*President.*] "Now D.r Last —" [*Dr. Last.*] I am come for my Shoes. Devil on two Sticks, Act 3.d Scene 2.d'

The painting also takes in the moment that immediately follows, as Last reels back on taking his leave, when faced with the President's abrupt recovery of his strength as he once again begins to rally his 'troops', exhorting them to chase the Licentiates up Fleet Street. Foote, for comic effect, is brandishing his own golden crutch, in place of the gold-headed cane that was the proper symbol of a Doctor of Physic. Foote mimicked the current President of the Royal College of Physicians, Sir William Browne, with such precision that Browne sent him a note of congratulation, pointing out that the only thing lacking was his muff, which he enclosed. It is prominently placed on the table.

RS

1. Black 2007, cat. 92. He also owned a version of its companion, *The Mayor of Garret*: Christie's sale, 29 Jan. 1794 (83, 104).
2. John Joseph Knight, 'Thomas Weston', *Dictionary of National Biography*, ed. L. Stephen and S. Lee, 1885–1900.

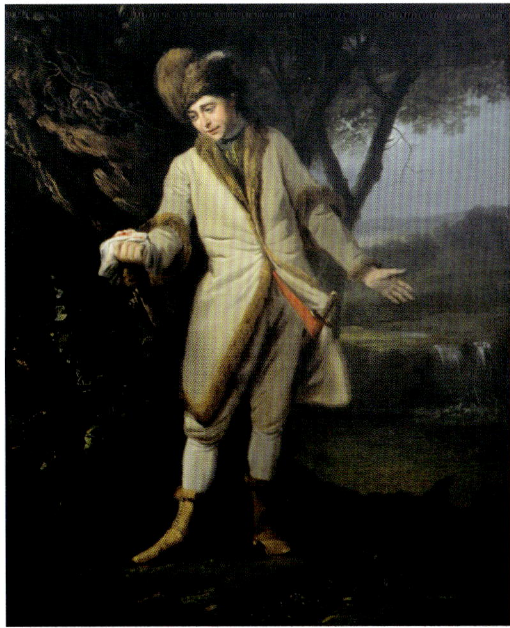

25

William Powell as Posthumus in 'Cymbeline'
*c.*1767

Oil on canvas, 91.4 × 71.1 cm (36 × 28 in)
Private collection

Provenance: Marchioness of Huntly (label 1885);
private collection until 1994; Philip Mould
Historical Portraits (as by Francis Wheatley)

Selected exhibitions: Hayward Gallery 1975, no. 26

Selected references: Treadwell 2009, 88–91

This painting shows William Powell, a veritable
shooting star of the Georgian theatre, whose career
lasted barely six years. During that time Powell
rose from 'stage-door johnny' to becoming one
of the most successful actors of the day, finally
becoming a quarter-owner of the patent at the
Theatre Royal Covent Garden which was bought
from John Beard and the widow of John Rich
(see cat. 27) for £60,000 on 1 July 1767. This
was one of the surest ways to make a fortune in
late-eighteenth-century London, and Powell
celebrated in style. He acquired a country house
and commissioned a number of paintings. At least
two, exhibited at the Society of Artists in 1768,
were by his friend and cricketing companion John
Hamilton Mortimer, one showing his family in
a conversation piece at their new house and the
other himself in the title role of *King John* (both
Garrick Club). The present painting, which exists
in two versions, must be another commission
dating from this period of new prosperity and
status.[1] The relative positions of the drapery
and sword show that the other version (where
the sword is inside rather than outside the coat)
was the one etched for Robert Sayer and Jonathan
Smith's publication, *Dramatic Characters, or
Different Portraits of the English Stage* (fig. 172).[2]

The Monday of 28 December 1767 was a royal
command performance in the presence of George
III and Queen Charlotte, which was probably
commemorated by this commission from Zoffany.

Powell had begun playing Posthumus at Drury
Lane, having taken it over from Garrick (first
performance 1 December 1763). Garrick had been
looking around for a young actor whom he might
train up in some of his roles while he went away to
the Continent, which he did on 15 September that
year. Powell was an astonishing success, first in
the title role of George Colman's adaptation of
Philaster by Francis Beaumont and John Fletcher
on 8 October, when the battle-hardened prompter
William Hopkins recorded: 'His Reception was
very great, he play'd the part amazingly well &
Seems to have Requisites to make a very Capital
Performer … A greater reception was never shown
to anybody … continued claps and huzzas of
bravo!'[3] In *Cymbeline* the reaction of the prompter
was more mixed: '[Powell was] very Wild &
Stampt too much with his foot receiv'd much
Applause.'[4] Despite the misgivings of colleagues
in the profession, including Garrick, Powell
remained a huge success with the audience until
his premature demise. The reason for his death
was the love of cricket that he shared with
Mortimer. He used to play and manage the theatre
in Bristol for the summer season, and caught
pneumonia after stripping off his cricketing clothes
and lying down on the grass in order to cool off.
After a month's illness he died on 3 July 1769.

Cymbeline is a play of improbable complexity
(Dr Johnson hated it) with a corresponding density
of language, even when heavily pruned in Garrick's
customary manner. What he thought of as an
'edition' was published in 1762 with a disclaimer:
'The Admirers of *Shakespear* must not take it ill that
there are some Scenes, and consequently many fine
Passages, omitted in this Edition of CYMBELINE.'
His version was first performed, with Garrick

himself as Posthumus, on 28 November 1761.
The present picture shows Posthumus at the
opening of Act V, Scene 2, when he enters 'with a
bloody handkerchief', the token he has asked for
as proof that his wife Imogen (whom he wrongly
believes to have been unfaithful) has been slain on
his orders. He addresses the handkerchief:

> Yea, bloody cloth, I'll keep thee; for I wisht
> Thou should'st be colour'd thus.

Cymbeline had a considerable hold on contemporary
audiences, perhaps on account of a fashionable
interest in the mythic world of ancient Britain. Its
locations move swiftly between Rome, the court of
Cymbeline ('King of Britain') and the mountains of
Wales, while the conflict between the Romans and
Britons carried a resonance of the concurrent Seven
Years War with France. Audiences warmed to the
appealing character of Imogen, while Posthumus
offered actors such as Garrick and Powell the
chance to revel in a character torn apart by extreme
emotions, like Jaffier in *Venice Preserv'd* (cat. 19), a
part that Powell had also taken over from Garrick
(first performed 22 November 1763). The *Public
Advertiser* of 3 December 1763 noted that Powell's
vivid playing of Posthumus was suited to the
strongly drawn character: 'The versatility of
Jealousy, Love, Tenderness, and Resentment, so
variously interspersed throughout this Tragedy,
are very strongly marked in the features of his face
and Tones of Voice; which, like the Strings upon
Musical Instruments, justly answered to the
Impressions made on them by the Mind.'

RS

1. It has previously been thought to date from *c.*1764
   (see Treadwell 2009, 90).
2. Aubrey M. Davidson, Sotheby's, 18 June 1969, no. 115,
   and Christie's, 20 June 1975, no. 89. It is slightly
   smaller at 88.9 × 69.8 cm (exhibited *Shakespeare in Art*,
   Nottingham University Art Gallery, 1961, no. 17,
   lent by Leger; Guildhall Art Gallery 1964, no. 7).
3. Diary of William Hopkins (20 Oct. 1763) in the
   London Stage (under 8 Oct. 1763) and see Highfill
   et al. 1973–93, vol. 12, 130–39.
4. Diary of William Hopkins in the *London Stage*
   (under 1 Dec. 1763).

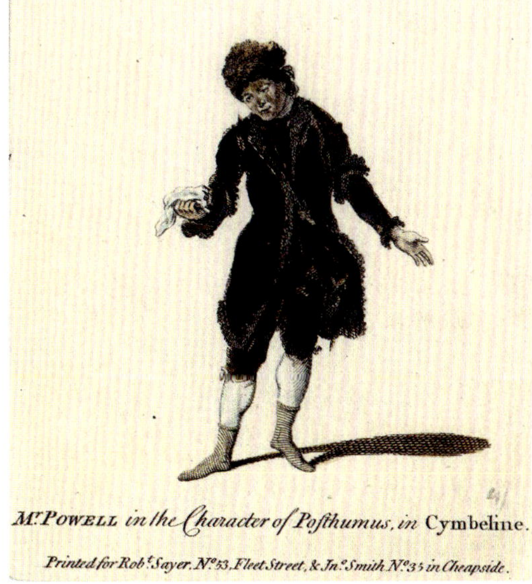

Figure 172
Jean Louis Faesch and ? Charles Grignion, after
Johan Zoffany, '*Mr Powell in the Character of Posthumus,
in Cymbeline*', *c.*1770–73, engraving and etching,
8.9 × 8.75 cm (3½ × 2⅞ in). University of Illinois
at Urbana-Champaign

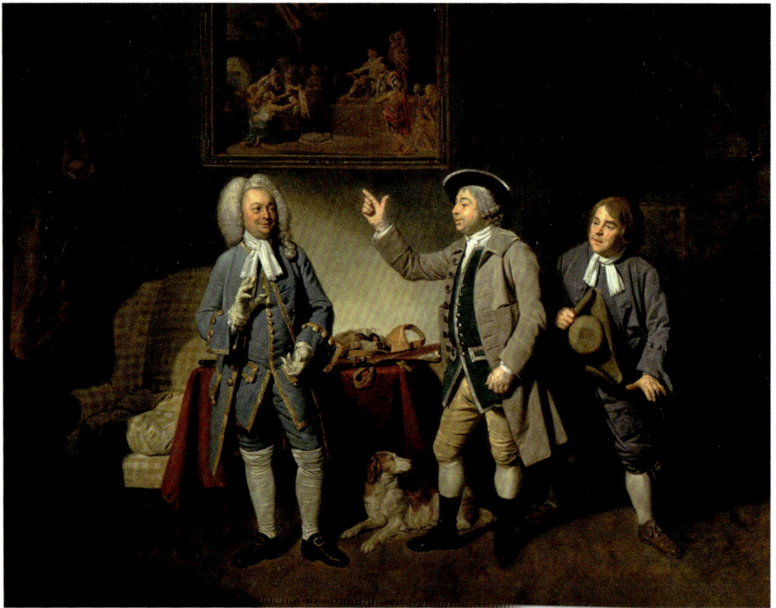

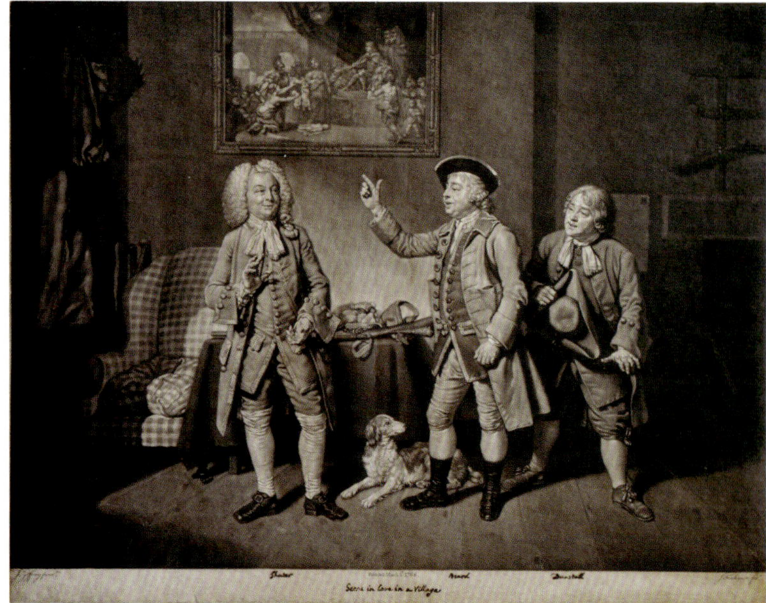

26

Edward Shuter, John Beard and John Dunstall in Isaac Bickerstaffe's 'Love in a Village'
1767

Oil on canvas, 130.2 × 165.1 cm (51¼ × 65 in)
Yale Center for British Art, Paul Mellon Collection

Exhibited at the Yale Center for British Art only

Provenance: Zoffany sale, Messrs Robins, 9 May 1811 (97)?; Acton Garle, *c.*1830; Christie's, 26 April 1985 (114); John Baskett; Paul Mellon, 1985

Selected exhibitions: Society of Artists, 1767, no. 194?; Society of Artists Special Exhibition, Sept. 1768, no. 138?; Society of Artists, 1768 (mezzotint), no. 240; South Kensington Museum 1867, no. 614; *British Comic Art 1730–1830*, Museum of Art and Archaeology, Univ. of Missouri, Columbia, 1988

Selected references: Manners & Williamson 1920, 17, 139; Mander & Mitcheson 1955, 24–36; Webster 2011, 181, 197–201

27

John Finlayson after Johan Zoffany, *Edward Shuter, John Beard and John Dunstall in Isaac Bickerstaffe's 'Love in a Village'*
1768

Mezzotint engraving,
41.7 × 45.5 cm (16⅜ × 17⅞ in)
Inscribed: 'J. Zoffany pinx.ᵗ Publish'd March 1ˢᵗ: 1768 J. Finlayson fec.ᵗ'; and in ink: 'Shuter | Scene in Love in a Village | Beard | Dunstall'
Private collection

Exhibited at the Royal Academy of Arts only

Love in a Village was one of the most popular theatrical productions of the eighteenth century. The actor in the centre playing Hawthorn is the famous singer John Beard, a tenor who starred in many of Handel's operas. Edward 'Ned' Shuter, playing Justice Woodcock on the left, was a renowned comic and singer, while the third actor is John Dunstall as Hodge (the contemporary term for a country bumpkin). All were in the original cast when the production began at Covent Garden on 8 December 1762, and the painting was commissioned to record their last performance together, on 9 April 1767. It also marked Beard's retirement from the stage.

Like the earlier *Beggar's Opera* and *Dragon of Wantley*, Isaac Bickerstaffe's *Love in a Village* was an example of a 'ballad opera', with new English words sung to the tunes of familiar songs. The plot is a lightly tangled tale of romance, disguises and mistaken identity, set in an archetypal English village. There are no dark shadows of any kind and the dialogue and action move along at a brisk pace. There are no fewer than forty-four songs, all short, rarely comprising more than two verses. The mixture of the fresh and the familiar was a winning formula first devised by John Gay in *The Beggar's Opera* in 1728. Beard himself was a celebrated Macheath in *The Beggar's Opera*, and *Love in a Village* was one of his first new productions at Covent Garden when the theatre came under his effective management after the death of his father-in-law John Rich in 1761. Beard sold the patent on 1 July for the staggering sum of £60,000, when a quarter share was bought by William Powell (see cat. 25).

Act I, Scene 5, is set in the hall of Justice Woodcock's house, where Hawthorn enters 'with a fowling-piece in his hand, and a net with birds at his girdle', both of which can be seen on the table in the centre, while the dog at his feet is referred to in the song he sings after the entry of Woodcock:

> Well, who cares a jot,
> I envy them not,
> While I have my dog and my gun.

Scene 6, identified on the print, follows immediately with the entrance of Hodge, who describes the goings-on at a fair for hiring servants on Woodcock's green. Woodcock hopes that he has powers, as a magistrate, to put a stop to it: 'I shall take measures for preventing it another year … by an act passed *Anno undecimo Caroli primi.*' Hawthorn, who likes the idea of the fair, then breaks into song, which is evidently the moment shown here:

> The greatness that would make us grave,
> Is but an empty thing;
> What more than mirth wou'd mortals have?
> The cheerful man's a king!

Three versions of the painting are known: one at the Detroit Institute of Arts; the present example; and one at the Holburne Museum, Bath. The first two, like the mezzotint, show a painting of the Judgement of Solomon on the back wall, the third, which is unfinished but of high quality, has Van Dyck's *Three Children of Charles I* in the background, in reference to Woodcock's words, quoted above, concerning an act passed in the time of Charles I.

RS

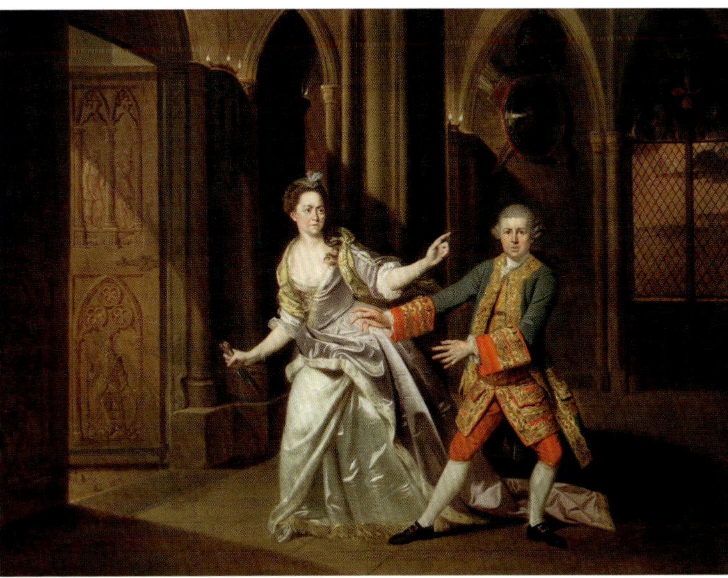

28
David Garrick and Mrs Pritchard in 'Macbeth'
1768

Oil on canvas, 102 × 127.5 cm (40⅛ × 50¼ in)
The Garrick Club, London

Provenance: Charles Mathews; acquired 1835

Selected exhibitions: Queen's Bazaar 1833, no. 57;
Tate 1951, no. 47; Guildhall Art Gallery 1964,
no. 15; Dulwich Picture Gallery 1997, no. 2;
Shakespeare in Western Art, c.1750–c.1910, Isetan
Museum of Art, Tokyo, Japan (and touring),
1992–3, no. 11; *Shakespeare in Art,* Palazzo dei
Diamanti Ferrara, Italy, and Dulwich Picture
Gallery, 2003, no. 34

Selected references: Lennox-Boyd 1994, 81–2;
Webster 2011, 183, 203–6

Figure 173
Henry Fuseli, *Garrick and Mrs Pritchard as Macbeth
and Lady Macbeth after the Murder of Duncan,*
*c.*1766, watercolour on paper,
32.3 × 29.4 cm (12¾ × 11⅝ in). Kunsthaus, Zurich

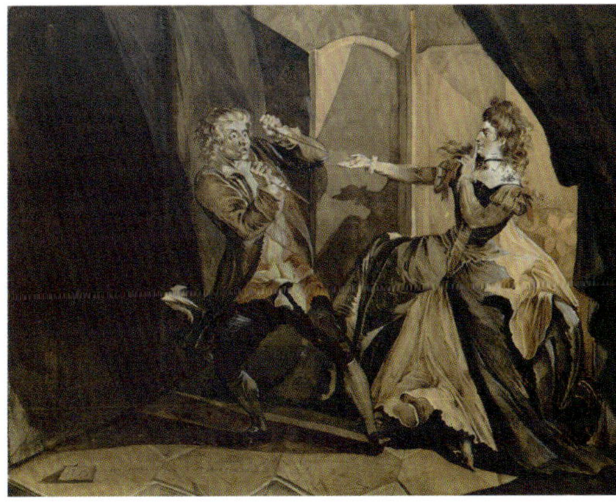

This picture was commissioned to mark the last
performance of Mrs Pritchard in the role of Lady
Macbeth, and her last appearance on stage, 25 April
1768. She died in August of the same year. The
scene here occurs in Act II, Scene 3, in Garrick's
production and shows the two main protagonists,
Macbeth and Lady Macbeth, immediately after the
murder by Macbeth of the sleeping king, Duncan.
The extraordinary intensity with which Garrick
and Pritchard played the scene, almost in whispers
throughout, established it as the turning point of
the whole play. Henry Fuseli, who saw them on
stage after his arrival in London in 1764, drew the
same scene (with some exaggeration) a little before
Zoffany did so (fig. 173). In his drawing we can see
how Lady Macbeth has her finger to her lips
reminding Macbeth to keep his voice down.[1]

There are two versions of Zoffany's painting,
both precisely modulated interpretations of
Garrick's text and production. One (Baroda
Museum and Picture Gallery) is that engraved by
Valentine Green, in which Lady Macbeth wears
black, whereas in the present version, which is not
a copy, she is in white. Among the other details that
distinguish this version from that in Baroda is the
position of the daggers: the two paintings represent
distinct moments in the action. The Baroda picture
shows Lady Macbeth ordering Macbeth to take the
daggers, with which he has stabbed Duncan, and go
back to the murder location, in order to incriminate
the grooms who sleep there:

> *Lady Macbeth.* Why did you bring these daggers
>   from the place?
> They must lie there: Go carry them, and smear
>   The sleepy grooms with blood.

She indicates with the index finger of her right
hand where he is to return. Garrick's own right
hand is still open, the daggers having just been
taken from his grasp. Immediately, Macbeth refuses
to comply with his wife's command:

> I'll go no more.
> I am afraid to think what I have done;
> Look on't again, I dare not.

In the present version the action has moved on,
while Garrick adopts a pose of 'repudiation' or
'aversion' and, with his mouth open, is clearly
speaking the lines just quoted.[2] But the precise
moment is poised between these and Lady
Macbeth's next words, as she adopts an attitude
of rebuke with her left-hand index finger.
She has taken the daggers and is about to say:

> Infirm of purpose!
> Give me the daggers; the sleeping and the dead
> Are but as pictures; 'tis the eye of childhood
> That fears a painted devil. If he do bleed,
> I'll gild the faces of the grooms withal,
> For it must seem their guilt. *Exit*[3]

Fuseli's drawing confirms that Zoffany's painting
is an imaginative recreation rather than an accurate
record of the staging. In Garrick's set Duncan's
chamber was stage left (to the right as we look), as
Fuseli shows it.[4] The double doors stage right (our
left) led to the rest of the castle, but in Zoffany's
composition, as is clear from the protagonists'
actions, they now lead back into Duncan's chamber.

RS

1. Fuseli called this 'the central moment … the crisis'
   of the play (John Knowles, ed., *The Life and Writings
   of Henry Fuseli, Esq., M.A. R.A.,* 3 vols., London, 1831,
   Aphorism 96, vol. 3, 94).
2. He averts his gaze, his face resolutely turned away
   from the object of his dislike, and with both his hands
   and his lower limbs pointing towards, while yet
   drawing away from, the location or action he is
   refusing to countenance. Discussed (in the context
   of *The Beggar's Opera*) in R. Simon 2007, 262.
3. The lines are taken from the publication of Garrick's
   version, 1773 (Bell edition, 'regulated from the
   Prompt Books').
4. Kalman Burnim, *David Garrick: Director,* Pittsburgh,
   1961, 111–14. Burnim did not note or resolve this
   inconsistency in the Zoffany image (p. 114).

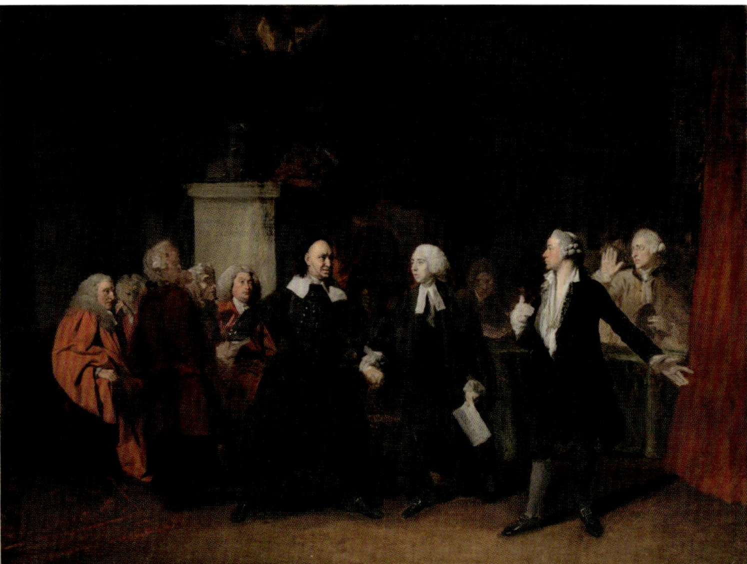

29

Charles Macklin as Shylock in *'The Merchant of Venice'*
*c.*1768, reworked ?1779

Oil on canvas, 116.2 × 151.1 cm (45¾ × 59½ in)
Tate, London; presented by the National Art Collections Fund, 1951

Provenance: Dominic Colnaghi; Lord Orford; Christie's (Wolterton House) 28 June 1856 (249); bt Farmer; Marquess of Lansdowne; presented to the Tate Gallery by the National Art Collections Fund, 1951

Selected exhibitions: Society of British Artists, 1832, no. 89; South Kensington Museum 1867, no. 806; *Exhibition of Works by the Old Masters and by Deceased Masters of the British School Including a Special Selection of Works by Paul Falconer Poole RA*, Royal Academy of Arts, 1884, no. 54; Park Lane 1930, no. 78; National Portrait Gallery 1977, no. 47

Selected references: Hughes 1981, 290–94; Mander & Mitchenson 1955, 56–63; Webster 2011, 210–13

Although Garrick is celebrated for revolutionizing the craft of acting in the middle years of the eighteenth century, he was not alone. The Irish actor Charles Macklin just preceded him in his transformation of Shylock from pantomime villain to a psychologically convincing character, first performed at Drury Lane 14 February 1741.[1] Macklin researched the part carefully, reading Josephus and visiting the Jewish quarter of London, as a result of which he adopted the costume we see here, the black 'Jewish gabardine' to which Shylock refers. The power of his performance was also captured by Zoffany in an individual portrait (Holburne Museum, Bath).

The four principal actors in the scene can be identified, the others besides Macklin being Maria Macklin as Portia, centre; Matthew Clarke, chest bared, as Antonio, right; and Robert Bensley as Bassanio, far right. All played together on several occasions at Covent Garden in the 1767–8 season. The likelihood is that Zoffany began this picture on his own account rather than as a commission, as it remained in his possession for at least another decade, for much of which he was away in Italy. The painting must have been worked on and left unfinished on at least two separate occasions, the second in 1779.[2]

The moment is in Act IV, Scene 1, as Shylock advances to cut off a pound of Antonio's flesh, equipped with dagger and weighing scales ('I have them ready'). Portia, who stands between the two men and holds the bond to which she refers throughout, stops him, as we can see by her right hand on Shylock's left wrist. Her mouth is open,

Figure 174
James Newton after John Kitchingman, *Mr Macklin as Shylock*, 1784, stipple engraving, 16.5 × 14 cm (6½ × 5½ in). British Museum, Department of Prints and Drawings 1868,0822.7718

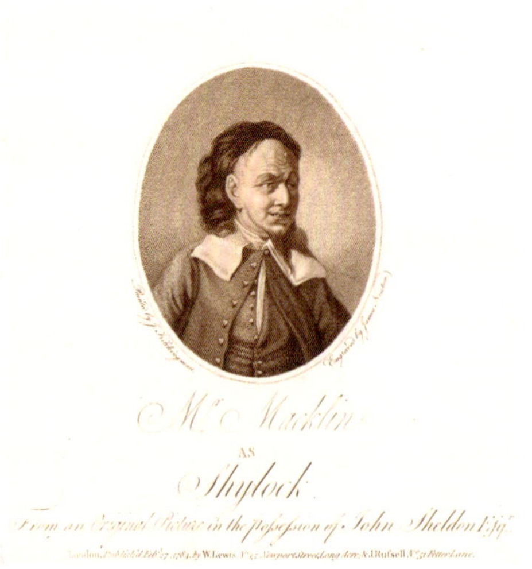

as she says:

> Tarry a little, there is something else;
> This bond doth give thee here no jot of blood.

The chief mystery of the painting is the topical presence, at the left-hand side, of the first Earl of Mansfield, the leading judge of the day.[3] Mansfield actually sat in a famous trial involving Macklin in 1775, congratulating the actor with the words: 'You have met with great applause today. You never acted better.'[4] Mansfield famously remained unmoved by the Earl of Chatham's collapse in the House of Lords, in April 1778, and he appears in John Singleton Copley's *The Death of Chatham* (begun 1779; National Portrait Gallery, London) in the same right-hand profile and similarly located as a spectator to the left. Zoffany returned to London in April 1779 and presumably saw Copley's study of Mansfield, which inspired him to include the judge in his own painting. The likelihood that 1779 was the year of Zoffany's alterations to his painting (begun in *c.*1768) is also indicated by the appearance in the Royal Academy exhibition of 1779 (no. 173) of a head of Macklin alone taken from the head as we see it in the present painting. That exhibit, by John Kitchingman, has been lost but is recorded in a print by James Newton of 1784 (fig. 174). In it Macklin bears the same fierce expression, gabardine and white collar, and even has the curious dark line along the right jaw, which is now unintelligible in the painting.

Mansfield's words to Macklin carried a double meaning, of course, and so does this painting, in which we are again confronted by a composition in which the actors are perceived both in and out of character at the same time (compare cat. 23). The viewer sees Macklin as Shylock but, partly because of the presence of Mansfield (and the Macklin trial was still famous), knows that he is also just Macklin. Equally, Mansfield is perceived both as a judge in eighteenth-century London and as a judge of the Venetian republic. This scene of *The Merchant of Venice* was also pertinent because Macklin had exercised clemency in Mansfield's court, only asking for a fraction of the damages to which he was entitled.

RS

1. He also pioneered the use of 'Caledonian' costume for *Macbeth* in 1773: Taylor 1833, 248. The same source (p. 250) records that Macklin had first acted Shylock in Lord Lansdowne's adaptation (*The Jew of Venice*, 1701). At Drury Lane Macklin returned to Shakespeare's text.
2. As suggested in Hughes 1981. The technical report by Helen Brett reveals its condition: John Schaeffer Nevill Keating Conservation Project, http://www.tate.org.uk/conservation/painting/zoffany.
3. The other contemporary judge portrayed here (behind Macklin's right arm) is Sir Richard Aston (1717–78) (not Lord Aston as Hughes had it), also of the court of King's Bench.
4. J.T. Kirkman, *Memoirs of the Life of Charles Macklin*, 2 vols., 1799, vol. 2, 256. A slightly different version is recorded in Taylor 1833, 249.

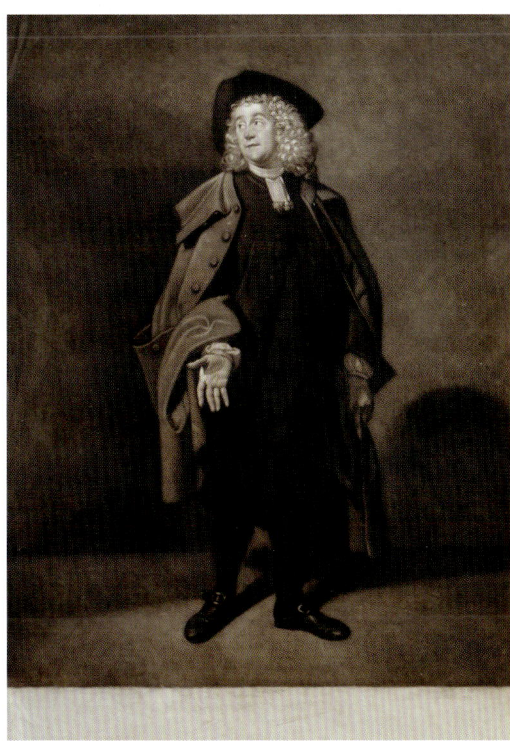

30
Giuseppe Marchi after Johan Zoffany, _John Moody as Foigard in 'The Beaux' Stratagem'_
_c._1769–71

Mezzotint engraving,
52.1 × 36.8 cm (20½ × 14½ in)
Private collection: exhibited Royal Academy
of Arts
Yale Center for British Art, Paul Mellon Collection:
exhibited Yale Center for British Art

Selected references: Lennox-Boyd 1994, 83–4 (cat. 35);
Webster 2011, 219–20

The painting from which this engraving was made was exhibited at the Society of Artists exhibition in April 1764 (no. 145). It shows the actor and singer John Moody (see fig. 52), who was born 'Cochran' in Cork and became one of Garrick's right-hand men, helping him on the business side and as a kind of talent-spotter.[1] Moody was included in a critique of contemporary actors published in 1788, when he had become fat and lazy:

> Dull, sluggish, cold, insensible and tame,
> He gives no pleasure, and deserves no fame.[2]

But he was praised in Charles Churchill's _Rosciad_ (1772), as the first to create credible Irish characters:

> At length, howe'er, the slavish chain is broke.
> And Sense, awaken'd, scorns her ancient yoke;
> Taught by thee, Moody, we now learn to raise
> Mirth from their foibles; from their virtues, praise.

Moody considered the ten lines accorded him in this poem 'his passport to the Temple of Fame'.[3]

Garrick trusted Moody as a friend as well as a colleague, not least because he bravely saved the theatre from being burned down during the 'Half Price' riots of 25 January 1763. Moody had been rescued by Garrick from his life as a 'stroller' in the provinces, after he had seen him as Lockit in _The Beggar's Opera_ at Portsmouth in the summer of 1759. He was a fixture at Drury Lane thereafter, playing a series of comic Irishmen, and, like King and Baddeley (see cat. 15), became a member of 'The School of Garrick'. His performance in the present role evidently pleased the Irish peer James Caulfeild, first Earl of Charlemont, enough for him to commission or, more probably, to buy the painting of Moody as Foigard, for which he paid the going rate for a single figure, 20 guineas, on 29 October 1764.

The part of Foigard offered Moody the opportunity to play almost entirely for laughs. Foigard, wearing a topcoat over clerical black, is the persona of a French priest adopted by a treasonous Irish priest, Macshane, who has enlisted as a chaplain in the French army. His speech shifts uncertainly between broad Irish and a cod French accent, which he is unable to control, and, to make things even more difficult, he is supposed to have been born in Brussels so that, when he is unmasked, he has to try to adopt a Flemish accent as well. In Act IV Foigard bribes the maidservant Gipsey to allow the French prisoner-of-war Count Belair into the bedroom of Mrs Sullen, daughter-in-law of the owner of the house, Lady Bountiful: 'Here is twenty _Lewidores_,[4] joy, for your shame; and I will give you an absolution for the shin.' It seems possible that Foigard's open-handed gesture refers to this transaction. Another possibility is the moment when Foigard is left alone on the stage, at the conclusion of a scene in Act V, when he ironically sums up the divorce agreement of Mr and Mrs Sullen: 'Upon my shoul, a very pretty sheremony.'

It is known that the composition was painted at Zoffany's studio in the Piazza, Covent Garden.[5] Since the painting was exhibited in April 1764 at the Society of Artists, it would have been inspired by one of the three performances by Moody of the part in the previous year, 22 September, 10 November and 27 December 1763, since he did not play it again until 18 September 1764. It must be possible that Moody's playing during this latter season inspired Charlemont to buy the picture.[6]

RS

1. Garrick 1963, nos. 592 and 677 (note), for example.
2. _The Modern Stage Exemplified, in an Epistle to a Young Actor_, London, 1788, 24.
3. Roberta Mock, 'John Moody', _ODNB_, http://www.oxforddnb.com/view/article/19084 (accessed 16 June 2011).
4. _Louis d'or_, French gold coins.
5. Angelo 1828–30, vol. 1, 147.
6. Another version of the painting is recorded, a little smaller, measuring 29 × 24 in (73.7 × 60.9 cm): fifth Earl of Cawdor's sale, 9 June 1939, no. 98 (photograph in Waterhouse archive, Paul Mellon Centre for Studies in British Art).

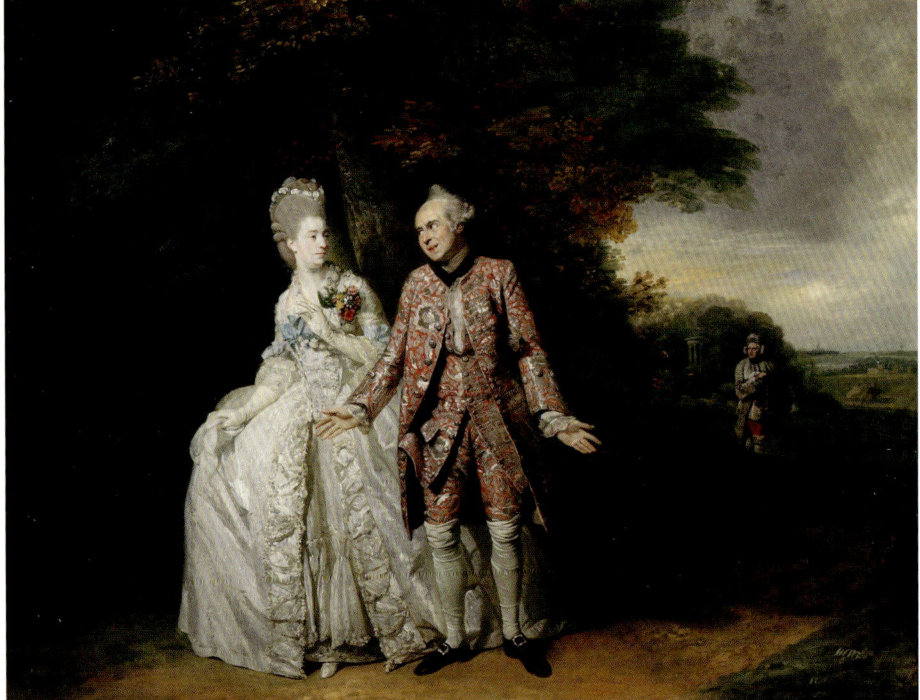

31

Sophia Baddeley and Thomas King in *'The Clandestine Marriage'*

1771

Oil on canvas, 94 × 125.5 cm (37 × 49⅜ in)
The Garrick Club, London

Provenance: James Grant Raymond sale (probably), Messrs Robins, London, 25 May 1825; Charles Matthews 1833; acquired 1835

Selected exhibitions: Queen's Bazaar 1833, no. 35; Royal Academy 1954–5, no. 125; National Portrait Gallery 1977, no. 57; Dulwich Picture Gallery 1997, no. 38

Selected references: Manners & Williamson 1920, 143–4; Ashton *et al.* 1997, cat. 23; Webster 2011, 183, 216–19, 227, 414

Engravings: Mezzotint by Richard Earlom, 1772; mezzotint (head of Sophia Baddeley only) by R. Laurie, published by Robert Sayer, 1 Sept. 1772

The Clandestine Marriage, first performed at Drury Lane on 20 February 1766, was written by Garrick and George Colman. The Prologue announced that it was inspired by Hogarth's *Marriage A-la-Mode*:

> Poets and painters, who from nature draw
> Their best and richest stores, have made this law:
> That each should neighbourly assist his brother,
> And steal with decency from one another.
> Tonight, your matchless Hogarth gives the
>   thought,
> Which from his canvas to the stage is brought …
> Each, as it suits him, takes a separate road,
> Their one great object, Marriage-a-la-mode!

The complicated plot turns on marriage as a financial transaction between impoverished aristocracy and the vulgar rich. Lord Ogleby, seen here in the foreground, was played by one of Garrick's favourite comedians, Tom King (see cat. 32). He is a vain and aged rake, who finds himself in the middle of negotiations for the marriage of the elder of a city merchant's two daughters to Ogleby's associate, Sir John Melvil. Ogleby finds both daughters attractive, but the younger, Fanny, 'delectable'. Having put the finishing touches to his rouge, he announces: 'If they are for a game of romps, me voilà prêt.' The clandestine marriage in question involves Fanny (seen here, played by Sophia Baddeley), who is secretly married to Lovewell. Complications arise, and in Act IV, Scene 1, Lovewell asks Fanny to get Ogleby to intercede on their behalf in making their marriage public, in order to solve the problem of Sir John Melvil's having broken off his engagement to the older sister in order to marry Fanny. Lovewell exits. Fanny is left alone. Enter Ogleby and his Swiss servant, the mischief-making Canton. Fanny is in confusion about how to broach the subject. Ogleby immediately mistakes it for evidence that she is attracted to him, and sends Canton away. In the subsequent scene of double-entendres, Ogleby believes that everything Fanny says about being devoted to Lovewell applies to himself. It reaches the climax shown here, when she confesses: 'I am entirely devoted to another.' Ogleby, thinking the way is now clear for their liaison, says: 'But tell me, my dear Miss Fanny, for I must know, tell me the how, the when, and the where –Tell me –.' At this very moment, to his fury, his servant Canton (played by Robert Baddeley; see cat. 15), who can be seen approaching in the background, re-enters with an urgent message.

The painting is notable for its extensive landscape, which allowed Zoffany to suggest that this is a scene of gallantry in the open air and not only a theatrical record. Sophia Baddeley's performance in this scene is supposed to have so inspired George III that he sent a message on the morning after the performance instructing her to take a sitting from 'Mr Zophany' showing her in this part 'and in this situation'.[1] There is no evidence to suggest that the present picture was ever in the Royal Collection, but the *General Evening Post* of 19–21 March 1772 reported:

> As one of this morning's papers have mentioned that Mr. Zoffani is busy on a picture of Mrs. Baddeley, for his Majesty's collection, we think it necessary to improve this intelligence by adding, that she is to be drawn in the character of Fanny, in the Clandestine Marriage, in the fine confusion scene of the fourth act, with Mr King, in the character of Lord Ogleby.[2]

There was a performance of the play by command of the king and queen on 12 October 1768 and the same cast continued to appear together well into the 1771 season.[3]

RS

1. Elizabeth Steele, *The Memoirs of Sophia Baddeley*, London, 1787, 15.
2. The earlier report appeared in the *Middlesex Journal or Chronicle of Liberty*, 19–21 March 1772: 'It is … said that his Majesty has ordered Mr. Zoffany to paint for him the picture of Mrs. Baddeley the Actress.'
3. The Royal Command performance on 24 October 1771 featured another actress as Fanny, Mrs Morland on her debut, and so cannot have occasioned the king's reaction.

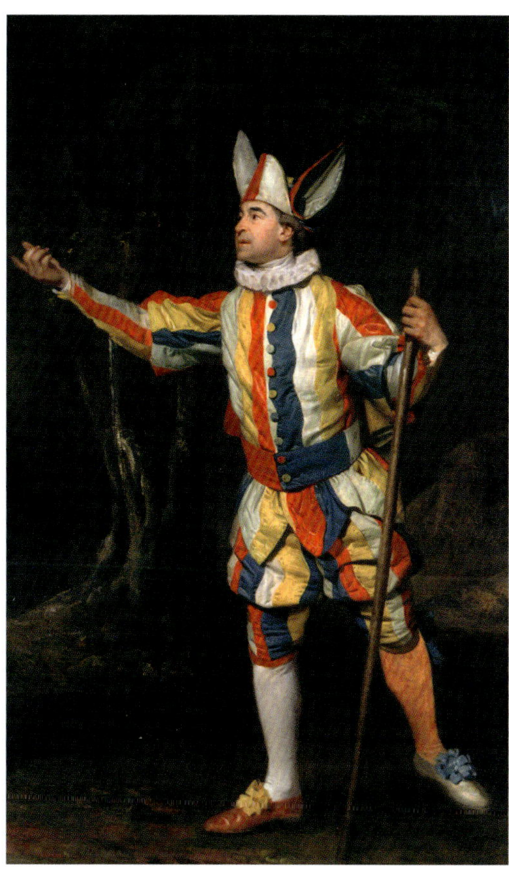

32

Thomas King as Touchstone in 'As You Like It'
1780

Oil on canvas, 91 × 55.5 cm (35⅞ × 21⅞ in)
The Garrick Club, London

Provenance: Zoffany sale, Messrs Robins, 9 May
1811, no. 91; Charles Mathews; acquired 1835

Selected exhibitions: Queen's Bazaar 1833, no. 60;
Tate 1951, no. 46; Guildhall Art Gallery 1964,
no. 36; *British Painting*, Palazzo Reale, Milan, 1975,
no. 102; Dulwich Picture Gallery 1997, no. 14;
Munich 2003, no. 176

Selected references: Ashton *et al.* 1997, cat. 401;
Webster 2011, 414–16

The picture has been cut down, and during cleaning
in 1976 an arm was revealed on the left-hand side.
The figure of Thomas King (see also cat. 31) is not
quite finished, which accords with the implication
of the description of the then entire canvas at
Zoffany's posthumous sale of 1811: '*As You Like It*,
Mr. King in Touchstone, and the celebrated
Mrs Robinson in Rosalind. The countenances
completely finished in Mr. Zoffany's happiest
manner.' The Mrs Robinson in question was
Mary 'Perdita' Robinson, actress, poet, novelist
and courtesan, immortalized in Gainsborough's
portrait of 1781 (fig. 175). She played Rosalind in
As You Like It three times at Drury Lane when
King was Touchstone, on 28 January, 7 April and
2 May 1780. She retired from the stage shortly
afterwards and so this painting was presumably
commissioned to mark that event, although it was
never finished and remained on Zoffany's hands.

The fate of the painting may be connected with
the hectic life Robinson was now leading and the
reason for her leaving the stage, which was her
affair with George, Prince of Wales, the future
Prince Regent and later George IV.[1] The prince
fell for Robinson when she appeared as Perdita in
a command performance of *The Winter's Tale* at
Drury Lane on 3 December 1779, and pursued her
as 'Florizel', Perdita's faithful swain in the play. He
promised to set her up in her own establishment on
condition that she left the stage, and they became
lovers in June 1780 after he had sent her a note for
£20,000, payable when he should come of age.
Robinson now lived it up with renewed enthusiasm
as a celebrity figure on the London scene, taking

a house in Cork Street and spending money like
water, not least on paintings. Commissioning this
picture from Zoffany would fit well with this brief
period in 1780, while what happened next would
explain why she never paid for it. Prince George
abandoned her in December the same year, and
repudiated the promise of money.[2]

The scene depicted here is from early in
Act III, where Rosalind (in disguise as Ganymede)
has discovered the dreadful trot-along verses
written about her by the lovelorn Orlando, which
he has hung up on a tree in the Forest of Arden.
Touchstone points out how bad these mysterious
rhymes are and proceeds to chant similar verses
impromptu, which must be what he is doing in this
painting, where both his pose and the gesture of
his right hand indicate that he is declaiming:

> If a hart doth lack a hind,
> Let him seek out *Rosalind*.
> If the cat will after kind,
> So be sure will *Rosalind*.

King appears in the same extravagant costume in
the second frontispiece of the 1774 edition of the
play,[3] and William Hazlitt described him wearing it:

> His acting … left a taste on the palate sharp and
> sweet like a quince. With an old, hard, rough,
> withered face, like a John-apple, puckered up into
> a thousand wrinkles; with shrewd hints and tart
> replies … he was the … true, that is, pretended
> clown in Touchstone, with Wit sprouting from his
> head like a pair of ass's ears, and Folly perched on
> his cap like the horned owl.

After Garrick's death in 1779 Richard Brinsley
Sheridan created for King the parts for which he
became most famous, Sir Peter Teazle in *The School
for Scandal* (1777) and Puff in *The Critic* (1779).

RS

1. See Martin J. Levy, 'Robinson, Mary (Perdita)',
   ODNB, http://www.oxforddnb.com/view/article/
   23857 (accessed 16 June 2011).
2. After many threats in December 1781 Robinson
   finally gained £5,000 from the king in exchange
   for the prince's love letters.
3. In the scene following, with 'Audrey'. The etching is
   entitled 'Mr King, in the Character of Touchstone |
   Come apace, good Audrey, I will fetch up your
   Goats, Audrey'. *As You Like It … as performed at
   the Theatre-Royal, Drury-Lane. Regulated from the
   Prompt-Book …*, published by John Bell, London, 1774.

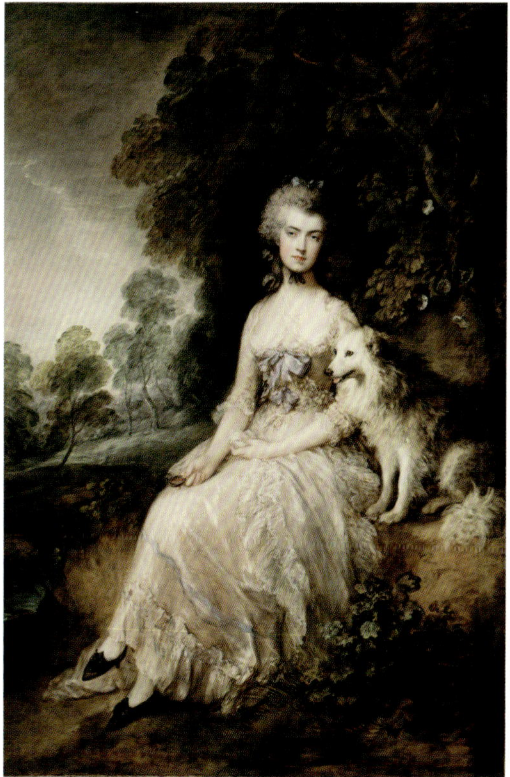

Figure 175
Thomas Gainsborough, *Mary Robinson*, 1781,
oil on canvas, 233.7 × 153 cm (92 × 60¼ in).
The Wallace Collection, London

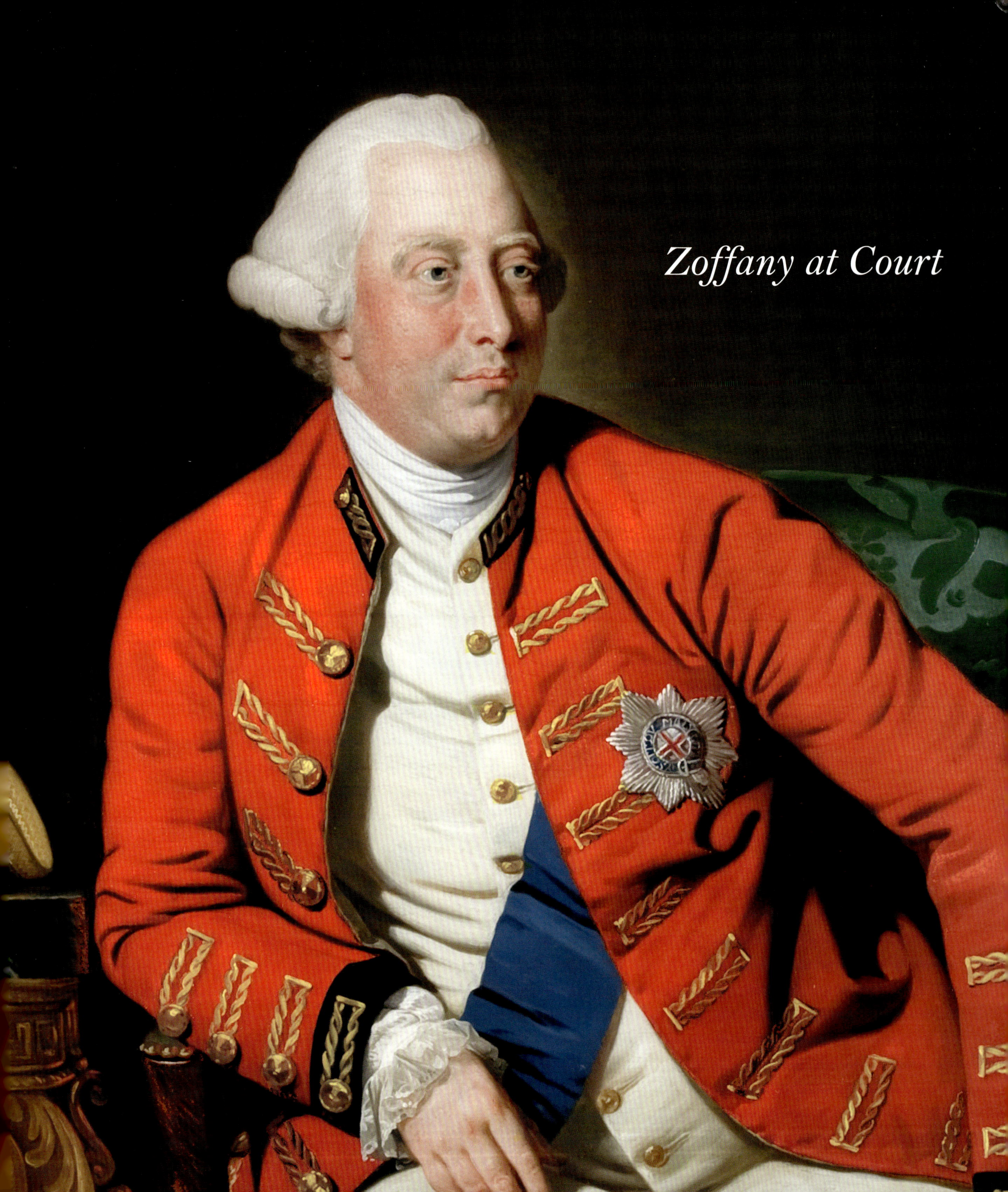
Zoffany at Court

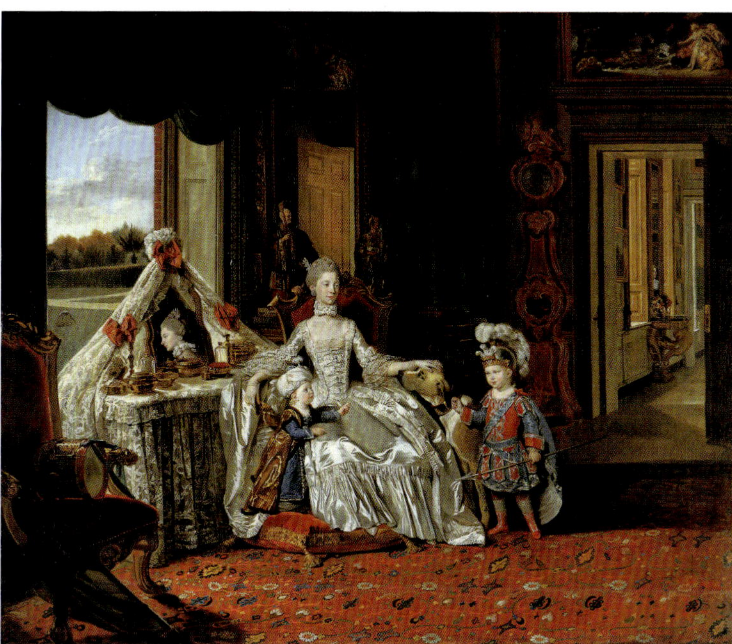

33

Queen Charlotte with her Two Eldest Sons
1764–5

Oil on canvas, 112.4 × 129.2 cm (44¼ × 50⅞ in)
The Royal Collection, Her Majesty Queen
Elizabeth II

Exhibited at the Royal Academy of Arts only

Provenance: Presumably commissioned by
George III or Queen Charlotte; first recorded
in the possession of the Prince of Wales in 1794

Selected exhibitions: Royal Academy 1934, no. 242;
Royal Academy 1946–7, no. 63; Royal Academy
1954–5, no. 105; National Portrait Gallery 1977,
no. 25; Queen's Gallery 2004, no. 4; _Portraits Publics,
Portraits Privés 1770–1830_, Galeries nationales
du Grand Palais, Paris 2006–7; _Citizens and Kings:
Portraits in the Age of Revolution 1760–1830_, Royal
Academy of Arts, London, and Solomon R.
Guggenheim Museum, New York, 2007, no. 87;
Queen's Gallery and Holyrood House 2009, no. 20

Selected references: Manners & Williamson 1920,
36–7, 210; H. Clifford Smith, _Buckingham Palace_,
London, 1930, 86–7; Collins Baker 1937, 329;
Millar 1969, vol. 1, 148–9, no. 1199; K.M. Walton,
'Queen Charlotte's Dressing Table', _Furniture
History_, XI (1975), 112–13; Treadwell 2009, 109,
111–12, 114; Webster 2011, 124, 133, 135–8

This painting was Zoffany's first royal commission.
He has portrayed Queen Charlotte as a ravishingly
pretty young princess, yet already the mother of
an heir and a 'spare' – George, Prince of Wales,
and Frederick, Duke of York – after only four years
of marriage. The pearly white satin dress with its
bows and flounces, and elaborate lace-trimmed
sleeves, emphasizes her slenderness and youth.
Frederick, aged only one, stands on a red velvet
cushion, nestling against his mother's knee; a
boarhound looks adoringly at the queen, while she
caresses its head. Queen Charlotte was extremely
fond of dogs of all sizes. Prince George, aged three,
displays a more grown-up confidence. As was
customary, boys before the age of six were kept
predominantly within a female world; the figure
just glimpsed in a mirror in the rear enfilade is
assumed to be the royal governess, Lady Charlotte
Finch.

The room represented is in Buckingham House,
bought for the queen on her marriage. Zoffany
has reorganized it and added the valuable oriental
carpet for the purposes of the picture.[1] The
dressing-table lace cover alone cost £1,079 14s
when purchased. The silver-gilt Augsburg toilette
service may have come over with the queen at her
wedding.[2] Zoffany has excelled himself in providing
a sumptuous depiction of the young consort as well
as demonstrating his virtuosity in perspective and
in representing the interplay of light, reflected in
the mirrors on the dressing table and the nearby
wall. It succeeded in gaining him twenty other
royal commissions.

The young princes' costumes show that they are
being schooled in the performative art of monarchy.
Acting in plays and tableaux was an element of
royal and aristocratic education; Lady Charlotte
acted in plays as a child,[3] and she ordered the
costumes in readiness for this picture.[4] The Prince
of Wales is dressed as Telemachus in a Baroque
version of ancient classical warrior dress, while
his helmet has the three feathers of the Wales
insignia. Telemachus was the son of the Greek
hero Odysseus, and in _The Adventures of Telemachus_
(1699) by François Fénelon, who taught
Louis XIV's grandson, Telemachus tours the
Mediterranean with his tutor, the original Mentor,
to observe good and bad types of rule. Fénelon's
book was widely read by British and European
princes and nobles; Zoffany's mother possessed a
copy of it.[5] It was also familiar to George III's own
governor, James, second Earl Waldegrave, who
wrote an allegory based on it, figuring George as
Telemachus.[6] In 1768 John Hawkesworth published
a new, stylistically praised, lavishly presented
translation of _The Adventures of Telemachus_,
dedicated to the soldier and politician William
Petty, second Earl of Shelburne, whose wife was
Lady Charlotte Finch's niece Sophia Carteret.[7]
Queen Charlotte's own bookish tendencies are
hinted at in the books grouped on the console in
the background.

Prince Frederick's Turkish costume anticipates
his military career as a British commander-in-chief
and also a ruling German prince in his own right,
signalled by the banner and drum on the chair to
the left. The electors of Hanover could nominate
the Prince-Bishop of Osnabrück alternately with a
Catholic ruler, and in 1764 young Frederick was
given this role. Charlotte's maternal great-uncle,
Joseph Fredrick of Saxe-Hildburghausen, was
an imperial field marshal, who reorganized the
military frontier with the Turks in the 1740s.
This link to the Habsburgs put Charlotte's family
into a more significant orbit. As the Turks became
less threatening, so their dress became more
fashionable for relaxed costume among the male
and female elite. Here it adds to the exoticism of
other decorative features in the picture, such as
the chinoiserie figures.

CCO

1. Webster 2011, 135.
2. Roberts 2004, 26.
3. Jill Shefrin, _Such Constant Affectionate Care: Lady
   Charlotte Finch, Royal Governess & the Children of
   George III_, Los Angeles, 2003, 63–4, 124–7.
4. Roberts 2004, 27.
5. Webster 2011, 16.
6. J.C.D. Clark, ed., _The Memoirs and Speeches of James,
   2nd Earl Waldegrave, 1742–1763_, Cambridge, 1988,
   226–37 ('An Allegory of Leicester House').
7. Clarissa Campbell Orr, 'The Queen of the Blues,
   the Bluestocking Queen, and Bluestocking
   masculinity', in Elizabeth Eger, ed., _Bluestockings
   Displayed: Portraiture, Performance and Patronage,
   1730–1830_, Cambridge, forthcoming, 2012.

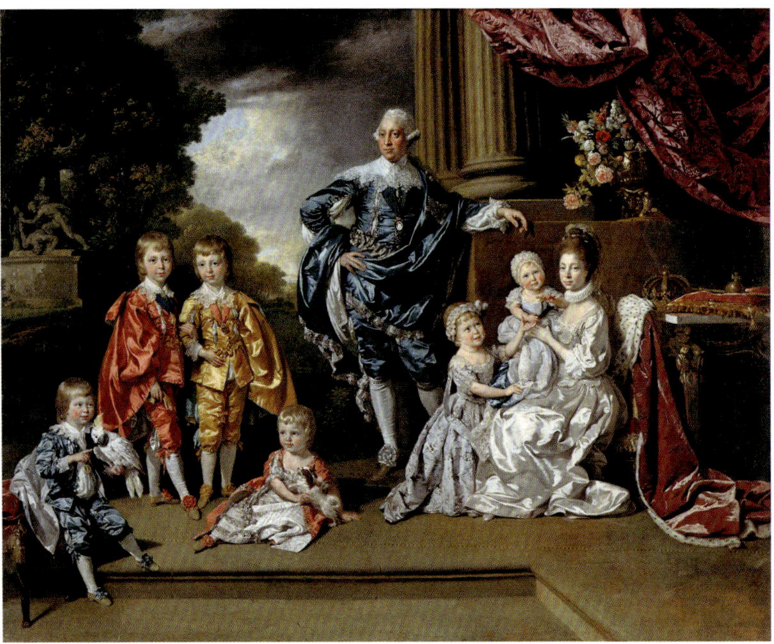

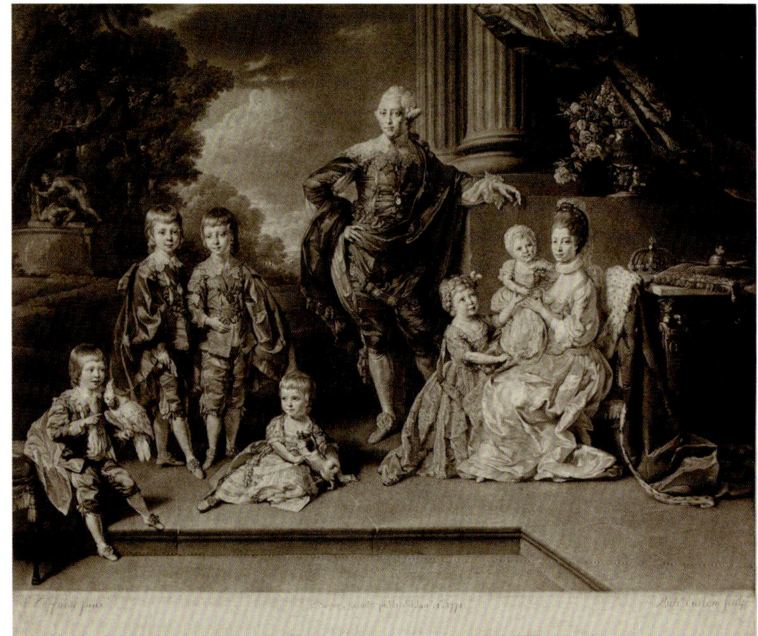

34

*George III and Queen Charlotte with their
Six Eldest Children*
1770

Oil on canvas, 104.9 × 127.6 cm (41¼ × 50¼ in)
The Royal Collection, Her Majesty Queen
Elizabeth II

Exhibited at the Royal Academy of Arts only

Provenance: Presumably commissioned by George
III or Queen Charlotte; listed in Princess Amelia's
bedroom at Kew, *c.*1800

Selected exhibitions: Royal Academy of Arts, 1770,
no. 211; Royal Academy 1946–7, no. 61; Queen's
Gallery 2004, no. 7; Queen's Gallery and Holyrood
House 2009, no. 21

Selected references: Manners & Williamson 1920,
24–6, 211; Collins Baker 1937, 328; Millar 1969,
vol. 1, ix–xv, no. 1201; Webster 1976, 52; Ribeiro
1995, 208; Treadwell 2009, 113–15; Webster 2011,
228–31

35

Richard Earlom after Johan Zoffany, *Their Most
Sacred Majesties George III and Queen Charlotte*
1771

Mezzotint engraving,
50.6 × 58.1 cm (19⅞ × 22⅞ in)
Inscribed below image in scratched lettering:
'J Zoffany pinxt | R Sayer, excudit publish'd,
Janry. 1st, 1771 | Richd. Earlom sculpst'
British Museum, Department of Prints and
Drawings, 1939,0211.4

Exhibited at the Yale Center for British Art only

Zoffany's group portrait of the Royal Family was
exhibited at the Royal Academy in the spring
of 1770, Horace Walpole noting in his copy of
the exhibition catalogue, 'In Vandyke dresses,
ridiculous – a print of it', a reference evidently to
Richard Earlom's mezzotint (cat. 35).[1] 'Vandyke
costume' had been fashionable among aristocratic
sitters for at least thirty years. It was also the
costume worn by Gainsborough's so-called 'Blue
Boy', which also featured in the Academy exhibition
of 1770. Yet for the royal family to wear dress
associated with Sir Anthony Van Dyck's early
patron, King Charles I, was problematic. Charles I
had been beheaded in 1649 by the Parliamentarians
at the conclusion of the English Civil War. After
this it was impossible to imagine the monarchy as
divinely ordained; and the mistakes made by his son
James II (reigned 1685–88) in trying to strengthen
the monarchy at the expense of Parliament,
triggered aristocratic and popular resistance and
forced his abdication. Thereafter, monarchs and
loyalists regarded the changes as providentially
ordained, but hereditary kings were now obliged
to share power with Parliament and could not
proclaim themselves divine right rulers answerable
only to God.

It is unlikely that Zoffany is alluding to these
aspects of Charles I's history: rather, there are
resonances between the two monarchs relating to
ancestry, connoisseurship and royal domesticity.
The Hanoverians traced their hereditary claim to
the throne to Charles I's sister Elizabeth, who had
married the Elector of the Palatinate, a German
principality equal in status to that of Hanover. The
Hanoverians, then, were not merely invited to rule
by Parliament, even if the succession had been
regulated by parliamentary law in 1701, but had a

prior and inherited claim. Emphasizing dynastic continuity was a way of implying Parliament could not again destroy the monarchical principle. George II's wife Queen Caroline (consort 1727–37) had helped reorganize the royal collections, including Tudor and Stuart treasures, as part of a strategy emphasizing this deep ancestry.[2] Charles I (reigned 1625–49) was known to have been one of the greatest royal patrons of art, and although his collections had been dispersed during the republican era (1649–60), some of the treasures had been reacquired. George III was very conscious of the monarchy's artistic inheritance and had rehung some of the Van Dycks in Buckingham House, while also re-acquiring paintings such as *The Five Eldest Children of Charles I* (fig. 176).[3] Not only had he restituted some of his ancestor's collection, he also restituted the idea of the royal family as a model of morality. Charles I was known as an uxorious husband to his wife Henrietta Maria and as a tender father. George III was perceived as following in his footsteps, given his wide-ranging connoisseurship as well as his familial rectitude and affection. When John Adams visited the court in 1783 as the first ambassador of the newly independent United States of America, he considered him 'the most accomplished courtier in his dominions. With all the affability of Charles the Second he has all the domestic virtues and regularity of Charles the First.'[4]

Included in the portrait are George, Prince of Wales, wearing the blue-ribboned Order of the Garter; Frederick, wearing the red-ribboned Order of the Bath (revived by George I); Prince William, the third son, on the left with a cockatoo, wearing the Scottish Order of the Thistle (the Stuarts were a Scottish dynasty); and Edward, the young Duke of Kent, the fourth son, playing with a spaniel – another Stuart echo, as Charles II popularized the breed.[5] He is not yet old enough to be breeched. The queen holds Princess Augusta, and beside her stands Princess Charlotte, the Princess Royal. The symmetry of the two groups projects family unison, but also playful affection alongside royal dignity, as children play with their pets and the girls nestle close to their father's protective shadow.

CCO

1. Graves 1905–6, vol. 8, 412. The earliest impression of the engraving in the British Museum is dated 29 October 1770 (1902,1011.883), although it was not published by Robert Sayer until the following January. Since the picture was only completed just before the opening of the exhibition in April 1770, Walpole's catalogue annotation was evidently made after the event, although he would have seen the painting itself at the Royal Academy exhibition.
2. Joanna Marschner, 'Queen Caroline of Anspach [*sic*] and the European princely museum tradition', in Campbell Orr 2002, 130–42.
3. Lloyd 2005.
4. Hibbert 1999, 165.
5. Edward was father of the future Queen Victoria, b. 1819.

36

Duesbury & Co., *Set of three figure groups of the royal family*
*c.*1773

Biscuit porcelain, heights: 'George, Prince of Wales, Prince Frederick, Prince William and Prince Edward' 22 cm (8⅝ in), 'George III' 30 cm (11¾ in), 'Queen Charlotte with the Princess Royal and Princess Augusta' 23.5 cm (9¼ in)
The Royal Collection, Her Majesty Queen Elizabeth II

Exhibited at the Royal Academy of Arts only

Provenance: 'George, Prince of Wales, Prince Frederick, Prince William and Prince Edward' and 'Queen Charlotte with the Princess Royal and Princess Augusta' (?) Princess Sophia (d.1848); Lady Carrington; by descent to third Lord Carrington, later Marquess of Lincolnshire; Albert Amor Ltd; from whom purchased by Queen Mary 1920; 'George III' purchased by Queen Mary, 1920

Selected exhibitions: Burlington House Antiques Fair, London, 1985

Selected references: William Bemrose, *Bow, Chelsea, and Derby Porcelain*, London, 1898, 54; R.L. Hobson, *Catalogue of the Collection of English Porcelain in the British Museum*, London, 1905, no. 1130; Frank Tilley, 'Some Royal Portraits on English Pottery and Porcelain', *Apollo*, vol. 35, June 1953, 196–7, fig. XIII; Arthur Lane, *English Porcelain Figures of the Eighteenth Century*, London, 1961, 8; Millar 1969, vol. 1, no. 1201, 149–50, vol. 2, pl. 32; Clifford 1985; Jane Roberts, ed., *Royal Treasures: A Golden Jubilee Celebration*, London, 2002, 185; Roberts 2004, 305–6; Felicity Marno, 'A Derby Bust of George III', *English Ceramic Circle: Transactions*, vol. 19, part 3, 2007, 527–32

Figure 176
Sir Anthony Van Dyck,
The Five Eldest Children of Charles I, 1637,
oil on canvas, 163.2 × 198.8 cm (64¼ × 78¼ in).
The Royal Collection, Her Majesty Queen Elizabeth II

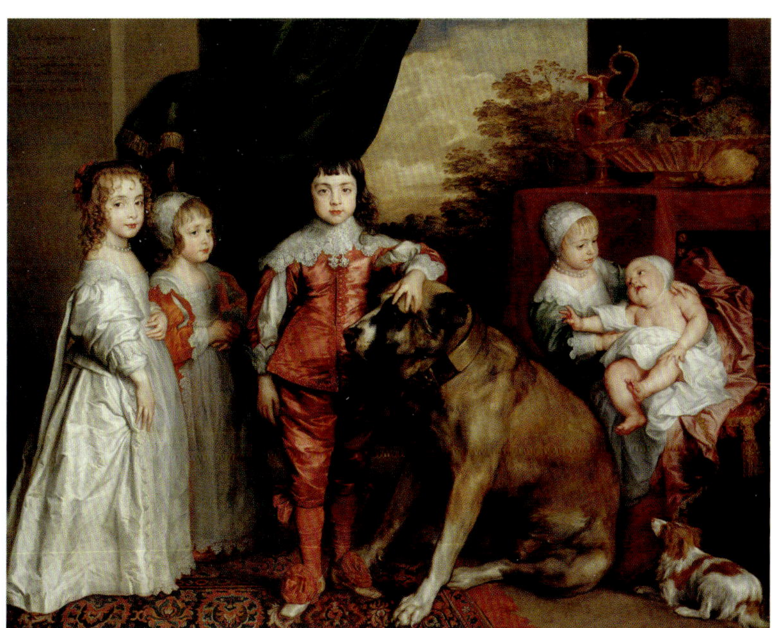

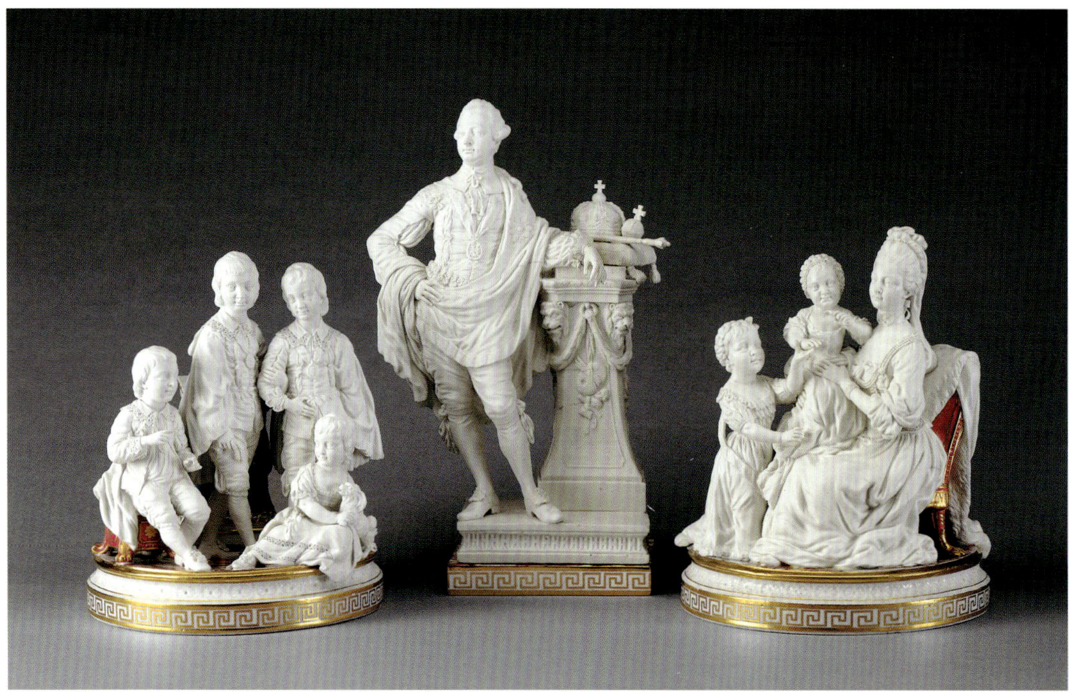

This elegant group of porcelain figures is modelled on Zoffany's portrait of George III, Queen Charlotte and their six eldest children (cat. 34), exhibited at the Royal Academy in 1771. The three groups were probably based on Richard Earlom's mezzotint engraving of Zoffany's royal portrait (cat. 35), rather than the original painting. Comparison between the painting, the print and the present porcelain group reveals a number of slight differences. In the porcelain group of the princes, George, Frederick and William are brought closer together, the cockatoo is missing, and Prince William's legs are repositioned. The single figure of George III, who here sways towards the left, rests his arm on a pedestal surmounted by a crown, orb and sceptre. Originally, the figure of the king would have been even higher, his base mounted on a cruciform plinth with lions and laurel festoons, of which there is an example in the British Museum (1887,0307,II.300).[1] The present base, with a Greek key pattern, is modern, having been made in 1924 to match the other two statuettes already in the Royal Collection. Compared with Zoffany's original painting or even Earlom's engraving, the countenances of the royal family in the porcelain figures are quite generic and expressionless, while their physical separation into three discrete groups emphasizes the hierarchical nature of Zoffany's composition.

The figures were made in one of the porcelain factories belonging to William (II) Duesbury, either in Derby or Chelsea. Duesbury, who had been operating in Derby since 1756, purchased the Chelsea porcelain factory in February 1770. The three statuettes of the royal family were advertised in Duesbury's catalogue to coincide with the opening of a 'commodious warehouse' in Covent Garden in the summer of 1773:

> THEIR present majesties the king and queen, and the royal family, in 3 grouped pieces in biscuit – the center piece represents the king in a Vandyke dress, on a blue and gold basement, supported by four lions, leaning on an altar richly ornamented in blue and gold, with hanging trophies of the polite arts and sciences. The crown, munde, and sceptre reposing on a cushion of crimson, embroidered, fringed, and tasselled in gold. 14 in.[2]

The statuettes in the Royal Collection, it has been suggested, are later, modified replicas of the statuettes advertised in 1773. Although these figures were mass-produced, they are nonetheless very rare. Indeed, as Timothy Clifford has observed, their 'shelf life' was probably quite short, production being limited to the period before the royal children reached adulthood, between about 1774 and 1780. Factory stock lists of 1795 mention, among existing moulds, only 'Fragments of the Royal Family', suggesting that these particular statuettes had long since been discontinued.[3]

The models on which the present figure groups were based may well have been made by the sculptor John Bacon, who in 1770 had produced a marble bust of George III, attracting further patronage from the king.[4] Bacon had been apprenticed to Nicholas Crisp, a jeweller and watchmaker, who also owned a porcelain factory in Vauxhall, where Bacon evidently made his first models.[5] By 1769, when he enrolled in the Royal Academy Schools, Bacon was an experienced and successful model maker, who between October 1769 and November 1770 was paid over one hundred pounds by William Duesbury for various models.

MP

1. The British Museum also owns the related statuette of Queen Charlotte with the Princess Royal and Princess Augusta, reg. no. 2005,0103.1. This group also once belonged to Queen Mary, who swapped it for the statuette now in the Royal Collection and exhibited here.
2. Clifford 1985, 13.
3. Clifford 1985, 13.
4. See Roberts 2004, 247–8, no. 254.
5. For the production of models for porcelain figures by sculptors, including Bacon, see Hilary Young, *English Porcelain 1745–95: Its Makers, Design, Marketing and Consumption*, London, 1999, 94ff.

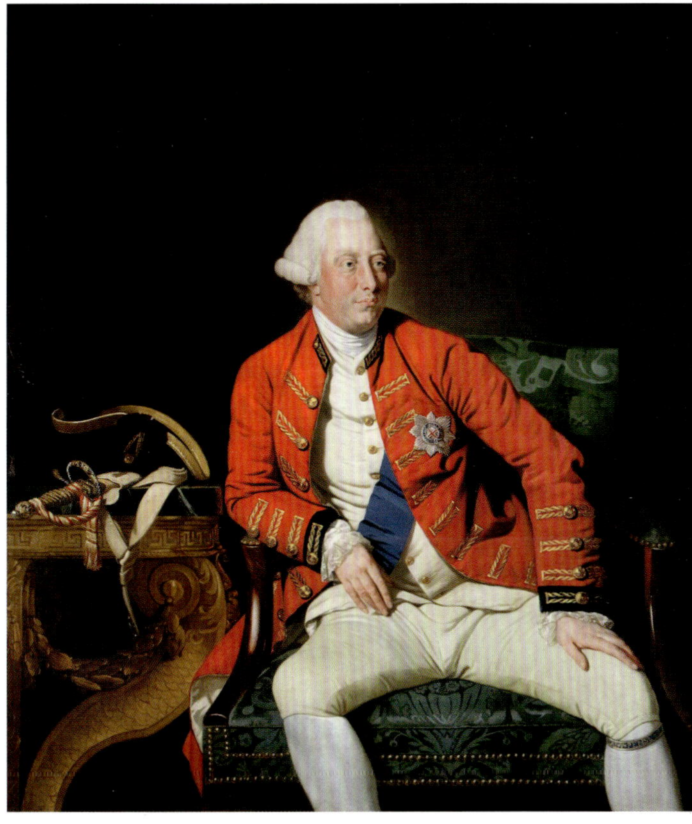

37

George III
1771

Oil on canvas, 161.9 × 138.5 cm (63¾ × 54½ in)
The Zetland Collection

Provenance: Commissioned by Sir Lawrence
Dundas; by descent

*Selected exhibitions: Masterpieces from Yorkshire and
Durham,* Leeds City Art Gallery, 1936, no. 34;
Barnard Castle 1962, no. 12

Selected references: Manners & Williamson 1920,
247; Millar 1969, vol. 1, 148, no. 1195; Webster
2011, 156–7

The present version of *George III* is a replica made
for Sir Lawrence Dundas (cat. 71), who in 1771 had
been made a privy councillor by the king. Dundas
paid Zoffany £74 15s for the portrait, which in
terms of quality is on a par with the original version
commissioned by the king.[1] Modern viewers are
likely to find this a surprisingly accessible and
informal image of a king. This was also Horace
Walpole's view; he sneered that it was 'Very like,
but most disagreeable and unmeaning figure'.[2]
It should be borne in mind, however, that in 1771
Walpole was affecting an anti-court stance. The
king is portrayed not in robes of state but in the
uniform of a general officer, in a pose that could be
that of any officer in the mess-room, or, indeed, a
landowner in his study. The background space is
left undelineated, and only the fine gilded console
suggests that this is a gentleman of high rank.

This perception is confirmed by the fact that
the king wears the star riband and garter of the
Order of the Garter, the chivalric order dating
back to 1344. When resident at Windsor, the
king worshipped daily in the order's chapel, and
commissioned a series of pictures from Benjamin
West on the order's history.[3]

The sword and hat are left in an attractive
clutter beside him, as if they have been put down
casually on coming inside from some unspecified
military duty. The king is both 'off-duty' and alert,
suggesting he is ready at any moment to finish the
sitting and get on with something else: his unseen
right foot might be imagined to be tapping the floor
slightly impatiently. Yet his right hand is relaxed
and composed. The king is not smiling, but
nevertheless radiates the affability of a busy man,
possessed of concentrated energy. The triangle of
his forehead and nose is balanced in the inverted
triangle of his loins, to which his right hand
unostentatiously gestures. It is an unmistakeably
masculine pose, a little startling to the viewer, but
the balanced diagonals of his right and left arms
and legs, the sash of the garter riband and the
complementary diagonals of his open red coat
also suggest the containment of libido within
the discipline of holy wedlock. The king, aged
thirty-three in this picture, was already the father
of seven children.

The portrait conjures up several overlapping
aspects of kingship. George III was commander-
in-chief of the army in a country at the zenith of

European and imperial power, before the loss of
the thirteen American colonies caused national
soul-searching over the possible effeminacy of its
men.[4] Like many European monarchs, he wears
uniform regularly as a form of working dress; in
1777 he designed a Windsor uniform for all male
members of his royal household.[5] This did not
suggest that kings were military dictators. Most
peers of the realm saw it as their vocation to offer
military or naval service to the crown; the king is
showing himself as merely the first gentleman of
his county, Berkshire. Nonetheless, assimilating
George's image too far into that of a mere
gentleman displeased the critic Robert Baker,
who wrote after seeing the portrait at the Royal
Academy: 'The posture, though it might do well
enough for the picture of a country-squire, is not
quite suited, I think, to the dignity of the person
represented.'[6]

The king's red coat is also a sign of patriotism,
and his pose is identical, surprisingly, with that
of William Hogarth's caricature of the rakish-
gentleman radical, John Wilkes (see fig. 199),
whose political opposition to the king and his
ministers had caused great controversy in the first
decade of George III's reign. The controversy
was conducted through differing interpretations
of the meaning of patriotism and the role of the
monarch in the British system, and referred back
to George III's father, Frederick Prince of Wales,
the figurehead in the late 1730s for politicians
known as 'Patriots' who urged war with Britain's

imperial rival, Bourbon Spain. Frederick's circle also admired the ideas of Henry St John, Viscount Bolingbroke, in his *Idea of a Patriot King* (1738), which argued that a king should rule above political factions. The war of 1756–63 delivered the Patriot agenda.

Early in his accession George III began peace negotiations. In a new phase of Patriot criticism, Wilkes led the attack on the king and his favourite minister, Lord Bute, accusing them of trying to restrict English liberty and reinstate royal absolutism. Wilkes's ability to work the London crowd turned him into 'the malicious court jester at the court of George III'.[7] As Celina Fox has suggested, Zoffany's portrait of the king as affable country gentleman implies that he, not the libertine demagogue, Wilkes, is the true patriot.[8]

CCO

1. See Webster 2011, 156–7.
2. Roberts 2004, 31.
3. Lloyd 2005.
4. Sylvia Harstock Myers, *The Bluestocking Circle*, Oxford, 1990.
5. Sasha Llewellyn, 'George III and the Windsor Uniform', *Court Historian*, 1996, vol. 1, no. 2, 12–16; Mansel 2005.
6. Cited in Fox 2010, 339.
7. Brewer 1976, 108.
8. Fox 2010, 338–9.

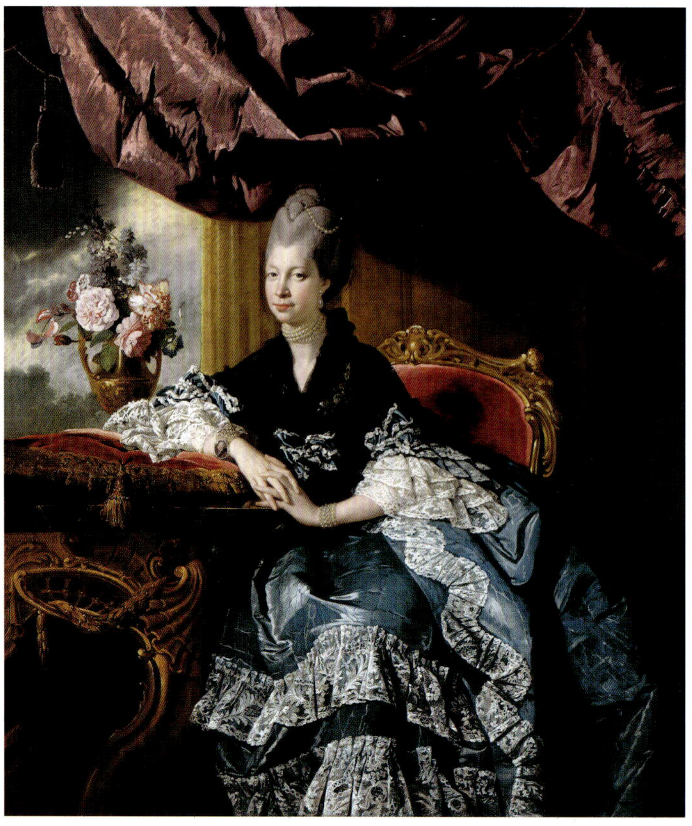

38

Queen Charlotte

1771

Oil on canvas, 163.8 × 137.5 cm (64½ × 54⅛ in)
The Royal Collection, Her Majesty Queen Elizabeth II

Provenance: Presumably commissioned by George III or Queen Charlotte

Selected exhibitions: Royal Academy 1946–7, no. 64; Arts Council 1960–61, no. 4; Queen's Gallery 2004, no. 9

Selected references: Manners & Williamson 1920, 209; Collins Baker 1937, 327; Millar 1969, vol. 1, no. 1196; Treadwell 2009, 118–19; Webster 2011, 237, 240–41

If Zoffany's portrait of George III, by presenting him standing out against a plain and dark background, suggests the isolation of a monarch who must be genial to all yet favour no one, the pendant portrait of his queen demonstrates that the ruler's heavy responsibilities are alleviated by the company of a devoted spouse. The logical way to hang these portraits would be to place them side by side with the queen on the viewer's right, where she is plainly leaning in towards the more uprightly seated king. This is perhaps the purpose behind an otherwise asymmetrical treatment of the couple's setting. She is portrayed with a more typical, stylized backdrop involving sumptuous folds of aubergine drapery suspended above a pillared window wall, with a vase of flowers silhouetted in front of the late afternoon sun, similar to the background of the 1770 group portrait. The sun highlights her face and upper body. Light falls clearly onto her right wrist, on which she wears a six-stranded pearl bracelet with an oval medallion portrait of the king, painted by Jeremiah Meyer. On her left wrist she wears its pair, which had a cipher in diamonds and a strand of his hair. These were a wedding present from the king and, touchingly, were a widely fashionable gift, not a unique commission, as if the royal couple were a well-to-do couple like any other.[1]

Queen Charlotte rests her elbow on a velvet cushion, placed on a marble topped and carved gilded console that had been used in the background of the 1765 portrait of her with her

two sons (cat. 33). Yet the cushion does not bear
a crown: this is a glimpse of the private role of a
consort, as helpmeet to her husband. In *The Idea
of a Patriot King* (1738) Henry St John, Viscount
Bolingbroke, had made it clear that the twin
dangers in a monarchy are a mistress or a favourite.
Therefore, the person most intimate with a king
must be a lawful wife, who will not be so glamorous
as to attract the erotic attention of others, will be
feminine enough to take her cue from the head
of the household, and never meddle in politics.[2]
Although Queen Charlotte was a mother seven
times over, there are no children in this picture to
distract her from this devotion. Her femininity is
enhanced by the expensive silk and lace of her
dress, but her black lace *fichu* jacket adds a note of
sobriety. The flowers also indicate her interest in
botany, regarded increasingly as a suitable form of
natural history for educated and polite women.[3]

CCO

1. Judy Rudoe, 'Queen Charlotte's Jewellery:
   reconstructing a lost collection', in Marsden 2005,
   179–215.
2. Clarissa Campbell Orr, 'Making a new start: Queen
   Charlotte, Popular Politics, and the fear of "Petticoat
   Power" in Britain c.1760 1770', in *Moving Elites:
   Women and Cultural Transfers in the European
   Court System* (European University Institute Paper
   HEC 2010/02), ed. G. Calvi and I. Chabot,
   http://cadmus.eui.eu/handle/1814/14234 (accessed
   22 June 2011), 33–49.
3. Clarissa Campbell Orr, 'Queen Charlotte, "Scientific
   Queen"', in Campbell Orr 2002, 236–66.

39

Queen Charlotte with her Brothers Prince Charles and Prince Ernest of Mecklenburg-Strelitz and Three of her Children

1771–2

Oil on canvas, 105 × 127 cm (41⅜ × 50 in)
The Royal Collection, Her Majesty Queen
Elizabeth II

Exhibited at the Royal Academy of Arts only

Provenance: Presumably painted for Queen
Charlotte, possibly as a gift for her brother, Prince
Ernest of Mecklenburg-Strelitz; first recorded in
the Royal Collection 1862

Selected exhibitions: Royal Academy 1946–7, no. 65;
English Portraits in the Landscape Park, Norwich
Castle Museum, 1948, no. 21; Queen's Gallery
2004, no. 10; Queen's Gallery and Holyrood House
2009, no. 22

Selected references: Manners & Williamson 1920,
35–6, 210–11; Collins Baker 1937, 332; Millar
1969, vol. 1, 151, no. 1207; Webster 2011, 234–7

Here, Zoffany apparently presents leading
members of the aristocracy as gentlefolk in a
rural setting, yet all but one of them are actually
of royal blood. Charlotte and her two brothers,
Princes Charles and Ernest, were attracted by
gardening and natural history, and they are
portrayed as pausing for a rest on a walk around
either Kew or Richmond. Charlotte inherited her
mother-in-law's interest in Kew and later created
a garden at her private Windsor retreat, Frogmore.
Charles made an English-style garden after he
inherited Mecklenburg-Strelitz from his eldest
brother, Adolf Frederick IV, in 1794, while Ernest
(see fig. 83) had a small manor in Celle, Hanover,
and created a park admired in its day. These
interests were strengthened in dialogue with the
ideas of Jean-Jacques Rousseau, the unconventional
citizen of Geneva, ideas that Charles had
encountered when he studied at the Académie
there.[1] Charlotte appointed as her Reader in 1773
the Genevan geologist and instrument maker,
Jean-André Deluc, a friend and critic of Rousseau.[2]
Deluc's role was to read out loud to her in French
and also to be her scientific adviser.

In the eighteenth century the term 'family'
also meant household, which included officials
and servants as well as resident or visiting kin.[3]
Included in this composition, therefore, is one of
Charlotte's most valued officials, Lady Charlotte
Finch, the Royal Governess. Lady Charlotte came
from, and married into, families of court insiders
and politicians. Her mother, Henrietta Fermor,
first Countess of Pomfret, was a lady-in-waiting
to Queen Caroline, consort of George II, and her
sister-in-law, Lady Isabella Finch, was the key
figure in the household of the king's aunt, Princess
Amelia. They were patrons of art, literature,
architecture and design – 'Bluestockings' *avant*

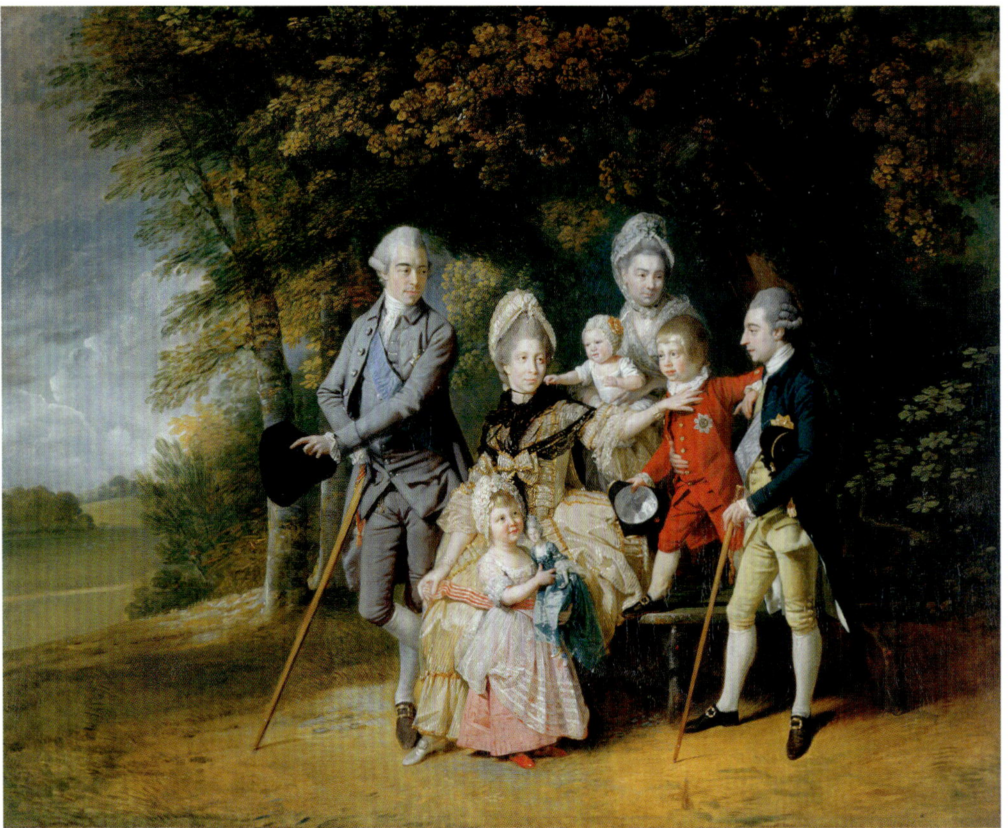

la lettre. Lady Charlotte linked the queen and bluestocking circles in her reign. She spent time in France and Italy with her parents and older sister in 1737–9, so, unusually for a woman, had experienced a kind of Grand Tour. Her knowledge of Florence probably informed Queen Charlotte's urge to commission Zoffany to paint a 'virtual' representation of the Uffizi. Lady Charlotte's eldest son, George Finch, ninth Earl of Winchilsea, is included in the finished composition, eyeing the *Venus de' Medici*. He was later to become Gentleman of the Bedchamber and, ultimately, Groom of the Stole.[4]

Queen Charlotte's brothers, who visited in 1771, benefited from their sister's marriage by joining the Hanoverian service, Charles as military and civil governor of Hanover, and Ernest as military governor of Celle. On this garden tour the children are getting distracted by their uncles. Charlotte, Princess Royal, wants to show off her fashionably attired doll: but she grew up to be rather uninterested in fashion.[5] Prince William, the future naval officer (and in 1830 King William IV), is being boisterous and is restrained by his mother. The baby is usually identified as Prince Ernest, to whom his uncle Ernest stood as god-father during this visit. Poignantly, as a grown man, Prince Ernest visited his uncle in 1804 in Hanover when the latter was dying. He later married Frederica, a daughter of his uncle Charles.[6]

Following her brothers' visit, Queen Charlotte seems to have corresponded more than previously with them, judging by surviving letters in the Mecklenburg archives.[7] Charles became a close confidant, and there are wistful references to the arduous nature of British court life, compared to the smaller German courts. Queen Charlotte sent and received books and advised Charles on the education of his daughters when he was widowed, recommending that they should be versed in the natural sciences. She also followed the travails of Ernest in trying to find a wife: he was not a 'good catch' because his fortune was small, and never married.[8]

CCO

1. Like Zoffany, Prince Charles was a Freemason.
2. Marcus Kohler, 'The courts of Hanover and Strelitz', in Marsden 2005, 60–81; Clarissa Campbell Orr, 'Charlotte, Scientific Queen' and 'Charlotte of Mecklenburg-Strelitz, Queen of Great Britain and Electress of Hanover, Northern Dynasties and the Republic of Letters', in Campbell Orr 2004, 368–402.
3. Naomi Tadmor, *Family and Friend in Eighteenth Century England: Household, Kinship and Patronage*, Cambridge, 2001.
4. Shawe-Taylor 2009, 129; R.O. Bucholz, Database of Court Officers 1660–1837, http://luc.edu/history/fac_resources/bucholz/DCO/DCO.html (accessed 16 June 2011).
5. James Home, ed., *Letters of Louisa Stuart to Miss Louisa Clinton*, 2 vols., Edinburgh, 1901, vol. 1, 72; Clarissa Campbell Orr, 'Charlotte of Mecklenburg-Strelitz', in Campbell Orr 2004, 368–402.
6. The electorate of Hanover became a kingdom in 1815 after the Napoleonic Wars. After 1837 possession of the two thrones in a single branch of the family ended.
7. The Hausarchiv des Mecklenburg-Strelitzschen Fürstenhauses/Briefsammlung is in Schwerin. There are only a few letters between Queen Charlotte and Charles before 1771 and a more consistent pattern of correspondence afterwards, but it is impossible to tell if this is just an accident of survival rather than a reflection of the number of letters written. My hunch is that it is the latter.
8. Clarissa Campbell Orr, 'Charlotte of Mecklenburg-Strelitz', in Campbell Orr 2004, 368–402; Clarissa Campbell Orr, 'Dynastic Perspectives', in Brendan Simms and Torsten Riotte, eds., *The Hanoverian Dimension in British History 1714–1837*, Cambridge, 2007, 213–51.

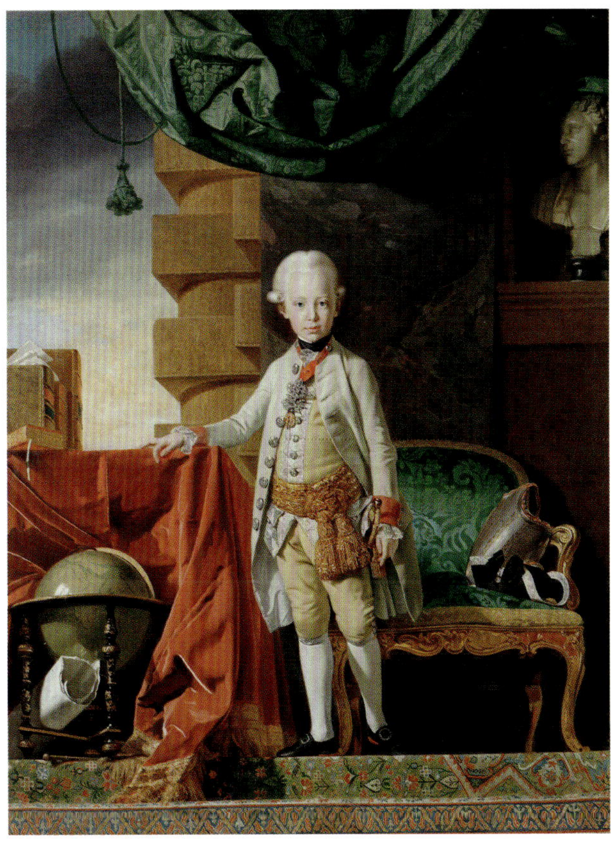

40

Archduke Francis
1775

Oil on canvas, 198 × 145 cm (78 × 57⅛ in)
Kunsthistorisches Museum, Vienna

Provenance: Commissioned by Archduchess Maria Theresa, 1775; Habsburg Dynasty Collection at Belvedere Summer Palace, subsequently Kunsthistorisches Museum, Vienna (currently Schloss Ambras, Innsbruck)

Selected exhibitions: National Portrait Gallery 1977, no. 80

Selected references: M. Zweig, 'Royal Portraits by Zoffany in Vienna', *The Connoisseur*, vol. 104, 1939, 80–81; Treadwell 2009, 246–7; Webster 2011, 322, 324–6

This portrait of Archduke Francis, the eldest son of Archduke Peter Leopold of Tuscany, was Zoffany's first commission from the Habsburg family and initiated a series of portraits that interrupted his work on the *Tribuna of the Uffizi* for Queen Charlotte. The young duke's birth occasioned great rejoicing by his grandmother Maria Theresa, as he was her first grandson. Since her eldest son, Joseph, was determined not to marry a third time in the attempt to beget male heirs, Francis was destined to inherit the Habsburg lands in Austria, together with the crowns of Bohemia and Hungary and their other territories, while Tuscany went to his next brother, Ferdinand. Their father had no choice but to acquiesce, as his

fortune was not large enough to provide for all thirteen of his surviving children.[1]

As in his portrait of the Prince of Wales (see cat. 33), Zoffany shows young Francis already being groomed to play the part of a ruler and soldier. Since he is nearly seven, he has already begun wearing breeches; he also sports a magnificent gold-braided sash for his sword and is wearing the highest chivalric order in Europe, the Order of the Golden Fleece, which was in the gift of the Habsburg family. The buttons of his white uniform are made of pearls. Zoffany has positioned him as though on a raised dais so that he can look directly at the viewer from a commanding position. Behind him is a monumental pillar of the Tuscan order, which was classified as a masculine architectural order. On his right is a globe and maps, with books above and further to his right; on his left the cuirass from his armour, borrowed for Zoffany from the state armoury. All symbolize aspects of government. Behind him to the right is a bust of the Roman emperor Marcus Aurelius, renowned for his wisdom and statecraft.[2] Seen close to, the young prince looks confident, but from a distance his slight shoulders and stiff neck suggest his anxiety to please, to live up to family expectation. He indeed matured into a phlegmatic, imperturbable man. Here, poignantly, he is still a child, as well as a royal prince.

While Zoffany was painting this portrait, he was invited to let his own baby son join the royal nursery. The artist must have been overjoyed that

his son would repeat his own experience of being absorbed for a time into a princely household, but tragedy soon followed when the infant died after an accident.[3] The portrait suggests the vulnerability of childhood, counterpointing the soft rounded limbs and the pale cream and buff uniform with the angularity and sober, dark grandeur of the background. Francis's education was regulated in detail by his uncle Joseph, and in 1781, when he was only thirteen, it was decided that he should marry Elizabeth, Princess of Württemberg, aged fourteen, whose elder sister was already married to the heir of Catherine the Great of Russia, Grand Duke Paul. Both children went to live in Vienna, to accustom themselves to their future roles, and were married in 1788.[4] Within two years Elisabeth died after a protracted childbirth. Francis married three more times, each time to cousins. It was he who was forced to dissolve the Holy Roman Empire in 1806 and to let his daughter Louisa become Napoleon's second wife, but he presided over the successful evolution of the Habsburg Austrian lands into the Austrian Empire.

CCO

1. Beales 1987–2009, vol. 1, *In the Shadow of Maria Theresa, 1741–1780*, 1987, 176–7; Beales 1987–2009, vol. 2, *Against the World, 1780–1790*, 2009, 355–6, 359–60.
2. Treadwell 2009 246; Webster 2011, 326.
3. Treadwell 2009, 248–9.
4. Beales 1987–2009, vol. 2, *Against the World, 1780–1790*, 124–32, 358–60, 370–71, 673.

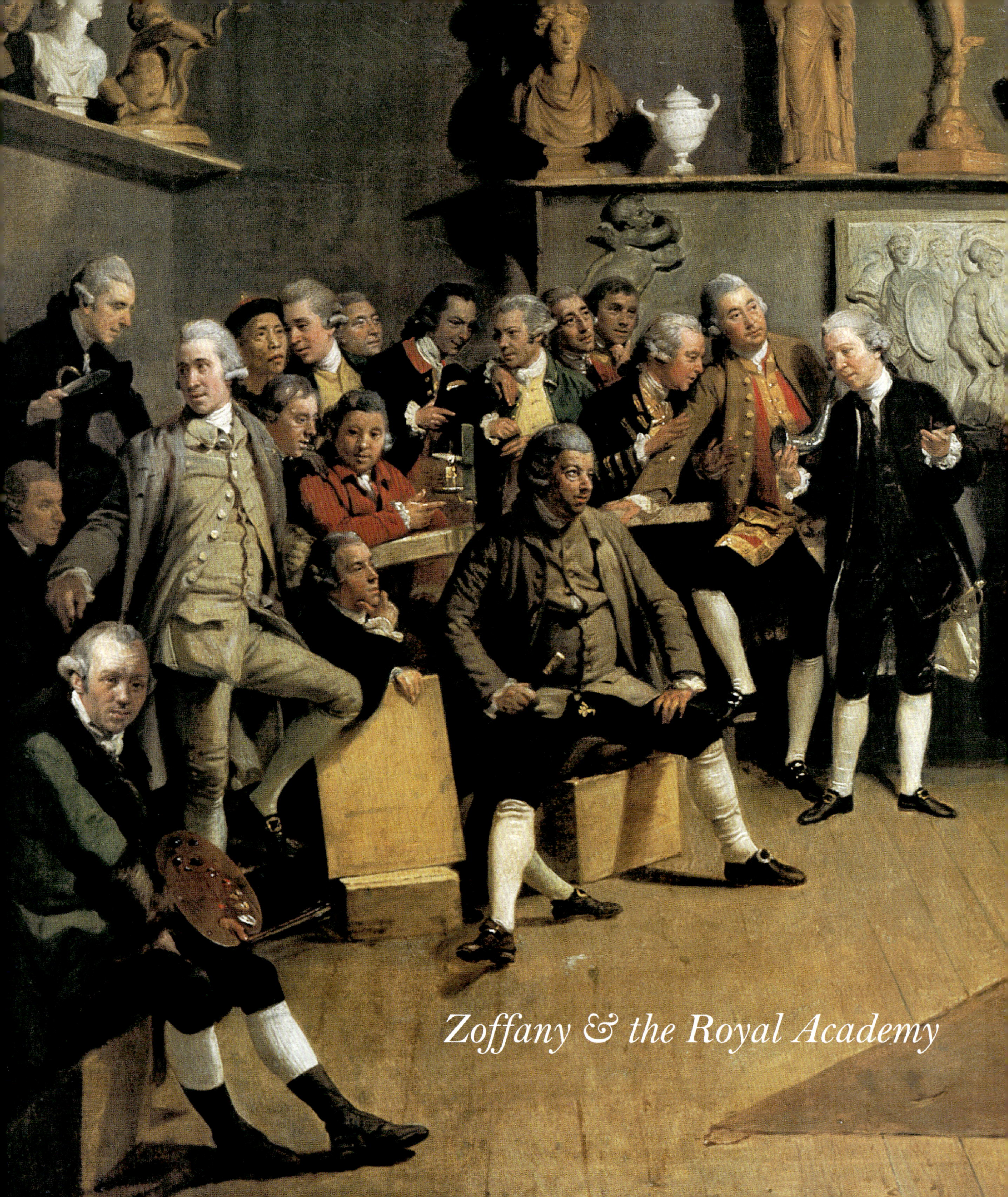
Zoffany & the Royal Academy

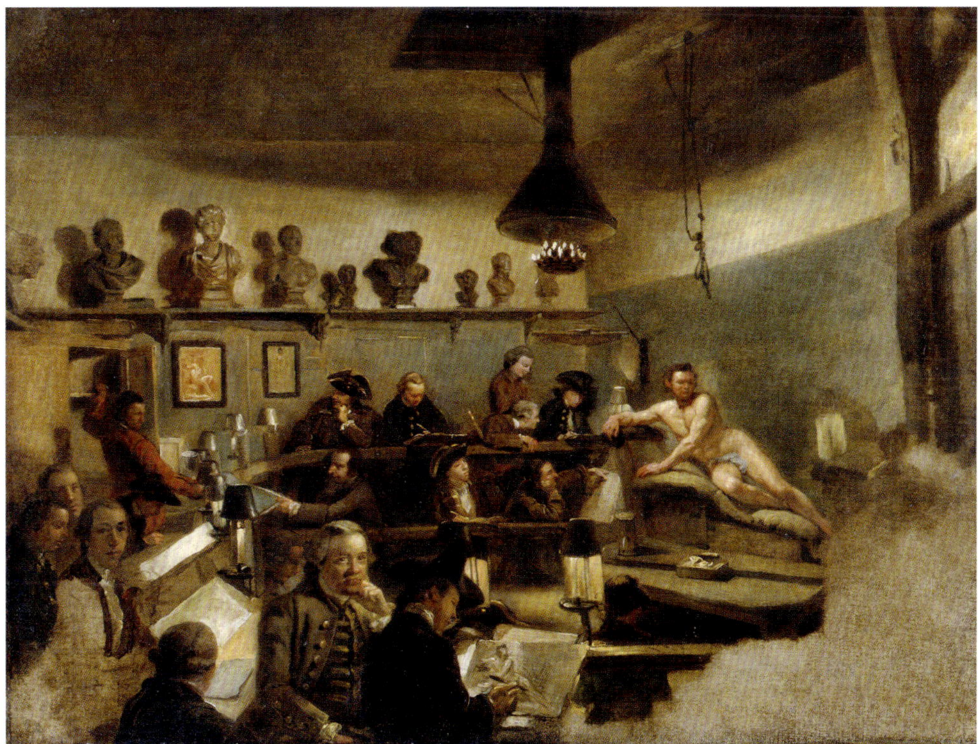

*An Academy by Lamplight, a Life Class at
St Martin's Lane Academy*
1761–2

Oil on canvas, 50.5 × 66 cm (19⅞ × 26 in)
Royal Academy of Arts, London; given by
William Smith, 1871

Provenance: Nicholas Thomas Dall; John Inigo
Richards by 1777; his sale, George Squibb, London,
14 March 1811, no. 66, 'The Life Academy, a highly
esteemed Picture'; given to the Royal Academy of
Arts by William Smith, 1871

*Selected exhibitions: Bi-Centenary Exhibition of
Paintings by Joseph Wright, A.R.A.,* Corporation Art
Gallery, Derby, 1934; Graves Art Gallery, Sheffield,
1934; Diploma Gallery, Royal Academy of Arts,
1939, no. 150; Royal Academy 1951–2, no. 1;
*Diploma Works and Other Paintings by the Early
Members of the Royal Academy,* Nottingham
University Art Gallery, 1959, no. 52; *Diploma
and Other Pictures from the Collections of the Royal
Academy, 1768–1851,* Arts Council Touring
Exhibition, City Art Gallery, Birmingham (then
to Sheffield, Bolton, Swansea and Plymouth),
1961–2, no. 47; *Paint & Painting: An Exhibition and
Working Studio Sponsored by Winsor & Newton to
Celebrate their 150th Anniversary,* Tate Gallery, 1982;
Buxton Festival, Derbyshire Museum and Art
Gallery, 1984, no. 92 ; Nottingham and Kenwood
1991, no. 4; *Dreihundert Jahre Hochschule der Künste,*
Akademie der Künste, Berlin, 1996; *Creative
Quarters: The Art World in London from 1700–2000,*
Museum of London, 2001

Selected references: Martin Postle, 'The St Martin's
Lane Academy. True and false records', *Apollo,*
vol. 134, no. 353, July 1991, 33–8; Webster 2011,
250–52

The painting is the only known depiction of the
St Martin's Lane Academy, which Zoffany joined
shortly after his arrival in London in 1760.[1]
Although unfinished, it is a unique visual record
of the appearance and activities of the precursor to
the Royal Academy of Arts, founded less than a
decade later. The St Martin's Lane Academy was
established as a life class by subscription in October
1720 by the artists Louis Cheron and John
Vanderbank. It was situated from this time onwards
in Russell's Meeting House, a former Presbyterian
chapel in St Peter's Court, an alley off the lower
west side of St Martin's Lane. The first St Martin's
Lane Academy closed in 1724, when the treasurer
embezzled the funds, and the furnishings and
equipment were seized in lieu of rent. In 1735 the
Academy reopened under the leadership of William
Hogarth, using equipment that he had inherited
from his father-in-law Sir James Thornhill, 'a
proper table for the figure to stand on a large lamp
iron stove and benches in a circular form'.[2] The
second St Martin's Lane Academy continued until

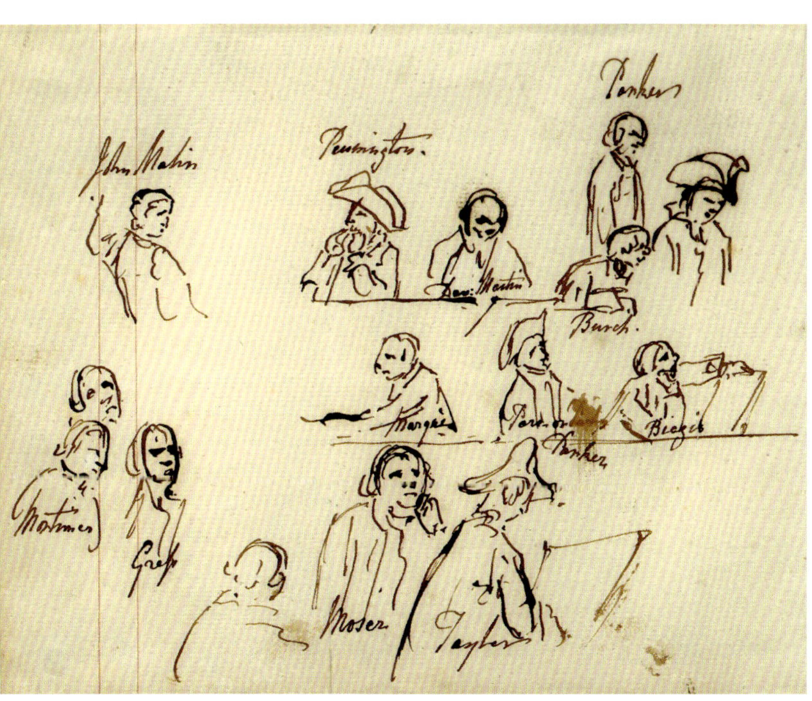

Figure 177
Unknown artist, *Key to St Martin's Lane Academy,*
*c.*1762, pen and brown ink on paper,
17.3 × 26.8 cm (6¾ × 10½ in). British Museum,
Department of Prints and Drawings

1767 when the furnishings and equipment were transferred to a former print warehouse in Pall Mall to form the basis of the life class of the embryonic Royal Academy. A number of items depicted in the present painting, including the oil lamp, the students' shaded candle-lamps, the semi-circular bench, and one of the classical busts on the mantelshelf, can also be identified in Zoffany's later painting of the Academicians of the Royal Academy.

The first recorded owner of the painting was the landscape and scenery painter Nicholas Thomas Dall, who from 1757 worked as a scenery painter at the Covent Garden Theatre. On Dall's death in December 1776 it passed to John Inigo Richards, secretary of the Royal Academy, who had worked with Dall as a scenery painter at Covent Garden.[3] It is quite possible that Dall acquired the painting directly from Zoffany, who, through his employment as a drapery painter for the artist Benjamin Wilson (also a theatre manager), had formed close ties with London's theatrical community by the early 1760s. Zoffany left the painting unfinished, perhaps because it was painted as a speculation or because he needed to concentrate on other more pressing professional commitments – intensified by his precarious finances at the time.

The painting was presented to the Royal Academy in 1871 as a depiction of 'the Life School at St Martin's Lane', although it was subsequently described as 'An Academy by Lamplight' and was attributed to Joseph Wright of Derby until the 1980s. However, close examination and comparison with other pictures made by Zoffany shortly after his arrival in London, notably the portrait of an artist (cat. 42), and *Time Clipping the Wings of Love* (cat. 9), reveal handling and tonal range that are entirely characteristic of his art at that period in his career.[4] It is also surely significant that in 1826 the picture was described in the *Literary Gazette* as by Zoffany:

> He painted a group of the members of the St. Martin's Lane Academy, and made the studies from the individuals on the spot. Moser, who is represented as the foreground principal figure, was looking over the drawing of a student, Mr. Taylor, then a young man; and several are therein introduced, who afterwards became distinguished members of the Royal Academy.[5]

The student in question, 'Mr. Taylor', was John Taylor, a professional drawing master, subsequently known as 'Old Taylor', who was himself the source of information on the picture's history, as well as other first-hand biographical information on Zoffany.

The presence of George Michael Moser and John Taylor in the present picture is confirmed by a pen-and-ink key to the present picture (fig. 177), which identifies most of the artists present and was possibly made by Zoffany, one of the artists featured in the painting, or perhaps by Dall or Richards. Moser, who had played a leading role in organizing life classes in London since the 1730s and was a director of the St Martin's Lane Academy, is depicted in the role of teacher. Behind and to the left of Moser are John Hamilton Mortimer and his friend John Alexander Gresse. Immediately behind them, although unidentified in the key, is Zoffany – who was also a close friend of Mortimer. The figure in red, by the cupboard, is John Malin, porter and occasional model at the St Martin's Lane Academy. He also served briefly as the first porter at the Royal Academy. The three artists in the middle row are, from left to right, Giuseppe Marchi, who had accompanied Reynolds to England in 1752 and worked as his lifelong studio assistant (see also cat. 42); probably William Pars or one of two artists named John Parker (a history painter and a landscapist, who won premiums for drawing at the Society of Arts at this time); and Biaggio Rebecca, who had travelled to London from Rome in 1760. The four artists in the back row of the life class can be identified as an otherwise unknown pastellist named Pennington, who exhibited portraits at the Free Society of Artists in 1764; David Martin, who in the 1760s worked as principal assistant to Allan Ramsay; the gem-engraver and medallist Edward Burch, and an unnamed artist. The artist in the brown coat, standing at the back of the room to the right, is perhaps one of the two Parkers already referred to. Collectively, the young artists represented in the painting – all aged between twenty and thirty – reflect the professional world of Zoffany in London in the early 1760s. His decision to produce such a picture also reflects his close allegiance to the Academy, which was to remain an important institution throughout his life.

MP

1. Ilaria Bignamini, 'George Vertue, Art Historian, and Art Institutions in London, 1689–1768', *Walpole Society*, vol. 54 (1988), 140.
2. Michael Kitson, 'William Hogarth's "Apology for Painters"', *Walpole Society*, vol. 41 (1968), 94.
3. *The Literary Gazette, and Journal of the Belles Lettres*, 1826, 429.
4. In her recent book Mary Webster resists an attribution to Zoffany, noting that the painting's technique 'seems to reflect a painter acquainted with the mannerisms of German rococo painting, for instance, the broken pink of the flesh tints in certain passages'. Webster 2011, 252.
5. *The Literary Gazette, and Journal of the Belles Lettres*, 1826, 429.

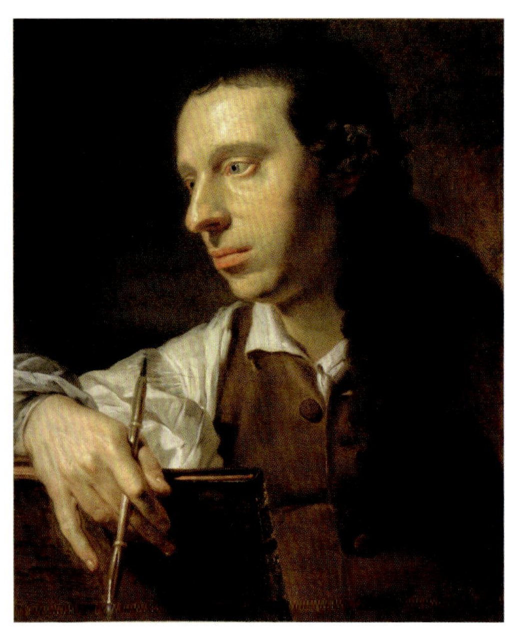

42

Portrait of an Artist
1761

Oil on canvas, 52.7 × 41.3 cm (20¾ × 16¼ in)
Signed: 'Zoffany pinx. | 1761'
National Portrait Gallery, London

Provenance: J. Scotcher (a broker), Ealing 1873; bt William Bean, from whom purchased 1875

Selected references: Manners & Williamson 1920, 221; Pressly 1987, 86–101; Pressly 1995, 49–55; Ingamells 2004, 498, no. 399; Treadwell 2009, 18–19

This intimate portrait of a young artist has long been considered by some authorities to be a self-portrait by Zoffany, painted shortly after his arrival in London. However, while the painting is certainly by Zoffany, who signed and dated the work, it is probably the portrait of a fellow artist, quite possibly a friend or associate at the St Martin's Lane Academy. That the portrait was made at the same time as Zoffany's painting of the St Martin's Lane Academy (cat. 41) is indicated by the date of the present work, the similar muted tonal range and the subject: a young artist at work.

The artist in the portrait appears to be in his mid-twenties. He is dressed informally in a waistcoat and white shirt, his right hand resting on his portfolio of drawings. The warm flesh tones are highly reminiscent of Zoffany's subject painting, *Time Clipping the Wings of Love* (cat. 9), also signed and dated 1761, and revealing the same virtuosity and close attention to anatomical detail, notably in the veins and clearly articulated bone structure of the hand. Cradled elegantly in the hand is the artist's brass, double-ended porte-crayon, designed to hold drawing materials. The prominence of the hand and the porte-crayon is perhaps significant, as it not only alludes to the individual artist but the

concept of 'disegno', wherein the hand not only performs, quite literally, the manual operation but translates an idea into physical form, as expressed in the celebrated anagram 'Disegno, segno di Dio' (Design, the sign of God). A concept developed in sixteenth-century Italy, it would have been familiar to Zoffany through his academic training there in the previous decade. Here, in this seemingly modest portrait, the hand takes on a renewed significance, as it acts as a virtual manifesto for the role of drawing in art.

The suggestion that the artist featured in the portrait is Zoffany has been put forward on the grounds that the facial features resemble his own, as seen for example in the painting of *David with the Head of Goliath* (cat. 3), although that picture probably does not depict Zoffany either. Indeed, the structure of the face, the nose and even the colour of the eyes in the present portrait differ considerably from Zoffany's features as they appear in known self-portraits. A possible sitter for this portrait is the Italian artist, Giuseppe Filippo Liberati Marchi, who also features in Zoffany's painting of the St Martin's Lane Academy. Although Marchi appears as only a small figure in the St Martin's Lane painting, he has the same high forehead and significantly, like the present artist, is distinguished by a striking queue of dark hair that trails down his back. In addition, a comparison between the present portrait and Joshua Reynolds's earlier portrait of Marchi (fig. 178), painted in 1753 shortly after his arrival from Italy, reveals a similar physiognomy,

notably the long straight nose, arched eyebrows, almond shaped eyes and full lips. Although there is no evidence of a particular bond of friendship between Zoffany and Marchi, their status as foreigners, a shared language and their common experience of Italy may have drawn them together at this time. Marchi also produced engravings of several of Zoffany's paintings of the 1760s, including *John Moody as Foigard in The Beaux' Stratagem* (cat. 30) and *Hester Maria Thrale* (see cat. 68).

MP

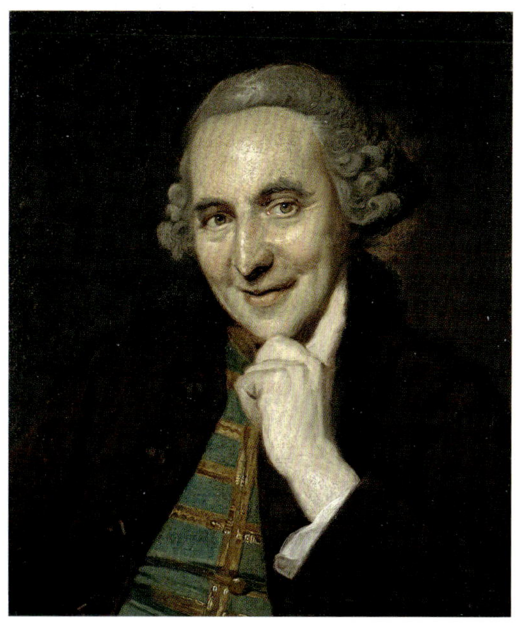

43

Simon-François Ravenet
1762–3

Oil on canvas, 52.7 × 43.2 cm (20¾ × 17 in)
Private collection

Provenance: London art market, 1990s; Bonhams, Knightsbridge, 11 July 2001, no. 155, bought in; purchased subsequently by the present owner

Selected exhibition: Society of Artists, 1762, no. 138 ('A gentleman's head')

Selected references: Webster 1976, 29; Treadwell 2009, 56, 198–9; Webster 2011, 61–2

This captivating image of the engraver Simon-François Ravenet is among the most intriguing portraits made by Zoffany following his arrival in England. Until its recent rediscovery the image was known only through the engraving of it in reverse by Ravenet himself, which he inscribed: 'S.F. RAVENET. Peint par son Ami Zaffanii et Gravé par lui même, en 1763' (see fig. 58). Simon-François Ravenet was born in Paris, and trained there as an engraver. In 1743 William Hogarth visited Paris, inviting Ravenet to London to make engravings for his series, *Marriage A-la-Mode*; Ravenet engraved plates IV ('The Toilette') and V ('The Bagnio'), published in 1745. Indeed, it may well have been Ravenet who first introduced Zoffany to Hogarth's work, which was to have such a profound effect on him. Following the initial commission for Hogarth, Ravenet remained in London where he made his home and established a successful career. Commissions included, in 1745–6, a series of prints of classical sculptures for Richard Dalton and, in the early 1750s, two plates for William Hunter's *Anatomy of the Human Gravid Uterus*, after drawings by Jan van Rymsdyck. By the 1760s he was employed on a broad range of images after contemporary British artists, including

Figure 178
Joshua Reynolds, *Portrait of Giuseppe Marchi*, 1753, oil on canvas, 77.2 × 63.6 cm (30⅜ × 25 in).
Royal Academy of Arts, London

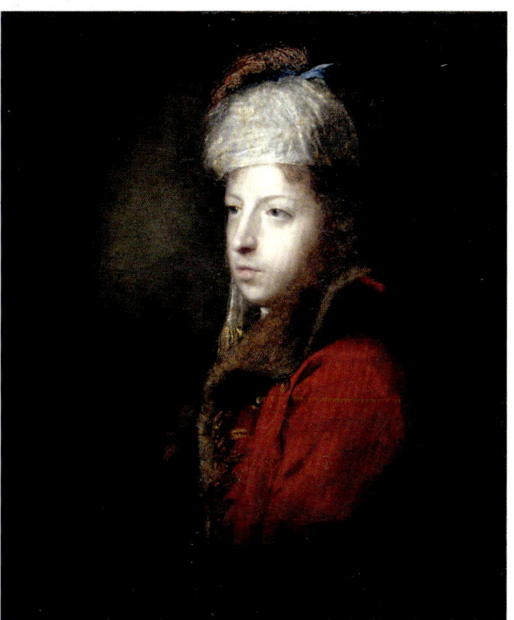

Benjamin Wilson, Francis Hayman and John Hamilton Mortimer. Much of his work was commissioned by leading print-publishers, notably Robert Sayer (the publisher of prints after Zoffany) and John Boydell, to whose three-volume *Sculptura Britannica: A Collection of Prints, Engraved from the most Capital Paintings in England* (1769–73), he contributed a large number of engravings, including 'An Academy' after Mortimer, which formed the frontispiece of volume two. In addition to his work as an engraver, Ravenet was active in London's art institutions: in 1767 he was a member of the committee of the Society of Artists and on 26 February 1770 he was made an Associate Academician of the Royal Academy, one of only a handful of engravers to be admitted.

In the present portrait Ravenet smiles mischievously at the viewer, his hand resting on his chin, with his forefinger extended towards his ear. An important pictorial influence on Zoffany's portrait must surely have been Joshua Reynolds's portrait of Laurence Sterne (fig. 179), painted in 1760 on the publication of the first two volumes of his groundbreaking satirical novel, *The Life and Opinions of Tristram Shandy*. Ravenet himself had an intimate knowledge of Reynolds's portrait since he had engraved it for the frontispiece of the first two volumes of Sterne's *Sermons of Mr Yorick*, published in May 1760 to great acclaim. In both Reynolds's *Sterne* and Zoffany's *Ravenet* the sitter's smile is not simply an indication of amiability but something more unsettling, a half-secretive smile that in Sterne's case refers to his wicked wit. More generally, both images can be considered in the context of the 'laughing philosopher', a tradition going back to the Greek philosopher, Democritus, who laughed at mortality and human folly. It was, moreover, an attitude that Zoffany was to adopt in

his own later self-portrait painted for the Uffizi Gallery (cat. 58). A more recent philosophical and visual influence on Zoffany's portrait may have been a celebrated print by the German painter and engraver Georg Friedrich Schmidt of the materialist philosopher Julien Offrai de la Mettrie (fig. 180). La Mettrie had scandalized French society through his libertinism and atheistic writings, expressed in his notorious masterpiece, *L'Homme machine* of 1747. As a result he fled France to escape persecution, finding protection in Berlin under Frederick II. As it has been observed, Schmidt's print was conceived not merely as a likeness but as propaganda, celebrating La Mettrie's Epicurean enjoyment of the pleasures of life, while disavowing the existence of God and the afterlife.[1] In his engraving of Zoffany's portrait Ravenet adopted the same format as Schmidt's print of La Mettrie, where the oval frame 'places the writer … at a remove from us, its cracked masonry speaking of transience and mortality'.[2] While Ravenet may not have adopted the extreme views of La Mettrie, he clearly endorsed the pleasure principle, as his engravings after Hogarth indicate.[3] There can be no doubt that he and Zoffany were kindred spirits.

Ravenet evidently proved a loyal friend to Zoffany following the latter's arrival in England in 1760. Although the precise circumstances surrounding their first acquaintance are not known, it was suggested some years later that Ravenet, aware that Zoffany had 'soon found himself in that distress which many Foreigners with great talents have experienced in this country', advised him to take up portraiture.[4] The same source stated that Zoffany was recommended to the portraitist Benjamin Wilson as a potential studio assistant by an artist who had seen his portrait of Ravenet.

It was also Ravenet who apparently rescued Zoffany from destitution when he absconded from Wilson, tracking him down to an ale-house near St Anne's, Soho, where he was making chalk drawings for the tap-room in exchange for beer. Whether the story is true, it is quite possible that Ravenet was responsible for introducing Zoffany to Benjamin Wilson and David Garrick, since he had in 1753 engraved 'Mr Garrick and Miss Bellamy in the Characters of Romeo and Juliet' after Wilson's original oil painting (fig. 59), a print that was reissued on several occasions afterwards. The present portrait, which was clearly well known at the time and is the only known one of its size dating from this period in Zoffany's career, may have been the picture entitled 'A gentleman's head', exhibited by 'Mr Zaffanii' at the Society of Artists in 1762. The picture may have been exhibited and presented to Ravenet as a token of Zoffany's friendship and gratitude. Although Zoffany was in Italy when Ravenet died in London in 1774, he would have been well acquainted with his son Simon-François Ravenet the Younger, who at that time was engraver to the Duke of Parma and Director of the Academy to which Zoffany himself gained admission as an honorary member in June 1778.

MP

1. Hilliard 2010.
2. Hilliard 2010, 131.
3. In addition to his engravings after *Marriage A-la-Mode*, Ravenet engraved several plates after Hogarth in volumes 1 and 3 of *The Life and Opinions of Tristram Shandy.*
4. Anon. 1781, iv–vi.

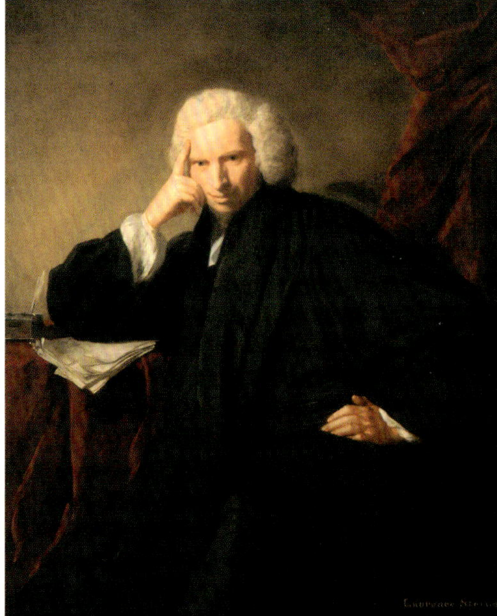

Figure 179
Joshua Reynolds, *Laurence Sterne*, 1760, oil on canvas, 127.3 × 100.3 cm (50⅛ × 39½ in). National Portrait Gallery; purchased with help from Mr and Mrs Lewis Golden, The Art Fund, the Pilgrim Trust, HM Government and the results of a public appeal, 1975

Figure 180
Georg Friedrich Schmidt, *Julien Offrai de La Mettrie*, 1757, line engraving, 25.2 × 19.2 cm (9⅞ × 7½ in). British Museum, Department of Prints and Drawings, 1838, 1215.129

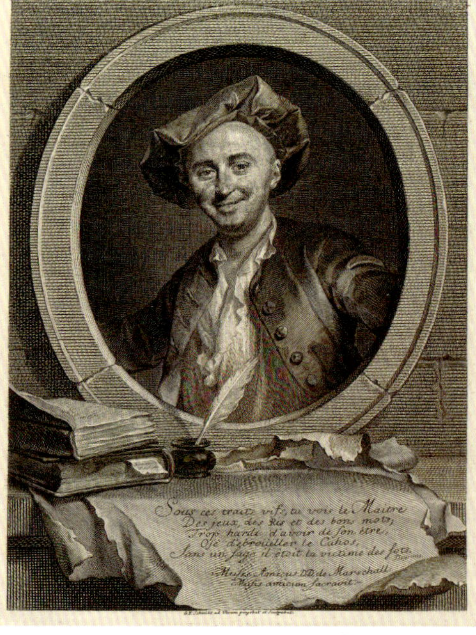

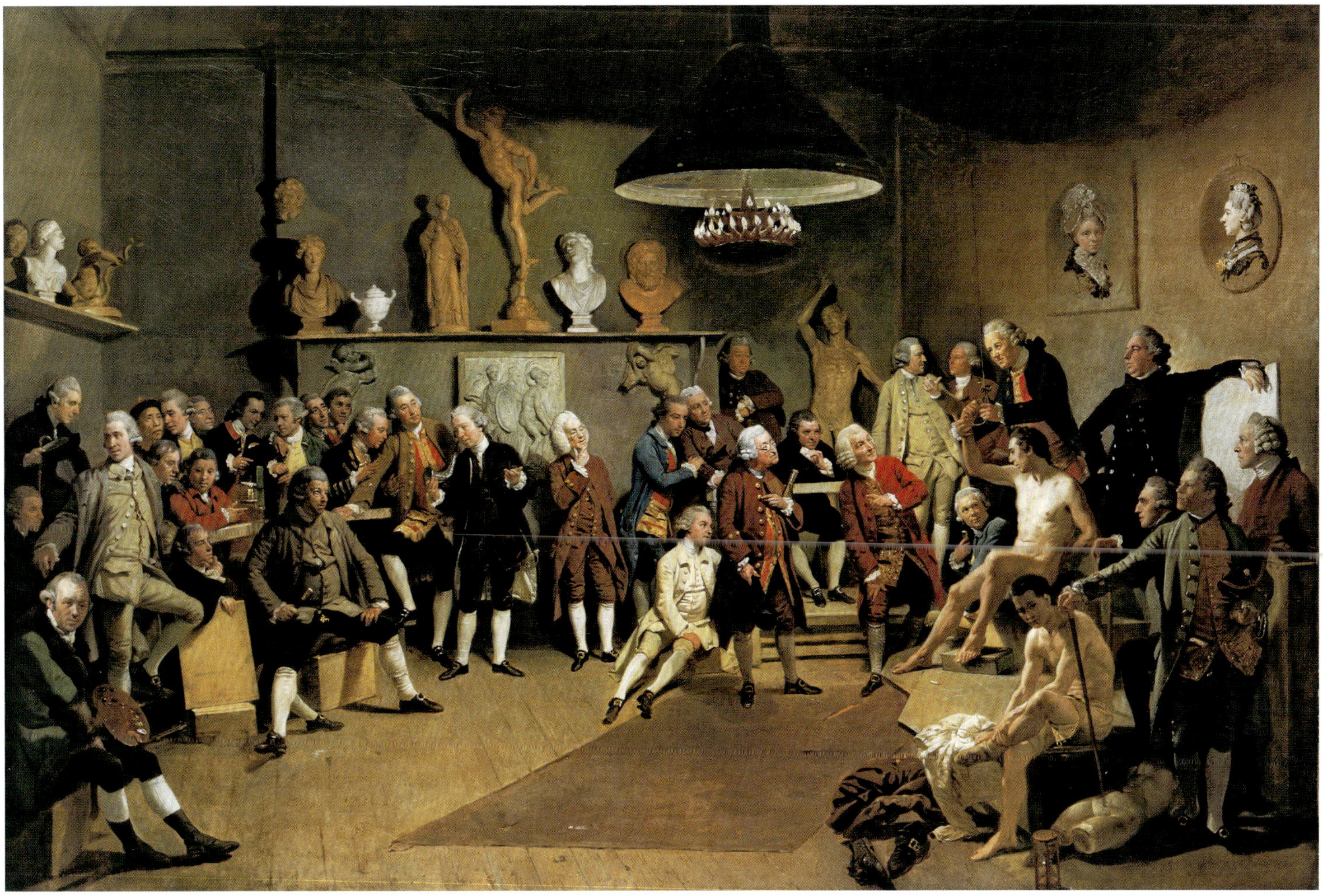

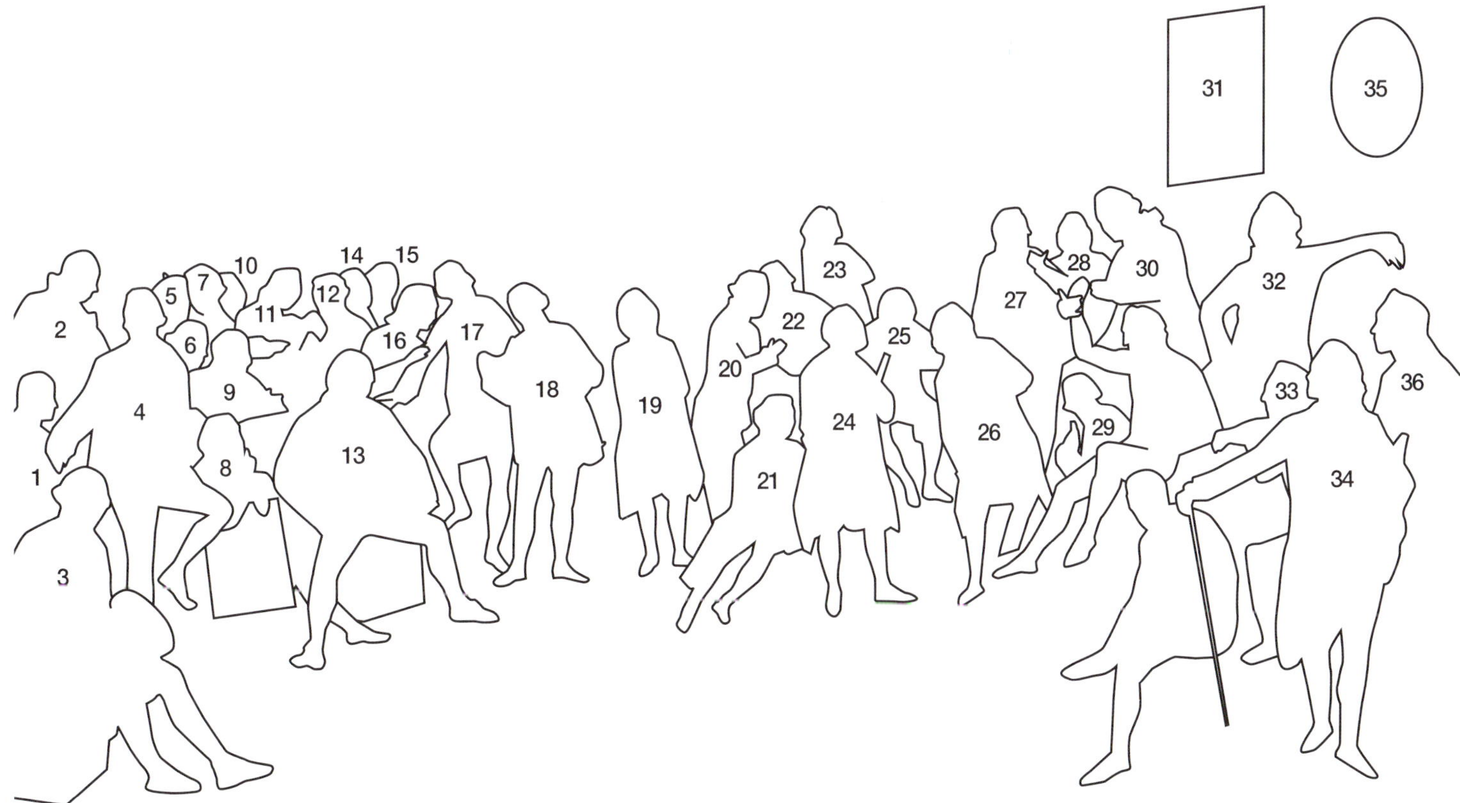

***The Portraits of the Academicians of
the Royal Academy***
1771–2

Oil on canvas
100.1 × 147.5 cm (39¾ × 58 in)
The Royal Collection, Her Majesty Queen
Elizabeth II

Provenance: Purchased by George III from
the artist, 1772

Selected exhibitions: Royal Academy of Arts, 1772,
no. 290; Royal Academy 1968–9, no. 12; Queen's
Gallery 1974–5, no. 34; National Portrait Gallery
1977, no. 74; Nottingham and Kenwood, 1991,
no. 5; Queen's Gallery 2004, no. 159

Selected references: Millar 1969, no. 1210; Treadwell
2009, 174–83, 192, 256, 281, 363, 397, 163;
Webster 2011, 252–61

Key to *The Portraits of the Academicians of
the Royal Academy*

1. John Gwynn
2. Giovanni Cipriani
3. Johan Zoffany
4. Benjamin West
5. Tan Chitqua
6. George Barret
7. Jeremiah Meyer
8. Mason Chamberlin
9. Joseph Wilton
10. Dominic Serres
11. Paul Sandby
12. Thomas Sandby
13. Francis Hayman
14. William Tyler
15. John Inigo Richards
16. Francis Newton
17. Sir William Chambers
18. Sir Joshua Reynolds
19. Dr William Hunter
20. Francesco Bartolozzi
21. Charles Catton
22. Agostino Carlini
23. Richard Wilson
24. Richard Yeo
25. Samuel Wale
26. Francesco Zuccarelli
27. Edward Penny
28. Peter Toms
29. Edward Burch
30. George Michael Moser
31. Angelica Kauffman (*portrait*)
32. Nathaniel Hone
33. Joseph Nollekens
34. Richard Cosway
35. Mary Moser (*portrait*)
36. William Hoare

This group portrait, together with *George III
and Queen Charlotte with their Six Eldest Children*
(cat. 34), was Zoffany's most ambitious to date.
It shows thirty-six individuals, thirty-four of
whom were Royal Academicians, engaged in, or
variously observing, the setting of the life model at
the Royal Academy. Three Academicians, Thomas
Gainsborough, George Dance and his brother
Nathaniel, are absent, possibly due to discontent
with the nascent institution (see cat. 45). Decency
demanded that the two female Foundation
Academicians, Angelica Kauffman and Mary
Moser, could only appear as portraits on the right
wall (31 and 35). The two non-Academicians are
the Cantonese sculptor, Tan Chitqua (5), and the
Royal Academy's first Professor of Anatomy,
William Hunter (19).

The painting was first exhibited at the Royal
Academy in 1772. Previously considered to have
been commissioned by George III as a record of the
Academy that he had instituted in December 1768,[1]
it was in fact a speculative work: Zoffany sold it to
the king for 500 guineas during the exhibition
(see cat. 51). It has been assumed that the work was
made between early 1771 and early 1772,[2] possibly
to record the move in January 1771 of the Royal
Academy's plaster and life schools, library and
administration from their temporary home on
Pall Mall to Old Somerset House.[3] However, an
annotation on the verso of the pencil outline copy
of the group portrait made by John Sanders, who
had entered the Royal Academy Schools in 1769,
records that Zoffany's painting had been started
in 1770 'in the room that was that of the Royal
Academy in Pall Mall'.[4]

Sanders's note raises the question of both the
date of execution and location of the scene. There
is no record of the appearance of the life school in
Old Somerset House.[5] However, two accounts
survive of the accommodation at 125 Pall Mall,
which had initially been accorded to the Royal
Academy by the king through his librarian
Richard Dalton, the lessee of the property.[6] If the
group portrait had indeed been started in 1770,
then it would be logical to conclude that the room
portrayed was in Pall Mall. Accepting Sanders's
assertion, William Hauptman[7] has argued that the
room in the painting must be the Great Exhibition
Room at 125 Pall Mall on the grounds of its
amplitude, unpanelled walls and great lamp
(see cat. 46).[8] However, given the absence of green
baize on the walls and the distinctive clerestory
windows above the Great Exhibition Room's
cornice,[9] together with the presence of a chimney
breast without a chimney piece, this identification
is not tenable. The wall colour, the splayed
perspective and the inclusion of shelves to
accommodate plaster casts would suggest that
Zoffany, as elsewhere, adopted a non-specific
space as a neutral platform for a programmatic
presentation of his fellow Academicians.

Zoffany's group portrait has traditionally been

read as a record of a central activity of the Royal
Academy, namely the setting of the life model in
the Life School by the assembled ranks of the
institution's membership. Such an event, however,
is a construct. According to the Academy's
Instrument of Foundation (1768), the life model
was neither to be set by all the Academicians nor
by the Keeper – as is the case in Zoffany's painting –
but rather by one of the nine annually elected
Visitors to the Schools.[10] Furthermore, the title
printed in the 1772 Annual Exhibition catalogue
reads, 'The Portraits of the Academicians …',
indicating that the work was primarily a record of
the distinguished painters, sculptors, architects and
engravers who constituted the institution's initial
membership. However, as Mary Webster has
argued, the focus on the setting of the life model
and the presence of plaster casts define another
fundamental aspect of the institution, namely its
aesthetic programme. To draw from the life model,
after mastering the delineation of the plaster cast
after the antique, was to understand the ideal
human form, which was fundamental for the
production of history paintings, the highest genre
of art, that was capable of appealing to the intellect
as well as to the sentiment. By bringing the life
model into direct contact with the complement
of Royal Academicians, the painting declared
unequivocally the Academy's affinity with other
European academies and its unique position in
Britain in providing professional training for
its students.

Sanders's annotated key of the early 1770s,
subsequently supported by the key published by
Laurie and Whittle in 1794, has to date supplied
the identity of the figures represented in the
group portrait.[11] Recently, Penelope Treadwell
has suggested the re-identification of four of the
protagonists, but careful study of the relevant
physical likenesses suggests that these cannot
be sustained.[12]

Horace Walpole claimed that Zoffany 'made no
design for [the painting], but clapped in artists as
they came to him, and yet all are easy and natural,
most of the likenesses strong'.[13] This statement,
implying an unplanned process of execution, is in
part countered by the existence of the oil sketch
of the head of Gainsborough (cat. 45). However
no preliminary drawings or other oil studies
survive. Yet the addition of a 19 cm (7½ in) strip
of canvas on the right-hand side to accommodate
Nathaniel Hone (Nominated Member, 32) and
two new Academicians, Richard Cosway (34),
elected in 1771, and Joseph Nollekens (33),
elected in February 1772 – and probably Thomas
Gainsborough – is evidence that the work evolved
over a period of time.

Despite the informality and shared intent
conveyed by Zoffany, the arrangement of the
figures is premeditated and articulates both
primary and secondary narratives. There are two
dominant foci within the composition. Right of

centre, focusing on the setting of the model, are those Academicians whose primary responsibilities lay in the professional training of the artist: Zuccarelli (26), one of the nine elected Visitors of the Life Academy in 1770, directs George Michael Moser (30), first Keeper of the Schools, as he sets the nude model, while Edward Penny (27) and Samuel Wale (25), Professors of Painting and Perspective respectively, give the process their close attention. To the left of centre the narrative focuses on the origins and establishment of the Royal Academy: Sir Joshua Reynolds (18), as first president, appears to hold centre stage, underlying the importance of the life drawing through the gesture of his left hand. Yet he defers to the portly, seated Francis Hayman (13), with Sir William Chambers (17), first treasurer, and Francis Milner Newton (16), first secretary, on his right. These latter two, with Reynolds, represent the official authority of the new Academy. The presence of Newton and Hayman within a wider triangular arrangement, whose apex is the figure of William Chambers, makes reference to the Academy's important antecedents. Hayman had been elected President of the Incorporated Society of Artists in 1765 but was defeated three years later, whereupon he led a group of sixteen dissident artists to form the Royal Academy. Newton was Secretary of the Society of Artists and had been centrally engaged in earlier abortive attempts to establish a professional body of artists. Chambers, member of the Society of Artists and architectural tutor and adviser to the king, was also the author of the memorandum that determined George III to establish the institution in December 1768. Finally, William Hunter (stroking his chin) (19) stands as a

pivot between the two groups, implying that, as first Professor of Anatomy (see cat. 46) he was entrusted to communicate the general principles of the science of anatomy to the practical needs of the students, a clear demonstration of the Academicians' appreciation of the importance of High Art to be informed by knowledge of relevant intellectual disciplines. There is one further figure, Richard Yeo (24), whose dominant position to the left of William Hunter suggests that he was an Academician of considerable authority, at least within the Royal Academy Schools. However, Yeo held neither a formal professorship nor a Visitorship during the period of the painting's execution.[14] He was, however, a distinguished medallist as well as engraver at the Royal Mint and of the king's seal. Does he stand as a proxy for the monarch himself?

Zoffany has positioned himself, palette in hand, at the lower left-hand corner of the composition. From this vantage point he is commentator not only on the work's primary narratives but also on its secondary ones. These include observations on his fellow Academicians: the two Sandby brothers, Paul (11) and Thomas (12), caught in conversation and placed beside Dominic Serres (10), their close neighbour in London; Mason Chamberlin (8), with drawing board in hand alluding to his recently completed portrait of Hunter; the dapperly dressed Charles Catton (21) in a prominent position; the ailing, morose Richard Wilson (23) relegated to a gloomy corner by the chimney breast; the miniaturist Jeremiah Meyer (7) placed beside the modeller of small, clay portrait busts, Tan Chitqua;[15] and the dandy Cosway in the pose of the Apollo Belvedere, his cane resting on the torso of

a female plaster cast after the antique.

The elevated subject of the painting's primary narratives, taken together with the orchestration of a multi-figure composition, suggests that Zoffany drew on the organization and iconography of Rapahel's fresco in the Vatican Stanze, *The School of Athens* (fig. 182). Zoffany could have studied this during his period in Rome from 1750 to 1756 and was probably familiar with the copy (Victoria and Albert Museum) made in 1755 for the Duke of Northumberland by Anton Raphael Mengs, with whom Zoffany had gone to study in the summer of 1753. Certainly, the formal structure of Raphael's composition accords with that of Zoffany: two groups of figures arranged in triangular form on either side of a central pivot. With two possible exceptions, the poses of Zoffany's figures do not echo Raphael's. However, the overarching iconographic programme of *The School of Athens* is germane to that of *The Portraits of the Academicians*. Raphael's celebration of an 'academy' of philosophy is summarized in the central figures of Plato on the left, who points heavenwards to indicate the world of the abstract idea, and of Aristotle on the right, who gestures earthwards to underscore the empirical, material source of his thought. Zoffany's Royal Academicians are grouped in such a way that they echo these two intellectual worlds: the ideas and underlying principles of the Academy on the left, and their practical, tangible realization on the right. And in so far as both facets are concerned with the making of high art, this recourse to Raphael as its primary exemplar, as expounded by Reynolds in his presidential Discourses, would have been wholly appropriate.

When exhibited in April 1772, the painting

Figure 181
Henry Singleton, *The Royal Academicians in General Assembly* (detail), 1795, oil on canvas, 198.1 × 259 cm (78 × 102 in).
Royal Academy of Arts; given by Philip Hardwick, R.A., 1861

Figure 182
Raphael, *The School of Athens*, 1510–11, fresco,
Stanza della Segnatura, Vatican Palace

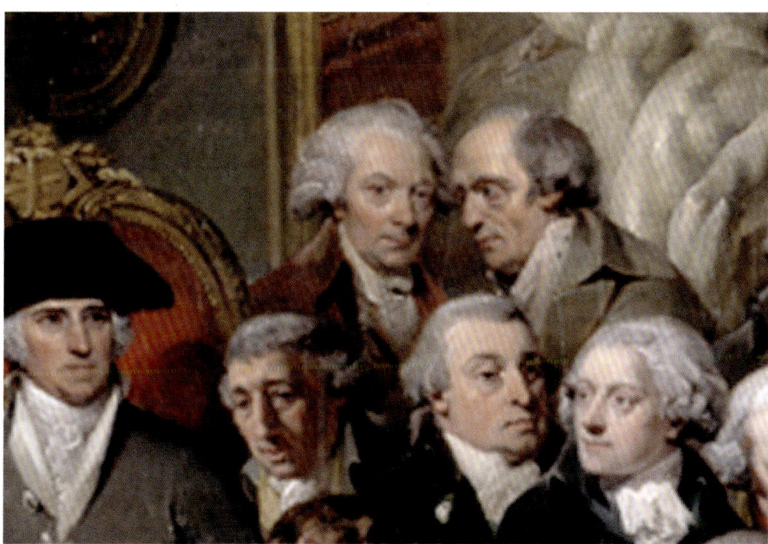

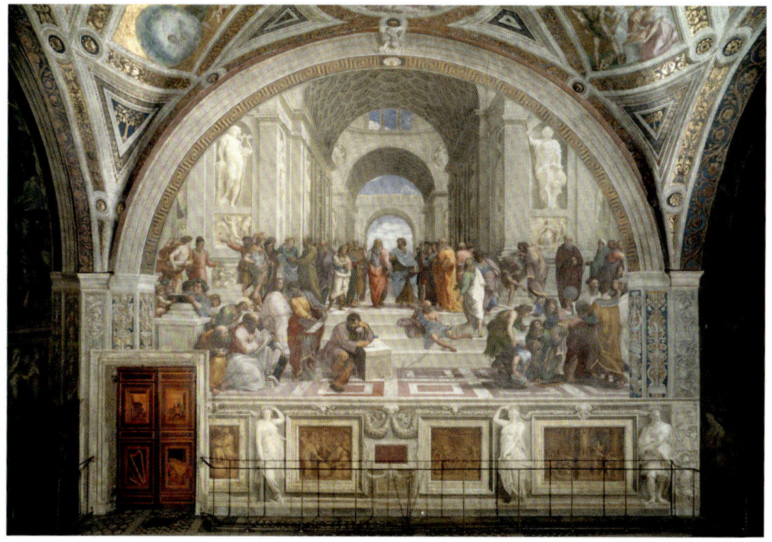

drew 'the densest crowd about it'.[16] Richard Earlom published a print of the work on 2 August 1773, but despite its success, Zoffany was little impressed. Writing to Joseph Banks from Florence on 15 January 1774, he declared: 'I saw a print of the Academy which very little pleased me, as there is no likeness in the heads, and I very much wonder at the success of it.'[17]

Zoffany was to appear in one other group portrait of the Academicians of the Royal Academy, Henry Singleton's painting of 1795 (fig. 181). Here, however, in this more conventional and hierarchical image, Zoffany featured merely as a face in the crowd.

MAS

1. No record of a commission from the king survives.
2. The painting has normally been dated as *c.*1771–2; see Roberts 2004, cat. 159; Treadwell 2009, 174; Webster 2011, 253.
3. RA Council Minutes, vol. 1, 95 (7 Jan. 1771): 'Notice is hereby given to the Members and Students that the Academy is removed to Somerset House, and will open on Monday, next 14th inst, at 5 o'Clo: in the afternoon.' The new spaces, providing seven apartments, had been put at the disposal of the Academy by George III, who paid £600 towards the cost of their refurbishment (Hoock 2003, 34).
4. National Portrait Gallery, London (NPG 1437). The drawing must have been made after the completion of the painting since it, like Zoffany's watercolour (British Museum 1923,0714.10), includes the three figures inserted late on the extreme right.
5. Edward Burney made a record of *The Antique School at Old Somerset House* (1779; Royal Academy, MS 03/7485).
6. One account, made in 1765 by Josiah Wedgwood, is in J. Wedgwood, *The Letters of Josiah Wedgwood*, 3 vols., London, 1903, vol. 1, 144–5, and the other is in James Christie's lease of part of 125 Pall Mall drawn up in 1771 (National Archives, London: CRES 38/1203). Further evidence specific to the Great Exhibition Room is given in William Chambers's plan of the room (Sir John Soane Museum, London: drawer 42, set 2, no. 11). See Hauptman 2011.
7. See note 6.
8. The 'great lamp' formed part of the equipment of St Martin's Lane Academy that had been moved, together with 'anatomical figures, bustoes, statues, lamps and other effects', to 125 Pall Mall under the aegis of Richard Dalton and Michael Moser in 1767; see Nicholas Savage, 'The "Viceroy" of the Academy: Sir William Chambers and the Royal Protection of the Arts', in John Harris and Michael Snodin, ed., *Sir William Chambers, Architect to George III*, exh. cat., Courtauld Gallery, London, 1997, 193.
9. See Michel-Vincent Brandoin, *The Exhibition of the Royal Academy of Painting in the Year 1771* (coloured drawing, Huntington Library and Art Gallery, San Marino, inv. no. 63.52.23), engraved by Richard Earlom and published by Robert Sayer, 20 May 1772.
10. The Visitors were 'to attend the Schools by rotation, each a month, to set the figures, to examine the performances of the Students'. Each Visitor was to receive 10s 6d for each attendance, which would last at least two hours (Instrument of Foundation, 10 Dec. 1768, Rule IX).
11. See note 4: the key derived from Sanders's drawing.
12. Treadwell 2009, 174–80.
13. Webster 2011, 253.
14. Visitors elected on 11 December 1769 were Bartolozzi, Carlini, Cipriani, Nathaniel Dance, Penny, West, Wilton, Zoffany and Zuccarelli; those elected on 10 December 1770 were Bartolozzi, Carlini, Chamberlin, Cipriani, Meyer, Penny, Toms, Wilson and Wilton; and those elected on 10 December 1771 were Birch, Catton, Chamberlin, Nathaniel Dance, Hayman, Meyer, Toms, West and Wilson.
15. Tan Chitqua arrived in London in August 1769. He exhibited at the Royal Academy Annual Exhibition, 1770, and was invited to attend the first Annual Dinner held on 23 April 1770. He was summoned to meet the king and queen, who 'were much pleased with him', which may explain his inclusion in the group portrait commissioned by the king. He returned to Canton in 1771. In *The Portraits of the Academicians* he stands on the left in close proximity to Benjamin West (1738–1820), also favoured by the monarchs since he had recently received his first royal commission for a history painting (1768); see Webster 2011, 253.
16. Quoted Roberts 2004, 186.
17. Webster 2011, 315.

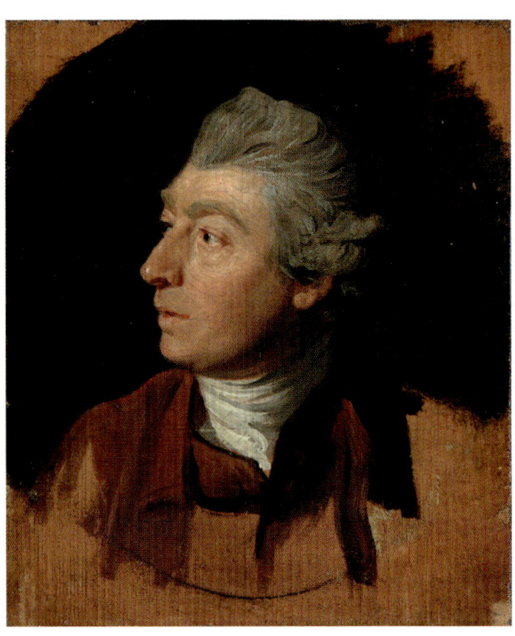

45

Thomas Gainsborough

*c.*1772

Oil on canvas, oval, 19.7 × 17.1 cm (7¾ × 6¾ in)
Tate, London; presented by the family of Richard J. Lane, 1896

Provenance: ?Presented by Zoffany to Gainsborough or his daughter Margaret; ?'Mr Briggs' (Henry Perronet Briggs); Miss Clarke; Richard Lane ARA (great-nephew of Gainsborough), the Misses Lane, by whom presented to the National Gallery 1896; transferred to the Tate Gallery on 4 January 1955

Selected exhibitions: British Institution, 1859, no. 166; *Works by the Old Masters and by Deceased Masters of the British School; including a Collection of Water-colour Drawings by Joseph M. W. Turner RA*, Royal Academy of Arts, 1887, no. 19; National Portrait Gallery 1977, no. 73

Selected references: Treadwell 2011, 176–7; Webster 2011, 259–60

In a letter dated 13 February 1772 to one of his patrons, Thomas Gainsborough informed the Hon. Constantine John Phipps (later second Baron Mulgrave) that Zoffany had been visiting Bath and was returning to London with some large drawings for Phipps: 'I have been trying a large Cartoon Landskip in the way of the Drawings I sent by Zaffani [*sic*] as they run off so quick, & intend two spanking ones for the Exhibition, if I succeed in getting large paper made for the purpose.'[1] This study of the portraitist, landscape painter and Foundation Member of the Royal Academy was almost certainly made on this visit to Bath, where Gainsborough had been in residence since 1759. The immediacy with which the turn of his fellow Academician's head has been captured and the relative lack of finish suggest that this was a study

for Gainsborough's presence in Zoffany's major programmatic group portrait, *The Portraits of the Academicians of the Royal Academy* (cat. 44), which was to be shown at the fourth Royal Academy Annual Exhibition in April 1772. Given the leftward cast of the head and the fact that the study was made within a few months of the exhibition of the work, it can be assumed that Gainsborough would have taken his position in the large group portrait towards the extreme right of the canvas, where he would have joined three other late insertions: Joseph Nollekens (elected RA in February 1772), Richard Cosway (elected 1771) and Nathaniel Hone (a Nominated Member of 1769, as was Zoffany).

Gainsborough was one of three Foundation Members who were not included in Zoffany's group portrait of the Royal Academicians, the other two being George Dance, the architect, and his brother Nathaniel, a painter. While it is unclear what prevented George Dance from being included, it has been suggested that neither Nathaniel Dance nor Gainsborough wished to appear on account of their growing disquiet with the treatment of their works by the Hanging Committee of the Royal Academy.[2] Gainsborough viewed Royal Academy exhibitions as public platforms from which he could proclaim his artistic pre-eminence and secure the attention of clients. Indeed, he was willing to put commissions on one side in order to complete work intended for this end. Less than satisfactory positioning of his works by the Hanging Committee jeopardized this goal. Despite his avowal to produce 'two spanking [large Cartoon landskips] for the Exhibition', Gainsborough's disaffection caused him to boycott the Royal Academy's Annual Exhibitions from 1773.[3] He only returned in 1777, having settled in London from 1774 and established a reputation that ensured support external to the Royal Academy itself.

MAS

1. Hayes 2001, 94, letter 56.
2. Rosenthal 1999, 73; Treadwell 2009, 177. George Dance exhibited only intermittently at the Royal Academy Annual Exhibition (1770, 1771, 1785, 1795, 1798–1800). Nathaniel Dance exhibited from 1769 to 1772 and in 1774, 1776, 1792, 1794 and 1800.
3. Rosenthal (1999, 73) quotes Walpole's comment that in 1773 'Gainsborough and Dance having disagreed with Reynolds did not send any pictures to this exhibition'.

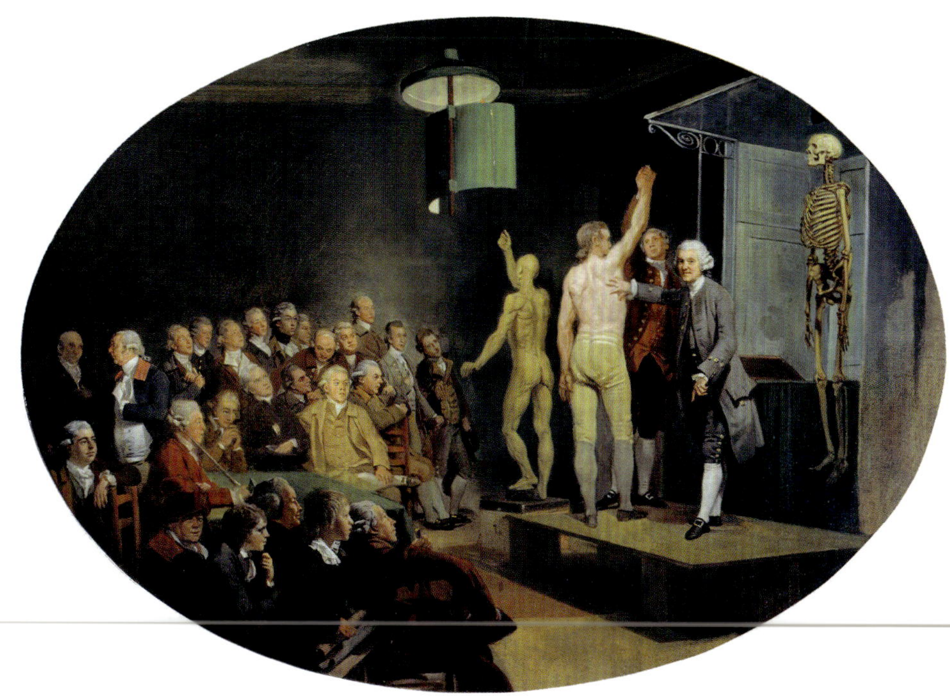

46

Dr William Hunter Teaching Anatomy at the Royal Academy

*c.*1772

Oil on canvas (oval),
77.5 × 103.5 cm (30½ × 40¾ in)
Royal College of Physicians, London

Provenance: bequeathed to William Hunter's nephew and heir, Dr Matthew Baillie; presented by Mrs Baillie 1823

Selected exhibitions: International Exhibition, London, 1862, no. 36; *National Portrait Exhibition*, South Kensington Museum, London 1867, no. 506; Royal Academy, London (Winter Exhibition), 1871, no. 265; *Georgian England*, Whitechapel Gallery, London, 1906, no. 23; *The Eye of Thomas Jefferson*, National Gallery of Art, Washington DC, 1976, no. 111; National Portrait Gallery, 1977, no. 75; *Georgian Canada: Conflict and Culture 1745–1820*, Royal Ontario Museum, Toronto, 1984, no. 181; Nottingham and Kenwood, 1991, no. 75; *The Anatomy Lesson: Art and Medicine. An exhibition of art and anatomy to celebrate the tercentenary of the Royal Charter of 1692 of the Royal College of Physicians of Ireland*, National Gallery of Ireland, 1992, 32; *L'âme au corps: arts et sciences 1793–1993*, Galeries nationales du Grand Palais, Paris, 1993–94, no. 73; *Die Kunst hat nie ein Mensch allein besessen Akademie der Künste*, Berlin, 1996, no. 1.4/5; Glasgow, 2007, no. 102

Selected references: Annals of the Royal College of Physicians of London, 22 December 1823, 219–20; *A List of Portraits &c., in the Royal College of Physicians of London*, London 1864, 12; *The Roll of the Royal College of Physicians of London*, London, 1878, vol. 3, 397; *A List of Portraits &c., in the Royal College of Physicians of London*, London, 1900, 5; R. Hingston Fox, *William Hunter, Anatomist, Physician, Obstetrician (1718–1783)*, London, 1901, 65; Manners & Williamson, 1920, 226; Gordon Wolstenholme, ed., *The Royal College of Physicians*, London, 1964, 232–3; Geoffrey Davenport, Ian McDonald and Caroline Moss-Gibbons, *The Royal College of Physicians and its Collections. An Illustrated History*, London, 2001, 133, 135; Helen McCormack, 'A Collector of the Fine Arts in Eighteenth-Century Britain: Dr William Hunter 1718–1783', unpublished Ph D thesis, University of Glasgow, 2009, 144–55; Treadwell 2009, 180; Webster 2011, 396–8

This work, probably a commission from Dr William Hunter, was first recorded in the collection of Hunter's heir, the physician, Mathew Baillie. It is unfinished, and its oval format (unusual for Zoffany's conversation pieces), confirmed during recent conservation, indicates that it was cut down from an original rectangular format.

The work was dated '*c.*1772' by Mary Webster (1976) but revised in 2011 to '1781–3' on the evidence of the reference to the painting in Samuel Foart Simmons, *An Account of the Life and Writings of the late William Hunter M., FRS, and SA* (London 1783): 'This picture is in the possession of Mr Baillie. The portrait of Dr Hunter is the only part of it that is finished. Of the other figures, Mr Zoffany had only traced the out-lines, when he embarked

for the East Indies.' (p. 66).[1] However, given Zoffany's engagement with the initial years of the Royal Academy (see cat. 44), the location of the lecture itself (see below), and the possible desire to mark the inauguration of Hunter's important contribution to the Academy's pedagogic programme from 1769 (see below), a date of *c.*1770 would seem more acceptable, with its lack of completion due to Zoffany's departure to Italy in 1772.

William Hunter was born in East Kilbride, near Glasgow; he trained in Glasgow, Edinburgh, London and Paris. He eventually established himself in London as a leading physician, gynaecologist, anatomist, and teacher, as well as a passionate art collector and bibliophile. In 1762 Hunter was appointed Physician in Extraordinary to Queen Charlotte.

In the Royal Academy's 'Instrument of Foundation', approved by George III on 10 December 1768, it was stated: 'There shall be a Professor of Anatomy, who shall read annually six public lectures in the Schools, adapted to the Arts of Design; his sallary [*sic*] shall be thirty pounds a year; and he shall continue in office during the King's pleasure'.[2] The inclusion of Anatomy in the Royal Academy's programme for the professional training of artists not only reflected practice in Continental Europe but also provided the essential foundation for drawing from the Life Model, the mastery of which led to the production of High Art (see cat. 44). At the Council Meeting of 17 March 1769, which Hunter attended, it was agreed that he should commence his series of six lectures on the '4th Monday in October next, to begin at one o'clock and end at two', the first three being devoted to the skeleton, while the 'other Lectures on the Muscles to be at such times as a Body can be procured from the Sherrifs, to whom he recomded [*sic*] that application should be made'.[3] Manuscript notes, made between 30 October 1769 and 21 September 1772, indicate Hunter's intentions to inform on all aspects of anatomy as it pertained both to nature and to the visual arts.[4]

As with his *Portraits of the Academicians of the Royal Academy* (cat. 44), Zoffany here presents a combination of the theatrical and the conversational. Dr Hunter stands before the Royal Academicians, their first President, Sir Joshua Reynolds, clearly visible in profile, sporting a red frock coat and an ear trumpet. Two students, representative of over 70 currently studying in the Schools, are shown at the lower left, a reference to the fact that, as Hunter himself had remarked in his lecture notes: 'Sirs, whatever company may happen to honour this place with their presence, it must be remembered that the lectures are calculated for the students, and addressed to them only.'[5] Unlike his group portrait of the Royal Academicians setting the life model, however, this is not a group portrait of readily identifiable sitters. To be sure, in addition to Reynolds, three other

Academicians can be fairly securely identified: Benjamin West, his hand in his hat, sits two figures to the right of Reynolds with Joseph Nollekens, seen in profile, immediately to his right; and the figure sporting a red flat hat set at a somewhat rakish angle in the lower left foreground, traditionally identified as Zoffany himself, is almost certainly George Michael Moser, who, as Keeper of the Schools, invites the spectator to engage in this exposition of one important element of the professional pedagogic activity of the institution. As in both his *Portraits of the Academicians* (cat. 44) and *An Academy by Lamplight* (cat. 41), Zoffany could have included himself, possibly as the figure who leans towards Nollekens as if engaged in passing a comment to one of his closest associates within the Royal Academy Membership. Given the difficulty of identifying other Academicians, it is possible that several of the figures included were not Academicians, but rather 'persons of rank', who would be invited to attend both presidential Discourses and the professors' lectures.

Hunter had begun delivering lectures to artists as early as 1751, when he gave a course on anatomy to artists at the St Martin's Lane Academy. Although he ended these lectures in 1761, he continued to deliver public lectures, which, from 1768, took place in his newly constructed house, museum and anatomy theatre in Great Windmill Street. In Zoffany's painting, the animated, intensely charismatic Hunter is shown on a temporary platform, set within a lofty, green hall. It has generally been supposed that Zoffany has placed Hunter in the lecture room at Old Somerset House, one of the seven apartments made available by George III and into which the Academy moved its Schools and Library in January 1771.[6] However, the setting was quite probably the Great Exhibition Room, the first 'home' of the Royal Academy, at 125 Pall Mall.[7] This would then suggest that, even if the work was not specifically created between October 1769 and January 1771, it was intended to celebrate the inception of this important component of the Royal Academy's pedagogic programme. As Hunter himself noted:

> This Institution carries within itself the strongest proof of its Utility. It is the Institution of a Prince who has relished and cultivated the Fine Arts; who, with the advice of some of the best living Artists, and all the experience arising from the knowledge of what has been found to be useful in other countries, has made the study of Anatomy a part of the plan of Education in this Academy.[8]

As lecture props, Hunter uses a skeleton, an écorché plaster standing figure (made in 1751 to support Hunter's lectures at the St Martin's Lane Academy; now lost) and a male model stripped to the waist, whose pose echoes that of the écorché figure. While Hunter would intermittently teach from a dissected body, he more often relied upon the demonstration materials shown here. Hunter's manuscript notes reveal that, although he addressed the need for his

audience to understand the totality of the human anatomy, he recognized the importance of a thorough understanding of the skeleton and the muscles, declaring that, of the 'Five Systems of the Body', the study of the

> Bones and the Muscles [the fourth and fifth 'Subordinate and general Systems'] will be allowed to be very essential to painters and sculptors … Every varied attitude, action and gesture, every change of face, is no other than varied muscular motion. Everything that we have seen acted in reality at Boughton's Amphitheatre at Saddlers Wells, and such places, and every thing that we see done on the Stage, in the way of imitation by the Comedian or the Tragedian, is nothing but a skilful exercise of muscular motion. We shall therefore consider the Bones and Muscles as our principle subjects; and after having explained them we shall make some remarks upon the cellular substance, and skin…'.[9]

This work directly compliments the aspirations and central pedagogic practices of the Royal Academy which Zoffany had celebrated in *The Portraits of Academicians of the Royal Academy*. By demonstrating current practice and making reference to antecedent practices and institutions, Zoffany has encapsulated within these two works the early history of the King's newly created Academy, and its precedents, both ancient and modern.

MAS

1. Webster 2011, 397, n. 31.
2. Instrument of Foundation, 10 December 1768, Rule X.
3. RA Council Minutes, I, 17.
4. Special Collections Department, Glasgow University Library, published in an edited version by Martin Kemp, *Dr William Hunter at the Royal Academy of Arts*, Glasgow, 1975
5. 'William Hunter's Lectures on Anatomy to Students at the Royal Academy Schools', in Black 2007, 170.
6. RA Council Minutes, I, 95: 'Notice is hereby given to Members and Students that the Academy is removed to Somerset House, and will open on Monday next 14th inst, at 5 o'Clo: in the afternoon.'
7. In the 1771 lease document drawn up for James Christie for 125 Pall Mall, the Great Exhibition Room is described as being 'hung in green bays [*sic*] (i.e. green baize, a colour used for exhibition spaces both in Paris and earlier in London for the exhibition rooms of the Incorporated Society of Artists), and as having a wooden cornice and being illuminated by a four-sided clerestory, NA, CRES, 38/1203; see Hauptman ms, and Vincent-Michel Brandoin, *The Exhibition of the Royal Academy of Painting in the year 1771* (coloured drawing, Huntington Library and Art Gallery, San Marino [inv. No. 63.52.23]), engraved by Richard Earlom and published by Robert Sayer, 20 May, 1773.
8. Glasgow 2007, 168
9. Glasgow 2007, 169

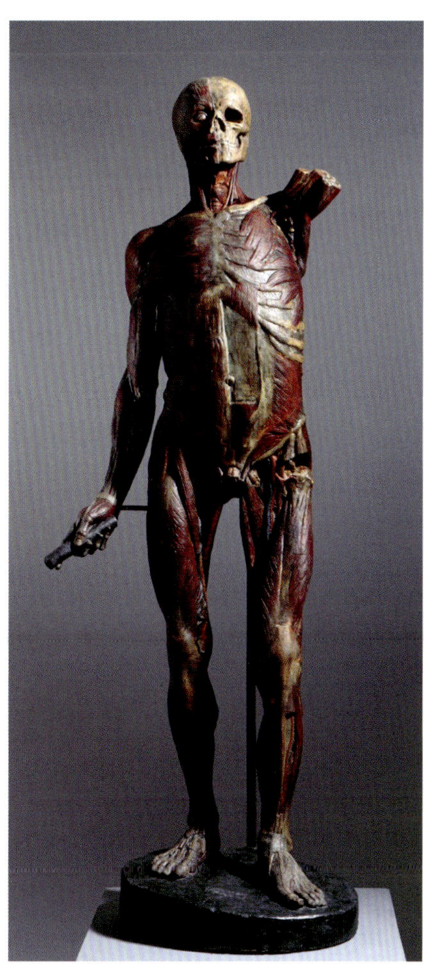

47

Unknown artist, Écorché figure,
probably 1771

Polychromed plaster,
171.5 × 61 × 47.5 cm (67½ × 24 × 18¾ in)
Royal Academy of Arts

Exhibited at the Royal Academy of Arts only

Selected exhibitions: Spectacular Bodies: The Art and Science of the Human Body from Leonardo to Now, Hayward Gallery, 2000–2001, no. 142; *The Body Politic: Anatomical Drawings by Benjamin Robert Haydon*, Royal Academy of Arts (Tennant Gallery), 2007; *No New Thing under the Sun*, Royal Academy of Arts (Tennant Gallery), 2011

Selected references: Kemp 1975, 16–17; Jehannine Mauduech, 'The Écorché', *Conservation News*, no. 47, March 1992, 21–2 ; Postle 2004, 58–9; James Fenton, *School of Genius: A History of the Royal Academy of Arts*, London, 2006, p. 81

The *écorché* figure, a plaster cast taken from a flayed body to reveal the underlying musculature and bone structure, was an essential piece of equipment in the anatomical education of the artist and was to be found in art academies throughout Europe. In his youth Zoffany, who underwent a thorough academic training, would have encountered the *écorché* figure in studios and academies in Germany and in Rome. Some of the most innovative *écorché* figures of the eighteenth century, however, were produced in England from the early 1750s under the direct supervision of the brilliant surgeon, obstetrician and anatomist, William Hunter. The first of Hunter's *écorché* figures was made in the 1750s for the Society of Artists in St Martin's Lane and was subsequently removed to the Royal Academy of Arts. This particular *écorché* figure proved very popular and was replicated in a small-scale version made from bronze.[1] Although the original plaster *écorché* has been lost, presumably destroyed, it features in two paintings by Zoffany. In *The Portraits of the Academicians of the Royal Academy* (cat. 44) it is partially visible against the back wall, while in *Dr William Hunter Lecturing at the Royal Academy* (cat. 46), it stands on a dais adjacent to the living model, who adopts its pose under Hunter's supervision. Zoffany, who clearly had a close interest in anatomy, as well as other branches of scientific enquiry, and who was a friend of John and William Hunter, also featured an *écorché* figure in the self-portrait he presented to the academy in Florence (see cat. 58) – in that instance a reduced version of the celebrated anatomical figure made in Rome by Antoine Houdon.

The *écorché* figure shown in the present exhibition was probably made under the supervision of William Hunter in December 1771. At that time, as noted by the artist James Northcote, the body of a Jew recently hanged for robbery and murder was used by Hunter in two anatomical demonstrations at the Royal Academy, before being used to cast an *écorché* figure.[2] Its identification with the present *écorché* is affirmed by an account of 1819 in Abraham Rees's *Cyclopaedia*, which notes that in the Royal Academy

> will be seen … [a] muscular figure, prepared by Dr. Hunter, one side of which has the skin, fat, &c., taken off, that a comparison may be made with the other side of the figure, in which it may be seen how much thicker some parts of the human body are covered than others.[3]

Indeed, it is possible that the process of revealing two successive layers of the body's underlying tissue may have related specifically to the two lectures given by Hunter prior to the production of the cast.

Recent conservation of the present *écorché* figure at the Royal Academy has revealed a removable section in the abdomen, beneath which, as x-rays indicate, are plaster reproductions of the internal organs. The sophisticated structure of the present *écorché* and its painted polychrome surface are entirely consistent with the meticulous practice of Hunter, who, as his brother John noted, 'was probably the first that made molds of parts of the human body, and to make them appear as like nature as possible he had them painted from the subject'.[4] In the lectures he was then presenting to the Royal Academy, Hunter, whose discourse was centred on the role of imitation in art, emphasized the importance of painted or coloured wax figures in understanding anatomy. Hunter noted that such figures were looked upon as 'disagreeable or painful objects', although they were disagreeable not because 'they are *too* like but because they are not enough'.[5] While Hunter's views were diametrically opposed to those expressed in the Discourses of the Academy's president, Joshua Reynolds, they were endorsed by Zoffany's painting practice in his fidelity to detail and close observation of nature.

MP

1. Postle 2004, 58.
2. MS letter from James Northcote to his brother, Samuel, 19 Dec. 1771, Royal Academy archives, RA NOR/6. The condemned criminals, Levi Weil (himself a physician), Asher Weil and Solomon Porter, were hanged at Tyburn on 9 December 1771. 'After they had hung the usual time, their bodies were taken down, and carried to the Surgeon's Hall for dissection. Levy Weil (the physician) is to be anatomized, and hung up in Surgeon's hall' (*The London Magazine: or Gentleman's Monthly Intelligencer*, 1771, vol. 39, 618–19). Details of the trial can be found at The Proceedings of the Old Bailey, London's Central Criminal Court, 1674 to 1913, http://www.oldbaileyonline.org, ref. no. t17711204-39.
3. Postle 2004, 59.
4. C.H. Brock, ed., *William Hunter 1718–1783: A Memoir by Samuel Foart Simmons and John Hunter*, Glasgow 1983, 20.
5. Martin Kemp, 'True to their natures: Sir Joshua Reynolds and Dr William Hunter at the Royal Academy of Arts', *Notes and Records of the Royal Society*, London, no. 46 (1), 77–88 (1992), 81.

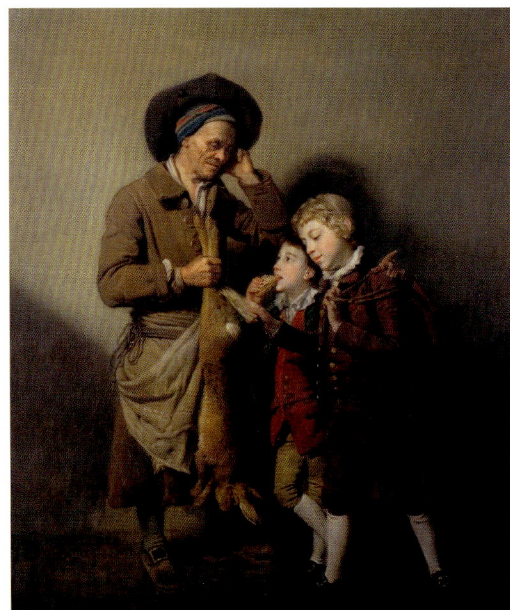

48

A Porter with a Hare
1768

Oil on canvas, 76.2 × 63 cm (30 × 24¾ in)
Inscribed on the label attached to the hare:
'Zu Zaffely'; on the back of the stretcher: 'Zafani'
Herbert Art Gallery & Museum, Coventry

Exhibited at the Royal Academy of Arts only

Provenance: Robert Sayer by 1774; James Sayer;
James Sayer sale, Christie's (auction held at Sayer's
house, Richmond Hill, Surrey), 24 May 1802 (71) as
'Zoffani. A porter with the hare, well known by the
print of it, 3 ft × 2¾ ft', bt Cooke; Christie's, 25 Feb.
1905 (110), as 'Two Boys, and Porter Carrying a
Hare' (76.2 × 63.5 cm/30 × 25 in) anonymous donor,
bt Colnaghi for £54 12s 0d. Col. Baskerville;
'Messrs Gooden & Fox; Ernest Cook', by whom
bequeathed to the NACF, 1955; presented to the
Herbert Art Gallery and Museum, Coventry

Selected exhibitions: Society of Artists, 1769, no. 213,
as 'A porter with a hare'; *Gifts to Galleries from the
National Art Collections Fund*, Walker Art Gallery,
Liverpool, 1968, no. 97; National Portrait Gallery
1977, no. 45; Nottingham and Kenwood 1998,
no. 59

Selected references: Manners & Williamson 1920,
19–20; Postle 1998, 80–81; Treadwell 2009, 184,
191, 204; Webster 2011, 263–5

49

Richard Earlom after Johan Zoffany,
The Porter and Hare
1774

Mezzotint engraving, 60.7 × 43.2 cm (23⅞ × 17 in)
Inscribed: 'From a most capital picture of Mr.
Zoffany, in the possession of Mr. Sayer | London,
Printed for Robt. Sayer, No. 53 in Fleet-Street;
Published as the Act directs 10 March 1774'
British Museum, Department of Prints and
Drawings, 1869,0710.146

Exhibited at the Yale Center for British Art only

Zoffany exhibited *A Porter with a Hare* at the annual
exhibition of the Society of Artists in 1769, one
of ten pictures he showed there that year.[1] It was
noticed by several critics, including Horace
Walpole who made a terse, but appreciative jotting
in his exhibition catalogue: 'admirable | Nature:'.[2]
According to an uncorroborated source, the picture
was a spontaneous composition: 'Zoffany from his
window witnessed the scene, and at once committed
it to canvas.'[3] Even if this was the case, the painting
involves a great deal of artifice. Characteristically,
Zoffany uses his skills in capturing the nuances of
facial expression and details of costume to enrich
the narrative. He contrasts the coarse apparel of
the porter with the fashionable attire of the boys.
To add to the comic potential of the scene, just as
the porter cups a deaf ear to listen, the younger boy
opens his mouth to take a bite from his sandwich,
a foodstuff named after John Montagu, fourth Earl
of Sandwich, Zoffany's friend and patron. Given the
particular cast of Zoffany's wit, it is possible that
the allusion was deliberate.

A Porter with a Hare was the first of several
paintings featuring scenes and subjects taken
from everyday modern life, a genre known in the
eighteenth century as the 'fancy picture'.[4] Such
images made a calculated appeal to the popular
market. Their commercial success was allied to
the market for popular prints, and artists worked
closely with engravers and print publishers to
produce images that would reach a broad public.
It is not surprising, therefore, that the first-
known owner of the present picture was the
print publisher, Robert Sayer, who published
the engraving by Richard Earlom in 1774 and
proclaimed his ownership of the original painting
on the print's inscription. Evidence of the
popularity of Earlom's print is revealed in its
adaptation in a pantomime entitled *Harlequin at
All* at the Covent Garden Theatre in 1778. 'Among
the new business,' it was reported, 'was the porter
and hare from Zoffani's print, in which one of the
school-boys strips and beats the French lover, to
the tune of Briton's Strike Home, which appeared
to give general disgust.'[5]

The popularity of Zoffany's painting, as well as
the ensuing print, is confirmed by the existence of
at least two other versions, with minor variations,

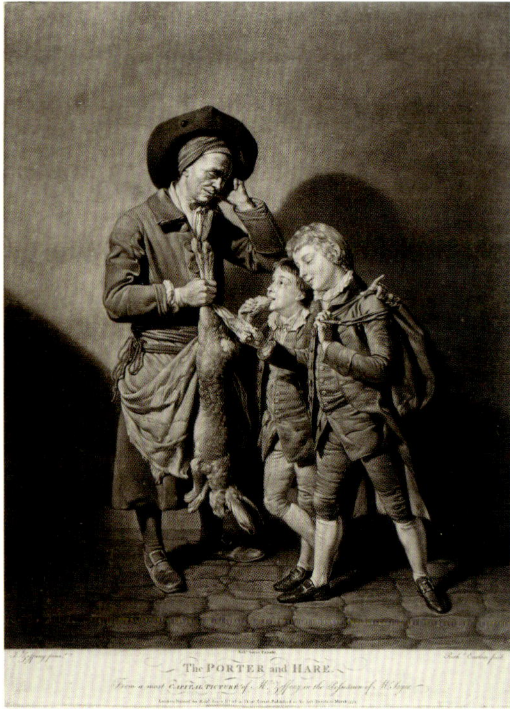

notably in the inscription on the label attached to
the hare. In the present picture the label in German
reads 'zu Zaffely', indicating possibly that the game
was the gift of a German friend or patron.[6] Given
his penchant for visual jokes, it is quite possible
that Zoffany included a former spelling of his name,
and the instruction *zu* (to) in order to intensify
the perplexity of the porter. In another version,
however, the label reads 'Mr Zoffany L[incoln's]
Inn Fields',[7] a more helpful instruction, since
Zoffany was then living in Portugal Row, on the
south side of Lincoln's Inn Fields.

MP

1. For a second version, see Webster 1976, 44, no. 46.
   Since the present painting belonged to Zoffany's
   friend and business partner, Robert Sayer, who
   published the engraving, it may well have been the
   prime, exhibited version.
2. Hugh Gatty, 'Notes by Horace Walpole, fourth Earl
   of Orford, on the exhibitions of the Society of Artists
   and the Free Society of Artists, 1760–1791', *Walpole
   Society*, vol. 27 (1938–9), 83. The picture was also
   flagged up as deserving attention by *Lloyd's Evening
   Post*, 3–5 May 1769.
3. Manners & Williamson 1920, 19.
4. See Postle 1998, *passim*.
5. *The Gazetteer and New Daily Advertiser*, 15 Oct. 1778.
   Britons Strike Home, or the Sailor's Rehearsal was a
   nautical farce written by Edward Phillips in 1739,
   the title inspired by the popular patriotic song that
   had originated in John Fletcher's tragedy *Bonduca*,
   first published in 1647, with later incidental music
   by Henry Purcell.
6. Webster 2011, 264.
7. Webster 1976, 44, no. 46.

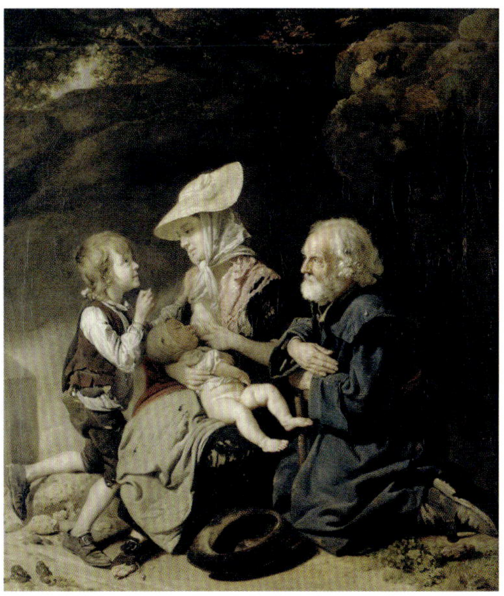

50

Beggars on the Road to Stanmore
*c.*1769–70

Oil on canvas, 91.5 × 76 cm (36 × 29⅞ in)
Private collection

Provenance: By descent

Selected exhibitions: Royal Academy, 1771, no. 232;
British Institution, 1840, no. 101; *Treasures and
Curiosities: Drummonds at Charing Cross, 1717–1967*,
National Portrait Gallery, 1968; National Portrait
Gallery 1977, no. 55; Nottingham and Kenwood
1998, no. 89

Selected references: Treadwell 2009, 148–50; Webster
2011, 265–6

'A beggar's family', as it was entitled at the Royal
Academy exhibition of 1771, was probably
commissioned or purchased from Zoffany by the
banker Robert Drummond, whose uncle Andrew

Drummond and his family Zoffany had recently
painted in two separate portraits (see cat. 69). The
present title of the picture, 'Beggars on the Road
to Stanmore', is derived from a tradition in the
Drummond family that the group was painted by
Zoffany from beggars encountered on the road
to Stanmore, Middlesex, where the Drummonds
owned a country house and substantial estate,
although by 1772 the picture was hanging in
Robert Drummond's newly acquired house
at Cadland Park, Hampshire.[1] As Zoffany's
contemporaries would have been aware, the secular
subject matter depicted here is dependent on the
traditions of sacred art, as the beggars evoke the
Holy Family: at the centre, suckling the Christ
child, the Virgin looks towards the suppliant figure
of the young John the Baptist, while to the right the
kneeling figure of St Joseph leans with one hand
on his staff, while placing the other across his chest
in a gesture of veneration. And yet, the real life
circumstances of the beggar family were quite
different. The grey-haired old man is clearly not
the woman's husband, but presumably her father.
Deserted by the father of her children, the young
woman is a single mother, reliant for the survival
of her family on the enlightened philanthropy of
families such as the Drummonds, who in
recognition of their own privileged position and
wealth practise Christian charity. Indeed, the
presence of the philanthropic patron is subtly
implied by Zoffany in the picture: firstly by the
silver coin that the boy holds up to his mother,
its value contrasted by the copper coin lying in
the beggar's hat; and secondly by the fresh horse
dung and carriage tracks in the left foreground,
indicating that the family's benefactors have
recently passed by – perhaps on their way to the
Drummond residence at Stanmore.

The models for Zoffany's beggars, here viewed
in the countryside, were paid professionals from
the metropolis, rather than individuals casually

encountered by Zoffany on a country road. The old
man was apparently a 'Beggar who frequented the
Bird-Cage Walk in St James's Park', who was also
painted in 1771 by Nathaniel Dance (fig. 183).[2] The
young woman, although her identity is unknown,
was the same model who sat for Zoffany's subject
picture, *Caritas Romana* (fig. 184), together with the
celebrated model and street paviour George White.[3]
Although they are not the same size, it is quite
possible that Zoffany conceived of *Beggars on the
Road to Stanmore* and *Caritas Romana* as pendants,
since they share the common subject of the gift
and receipt of charity, and a common motif, as the
woman offers her breast in the former painting to
her child and in the latter to her imprisoned father.

When he was employed in Zoffany's studio,
around 1770, Henry Walton made a copy of the
present picture.[4] Decades later, Zoffany himself
returned to the subject of beggars in a picture also
entitled 'A Beggar's Family', which he exhibited at
the Royal Academy in 1797. It may be identified as
the picture by Zoffany currently in a British private
collection, which shows a seated male beggar with
a staff and outstretched hat, flanked on the left by
a little girl holding a basket and on the right by
a bare-foot woman in a red shawl and bonnet
cradling a naked child. Technically and conceptually,
it falls short of *Beggars on the Road to Stanmore*,
revealing a marked decline in Zoffany's powers at
this late stage in his career. One reviewer, who saw
'A Beggar's Family' at the Royal Academy in 1797,
observed that it was 'greatly inferior to former
productions of this Artist; there is however much
expression in the faces of the different mendicants,
and the figures are prettily grouped, but the grand
objection lies against the general effect of the
picture; the colouring moreover is foul.'[5]

MP

1. See Webster 2011, 265–6. For Cadland House, see
   Clive Aslet, 'Manor of Cadland, Hampshire. Home
   of Mr and Mrs Maldwin Drummond', *Country Life*,
   1 Oct. 1987, 140–45.
2. See Webster 2011, 266; Henry Bromley, *Catalogue of
   British Engraved Portraits from Egbert the Great to the
   Present Time*, London, 1793, 450.
3. See Martin Postle, 'Patriarchs, Prophets and Paviours:
   Reynolds's images of old age', *Burlington Magazine*,
   vol. 130, no. 1027 (Oct. 1988), 735–44.
4. See Evelynne Bell, 'The Life and Work of Henry
   Walton', *Gainsborough's House Review*, 1998/9, 75,
   no. 187.
5. *London Packet or New Lloyd's Evening Post*, 19–22 May
   1797.

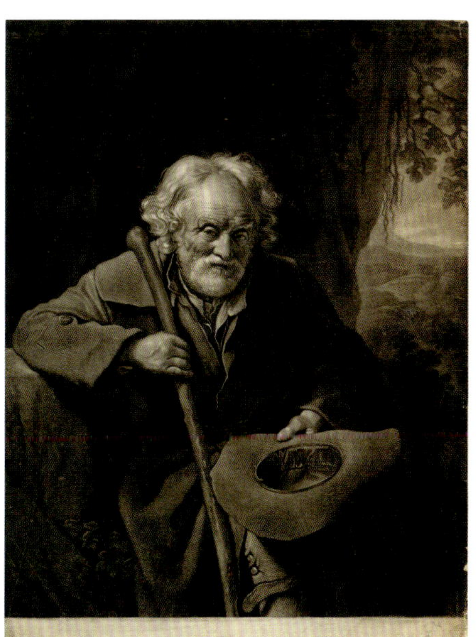

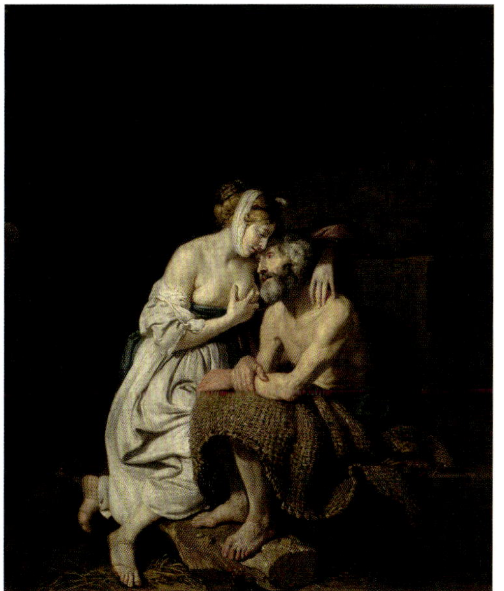

Figure 183
Charles Townley after Nathaniel Dance, *A Beggar who
Frequented the Bird Cage Walk, c.*1761–1800, mezzotint
engraving, 48.5 × 35.6 cm (19⅛ × 14 in). British
Museum, Department of Prints and Drawings,
1870,0625.1161

Figure 184
Caritas Romana, ?1769–71, oil on canvas,
76.3 × 63.5 cm (30 × 25 in). National Gallery of
Victoria, Melbourne; Felton Bequest, 1932 (4614-3)

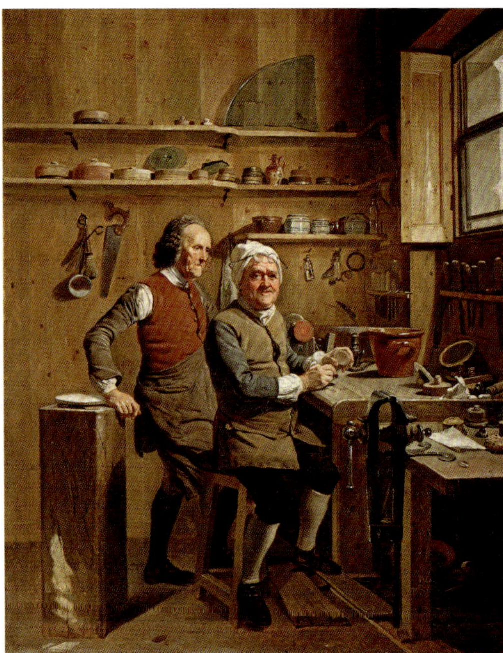

51

John Cuff and his Assistant
('An Optician, with his Attendant')
1772

Oil on canvas, 89.5 × 69.2 (35¼ × 27¼ in)
Signed (on the leg of the bench): 'Zoffanÿ pinx |
1772'
The Royal Collection, Her Majesty Queen
Elizabeth II

Provenance: ?Richard, first Earl Grosvenor;
acquired by George III by *c.*1800–05

Selected exhibitions: Royal Academy, 1772, no. 291;
National Portrait Gallery 1977, no. 71; *Treasures
from the Royal Collection*, The Queen's Gallery,
Buckingham Palace, 1988–9, no. 33; *The Queen's
Pictures: Old Masters from the Royal Collection*,
Museum of New Zealand/Te Papa Tongarewa,
Wellington, National Gallery of Australia,
Canberra, National Gallery of Canada, Ottawa,
1994–5, no. 24; *The Quest for Albion: Monarchy and
Patronage of British Monarchy*, The Queen's Gallery,
Buckingham Palace, 1998, no. 19; *George III and
Queen Charlotte: Patronage, Collecting and Court Taste*,
The Queen's Gallery, Buckingham Palace, 2005,
no. 160; Queen's Gallery and Holyrood House
2009, no. 23

Selected references: Millar 1969, vol. 1, no. 1209;
Nicholas Goodison, *English Barometers 1680–1860*,
London, 1969, 124–5; E.D.H. Johnson, *Paintings
of the British Social Scene from Hogarth to Sickert*,
London, 1986, 65–6; Fox 1987, 111, 266 (note on
pl. VI); G. Clifton, *Directory of British Scientific
Instrument Makers 1550–1851*, London, 1995, 73;
Hanson 2010–11; Webster 2011, 243–4

In the spring of 1772 Zoffany exhibited three works
at the annual exhibition of the Royal Academy.
They included 'An optician, with his attendant'
and 'The portraits of the Academicians of the Royal
Academy' (cat. 44). Shortly after the exhibition's
opening, it was reported in the press that 'Mr.
Zoffani has sold his picture of the Royal Academics
to a Great Personage for the sum of five hundred
guineas; and his piece of Mr. Cuff, the Optician,
at work in his shop, to Lord Grosvenor, for two
hundred pounds'.[1] Among other things, this
significant piece of intelligence – which has not
hitherto been noted – suggests that the King
(the 'Great Personage') paid Zoffany 500 guineas
for the *Academicians*. It also opens up the intriguing
possibility that the initial owner of *John Cuff and
his Assistant* may not have been George III, as has
been supposed, but the aristocrat and art collector
Richard, first Earl Grosvenor (1731–1802), who
also owned other paintings by major contemporary
artists, including Benjamin West's *Death of General
Wolfe*, exhibited at the Royal Academy in 1771.
Finally, it confirms the identity of Zoffany's
optician as John Cuff, which had been questioned.

Exactly when *John Cuff and his Assistant* entered
the Royal Collection is not known. It was first
mentioned in the rough draft of an inventory of
Kew Palace of around 1800–1805, when it hung in
Princess Augusta's bedroom. Here it was described
as 'Mr Cuff – Optician – Zoffany'.[2] When shown at
the British Institution in a retrospective exhibition
of Zoffany's work, the sitter was identified as
'Mr Cuffs', although when exhibited there in
1827 it was simply entitled 'Two Old Men'. To
complicate matters further, in his royal inventory
of 1859 Richard Redgrave, who described the
picture as 'The Lapidaries', recorded a pencil note
on the stretcher: 'Dollond the Optician in the
Strand London'.[3] As the association with John
Cuff was gradually erased, it is little wonder that
his identification as Zoffany's optician has been
doubted in recent times.[4] Yet, quite aside from the
evidence provided by the contemporary newspaper
report, the trajectory of Cuff's career and his close
association with royal circles suggest that he must
have been the focus of Zoffany's attention in the
present picture.

John Cuff was born in London, the son of a
watchmaker. In 1722 he was apprenticed to an
optical instrument maker and in 1730 was formally
admitted into the Spectacle Makers' Company.
From the late 1730s Cuff occupied a shop in Fleet
Street at the sign of the Reflecting Microscope
and Spectacles, where he established a reputation
especially as a maker of microscopes, his solar
microscope being described in Henry Baker's
The Microscope Made Easy in 1742. In 1750, despite
support from Baker, Cuff was declared bankrupt.
He also faced increased competition, notably when
the instrument maker Benjamin Martin moved
into the shop next to Cuff 'and by advertising, and
puffing, and by the Mistakes of many who took one

shop for the other, did him much Disservice'.[5]
Eventually, Cuff was forced to sell his entire stock.
Although he struggled financially in later years,
Cuff continued to take on assistants and maintain
a public profile. The King, who was fascinated by
scientific instruments, purchased microscopes from
Cuff, and when, on 5 June 1769, he watched the
transit of Venus from his newly constructed
observatory in the Old Deer Park in Richmond,
Cuff was invited to attend. And in the years leading
up to Cuff's death, probably in 1772, George III
supplied him, out of his own pocket, with the tools
of his trade.[6]

Zoffany's decision to paint Cuff with his
assistant in his workshop was speculative. He may
have been inspired by royal interest in Cuff, but the
painting also stemmed from his own penchant for
scientific matters, viewing the subject not so much
as the portrayal of a specific individual but as a
genre painting, an evocation of superannuated
craftsmen in an antiquated workshop at a time
when traditional work practices were being
eclipsed by modern, and more ruthless, methods
of mass production. Another point to be borne in
mind, in considering the present picture as the
'portrait' of a particular optician, is that it differs
considerably from Zoffany's other depictions
of scientific and professional men, such as the
botanist Benjamin Stillingfleet or the surgeon John
Heaviside, whose status as gentlemen rather than
artisans merited the respect accorded by formal
portraiture.

In his painting Zoffany exhibits with great
sensitivity two ageing craftsmen in a cluttered
workshop, surrounded by their lathe, lenses,
grinding tools and chisels; a scene reminiscent of
seventeenth-century Dutch paintings of alchemists,
albeit in a more orderly environment.[7] As the
sunlight streams into the shop's interior, casting
reflections onto the open shutters and work
surfaces, and glinting on the various implements,
Zoffany opens a window into an everyday scene of
enlightened industry, otherwise ignored or taken
for granted by the general populace. Horace
Walpole, an admirer of Zoffany, noticed the picture,
writing in his exhibition catalogue: 'Extremely
natural, but the characters too common nature,
and the chiaroscuro destroyed by his servility in
imitating the reflexions of the glasses'.[8] While
Walpole was dismissive of the 'common nature'
of the opticians, Zoffany, who himself owned an
assortment of clocks, watches, thermometers,
barometers and a 4ft telescope, would have been
aware that English instrument makers were
renowned for their skill and craftsmanship.[9]

Zoffany's awareness of the sea change in the
sphere of the professional optician probably
stemmed from his arrival in England in 1760.
The previous year, John Dollond had opened a shop
at the Golden Spectacles and Sea quadrant, near
Exeter Exchange in the Strand. Dollond was a
noted optician and maker of telescopes, who, in

recognition of his work on achromatic lenses, was appointed optician to George III in December 1760 and the following year a fellow of the Royal Society. In 1761, at the very time Zoffany was working in his studio, Benjamin Wilson – also a fellow of the Royal Society – exhibited Dollond's portrait at the Society of Artists.[10] At the time Dollond emerged on the scene, opticians continued to operate in small unpretentious workshops: a master attended by a few specialized mechanics who not only made but invented, developed and refined a range of scientific instruments, including microscopes, telescopes, quadrants, barometers, thermometers and, of course, spectacles. Yet, the 1760s also witnessed the development of larger workshops in London with as many as fifty artisans, many of whom were proficient only in the more basic manufacturing tasks. And by 1770 the perceived deterioration in quality caused by such mass-production methods was commented on by visitors from Europe. Among the chief culprits was John Dollond's son Peter, who, although lacking in technical skill, was a ruthless businessman and who, in order to protect the patent on his father's achromatic lens, had fought a fierce court battle in the 1760s with a number of other London opticians, some of whom were ruined as a result and forced to close their workshops.[11] Zoffany, perhaps conscious of the problems that plagued the otherwise serious minded sphere of the optician, may have conceived his picture not only as an affectionate tribute to the ageing Cuff but as a memorial to the vanishing world that he epitomized.

MP

1. *The Middlesex Journal or Chronicle of Liberty,*
   30 April–2 May 1772.
2. In the final inventory it was described, somewhat curiously, as 'A Methematitian. Zoffani'. See Millar 1969, vol. 1, 152.
3. Millar 1969, vol. 1, 152.
4. See Fox 1987, 266; Giles Hudson, 'Cuff, John (1708?–1772?), optician and microscope maker', *ODNB,* http://www.oxforddnb.com/view/article/48255, accessed 11 Oct. 2010; Hanson 2010–11, 408.
5. J.R. Millburn, *Benjamin Martin: Author, Instrument-Maker, and Country Showman,* Leyden, 1976, 108.
6. See Webster 2011, 244.
7. See Shawe-Taylor 2009, 20–23, who views Zoffany's painting as a parodic recreation of the paintings of alchemists by artists such as David Teniers II.
8. Cited in Webster 2011, 245.
9. For Zoffany's ownership of technical instruments see his house sale, Christie's 17–18 Aug. 1772, lots 5–12, 22–3, in Webster 2011, 642.
10. Dollond's portrait was also engraved by John Raphael Smith. See D'Oench 1999, 8, fig. 5, 188–9, no. 14.
11. See Maurice Daumas, *Scientific Instruments of the Seventeenth and Eighteenth Centuries and their Makers,* London, 1972, 233–40.

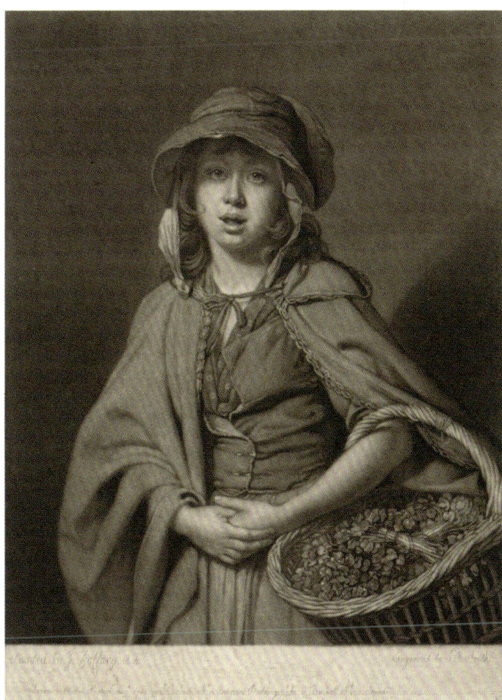

52

John Raphael Smith after Johan Zoffany,
The Watercress Girl
1780

Mezzotint engraving, 38.1 × 27.6 cm (15 × 10⅞ in)
Inscribed lower left: 'Painted by J. Zoffanÿ R.A.';
lower centre: 'London Publishd Septem.r the 9th 1780 by J R Smith, Nº 10 Batemans Buildings Soho & Birchall Nº 473 Strand'; lower right: 'Engraved by J.R. Smith'
Yale Center for British Art, Paul Mellon Fund

Exhibited at the Yale Center for British Art only

Selected references: Chaloner Smith 1878–84, vol. 3, 1320, no. 200; Manners & Williamson 1920, 259, 308; Webster 1976, 70, no. 89; Postle 1998, 79–80, no. 57; Webster 2011, 400–401

The original painting on which the present mezzotint engraving is based (see fig. 28) was exhibited by Zoffany at the Royal Academy in 1780 as 'Girl with water-cresses'. The picture, and its pendant, *The Flower Girl* (*c.*1780; private collection), were representative of a type of character portrait or vignette, known as the 'fancy picture', that had spread to England from France and the Low Countries in the earlier eighteenth century and was widely disseminated in the form of mezzotint and stipple engravings. Among those who featured prominently in fancy pictures were serving maids, street vendors, old beggars and ragged urchins. The popularity of fancy pictures depicting street vendors – to which *The Watercress Girl* belongs – was stimulated by the publication of Marcellus Laroon's *Cryes of the City of London Drawn after Life* in 1687, which in turn spawned a lucrative print industry featuring a range of

colourful street characters. And, in the case of pretty young women, the commodities they touted were associated inextricably with their sexual allure, even if, as in the present instance, the open-mouthed street vendor appears to be, disturbingly, little more than a child.[1] The painting proved popular at the Royal Academy exhibition, one reviewer noting that Zoffany 'has been very fortunate in a choice of a most beautiful Girl for his subject and he has copied nature so exactly, that it is not easy to determine whether it is real life or a painting'.[2] Indeed, the painting's popularity at exhibition must have prompted the production of the present engraving.

The Watercress Girl was first engraved in September 1780 by John Raphael Smith, by this time one of London's foremost mezzotint and stipple engravers, as well as a painter of genre pictures in oils and pastels. Although the identity of the young girl who modelled for Zoffany's picture is unknown, an impression of Smith's engraving, now in the collection of the British Museum (1902,1011.5086) is inscribed in ink, in the margin below the image, 'Jane Wallis', an inscription made possibly by the engraver. Mary Webster has suggested that Jane Wallis was perhaps a niece of David Garrick's lawyer, Albany Wallis.[3] An alternative suggestion is that she was the actress Tryphosa Jane Wallis, who, although she did not make her Covent Garden debut until 1789, was certainly treading the boards in Dublin and in England as a child. Certainly, Zoffany's model is a 'girl' rather than a young woman. If he had not already embarked on a pendant picture, the success of both the painting and the print of *The Watercress Girl* perhaps prompted Zoffany to paint *The Flower Girl*, which features a different and rather older model. Both pictures were engraved in January 1785 by John Young, a pupil of John Raphael Smith. As the inscriptions on the engravings indicate, the original paintings then belonged to Zoffany's friend Jacob Wilkinson, a Director of the East India Company, who had supported his petition to travel to India. Before his departure Zoffany painted Wilkinson's portrait (1782–3; Chequers Trust). He may also at that time have given him *The Watercress Girl* and *The Flower Girl*.

MP

1. See Postle 1998, 17–20.
2. *A Candid Review of the Exhibition (being the twelfth) of the Royal Academy. MDCCLXXX. Dedicated to His Majesty. By an artist,* London, 1780.
3. Webster 2011, 400.

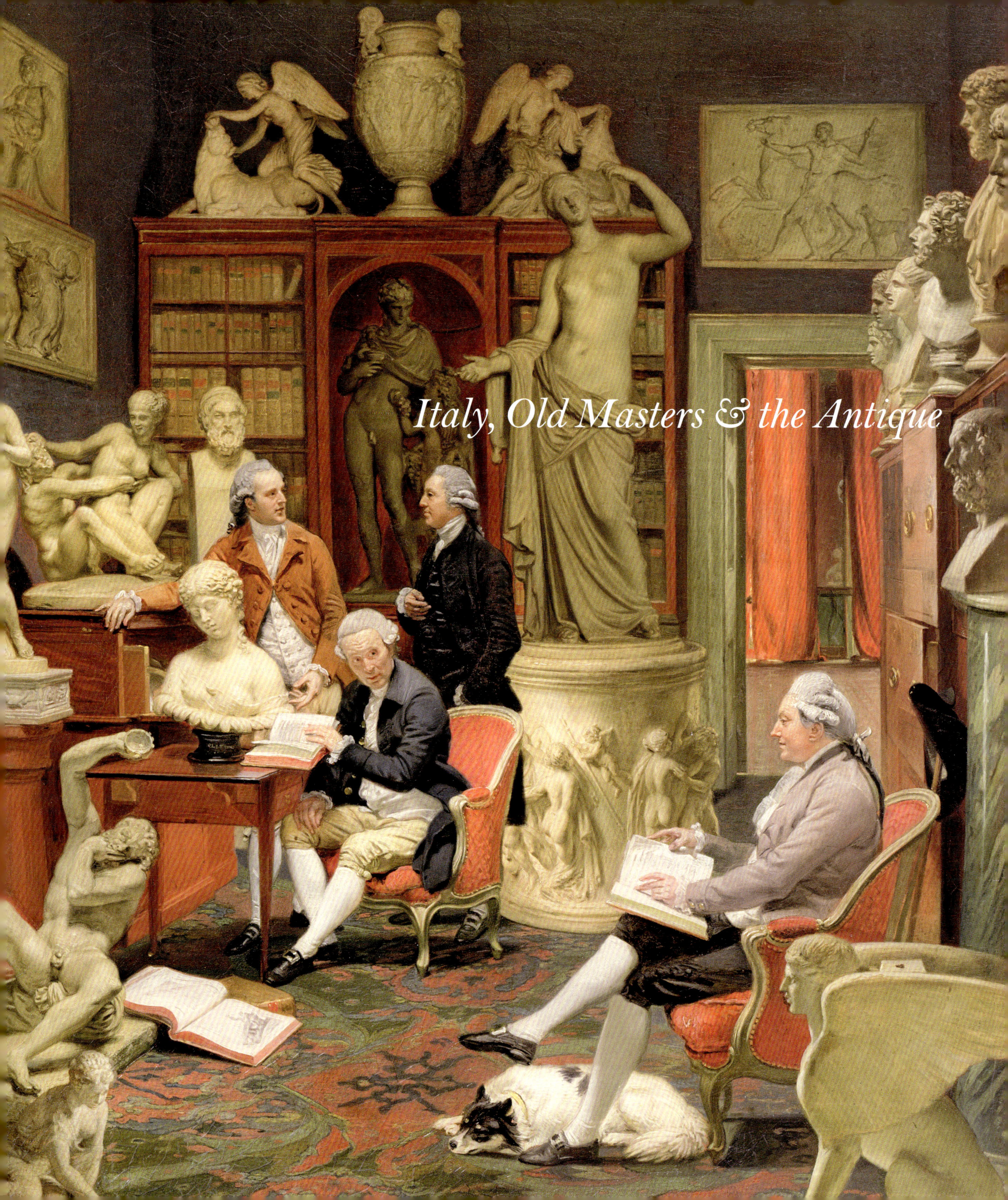

Italy, Old Masters & the Antique

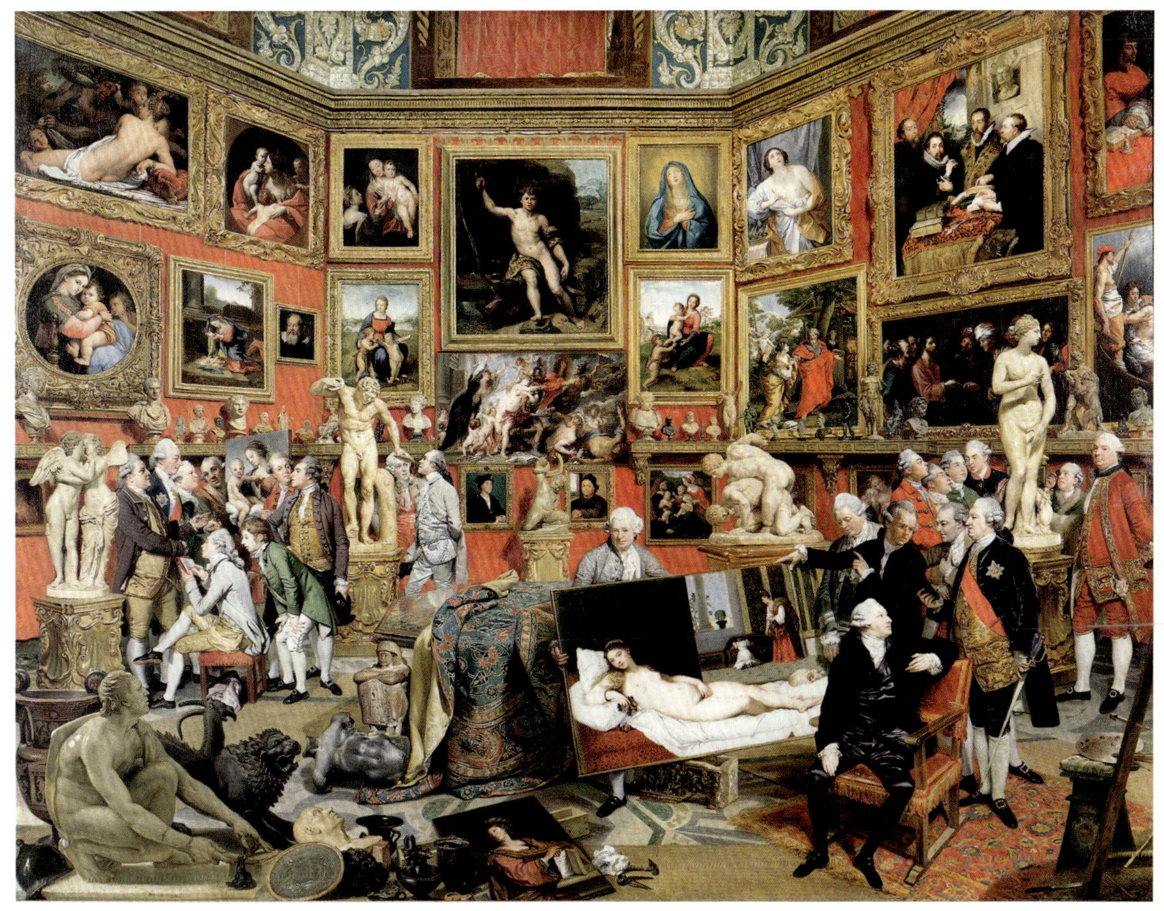

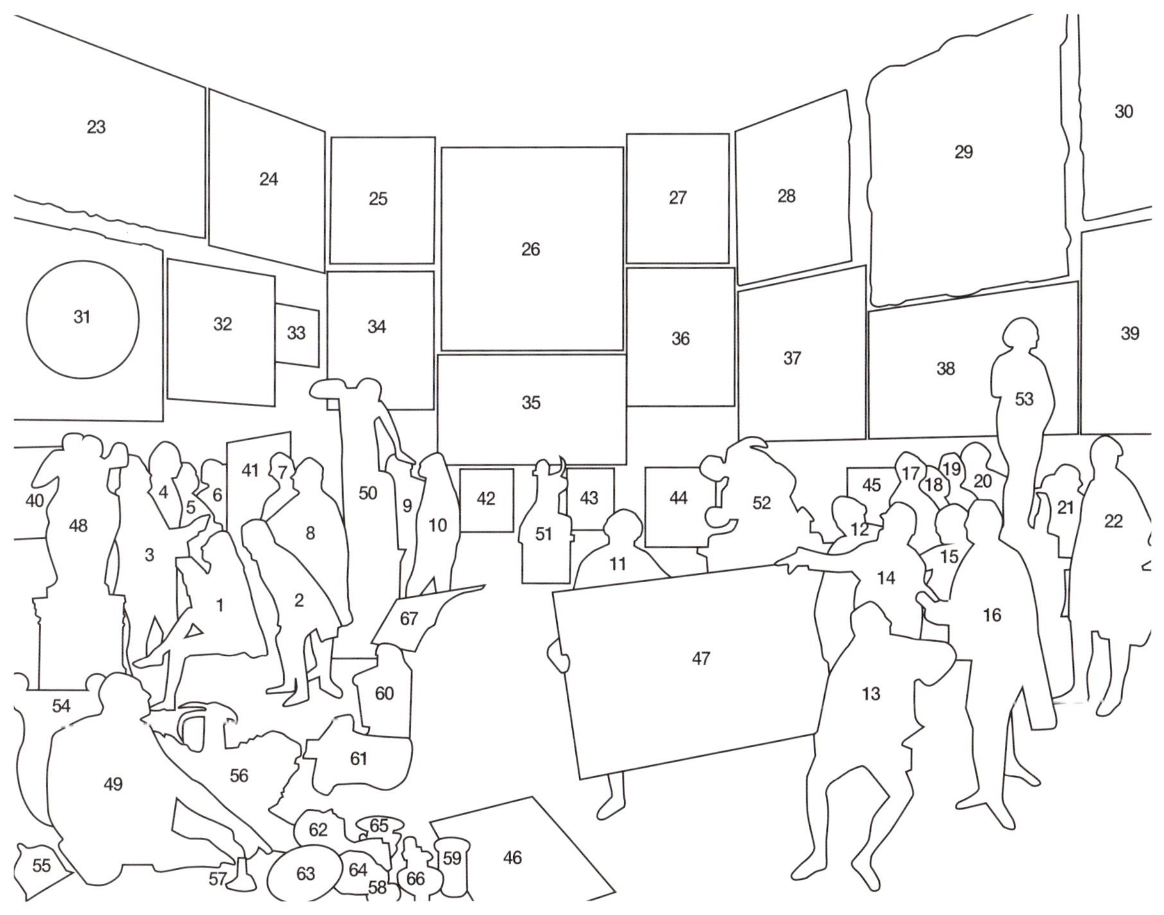

23
24
25
26
27
28
29
30
31
32
33
34
35
36
37
38
39
40
48
4
5
6
41
7
50
9
10
42
43
44
45
17
19
18
20
52
21
22
3
8
51
1
2
67
11
14
15
16
13
54
60
47
49
56
61
55
62
65
57
63
64
58
66
59
46
53
12

Figure 185
Key to the Tribuna of the Uffizi

Visitors
1. Charles Loraine Smith
2. Richard Edgcumbe, later 2nd Earl
   of Mount Edgcumbe
3. George, 3rd Earl Cowper
4. Sir John Dick
5. Other Windsor, 6th Earl of Plymouth
6. Johan Zoffany
7. Mr Stevenson
8. George Legge, Lord Lewisham,
   later 3rd Earl of Dartmouth
9. Unknown man
10. Valentine Knightley of Fawsley
11. Pietro Bastianelli
12. Mr Gordon
13. Hon. Felton Hervey
14. Thomas Patch
15. Sir John Taylor Bt.
16. Sir Horace Mann
17. George Finch, 9th Earl of Winchilsea
18. Mr Wilbraham, probably Roger
19. Mr Watts
20. Mr Doughty
21. T. Wilbraham, probably Thomas
22. James Bruce

Paintings
23. Annibale Carracci, *Venus and Satyr*
24. Guido Reni, *Charity*
25. Titian (school), *Madonna and Child with
    St Catherine*
26. Raphael, *St John the Baptist*
27. Guido Reni, *Madonna*
28. Guido Reni, *Cleopatra*
29. Rubens, *Justus Lipsius with his Pupils*
30. Raphael, *Pope Leo X with Cardinals
    Giulio de' Medici and Luigi de' Rossi*
31. Raphael, *Madonna della Sedia*
    (*Madonna of the Chair*)
32. Correggio, *Madonna and Child*
33. Justus Sustermans, *Galileo*
34. Raphael, *Madonna del Cardellino*
    (*Madonna of the Goldfinch*)
35. Rubens, *Allegory Showing the Effects of War*
36. 'Raphael', *Madonna del Pozzo*
    (*Madonna of the Well*)
37. Pietro da Cortona, *Abraham and Hagar*
38. Caravaggio (school), *Tribute Money*
39. Cristofano Allori, *Miracle of St Julian*
40. Unidentified painting in the style of Rembrandt
41. Raphael, *Niccolini-Cowper Madonna*
42. Holbein, *Sir Richard Southwell*
43. *Portrait* (then thought to be a Holbein
    portrait of Martin Luther, now possibly
    a Raphael portrait of Perugino)
44. *Holy Family* (then attrib. Perugino,
    now Niccolò Soggi)
45. Unknown artist, *Roman Charity*
46. Guercino, *Samian Sibyl*
47. Titian, *Venus of Urbino*

53
The Tribuna of the Uffizi
1772–7

Oil on canvas, 123.5 × 155 (48⅝ × 61 in)
The Royal Collection, Her Majesty Queen
Elizabeth II

Exhibited at the Royal Academy of Arts only

Provenance: Painted for Queen Charlotte
Selected exhibitions: Royal Academy, 1780, no. 68;
Royal Academy 1946–7, no. 48; Royal Academy,
1960, no. 125; *George III: Collector and Patron*,
The Queen's Gallery, Buckingham Palace, 1974–5,
no. 47; National Portrait Gallery 1977, no. 76;
*Norfolk and the Grand Tour: Eighteenth-Century
Travellers Abroad and their Souvenirs*, Norwich
Castle Museum, 1985, no. 109; *The Queen's Pictures:
Royal Collectors through the Centuries*, National
Gallery, London, 1991, no. 61; *Royal Treasures:
A Golden Jubilee Celebration*, The Queen's Gallery,
Buckingham Palace, 2002, no. 24; Queen's Gallery
2004, no. 161; Queen's Gallery and Holyrood
House 2009, no. 25

Sculpture
48. *Cupid and Psyche*
49. The '*Arrotino*' (Knife-Grinder)
50. *Dancing Faun*
51. *The Infant Hercules Strangling the Serpents*
52. *The Wrestlers*
53. *Venus de' Medici*

Other Objects
54. South Italian crater
55. Etruscan helmet
56. *Chimera*
57–8. Roman oil lamps
59. South Italian situla
60. Egyptian ptahmose
61. Greek bronze torso
62. Bust of Julius Caesar
63. Roman silver shield
64. Head of Antinous
65. South Italian crater
66. Etruscan jug
67. Octagonal table with *pietra dura* top

Selected references: Millar 1966, *passim*; Millar 1969,
vol. 1, 154–7, no. 1211; Stella Rudolph and Anna
Biancalani, *Mostra Storica della Tribuna degli Uffizi*,
Quaderni degli Uffizi, I, Florence 1970; Paulson
1975, 138–48; Andrew W. Moore, *Norfolk and the
Grand Tour: Eighteenth-Century Travellers Abroad
and their Souvenirs*, exh. cat., Norwich Castle
Museum, 1985, 17, 66, 95–6, 153–4; Christopher
Lloyd, *The Queen's Pictures: Royal Collectors through
the Centuries*, London, 1991, 170–3; Pressly 1999,
9–10, 14, 160; David H. Solkin, *Art on the Line:
The Royal Academy Exhibitions at Somerset House
1780–1836*, New Haven and London, 2001, 1–6;
Treadwell 2009, 214, 218, 223–4, 229–37, 240–1,
248–50, 252, 256, 269, 270–71, 272, 293, 298–9,
300, 308, 313, 318, 321, 324, 362, 477n; Webster
2011, 281–301, 381–3

Following an abortive attempt to join Captain
Cook's second voyage to the South Seas, in the
summer of 1772 Johan Zoffany headed instead
for Italy where, at the behest of Queen Charlotte,
he was instructed to record the collection of the
Grand Duke of Tuscany in the Tribuna of the Uffizi
Gallery in Florence, the intention being apparently
to produce a worthy pendant to Zoffany's
Academicians of the Royal Academy (cat. 44), another
recent royal commission.[1] His commission may
not have involved the physical dangers that Cook
encountered during his voyage, but it proved,
nonetheless, something of an odyssey, preoccupying
Zoffany for six years and resulting ultimately in
the termination of his royal patronage. Even so,
Zoffany set out with the full confidence of the
queen, as revealed by Lady Spencer's letter to her
nephew Lord Cowper, who was to liaise with the
grand duke on her behalf:

> I have the Queens commands to recommend
> Zoffani a Painter & a very ingenious Man to your
> Lordships protection, Her Majesty sends him to
> Florence & wishes to have him admitted into the
> Great Dukes Gallery this I have no doubt will
> be a sufficient Motive for your Lordships gaining
> him every advantage in your power, but I cannot
> in justice to the Man help adding that he has
> uncommon Merit & has distinguish'd himself
> very much in his stile of Portrait Painting.[2]

With the authority of the queen behind him, every
door was duly opened to Zoffany through the
agency of Lord Cowper and Horace Mann, British
Resident in Florence. And, in the course of his
commission, Zoffany himself became something
of a celebrity, his painting a talking point among
all who visited the Uffizi. Yet, when in 1779
Zoffany returned to England with the picture,
it was accepted reluctantly, paid for eventually
and consigned to a room used by the king in Kew
Palace. It was also there in 1788 during a bout
of illness that George III pulled the picture to
the floor. He was 'perceived to be busy with it',
possibly scratching at the area containing Titian's

Venus (47), a painting that, Horace Mann had noted, 'will not please her Majesty so much as it did the young men to whom it was showed'.[3] Many years later, in conversation with the artist William Beechey, the king returned once more to the picture and 'expressed wonder at Zoffany having done so improper a thing as to introduce the portraits of Sir Horace Man[n], [Thomas] Patch, & others, who were considered as men addicted to improper practises. – He sd. the Queen wd. Not suffer the picture to be placed in any of Her apartments'.[4] One of the reasons why Zoffany's picture remains so admired is the lively presence of the assorted connoisseurs, artists and travellers, twenty-two men in total, whom Horace Walpole was to refer to memorably as a 'flock of travelling boys'.[5] Yet, it may have been the 'improper' behaviour of certain individuals in Zoffany's picture, as much as their mere presence, that offended his royal patrons' sense of propriety.

The Tribuna of the Uffizi is an octagonal room, designed in the late 1580s by Bernardo Buontalenti to house works of art in the collection of Francesco de' Medici. Since 1737 it had been in the possession of the Habsburgs, represented in 1772 by Pietro Leopoldo, Grand Duke of Tuscany. It was not surprising that Zoffany took considerable pains over his commission to paint what was regarded as possibly the greatest art collection in Europe. Already, early in 1773, Lord Winchilsea (17), who features in Zoffany's painting, noted the laborious nature of the task; copying pictures, frames, bronzes, the octagonal table, and

> beside that he is obliged to put several of the pictures in perspective, & to make a distinction between the life & the heads in the Pictures, & what is most difficult of all to make them appear as if they were painted on different Kinds of canvass as in the Originals.[6]

To do justice to the Tribuna, and to produce a viable composition that was more than a mere pictorial replica, Zoffany altered the perspective in the octagonal gallery and, in order to incorporate the various pieces of antique statuary, reduced their relative size. According to Horace Mann, Zoffany was criticized at the time for the liberties that he had taken with the room's perspective 'and tried to get assistance to correct it; but it was found impossible, and he carried it away as it was'.[7] Zoffany was also aware, as he worked on his painting of the Tribuna, that plans were already afoot to reorganize the entire mode of display and collections in the Uffizi gallery, giving him further freedom to make his own decisions as to what he would include. At the same time his picture reflected the reforming spirit of Duke Pietro Leopoldo in its taxonomic concern with the distinction of the various branches of art, rather than a cabinet of miscellaneous curiosities.[8] Although he followed the general hang of the pictures in the gallery, Zoffany omitted certain pictures and introduced works from other rooms, including Titian's *Venus of Urbino*, as well as old masters from the Pitti Palace such as Guido Reni's *Charity* (24) and *Cleopatra* (28), Raphael's *Madonna della Sedia* (31) and Rubens's *Allegory Showing the Effects of War* (35), these works being physically transported to the Uffizi for Zoffany's benefit. It is also notable that several of the paintings are unframed: the Rubens, Titian's *Venus of Urbino* and Guercino's *Samian Sybil* (46), which is propped up on the floor next to a bunch of picture-hanging tools (a hammer, nails and pincers). The unframed *Venus of Urbino* is of particular interest since after 1771 the duke would not allow the picture to be removed for copying, an exception being made eventually for Zoffany in November 1777, when it was taken down expressly for him; Pietro Bastianelli (11), the gallery's custodian, presumably supervised the operation, as he is shown doing in Zoffany's picture.[9]

Zoffany's idiosyncratic agenda for populating his picture with miscellaneous Grand Tourists emerged at an early stage in its composition, Lord Winchilsea observing in December 1772 that it already included portraits of George, third Earl Cowper (3), Horace Mann (16), the Earl of Plymouth (5), the Hon. Felton Hervey (13), 'Mr Wilbraham' (Thomas or Roger) (18), 'Mr Dashwood' (Thomas), as well as 'two men that Shew the Pictures', one of whom was the already mentioned Pietro Bastianelli, standing in the centre holding the *Venus of Urbino*, and the other, the current Soprintendente, Giuseppe Querci, whose portrait was removed after his death in 1773.[10] Zoffany routinely added and removed portraits in his picture, Mann telling Walpole in 1779 that Zoffany had been in the habit of telling young travellers to Florence that the king had expressly ordered him to include their portraits.[11] Yet, even by the summer of 1774 Mann, who sat to Zoffany on several occasions for the picture, was complaining that the picture was 'too much crouded with (for the most part) uninteresting portraits of English travellers then here'.[12] By now, however, Zoffany was clearly enjoying himself, adding (and removing) figures, irrespective of their relevance to his royal patron's interests. He also adopted a high-risk strategy of incorporating a series of lewd visual jokes, one reason why women, although they were frequent visitors to the Tribuna, are excluded entirely from this resolutely homosocial assembly.

To the right of the composition a huddled group ogles the posterior of the *Venus de' Medici* (53). The sculpture was a recognized focus for sexual as well as artistic banter among male Grand Tourists, Charles Townley being informed in 1767 that 'the sight of the Venus in the Florence Gallery will give you some yammering after a Tuscan Whore'.[13] In front of this robustly heterosexual clique, by way of contrast, the artist Thomas Patch (14) – who had been expelled from Rome for homosexual behaviour – points out to Horace Mann, a fellow 'finger-twirler' (to borrow Mrs Piozzi's phrase), the physical attractions of the statue of *The Wrestlers* (52).[14] In addition, at one point Zoffany had apparently also painted a black patch on one of the wrestler's buttocks, as a visual pun at the expense of his fellow artist.[15] In a similar vein, to the left of the composition, Richard Edgcumbe (2) (in the green coat) bends over to take a closer look at the sketch being made of *Cupid and Psyche* (48) by the artist in front of him, while George Legge, Viscount Lewisham (8), presses uncomfortably close to the young Edgcumbe, wearing an ambiguous expression of elation. Facing him, Earl Cowper gestures pointedly at the tip of Sir John Dick's (4) gold-topped cane, while ostensibly admiring his painting of Raphael's Madonna (41), being held aloft by Zoffany. And, as Dick grasps the tip of the phallic cane, 'Other' Windsor, sixth Earl of Plymouth, in profile to the right, wears a startled expression, as he, too, is incorporated into the double entendre. In the left foreground the crouching statue of the *Arrotino* (knife grinder) (49) takes on a renewed significance, performing the traditional role of spy and the Scythian flayer of Marsyas, in this case watching covertly the antics of modern British tourists, who are being 'flayed' alive by Zoffany.[16] Given the multiplicity of jokes – including some heavily weighted homosexual innuendoes – it was little wonder that George III fretted over the presence of individuals 'addicted to improper practises' or that the picture was perceived as an affront to the sensibilities of the queen. Nor was it surprising that in 1826, in an article in the *Literary Gazette*, the author made particular reference to the ribald humour exhibited in the picture by its 'waggish narrator'.[17]

MP

1. Millar 1966, 42.
2. Millar 1966, 10.
3. Lewis 1937–83, vol. 24, 540, Horace Mann to Horace Walpole, 10 Dec. 1779. See also Millar 1966, 33; Webster 2011, 383.
4. Farington 1978–84, vol. 6, 2471.
5. Lewis 1937–83, vol. 24, 527, Horace Walpole to Horace Mann, 12 Nov. 1779.
6. Millar 1966, 13.
7. Lewis 1937–83, vol. 24, 539, Horace Mann to Horace Walpole, 10 Dec. 1779.
8. Webster 2011, 281–5.
9. Webster 2011, 299.
10. Millar 1966, 13; for the removal of Querci, see Webster 2011, 294. Dashwood, who did not appear in the final painting, had also evidently been erased.
11. Lewis 1937–83, vol. 24, 539, Horace Mann to Horace Walpole, 10 Dec. 1779.
12. Lewis 1937–83, vol. 24, 34, Horace Mann to Horace Walpole, 23 Aug. 1774.
13. Coltman 2009, 180.
14. Piozzi 1942, vol. 2, 875 n.1.
15. *Literary Gazette and Journal of the Belle Lettres*, 1826, 442; Manners & Williamson 1920, 63.
16. See Paulson 1975, 140; Webster 2011, 286.
17. *Literary Gazette and Journal of the Belle Lettres*, 1826, 442.

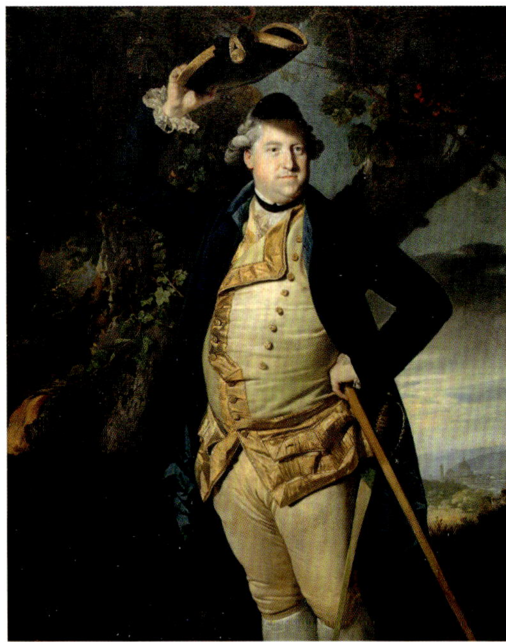

54

George Nassau, Third Earl Cowper
1772–3

Oil on canvas, 142.2 × 111 cm (56 × 43¾ in)
Trustees of the Firle Estate Settlement

Provenance: By descent

Selected exhibitions: Royal Academy 1954–5, 42,
no. 97; National Portrait Gallery 1977, no. 77

Selected references: Boyle 1885, 148–51, 404;
Manners & Williamson 1920, 51–3, 236; Sutton
1956, 80–84; Treadwell 2009, 223–6, 242;
Webster 2011, 305

Just before Zoffany set out for Italy from London,
Lady Spencer wrote a letter to her stepson, George
Nassau Clavering Cowper, third Earl Cowper
(1738–89), an expatriate living in Florence. At 'the
Queens Commands', she recommended the artist
to Cowper's protection, and asked for his assistance
in gaining an entrée to the Grand Duke's gallery:
'This I have no doubt will be a sufficient Motive for
your Lordships gaining him every advantage in
your power, but I cannot in justice to the Man
help adding that he has uncommon Merit & has
distinguish'd himself very much in his stile of
Portrait Painting.'[1] The earl was a great favourite
at the Grand Ducal court and thus an obvious
candidate to approach for such help. Cowper not
only clearly obliged his stepmother in her request
but also, within a year or so of Zoffany's arrival in
the Italian city, had come to agree with her verdict
on the painter's merits as a portraitist,
commissioning this three-quarter-length likeness.
If, as Mary Webster has suggested, the sitter's blue
velvet coat and pale yellow waistcoat represent
Tuscan court dress, then the picture pays testimony
to Cowper's position in Pietro Leopoldo's circle.[2]

Cowper had first visited Florence on a Grand

Tour in July 1759 and had become so enamoured of
the place that he took up residence there at the first
opportunity, escaping what he termed 'the dull
melancholy of England'.[3] He became the life and
soul of Florentine society, and the *Gazzetta Toscana*
regularly featured the supper parties, concerts, balls
and fêtes he threw at his home in Fiesole, the Villa
Palmieri. The distant view of Florence in the right
background of Zoffany's portrait suggests that
Cowper is taking the air in the grounds of this
property, where he had been resident since 1761.

The portrait marked the beginning of a long and
fruitful relationship, which endured after Zoffany's
return to England. In 1779 the artist wrote to
thank Cowper for a recent letter, which had given
him 'the Gratest pleasure as it convinced me
I Still retained a place in your good opinion, which
I Schall ever highly Value; & hope never to forfeit'.[4]
As well as painting a number of portraits for the
earl while in Florence (see cats. 55, 56), Zoffany
also provided advice on the acquisition of works
of art. Zoffany's crucial role in developing the earl's
collection is signified, as Hugh Belsey has pointed
out, by the fact that Cowper added few works
after the artist's departure from Italy.[5]

Zoffany depicts Cowper as a rather portly
figure, the 'solitaire' or black ribbon at his neck
serving to accentuate the ample flesh below his
chin. He lifts his gold braided hat, casting a strong
directional shadow across his forehead. Cowper's
portrait treads a fine line between characterizing
an expansive host and capturing some of the earl's
renowned vanity and pomposity. Earl Cowper's
constant striving after honours and distinctions
earned him much scorn from contemporary
commentators. It was ignored by George III but
rewarded by Emperor Joseph II, who bestowed on
him the title of Prince of the Holy Roman Empire
in 1778. As Penny Treadwell has noted, the way in
which Cowper's sword hangs across his body, with
the clear potential to stab him in the calf, enhances
the suggestion of something a little subversive
here.[6] It is, perhaps, a gentle dig from an artist
whose own fondness for lavish costume, orders
and titles could rival that of his sitter. One source,
recounting an incident which says much about
both men, states that Cowper raised an objection
to Zoffany going about Florence in a pale pink
coat, that being the prerogative of an earl.[7]

KR

1. Hertfordshire Archives, D/EP F296/A/227,
   Lady Spencer to Lord Cowper, 23 June 1772.
2. Webster 2011, 305. A head and shoulders version of
   this portrait is in the Walker Art Gallery, Liverpool.
3. Sutton 1956, 81.
4. Hertfordshire Archives, D/EP F310/129, Zoffany
   to Lord Cowper, 21 Oct. 1779.
5. *ODNB* George Nassau Clavering.
   I am grateful to Hugh Belsey for his help with this
   and related entries.
6. Treadwell 2009, 225.
7. Manners & Williamson 1920, 54.

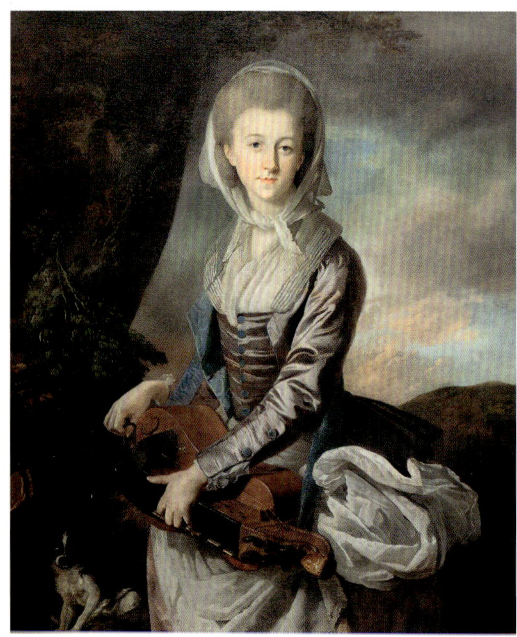

55

Miss Anne Gore as a Savoyarde
1774

Oil on canvas, 121.9 × 97.8 cm (48 × 38½ in)
Trustees of the Firle Estate Settlement

Exhibited at the Yale Center for British Art only

Provenance: By descent

Selected exhibitions: Arts Council 1960–61, no. 14;
National Portrait Gallery 1977, no. 78

Selected references: Boyle 1885, 308–9, 372–3;
Manners & Williamson 1920, 51–3; Leppert 1988,
168–71; Treadwell 2009, 242–3; Webster 2011,
305–7

Hannah Anne Gore (1758–1826) arrived in
Florence early in 1774, travelling with her family
in search of an environment that would benefit her
mother's health. She quickly caught the eye of
George, third Earl Cowper (see cat. 54), who wrote
to a cousin on 24 June:

> The youngest of the daughters I like very much, &
> should I find in the progress of time that she should
> have no objection to me I shall certainly have none
> to here [*sic*] they are … very accomplished in every
> respect, and as unassuming as Girls of eight years
> … I hear they have fifty thousand pounds a piece,
> which would be very well.[1]

In September Horace Mann, British envoy to the
Tuscan court, informed a friend:

> Lord Cowper has declared his intention of
> marrying the youngest daughter of Mr Gore, a
> gentleman of Lincolnshire, who with his wife and
> two other daughters has been here some months.
> The young lady is not quite sixteen years of age,
> the marriage therefore will not be celebrated till
> this time twelvemonth.[2]

Zoffany depicts the earl's fiancée, described by
Mann as 'very young and pretty',[3] on a similar size
canvas to that used for Cowper the previous year.
In both portraits the sitters are posed against a
distant landscape, framed against a tree, which
leans into the canvas from the left. However, while
George looks out across his domain, Hannah shyly
meets our gaze. More remarkably, Hannah wears
the costume of a Savoyard, as she turns the crank
and depresses the keys of a hurdy-gurdy. In
February 1775 Mrs Delany met Lady Cowper, and
found her 'full of … her commissions from Lord
Cowper for jewells for his lady elect, whose picture
in water-colours he has sent her (like a Savoyarde,)
pretty eno' tho' not ans[g] [answering] her character
for beauty, but I supposed it does not do her
justice.'[4] The present painting was probably the
original of the watercolour that Cowper sent his
stepmother in England.

In reality, Savoyards were poor, itinerant
musicians from the north of Italy, who travelled
throughout France scraping a living. These may
seem rather unlikely people with whom to associate
the genteel Hannah Gore, soon to be Lady Cowper.
However, Savoyards – particularly women and
boys – had become the stuff of picturesque genre
pieces. They were associated with values of
simplicity and innocence, and renowned for their
attachment to family and homeland thanks in part
to the characterization of Jean-Jacques Rousseau.[5]
All were suitable qualities with which to associate
this maiden on the verge of wedlock.

Hannah's lapdog both adds the virtue of loyalty
(*semper fidelis*) and, as the standard accompaniment
of the refined English lady, underlines the
fictiveness of Hannah's costume. Despite the
humble scarf thrown over her head, her dress is
notably ornate, a masquerade version of Savoyard
garb. Costumes worn at masquerades were
multifarious, but there was a distinct trend in the
1770s in favour of what Aileen Ribeiro has termed
'the pastoral theme'.[6] At a private masquerade
held in 1770, for example, the young Fanny
Burney encountered 'a very complete Shepherdess'
together with 'two or three young pastoral
nymphs'. Fanny attended this event in *'fancy dress'*,
and her sister Hetty joined in the rustic theme as
'a Savoyard, with a *hurdy gurdy* fastened round her
waist. Nothing could look more simple, innocent, or
pretty … Both our dresses met with approbation.'[7]
The kind of outfit worn by Hannah Gore, seen to
convey a pleasing purity and wholesomeness was
thus deemed highly flattering by contemporaries.

In eighteenth-century France the hurdy-gurdy,
or vielle, had become a favoured prop in the
Arcadian pastimes of the aristocracy. Although
the instrument was only occasionally played by
members of the propertied classes in Britain,
Hester Thrale noted in 1777 that Lady Hereford
would play 'on the Vielle to amuse her Friends'.
The verdict of a certain Dr Parker suggests limited

success: 'When he had listened a while, [he] said
very gravely – if your Ladyship will give me leave
I'll go to the Door & hearken, for I have a Notion
'tis best at a Distance.'[8] Hurdy-gurdies make a raw
and intense sound and are, as a result, very much
an outdoor instrument. It is thus perhaps fortunate
that Zoffany's whimsical portrait shows Hannah
playing her vielle in a mountainous Italian
landscape, a setting that makes reference to both
the homeland of the Savoyards and the country
where she was to spend the rest of her life.

KR

1. Cowper and Newton Museum, Olney MS, Box 5,
   no. 790, Lord Cowper to Colonel Cowper, 24 June
   1774, quoted Wilton & Bignamini 1996, 92.
2. Lewis 1937–83, vol. 24, 38, Horace Mann to Lord
   Rochford, 13 Sept. 1774.
3. Lewis 1937–83, vol. 24, 40, Horace Mann to Horace
   Walpole, 20 Sept. 1774.
4. Llanover 1862, vol. 2, 111, Mrs Delany to Mrs Port,
   21 Feb. 1775.
5. For the Savoyards, see Leppert 1988, 169 and Richard
   Leppert, *Arcadia at Versailles: Noble Amateur Musicians
   and their Musettes and Hurdy-gurdies at the French Court
   (c.1660–1789): A Visual Study*, Amsterdam and Lisse,
   1978, 78, 92–6, 100. See also Webster 2011, 307.
6. Ribeiro 1984, chap. 4, part I, 249ff.
7. Anne Raine Ellis, ed., *The Early Diary of Frances
   Burney, 1768–1778*, 2 vols., London, 1889, vol. 1, 64–8,
   10 Jan. 1770.
8. Piozzi 1942, vol. 1, 129.

56

***The Gore Family with George,
Third Earl Cowper***
*c.*1775

Oil on canvas, 78.7 × 97.8 cm (31 × 38½ in)
Yale Center for British Art, Paul Mellon Collection

Provenance: Commissioned by either Charles Gore
or George, third Earl Cowper; Lady Cowper;
purchased in Florence by Hon. Spencer Cowper
in 1845; given to his brother George, sixth Earl
Cowper; by descent to Rosemary, Lady Ravensdale;
with Agnew in 1977; purchased by Paul Mellon,
1977

Selected exhibitions: South Kensington Museum
1867, no. 5; Whitechapel 1908, no. 157; *Woman
and Child in Art*, Grosvenor Gallery, London,
1913–14, no. 80; Royal Academy 1934, no. 240;
Royal Academy 1954–5, no. 122; *Pittura Inglese
1660–1840*, British Council, Milan, 1975, no. 62;
National Portrait Gallery 1977, no. 79; *Arthur Devis
and his Contemporaries*, Yale Center for British Art,
1980, no. 61; Tate 1996, no. 47; *This Other Eden*,
Yale Center for British Art, 1998, no. 20

Selected references: Boyle 1885, 148, 308–9; Manners
& Williamson 1920, 51–3, 191–2; Williamson 1931,
17–18; Sitwell 1936, 30; Sutton 1956, 81; Paulson
1975, 141; Webster 1976, 62–3; Retford 2006,
187–9; Treadwell 2009, 242–4; Marcia Pointon,
*Brilliant Effects: A Cultural History of Gem Stones
and Jewellry*, New Haven and London, 2009, 33–4;
Webster 2011, 302, 308–10

This conversation piece heralded the marriage of
George, third Earl Cowper (see cat. 54) and Hannah
Anne Gore (see cat. 55) in a private ceremony in
Florence on 2 June 1775.[1] It both emphasizes the
earl's proposed union with his young fiancée and
testifies to his new-found association with the Gore
family. The engaged couple are standing, Cowper
posed just right of centre, as he both points and
looks towards his betrothed. Hannah Gore returns
his gaze coyly, holding some sheet music that links
her to the duet taking place between them. Her
father Charles Gore plays the violincello, while
her sister Emilie provides accompaniment on the
square piano. Charles Gore was a gentleman from
Lincolnshire whose considerable wealth enabled
him to enjoy a life of leisure, devoting himself to the
study of navigation, building yachts after his own
models, and his practice as an amateur artist.[2]
Farington, some years later, referred to Gore's
prowess in 'sketching vessels & Sea views in which
He so much excelled as to be very generally spoken
of for His superior taste in art'.[3] Such a 'Sea view' is
casually displayed on the chair to the left. On the
opposite side, Charles's wife, Mary, sits looking out
of the canvas to meet and draw in our gaze to the
newly expanded family unit. She is accompanied by
her eldest daughter Elizabeth, who is perhaps
engaged in sketching her mother's likeness.

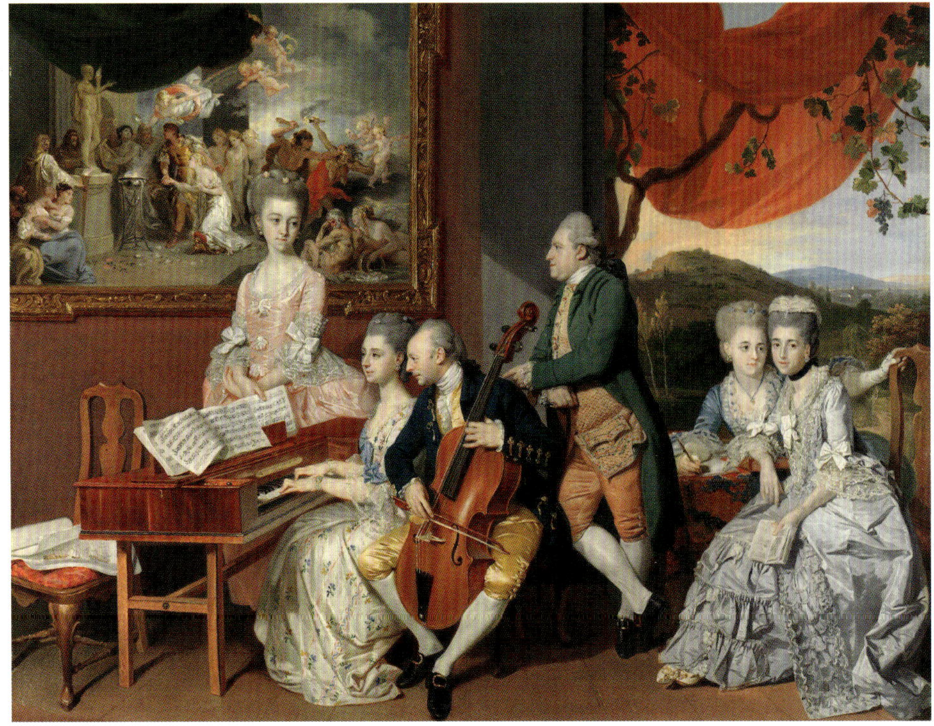

The painting provides a virtuoso display of Zoffany's considerable ability in capturing the details and textures of fashionable costumes and objects. The wood of the musical instruments glows softly, Charles's bright yellow breeches have an extraordinary sheen, and the quilted patterning of Cowper's waistcoat is beautifully rendered. In its meticulous recreation of the material world, Zoffany builds on the early eighteenth-century tradition of the conversation piece. However, he also breaks with that tradition in significant ways. While the Tuscan hills behind Mary and Elizabeth are as carefully rendered as the furnishings among which the sitters are posed, the way in which the room abruptly and unfeasibly opens onto that landscape – a liminal space that is neither interior nor exterior – is much more characteristic of Reynolds. Zoffany further plays with convention by adopting the great swathe of red drapery so typical of the grand manner portrait, yet draping it across a tree, rather than entwining it around a column.

The unusual quality of this portrait is most pronounced, however, when one's attention turns to the painting prominently displayed behind Hannah Gore. It was entirely standard to include paintings within conversation pieces, and both Zoffany and his contemporary John Hamilton Mortimer were fond of including internal images partially cut off by the frame of the actual portrait. A conversation piece artist such as Arthur Devis would have included, perhaps, a suitable classical landscape to suggest his sitters' taste, but Zoffany shows a complex, Baroque allegorical scene set in the Temple of Hymen, God of Marriage. The image, as Mary Webster has pointed out, is characteristic

of Zoffany's work prior to his arrival in England.[4] A young couple pay their respects to a statue of the God, and the Three Graces, a musician playing his lyre and a mother with her baby, anticipating the fruits of the union, are in attendance. The conceit is apt, yet, directly above Hannah Gore's carefully arranged coiffure, we see Hercules raising his club threateningly as he evicts the figure of Calumny, her ghastly, haggard face revealed by the cupids who have just removed her mask. Zoffany may have had in mind Botticelli's famous rendition of Calumny, in which she is shown as a beautiful woman, dragging a praying man towards a judge who is likely to be swayed by her physical attractions.[5] He could have seen the picture at the Galleria della Gran Duca, where he was of course engaged in perhaps the ultimate exercise in representing pictures within a picture (cat. 53).

The logical interpretation of Zoffany's own allegory is that malicious gossip has been warded off; that defamation has been averted in order for the ceremony in front of the altar to proceed. This only makes sense in the context of Lord Cowper's chequered past, and the scandal that had followed various romantic entanglements prior to his relationship with Hannah. Most notoriously, when first in Italy, George had 'los[t] his whole time by acting the cicisbeo [companion or lover]' to one Marchesa Corsi.[6] His attachment had been such that he had notoriously resisted attempts by his dying father to get him to return to England. This tryst was followed by at least one more affair, before marriage negotiations with the family of a Florentine noblewoman, conducted only a few years before Hannah's arrival, broke down over a

religious dispute. Each of these liaisons had been accompanied by considerable gossip, and, when the engagement with Hannah was announced in 1774, Mrs Delany expressed her satisfaction that there would have to be a year's delay in deference to the bride's young age: '*If* his lordship continues constant, he will be *more* worth her acceptance!'[7]

Some debate has taken place over whether this picture was commissioned by Lord Cowper or Charles Gore.[8] However, the references tailored to Earl Cowper's fraught personal history suggest that it was his commission. Although the allusions to Cowper's private life explain the narrative of the internal painting, it remains a startling inclusion, a dramatically personal declaration that offsets a conventional statement about the yoking of two families through intermarriage.

KR

1. I am most grateful to Hugh Belsey for his help with this entry and with Lord Cowper more generally.
2. R.C.B. Oliver, 'Charles Gore: A Lincolnshire-born High Sheriff of Radnorshire', *Transactions of the Radnorshire Society*, XLVII (1977), 32–51.
3. Farington 1978–84, vol. 10, 3622, 31 March 1810.
4. Webster 2011, 308.
5. Retford 2006, 187–9.
6. Lewis 1937–83, vol. 21, 415, Horace Mann to Horace Walpole, 14 June 1760.
7. Llanover 1862, vol. 2, 42, Mrs Delany to Mrs Port, 14 Oct. 1774.
8. For Cowper as the patron, see Webster 2011, 308; Webster 1976, 62. For Gore as the patron, see Wilton & Bignamini 1996, 91; Malcolm Warner and Julia Marciari Alexander, *This Other Eden: Paintings from the Yale Center for British Art*, New Haven and London, 1998, 64.

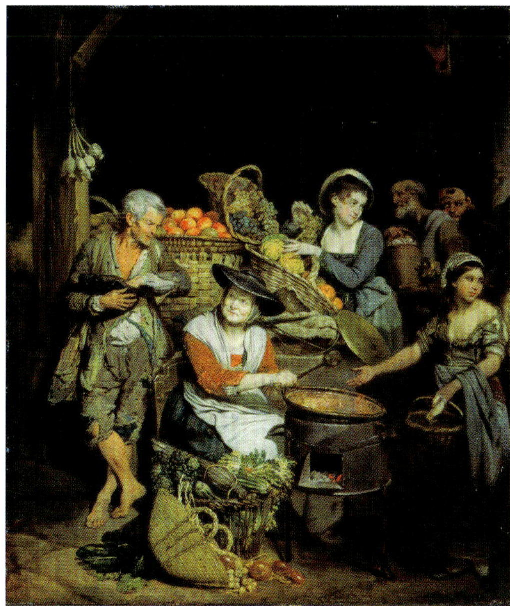

57

A Florentine Fruit Stall

*c.*1777

Oil on canvas, 57.8 × 49.2 cm (22¾ × 19⅜ in)
Tate, London; purchased 1955

Provenance: Zoffany's sale, Messrs Robins, 9 May
1811 (90); Sir William Proctor; Mrs Beverley
before 1913, by descent, Christie's, 12 June 1931
(47) as Henry Walton; Ernest Cook, bequeathed
through the National Art Collections Fund 1955

Selected exhibitions: National Portrait Gallery 1977,
no. 84

Selected references: Treadwell 2009, 278–80; Webster
2011, 348–9

This is one of two known genre paintings made by
Zoffany during his time in Italy, the other being
The Festival of the Maize Harvest (cat. 62). While
the latter painting entered the collection of the
Duke of Parma, Zoffany retained the present
picture. It can be identified as 'A Florentine Fruit
Stall; a most excellent groupe, very highly finished,
and one of his best performances', which featured
in his posthumous studio sale in 1811. Zoffany had
painted several genre pictures before his departure
for Italy, notably *Beggars on the Road to Stanmore*
(cat. 50), *A Porter with a Hare* (cat. 49), and *John
Cuff and his Assistant* (cat. 51). As with the previous
pictures, the present work may have been made by
Zoffany as a speculation, generated by his own
interest in the subject matter. Although the work is
highly finished, Zoffany did not exhibit it during his
lifetime. However, it may have been displayed in his
studio or home, as a souvenir of his time in Italy.
Among those who may have seen it was his patron,
Mrs Thrale, who was, in any event, a great admirer
of his work. In 1784 Mrs Thrale, recently widowed,
travelled through Europe with her new husband
Gabriel Piozzi, publishing an account of her

experiences a few years later.[1] In Alessandria her
principal 'amusement', as she noted, 'was to look
out upon the huddled market-place, as a great
dramatic writer of our day has called it; and who
could help longing there for Zoffani's pencil to
paint the lively scene?'[2]

   To the left of the painting an elderly beggar
leans against a wooden post, his tattered clothes
and bare feet proclaiming his profession. In marked
contrast, the woman tending the brazier, who
throws him an enquiring glance, is neatly, if simply,
dressed. At her side Zoffany has painted an
exquisite still life composed of baskets, artichokes,
onions and brassica. The right-hand side of the
composition is more complex, and slightly difficult
to comprehend, not least because at some stage in
the picture's history a strip of canvas has been cut
away, removing one or perhaps two figures from
the scene who were vital to understanding the
narrative. Even so, the gestures and expressions
of the young woman and girl have a strong sexual
undercurrent, suggesting that the missing figures
are male. The young woman, her bosom partially
exposed, smiles coyly as she plucks a grape, while
placing her other hand on the two melons in the
basket. The girl, who appears slightly wary,
gestures towards the brazier with her right hand,
her left partially wrapped in a rag, perhaps to hold
hot chestnuts from the brazier. Her dress falls away
from her shoulder, revealing her bare breast. In the
shadows a nervous looking peasant cradles a bag
of eggs. Directly behind him lurks the figure of a
Capuchin monk, intent on begging, if not theft.
Above him Zoffany has placed a holy-water stoup
and the image of the Madonna. The narrative is
resolutely Hogarthian in its focus on the minutiae
of everyday life and the inclusion of sexual
innuendo. The market girls, in their behaviour and
appearance, also relate to images found in popular
prints, where the sale of commodities – flowers,
fruit, shrimps and oysters – was compared closely
to prostitution, so the real commodity on offer was
the woman herself. It was a genre that Zoffany was
to explore on his return to England, too, in the
pendant fancy pictures he made of *The Flower Girl*
and *The Watercress Girl* (see cat. 52).

MP

1. Piozzi 1789.
2. Piozzi 1789, vol. 1, 57.

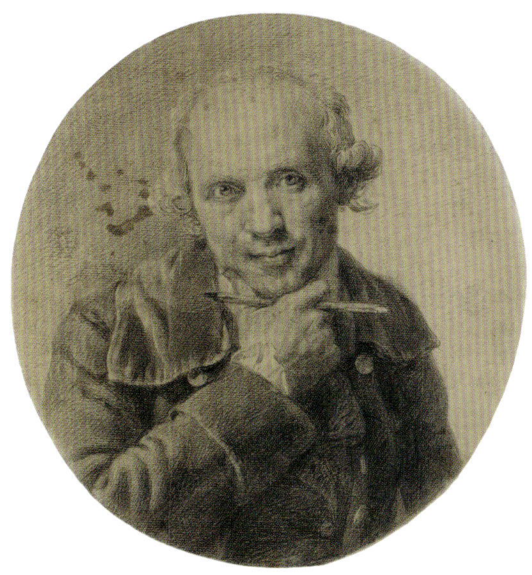

58

Self-Portrait

*c.*1775–6

Black chalk on white paper, oval,
30.5 × 28 cm (12 × 11 in)
British Museum, Department of Prints and
Drawings, 1927,0419.1

Provenance: Presented by Zoffany to Gabriel
Mathias; by descent to Miss Lettice A. MacMunn,
from whom purchased by the British Museum,
1927

Selected exhibitions: National Portrait Gallery 1977,
no. 122; *The Intimate Portrait: Drawings, Miniatures
and Pastels from Ramsay to Lawrence*, National
Portrait Gallery, Edinburgh, and the British
Museum, 2008–9, no. 56

Selected references: C. Dodgson, 'John Zoffany RA,
1733–1810', *Old Master Drawings*, vol. 2, 1928, 64;
Pressly 1987, 86–101; Pressly 1995, 49–55;
Ingamells 2004, 499; Treadwell 2009, 272–3;
Webster 2011, 350

This refined drawing can be related to the
self-portraits Zoffany made in Florence during
the mid-1770s. In particular, it relates to the
self-portrait with a dog, in which the artist holds
his hand to his chin (Uffizi Gallery, Florence).
It cannot, however, be regarded as a study for that
portrait, since the expression in the present work
is quite different, and with its high degree of finish
it does not resemble a preparatory drawing but
seems to be a complete work of art in its own
right. Indeed, the existence of what appears to be
a preliminary sketch for this drawing (Sotheby's
10 July 1997, no. 15) suggests that it was quite
carefully considered. Zoffany's expression in the
drawing is contemplative and introspective. He
strokes his chin, porte-crayon in hand, as though
he has paused briefly to consider the composition
at hand. The expression is also perhaps tinged with

an air of melancholy, which, as has been pointed out in relation to the present drawing, had been a means of conveying genius in artists' self-portraits since the Renaissance.[1] However, Zoffany's expression may also have been associated with his personal circumstances at the time, since he is known to have suffered greatly following the death of his infant son in a tragic accident around this time.

Zoffany presented the drawing to Gabriel Mathias, a portrait and genre painter who was of German origin and had studied in Rome during the 1740s with Batoni. In addition to producing his own art, he also worked as an art dealer, importing from France marine paintings by Joseph Vernet. Zoffany may have known him through a court connection since Mathias had a post in the Privy Purse and administered George III's payments to the Royal Academy. Zoffany is supposed to have painted a portrait of Mathias with a bust of his brother, although the portrait, if it was indeed by Zoffany, is lost.[2]

MP

1. Lloyd & Sloan 2008, 102.
2. Manners & Williamson 1920, 64–5, 218.

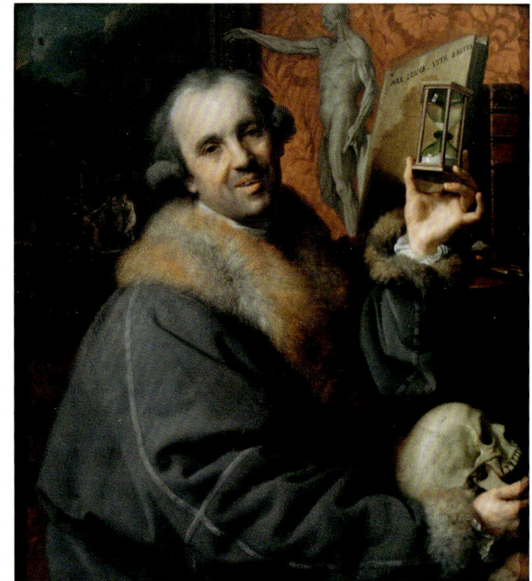

59

Self-Portrait

1778

Oil on panel, 87.5 × 77 cm (34½ × 30⅜ in)
Inscribed: 'ARS LONGA. VITA BREVIS'
Uffizi Gallery, Florence

Provenance: Presented by the artist to the Royal Collection in Florence, 30 March 1778

Selected exhibitions: Firenze e l'Inghilterra: Rapporti artistici e culturali dal XVI al XX secolo, Palazzo Pitti, Florence, 1971, no. 67; *Artists' Self-Portraits from the Uffizi*, Dulwich Picture Gallery, 2007, no. 19

Selected references: Millar 1966, 30–31, pl. 32; Paulson 1975, 138–48; Webster 1976, 13; Pressly 1987, 88–101, 91ff.; Treadwell 2009, 274–8; Webster 2011, 344, 353–5

Engraved: Carlo Lasinio, *Serie di ritratti di pittori che da se stessi si dipinsero esistenti nella R. Galleria di Toscana*, Florence 1796, no. 231

This arresting image, presented by Zoffany to the Grand Duke Pietro Leopoldo of Tuscany on 30 March 1778, contains elements of self-portraits in the *vanitas* tradition, with a Latin quotation inscribed on the vellum-covered book: 'Life is short but art is long.' Zoffany gives the picture an allusiveness that was personal and appropriate to the painting's destination: the Galleria degli Uffizi among a collection of artist's self-portraits from all over Europe. The *écorché* statuette behind the artist suits the Latin quotation, alluding not only to Zoffany's 'life' but also his 'art', while reinforcing the more familiar memento mori of the skull and also representing the teaching of art.[1]

There are other reasons for the inclusion of the *écorché*, a celebrated plaster by Jean-Antoine Houdon dated 1767 (fig. 186), which was created for his lost plaster sculpture *St John the Baptist* for Santa Maria degli Angeli, Rome.[2] It appears to

'baptize' the artist,[3] the fuller significance of which has not been appreciated: first, Zoffany was baptized John, and so the Baptist was the Zoffany's 'name saint'; secondly, St John the Baptist is the patron saint of Florence and, since a lamb was the animal associated with the Baptist, Zoffany's decision to show himself in a sheepskin coat was not merely due to his painting the picture in winter. In a most elegant allusion Zoffany shows himself in this presentation portrait being 'baptized' by Florence – and by art.[4]

The title of the red book reads 'HISTORIA | NATURALI | TOM I', identifying it as the first volume of *Historia Naturalis* by Pliny the Elder. The first volume contains the preface that includes the famous phrase, heavy with significance for Zoffany's picture, 'homines enim sumus' ('for we are only human'). An incident in the background at the left involves a friar, and Zoffany was shortly to depict himself with a friar's habit in the Parma *Self-Portrait* (cat. 60). The friar (a Capuchin?) is leaning over a prie-dieu, beside a fire, his right arm outstretched, but he is being touched on the left shoulder by one of the Three Graces and turns to look at them.[5] These are, however, the Three Graces in frisky mood, and they are evidently teasing the friar with sexually provocative poses. There may be a message here concerning the temptations of sex. But there is not much angst in it – Zoffany was no hermit or friar. Instead, this scene indicates his feeling that, unlike the man in the habit, much was to be gained from following the Three Graces, whom he had painted in one of his earliest works (cat. 1). They were traditionally

Figure 186
Jean-Antoine Houdon, *L'Écorché*, 1767, white plaster with self base, 181 × 59 × 71 cm (71¼ × 23¼ × 28 in). Académie de France, Rome

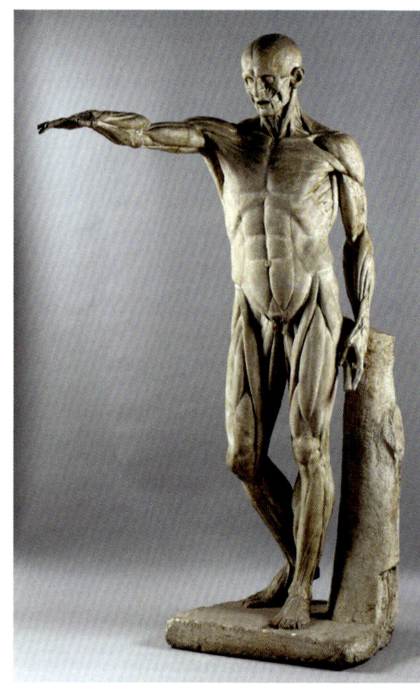

an inspiration to artists, while bringing joy to
mortals and gods alike and presiding over
social celebrations. The Three Graces, Aglaea
(Splendour), Euphrosyne (Mirth) and Thalia
(Cheerfulness), were associated with Aphrodite
(Venus), the goddess of Love. And so, in attempting
to interpret this particular allusion, there is no
reason to identify the figure in a habit as either
St Anthony or St Jerome, and above all no reason
to think of him as representing Zoffany.[6] He is
merely a monk-like figure and, in this context,
representative of a pointless attempt to retreat
from life.

The rather forced expression on Zoffany's face –
which has been called a *rictus* – may be suggestive of
the classical philosopher Democritus, he of 'cheerful
wisdom and instructive mirth', who laughed rather
than wept at the follies of mankind.[7] But there is
surely a related message conveyed in the skull that
Zoffany holds, because he is forcing down its lower
jaw in order to make it grin. Like Zoffany, the skull
is being compelled to smile in the face of mortality.
Zoffany's *sprezzatura* – his apparently effortless
creation of a painting full of wit and learned
allusions – must have been a principal reason for
the painting's instant celebrity in Florence.

RS

1. From the time of Zoffany's arrival in Florence it was
   understood that his *Tribuna* (cat. 53) was to form a
   pendant with his painting of the Royal Academicians
   (cat. 44), already in the Royal Collection, a composition
   explicitly focused on artistic training and instruction:
   see Millar 1966, 42.
2. The intended marble appears never to have been made
   (Poulet 2003, 63ff., 73ff.). A life-size plaster for the lost
   statue (destroyed 1894) was found in 1921 in the store
   of the Museo Nazionale, Rome. It is now in the Villa
   Borghese (Poulet 2003, cat. 3). Zoffany had visited
   Rome in 1772 (Lindsay Stainton, 'Hayward's List:
   British Visitors to Rome 1753–1775', *Walpole Society*,
   vol. 49 (1983), 3–36, 14, 15, 36), and in fact the *écorché*
   he shows in the *Self-Portrait* must be the one he saw
   there in the Académie de France. Houdon abandoned
   the tree-trunk support (originally for a marble) in his
   replica casts once he had returned to Paris, and the
   only other cast that matches the one seen here was
   sent to Schloss Friedenstein, Gotha, in 1772 (Poulet
   2003, 64).
3. Pressly 1987, 96.
4. Zoffany had already been made a member of the
   Florentine Academy on 19 August 1773: Florence,
   Archivio di Stato, Accademia delle Belle Arti 22,
   Giornale della Reale Accad:ma del Disegno dal 1771 al
   1778, ff.14, 14v (cited in Webster 2011, 320, 665 n.74).
5. There is a very odd coincidence here, in that Houdon
   recorded using the head of 'a kind of hermit …
   wearing a sort of cape of a Capuchin friar' for the
   head of his Baptist *écorché*. The hermit had refused to
   cooperate, saying he was not worthy to represent a
   saint, but Houdon used his head anyway (Poulet 2003,
   74). One of Houdon's closest friends, incidentally,
   was Johann Christian von Mannlich, who also
   visited Parma.
6. Webster 1976, 13 (St Anthony); Pressly 1987, 92 (St
   Anthony); Paulson 1975, 144 (St Jerome); Treadwell
   2009, 278 (St Jerome).
7. Pressly 1987, 93ff.

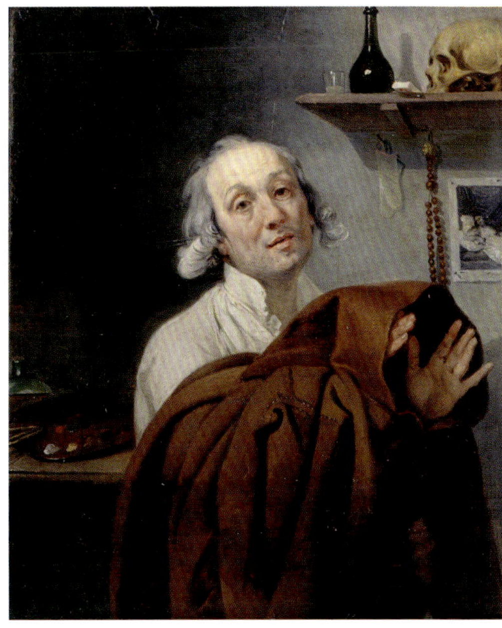

60

Self-Portrait with Friar's Habit
1779

Oil on panel, 43 × 39 cm (16⅞ × 15⅜ in)
Signed and dated lower left: 'Cav.re J. Zoffanij. |
Parma 1779 | 13 Marzo'
Galleria Nazionale di Parma

61

Repose on the Flight into Egypt
1779

(On the reverse of *Self-Portrait with Friar's Habit*,
cat. 59)
Oil on panel, 43 × 39 cm (16⅞ × 15⅜ in)
Galleria Nazionale di Parma

Provenance: Acquired 1917

Selected exhibitions: Parma 1979, no. 122

Selected references: A.O. Quintavalle 1939, 230; A.G.
Quintavalle 1955a, I (Jan.–March), 7–15, figs. 1, 2;
Millar 1966, 31–3, pls. 33, 34; Paulson 1975,
138–48; Webster 1976, 13; Pressly 1987, 88–101,
figs. 4, 5; Schianchi 2000, cat. 789; Treadwell 2009,
289–93; Webster 2011, 367–9

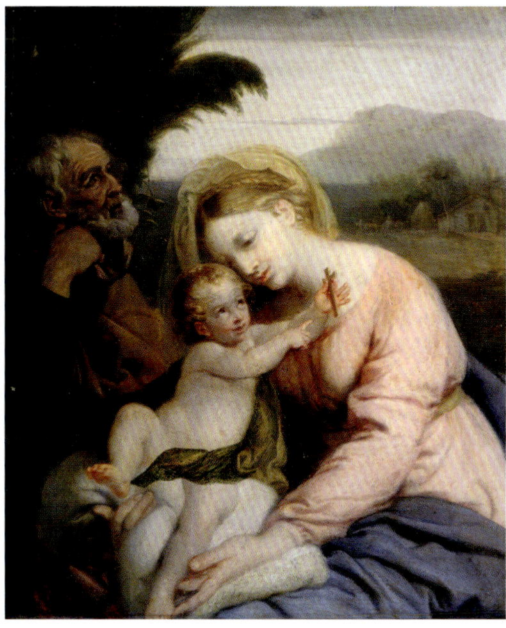

Zoffany's decision to paint on panel rather than
canvas must have been dictated by his desire that
each image on this double-sided work would inform
the meaning of the other. The panel on which the
works are painted is of the same, non-standard,
small dimensions as those of the *Festival of the
Maize Harvest* (cat. 62), and it is probable that the
two works were formed from one 'kit-kat' panel
(approximately 36 × 28 in / 91 × 71 cm), cut in half.[1]
The signature on the *Self-Portrait* dates the work to
a single day, '13 March 1779', Zoffany's forty-sixth
birthday. The *Repose on the Flight into Egypt* is a
free imitation of the style of Correggio, Parma's
most celebrated artist, and refers to the travels of
Zoffany himself and his wife and children, who
were at that very moment on their way out of Italy
towards England. Zoffany had discovered on
12 March, the day before he signed this painting,
that they were now free to go.[2]

The *Self-Portrait* was presumably created for
someone in Parma who shared Zoffany's sense of
humour. The most appropriate recipient would
have been the engraver Simon-François Ravenet
the Younger, as the style of the *Repose* would have
referred to his engraving of a set of Correggio's
paintings.[3] His father Simon-François Ravenet
the Elder was Zoffany's friend (cat. 43), while the
younger Ravenet, who had been in Parma since
1759,[4] engraved Zoffany's portrait of Ferdinando,
Duke of Parma, as the frontispiece to his set of
Correggio prints.[5] The most celebrated Correggio
painting in Parma, engraved by Ravenet, was the
Madonna of St Jerome in the Academy (fig. 187),
elements of which appear in Zoffany's pastiche.[6]

Zoffany's satirical double painting was inspired
by the unusual circumstances of the ducal court at
Parma. In June 1769 Ferdinando (Duke of Parma
from 1765, see fig. 79) had married Maria Amalia
of Austria (see fig. 78), daughter of the Emperor

Francis and Empress Maria Theresa, Zoffany's patron, and sister of Grand Duke Pietro Leopoldo of Tuscany, for whom Zoffany had worked in Florence. It was only on 1 November that year that Ferdinando was able to consummate the marriage, owing to a painful medical condition.[7] Having achieved consummation, Ferdinando remained overawed by his wife and retreated into a kind of infantilism. Shortly after the marriage his father's prime minister, Guillaume du Tillot, reported to Versailles: 'You can see that he is afraid of [his wife].'[8] Although the duke and duchess were on good terms, from 1775 they were separated. The duchess thenceforward lived at what had been the summer palace of Castello di Sala Baganza,[9] 6 miles (10 km) to the south of the city, while he preferred the palace at Colorno 9 miles (14 km) to the north of it. Although Ferdinando found time to make his wife pregnant on nine occasions between 1770 and 1788 (the last two children, twins, were stillborn in May 1789), Amalia was ultimately driven to find satisfaction in liaisons conducted in the discretion of a hunting lodge, 'Il Casino dei Boschi', which she had built in 1775 in the beechwoods at Sala. Meanwhile, Ferdinando was possessed by what has been described as 'a maniacal attachment to religion',[10] which scandalized his royal relations in France and Spain. Louis XV wrote to him on 4 November 1769: 'One may be a monk when no longer a prince; but for a prince to be a monk is mere folly.'[11]

Figure 187
Antonio Correggio, *Madonna of St Jerome*, 1527–8, oil on canvas, 205.7 × 141 cm (81 × 55½ in). Galleria Nazionale di Parma

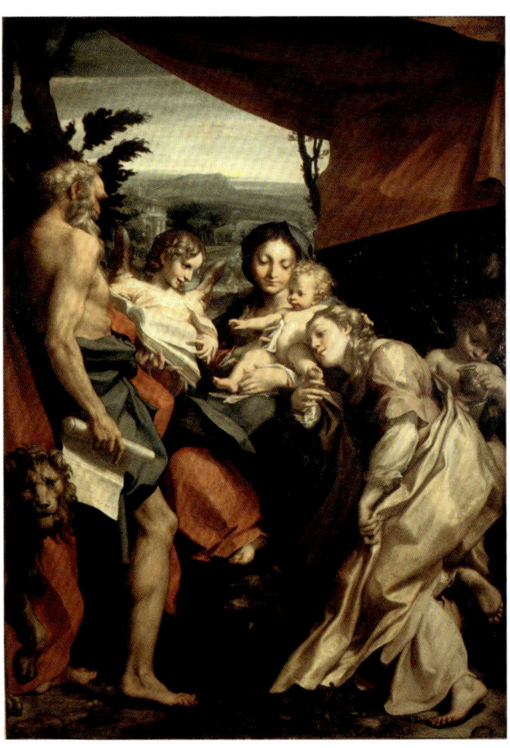

But there was another side to Ferdinando's religiosity: he was very fond of young peasant women. Giuseppe Gorani, on a visit to Colorno, saw the duke at mass and then visited the garden. He was told that, although the duke would process devotedly around the fourteen chapels that he had built, 'he knew how to combine his devotions with a pinch of debauchery'. At each chapel, Gorani was intrigued to hear, 'a pretty peasant girl was voluptuously positioned … the Duke would warm up with one of these goddesses, receive a kiss from another, explore the charms of a third; and finally … reach the fourteenth [station] where [like a Sultan[12]] he chose which one he would enjoy'. When Gorani was about to leave the garden, the story appeared to be confirmed in dramatic fashion, as he saw 'a great covered carriage' drawing up before his eyes: 'Seven peasant girls, gallantly dressed, nimble, frisky and pretty [were] getting down; they were followed by several manservants and finally the Duke, who honoured me with an obliging greeting.'[13] Ferdinando's modern historian concluded that the duke was a 'libertine monk'.[14]

And so Zoffany's double painting mirrors the two-sided world in which he found himself. Outwardly, the court in Parma wore a face of Roman Catholic devotion and family unity, which he represents by an episode specifically associated with family devotion. The other side of court life, the private pursuit within the ruling family of adulterous sex, is suggested by Zoffany's insinuating *Self-Portrait* on the verso (although signed, it must function as the back of the panel). The *Self-Portrait* is also ostensibly religious. It presents the image of a man taking the habit of a Franciscan friar, a gesture that usually symbolized the rejection of the world and its delights, and indeed the painting has been interpreted as meaning just that.[15] In a reflection of the duke's practices, the habit Zoffany is putting on is specifically Capuchin, an order to which the duke was devoted. It has the distinctive, long, pointed hood: the nickname 'Cappuccini' ('hoodies') arose from this feature.

A moment's reflection reveals to the viewer, however, that, far from retreating from the pleasures of the flesh, the reason the artist is taking the habit is to make ready to enjoy them. Zoffany is actually donning a popular masquerade costume,[16] and so he is making ready for a night's entertainment, when he will be taking with him a condom (or two) from the peg on the wall in the background. There are precedents for this double entendre, especially in the work of Zoffany's key source of inspiration, William Hogarth. Zoffany's painting shares several elements with Hogarth's portrait *Sir Francis Dashwood at his Devotions* (private collection), which reflects the penchant of Dashwood and his circle for dressing up as friars and nuns in order to take part in orgies.[17] Both pictures exhibit a Franciscan habit and rosary, and Hogarth obliquely refers to a condom in the

tying of the rosary beads by means of a ribbon to a phallically erect branch. Zoffany shows actual condoms with, of course, their customary ribbon attachment. Hogarth puts a masquerade mask in place of the skull that would normally be present as a memento mori in an image of a saint at his devotions, while Zoffany shows the skull itself, although juxtaposed with a pack of cards and a carafe of wine. Hogarth replaces the crucified Christ on the Cross with a naked Venus, but Zoffany places, near the condoms, a print of the *Venus of Urbino*, which is at the same time damaged in the genital area by a tear in the shape of a condom. The rosary in Hogarth's picture, together with its cross, dangles directly over a suggestive still life of fruit, while Zoffany shows the rosary on its own, yet also gives it the shape of a vagina.

RS

1. The kit-kat was a standard European size dating back to the Renaissance, and used both for panels and canvases: Robin Simon, *The Portrait in Britain and America*, Oxford, 1987, 111 (and note). The dimensions of the two panels differ, if at all, by a matter of a half to one centimetre in either direction. The *Maize Harvest* was recorded in inventories of the royal collection in Parma in 1791 and 1805–6 but these inventories do not make any mention of the *Self-Portrait*, which did not enter the Gallery at Parma until 1917. See A.G. Quintavalle 1955a, I (Jan.–March), 12; A.O. Quintavalle 1939, 230 (inv. 1118).

2. This was in the form of a *gratificazione*, a final payment which also indicated that the artist might expect no more from the court: A.G. Quintavalle 1955b, III (July–Sept.), 201, 'Zoffany Cav. Giovanni pittore: Gratificazione. Direttore Obach per le provvidenze' (Register of the 'Azienda e Real Casa' for 12 March 1779).

3. The contract is referred to as established in a letter of 1 November 1778 requesting permission to include the name of Louis XV among those of the subscribers: Campagnola 1978, vol. 1 (March–June), 25. The Duke of Parma's affection for Ravenet is specifically mentioned.

4. The biographical dates of the younger Ravenet and of his residence in Parma were established, on the basis of Ravenet's own account given in 1797 to the post-revolutionary French government, in Campagnola 1978, vol. 1 (March–June), 22–9 (Paris, 'Archive des affaires étrangères: *Parme*', vol. 40, 353rv, vol. 46, 405–406r). Ravenet stated in 1797 that by that date he had been in Parma for thirty-eight years and that he was now aged sixty. (His father's dates also need to be revised: he was born in 1704.) Further clarification comes from Roberto Lasagni, *Dizionario biografico dei Parmigiani*, 1999, http://www.parmaelasuastoria.it (accessed 26 Nov. 2010). Ravenet the Younger was born Simon Jean François Ravenet on 18 May 1737 in Paris and died in Parma on 16 April 1821.

5. His print of the *Madonna della Scudella* of 1778 (British Museum 1837,0408.116) initiated the series, which continued until 1797, when fifteen plates had been made. For his 1782 print after Zoffany's portrait of Don Ferdinando, see Adorni *et al.* 1979, cat. 759; and especially Davide Gasparotto and Mariangela Giusto, ed., *Principi in Posa, Rittratti del Settecento alla Galleria Nazionale di Parma. Nuove acquisizioni e restauri*, exh. cat., Galleria Nazionale, Parma, 20 Jan.–17 April 2006,

pub. Milan, 2005, 82 (fig. 27), where the important
point is made that the Ravenet is after the (presumably
autograph) version of the portrait on canvas in a
French private collection (sold in New York in 1998),
rather than after that attributed to Zoffany (and on
panel) in the Galleria Nazionale, Parma, which appears
to post-date Zoffany's visit.

6. It also bears some resemblance in reverse to Raphael's
Orléans Madonna (1506) at Chantilly.

7. Badinter 2008, 90–91, and see 91 n. 1 for a medical
assessment of the problems of the duke's penis.
See cat. 62 for details of the expulsion of the French
courtiers.

8. Badinter 2008, 93: 'On s'aperçoit qu'il craint l'infante.'
As the grandson of Philip V of Spain, Ferdinando
was correctly titled (in Spanish) 'Infante' and his
wife 'Infanta', in French 'Infant' and 'Infante'.

9. J.J. Lefrançois de Lalande, *Voyage en Italie & les
anecdotes les plus singulieres de l'Italie …*, Venice 1769,
2nd ed. (corrigée et augmentée), 9 vols., Paris, 1786,
vol. 2, 127.

10. Giuseppe Bertini and Francesco Sandrini, eds.,
Il Bigotto Illuminato (Quaderni del Museo no. 5),
exh. cat., Museo Glauco Lombardi, Parma, 2002.

11. 'On peut se faire moine et n'être plus prince, mais
quand on est prince, on ne peut sans ridicule être
moine' (quoted in Badinter 2008, 104–5.)

12. Gorani uses the term 'jeter le mouchoir', which refers
to the supposed habit of a sultan in his harem, who
would throw a handkerchief at the woman he had
chosen to sleep with.

13. G. Gorani, *Mémoires secrets et critiques des cours, des
gouvernements et des moeurs des principaux Etats en Italie*,
1793, vol. III, 296–7 (quoted in Badinter 2008,
150–51.)

14. 'Ce moine libertin' (Badinter 2008, 155).

15. Webster 2011, 367.

16. A notably lavish masquerade in Parma, attended
by the duchess 'ed altri cavalieri', took place on
22 February 1778: Cusatelli *et al.* 1997, 372.

17. See R. Simon 2007, 204ff., for masquerades and a
full account of Hogarth's picture.

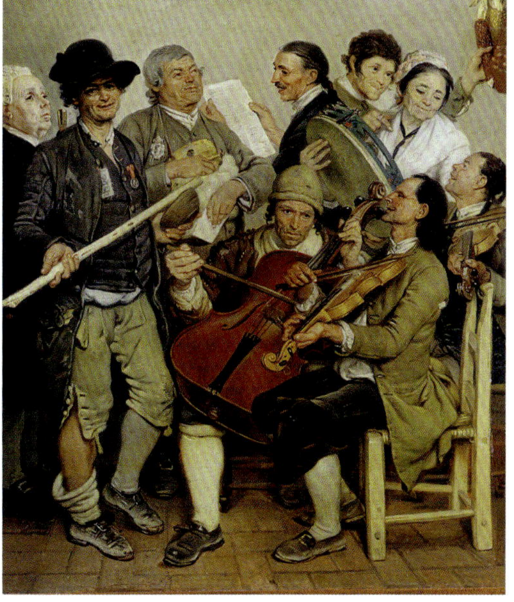

62

'La Scartocciata', the Festival of
the Maize Harvest
1778

Oil on panel, 43.5 × 38 cm (17⅛ × 15 in)
Galleria Nazionale di Parma

Provenance: Probably painted for Ferdinando,
Duke of Parma; Inventory, Royal Collection,
Parma, 1791; recorded again 1805–6; given by
Maria Luigia, Duchess of Parma, to the gallery,
1821; taken back 1851 by Luisa Maria di Borbone,
Duchess Regent of Parma (exiled 1859);
Guardamobili ducale, Parma, until 1865 when
placed by the state in the Pinacoteca (Ricci 1896)

Selected exhibitions: National Portrait Gallery 1977,
no. 85; Parma 1979, no. 123; *L'anima e il Volto:
Ritratto e fisiognomica da Leonardo a Bacon*, Milan,
1998, 364–7 (ill.); *Il Gran Teatro del Mondo; l'Anima e
il Volto del Settecento*, Palazzo Reale, Milan, 2003–4,
no. II.171

Selected references: Ricci 1896, 15; A.O. Quintavalle
1939, 230; A.G. Quintavalle 1955a, I (Jan.–March),
7–15, 12, 15 n. 11, fig. 7; Schianchi 2000, cat. 790;
Treadwell 2009, 284–6; Webster 2011, 356, 364–7

The festival of stripping the maize took place at
Parma in October each year and so Zoffany would
have seen it in 1778.[1] It took place in the evening,
under the eye of the farm's proprietor who would
serve a meal at about eleven or midnight, followed
by music and dancing, accompanied by 'one or
two violins'.

In Zoffany's painting, as so often, things are
not quite as they seem. The proprietor, the eminent
French architect Ennemond-Alexandre Petitot,
stands at the extreme left of the composition,
holding a gold-topped cane.[2] His country house was
in Marore, just south of Parma, and so we imagine
that is the purported location of the festival. One
problem, however, is that Petitot does not seem to
be enjoying the occasion.[3] Another is why, since
the picture was in the royal collection, Petitot is
represented, because by the time of Zoffany's
arrival in Parma he had long since been dismissed
from the court. The explanation must be that this
kind of entertainment was very much to the taste
of Ferdinando, Duke of Parma (see fig. 79), and not
at all to that of Petitot, whose expression is one of
foppish distaste: indeed, he holds the top of his cane
up to his mouth, a gesture that was a contemporary
'signifier' of a fop.[4] Petitot had joined the court
under Ferdinando's father Filippo, as one of a group
of French Enlightenment stars overseen by the
prime minister Guillaume du Tillot. One of their
principal tasks was to educate the young
Ferdinando as a 'prince des lumières'. They failed
and were horrified by his preference for the
company of peasants and for speaking the dialect of
Parma instead of French. In particular, Ferdinando
developed a taste for nocturnal festivities of
precisely the kind shown in this picture, which he
would encourage in a building adjoining his palace
at Colorno called 'the pheasantry'. These events
also indulged his preference for peasant women
over his wife.[5]

Following his marriage in 1769, Ferdinando and
his wife had, however, been united in their desire to
get rid of the French courtiers, which they achieved
with the dismissal of du Tillot, who left Parma
on 19 November 1771 to the sound of the crowd,
whipped up by the duchess, shouting 'Death to the
tyrant Dutillot'.[6] Petitot was 'marginalized' the
same month[7] and in 1773 was formally replaced
as court architect. When Zoffany painted the
Maize Harvest in late 1778 or early 1779, Petitot's
energies had been redirected to teaching in the
Parma Academy,[8] and he was stuck in the country.[9]
The picture records an entertainment of which the
duke was especially fond; in fact Pietro Martini,
secretary of the Parma Academy from the 1860s,
stated that the picture had been 'painted at
Colorno where these poor musicians cheered
Duke Ferdinando … with their instruments',
and Quintavalle remarked that it 'calls to mind
the frequent delight of the Duke at Colorno'.[10]
Meanwhile, Petitot's disapproving presence
records the reaction of one of the discomfited –

but surviving – French 'Lumières' towards such unseemly goings-on.[11]

Zoffany's remarkable freedom of brushwork aids the impression of an impromptu performance, but each individual is depicted with great precision, as he indicates the clash of classes apparent on such occasions. Although Petitot has a gold-topped cane, he is apparently affected by the low company he is forced to keep: his feet are clumsily positioned like those of a peasant, rather than at an angle of ninety degrees, as courtly deportment demanded.[12] Indeed, the seated blind musician in the right foreground, facing Petitot across the picture's space, has his feet more correctly positioned, although he gives the game away by squashing his hat onto his knee: a gentleman would have it tucked under his arm.

RS

1. Médéric Louis Élie Moreau de Saint-Méry, quoted in Webster 1976, 67–8, and Webster 2011, 366–7. The title refers to the act of stripping the ears of corn: *scartocciare* means to take a wrapping off.
2. The likeness is confirmed by comparison with Petitot's watercolour *Self-Portrait*; see Cusatelli *et al.* 1997, pl. 7.
3. Treadwell 2009, 284, notes the oddity of the portrait.
4. R. Simon 2007, 265ff., and see figs. 235, 236, 238, 240.
5. Badinter 2008, 149.
6. Giorgio Cusatelli and Fausto Razzetti, *Il Viaggio a Parma, visitatori stranieri in età farnese e borbonica*, Parma, 1990, 76–7.
7. Cusatelli *et al.* 1997, 371.
8. Where Ravenet taught engraving and was shortly to become director. The joke is mild enough to have been one that Zoffany, Ravenet and Petitot (whom we must presume was also well known to Zoffany, an *accademico d'onore*) could share.
9. In a letter of 27 August 1776 Petitot wrote: 'Here [at his *maison de campagne* at Marore] is Petitot, he who would not exchange the fortune he presently enjoys for that of a [court] favourite; he finds himself in a house in the country, as you know, where he cultivates a little land decked out with vegetables and flowers.' (Cusatelli *et al.* 1997, 372.) The French original is quoted in full by Roberto Tassi, 'Ennemond-Alexandre Petitot', in Adorni *et al.* 1979, 261, who affirms that there are no works documented as carried out by Petitot for the court in Parma after 1771, his last having been the design of the 'Mascarade à la Grecque' that year.
10. A.G. Quintavalle 1955a, I, 12. Martini catalogue of the collection (1872), quoted Ricci 1896, 15–16.
11. Petitot was out of sight but not out of mind, as his pre-existing designs were still being implemented at Colorno during the 1770s, for example, the chapels of S. Liborio and S. Bernardo in 1775. Marco Pellegri, *Colorno: Villa Ducale*, Parma, 1981, e.g. 102, 104–5. Cusatelli *et al.* 1997, 372. See also Marco Pellegri, *Ennemondo Alessandro Petitot 1727–1801: architetto francese alla real corte dei Borboni di Parma*, Parma, 1965. Schianchi sensed the oddity of Petitot's presence in this painting, in 'Le ricche spoglie dell'arte a Parma nel Settecento', Schianchi 2000, xiii–liv: li.
12. This was one of the most conscious indications of social rank throughout Europe in the eighteenth century: R. Simon 2007, 161ff.

Charles Townley's Library, No. 7 Park Street, Westminster

1781–3, 1792, 1798

Oil on canvas, 123.5 × 99.5 cm (48⅝ × 39⅛ in)
Burnley Borough Council, Towneley Hall Art Gallery & Museums, purchased with the Assistance of the National Art Collections Fund, 1939

Provenance: Given by Zoffany to Charles Townley; by descent to the third Lord O'Hagan; Christie's, 19 May 1939 (92); purchased by Burnley Corporation with funds from the Edward Stocks Massey Bequest

Selected exhibitions: Royal Academy of Arts, 1790, no. 191; British Institution, 1814, no. 92*; British Institution, 1849, no. 124; Victoria and Albert Museum, 1868; Burlington Fine Arts Club, 1904; International Fine Arts Exhibition, Rome, 1911; British Empire Exhibition, 1924–5; *English Taste in the Eighteenth Century*, Royal Academy of Arts, 1955; Arts Council 1960–61; *Pictures from the Provinces*, Royal Academy of Arts, 1961–2; Royal Academy and V&A 1972, no. 285; National Portrait Gallery 1977, no. 95; *Pinturas Britanicas: Obras Maestras de Hogarth a Turner*, Prado, Madrid, 1988–9; *The Portrait in British Art*, National Portrait Gallery, 1991, no. 36; Tate 1996, no. 215; *Art Treasures of England: The Regional Collections*, Royal Academy of Arts, 1998, no. 8; *2000 ans de création, d'après l'Antique*, Louvre, Paris, 2000–2001; *Ricordi dell'Antico. Sculture, porcellane e arredi all'epoca del Grand Tour*, Capitoline Museum, Rome, 2008, no. 10.

Selected references: Manners & Williamson 1920, 121–4; Mary Webster, 'Zoffany's Painting of Charles Towneley's Library in Park St. Westminster', *Burlington Magazine*, vol. 106, no. 736 (July 1964), 316–23; Paulson 1975, 152–3; B.F. Cook, *The Townley Marbles*, London, 1985, 30–37; Gerard Vaughan, 'Reflections on "Charles Towneley and his friends"', *Apollo*, vol. 144, Nov. 1996, 32–5; Colette Crossman, 'Priapus in Park Street: Revealing Zoffany's Subtext in "Charles Townley and Friends"', *British Art Journal*, VI, no. 1, Spring 2005, 71; Viccy Coltman, 'Representation, replication and collecting in Charles Townley's late eighteenth-century library', *Art History*, April 2006, vol. 29, issue 2, 304–24; Viccy Coltman, *Fabricating the Antique: Neoclassicism in Britain, 1760–1800*, Chicago and London, 2006, 19, 22, 54–5, 165–72, 182–3, 188, 196; Coltman 2009, 164–71; Treadwell 2009, 256, 321–5, 396; Webster 2011, 419–43

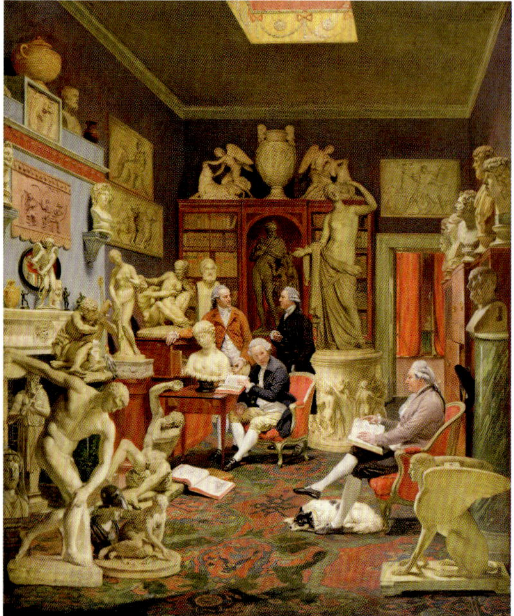

In 1780 Zoffany exhibited the *Tribuna of the Uffizi* at the Royal Academy. The following year, on 16 August, Charles Townley wrote to James Byres in Rome: 'Mr. Zoffany is painting, in the Stile of his Florence tribune, a room in my house, wherein he introduces what Subjects he chuses in my collection. It will be a picture of extraordinary effect and truth.'[1] A month later, Townley's younger sister Cecilia wrote from his house at 7 Park Street, Westminster: 'Zoffany has been here at yᵉ picture some days this last week, I wish much to see it finished.'[2] On 23 November 1782 the *Morning Herald* reported: 'Zoffani is now at work on a picture, the plan of which is similar to that painted for the King, the gallery at Florence. – A groupe of portraits in small whole length, and the noble collecion of Mr. Townley's statues, busts &c. in the background.' Following his return to England, having worked on it again, Zoffany exhibited the picture at the Royal Academy as 'A nobleman's collection'. Zoffany's painting of Charles Townley and his friends at his London home in Park Street, Westminster, was not a commission in the routine manner. Rather, it was conceived as a labour of love, a microcosm of the enlightened antiquarian culture to which Zoffany had a deep personal attachment. And, although he is not in this instance depicted in the picture, it reveals as much about Zoffany's taste and cultural interests as those of the four men portrayed.

The room depicted is a top-lit room on the first floor of Park Street, where Townley kept his library. Townley sits, cross-legged, in the right foreground, his profile echoing the bust of Homer above, while his dog Kam, snoozing on the carpet at his feet, echoes the marble sphinx at his side.[3] Kam, like Townley, was something of a traveller and celebrity, having served on Captain Cook's third and final voyage as a sled dog.[4] Occupying

the armchair at the centre of the composition
is Pierre-François Hugues, the self-styled 'Baron
d'Hancarville'. Hugues, who had arrived in London
from Italy in 1776, was a notorious figure who had
hitherto enjoyed a chequered career as a classical
scholar, book publisher, art dealer, pornographer
and all round 'adventurer'. Compelled to resettle in
Florence in 1770, he also probably first met Zoffany
there. The man standing behind d'Hancarville to
the left, in the light brown coat, is Charles Francis
Greville, younger son of the Earl of Warwick, who
had already established a reputation as a mineral
collector and who had in 1772, probably through
the agency of Sir Joseph Banks, been elected a
Fellow of the Royal Society. At the time he was
painted by Zoffany, Greville was also conducting
an affair with the sixteen-year-old Emma Hart
(née Lyon), which may explain his close proximity
to the celebrated bust of the nymph Clytie,
Townley's favourite sculpture and the one he had
engraved on his calling card. Listening to Greville
to the right, in profile and dressed in black, is
Thomas Astle, an authority on ancient manuscripts
and, like Greville, a Fellow of the Royal Society.
Astle, a noted palaeographer and Keeper of Records
at the Tower of London, was at this time engaged
on what was to be his most important work,
The Origin and Progress of Writing, published in
1784. Collectively, the four men assembled in the
painting represented the kind of informed, liberal
(even libertine) homosocial company that Zoffany
relished most.

Born at the family's country seat, Towneley Hall
near Burnley, Lancashire, and tutored at a Jesuit
college in France, Charles Townley travelled to
Italy in 1767 on the first of three visits. A dedicated
Grand Tourist, in pursuit of sexual conquests
and art in equal measure, Townley assembled an
impressive collection of antiquities, vases, gems,
coins, books, old master drawings and paintings.
It was in Italy also that Townley probably first

met Zoffany, who was to become a lifelong friend.
Following his return from Italy in 1774, Townley
had purchased the lease on a newly constructed
house at 7 Park Street (now 14 Queen Anne's Gate,
according to the Survey of London, 1926), which he
developed and decorated specifically to display his
collection of antique sculpture, coins, vases, old
master drawings, paintings and manuscripts.
The collection was open to visitors and artists who
wished to study and copy the objects on display, as
shown in two watercolours by William Chambers
(fig. 188). Townley himself entertained company
there on Sundays, when it was noted that 'Sir
Joshua Reynolds and Zoffany generally enlivened
the circle'.[5] Zoffany, as he worked on his own
painting, must have also made frequent visits to
Park Street to make copies of the various objects,
Townley noting early in 1783 a payment to his
mason for 'moving figures for Zoffany'.[6] Indeed,
it is almost certain that the picture was created
almost entirely, and retained, in Townley's house
rather than in Zoffany's studio. As it has often
been noted, Zoffany took considerable liberties in
the manner in which he represented Townley's
collection, altering their size and colour (toning
down their whiteness), as well as bringing them
together in a single space, when in reality the
majority were disbursed over various parts of
the house, the larger ones immoveable in the
ground-floor dining room. His continuing
attention to the picture well into the 1790s was
conditioned by Townley's expanding collection.
The figure of the Discus Thrower (Discobolos)
in the left foreground, acquired from the dealer
Thomas Jenkins in 1793, was the final sculpture
to be introduced – somewhat uncomfortably – in
the summer of 1798, Townley noting in his diary
on 19 July that Zoffany 'finished & varnished his
picture'.[7] Shortly afterwards Zoffany presented
the painting to Townley, who appears to have been
gratefully surprised by the gift. On acquiring
Zoffany's picture, Charles Townley took it on
himself to have it engraved. In the event, it proved
to be an extraordinarily contracted process, the
final engraving by William Henry Worthington
being published in 1833, with a key to the
individuals and objects. Following Townley's
death in 1805, his collection of antiquities was
purchased by the British Museum.

That Zoffany, as artist, played the pivotal role
in orchestrating the display of objects in his
picture is clear. The relative roles of Townley and
d'Hancarville in the evolution of Zoffany's pictorial
space are more speculative and relate to perceptions
of the manner in which the 'Baron' was influencing
his protégé's liberal attitude towards pagan cults
and rituals, a heady cocktail of primitive mysticism
in which antique art was related to even more
ancient mythologies, rife with sexual imagery and
symbolism. At the very time Zoffany was working
on the picture, d'Hancarville was immersed in the
research that was to result in his *Recherches sur*

l'origine, l'esprit et les progrès des arts de la Grèce,
published in three volumes in 1785–6. It is
therefore no coincidence that those sculptures that
best conform to d'Hancarville's sexually fuelled
theories are also prominent in Zoffany's picture:
the *Venus*, the bust of Clytie, the Drunken Silenus,
the grappling figures of the Nymph and Satyr,
as well as the Bacchanalian wall reliefs and the
so-called 'Townley vase', depicting priapic rituals.[8]
Viewed in such a context, the licentious antics of
the sculptures to the left of the painting are all the
more notable when confronted by the solemn row
of profiled busts of philosophers and dignitaries
lined up against the right-hand wall. It is also
significant, in the context of d'Hancarville's
theories, that the room chosen as the setting for
Zoffany's picture was Townley's library. For, as
Viccy Coltman has observed, Townley's book
collection and his collection of antiquities were
inextricably related. The point is demonstrated
by the tomes that Townley and d'Hancarville pore
over, as well as the book on the floor by the statue
of the Drunken Silenus, volume 6 of *Antichità di
Ercolano esposte* (1771), which lies open at plate 42,
depicting a similar bronze sculpture recently
excavated at Herculaneum and then on display at
the Royal Museum in Naples.[9] This extraordinary
picture was, then, an imaginative visual record
of an ongoing intellectual dialogue between the
present and the ancient past, and an emblem of
Enlightenment enquiry shaped by the collection
of Townley, the ideas of d'Hancarville and the
pictorial genius of Zoffany. It was a 'conversation
piece' to surpass all others.

MP

1. Vaughan 1996, 32.
2. Webster 1976, 72.
3. I am grateful to Jonathan Yarker for this observation.
4. Kam's name related to a particularly breed of sled dog
   used by the natives of Kamchatka, and also to his role
   in conveying the king's dispatches to the Russian
   commander of the Kamchatka peninsula in Siberia.
   See Smith 1828–30, vol. 1, 259; Vaughan 1996, 35 n. 6;
   Webster 2011, 439.
5. Smith 1828–30, vol. 1, 258.
6. Webster 2011, 429.
7. Webster 2011, 434.
8. Vaughan 1996, 33; Webster 2011, 433.
9. Coltman 2006, 23, 54–5.

Figure 188
William Chambers, *The Sculpture Collection of Charles
Townley, Park Street*, 1794, pen and grey ink and
watercolour, with some bodycolour, on washline
mount, 39 × 54 cm (15⅜ × 21¼ in). British Museum,
Department of Prints and Drawings

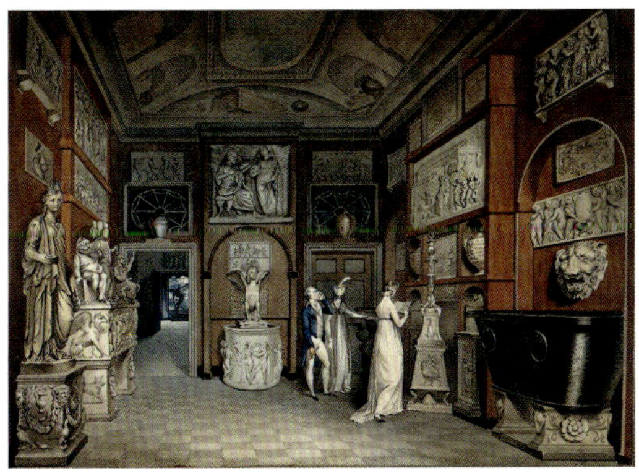

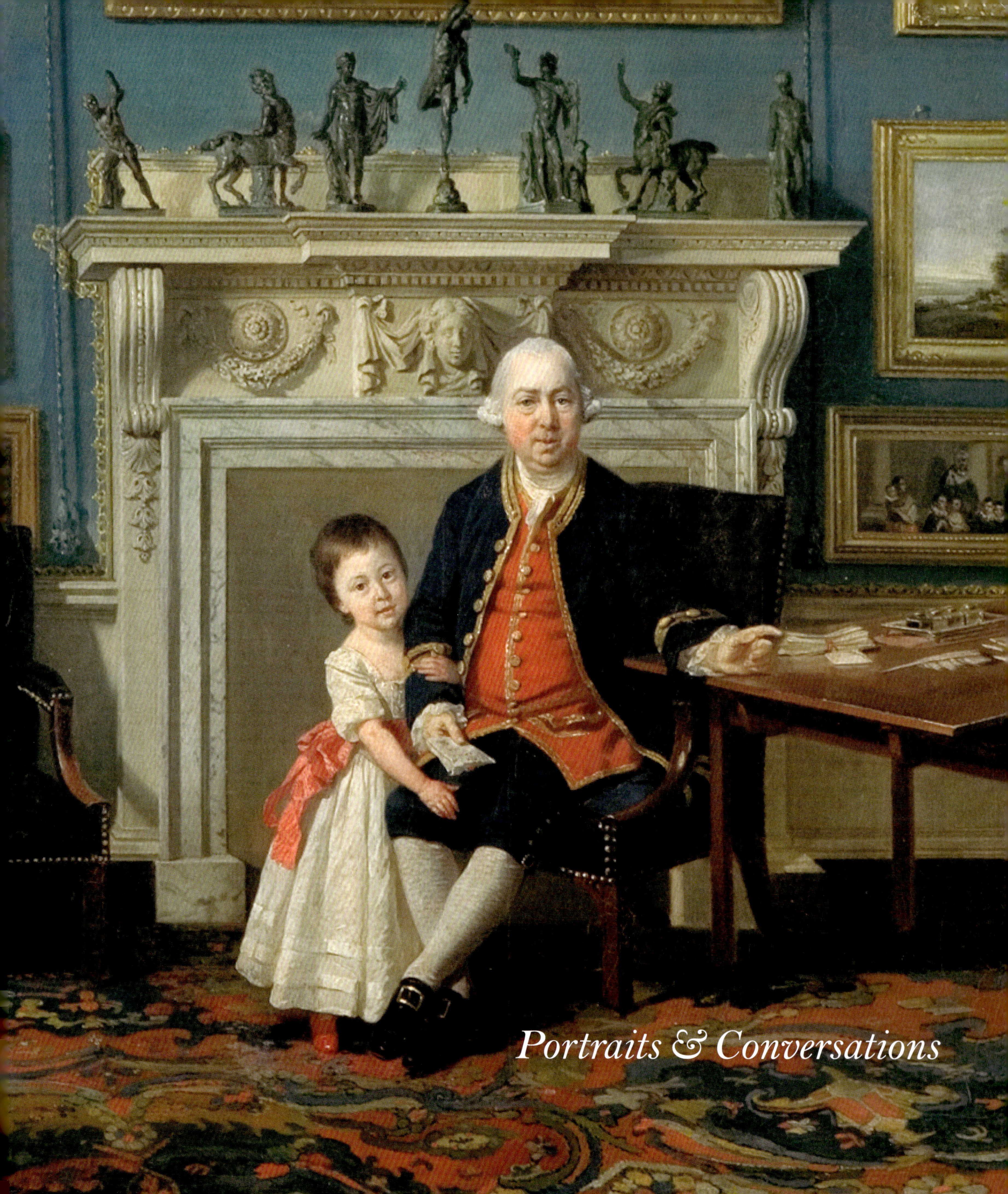
Portraits & Conversations

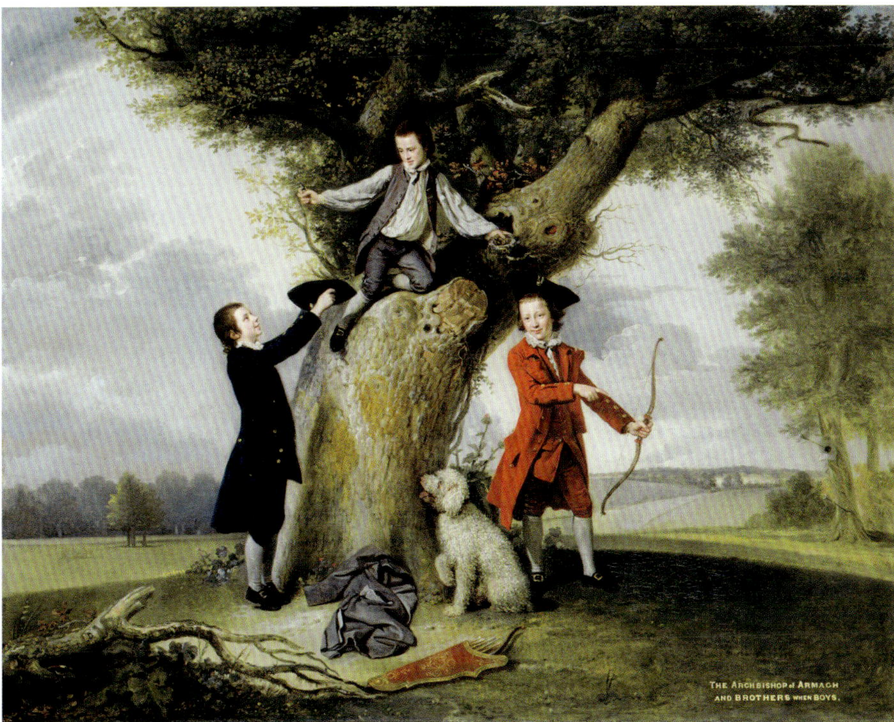

64

Three Sons of John, Third Earl of Bute
1763–4

Oil on canvas, 100.9 × 126 cm (39¾ × 49⅝ in)
Tate, London; accepted by H.M. Government in
lieu of tax with additional payment (General
Funds) made with assistance from the National
Lottery through the Heritage Lottery Fund,
the National Art Collections Fund and Tate
Members 2002

Selected exhibitions: National Portrait Gallery 1977,
no. 20; Bath 2005, no. 12

Selected references: Manners & Williamson 1920, 17;
Webster 1976, 30; Treadwell 2009, 97–8, 103–5;
Webster 2011, 127–30

Accounts of how Zoffany met one of his most
important and influential early patrons, John
Stuart, third Earl of Bute, vary. Some sources
suggest that he was introduced by another client,
Lord Barrington; others that Bute had known and
approved of Zoffany's work for David Garrick in
1762.[1] The fact that Bute's art collection contained
a number of Dutch and Flemish works reveals him
to have had a taste for the kind of intricate detail
and high finish that Zoffany offered.[2] The stylistic
qualities that Zoffany shared with such artists as
Adriaen van Ostade, Gabriel Metsu, Frans van
Mieris and Aelbert Cuyp are richly apparent in
the three paintings of Bute's children he executed
around 1763–4: one of the earl's eldest son, John,
Lord Mountstuart (see fig. 108); one of his three
youngest daughters (cat. 65); and the present,
pendant portrait of his three youngest sons. These
commissions mark a crucial moment in Zoffany's

career, as it must have been Bute, trusted friend
and mentor of George III, who introduced Zoffany
to the king and queen.

Charles Stuart (1753–1801) perches
precariously in the branches of a large oak, having
ascended the tree on a mission to raid a bird's nest.
He holds the nest full of cheeping chicks in one
hand, as he passes the parent down to his younger
brother, William. Meanwhile, the eldest brother,
Frederick, is engaged in archery practice.[3]
He invites our admiration for his skill, proudly
gesturing to a bull's eye pinned to a brightly lit
tree. While his first arrow has gone badly astray,
hitting the trunk near the base, his second has
scored a direct hit.

The painting is redolent with the theme of
elite, landed, masculine privilege. Indeed, archery
had recently experienced a resurgence within
aristocratic culture. Frederick's eldest brother,
Lord Mountstuart, had earlier been painted by
Allan Ramsay in the pink satin uniform of the
Harrow Archers.[4] The figure of Frederick
practising with his bow may recall that earlier
portrait – and perhaps also a painting by Nicolas
Lancret entitled *Four Ages of Man: La Jeunesse*,
owned by Bute and now in the National Gallery,
which prominently features two archers.

The motif of bird nesting was a popular one
for portraits of young boys, to be reused by Zoffany
in *The Drummond Family* of 1769 (cat. 69). It was
not without problematic connotations, as writers
at this time emphasized the importance of teaching
children to be kind to the animal world.[5] But bird
nesting could also be seen to reveal properly male
urges that could be shaped into appropriate adult

activities, primarily hunting. This is suggested by
the three fallow deer grazing in the background.

This narrative conceit may well have also had
particular significance in light of recent dramatic
events in Bute's career. He had swiftly risen to be
First Lord of the Treasury in May 1762, but it
had not been a happy ascendance. As John Brewer
has observed: 'Few politicians can have been
as maligned, insulted and manhandled as John
Stuart.'[6] Bute was castigated for apparent undue
influence over George, popularly rumoured to be
amorously entwined with George's mother and
vilified for his nationality in an era of rampant
Scottophobia. He was also seen as overly full of his
station. Matters got worse when the Peace of Paris,
the resolution to the Seven Years War towards
which Bute had strived for some time, was formally
ratified in February 1763. The treaty was widely
criticized as being unfavourable to Britain.

Bute resigned and went into rural retirement at
his Bedfordshire estate, Luton Hoo, around the time
that Zoffany painted the pendant portraits of his
children in its grounds. The image of Bute's sons
focuses on aristocratic privilege, landownership
and the right to hunt, the positive values of life on
a large country estate. It emphasizes martial spirit
and those masculine qualities popularly seen to
secure a future generation of leaders and heroes.
It thus appears to take an assertive tone in the face
of popular criticism of Bute and his career.

KR

1. See Webster 2011, 125.
2. For Bute's collection, see Francis Harris, *John, Third
   Earl of Bute: Patron and Collector* (London, 2004),
   esp. 183–4, 197–8. See also G.F. Waagen, *Works of
   Art and Artists in England*, 3 vols. (London, 1838),
   vol. 3, 357–77.
3. There is some inconsistency in the identification of
   the brothers. This entry follows the most recent
   interpretation provided in Bath 2005, 41, and
   Webster 2011, 43–4.
4. Alastair Smart, *Allan Ramsay: A Complete Catalogue
   of his Paintings* (New Haven and London, 1999),
   85–6, cat. 70.
5. A point also made in the first scene of William
   Hogarth's *Four Stages of Cruelty*, 1751.
6. John Brewer, 'The Misfortunes of Lord Bute:
   A Case-Study in Eighteenth-Century Political
   Argument and Public Opinion', *The Historical
   Journal*, 16, 1 (March 1973): 3.

65

Three Daughters of John, Third Earl of Bute
1763–4

Oil on canvas, 101.2 × 126.5 cm (39⅞ × 49¾ in)
Tate, London; accepted by H.M. Government
in lieu of tax with additional payment (General
Funds) made with assistance from the National
Lottery through the Heritage Lottery Fund,
the National Art Collections Fund and Tate
Members 2002

Provenance: Commissioned by John Stuart,
third Earl of Bute; by descent; Tate

Selected exhibitions: National Portrait Gallery
1977, no. 21; Bath 2005, no. 13

Selected references: Treadwell 2009, 103–5;
Webster 2011, 127, 130

Zoffany's paired portraits of the youngest
daughters and sons (cat. 64) of John Stuart,
third Earl of Bute, complement one another in
their similarities and differences. Each depicts
three children, painted on the same-size canvas.
Each is dominated by a large, central tree, shown
against a low horizon. In each, Zoffany has elevated
one figure through a suitable narrative device in
order to create a broadly triangular grouping.
However, the activities of the two sets of children
are contrasted through opposing characteristics
associated with their respective genders. While
bird nesting and archery are 'proper' occupations
for Bute's sons, his daughters are engaged in
activities that suggest their nurturing qualities.

Louisa reaches up to encourage her squirrel to
descend from the tree, while her sister Caroline has
managed to keep hold of her own pet. Caroline's
more senior years are not only indicated by her
greater level of responsibility but also by her deep
blue satin robe, contrasting with Louisa's childish
costume. Anne, seated between her sisters, is the
eldest of the three and adopts the role of substitute
mother, raising a warning hand to Louisa while
looking back over her shoulder to attend to
Caroline's welfare. Her presence in the portrait
helps to pinpoint a date of execution before the
summer of 1764, when Anne married Hugh
Percy, Lord Warkworth.

The Palladian building on the right can be
identified as the gateway to the park at Luton Hoo,
as it also appears in one of a series of drawings of
the extensive grounds executed by Paul Sandby at
around the same time (fig. 189).[1] Indeed, Zoffany
may have used this image as a model.[2] The painting
predates work done on the house and grounds by,
respectively, Robert Adam and Capability Brown,
although discussions over the development of
Luton Park are likely to have been in progress.[3]
Since the sale of Cane Wood (now Kenwood) in
1754, Bute had not possessed a country estate.
A boost to his wealth in 1761, thanks to the death
of his father-in-law and the advantageous marriage

of his eldest daughter, combined with the decline
of his political fortunes, encouraged him to look for
a new seat near London. He settled on Luton Hoo,
being sold by Francis Hearne, the following year
and retreated to the estate in the autumn of 1763.

It seems likely that the portraits of Bute's
children were conceived before the novelty of life
outside London wore off. By the following March
the earl was declaring to John Home: 'You will
probably find me in town, not from any business
that I can have there, but from its suiting better my
age and spirits than a country life, which I have now
six months of.'[4] The property provided yet more
ammunition for his critics. In 1765 a diatribe by
'Anti-Sejanus' in the *Public Advertiser* complained:
'Have we not seen him for a long Time displaying
his exorbitant Treasures, in every kind of princely
Profusion? Has not he purchased Estates, built
and adorned Villas, erected Palaces, and furnished
them with sumptuous Magnificence?'[5]

KR

1. Sold Christie's, 3 July 1996, lot 109. The series of
   Sandby views were sold as lots 103–14. I should like to
   thank John Bonehill for discussions on Luton Park and
   the Sandby pictures. See John Bonehill and Stephen
   Daniels, eds., *Paul Sandby: Picturing Britain* (London,
   2009), 211–14, cats 89–91.
2. For this suggestion see Webster 2011, 130, fig. 121.
3. A first contract was agreed with Brown for work
   begun in October 1764. See Russell 2004, 167.
4. Earl of Bute to John Home, 9 March 1764, quoted in
   Russell 2004, 69.
5. *Public Advertiser*, 3 Aug. 1765.

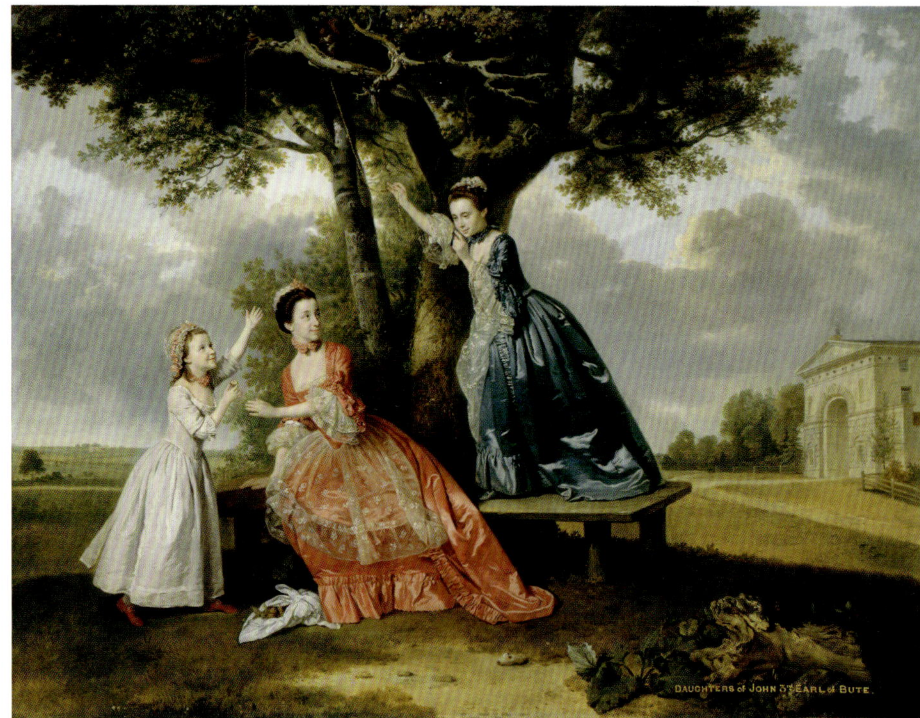

Figure 189
Paul Sandby, *Cattle and Figures with an old Man on a
Horse selling Cherries, before a Palladian Gatehouse, in the
Park at Luton*, date unknown, pencil, pen and ink and
watercolour with touches of white heightening,
45.1 × 101 cm (17¾ × 39¾ in). Private collection

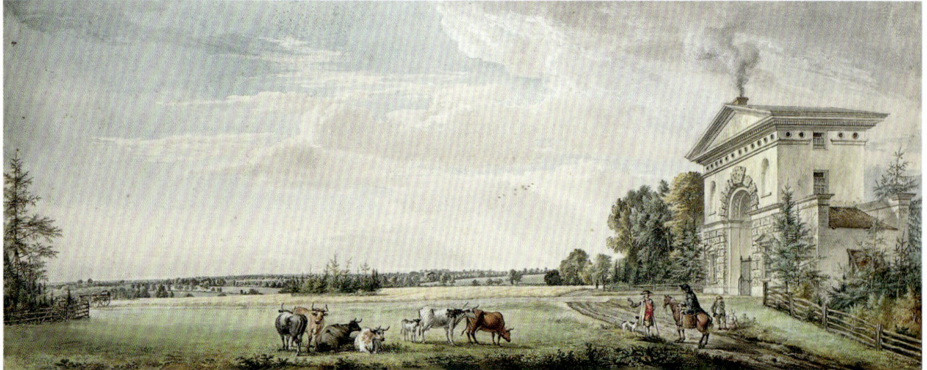

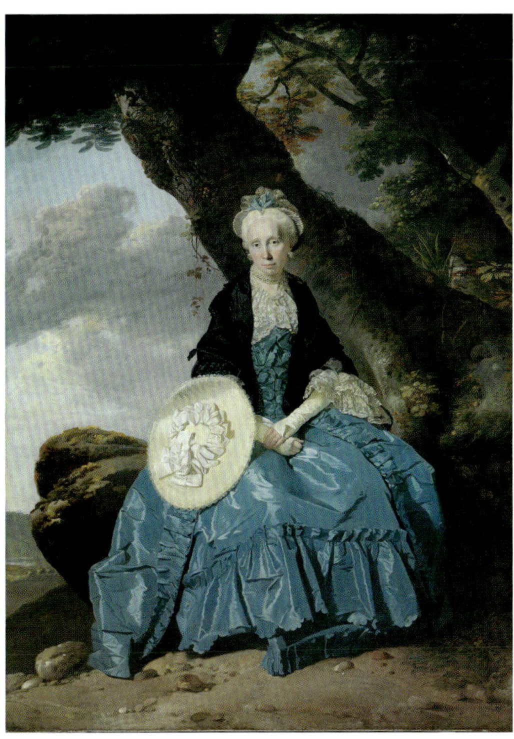

66

Mrs Oswald
1763–5

Oil on canvas, 226.5 × 158.8 (89⅛ × 62½ in)
National Gallery, London; bought 1938

Exhibited at the Yale Center for British Art only

Provenance: Presumably commissioned by Richard Oswald; following the sitter's death in 1788, passed to Oswald's nephew and heir, George Oswald; by descent to Richard Alexander Oswald of Auchincruive (d. 1921), by whose executors sold Sotheby's 14 June 1922 (106); purchased by Leggatt Brothers for Lord Lee of Fareham, from whom purchased by the National Gallery in 1938

Selected exhibitions: Glasgow Institute, 1914, no. 430; Royal Academy 1934, no. 271; National Portrait Gallery 1977, no. 28

Selected references: Manners & Williamson 1920, 159, 166 n. 2, 224–5; Tancred Borenius, *A Catalogue of Pictures, Etc. … Collected by Viscount and Viscountess Lee of Fareham*, Oxford, 1923, 111–12; Davies 1959, 111–12, no. 4931; Egerton 1998, 350–55; Treadwell 2009, 141–2; Webster 2011, 106–9

Mary Oswald was around fifty years old, and very rich, when Zoffany painted her portrait. The only daughter of a Scottish merchant and plantation owner, she had inherited several fortunes before her marriage, in 1750, to the slave trader and ship owner Richard Oswald. At this time she placed in trust her 'Land Tenements Hereditaments … Goods, Chattels, Real or personal, Negroes … or effects Whatsoever & wheresoever belonging to her … either in the Island of Jamaica or in Great Britain'.[1] Following their marriage, the Oswalds lived in Great George Street, Westminster, although in the early 1760s Mr Oswald, who aspired towards gentrification, acquired a fortified manor house and estates at Auchincruive, in South Ayrshire. Using plans made by Robert Adam for the previous owner and commissioning new designs from him, Oswald set about improving and modernizing the property, which was completed in the late 1760s. It was for Oswald's new house that the present portrait was no doubt commissioned. And it was there, until the 1920s when the family gave up the house, that it remained.

Money was no object when it came to commissioning Mrs Oswald's portrait. It is therefore worth speculating why her husband chose Zoffany – who at this time had no track record in painting full-length portraiture – as opposed to Reynolds, Cotes or Ramsay, all top-flight, London-based society portraitists. A Scottish connection may have been a factor, for by this time Zoffany's patrons included prominent Scottish aristocrats, including the Earl of Bute and the Duke of Atholl. By now Zoffany was also patronized by the king and was generally admired for the pictures he exhibited at the annual Society of Artists' exhibitions. Oswald himself was known as a man of some taste and over the years acquired an art collection, including Dutch and Italian baroque paintings.[2] Thus, even though Zoffany had yet to produce a work on this scale, Oswald must have had confidence in his network of influential patrons and his technical ability; confidence that was amply rewarded by Zoffany's assured performance in the present portrait.

In Zoffany's portrait Mrs Oswald is seated on a wooded promontory, intended presumably to overlook her husband's newly acquired estate, with in the distance, to the left, the River Ayr and a suggestion of the recently remodelled house with its battlemented tower. According to family tradition, Mr Oswald had originally also been included in the picture, although he had objected, compelling Zoffany to cover him with a cloud. Technical investigation, however, has revealed little evidence to support such an assertion.[3] Mrs Oswald is dressed in the height of fashion in a blue taffeta dress with bows and lace sleeve ruffles. Around her neck hang rows of pearls and below, a lace 'modesty piece', consistent with her self-contained pose and steely gaze. The principal glory of the portrait is Mrs Oswald's bright blue taffeta sacque dress,

a dazzling display of painterly virtuosity. In full-length portraits of the period it was common practice, in the painting of elaborate dresses with bows and ruches, to employ a professional drapery painter. And, indeed, it has been suggested that Zoffany at times used the services of Peter Toms, a prominent drapery painter employed by Reynolds and Cotes among others.[4] However, the liveliness of touch in the present draperies, the way in which, for example, the blue of the dress is reflected in the cream silk glove, or the shadows play across the straw hat, suggests that Zoffany himself was responsible for the entire composition. It is also worth recalling that shortly after his arrival in England Zoffany had been offered a three-year contract as a drapery painter to the portraitist Benjamin Wilson. According to one source, Wilson gave him 'a drapery of satin to decorate a female portrait', although Zoffany, 'not having been used to paint modern drapery, made many unsuccessful attempts – he grew peevish & piqued &c'.[5] By the time he tackled Mrs Oswald's portrait, Zoffany had mastered the technique.

MP

1. Egerton 1998, 352.
2. Webster 2011, 108.
3. For the assertion concerning the presence of Mr Oswald, see Manners & Williamson 1920, 224. See also Davies 1959, 112 n. 1. I am grateful to Larry Keith, Painting Conservator at the National Gallery, who recently restored *Mrs Oswald*, for sharing his observations on technical aspects of the present painting.
4. See Whitley 1928, vol. 1, 279.
5. Anon. 1781, iv–vi.

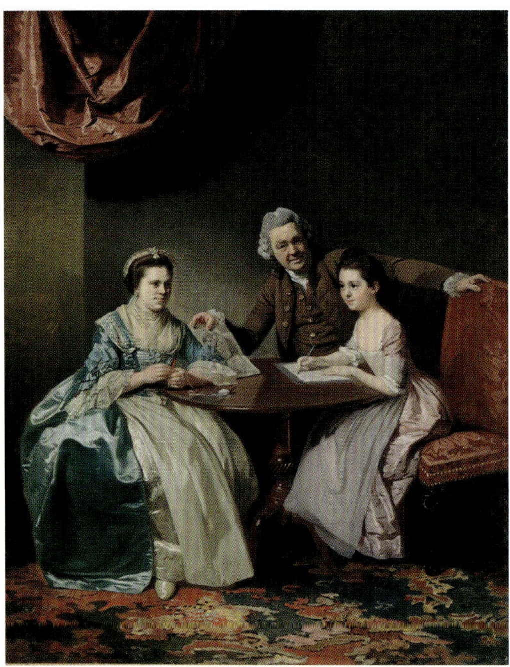

67

**Mr and Mrs Dalton and their
Niece Mary Deheulle**
*c.*1765–8

Oil on canvas, 90.8 × 71.1 cm (35¾ × 28 in)
Tate, London; bequeathed by Alan Evans, 1974

Exhibited at the Yale Center for British Art only

Provenance: Presumably painted for Richard Dalton,
and first recorded in the will of his brother-in-law
John Landon, who bequeathed it to his brother
James Landon; Captain Samuel Landon, by descent
to the Revd John Primatt Maud; sold Christie's,
31 May 1902 (68), as 'The Drawing Lesson';
bt. 'A.W.'; the Hon. Frederick Wallop by 1920, by
descent to Alan Evans, by whom bequeathed to
the National Gallery, 1974; transferred to the
Tate Gallery

Selected exhibitions: Park Lane 1930, no. 58; National
Portrait Gallery 1977, no. 32

Selected references: Manners & Williamson 1920,
154 (repr. opp.), 155, 242, 308; Williamson 1931,
22, pl. LXV; *The Tate Gallery 1974–6: Illustrated
Catalogue of Acquisitions*, London, 1978, 44–5;
Landon 1992, 331–2, 337–8, pl. XXVI(c); Webster
2011, 165–7

Richard Dalton had a great deal in common with
Zoffany in terms of their artistic education and
knowledge of the traditions of European art, and
by the mid-1760s, around the time this portrait
was made, the two men were clearly on close
terms. And, although nothing is known about the
circumstances surrounding the production of this
portrait, it may well have evolved as a result of
their friendship, rather than an official commission,
and as x-ray photographs reveal, it underwent
considerable changes before Zoffany arrived at
the final composition (see fig. 190). In the x-ray
two figures are visible above and to the right of
Richard Dalton. The figure above appears to be
Dalton himself, while the figure to the right is a
quite different, unidentified, male.

Richard Dalton had first visited Italy in 1739,
studying in Rome under Agostino Masucci – as
Zoffany was to do a decade or so later. A second
visit to Europe from 1747 to 1751 took Dalton
not only to Italy but to Malta, Turkey, Egypt and
Greece, where he made drawings of monuments
for the Earl of Charlemont. Dalton continued to
make regular visits to the Continent into the 1770s,
principally to purchase works of art for the king
and other British aristocrats. By the time of
Zoffany's arrival in London Dalton was established
as a major figure in the metropolitan art world, as
an art dealer and librarian to George III. In 1764
Dalton, then approaching fifty, married Esther
Deheulle, the daughter of a wealthy Spitalfields
silk weaver. The couple, who had no children of
their own, adopted Esther's niece Mary Deheulle,
orphaned following the death of her father in
1763. Zoffany's picture, therefore, celebrates the
establishment of Dalton's new family.

At the time of this portrait Dalton was
occupying apartments in St James's Palace,
although in this instance Zoffany has opted for a
neutral studio setting, restricting the furnishings
to the richly woven carpet, polished table, chair
and the theatrical swag of drapery. To the left
Mrs Dalton, fashionably dressed, looks towards
her niece, while engaging her hands with a knotting
shuttle and thread used in making embroidery.
Dalton, in the centre, holds up a chalk drawing
of the celebrated classical statue, known as the
Spinario, of a boy taking a thorn from his foot.
Dalton was himself an accomplished draughtsman
and during his visit to Italy in 1741 had made a
series of meticulous red chalk drawings of classical
statues, several of which passed into the Royal
Collection.[1] Dalton's niece is posed at the table,
porte-crayon in hand, as she makes a copy of the
drawing. For professional artists drawing from
antique statuary formed the basis of all future study,
and, in addition to drawing directly from statues
and plaster casts, it was expected that students
would copy from 'master' drawings in order to form
a correct technique. For amateurs, too, including
young ladies, drawing was considered an essential
accomplishment.

After Mary Deheulle's death Zoffany's portrait
passed to another branch of the family. In the
course of time the identity of the sitters was lost,
until by the twentieth century it was thought to
be a portrait of Philip Palmer of Dorney Court,
Buckinghamshire, with his wife and daughter.
In 1902, when it left the family's possession, it
was described at auction simply as 'The Drawing
Lesson', while in 1920 Manners & Williamson
entitled it 'Group of Mr. and Mrs. Palmer and
their daughter, afterwards Mrs. Landon of Dorney
Court, Bucks'.[2] The true identity of the sitters was
not recovered until 1975, once the picture had
entered the collection of the Tate Gallery. At that
time a descendant of the Deheulles discovered a
letter written in the 1840s by a member of the
family, John Landon, who provided the correct
identification. Landon, who had as a child met
Dalton, noted that Zoffany's likeness was
'wonderful'.[3]

MP

1. See Oppé 1950, 38, no. 163.
2. Manner & Williamson 1920, repr. opp. 154.
3. Landon 1992, 337.

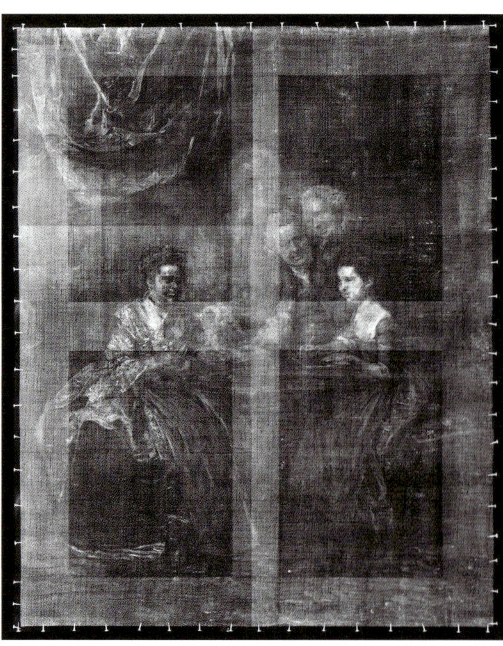

Figure 190
X-radiograph of *Mr and Mrs Dalton and their
Neice Mary Deheulle*, courtesy of the Conservation
Department, Tate

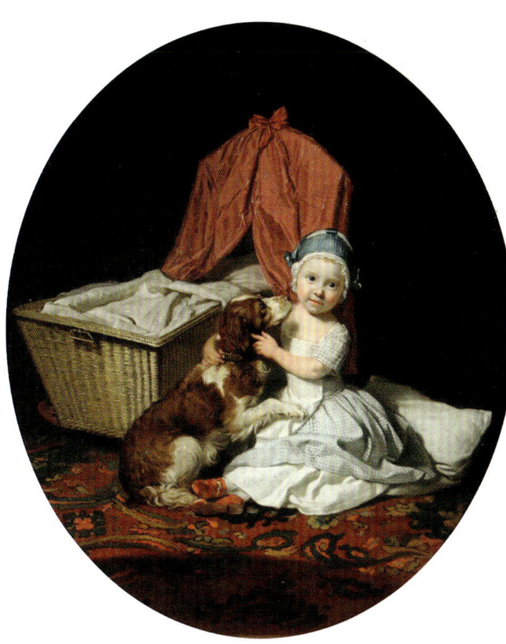

68

Hester Maria Thrale, 'Queeney'
1766

Oil on canvas, oval, 73.7 × 61 cm (29 × 24 in)
Alice and Douglas Hyland

Exhibited at the Yale Center for British Art only

Provenance: Hester and Henry Thrale; Hester
Maria Thrale; Daniel H. Farr; purchased from
Daniel H. Farr in 1924 by Keith Merrill, Avalon,
Massachusetts; by descent

Selected references: Chaloner Smith 1878–84, vol. 2,
916, no. 13; Webster 1976, 41, no. 37; Treadwell
2009, 144; Webster 2011, 99–100

Engraved: Giuseppe Marchi, *c.* 1766–8

'My eldest Daughter's Birth', wrote Mrs Thrale,
'was an Event of seemingly great Joy, for
Mr Thrale had somehow a Notion we were to
have no Children, & even doubted of my Pregnancy
till it became quite past all Question.'[1] Hester
Maria Thrale was born on 17 September 1764,
the first of thirteen children, and only one of
four to survive into maturity. Hester Maria's
mother was the redoubtable bluestocking and
socialite, Hester Lynch Thrale, (née Salusbury),
her father, the London brewer Henry Thrale,
a rather dour individual who, yet, counted
among his friends leading lights in the capital's
intellectual and artistic community, including
Samuel Johnson, Oliver Goldsmith, Charles
Burney and Joshua Reynolds. Hester Thrale,
whom Johnson nicknamed 'Queeney', was by all
accounts a precocious child. Mrs Thrale, who
recorded in detail her children's accomplishments
in her 'Family Book', noted that by the age of
two-and-a-half she had

> learned to distinguish Colours, & to name them:
> as also to tell a little Story with some Grace &
> Emphasis, as the Story of the Fall of Man, of
> Perseus & Andromeda of the Judgment of Paris
> & two or three more. These are certainly
> uncommon performances of a Baby 2 Years &
> 6 Months only; but they are most strictly true.
> She cannot however read at all.[2]

Zoffany, who painted Hester's portrait in the
spring of 1766, at the age of twenty months, was
apparently astonished by Hester's precocity and,
according to Mrs Thrale, even informed the king
about her 'odd performances'.[3] Hester, clearly a
lively child, looks directly at the viewer. Seated
on a Turkey rug, she would seem to have already
outgrown the cradle behind her. On her head she
wears a 'pudding' hat, a sort of padded crash
helmet designed to protect toddlers from accidents.
Mrs Thrale noted that she could not only walk
and run but was 'strong enough to carry a Hound
puppy two Months old quite across the Lawn at
Streatham'.[4] Hester's companion in the portrait
is, fittingly, Mrs Thrale's pet spaniel, named Belle,
who also appears in Zoffany's portrait of Hester's
widowed maternal grandmother, Mrs Salusbury
(1764; The Trustees of the Bowood Collection).
Aside from the dog's prominent appearance in
these portraits, Belle's other principal claim to fame
was to eat Dr Johnson's toast surreptitiously while
he was engaged in conversation with Mrs Thrale.[5]

The Thrales were evidently pleased with
Zoffany's portrait, and a mezzotint engraving
(fig. 191) was made from the picture by Reynolds's
studio assistant Giuseppe Marchi, who was also
a member, with Zoffany, of the St Martin's Lane
Academy (see cat. 41). The engraving is undated
but must have been made by early 1768, at which
time the three-and-a-half year old Hester was
using the print to make cards to send to her
friends.[6] While Hester continued to amaze adults
by her intelligence, she became increasingly
reserved and proud, Mrs Thrale observing that
she had 'a Heart void of all Affection for any Person
in the World'.[7] In 1808, at the age of forty-four, in
her determination to gain a title, Hester married a
widowed admiral, Baron Keith. The following year,
now Lady Keith, she gave birth to her only child,
a daughter.

MP

1. Piozzi 1942, vol. 1, 308.
2. Hyde 1977, 24.
3. Piozzi 1942, vol. 1, 308 n.3.
4. Hyde 1977, 21.
5. Webster 2011, 99.
6. Hyde 1977, 29.
7. James L. Clifford, *Hester Lynch Piozzi (Mrs Thrale)*,
   Oxford, 1941, 79.

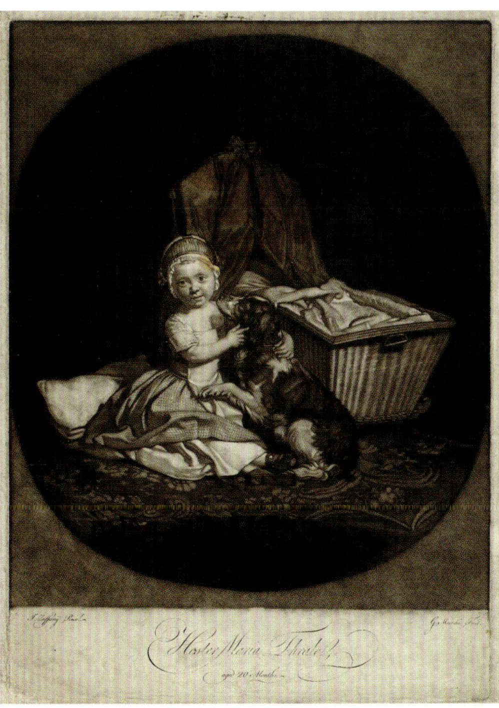

Figure 191
Giuseppe Marchi after Johan Zoffany,
*Hester Maria Thrale Aged Twenty Months, c.*1766,
mezzotint engraving, 50.5 × 35.6 cm (19⅞ × 14 in).
British Museum, Department of Prints and Drawings,
1873,1213.800

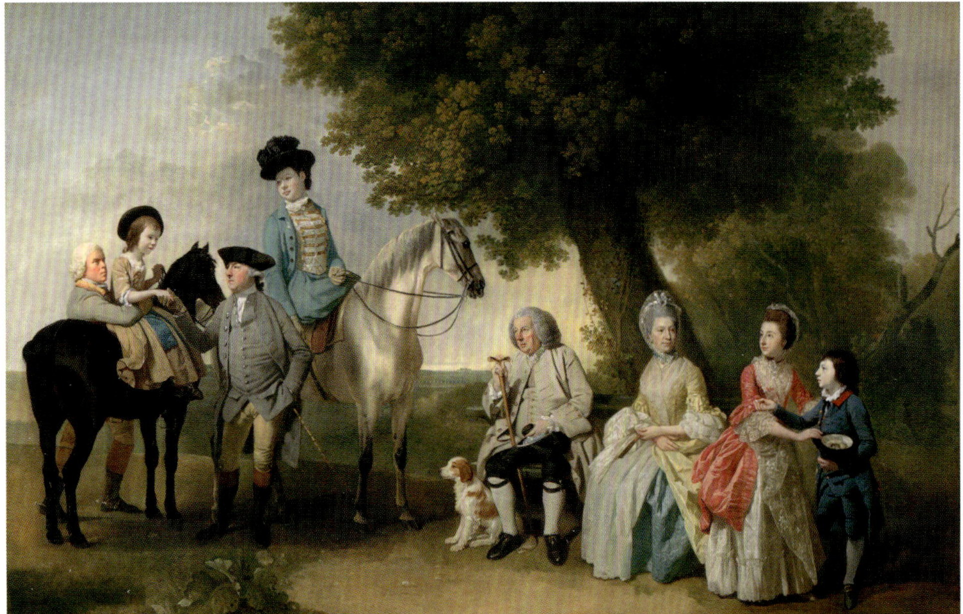

69

The Drummond Family

*c.*1769

Oil on canvas, 104.1 × 160 cm (41 × 63 in)
Yale Center for British Art, Paul Mellon Collection

Exhibited at the Yale Center for British Art only

Provenance: Commissioned by either Andrew or
John Drummond; by descent to 1959; Leggatt Bros,
1959; Agnew 1959; Ackerman and Johnson, 1962;
purchased by Paul Mellon, 1962

Selected exhibitions: Park Lane 1930; *Paintings,
Sculpture and Drawings Collected by Yale Alumni,*
Yale University, 1960, no. 29; *Painting in England,
1700–1850*, Virginia Museum of Fine Arts,
Richmond, Virginia, 1963, no. 235 (pl. 229);
*Treasures and Curiosities: Drummonds at Charing
Cross 1717–1967*, National Portrait Gallery, 1968;
Paul Mellon's Legacy: A Passion for British Art, Yale
Center for British Art, New Haven, and Royal
Academy of Arts, 2007–8, no. 39

Selected references: Manners & Williamson 1920, 20,
192–3; Williamson 1931, 16–17; Sitwell 1936, 38;
John Cornforth, 'At the sign of the Golden Eagle:
250 years of Drummonds of Charing Cross',
Country Life, 23 May 1968, vol. 143, no. 3716,
1379–80; Paulson 1975, 155, 157; Yale Center for
British Art, *Selected Paintings, Drawings and Books,*
foreword by Paul Mellon, New Haven, 1977, 24;
Denis Cosgrove and Stephen Daniels, eds., *The
Iconography of Landscape: Essays on the Symbolic
Representation, Design and Use of Past Environments,*
Cambridge, 1988, 48–50; Tobin 2004, 98–9, 220
n. 40; Treadwell 2009, 145–6; Webster 2011,
148–52

The figure at the heart of this conversation piece
is Andrew Drummond, founder of Drummonds
Bank. The painting was executed either just before
his death on 2 February 1769, aged an impressive
eighty-one years, or, more probably, soon
afterwards (see p. 172). The likelihood that this
is a posthumous image is strengthened both by his
rather isolated position and, more significantly, by
Zoffany's reliance on the life-sized portrait that
he had painted around 1765–6 (see fig. 162). Here,
Zoffany has moved the dog, but everything else
is virtually identical to that previous image. The
walking stick and snuffbox included in both survive
to this day in the board room at Drummonds, now
part of the Royal Bank of Scotland.[1] The cane
plays a crucial part in the legend of Andrew's early
years, apparently assisting him in a long walk from
Edinburgh to London, where he arrived soon
after the Act of Union with only ten guineas in his
pocket. This tale has to be taken with a pinch of salt,
but Andrew's rapid success after setting himself
up as a goldsmith in Charing Cross, the heart of
the Scottish community in London, was clearly
remarkable. He opened a ledger as a banker in 1717,
and his clientele quickly expanded to include many
notable customers, including Zoffany himself, who
started an account in December 1765. It could
well have been this event that led to the artist's
sustained patronage from the Drummonds. They
also owned *Beggars on the Road to Stanmore* (cat. 50),
executed around the same time as this group
portrait, and another conversation piece of
Andrew's nephew, Robert, surrounded by his family
(*c.*1781–3, now destroyed).

If Andrew's likeness is indeed posthumous,
then the portrait must have been commissioned by
his sole surviving offspring, John Drummond, a
partner in the bank and MP for Thetford, towards
whom he looks in the painting. John, assisted by
a groom wearing the grey Drummond livery, is
absorbed in helping his infant son, also John,
down from a horse. The second mounted sitter is
John's daughter Jane Diana. *The Drummond Family*
thus encompasses three generations and clearly
expresses satisfaction in the family's notable
success and social status. John's wife, the
Honourable Charlotte Beauclerk, granddaughter
and heiress to the Duke of St Albans, sits beside
her father-in-law on the bench (Andrew's own
wife Isabella had died in 1731). Charlotte plays a
role in the second narrative conceit included in the
painting. Her other son George has, like Charles
in *Three Sons of John, Third Earl of Bute* (cat. 64),
been bird nesting. His upturned hat contains three
eggs, and he offers a fourth to his mother, while his
sister Charlotte moves as if to restrain him.

Symbolically, the oak signifies the family tree –
the 'colony of Drummonds' Andrew was proud
to have 'planted' – and was a trope favoured by
Zoffany in the 1760s.[2] He reused it in both *William
Berry Introduced as Heir to Raith* (cat. 70) and *The
Bradshaw Family* (fig. 19).[3] Here, the tree also forms
part of the grounds of the family home at Stanmore,
and the town of Harrow-on-the-Hill is just visible
in the distance. Andrew had purchased the estate
in 1729, but it was only in recent years that the
family had taken steps to improve the property.
They had commissioned Capability Brown to
develop the grounds, and a new house, designed
by John Vardy and William Chambers, began to
be erected in 1763.

KR

1. I would like to thank Philip Winterbottom of the
Royal Bank of Scotland for information relating to
this point.
2. J. Ramsay, *Scotland and Scotsmen in the Eighteenth
Century, from the MSS of John Ramsay, Esq. of
Ochtertyre*, ed. A. Allardyce, 2 vols. (Edinburgh and
London, 1888), vol. 2, 304.
3. For the device of the tree, see Paulson 1975, 154–5.

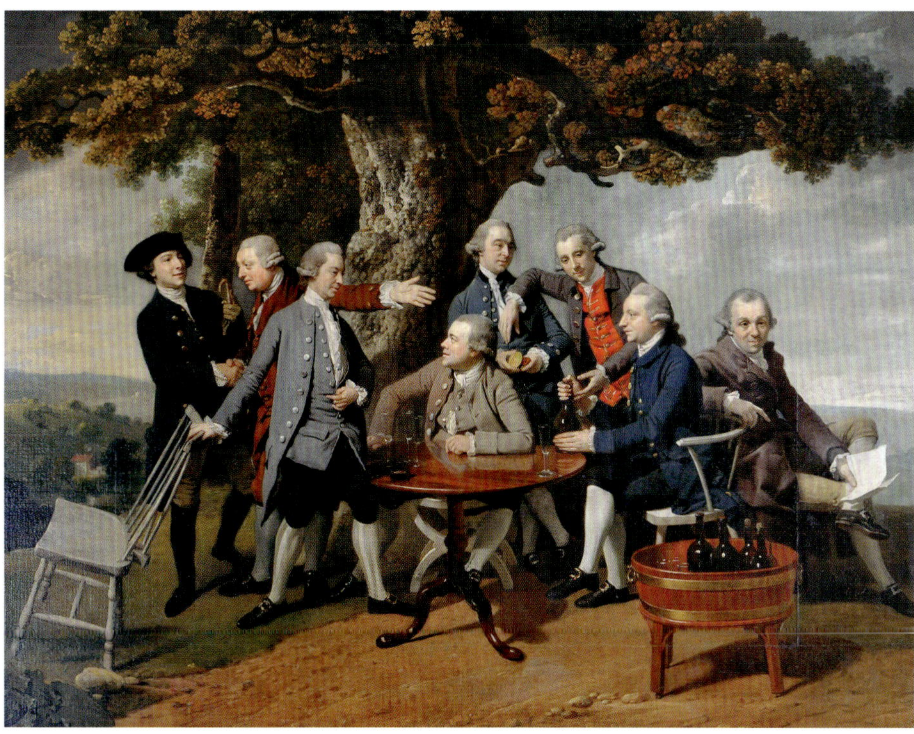

70

William Berry Introduced as Heir to Raith

1769

Oil on canvas, 106 × 131.5 (41¾ × 51¾ in)
Private collection

Exhibited at the Royal Academy of Arts only

Provenance: By descent

Selected exhibitions: National Portrait Gallery 1977,
no. 52

Selected references: Webster 1976, 47; Treadwell
2009, 155, 157–61; Webster 2011, 152–4

The event celebrated in the present picture is very
specific, and although the atmosphere is one of
conviviality, it may have been painted to gloss
over an issue that was the cause of considerable
discontent within the family concerned: the
confirmation of William Berry as the sole heir
of his uncle's estate and fortune. The main
protagonists in the picture are William Berry and
his uncle Robert Ferguson. Berry, the young man
in the hat and dark blue coat, enters at the extreme
left, his boots and the riding crop tucked under
his arm indicating that he has just dismounted from
his horse. Ferguson, dressed in a russet brown coat,
greets him with an avuncular handshake, while
introducing him to the assembled company. None
of the other figures have been positively identified,
other than Zoffany himself, who is seated at the
extreme right of the picture, a curiously remote
presence. The imminent celebration is indicated
by the empty wine glasses and the action of the
seated gentleman in blue, who is about to uncork
the first of several bottles of wine. As heir, Berry
was apparently noted for his generous hospitality,
a friend 'minded the day when eleven hogsheads
of one particular kind of claret came to the port of
Leith; and ten of them went to Raith'.[1] The type
of glasses on the table and bottles depicted by
Zoffany suggest that on this occasion the toast
to the heir was to have been champagne.

Robert Ferguson was a wealthy Scottish
merchant, whom Zoffany presumably met in
London, where his business was based. Ferguson,
who had a fortune derived from the East India
Company, also owned estates at Raith in Scotland
and, since he was childless, he decided to leave his

considerable assests to his sister's son William
Berry. The decision was the cause of considerable
acrimony within the family, since, in the ordinary
course of events, the heir to the estates ought to
have been William's elder brother Robert, who
had, however, offended his uncle by making an
unsuitable marriage, as well as his 'careless
disposition and literary interests'.[2] William, by
contrast, evidently had a sharp business mind and
proven ability in managing his uncle's Scottish
estates *in situ*. In November 1768 Robert Ferguson
confirmed his decision in his will, wherein his
Scottish estate was entailed upon William and
his male heirs. In 1782, following his uncle's death,
William changed his name from Berry to Ferguson.
In the meantime, his brother Robert had a
considerable smaller legacy, much to the disgust
of his daughters Mary and Agnes Berry, who felt
cheated out of their birthright. The Berry sisters,
who never married, did, however, go on to attain
a certain celebrity as society hostesses in London.
Zoffany also painted their portrait, suggesting
that he remained on good terms with both branches
of the family.[3]

The setting for Zoffany's picture was
presumably intended to refer to Robert Ferguson's
estate at Raith, the house in the distance bearing
a resemblance to Raith House, set in the rolling
Scottish hills. In such a context the three-legged
table appears somewhat incongruous. Indeed, on
close inspection it would appear to be the same
table that features in Zoffany's earlier portrait
of Mr and Mrs Dalton and their niece (cat. 67),
a reminder that the picture was conceived and
executed in Zoffany's London studio, then in

Portugal Row, on the south side of Lincoln's Inn Fields. (Ferguson's own business premises were in Austin Friars in the City.) The brass-bound wine cooler in the right foreground may also have been modelled on one belonging to Zoffany, although William Ferguson's descendants still own a cooler identical to that which features in Zoffany's painting – a common enough object at the time.

Aside from Ferguson and his nephew, Zoffany is the only other figure in the painting who can be positively identified, the other gentlemen being, presumably, Ferguson's business friends and associates. (There is no evidence, as has been suggested, that the man seated next to Zoffany is Robert Berry, William's disinherited brother, since his presence could only have rubbed salt into the wound.[3]) As visible joins in the canvas indicate, the picture was at some stage extended on all sides, allowing for a wider view of the surrounding landscape and possibly for the inclusion of Zoffany, who may have been a late addition to this resolutely homosocial company. His detached role, as a recorder of the event rather than a participant, is underlined by the way he looks directly out at the viewer, his back turned towards the main group. In his hand he holds a large sheet of paper, to which he points. The sheet, although it appears to be blank, quite possibly refers to the legal documents that set out the terms of Ferguson's will and his nephew's good fortune. Zoffany's expression, like the piece of paper in his hand, is blank, indicating through a humorous twist his own disinterested role in the proceedings.

MP

1. James Ferguson and Robert Menzies Ferguson, eds., *Records of the Clan and Name of Fergusson Ferguson and Fergus*, Edinburgh, 1895, 313.
2. Webster 2011, 152.
3. For Zoffany's portrait of Mary and Agnes Berry, see Webster 2011, 121–3.
4. See Treadwell 2009, 159.

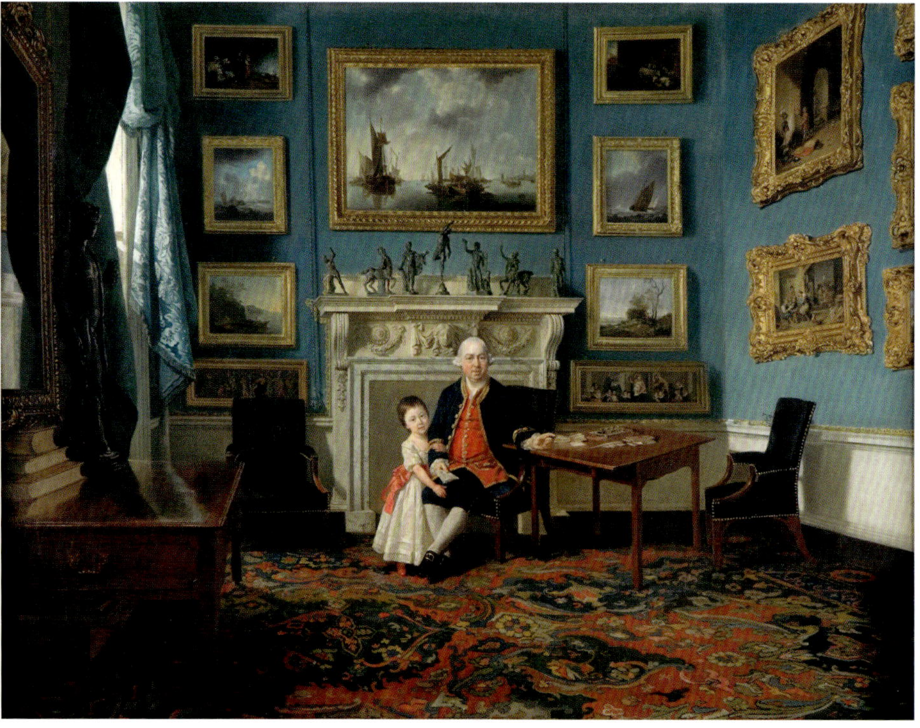

71

Sir Lawrence Dundas with his Grandson
1769–70

Oil on canvas, 101.6 × 127 cm (40 × 50 in)
The Zetland Collection

Provenance: Commissioned by Sir Lawrence Dundas; thence by descent

Selected exhibitions: Royal Academy 1954–5, no. 115; Barnard Castle 1962, no. 11; National Portrait Gallery 1977, no. 56; *The Treasure Houses of Britain: Five Hundred Years of Private Patronage and Art Collecting*, National Gallery of Art, Washington DC, 1985, no. 281; *Pintura Britanica de Hogarth a Turner*, Prado, Madrid, 1988–9; *Masterpieces from Yorkshire Houses: Yorkshire Families at Home and Abroad, 1700–1850*, York City Art Gallery, 1994, no. 28

Selected references: Manners & Williamson 1920, 247; Sitwell 1936, 40; Harris 1967, 170–79; Anthony Coleridge, 'Sir Lawrence Dundas and Chippendale', *Apollo*, vol. 86, Sept. 1967, 190–203; Sutton 1967a, 168–9; Sutton 1967b, 204–13; Saumarez Smith 1993, 262; Wilmot-Sitwell 2009; Webster 2011, 154–57

At the exact centre of this canvas the apparently genial and decidedly plump face of Sir Lawrence Dundas returns our gaze. He seems to be commenting, albeit none too seriously, that his grandson, also Lawrence, is distracting him from his paperwork. The decision to depict Dundas with his grandchild is surprising, particularly as the boy's father, Thomas, was very much alive and well. Lawrence, the fruit of Thomas's union with Lady Charlotte Fitzwilliam in 1764, may appear here on account of a particularly fond relationship. His presence may also emphasize the fact that Sir Lawrence's name, wealth and property were secured for two generations.

Descended from an impoverished branch of an old Scottish family, Dundas had set himself up as a merchant and contractor with remarkable success. Through speculation on the Stock Exchange and, most notably, as Commissary-General and Paymaster to the Army in Scotland, Flanders and Germany during the Seven Years War, he had amassed a large fortune. Dundas was quick to translate these material gains into the suitable accoutrements of elevated social position. In 1762 Lord Shelburne noted: 'Dundas, the Nabob of the North, writes me to desire I'll get him made a baronet.'[1] His request was granted two months later, as was his wish to purchase a parliamentary seat by the end of the year. At the same time Dundas turned his attention to acquiring a large number of properties, including, in 1763, Moor Park in Hertfordshire for £25,000 and 19 Arlington Street in London for £15,000.[2] He quickly set about commissioning major improvements to and furnishings for these

properties, patronizing Robert Adam, John Carr and Thomas Chippendale.[3]

There is a persistent idea that the setting represents the library or pillar room at Arlington Street, recently altered by Adam and newly furnished.[4] However, through the recent rediscovery of the inventory of the house, drawn up on 12 May 1768, Caddy Wilmot-Sitwell has demonstrated that it is in fact the room next door – Sir Lawrence's dressing room.[5] The tension between the itemized contents of the library and the room portrayed in Zoffany's painting had previously led art historians to conclude that, as in works like *George, Prince of Wales, and Frederick, Later Duke of York* (1764–5; Royal Collection) or *Charles Townley's Library* (cat. 63), mimetic transcription had been tempered by artistic licence. It seemed that bookcases had been removed and pictures and sculptures relocated, the better to emphasize Dundas's achievements as a connoisseur. In this case, however, Zoffany made only minimal adjustments to the depicted space, providing a remarkably faithful record of an interior in Dundas's town house. '2 Blue damask window Curtains', '2 French Elbow Chairs in horse hair' and Dundas's 'large rosewood writing Table' bearing a 'figure of Bacchus' with a 'Pier glass in a gilt frame' hung above, all are included in the 1768 record. We see seven of the '8 Antique figures on the Chimney' – bronzes crafted by Giacomo and Giovanni Zoffoli – identified in the inventory.[6] Zoffany has also recorded one of the '3 mohogany [*sic*] writing 2 flap Tables' cited in this room and fourteen of the '29 Pictures', eleven clearly visible and three more suggested by their frames.[7]

Dundas is thus depicted in his 'cabinet', surrounded by his collection, which included a substantial number of works from the seventeenth-century Netherlandish School. He had a particular fondness for Aelbert Cuyp, represented here by two farmhouse interiors, and David Teniers, whose *Corps du Garde* and *Journeymen Carpenters* can be seen on the right-hand wall. The latter painting is cited in a 1763 invoice sent by the dealer John Greenwood and, like every other picture depicted here, was included in the 1794 sale of Dundas's collection.[8] Pride of place is given to Jan van de Cappelle's *Shipping Becalmed*, displayed over the fireplace.[9] This picture stayed in the family until very recently, when it was sold to the National Museum of Wales.

Zoffany's portrait is an extraordinary record of Dundas's achievements as a collector, foreshadowing the *Tribuna* and *Charles Townley's Library* (cats. 53 and 63). The level of detail and intense finishing of the surface of the canvas enabled Zoffany to record Dundas's Netherlandish masterpieces, and to reveal his indebtedness to their painterly qualities. The descriptive phrases used by Greenwood to entice Dundas into purchasing works by artists such as Cuyp could equally well be applied to pictures by Zoffany himself: 'a most high finished piece', 'so highly finish'd as if it were enamled', 'so small & highly finish'd'.[10] In light of Dundas's fondness for such paintings, it is not surprising that he chose Zoffany to execute this portrait commission. Their relationship was to continue, Zoffany providing him with a version of his portrait of George III only a few years later (cat. 37).

KR

1. Lord Shelburne to Henry Fox, 19 Aug. 1762, quoted in Namier & Brooke 1985, vol. 2, 358.
2. See R.P. Fereday, 'Dundas family of Fingask and Kerse (per. 1728/9–1820)', *ODNB*, http://www.oxforddnb.com/view/article/64103 (accessed 5 July 2011).
3. See Harris 1967, 170–9.
4. Webster 1976, 49–51; *Masterpieces from Yorkshire Houses: Yorkshire Families at Home and Abroad, 1700–1850*, exh. cat., York City Art Gallery, 1994, no. 28; Webster 2011, 154–7.
5. Wilmot-Sitwell 2009 (inventory reproduced in full on pp. 89–99).
6. This arrangement has inspired the display of the four bronzes that remain with the family today beneath the portrait. They were exhibited alongside the portrait in the exhibition, *The Treasure Houses of Britain: Five Hundred Years of Private Patronage and Art Collecting* (Jackson-Stops 1985, 359, 361, cats. 284–6, 289).
7. Wilmot-Sitwell 2009, 94–5.
8. Greenwood 1794; see Jackson-Stops 1985, 357, cat. 281. For the *Journeymen Carpenters*, see invoice from John Greenwood, 28 Aug. 1763, reproduced in Sutton 1967b, 212; Greenwood 1794, 17, 2nd day, lot 36.
9. Greenwood 1794, 22, 3rd day, lot 13.
10. John Greenwood to Sir Lawrence Dundas, 10 Dec. 1762, reproduced in Sutton 1967b, 208.

72

Lord Willoughby de Broke and his Family
1766

Oil on canvas, 100.5 × 125.5 cm (39⅝ × 49⅜ in)
J. Paul Getty Museum, Los Angeles

Exhibited at the Yale Center for British Art only

Provenance: Commissioned by John Peyto-Verney, fourteenth Baron Willoughby de Broke; by descent to Dowager Lady Willoughby de Broke; sold Christie's, 1989; with Agnew's, 1989–96; purchased by the J. Paul Getty Museum, 1996

Selected exhibitions: Society of Artists, 1769, no. 215; *Illustrated Catalogue of a Loan Collection of Portraits*, City of Birmingham Museum and Art Gallery, Birmingham, 1903, no. 62; *Spring Exhibition: Illustrating Georgian England*, Whitechapel Art Gallery, London, 1906, no. 31; Royal Academy 1934, no. 242; *Two Centuries of British Art*, Stedelijk Museum, Amsterdam, 1936; Royal Academy 1954–5, no. 108; Royal Academy 1956–7, no. 360; *British Painting in the Eighteenth Century*, Museum of Fine Art, Montreal, National Gallery of Canada, Ottawa, Art Gallery, Toronto, Museum of Art, Toledo, Ohio, 1957–8, no. 85; Arts Council 1960–61, no. 5; *English Portraits*, Bucharest and Budapest, 1972–3, no. 32; National Portrait Gallery 1977, no. 35

Selected references: Manners & Williamson 1920, 153, 244–5; Williamson 1931, 14; Sitwell 1936, 24–5, 37, 45; Praz 1971, 104, no. 64; Saumarez Smith 1993, 261; Tyack 1994, 64–70; Webster 2011, 163–5

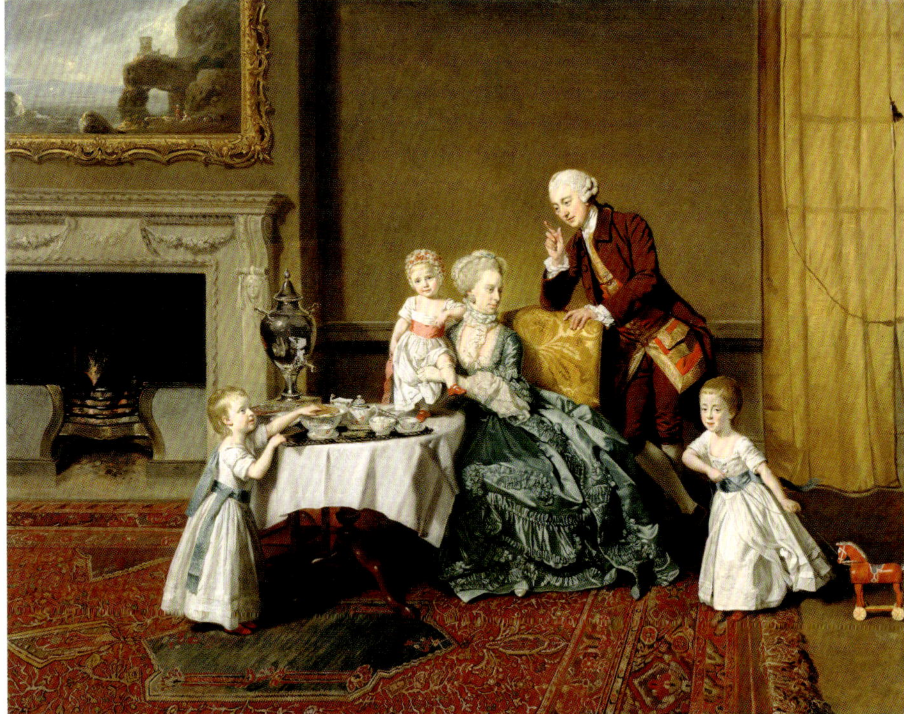

Zoffany exhibited the present picture with the Society of Artists in 1769 as 'a nobleman's family', having executed it three years earlier. John Peyto-Verney, fourteenth Baron Willoughby de Broke, in a brown frock suit and red waistcoat trimmed with gold, leans on the back of his wife's chair. Since 1763 he had enjoyed the position of Lord of His Majesty's Bedchamber, and this commission could well have been inspired by the recent conversation pieces Zoffany had executed for George III and Charlotte. Willoughby de Broke's attention is attracted by the sight of his little boy George clutching at the tray on the breakfast table and reaching up to take a piece of toast. In response he lifts a warning finger. His wife Lady Louisa has not observed George's antics. Their daughter Louisa, who casually stands on the breakfast table and rests her elbow against her mother's shoulder, needs to have her 'coats' kept out of the delicate porcelain arrayed on the tray. Meanwhile, their elder son John has just entered the room, dragging along his red wooden horse on wheels and drawing his mother's gaze. Both John and little Louisa look directly out of the canvas to meet our gaze, seeming to invite our collusion.

This beautifully observed display of domestic life, parental attentiveness and childish antics was entirely in tune with recent developments in family portraiture. The new sentimentality and emphasis on openly displayed affect evident here were also manifest in contemporary literature. In the same year as the Willoughby de Broke portrait was probably painted, the Reverend John Fordyce published his highly popular *Sermons to Young Women*, in which he described an ideal woman providing a softening influence on her necessarily sterner husband and tenderly nurturing her offspring: 'I think I behold you … casting your fond maternal regards round and round through the pretty smiling circle.'[1] Yet, such new emphasis on the display of domestic bliss did not supplant other, more traditional imperatives for the noble family. Lord Willoughby de Broke may be a concerned and attentive father, but he is also at the summit of a triangular composition, expressive of his position as *pater familias*. Furthermore, while neither son has yet been breeched, Zoffany provides a clear visual clue that John, on the right, is the eldest, the heir to the Willoughby de Broke name, estate and fortune, by placing him in close proximity to his father.[2]

This is another meticulously rendered interior, and the breakfast table, with the delicately patterned porcelain tea service and the large silver tea urn displaying the reflection of the cups, is a feat of virtuoso painting. When this portrait was attracting notice in the early decades of the twentieth century, it was repeatedly stated that this urn had survived among the family's possessions.[3] Although this has been queried, recent correspondence with the current generation of the family reveals that it remains in their collection.[4] The other assertion commonly made about this portrait – that the family are depicted in the morning or breakfast room at their country house, Compton Verney in Warwickshire – is more questionable. The outsize overmantel and the curious positioning of the chimneypiece (on the same wall as the window) cast considerable doubt on the idea.[5] However, the general design of the painted room must gesture towards the house that Lord Willoughby de Broke was then remodelling according to plans submitted by Robert Adam. An early Adam drawing for the new elevation of the east front is dated 1760, but work appears to have begun in earnest in 1762. This was not completed until 1768 and so was in full swing while Zoffany was executing the painting.[6]

The new house and grounds at Compton Verney attracted considerable attention and were given a fulsome write-up in Richard Jago's topographical poem, *Edge-Hill, or, The Rural Prospect Delineated and Moralized* of 1767. Jago swiftly moves from the 'stately Walls' to the family within, praising Lord and Lady Willoughby de Broke for their domestic virtues and their love of the retired life, using an idiom that cannot fail to evoke Zoffany's picture. While John Verney is formed 'Alike for Courts … or rural Pleasure', Jago praises in particular his 'Love of studious Ease, and sweet Domestic Bliss'. Both he 'and his Consort fair' resist the temptations of the fashionable world, enjoying the delights of their country seat: 'their sympathizing Hearts | in safer League unite, and, inly blest, | From Nature's Source draw purer Tides of Joy.'[7]

KR

1. John Fordyce, *Sermons to Young Women*, 4th ed., 2 vols., Dublin, 1766, vol. I, 24.
2. Retford 2006, *passim*.
3. See, for example, Manners & Williamson 1920, 153; *Exhibition of British Art*, exh. cat., Royal Academy of Arts, London, 1934, 67, cat. 242; Sitwell 1936, 37; *European Masters of the Eighteenth Century*, exh. cat., Royal Academy of Arts, London, 1954, 46, cat. 108.
4. I am most grateful to Amanda Herrin at the J. Paul Getty Museum for providing information on this matter.
5. See, for example, Williamson 1931, 14; *British Portraits*, exh. cat., Royal Academy of Arts, London, 1956–7, 113–14, cat. 360; *Johann Zoffany*, exh. cat., Arts Council, London, 1960, 12, cat. 5; Webster 1976, 40, cat. 35; http://www.comptonverney.org.uk/?page=about/house/18century.html, accessed 27 April 2010. I would like to thank Steven Parissien, Director of Compton Verney, for his observations on this matter.
6. Tyack 1994, 64–70; http://www.comptonverney.org.uk/?page=about/house/18century.html (accessed 27 April 2010).
7. Richard Jago, *Edge-Hill, or, The Rural Prospect Delineated and Moralized*, London, 1767, 14–15.

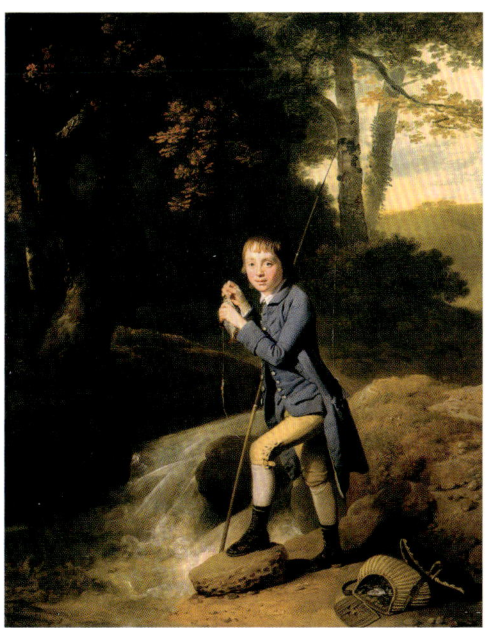

73

Master James Sayer

1770

Oil on canvas, 89 × 68.5 cm (35 × 27 in)
The Woolavington Collection

Provenance: By descent, Sotheby's, 31 July 1934 (118)

Selected exhibitions: National Portrait Gallery 1977,
no. 60

Selected references: Chaloner Smith 1878–84, vol. 2,
686, no.109; Manners & Williamson 1920, 26, 27,
37, 157, 232, 264; Walter Shaw Sparrow, *Angling in
British Art*, London, 1923, 191–3; Treadwell 2009,
202–3; Webster 2011, 103–4

James Sayer, depicted here at the age of thirteen, was
the son of the print publisher, Robert Sayer. Born
on 16 February 1757, he was baptized the following
month at the church of St Dunstan-in-the-West,
close to his father's business at 53 Fleet Street.
James was one of seven children of Robert and
Dorothy Sayer and the only one to survive infancy.
As Sayer's sole son and heir, James must therefore
have been the object of special affection. In the
present picture he is depicted as an angler,
unhooking his catch, Zoffany paying his customary
close attention to detail: the intricacies of the float
attached to the line, the wicker creel at the boy's
feet, his gold braided tricorne hat, muddy boots
and the fish on the end of the hook (which appears
on close inspection to be a roach). Fishing was a
popular pastime in the eighteenth century, enjoyed
by men, women and children from a wide range of
social backgrounds, and featured consequently in
numerous portraits, conversation pieces and fancy
pictures. Zoffany himself included fishing motifs
in a number of portraits, notably the 1762 portrait
of David Garrick and his family taking tea in the
garden of his house at Hampton (fig. 92), *John,
Third Duke of Atholl and his Family* (fig. 96), *The*

Rosoman Family (fig. 13) and even the portrait of
Claude Martin's Indian mistress, Boulone (fig. 123).
Robert Sayer, who commissioned the portrait, in
1772 also commissioned the engraver Richard
Houston to make a mezzotint, which he published
from his Fleet Street premises with the title,
'James Sayer. Aged 13 Years', indicating that the
painting was made in 1770, perhaps to mark his
son's birthday. Although the print must have had
a particular personal appeal to Robert Sayer, as an
astute businessman he would also have been aware
of its market value as a kind of 'fancy picture', not
only a portrait of his own son but also an attractive
generic image of boyhood.

Robert Sayer was by the early 1770s among
London's most successful print publishers. Born
in Sunderland, he had established his business in
London by the late 1740s, when he began trading
in maps and prints at the sign of the Golden Buck
in Fleet Street. In 1754 he married Dorothy
Careless (or Carlos), 'an agreeable young lady with
a handsome fortune'.[1] During the 1760s, as Sayer
expanded the remit of his print publishing business
into portraits and humorous 'drolls', he began to
publish engravings after Zoffany's theatrical
paintings. By the time Zoffany painted this portrait
of his son, he and Sayer were firm friends and close
business associates, sharing profits in prints after
a wide range of Zoffany's works, including royal
portraits, fancy pictures, and theatrical pictures.
Sayer also owned a number of original paintings by
Zoffany, including *A Porter with a Hare* (see cat. 49).
In 1780, following the death of his first wife, Robert
Sayer, who already had a home on the Green in
Richmond upon Thames, married a wealthy widow
who had recently been bequeathed a property in
Richmond, close to the newly built bridge across
the Thames.[2] Around that time Sayer commissioned
Zoffany to paint a portrait of himself, his wife and
his son James in the garden of Bridge House
(private collection). In 1794 Robert Sayer died
at Bath and was buried in Richmond. Shortly
afterwards, James married. In February 1797
James's own son was born, although his wife died
two weeks after the birth, the son being 'privately
christened over his mother's corpse'.[3] James Sayer
died six years later in 1803, leaving his son Robert
with a considerable fortune under the guardianship
of a female cousin, whose assets he was also in time
to inherit. The present picture passed eventually
to Robert Sayer's granddaughter, who sold it at
auction in 1934.

MP

1. *Daily Advertiser*, 19 July 1754.
2. John Cloake, 'Cardigan House and its architects',
   *Richmond History: The Journal of Richmond Local
   History Society*, May 1994, vol. 15, 18–26.
3. See 'The Work of J P Sayer, The Sayers of Richmond,
   Surrey' at http://www.bedfordpark.net/genealogy/
   sayer/jps_richmond.htm (accessed 28 Dec. 2010).

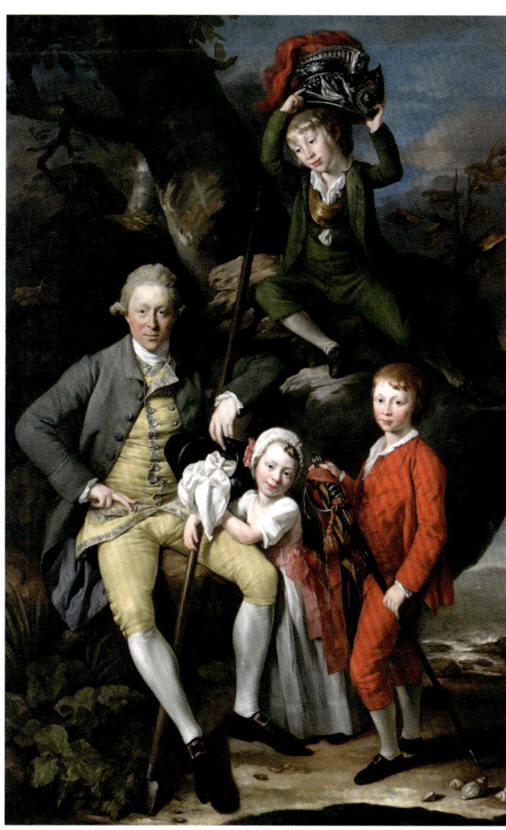

74

**Henry Knight of Tythegston with his
Three Children**

*c.*1770

Oil on canvas, 240.5 × 149 cm (94⅝ × 58⅝ in)
Amgueddfa Genedlaethol Cymru/National
Museum of Wales

Exhibited at the Royal Academy of Arts only

Provenance: Commissioned in 1770 by Henry
Knight of Tythegston Court, Glamorganshire; by
descent; sold Sotheby's, 8 June 1999 (14); purchased
by the National Museum of Wales through the
bequest of Miss June Tiley, with the assistance of
the National Art Collections Fund and the National
Heritage Memorial Fund

Selected exhibitions: On loan to the National Museum
of Wales, 1940–58

Selected references: John Steegman, *Portraits in South
Wales Houses*, 1962, vol. II, 119, no. 12, pl. 27D; John
Cornforth, 'Tythegston Court, Glamorganshire',
Country Life, 13 Oct. 1977, 1008–9; Webster 2011,
170–72, 659 n. 50

Zoffany's full-length portrait of Henry Knight and his children was produced in the midst of an expensive, messy and scandalous divorce case: a propagandist visual statement at a time of great personal turmoil. Henry Knight, a wealthy squire from Tygethston, Glamorganshire, married Catherine Lynch in March 1762 at the church of St Anne's, Soho. Catherine, a daughter of the pluralist Dean of Canterbury, John Lynch, and granddaughter of William Wake, Archbishop of Canterbury, came from a privileged background. At first all went well: their first child, a boy, was born in 1763, followed by two more boys and a daughter.[1] In 1765, during a sojourn with her husband near Deal in Kent, Catherine Knight became acquainted with John Norris, MP for Rye and Governor of Deal Castle. Norris, who was described as having 'such attachment to women of no character as is extraordinary', shortly afterwards formed an attachment to London's most celebrated courtesan Kitty Fisher, whom he married in December 1766.[2] A few months later, in March 1767, Fisher died.

The following year Norris began an affair with Catherine Knight, who in the spring of 1768 eloped with him, the couple setting up house under the assumed name of Johnson near Grosvenor Square. In November 1769 Catherine gave birth to a daughter, at which point Henry Knight instituted divorce proceedings through the Consistory Court of London. The divorce trial, as was the norm in cases dealing with adultery, provided salacious details of Catherine's relationship with Norris through the testimony of servants and neighbours. Indeed, the case proved interesting enough to be published in 1779 in a compendium of the juiciest divorce trials of the age, alongside the celebrated divorce proceedings taken by Lord Bolingbroke against Lady Diana Spencer.[3] Henry Knight won his ecclesiastical court case in June 1770, which allowed for him and his wife 'to be divorced and separated from bed, board, and mutual cohabitation'.[4] However, as this judgement alone could not provide an absolute divorce (or allow either party to remarry), Knight took the option open only to the very wealthy and applied for a divorce by Act of Parliament, employing as his barrister the eminent actor, playwright and lawyer, Arthur Murphy.[5] 'The bill to dissolve the marriage of Henry Knight, with his now wife, and enable him to marry again', was given royal assent by the king on Friday, 8 March 1771.[6] Four days later Catherine married her lover John Norris. Knight, who did not remarry, sued Norris for adultery, winning damages of £3,000.[7] Norris, who was already in financial difficulties, was now ruined, forcing him to sell his estates and in 1774 leave the country. Knight's retribution, and his expensive divorce case, was not simply to repay his wife for unfaithfulness, however, but to exclude her from any rights to his property and lands, which by 1769 included an unwanted entail.[8]

At the time of Zoffany's portrait Henry Knight was bringing up his children with the assistance of an aunt. The portrait of the father – and the absence of a mother – served therefore to reinforce Knight's close bond with his offspring, suggested by the playful nature of Zoffany's lively image. Knight's decision to commission a full-length portrait from Zoffany, rather than a conversation piece, which was Zoffany's more usual format, may also have related to the particular personal circumstances surrounding his impending divorce, as he sought to uphold his position as the moral and legal guardian of his offspring. Knight, as paterfamilias, is seated in the left foreground. Leaning on his knee is Knight's three-year old daughter Ethelreda, to the right, dressed in red, is her eldest brother Henry, while directly above is Robert. The figures are situated on a rocky outcrop by the sea, presumably a visual reference to Knight's estate at Tythegston, which lay a few miles from the coast between Bridgend and Porthcawl.

Henry Knight's family came from Bristol, where they had been prominent merchants in the seventeenth century. In 1732 Knight's grandfather Robert had inherited through marriage the manor of Tythegston in Glamorgan, which subsequently passed to Henry. As a young man, Henry had made his career as a soldier, and although he is dressed as a gentleman, Knight's previous military career has a strong visual presence in Zoffany's portrait. It is alluded to by the sword and belt held by his son Henry and by the long-handled weapon cradled by Knight in his arm, an infantry officer's spontoon (or half-pike), its sharp point embedded in the sand. The spontoon alludes presumably to Knight's commission as Captain in the 70th Regiment of Foot during the Seven Years War. The dragoon's helmet, held aloft by his younger son (who also wears his father's gorget, or throat armour), is emblazoned with the name 'Emsdorf', presumably recalling Knight's participation in the Battle of Emsdorf of July 1760, where Anglo-Hanoverian forces had defeated the French, owing in no small measure to the prowess of the British 15th Light Dragoons, in which Knight had evidently also served.

In addition to his military career, Henry Knight had developed during the 1760s an interest in drawing and architecture, his diaries referring to drawing lessons, as well as the purchase of drawing materials and books on architecture. At this time he began to remodel his Tudor manor house at Tythegston. Knight's diaries also refer to a number of transactions with Zoffany. On 27 April 1770 he noted a part-payment to Zoffany of £25, which may have been for the present picture. The following year, on 28 February, he noted: 'This day or yesterday my 2 Pictures the Holy Family by Rubens and a Landscape by Ruisdall were sent to the Bath Waggon to be forwarded to London to Mr Zoffanij to be cleaned.'[9] He wrote again to Zoffany on three separate occasions in 1771, their correspondence being curtailed by Knight's untimely death in 1772 at the age of thirty-four.

MP

1. Three children appear in the portrait, although in Mrs Knight's trial for adultery (see note 3 below) four children are mentioned, indicating that the third boy, born in 1765, had died in infancy.
2. Namier & Brooke 1964, vol. 3, 203.
3. See 'Henry Knight, Esq. against Catherine Knight. Libel given in the 17th of May, 1770', in *Trials for Adultery: or, the History of Divorces. Being select trials at Doctors Commons, for Adultery, Fornication, Cruelty, Impotence &c. From the Year 1760 to the present Time. Including the whole of the Evidence on each Cause. Taken in short-hand, by a civilian*, vol. 3, London, 1779, 1–25.
4. London Metropolitan Archives. Henry Knight divorce, Consistory Court of London, 1770: D/L/C555/133–135. I am grateful to Oliver Fairclough for sharing his notes on the case with me.
5. 'A bill is depending for dissolving the marriage of Henry Knight, Esq., with Catherine Lynch his wife', *Middlesex Journal or Chronicle of Liberty*, 24–6 Jan. 1771. For Murphy's involvement, see Jesse Foot, *Life of Arthur Murphy*, London, 1811, 354.
6. *Bingley's Journal or Universal Gazette*, 2–9 March 1771. See also Records of the House of Lords: Private Bill Office: Private Act, 11 George III, c. 29, Ref No: HL/PO/PB/1/1771/11G3n56.
7. Namier & Brooke 1964, vol. 3, 203.
8. See *Archaeologia Cambriensis: A Record of the Antiquities of Wales and its Marches, and the Journal of the Cambrian Archaeological Association*, vol. 4 (New Series), London, 1853, 249f. ('Line of Knight').
9. Entries from Henry Knight's diary are taken from Sotheby's sale catalogue, London, 8 June 1999, lot 14, p. 43.

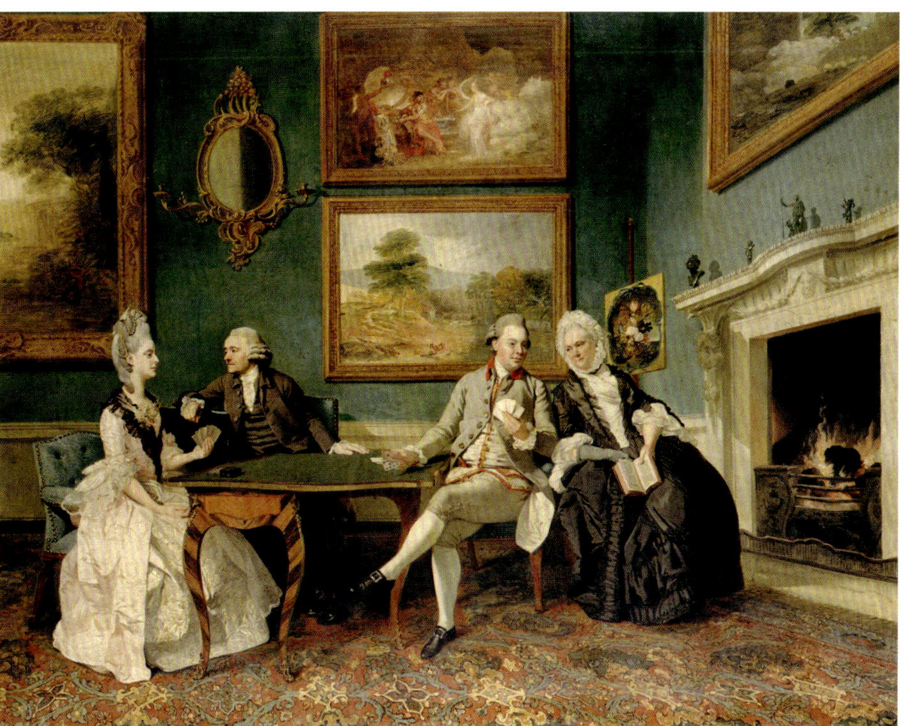

75

The Dutton Family
1771–2

Oil on canvas, 101.5 × 127 cm (40 × 50 in)
Private collection

Exhibited at the Royal Academy of Arts only

Provenance: Commissioned by James Lenox Dutton;
by descent to James Huntly Dutton, sixth Baron
Sherborne; sold Christie's 1929; bt Daniel Farr;
Walter Samuel, second Viscount Bearsted; Peter
Samuel, fourth Viscount Bearsted; by descent;
sold Sotheby's, 14 June 2001 (16)

Selected exhibitions: Royal Academy 1907, no. 143;
Park Lane 1930, no. 134; Royal Academy 1954–5,
no. 100; *Le siècle de l'élégance: la demeure anglaise au
XVIIIe siècle*, Musée des Arts Decoratifs, 1959, no.
215; *The Eye of Thomas Jefferson*, National Gallery
of Art, Washington DC, 1976, no. 76; *Rococo Art
and Design in Hogarth's England*, Victoria and
Albert Museum, 1984, no. M31

Selected references: Manners & Williamson 1920,
233, 277; Williamson 1931, 14–15; Sitwell 1936,
24–5, 36; Praz 1971; Paulson 1975, 156–7; *The
Dutton Family by John Zoffany*, sale cat., Sotheby's,
London, 2001, *passim*; Webster 2011, 172–3

The Dutton Family must have been one of the last
conversation pieces Zoffany painted before his
departure to Italy. It is also one of his finest
exercises in the genre. The grouping creates an
unusual rhythm across the canvas, with two pairs
of sitters seated either side of a fine Louis XV
Kingwood table. On the right, James Dutton,
the eldest son of the family, leans backwards in

his chair to consult his mother, Jane, about his
cribbage hand. She has lowered the book she
has been reading to attend to his request. They
incline affectionately towards one another, but
James's younger sister, Jane, sits bolt upright
across the other side of the table, awaiting her
sibling's decision and the opportunity to make
her next move. She seems not entirely engaged
with her father's attempt to proffer advice. He
points towards her cards, his figure accurately
foreshortened and almost seeming to come
forward into the viewer's space.

James Lenox Dutton is the head of this family,
but here Zoffany has not used his favoured
composition of a broadly triangular arrangement
for a family group, with the *pater familias* at the
summit. Only James's placement directly below
the mirror, reflecting the line of a corner of the
room, serves to accentuate his figure. He had been
born James Lenox Napier but had assumed the
surname of Dutton on taking over the estates of
his childless maternal uncle. James's first wife,
Catherine, had died some time previously, and their
son John had also passed away only the year before
the execution of this painting. James is thus shown
with his second wife and two of their children.

Zoffany shows himself, once again, to be a
master of narrative, utilizing the skills that had
already made him such a successful painter of
theatrical scenes. In its careful construction of a
plot the painting is reminiscent of Hogarth. The
way in which James displays his cards recalls the
central figure in Hogarth's *Assembly at Wanstead
House* of 1728–31 (Philadelphia Museum of Art),
while the relationship between his mother, the

polescreen protecting her face from the fire,
and the hearth evokes his *Picquet; or Virtue in Danger
(The Lady's Last Stake)* of 1759 (Albright-Knox
Art Gallery, Buffalo, New York). The sense of a
captured moment providing an insight into the
life of the Duttons is strengthened by the careful
depiction of the room. The rich Turkey carpet is
familiar from many of Zoffany's interiors; the
paintings consist of three landscapes and a scene
of the Forge of Vulcan; the rendition of the
breakfront chimneypiece is particularly successful.
Hearths are often unlit in conversation pieces, but
here the flickering flames illuminate the inside
of the fireplace, and the light catches the marble
surround.

This is a very different interior from that which
Zoffany had provided for Lawrence Dundas a
few years previously (cat. 71). The level of detail
varies notably across the canvas, from the carefully
rendered inlay of the table to the rather sketchily
depicted paintings on the wall. Furthermore,
although the painting was exhibited in 1930 as
'Mr and Mrs Dutton and Family, in the
drawing-room at Sherborne Park, Gloucestershire',
it is unlikely that it accurately depicts a room in
the old-fashioned, three-storey Jacobean house.[1]
This is probably the artist's invention, an amalgam
of objects and styles, carefully contrived to suggest
the wealth and taste of the Duttons.

KR

1. Leonard Willoughby, 'Sherborne House',
  The Connoisseur, vol. 30, May 1911, 3–13.

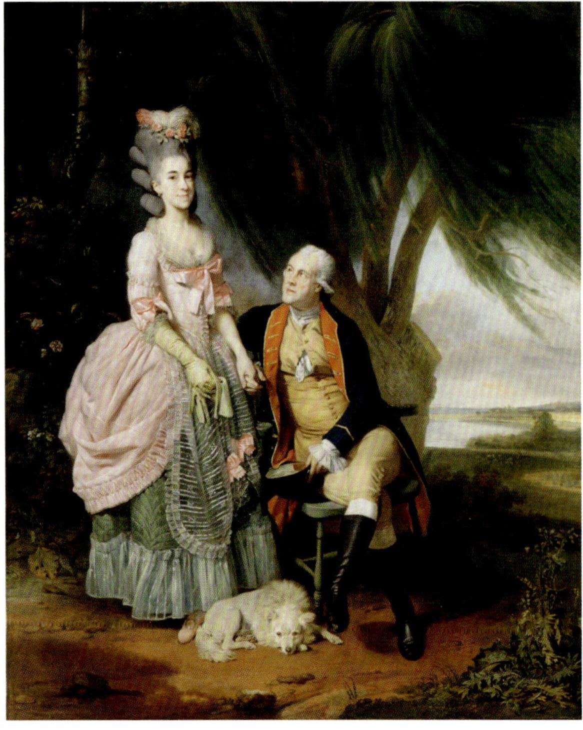

76

John Wilkes and his Daughter Mary (Polly)
1779

Oil on canvas, 126.4 × 100.3 cm (49¾ × 39½ in)
National Portrait Gallery, London; purchased with
help from the National Heritage Memorial Fund
and the National Art Collections Fund, 1991

Provenance: Commissioned by John Wilkes; by
descent to his niece Dinah Hayley, who married
Sir Robert Baker, first Baronet; by descent to
Sir Robert Sherston-Baker, seventh Baronet;
Sotheby's 1990; purchased by the National
Portrait Gallery, 1991

Selected exhibitions: Royal Academy 1782, no. 53;
Into View: British Paintings from Private Collections,
Gainsborough's House, Sudbury, 1986, no. 17;
Treasures for Everyone, National Art Collections
Fund, Christie's, 1997

Selected references: Manners & Williamson 1920,
73–4, 176–7; Webster 1990, 19; Ribeiro 2000,
133–5; Ingamells 2004, 484–6, cat. 6133; Retford
2006, 145–7; Treadwell 2009, 133–5; Webster
2011, 385–8

John Wilkes, as depicted here, was a rather different
character from the notorious radical politician of
the 1760s, vilified and worshipped in equal measure.
His scurrilous attacks on the Earl of Bute and
George III, his arrests and imprisonment, his exile,
the three occasions on which his election as MP had
been annulled, all were behind him. Over the course
of the 1770s he had carefully recovered his career in
London and its suburbs as a City dignitary. From
being elected Alderman in 1769, he became Sheriff
in 1771, Lord Mayor and MP for Middlesex in
1774, and was appointed Chamberlain of the City of
London on 1 December 1779, shortly after Zoffany
started work on the portrait. This last office, which
he had chased for a number of years, allowed Wilkes
to discharge his debts and provided him with some
security: 'After being harassed for so many years,
I cannot but earnestly desire to arrive in a safe
port.'[1] Wilkes's official looking garb in Zoffany's
portrait, the dark blue coat with gold trim and red
facings over a buff waistcoat and breeches, can
perhaps be associated with his post as chamberlain,
or with Whig colours more broadly, but it is
inconclusive.[2] The politician's newfound status was
enhanced when, the year the painting was placed on
display at the Royal Academy, he achieved another
strenuously sought-after recognition. In May 1782
the Commons finally voted to expunge from its
records the resolution expelling him from the
House.

Wilkes is seated, as he had been in William
Hogarth's famous satirical print of 1763 (fig. 192).
However, here his legs are crossed rather than
widely splayed in a manner suggestive of his rakish
character, and his famously crossed eyes are, in the
words of Horace Walpole, 'squinting tenderly at his
daughter'.[3] Mary, more commonly known as Polly,
clasps his hand in warm response. The portrait
was exhibited as 'A Conversation', emphasizing
the contact between the two figures and drawing
attention to their interaction. One critic, writing in

Figure 192
William Hogarth, *John Wilkes Esqr*, 1763, etching
and engraving, 34.2 × 22.2 cm (13½ × 8¾ in).
British Museum, Department of Prints and Drawings

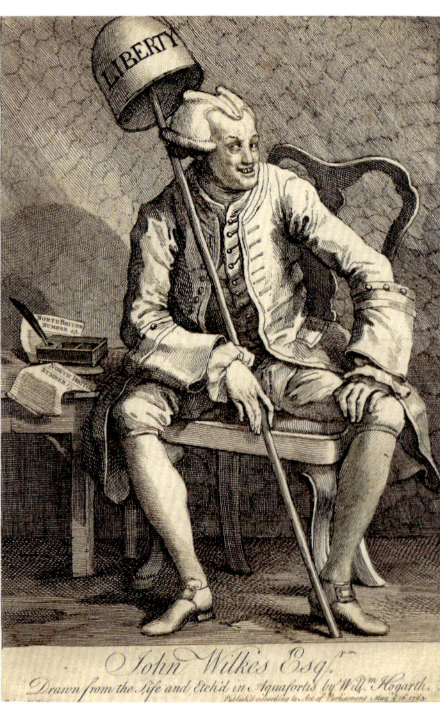

John Wilkes Esqr.
Drawn from the Life and Etch'd in Aquafortis by Will.ᵐ Hogarth.

the *London Courant*, described the painting thus:
'Mr Wilkes sitting in a garden, with his daughter
standing near his right side, he has hold of her
hand, and looking up to her, seems conversing
affectionately.'[4]

Polly was the sole offspring of Wilkes's
marriage in 1747 to a rich heiress by the name of
Mary Mead, a union terminated by a permanent
separation in 1757. It had been arranged to secure
the status of the Wilkes family, and although John
Wilkes doesn't seem to have raised much objection
at the time, he later wrote to a woman he was
pursuing: 'In my non-age, to please an indulgent
father, I married a woman half as old again as
myself of a very large fortune, my own that of a
gentleman. It was a sacrifice to Plutus, not to
Venus.'[5] After the breakdown of the relationship
Wilkes had continued to care for Polly and oversee
her education, pouring vast amounts of time, effort
and money into her wellbeing: 'One thing I insist
on, that my dear daughter does not deny herself
any pleasure of any kind she chuses, and let me
know what it is, and I will contrive it … I never
expend any [money] with so much pleasure to
myself, as for my dear girl.'[6] Polly's singularly
elaborate dress implies the fruits of her father's care
and generosity. She wears a pink and white striped
polonaise gown with pink bows over a green quilted
underskirt with a gauze flounce and a matching
apron adorned with yet more bows. To top off this
elaborate confection, her piled hair is ornamented
with foliage, pink silk roses and ostrich feathers.[7]
To one observer, at least, her upright figure,
seemingly straight out of a fashion plate, was a
little too rigid: 'She stands a perfect *Miss Prim*, as
stiff as the Queen of Diamonds.'[8]

Polly never married and lived with her father. As
John Sainsbury has recently noted, the relationship
'took on many features of a companionate
marriage', and Polly acted as Lady Mayoress in
1774 to great acclaim.[9] Wilkes was thus able to
temper his widespread reputation as a libertine,
constantly drawn on by his detractors, with his love
of the domestic life. His relationship with Polly
was an asset to his public image, and he was not
averse to advertising their close bond. Some of the
odes he wrote on her birthdays were published
in *The New Foundling Hospital for Wit* in 1784,
including:

> The noblest gift you could receive,
> The noblest gift to-day I'd give;
> A father's heart I would bestow,
> But that you stole it long ago.[10]

When he was confined in the Tower of London
in 1763, one of his first actions was to write to his
daughter to assure her that he had 'done nothing
unworthy of a Man of Honour, who has the
happiness of being your father'. However, he also
sent a copy of this letter to the press at the earliest
opportunity.[11]

This portrait of a loving father and dutiful
daughter was certainly in progress by November
1779, when Horace Walpole saw it in Zoffany's
studio, although it was not exhibited until three
years later. The fame of the sitters drew the
attention of many reviewers, most of whom praised
the strength of the likenesses. Walpole, too, thought
it 'like', but 'Horridly' so.[12] Never a fan of the
politician, he had thrown an unflattering analogy
at the painting on first viewing: 'It is a caricatura
of the Devil acknowledging Miss Sin in Milton.'
He also attacked the strangely exotic-looking
willow tree behind the sitters: 'I do not know why,
but they are under a palm tree, which has not
grown in a free country for some centuries.'[13]
It could be that the tree and the riverscape behind
were intended to suggest the Thames and the
garden of the Wilkes's house in Elysium Row,
Fulham, which John personally tended.[14] Even as
a rather more generic suggestion of a country
residence, it is an appropriate backdrop for a man
who clearly felt he had finally achieved some
security, both professional and financial, and who
was keen to advertise his domestic ties.

KR

1. British Library, Add. MS 30,871, f. 258, John Wilkes
   to Sir Stephen Janssen, 18 Nov. 1775.
2. Webster 2011, 388; Webster 1990, 19.
3. Lewis 1937–83, 33, 138, Horace Walpole to
   Lady Ossory, 14 Nov. 1779.
4. *London Courant*, 2 May 1782.
5. British Library, Add. MS 30,880B, f. 71, John Wilkes
   to Maria Stafford, 14 March 1778.
6. British Library, Add. MS 30,879, f. 126, John Wilkes
   to Polly Wilkes, 24 June 1768.
7. Ribeiro 2000, 133–5.
8. *Morning Post*, 2 May 1782.
9. Sainsbury 2006, 19.
10. John Almon, ed., *The New Foundling Hospital for Wit*,
    2nd ed., 6 vols., London, 1784, vol. 1, 389.
11. British Library, Add. MS 30,879, f. 13, John Wilkes
    to Polly Wilkes, 1 May 1763; *Public Advertiser*,
    7 May 1763.
12. Graves 1905–6, vol. 8, 413.
13. Lewis 1937–83, 33, 138, Horace Walpole to
    Lady Ossory, 14 Nov. 1779.
14. Sainsbury 2006, 26–7. The suggestion was made in
    Manners & Williamson 1920, 74.

The Sharp Family

1779–81

Oil on canvas, 115.6 × 125.7 cm (45½ × 49½ in)
By courtesy of the National Portrait Gallery,
London, and the Lloyd-Baker Trustees

Provenance: Commissioned by William Sharp; by
descent in the family of his only daughter, Mary
(1778–1812), who in 1800 married Thomas
Lloyd-Baker (1774–1841) of Hardwicke Court,
Gloucestershire; thence to his great-great-grand-
daughter, the late Miss Olive Lloyd-Baker

Selected exhibitions: Royal Academy 1781, no. 85;
Royal Academy 1934, no. 241; Royal Academy
1954–5, no. 120; Arts Council 1960–61, no. 13;
Royal Academy 1968–9, no. 62; National Portrait
Gallery 1977, no. 87; *Handel: A Celebration of his
Life and Times, 1685–1759*, National Portrait
Gallery, London, 1985, no. 228

Selected references: Manners & Williamson 1920,
70–72, 175–6; Williamson 1931, 18–19; Sitwell,
1936, 30–31; Paulson 1975, 54; John Kerslake,
'A Note on Zoffany's "Sharp Family"', *Burlington
Magazine*, vol. 120, no. 908 (Nov. 1978), 753–4;
J. Simon 1985, 239, 246–7; Leppert, 1988, 205–8;
Ribeiro 2000, 137–9; Crosby 2001, 1–118;
Treadwell 2009, 303–7; Webster 2011, 388–94

The Sharp siblings were a close-knit, highly
musical family, who gathered together regularly to
perform. Once a fortnight, the brothers would give
a Sunday concert of sacred music, and throughout
the summer months the entire family would
engage in what they termed 'Water Scheems'.[1]
The performances given by the Sharps on their
yachts, shallops (small open boats) and barges
were renowned,[2] attracting members of the royal
family, ambassadors and foreign ministers. They
would also venture beyond London, as far afield
as Lincolnshire and Norfolk.[3] As Zoffany was
working on this portrait of the Sharp family on
board a barge named *The Apollo*, a song about their
activities was published in *The Morning Chronicle*:

> In the golden barge we ride;
> Down the silver Thames we glide;
> Eternally picking
> Cold ham and cold chicken … Puff! puff! puff! –
> With flute, double-flute,
> And serpent to boot.
> Hum! hum! hum! Toot! toot! toot!
> With flats and with sharps,
> French horns and Welsh harps …[4]

The specific Thames location in the painting is
discernible from the strip of land visible behind the
mass of sitters. On the left is old Fulham church,
adjoining a cottage with bowed balconies that
belonged to William Sharp, owner of *The Apollo*.
The boat flying the Union Jack from its stern below
the church is *The Union*, a Sharp yacht built in 1775

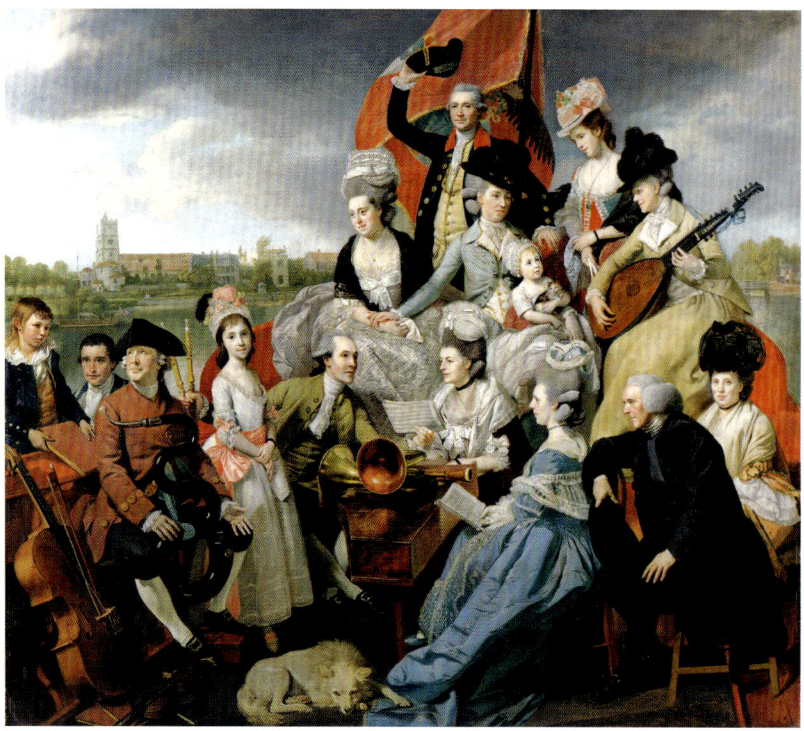

and also used for musical parties.[5] On the right of the canvas is the south end of the old wooden-railed Fulham Bridge with its tollhouse.

This representation of the 'pleasant moving Picture'[6] the family made on their watery expeditions was commissioned by William Sharp, surgeon to George III. Here, he raises his hat in much the same manner as Earl Cowper (cat. 54), with one hand firmly on the tiller of the boat and his wife Catherine and baby daughter Mary seated below. In his Windsor uniform, with the family standard made by his sister Judith[7] gently unfurling in the breeze behind and a dark, threatening cloud lowering overhead, his likeness seems almost a parody of military portraiture. A storm may be approaching, but the Sharps were well prepared for such eventualities. As well as bedrooms and a dining room below deck, *The Apollo* also had an awning. William's sister, Elizabeth, recalls a performance given for George III and Charlotte one August day being interrupted by a thunderstorm: 'The out Side House, was drawn over the Performers, & Instruments, in a moment. & seeing their Majestys had only the Tree to chelter them, my Bro:rs took the House of the little Boat, & in 2 minits lifted it up to the Taris [Trees].'[8]

The other Sharp brothers are posed in the lower half of the canvas. On the right is the eldest, Dr John Sharp, Archdeacon of Northumberland, wearing 'full Canonicals'[9], with his wife Mary seated behind. John and Mary's daughter, Anna Jemima, is the demure figure standing some way above her parents, grasping a fan. The most famous of the four brothers, Granville Sharp, philanthropist and abolitionist, holds up sheet

music for his sister Elizabeth and grasps his double flageolet. His ability to play this complex instrument attracted some attention, although verdicts differed on the results. While William Shield recalled his performances as 'to the delight and conviction of many doubters', R.J.S. Stevens remarked: 'From the impossibility of blowing two flutes in tune, at one time, the performance after the novelty of it was over, was rather disagreeable.'[10] In a distinctly subversive gesture, Granville holds this instrument so that it makes the unmistakable sign of the cuckold's horns above the head of James Sharp. This fourth brother sits with his serpent between his legs, gazing over his shoulder at the cabin boy who brings another book of music to the family, while the face of the boatmaster pops up comically between them. James's wife, Catherine, is the lady in the lilac dress and black shawl. She gazes rather mournfully towards her husband across the head of their daughter Catherine, clasps a handkerchief and is the recipient of a comforting gesture from William's spouse.

This section of the painting can be deciphered as an 'in joke', of the kind of which the Sharps were particularly fond. Their memoirs, letters and jottings have a distinctly jovial tone, filled with puns and witticisms, and often signed with just an initial and a '#'. James was a noted ironmaster, as well as an engineer, an inventor, a navigator and a member of the Thames committee. He was thus fondly known as Vulcan, the heavenly farrier and husband of Venus.[11] Zoffany here appears to be playing on the nickname, as Venus famously cuckolds her spouse after falling in love with Mars. This makes sense of both Granville's gesture and Catherine's indication of sympathy, the latter

perhaps also drawing on the fact that neither wife appears to have engaged much with her spouse's musical activities. It is the kind of humorous touch of which Zoffany was so fond, and a sympathetic bond with these sitters must have encouraged such banter. Zoffany was a great musical enthusiast, and good friends with J.C. Bach, Carl Friedrich Abel and Giacobbe Cervetto, who are among those identified as having performed on the Sharps' barge. Indeed, the artist himself was present at at least one of the Sharps' Sunday concerts, and he owned his own boat, a shallop staffed by servants in livery, which was used for musical parties.[12] The jest at James's expense was thus born of an amicable relationship, signed off with the inclusion of Zoffany's dog, Roma. Viewed in exactly the same pose as in the portrait of John and Mary Wilkes (cat. 76), Roma acts as a stand-in for the painter. The complex narrative, however, left the portrait open to other interpretations. One commentator fantasized that the Sharps had been shown

> grounding on a Shoal near Fulham … One of the Mr. *Sharps*, very *naturally* waves his Hat for Assistance from shore – The Ladies dread a general Leak – The Thames Committee Brother has his Eyes fixed toward Heaven, asking Forgiveness for not having removed the Shoals. – At the same Time a Serpent is gnawing at his Breast, as an Emblem of a hurt Conscience.[13]

The remaining members of the family are the three Sharp sisters. Judith, in a yellow riding habit and extraordinary black hat trimmed with ostrich feathers, plays a lute; Frances, in a blue silk *robe à l'anglaise*, holds some sheet music, while Elizabeth plays the fortepiano at the centre of the group.[14] Some debate has taken place over whether this

might rather represent a small harpischord.
However, the fact that she was presented with such
a piano by her late husband's sister in March 1780,
while Zoffany's canvas was in progress, is surely
significant.[15] Indeed, the musical instruments
scattered throughout the painting are notable
for their specificity and the accuracy of their
representation. Granville's flageolets survive in
the Bate collection at Oxford, as do his clarinets
and William's french horns, depicted on top of the
piano (fig. 193).[16] Much of our knowledge as to the
Sharps' activities comes from Elizabeth's diary, and
she records the lengthy process by which Zoffany
constructed the portrait. Work had begun by
12 November 1779, when she noted that 'all the
Party was siting to Zopheney for the Family
Picture, & when I go to Town am to be aded to
the Party'. On the 29th of that month she writes:
'Jud[ith] & I set out for London & my Picture
was aded to the Grupe.' Her portrait, however,
was still unfinished by December 1780, when
Zoffany made a trip to her home, Wicken Park
in Northamptonshire, in order to complete the
canvas in time for the Royal Academy exhibition
the following year.[17]

Elizabeth's account emphasizes the complex,
additive process by which the likenesses of the
various members of the family had to be combined
and organized by the artist. The composition, at
first sight, is rather overwhelming, the sitters
crammed into the canvas and juxtaposed in a melée
of elaborate costumes and contrasting poses.
Certainly, when reviewers came to pronounce their
verdicts on the portrait in the spring of 1781, most
felt the organization to be a failure: 'the effect of the
tout ensemble is abominable',[18] 'they are piled up in
a style of grouping that it is impossible to dwell
upon without pain'.[19] There was plenty of room
for punning witticism: 'how has he … jumbled
together, without the smallest attention to
harmony, the *flats* and *sharps* of one of the most
musical families in Great-Britain!'[20]

KR

1. Gloucestershire Record Office, D3549/14/1/2,
   Memoirs of Elizabeth Prowse, née Sharp, 5 Aug. 1770.
   For discussion of the family's musical activities, see
   E.C.P. Lascelles, *Granville Sharp and the Freedom of
   Slaves in England*, London, 1928, 119–26; Hoare 1828,
   vol. 1, 207–19, vol. 2, xviii–xxiv; Crosby 2001, 1–118.
2. For the vessels, see Gloucestershire Record Office,
   D3549/12/1/11.
3. Gloucestershire Record Office, D3549/12/1/5,
   D3549/13/4/2, D3549/14/1/2, D3549/12/1/1.
4. *Morning Chronicle*, 28 June 1780.
5. There is some disagreement over whether this
   belonged to William or James. See Crosby 2001,
   47–8, 77.
6. Gloucestershire Record Office, D3549/14/1/2,
   5 Aug. 1770.
7. Gloucestershire Record Office, D3549/12/1/2,
   notes removed from the back of the portrait.
8. Gloucestershire Record Office, D3549/14/1/2,
   8 Aug. 1770.
9. Gloucestershire Record Office, D3549/12/1/2.
10. Hoare 1828, vol. 2, xviii–xxiv, 'Appendix VI: Remarks
    on Mr G. Sharp's "Short Introduction to Vocal Music"
    by William Shield, Esq. Master of his Majesty's Band
    of Musicians [1816]', esp. xix; Mark Argent, ed.,
    *Recollections of R.J.S. Stevens: An Organist in Georgian
    London*, London and Basingstoke, 1992, 10.
11. C.S. Smith, 'James Sharp: Pioneer of Rolling Carts',
    Country Life, vol. CLII, 7 Dec. 1972, 1596.
12. Gloucestershire Record Office, D3549/12/1/5,
    'Visiting Book', 1773–83. 'Mr Zeffany' was present at
    a concert on 13 February 1780. For Zoffany's musical
    activities in general, see Webster 2011, 198, 272, 376,
    386, 391–2, 402, 603, 613. See also Webster 2011,
    Appendix 7, 640–41, the catalogue to the Christie's
    sale of Zoffany's effects, 17–18 Aug. 1772, which
    includes two violins, two guitars, a harpsichord and
    a music desk.
13. *Public Advertiser*, 3 May 1781. Reproduced in the
    Morning Herald, 4 May 1781.
14. For the costumes, see Ribeiro 2000, 137–9.
15. See Crosby 2001, 9–10, 55–6, for discussion.
16. J. Simon 1985, 239, 246–8, cats. 228–31.
17. Gloucestershire Record Office, D3549/14/1/2,
    12 Nov. 1779, 29 Nov. 1779, Dec. 1780.
18. Anon. 1781, 10.
19. *Morning Herald*, 10 May 1781; *Morning Chronicle*,
    10 May 1781.
20. *Whitehall Evening Post*, 1 May 1781; reproduced in
    Morning Herald, 2 May 1781.

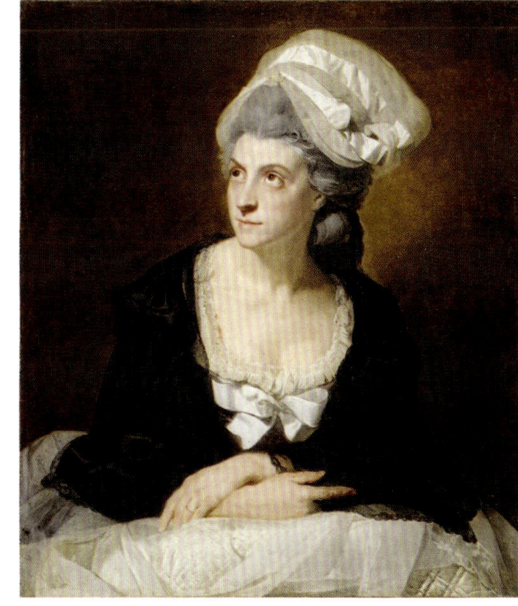

78

Mary Thomas (Mrs Zoffany)
*c.*1781

Oil on canvas, 75 × 61.5 (29½ × 24¼ in)
Ashmolean Museum, University of Oxford;
purchased with the assistance of the Museums
& Galleries Commission/Victoria & Albert
Museum Purchase Grant Fund, the National
Art Collections Fund and the Friends of the
Ashmolean, 1979

Provenance: By descent from the sitter to
Miss Claudine Roberts; purchased in 1979
(WA 1979.81)

Selected exhibitions: National Portrait Gallery
1977, no. 96

Selected references: Manners & Williamson, 1920,
205; Catherine Casley, Colin Harrison and John
Whiteley, eds., *The Ashmolean Museum: Complete
Illustrated Catalogue of Paintings*, Oxford, 2004,
248; Treadwell 2009, 316–17; Webster 2011,
372, 377

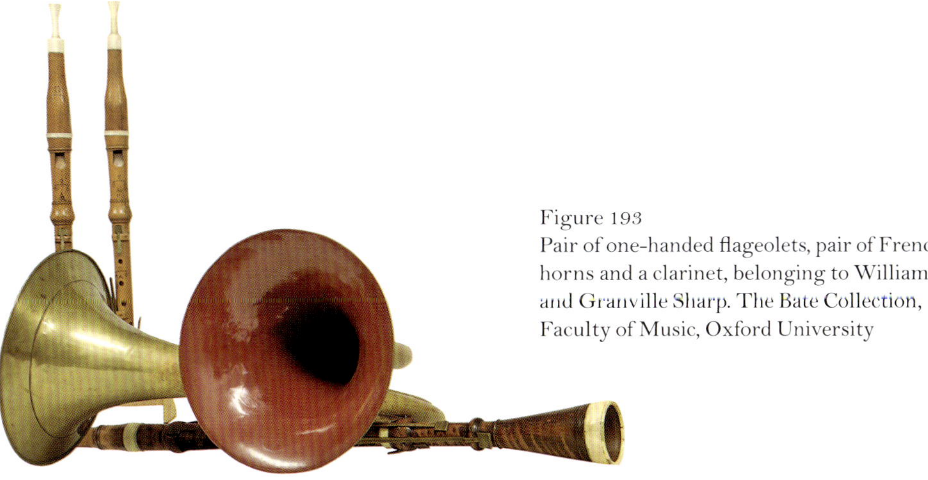

Figure 193
Pair of one-handed flageolets, pair of French
horns and a clarinet, belonging to William
and Granville Sharp. The Bate Collection,
Faculty of Music, Oxford University

Mary Zoffany (née Thomas) is seated, leaning slightly forward, her expression intelligent and alert, her gaze averted from the viewer. The dress is fashionable yet unostentatious, the sitter's arms folded modestly across the lap; a gesture reminiscent of Allan Ramsay's portraits of a decade or so earlier of ladies from polite society. Mrs Zoffany wears a wedding ring on her left hand. The prominence of the ring alludes to her status as a respectable wedded woman; yet it tells a lie, for in the eyes of the English law she and Zoffany were unmarried. Indeed, at the very time Zoffany painted this portrait, shortly after his return from Italy, he was dogged by rumours that Mary was not his only or, indeed, his real wife, and that the first Mrs Zoffany was alive and well. The rumours were true. Zoffany had married his first wife, the daughter of a Würzburg innkeeper, just before his arrival in England in 1760.[1] Although they quickly separated, Zoffany's German wife continued to cling to her married status and to pursue him for money for years to come. When Zoffany and Mary returned to England, it was even suggested in Italy that he had been hanged for bigamy.[2] And, while bigamy was not a hanging offence in England, gossip continued to surround their relationship and the legitimacy of their children. It is not surprising, therefore, that Mary Zoffany preferred to keep a low profile and seldom strayed beyond her intimate circle of friends.

Mary Thomas, the daughter of a London glove maker, first met Zoffany sometime in the winter of 1771 or early the following year.[3] Mary's own account of her early life with Zoffany was recorded in the memoirs of her friend Charlotte Papendiek. According to Mrs Papendiek, Mary had told her how Zoffany, who 'in his leisure hours prowled around for victims of self-gratification', had stalked her to her parents' 'humble dwelling'.[4] Shortly afterwards he left for Italy. On discovering that she was pregnant, Mary stowed away on the boat, making herself known to Zoffany during the voyage. On arrival in Italy, Zoffany apparently told Mary that he had discovered that his German wife had died a few months earlier, and so 'he married the object of his affection, who became a mother at fifteen'.[5] According to an unverifiable source, Zoffany and Mary were married 'according to the rites of the Catholic church' in Genoa, Zoffany having gained legal proof of his first wife's death in Koblenz. It was also asserted by the same source that on their return to England in 1779 Zoffany and Mary were married in a Protestant ceremony at Wood Street in Cheapside, after which all four of their daughters were born.[6] Aside from the possibility of a Catholic wedding ceremony in Italy (which may explain the ring on Mary's finger in the portrait), there would appear to be little truth to the story, since there is no record of any such a marriage having taken place in Wood Street.[7] Mrs Papendiek noted that before he introduced Mary to his friends on his return to England,

Zoffany 'should have married her according to the Protestant religion and our law'.[8] However, it can be verified that on 20 April 1805, on learning that his first wife had died in Würzburg earlier that year, the seventy-two-year-old 'Johan Zoffany of this Parish, Widower and Mary Thomas of the same Parish Spinster' were married in a private ceremony at the parish church of St Pancras, Camden. In signing the register, Mary had inadvertently begun to write her name 'Mary Zoff', indicating that to all intents and purposes she was already Mrs Zoffany.[9] At exactly what point in her relationship with Zoffany she became aware of the continued existence of his first wife is unrecorded. And, would she have worn a wedding ring in this portrait had she known?

By nature shy and retiring, Mary Thomas, who was known as Mrs Zoffany in Florence, blossomed in Italy. According to Mrs Papendiek, she learned to speak Italian, 'though still so young, and her beauty, good dressing, and a natural elegance of appearance, combined with the feeling of happiness which shone in her countenance, soon fitted her for any society'.[10] Her first child, a son, was born probably towards the end of 1772. He died, tragically, aged sixteen months after falling down a flight of stairs. In 1777 the couple's first daughter, Maria Theresa Louisa, was born, named after the empress who had recently ennobled Zoffany. A second daughter, Cecilia Clementina, was born in November 1780, following the couple's return to England.[11] During the early 1780s, at the time of the present portrait, Mary and Zoffany were living with their two young daughters in some style at their house in Albemarle Street and a country house at Strand-on-the-Green.

In 1783 Zoffany travelled alone to India, where he took an Indian mistress and fathered a son, whom he left behind on his return to England. On his return in 1789, he and Mary were reunited and had two further children, while Zoffany arranged for Mary's mother to live in one of the smaller houses he owned in Strand-on-the-Green. Mary Zoffany survived her husband by over twenty years and was later in life offered a proposal of marriage by the ageing sculptor Joseph Nollekens, whom she refused on the grounds that people would say that she had married him for his money. Nollekens did, however, leave her £300 in his will.[12] Mary Zoffany died with her eldest daughter in the cholera epidemic of 1832 and is buried with Zoffany in the churchyard of St Anne's Kew.

MP

1. For Zoffany's first wife, see Webster 2011, 50, 274–77.
2. 'So then it is not true that he was hanged for bigamy, as was reported among the Italians in spite of all I could say to convince them that with us, though he has two wives, it is not a hanging matter' (Lewis *et al.* 1937–83, vol. 24, 539, Horace Mann to Horace Walpole, 10 Dec. 1779).
3. Webster 2011, 276–7.
4. Papendiek 1887, vol. 1, 86.
5. Papendiek 1887, vol. 1, 87. According to Mrs Papendiek, on Mary Zoffany's own authority she was fourteen years old when made pregnant by Zoffany. However, her gravestone records that at her death, on 30 March 1832, she was seventy-seven years old, which would mean she was born in 1755 and would, therefore, have been around sixteen years old when she met Zoffany.
6. Manners & Williamson 1920, 48. The information may have come from Zoffany's descendants, who were apparently disinclined to believe Mrs Papendiek's version of events.
7. An online search, via the International Genealogical Index, of relevant parish records for the churches of St Michael and St Alban, Wood Street, London, has failed to reveal any record of Zoffany's marriage.
8. Papendiek 1887, vol. 1, 88.
9. Webster 2011, 598.
10. Papendiek 1887, vol. 1, 87.
11. See Treadwell 2009, 309.
12. Smith 1828–30, vol. 2, 18, 36.

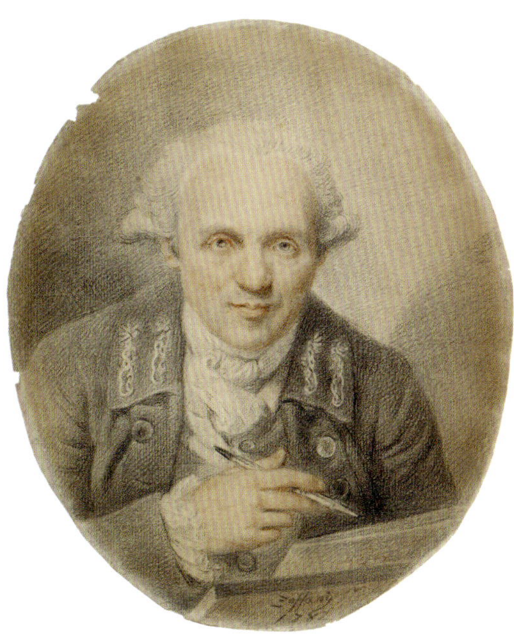

79
Self-Portrait
1782

Black and red chalk on paper,
29.7 × 24.2 cm (11¾ × 9½ in)
Inscribed: 'Zoffany 1782'
Ashmolean Museum, University of Oxford

Provenance: By descent to Miss S.J. Beachcroft,
great granddaughter of the artist; on loan to
the Fitzwilliam Museum, Cambridge, 1922–30;
Christie's, 9 Nov. 1934 (3); purchased 1934 by
the Ashmolean Museum (Hope Collection)

Selected exhibitions: British Self-Portraits, Arts
Council, 1962, no. 35; National Portrait Gallery
1977, no. 123

Selected references: Manners & Williamson 1920,
127; David Blayney Brown, _Catalogue of the
Collection of Drawings, Ashmolean Museum, Oxford_,
Oxford, 1982, vol. 4, no. 1919, 675; Ingamells 2004,
499; Treadwell 2009, 430; Webster 2010, 377

Zoffany presents himself here in an unusually
serious and straightforward manner, his powdered
wig and embroidered coat indicating his status as
a gentleman as well as an artist, for he was by now
a baron of the Holy Roman Empire, following the
honour conferred on him in 1776 by the Empress
Maria Theresa. In his right hand he holds his
porte-crayon, a double-ended drawing implement
(see cat. 42). However, assuming that he is drawing
himself in the mirror, it would appear that Zoffany
was actually left-handed. Zoffany holds his porte-
crayon in the same hand in the earlier self-portrait
drawing of _c._1775 (cat. 57). In the _Academicians
of the Royal Academy_ (cat. 44) and the Cortona
self-portrait (fig. 24) he holds his palette in his left
hand, while in the self-portrait with his daughter
and the Cervettos (fig. 31) he again appears to hold
his brush in his right hand. Assuming all these
self-portraits were made looking in the mirror, it
would confirm his left-handedness. Just to confuse
matters, in the late self-portrait with his family
(cat. 111) Zoffany holds the brush in his left hand.
However, this can be explained because that
portrait was conceived within the context of a
conversation piece – rather than as a self-portrait
per se – and for the sake of accuracy he appears to
have placed the brush in the correct hand.

As with the self-portrait painted in Parma
(cat. 59), the present drawing is dated, allowing
us to tie it precisely to a particular phase in his
career. Then aged forty-nine, Zoffany was living
in Albemarle Street and at his country house at
Strand-on-the-Green, near Kew, with his wife
and two daughters. He enjoyed a busy social and
professional life, although his lavish expenses
continued to stretch his financial resources, more
so since he had lost the influential patronage of
the king. Nonetheless, Zoffany was engaged in
a number of important paintings at this time,
including Charles Townley's Library in Park
Street, Westminster (cat. 63), and was closely
involved with Royal Academy, both as a member
of Council and as an exhibitor.

In November 1782 Zoffany applied to the East
India Company to visit India. Given the dangers
that such a journey involved, it is possible that
Zoffany made the present drawing as a keepsake
for his wife and family in the light of his imminent
departure. Certainly, the self-portrait has the
finished quality characteristic of a 'presentation'
drawing (see cat. 58) and it remained in the
possession of his family, at some point passing to
his third daughter Claudina.

MP

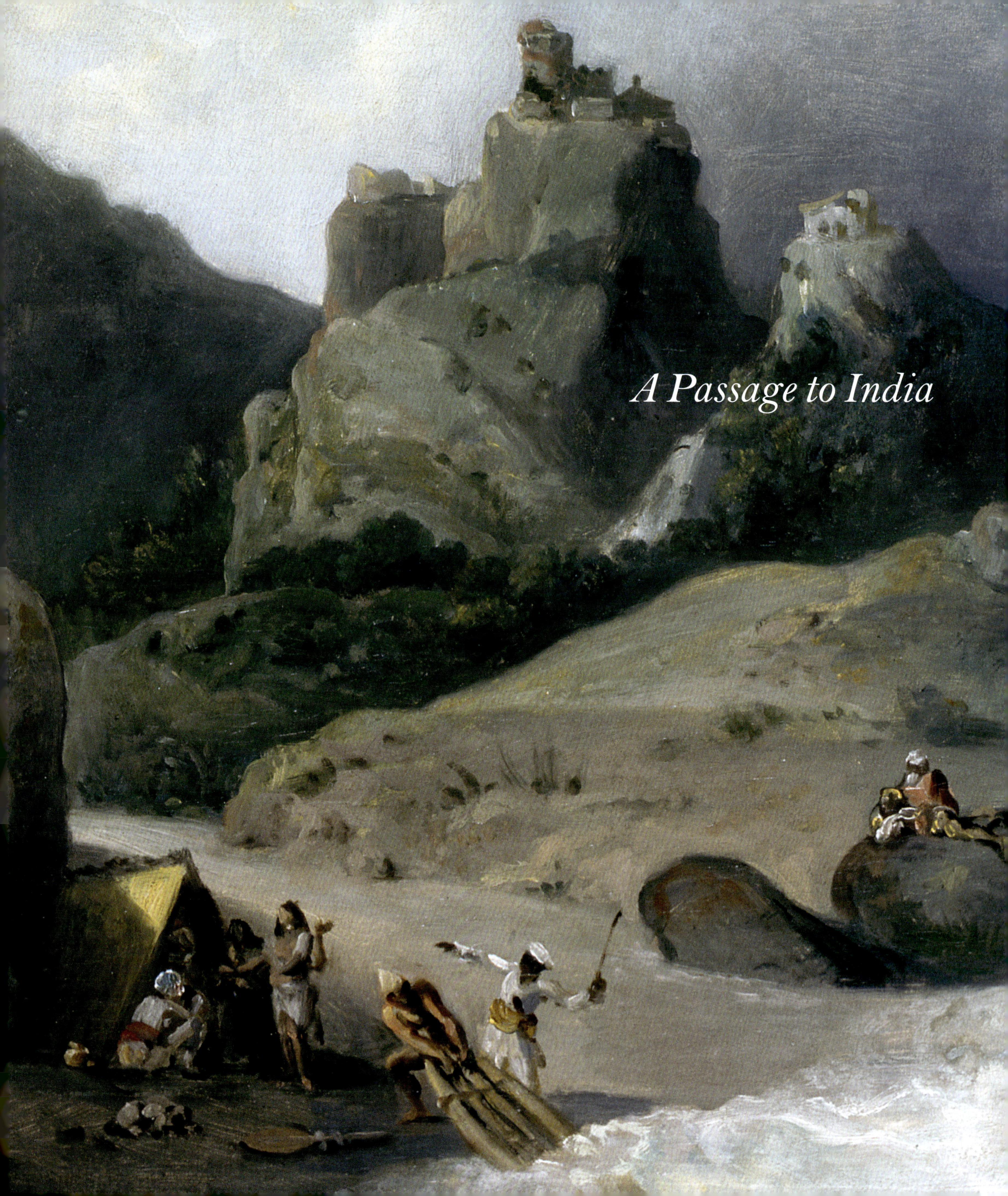
A Passage to India

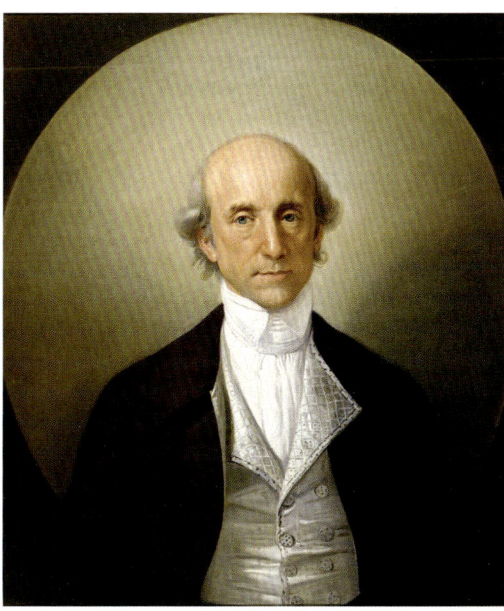

80

Warren Hastings

1783–4

Oil on canvas, 72.4 × 62.3 cm (28½ × 24½ in)
Private collection, UK

Provenance: Painted for Warren Hastings, 1783,
and presumably presented to Sir Elijah Impey,
Chief Justice in Calcutta; Colonel Archibald
Lovibond-Impey; by descent to Mrs M.A. Sanders,
Christie's, 31 July 1936, lot 203; bt H. Spiller
(frame dealer); sold H. Spiller, Christie's, 10 Dec.
1985, lot 38, as 'English School. A gentleman,
small half length, wearing a brown coat, a white
waistcoat and stock, in a painted oval, unframed';
bt the Leger Galleries and sold to the Hon. Simon
Sainsbury; private collection

*Selected exhibitions: English Pictures for the Country
House*, Leger Galleries, London, 1986, no. 18

Selected references: Manners & Williamson 1920,
98; Sir Arthur Knapp, *A Catalogue of the Known
Portraits of Warren Hastings (1732–1818), First
Governor General of Bengal*, London, 1935, no. 8;
Archer 1979, 135, 152; Treadwell 2009, 347;
Webster 2011, 465–6

The key to Zoffany's success in India was his
introduction to the Governor General, Warren
Hastings. Zoffany's arrival in Calcutta from Madras
on 15 September 1783 coincided with William
Hodges's return from up country before the latter's
departure for England on 3 December on board
the *Worcester*. The artists were old friends and it is
almost certain that the introduction to Hastings
came from this brilliant and enigmatic landscape
painter. Thereafter, the governor general become
Zoffany's chief benefactor in India and through
his munificence and patronage the artist was able
to travel extensively in Upper India.

Warren Hastings came from an old gentry
family from Worcestershire that had fallen on
hard times and lost their family estate at Daylesford
in the early eighteenth century. Brought up in
the vicarage nearby, Hastings was educated at
Westminster and held a lifelong ambition to
repurchase the family estate. To achieve this end
he fell back on the device used by numerous young
impoverished Englishmen to repair a fortune –
service in the East India Company. When Hastings
reached Calcutta in 1750 at the age of seventeen,
the Mughal Empire was already in an advanced
state of decay, but the British were still, in his own
words, 'humble … trading adventurers'.[1] Yet, by
the time Hastings departed India for the last time
thirty-five years later, they had transformed
themselves into rulers of Bengal and Bihar and
the most powerful presence in the subcontinent.
Hastings was both a witness and a participant in
this extraordinary metamorphosis, but to this day
his role remains a matter of some disagreement.

Hastings's appointment in 1772 as governor
general followed what must be the darkest period
in the British involvement in India. Following the
victories at Plassey in 1757 and Buxar seven years
later, the British became the effective rulers of the
rich Mughal provinces of eastern India. For most
of the individuals concerned, this assumption of
power merely provided an opportunity to make
as large a fortune as possible. Their rapaciousness
and greed brought about the destruction of the
economy of an entire province. It culminated in
the tragic Bengal famine of 1770 and the near
bankruptcy of the East India Company itself.
In contrast, Hastings's role during this period
seems to have been one of moderation. He alone
was held in such high esteem by Siraj-ud-daula
in 1756 that he was set at liberty in Murshidabad
during the sack of Calcutta. In the early 1760s
he supported the Nawab Mir Kasim as sovereign
prince against Clive, whose preoccupation seems
to have been the extraction of ever greater amounts
of cash from the depleted treasury in Murshidabad.

Warren Hastings's brief, on assuming power
in Calcutta, was to reform the administration of
government, to improve the Company's finances
and curb the excesses and blatant corruption of
the Europeans in Bengal. Over the next thirteen
years, despite the persistent opposition of Philip
Francis and Colonel Monson in the Council,
Hastings made significant reforms. Central to
this was the restoration of the crumbling Mughal
system of government in eastern India, which
effectively survived until 1947. He was responsible
for the codification of Muslim and Hindu law and
his local courts based on them were popular and
successful. He brought about a complete reform of
the customs to the considerable advantage of Indian
merchants. Less well known was his patronage of
Hindu learning, sponsoring translations of Sanskrit
texts and establishing with Sir William Jones the
Asiatic Society in Calcutta. Throughout his period
in office he was a generous patron of both European
and Indian artists. It is one of the ironies of history
that on Hastings's return to England it was he
who was impeached rather than his deeply corrupt
rival Sir Philip Francis. After a long and strenuous
trial Hastings was cleared on all charges.

Zoffany must have started this portrait of
Hastings soon after his arrival in Calcutta. It has
long been presumed that it remained in Calcutta
until at least August 1784, when it was engraved
and published in Calcutta by Richard Brittridge,
whose print was used as the frontispiece for
Hastings's Memoirs Relative to the State of India
published in 1786. However, it is more likely that
the portrait was presented to the Chief Justice,
Sir Elijah Impey, before his departure for England
on the same ship on which Hodges sailed back
to London. The engraving was probably based
on the fine chalk preliminary drawing (private
collection). The painting is among a small group
of intimate single portraits that survive from the
artist's Calcutta period. It is a study of the governor
general in an informal setting, dressed in a modest
suit of clothes. The full-face pose accurately
conveys the strain of office but at the same time
Hastings's decency and modesty, attributes that
endeared him to his old friend the Chief Justice.
The use of the old-fashioned and almost halo-like
device of a feigned oval conveys the importance
of Hastings and his position in India. Zoffany
painted at least three other, and probably larger,
single portraits of the governor general, which are
recorded in the bill of sale that Zoffany presented
to William Larkins for Hastings in February 1786.
All three are missing.

CG

1. Penderel Moon, *Warren Hastings and British India*,
   London, 1947, 1.

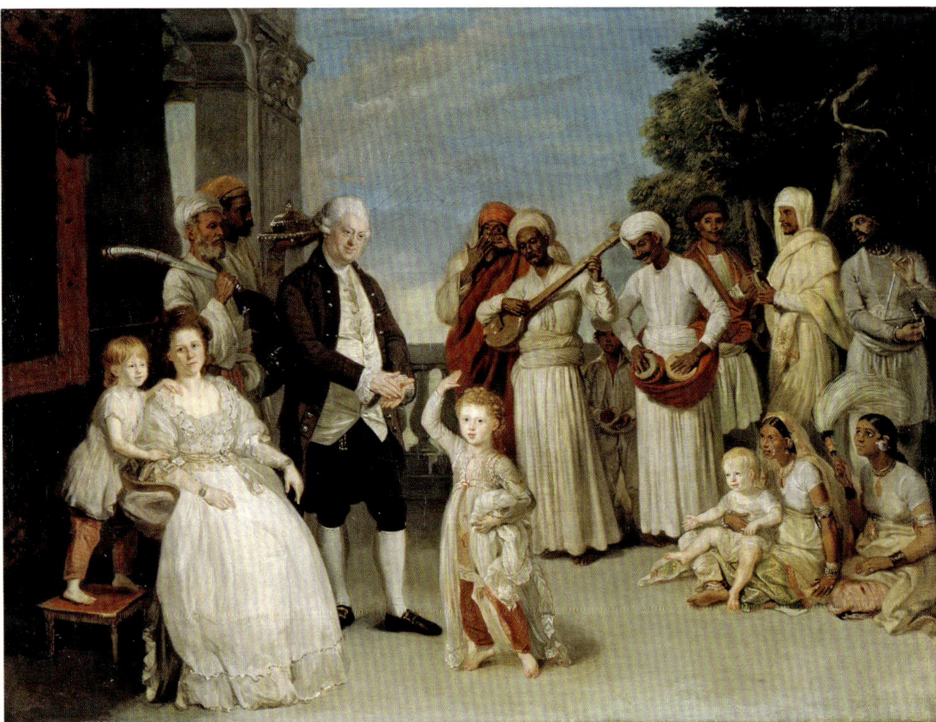

81

The Impey Family
1783

Oil on canvas, 91.5 × 122 cm (36 × 48 in)
Museo Thyssen-Bornemisza, Madrid

Exhibited at the Royal Academy of Arts only

Provenance: By descent; sold Christie's, 18 April
1986, lot 132, as 'Property of a Gentleman';
purchased Baron and Baroness Thyssen-
Bornesmisza

Selected references: Manners & Williamson 1920,
110, 207; Sitwell 1936, 32; Archer 1979, 136; Tobin
2004, 103–4; Ghosh 2006, 60–61; Treadwell 2009,
340–43; Webster 2011, 461–3

Zoffany arrived in Calcutta in September 1783,
having spent five productive weeks in Madras,
and was immediately inundated with commissions
from British residents eager to take advantage of
the presence of a portrait painter of such stature
and abilities. Zoffany was well suited to his new
environment and used his extensive experience to
construct new idioms for portraying the emerging
colonial society in both public and private spheres.
The artist's understanding of the rhetoric of court
portraiture proved invaluable for creating images of
East India Company officials that subtly conveyed
authority and probity, a pressing need given
escalating concerns in Britain about corruption and
mismanagement in India. Zoffany's family portraits
functioned as reminders of domestic life after their
subjects returned to Britain, as they invariably did,
as well as poignant memorials of those who had

not survived, a particular concern in India, where
mortality was high.

On arrival, Zoffany was immediately
commissioned to paint a portrait of Elijah Impey
(see fig. 117), the first Chief Justice of the Calcutta
Supreme Court, which had been established under
the Regulating Act of 1777, along with the Bengal
Supreme Council, in order to bring the Company
under greater control of the British government.
Impey was regarded as a man of mediocre abilities,
and his reputation had been severely damaged by
his involvement in the case of Raja Nandakumar,
a government agent who was tried and hanged in
1773 on charges of forgery, an incident in which
Warren Hastings was also implicated and which
was a key issue in the impeachment proceedings.
The consensus among recent historians is that
Impey's conduct of the Nandakumar trial was
equitable, however.[1]

Zoffany's full-length portrait of Impey was
commissioned by the 'Gentleman of the Supreme
Court',[2] presumably in an attempt to rehabilitate
the reputation of the Chief Justice, who had been
recalled by the British government in 1782
and was shortly to leave Calcutta. The portrait
still hangs in the Court House in Calcutta.[3]
A half-length portrait of Impey by Zoffany has
also survived,[4] while another portrait of Impey,
attributed to Zoffany, is in the National Portrait
Gallery, London.[5]

Cat. 81 is a family portrait commissioned by
Impey, showing his wife Mary, and three of the
four children born in Calcutta (left to right), Elijah,
Marian and Hastings. The Impeys had left their

first three children in Britain, as well as two
Impey had with Elizabeth Curbyshire before his
marriage, and their eldest child born in India had
died in infancy. The family is shown with a group
of musicians and flanked by their Indian servants.
The Impeys evidently were interested in music,
and as Jerry Losty has noted, one of the albums
in the extensive collection of Persian and Indian
manuscripts that they had assembled during their
time in Calcutta was a *Ragamala*, or series of
paintings illustrating the ragas of Indian music.[6]
Marian, wearing Indian dress, dances for the group,
encouraged by her father.

Mary Impey's expression of ennui may appear
to imply a role as long-suffering spouse passively
enduring the inconveniences of life in Calcutta,
but her engagement with India was much more
productive than Zoffany's portrayal of her might
suggest. A dedicated natural historian, Lady Impey
commissioned three Indian artists from Patna,
Shaik Zain al-Din, Ram Das and Bhawani Das, to
draw specimens from her collection of birds and
fauna, which are highly regarded for their scientific
and aesthetic significance.[7] Two images made by
indigenous artists seem to offer a more revealing
picture of domestic life in the Impeys' household
than Zoffany's staged family group: a remarkable
watercolour of Mary Impey and her servants
attributed to Shaik Zain al-Din,[8] and a companion
drawing of her children in their bedroom, which
may have been made by Ram Das or Bhawani Das.[9]

GF

1. T.H. Bowyer, 'Impey, Sir Elijah (1732–1809)', *ODNB*,
   http://www.oxforddnb.com/view/article/14371
   (accessed 10 March 2011).
2. Webster 2011, 464.
3. Repr. Archer 1979, 138, fig. 86.
4. Private collection. Archer 1979, 135, fig. 83; Webster
   2011, 462, fig. 345.
5. Ingamells 2004, 280 (repr.), no. 335.
6. *ODNB* Mary Impey. For British interest in Indian
   music in Calcutta in the 1780s, see Head 1985, 551–2.
7. *ODNB* Mary Impey.
8. Rosemary Crill and Kapil Jariwala, eds, *The Indian
   Portrait 1560–1860*, exh. cat., National Portrait
   Gallery, London, 2010, 150–51, no. 51 (repr.)
9. Stuart Cary Welch, *India: Art and Culture, 1300–1900*,
   exh. cat., Metropolitan Museum, New York, 1985,
   425, no. 281d.

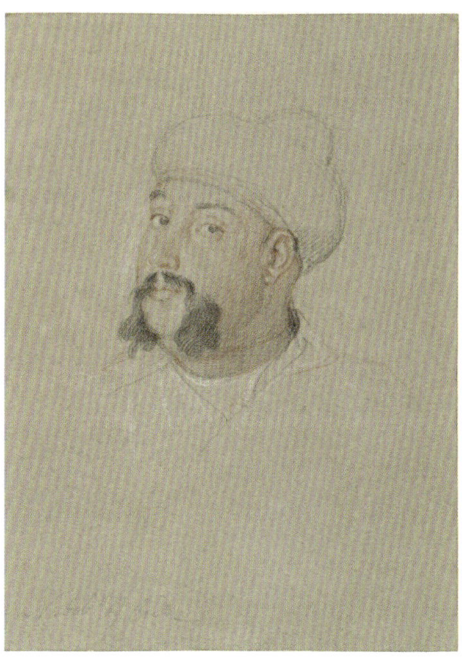

82

Asaf-ud-Daula

1784

Black, red and white chalk on paper,
21.7 × 15.2 cm (8⅝₆ × 6 in)
Inscribed, below at left: 'Nabab of Oude'
The Royal Collection, Her Majesty Queen
Elizabeth II

Exhibited at the Royal Academy of Arts only

Provenance: ?Zoffany sale, Messrs Robins, 9 May
1811, possibly part of lot 26; … Colnaghi, from
whom purchased by the Prince Regent, 5 June 1811

Selected exhibitions: Royal Academy 1947–8, no. 915;
National Portrait Gallery 1977, no. 124

Selected references: Oppé 1950, 105, no. 698; Webster
2011, 493–4

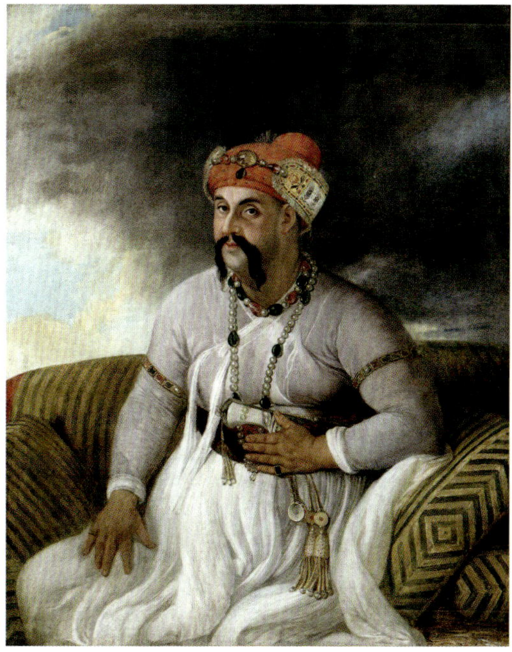

83

Asaf-ud-Daula, Nawab Wazir of Awadh

1784

Oil on canvas, 129.5 × 105.5 cm (51 × 41½ in)
The British Library, India Office Library &
Records, London

Exhibited at the Yale Center for British Art only

Provenance: Asaf-ud-Daula, by whom given to
Francis Baladon Thomas; … purchased by the
India Office Library, British Library, 1906

Selected exhibitions: Whitechapel 1908, no. 4;
Royal Academy 1947–8, no. 914; National Portrait
Gallery 1977, no. 103; National Portrait Gallery
1990–91, no. 78

Selected references: The Journal of Indian Art, XII,
vol. 12, no. 107 (July 1909), pl. 165; Manners &
Williamson 1920, 207; Foster 1924, no. 108; Archer
1979, 147–8; Archer 1986, 49, no. 65, pl. XI; Eaton
2004, 827–30; Webster 2011, 493–5

In the summer of 1784 Zoffany travelled from
Calcutta to Lucknow at Warren Hastings's
invitation, arriving on 3 June. Hastings had arrived
there two months earlier, and Zoffany's journey
of eight hundred miles evidently was not without
some difficulties, since Sir William Jones later
noted that he had been 'exposed … to a thousand
distresses on the way'.[1]

Hastings's visit had been prompted by the East
India Company's increasing inability to exert
control over the court of Awadh. Asaf-ud-Daula,
the nawab, was in chronic arrears with payment of
the enormous revenues levied by the British which
they desperately needed to finance the escalating
costs of the hostilities with the French in India, and
his resources were continually drained by the large
and ever-increasing retinue of British employees
foisted upon him by the Company. In 1781 Hastings
had articulated his strong disapproval of the latter
situation in a letter to his former personal agent
John Macpherson:

> Lucnow [*sic*] was the Sink of Iniquity. It was the
> School of Rapacity. What will you say of beardless
> Boys rejecting with Indignation the offer of
> monthly gratuities of 3000 and 5000 Rupees?
> What will you think of Clerks in Office clamoring
> for principalities, threatening those who hesitated
> to gratify their Wants with the Vengeance of
> Patronage? What will you think of Men receiving
> the Wages of Service from the Nabob, and
> disclaiming his Right to Command it; and what of
> a City filled with as many independent and absolute
> Sovereignties as there are Englishmen in it.
>
> Such was the true portrait of what Lucknow
> was. I was resolved to reform it. I made no
> distinction for my own friends.[2]

Hastings seems to have prevaricated over making a
direct intervention; however, by the end of 1782
diplomatic relations between Awadh and the British
had deteriorated to such an extent, damaged
further by Hastings's notoriously aggressive
extortion of funds from the court of Bahu Begam,
Asaf-ud-Daula's estranged mother, at Faizabad,
that he felt it critical to attempt to resolve the
situation in person.[3] Despite the tenacity with
which Hastings prosecuted his policies in Awadh,
Asaf-ud-Daula seems to have venerated the
governor general, attributing the humiliations
to which he was subjected by the Company to
the intransigent Resident, John Bristow, instead.
Hastings evidently considered that Zoffany, ever
alert to the role portraiture could play in the
dynamics of power, could assist in facilitating his
highly sensitive diplomatic mission. As Natasha
Eaton has suggested, Hastings had attempted
to institute a practice of giving portraits rather
than jewels or other costly objects for diplomatic
purposes to deflect criticisms of corruption.[4]
Hastings was not slow to make use of the artist's
presence in Lucknow, since Zoffany's first sitting
with the newly arrived refugee prince, Jawan Bakht
(cat. 85), took place the day after his arrival.

Hastings kept a detailed journal of his five-month sojourn in Awadh, and his diary entries provide an invaluable record of Zoffany's official commissions as well as a vivid picture of life at court.[5] On 21 June Zoffany began a series of four sittings with Asaf-ud-Daula, which Hastings attended.[6] Hastings's diary entries are brief but highly revealing of the extent to which politics and art were inextricably entwined. On Wednesday 23 June he noted, 'went w y[e] N[awab] to his 2[d] Sitt[g] to Zoffany and visited him in y[e] Ev[g] to take Leave, and to commission him to make my Peace w his Mother.'[7] Hastings's evening visit was followed by a high-profile reconciliation between Asaf and Bahu Begam's court at Faizabad, one of his key objectives for the Awadh mission and marking a significant shift in power politics that would be highly beneficial for the British, as well as offering the possibility that payment of some of the nawab's colossal debts might be forthcoming.[8] Hastings's diary entries did not chronicle the conversations that took place during the nawab's sittings to Zoffany, but it seems likely that they would have played a significant role in the diplomatic process. Hastings was to institute a number of 'reforms' in the wake of his visit to Awadh, reducing Asaf-ud-Daula's crippling debts to the Company, separating his personal from state finances, and withdrawing many of the Company troops and hangers-on.

Zoffany produced a number of portraits of Asaf-ud-Daula, including a chalk drawing (cat. 82), presumably made at one of the sittings, that Zoffany used as a basis for his paintings, including cat. 83. Many contemporary accounts of Asaf have survived, typically laden with Orientalist tropes and stressing his impotence, homosexuality, self-indulgence, corpulence, addiction to gaming, undiscriminating aesthetic taste, and legendary profligacy.[9] Lewis Ferdinand Smith, one of the nawab's retinue of British hangers-on, noted in a lengthy account sent to a friend in 1795 that his employer was

> fond of lavishing his treasures on gardens, palaces, horses, elephants, and above all, on fine European guns, lustres, mirrors, and all sorts of European manufactures, more especially English; from a two-penny deal board painting of ducks and drakes, to the elegant paintings of a Lorraine or a Zoffani … a curious compound of extravagance, avarice, candour, cunning, levity, cruelty, childishness, affability, brutish sensuality, good humour, vanity, and imbecility.[10]

While it is indisputable that Asaf had allowed the fiscally robust Awadh that he had inherited from his able father Shuja-ud-Daula to fall into decline, more recent revisionist accounts have argued persuasively that he was an astute politician who was deprived of agency by the British and dealt with his humiliating puppet status by strategically avoiding issues of governance and assuming the stereotypical attributes of the debauched and

infantilized oriental ruler. Maya Jasanoff has suggested in the present volume that Asaf's lavish cultural programme can be interpreted as an assertion of his autonomy. He was a devout Shiite, and his project to build the monumental Bara Imambara may have been conceived in part as a work creation scheme during a period of famine, but it was also an eloquent manifestation of his ambitious re-imagining of Lucknow as a pre-eminent Muslim centre.

Cats. 82 and 83 are sympathetic portrayals of Asaf-ud-Daula, which stress his princely dignity rather than his renowned corpulence, as does another, three-quarter-length portrait by Zoffany painted in 1786, for which the present drawing may have served as a preliminary sketch. Asaf gave the latter portrait, which measures only 41 × 32 cm (16⅛ × 12⅝ in), to Sir John Shore, the governor general, when he visited Lucknow in 1797, and Shore deemed it 'a strong resemblance of the Nabob'.[11] In cat. 83 Asaf is depicted seated on a *musnud*, or cushion throne, wearing a translucent white, Mughal-style muslin garment and a traditional Awadhi turban-cap adorned with a band fastened with a *sarpech*, or jewelled *aigrette*. As Mary Webster has noted, the portrait was probably intended to be semi-formal, since Asaf is not depicted clasping a sword or sitting upright as in fig. 194.[12]

Zoffany's portrayal of Asaf in Warren Hastings's version of *Colonel Mordaunt's Cock Match* (cat. 86) was much more ambiguous, however. It is undocumented how many portraits Zoffany produced of him, but two were recorded in the inventory of Claude Martin's collection (see cat. 90).[13] Zoffany presumably brought cat. 82 with him when he returned to England from India; it was not described in the catalogue for his 1811 posthumous sale, but may have been part of lot 26, which was described as 'Nine [sketches], Colonel Martin and other Portraits, &c.'[14] and was purchased from Colnaghi on 5 June of that year by the Prince of Wales.[15]

Asaf-ud-Daula's opinion of Zoffany's portraits is not recorded, but the nawab's preference for his 'own country pictures to any Mr Z. can do', noted by Ozias Humphry,[16] was borne out by Asaf's extensive collection of superlative examples of Mughal painting. Asaf also stimulated the formation of a 'Lucknow School' of indigenous artists working within the traditional Indian artistic conventions, who were, in turn, also influenced by visiting European artists, including Zoffany. It is likely that Asaf would have commissioned a number of such copies as gifts for Europeans, including fig. 194. Asaf gave cat. 83 to Francis Baladon Thomas, a Company employee who was his attending physician, together with Zoffany's portrait of his minister, Hasan Reza Khan. The two portraits have identical gilded frames embellished with a fish, the emblem of Awadh, which are presumably original. Baladon

Thomas was court-martialled and dismissed in 1784, and as Eaton has suggested, Asaf's gift of Zoffany's portrait to a disgraced Company employer could be read as a measure of how little he valued the portraits as well as a subtle subversion of Hastings's policy of exchanging portraits for diplomatic purposes.[17]

GF

1. See Webster 2011, 483.
2. Hastings to John Macpherson, 12 Dec. 1781, quoted in Henry Dodwell, ed., *Warren Hastings' Letters to Sir John Macpherson*, London, 1927, 106–7.
3. See Barnett 1980 for a detailed account of the complex and fraught relationship between the British and Awadh between 1720 and 1801.
4. Eaton 2004, 810ff.
5. Hastings papers, British Library Add. MSS 39,878–9.
6. Archer 1979, 145. Hastings papers, British Library Add. MS 39,879, ff. 30–34.
7. Hastings papers, British Library Add. MS 39,879, f. 30.
8. For Hastings's visit to Awadh and its outcomes, see Barnett 1980, 223–38.
9. The writers of these critiques were often poorly educated Company employees, who seldom seem to have appreciated the irony of the fact that they often were the beneficiaries of Asaf's generosity.
10. Quoted in Archer 1979, 144.
11. Webster 2011, 494.
12. Webster 2011, 494.
13. Archer 1979, 448.
14. Robins 1811, lot 26 (9 May); Webster 2011, 644.
15. Webster 2011, 493.
16. Quoted in Eaton 2004, 834.
17. Eaton 2004, 827.

Figure 194
Unknown Lucknow artist after Johan Zoffany, *Asaf-ud-daula*, *c*.1784, pencil, pen and black ink, watercolour and bodycolour with gum arabic, 44.8 × 31.8 cm (17⅝ × 12½ in). Private collection

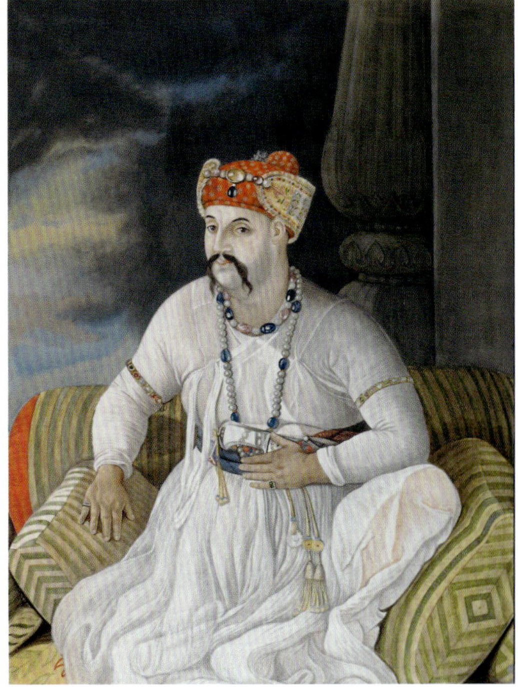

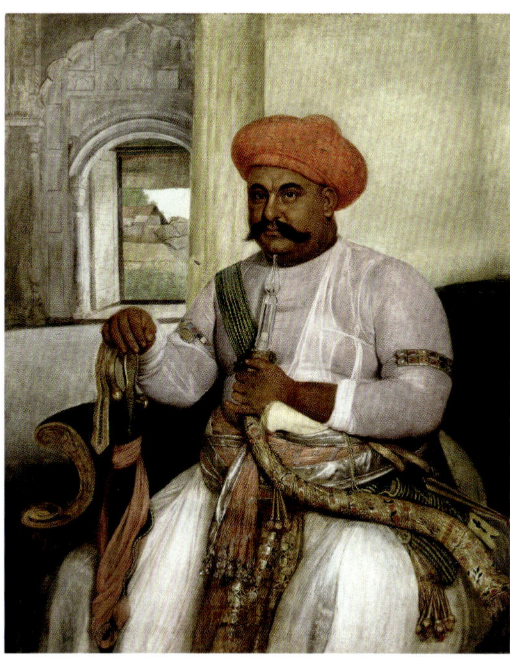

84

Hasan Reza Khan

1784

Oil on canvas, 129.5 × 105.5 cm (51 × 41½ in)
Inscribed verso: 'Joh. Zophany painted this Picture
at Lucknow, AD 1784, by desire of Hussain Reza
Caun, Nabob Suffraj Ul Dowlah, who gave it to
his friend Francis Baladon Thomas'
The British Library, India Office Library &
Records, London

Provenance: Given by the sitter to Francis Baladon
Thomas; by descent; purchased 1906

Selected exhibitions: Whitechapel 1908, no. 4; Royal
Academy 1947–8, no. 914; National Portrait
Gallery 1977, no. 103; National Portrait Gallery
1990–91, no. 140

Selected references: The Journal of Indian Art, XII,
no. 107, July 1909, pl. 166; Manners & Williamson
1920, 207; Foster 1924, no. 108; Denys Sutton,
'Sahib and Guru', *Apollo*, vol. 92, Aug. 1970, 90,
fig. 4; Archer 1979, 146–7; Archer 1986, 49–50,
no. 66, pl. XI; Webster 2011, 495–6

Hasan Reza Khan had been made chief minister
(*Naib-i-kull*, or absolute deputy) by Asaf-ud-Daula
soon after the beginning of his reign. He is said
to have already served as superintendent of
Shuja-ud-daula's kitchen, a position of importance
in an Indian court where so much emphasis was
placed on entertainment and Mughal and Persian
cuisine. He was a devout Shiite Muslim and came
from an old family that had been in the service of
the Mughals in Delhi before venturing to Faizabad
in the third quarter of the eighteenth century. His
grandfather had been a courtier under the Mughal
Emperor Aurangzeb and was a distant relative of
the founder of the Awadh dynasty, Sada'at Khan.

As chief minister, Hasan Reza Khan continued
to supervise Asaf-ud-Daula's private kitchen but
more significantly he was responsible for the
administration of the East India Company's
revenue assignment in Awadh. This often involved
tortuous and protracted negotiations with the
British through the various Residents. They in turn
relied heavily on him in their negotiations with the
nawab, despite the fact that he was largely illiterate
and had only a limited grasp of business matters.
He used his long tenure in office to promote the
Shiite faction and particularly his own relatives in
court, where over two hundred were present: after
Haider Beg's death in 1792 the Governor General
Sir John Shore recorded that Hasan Reza Khan
was using his position to monopolize the entire
administration through his family. In 1793, during
the short-lived second Rohilla War, he turned
his abilities to military matters, leading three
battalions of the nawab's sepoys together with
800 cavalry and eight guns.

Hasan Reza Khan was painted by a number
of European artists who visited Faizabad and
Lucknow, including Tilly Kettle, Ozias Humphry
and Charles Smith. Zoffany painted him on a
number of occasions. He appears as a dignified
figure dressed in a splendid blue brocade coat
standing behind Salar Jung in both versions of
Colonel Mordaunt's Cock Match (cats. 86 and 87).
This single portrait appears to be the sole survivor
of a number of such portraits of Hasan Reza Khan
that were done in Lucknow – three were listed
among the effects of Claude Martin after his death
in Calcutta on 13 September 1800. From the
evidence of surviving copies by Indian artists there
were probably others done for the sitter himself.

The first impression is of an immensely large
man, too many rich pulaos and too little exercise no
doubt contributing to his expansive girth. Here he
is shown seated on a sturdy gilt framed sofa covered
in dark green velvet. He wears a coat (*jama*) of fine
white muslin for which Lucknow was famous, a
vermilion turban, jewelled armlets (*buserbunds*),
a green sash and a broad cummerband which
supports an ivory hilted dagger (*khanjar*). His right
hand rests on the hilt of a sword with a green velvet
scabbard and his left hand holds the gold thread
and brocade-covered 'snake', or hose, of a hookah
(*huqqa*) with a cut-glass mouthpiece. Fine glass
was produced in India in the Mughal period at
Firozabad near Agra, in Hyderabad and in western
India, but glass was also imported from Europe.
The shape and cutting on Hasan Reza Khan's
mouthpiece suggests that it was made in England
as part of the luxury trade for the Indian market,
much of it destined for the court at Lucknow. The
hookah had been introduced into India in about
1600 from Persia. The earliest record dates from
1604 when a Mughal courtier Asad Beg acquired
tobacco and jewelled pipes in Bijapur and presented
one to the Emperor Akbar. By the late eighteenth
century Lucknow itself produced some of the finest

bell-shaped hookahs in precious metals and enamel.
The background is probably Hasan Reza Khan's
house on the opposite side of the river from the
Macchi Bhawan. There he had established a new
district, Hasanabad. The room, decorated in late
Mughal style, looks out through an arched window
to a rural village nearby. Other rooms in the house
were probably more European in style if we are to
believe Ozias Humphry's description. In 1786 after
dining with the minister, he wrote, 'If I looked no
further than the Tea-table, I could persuade myself
I was in London', to which the minister replied:
'For some years their interest had been so
connected and interwoven with the English that
they endeavoured in all matters that they could
with propriety to accommodate themselves to
these manners.'[1]

An inscription on the reverse of the picture
records the gift of the painting to Francis Baladon
Thomas. He had entered the Company's service
back in 1767, serving as surgeon to various
brigades. In May 1781 Asaf-ud-Daula had
requested his services to help develop a trade in
the products of his forests and hills, presumably
plants for medicinal purposes. A year later he was
again in attendance on the nawab, as physician.
In the following year he was appointed Surgeon
to the Lucknow Residency, paying his predecessor,
Dr Murchison, a year's salary to relinquish the
post. His departure from Lucknow in August 1784,
following his dismissal for demanding excessive
fees from the Resident, is mired in controversy.
Thomas drew the princely salary of £14,000 for
the combined services of Surgeon to the Nawab and
the Residency. Yet it appears that John Bristow, the
Resident, certainly one of the greediest Company
officials in an age when corruption was rampant,
seems to have been drawing much higher fees for
the Surgeon from the Company and pocketing the
difference for himself. This painting was probably
the parting gift from a grateful friend for medical
services and must have been one of the earliest
works completed during Zoffany's first visit to
Lucknow.

CG

1. Ozias Humphry's diary, Osborn Collection,
   Beinecke Rare Book and Manuscript Library,
   Yale University, f. 26.

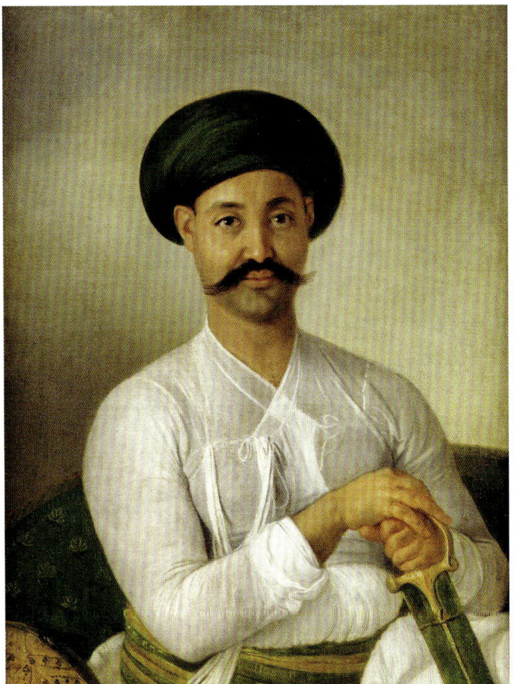

85

Prince Jawan Bakht (Jahandar Shah)
1784

Oil on canvas, 91.5 × 66.1 cm (36 × 26 in)
Private collection

Provenance: Painted in Lucknow for Warren
Hastings; by descent through Mrs Hastings's
family to Miss Winter, Nether Worton House,
Oxfordshire; acquired by the booksellers, Francis
Edwards, *c.*1920

Selected references: Manners & Williamson 1920,
112 (incorrectly identified as Beneram Das);
Archer 1979, 181 (incorrectly as by Charles Smith);
Treadwell 2009, 353; Webster 2011, 483–5

On the night of 14 April 1784 Prince Jawan Bakht
slipped out of his chamber and, with the aid of a
rope, climbed down a wall of the Red Fort (*Lal
Qila*), Delhi, to waiting companions below. Having
bribed the nightwatchmen to remain silent, he
passed through the old city and out through the
Ajmer Gate to open country. After crossing the
Jumna, the prince made his way to Rohilcund,
where he was welcomed by the ruler Faizullah
Khan and taken on in safety to Lucknow, the new
capital of Awadh.[1] Here the nawab, Asaf-ud-Daula,
ruled the province as a vassal of Shah Alam and as
vizier of the Mughal Empire. Such an escape by a
prince was not entirely exceptional.[2] But this was
no ordinary prince: Mirza Jawan Bakht was the
eldest son and royal heir of the Emperor Shah
Alam, and his flight came at a most critical and
dangerous moment for the Mughals. Delhi was
threatened by powerful enemies each of whom
sought to control the empire. At this time the
Nawab Afrasiyab Khan was in the ascendancy but

was bitterly opposed by the Mahrattas, led by
Mahadaji Scindia, and by the Sikhs and Afghans.
It seems probable that Jawan Bakht fled Delhi at
this moment to try to obtain the assistance of both
the British and Asaf-ud-Daula against these
competing enemies of the empire.

On 6 May the prince reached Lucknow and was
conveyed into the city, seated beside the Nawab of
Awadh (cat. 83) on an elephant. Warren Hastings
followed closely behind on another. The governor
general took an immediate liking to the young
prince. He wrote of him to the board of the East
India Company: 'I found him gentle, lively,
possessed of a high sense of honour, of a sound
judgement, an uncommonly quick penetration,
and a well cultivated understanding, with a spirit
of resignation and an equality of temper almost
exceeding any within reach of my own knowledge
and recollection.'[3] Hastings immediately persuaded
the nawab to grant the prince a monthly allowance
of 33,333 rupees. Thereafter the governor general,
through his agent in Delhi, Major Brown, tried to
negotiate the safe return of Jawan Bakht to his
father in Delhi, an assignment of land, the offer of
Company troops for his protection and the use of a
fortress for his security. But events moved fast in
Delhi, with the murder of Afrasayib Khan in Agra
late in 1784 and the rapid ascendancy and influence
of Mahadaji Scindia over the emperor. When it
became clear that the prince's security could never
be guaranteed, Hastings allowed him to move out
of the nawab's dominions to reside in Company
territory at Benares until his early and sudden
death in 1788. By then events had reached their
nadir in Delhi with the sacking of the palace by
the Rohilla chief, Ghulam Qadir, in the autumn of
1787, followed by the blinding of the emperor. The
Marathas reconquered Delhi in October of that
year and pursued the Rohilla chief for months until
his capture on 2 March 1789. Years later, back in
England, Zoffany painted the scene of Ghulam
Qadir's death. It featured in Zoffany's posthumous
studio of 1811 as 'The death of Gholaum Cawdor
by Elephants containing a numerous assemblage
of figures' and has never reappeared.

Zoffany arrived in Lucknow on 4 June 1784 after
an exhausting and difficult journey from Calcutta.
Immediately on the evening of his arrival, Hastings
arranged for Prince Jawan Bakht to sit for the
artist. Two days later Major Sweeney Toone,
commander of Hastings's bodyguard, accompanied
Zoffany to visit the prince. Further sittings took
place in the presence of the governor general.[4]
Zoffany charged Warren Hastings 900 rupees
(about £90 at the time).[5] He also made another
version for Colonel Claude Martin. Although this
painting is lost, there are several surviving small
copies by Mihr Chand and other Company painters.
A copy of the original Hastings version was done
for Colonel Polier for an album now in the Museum
für Asiatische Kunst, Berlin.

Zoffany painted the prince dressed in a simple

fine white muslin *jama*, fastened on his right side as
was customary for Muslims. He wears the Islamic
dark green turban and green and gilt sash normally
reserved for Sayyids, the descendants of the
Prophet, but here to show his status as a descendant
of Timur. He is seated on a *musnud* of embroidered
green cushions and his hands rest on the hilt of his
sword, both references to kingship. By showing the
prince so simply attired – without jewels of any
description – Zoffany emphasizes both the prince's
humility and his precarious situation in Lucknow as
a refugee from the troubles in Delhi. It is an oblique
reference to the straitened circumstances into
which the house of Timur had plunged by the
mid-1780s. At the same time Zoffany conveys, with
remarkable sensitivity, the prince's gravity and
dignity, qualities that the artist saw as singularly
lacking in the nawab.

An unfinished oil sketch (see fig. 147) is the
only other known surviving painting by Zoffany
recording these events. Here the prince is shown
under a moonlit sky, seated on a *musnud* and in
similar dress. Surrounding him are the nawab with
members of his court, and Warren Hastings with
various civil and military Europeans seated on the
ground. Beyond them nautch girls and musicians
are performing for the prince. Why it remained
unfinished is something of a mystery. Perhaps
it was a study for an intended full-scale composition
that never materialized when other commissions
took precedence.

CG

1. Prince Jawan Bakht, 'Bayaz Inayet Murshidzada'
   (Persian Memoirs), India Office Library, British
   Library, and K.K. Datta, *Shah Alam II and the East
   India Company*, Calcutta, 1965, 83.
2. Shah Alam's brother, Sulayman Shikoh, had escaped to
   Benares shortly before, and Mirza Ali Bakht fled from
   the confines of Salimgarh in 1789, leaving a detailed
   account of his flight and subsequent wanderings. See
   'Travels of a Mughal Prince in the late 18th Century –
   The Narrative of Mirza "Ali Bakht Azfari"', MS
   translation from the Persian by Simon Digby, 2001.
3. Bengal Secret and Military Consultations, India Office
   Library, British Library, P/B/4/p.40, Hastings to
   Board, 14 Dec. 1784.
4. 12, 16, 17, 21 June. Warren Hastings's Diary, British
   Library, Add. MS 39,879, ff. 27v–34; see also Webster
   2011, 484–5.
5. 'A Kit cat of the Prince of Delhy | Rs 900', 21 February
   1785. Invoice from Zoffany to Warren Hastings,
   submitted to William Larkins after Hastings's
   departure from India in 1785. British Library,
   Hastings Papers (Private Accounts), Add. MS 29,229,
   ff.154, 194.

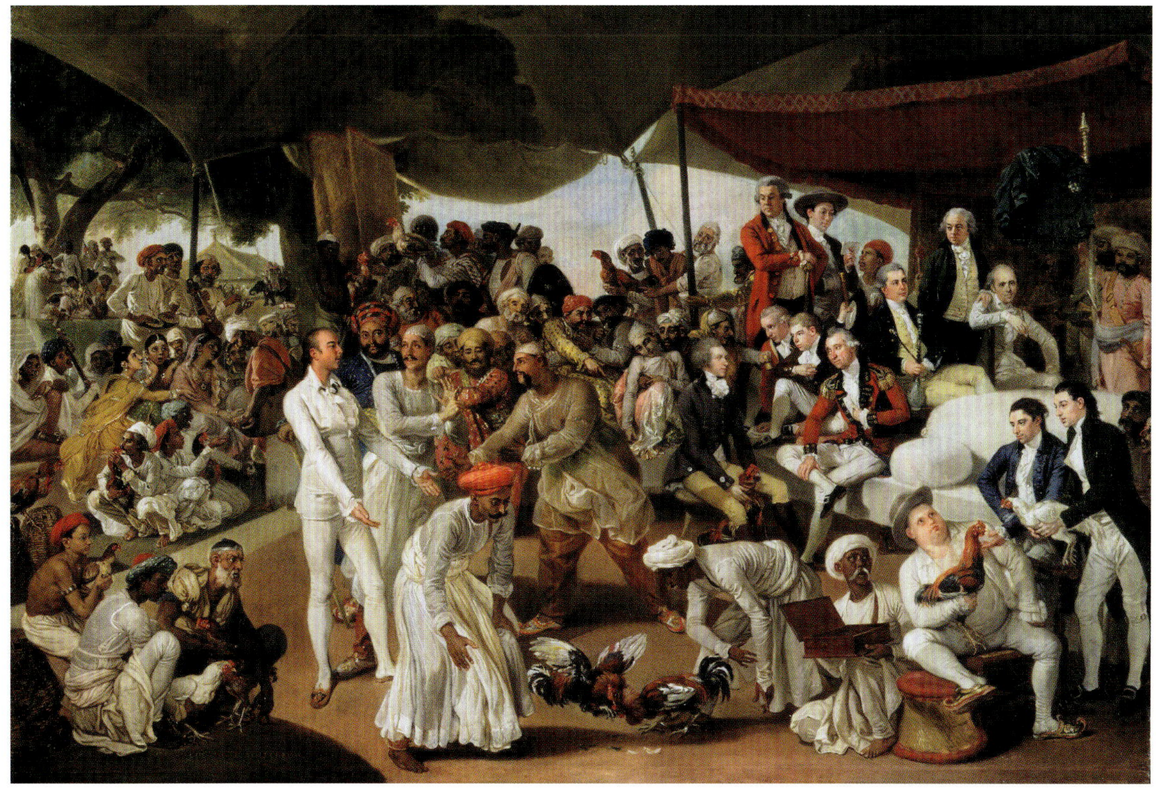

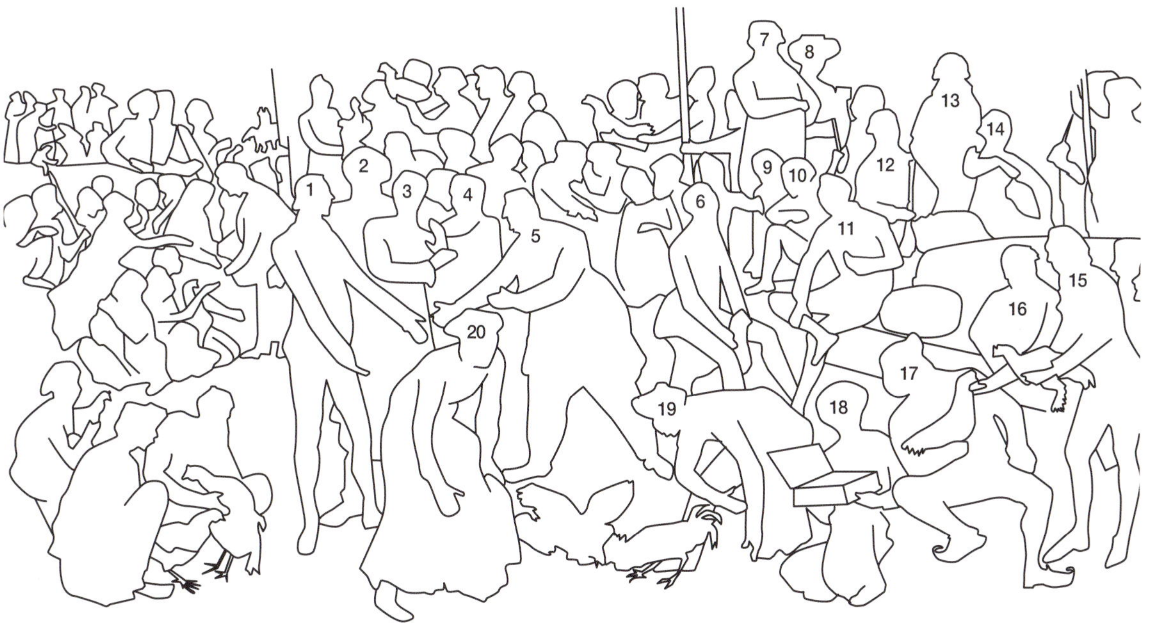

Figure 195
Key to *Colonel Mordaunt's Cock Match*

1. Lieutenant-Colonel John Mordaunt, Commander of the Nawab's Bodyguard
2. Hasan Reza Khan, Chief Minister to Asaf-ud-Daula
3. Salar Jung, uncle of Asaf-ud-Daula
4. Haidar Ali Khan, Deputy Minister to Asaf-ud-Daula
5. Asaf ud-Daula, Nawab Wazir of Awadh
6. Trevor Wheler, East India Company Assistant Resident, Lucknow
7. Probably Gabriel Harper, East India Company Resident, Lucknow (from 1785)
8. Sackville Marcus Taylor, East India Company Postmaster, Lucknow
9. Lieutenant John Pelling Pigot
10. Richard Johnson, former East India Company Resident, Lucknow
11. Major-General Claude Martin, Superintendent of Asaf-ud-Daula's Arsenal
12. John Wombwell, East India Company Accountant and Paymaster General, Lucknow
13. Ozias Humphry
14. Johan Zoffany
15. Robert Gregory, East India Company Senior Merchant
16. James Orr, Assistant to John Wombwell
17. Lieutenant William Golding
18. Indian assistant offering cockspurs to William Golding
19. Indian assistant to Asaf-ud-Daula
20. Indian assistant to Lieutenant-Colonel Mordaunt

Colonel Mordaunt's Cock Match

*c.*1784–8

Oil on canvas, 103.9 × 150 cm (40⅞ × 59 in)
Inscribed lower left: 'COCKFIGHT AT LUCKNOW
ZOFFANY [?Pinct] 1790'
Tate, London; purchased with assistance from the
National Heritage Memorial Fund, the National
Art Collections Fund, the Friends of the Tate
Gallery and a group of donors, 1994

Provenance: Commissioned by Warren Hastings;
Marian Hastings; her son, General Charles Imhof;
sale, Fairbrother, 26 Aug. 1853, lot 924, bt Colonel
Henry Dawkins, 215 guineas; sale, Christie's,
19 March 1898, lot 195, bt Agnews, 210 guineas;
Marquess of Tweedale; Sotheby's, 30 June 1926,
lot 115; Sir George Sutherland and by descent;
Christie's, 10 April 1992, lot 31, bt in; Tate

Selected exhibitions: British Institution, 1862,
no. 201; Whitechapel 1908, no. 9; Royal Academy
1947–8, no. 918; National Portrait Gallery 1977,
no. 104

Selected references: Manners & Williamson 1920,
83–91; Archer 1979, 148–54; Pollock 2003; Jasanoff
2005, 59–60; Treadwell 2009, 355–61; Webster
2011, 489, 490, 494, 497–509, 545

On 5 April 1784 Warren Hastings tersely noted in
his diary, 'At Mordaunt's Cock fight'.[1] Cock fighting
was a popular recreational activity in India, enjoyed
by both Europeans and Indians, but in Lucknow
it seems to have been regarded virtually as an art
form. Asaf-ud- Daula maintained at colossal
expense a vast menagerie of fighting animals,
an extravagance often remarked by Company
employees and cited as evidence of the nawab's
irredeemable moral degradation. Claude Martin
noted caustically in a letter to Ozias Humphry
(apropos of Asaf's reluctance to pay his debts):

> For what I know of his Character I think it such,
> that if one could read in his heart he would perceive
> it loaded with many dark sinister intentions and
> as you know those who compose his Court you
> then ought to know what a man he is. A man that
> delights in Elephant and Cocks fighting would
> delights [*sic*] in some thing worse if he feared
> nothing.[2]

Martin himself did not eschew the pleasures of
blood sports. As Rosie Llewellyn-Jones has noted,
cockspurs were listed in the inventory of his house,
Farhat Baksh, and, as Charles Greig shows in this
volume, he owned an opulent cockpit, the Kakori
Kothi, in the district of Khayaligunj (fig. 152).[3]
European women sometimes attended cock fights,[4]
but on the whole they were primarily homosocial
gatherings and may have played an important role
in the perenially fraught diplomatic negotiations
between court and Company at Lucknow.

Hastings, scholarly and retiring by nature, is
unlikely to have relished cock fighting. As he wrote
to a friend later that year, 'I neither drink, game,
nor give my vacant hours to music, and but a small
portion of them to other relaxations of society'.[5]
Even so, the match he attended clearly made a
vivid impression on him, since he commissioned
Zoffany to paint a picture on the subject for him.
No documentary evidence of the painting's genesis
is known, and Hastings did not chronicle it in
the diary he kept assiduously during his stay in
Lucknow. The resulting work, known as *Colonel
Mordaunt's Cock Match*, is probably the most
remarkable image engendered by the British
involvement in India, a provocative work of great
visual power, complexity and hybridity that raises
significant questions about power relations, race
and culture at a critical historical moment.

The central focus of the painting is the
encounter between Asaf-ud-Daula (5) and Colonel
John Mordaunt (1). Mordaunt, an illegitimate son
of the Earl of Peterborough, was a Protean figure
who has been documented only by a brief chatty
memoir published in 1808 and fragmentary
anecdotal information. Virtually illiterate, he
served, apparently without distinction, as an officer
in the Company army in Bengal. Even so,
Mordaunt seems to have ingratiated himself with
Hastings, who sent him to Lucknow to join the
large retinue of Company employees imposed on
Asaf-ud-Daula, and served intermittently as
commander of the nawab's bodyguard.[6] Mordaunt's
duties seem to have been somewhat nebulous, and it
is likely that his role (at least from the Company's
perspective) was that of minder and informant.[7]
Mordaunt and Asaf-ud-Daula were said to have
been close friends, a supposition supported by their
mutual love of blood sports and the lavishness of
the colonel's lifestyle in Lucknow, though the
enormous salary Mordaunt commanded on paper
typically went unpaid.[8] The exact nature of their
bond is difficult to ascertain, however, given Asaf's
complex and fraught relationship with the
Company and his contemporaries' tendency to view
him through
the filter of Orientalist stereotypes (he was said to
have 'wept like a child' on hearing of Mordaunt's
death in Cawnpore in 1790).

Zoffany's painting is charged with sexual
innuendo. Asaf's inability to father an heir was
common knowledge in Awadh, and, as Maya
Jasanoff has noted in this volume, the joke of the
illegitimate son encountering the impotent ruler
at a cock match may not have escaped Zoffany,
often susceptible to double entendre, as suggested
by the nawab's apparently aroused state. Asaf
was said to have enjoyed obscene and adversarial
banter, suggesting perhaps that the encounter
with Mordaunt involves a ritualistic exchange of
sexually charged insults.

Asaf-ud-Daula and Mordaunt are surrounded by
Europeans and Indians, a number of whom were
identified on the index to the engraving, which was
published in London in 1792 (cat. 88). Asaf's uncle,
Salar Jung (3), stands between the two
protagonists, counting the sum of Asaf's bet on his
fingers, flanked by the figures of Asaf's chief
minister, Hasan Reza Khan (2; cat. 84), to the left,
and his deputy minister, Haidar Beg Khan (4; see
cat. 101). To the right, in the foreground, the
corpulent figure with a vacant expression is
William Golding (17), a lieutenant in the Corps of
Engineers; he talks with Robert Gregory (15), a
senior merchant who holds a white cock, and James
Orr (16), who was John Wombwell's assistant, and
they are being offered cockspurs by an Indian. To
their left Claude Martin (11) sits on the white sofa
next to the empty seat presumably vacated by
Asaf-ud-Daula, speaking with the Assistant
Resident, Trevor Wheler (6), who holds a cock;
above them Richard Johnson (10), the former
Assistant Resident of Lucknow, crouches, watching
an Indian shake a dice box with Lieutenant John
Pelling Pigot (9). The figure above him resting on a
cane was identified in the index to the engraving as
Antoine Polier; Mary Webster has suggested that
this was an error, and the figure certainly does not
seem to correspond to Zoffany's portrayal of him in
Colonel Polier and his Friends (cat. 90). Webster
identifies the figure as Colonel Gabriel Harper (7),
who was appointed Resident in 1785,[9] and the
figure to his right receiving a letter is Sackville
Marcus Taylor (8), who was postmaster at
Lucknow. The triangulated group to the right
comprises John Wombwell (12; see cat. 90) seated
with the hookah, the miniature painter Ozias
Humphry (13), and Zoffany (14) himself. Hastings
is absent from the painting.

In her ground-breaking analysis of the painting,
Griselda Pollock has suggested that *Colonel
Mordaunt's Cock Match* thematizes the power-play
between the Awadh court and the British.[10]
The corpulent Asaf's gesture towards the taut,
statuesque figure of Mordaunt has been interpreted
as ingratiating and submissive, but an alternative
interpretation might be considered that would cast
the painting in a different light. There are striking
affinities between Asaf's pose and that
of Akbar in the painting from the celebrated
series, the *Akbarnama*, showing the Mughal
emperor supervising the construction of
Fatephur Sikri (Victoria and Albert Museum,
London). Akbar famously removed his court from
Delhi, establishing it at Agra, and the analogies
between this and Asaf's relocation from Faizabad
to Lucknow, as well as his ambitious building
programme, would not have been lost on an erudite
viewer, such as Warren Hastings, who himself had
an outstanding collection of Mughal paintings.[11]
Asaf owned the *Akbarnama*, and Zoffany may well
have seen it;[12] as Maya Jasanoff has noted in this
volume, the densely layered composition of *Colonel
Mordaunt's Cock Match* owes much to Mughal
miniature painting, as does its minute detailing.
On the invoice he presented to William Larkins,
Hastings's agent, Zoffany described the painting

as 'an Historical picture of a Cock pitt composed of a great number of small figures'.[13] Zoffany's designation of the work as a history painting implies his awareness of its political significance, as well as its ambition, but he also drew on other genres, including the conversation piece, the theatrical portrait and even caricature. In this respect, one of the key influences may have been Hogarth, an artist whom Zoffany greatly admired and whose engraving, the *Cockpit*, was included in Zoffany's posthumous sale, along with a considerable number of his other prints.

The history of the painting's production has been the subject of some speculation. Zoffany billed Hastings on 21 February 1785 for the large sum of 15,000 rupees, and when forwarding the invoice, Larkins justified the expense, noting that Zoffany had been 'extremely moderate in the sum which he has charged for the Cock Pit in which I understand there is about 90 figures'. Zoffany was paid in sterling on 14 October 1786 but by September of the following year Hastings's former Secretary George Nesbitt Thompson, who was handling the shipping of his pictures, still had not received it. Nesbitt Thompson noted in a letter to Hastings of 14 February 1788 that he had despatched 'five pictures', presumably all by Zoffany; one of these may have been the *Cock Match*.[14] Some fifteen years after Zoffany's death a rumour circulated that the painting had been lost at sea. In 1824 an anonymous correspondent ('Z') in the *Somerset House Gazette* published the story in a letter to the editor, W.H.Pyne.[15] It was repeated almost verbatim the following year by James Elmes in *The Arts and Artists*.[16] It is not completely out of the question that the painting was either unfinished, damaged (as was the portrait of Marian Hastings that the artist had packed carelessly) or lost, and that Zoffany had reconstructed it from sketches after his return to London, a theory supported by a notice in the *Public Advisor* of 11 March 1791 (see cat. 89) and the date inscribed on the painting, although this has generally been assumed to be inauthentic.

The picture hung in the library at Daylesford until the death of Hastings's stepson, Charles Imhoff. What significance the painting would have had for the former governor general is a matter for conjecture. He may have regarded it as a sentimental souvenir from his interlude in Lucknow, but it could also be interpreted as a celebration of the success of Hastings's diplomatic mission to Lucknow, as well as the fulfilment of his objective to effect the 'reconciliation' of 'the people of England to the natives of Hindostan'.[17]

GF

I am grateful to Holly Shaffer, Tamara Sears, Mark Aronson, Jessica David, Tim Barringer and Sylvia Houghteling for their helpful comments in preparing this catalogue entry.
 1. British Library, Add. MS 29, 879, f. 19.
 2. Llewellyn-Jones 2003, 172, letter 145.
 3. Llewellyn-Jones 1992, 136 n. 48.
 4. Jasanoff 2005, 260.
 5. Letter to J. Scott, 24 Nov. 1784, British Library, Add. MS 29,129, f. 270, quoted P.J. Marshall, 'Hastings, Warren (1732–1818)', *ODNB*, http://www.oxforddnb.com/view/article/12587 (accessed 19 June 2011).
 6. Mordaunt was replaced by Richard Chicheley Plowden in 1780 on Hastings's orders and travelled to Calcutta to plead for reinstatement (Chicheley Plowden 1914, 154).
 7. Anon. 1808, 141.
 8. Anon. 1808, 141–2.
 9. Webster 2011, 501. Harper did not become Resident until 1785, taking over from Palmer, who was appointed by Hastings in the aftermath of his visit to Lucknow and in the wake of the recall of the notorious John Bristow. For a helpful decoding of the complex history of the Lucknow Residents during the early 1780s, see Barnett 1980.
10. Pollock 2003.
11. I am grateful to Tamara Sears for this suggestion.
12. The *Akbarnama* was purchased by General John Clarke, the Commissioner of Oude between 1858 and 1862, and was acquired by the Victoria and Albert Museum from his widow in 1896. I am grateful to Holly Shaffer for supplying this provenance.
13. Archer 1979, 152.
14. As Archer (1979, 163) noted, the other four were probably the single portraits of Hastings, Impey and Jawan Bakht, and the portrait of Hastings, his wife and their Indian servant at Alipore.
15. *Somerset House Gazette and Literary Museum*, vol. XLVI, 1824, 315.
16. Elmes 1825, vol.1, 12–13. See also Archer 1979, 163; Webster 2011, 505.
17. P.J. Marshall, 'Hastings, Warren (1732–1818)', *ODNB*, http://www.oxforddnb.com/view/article/12587 (accessed 19 June 2011).

87

Johan Zoffany and a Lucknow artist,
Colonel Mordaunt's Cock Match
1786–*c.*1790

Oil on canvas, 119.1 × 86.6 cm (46⅞ × 34⅛ in)
White's Club, London

Exhibited at the Yale Center for British Art only

Provenance: Probably painted for Nawab Asaf-ud-Daula, thence to Nawab Ghazi-ud-din, who gifted the painting to Richard Strachey (Resident in Lucknow) in 1817, thence by descent; acquired by Robert Coe Esq., *c.*1955; bequeathed to White's

Selected references: Archer 1979, 149, pl. 91; Webster 2011, 507–9

With the publication of Manners and Williamson's biography of Zoffany just over ninety years ago, there began a long period of confused claims and counter-claims relating to the attribution of this so-called 'Ashwick' version of Colonel Mordaunt's Cock Match.[1] Williamson (correctly as it now seems) presumed that this was the version done for Asaf-ud-Daula, but almost everything else that she wrote on the subject was a misinterpretation. Mildred Archer, in 1979, attributed the painting to Robert Home, while other scholars dismissed it as a Company school copy. This bewildering range of opinions resulted in part from evidence given by Fanny Parkes that she had seen a painting of the Cock Match in the Daulat Khana in Lucknow on 24 January 1831, fourteen years after Strachey had brought his painting back to England.[2]

Recent detailed examination of the 'Ashwick' painting has revealed something rather unexpected. Various figures including Mordaunt, the nawab, Marcus Sackville Taylor and Lieutenant Golding were clearly painted by Zoffany himself. He sketched in much of the background: the view resembles the Rajmahal hills a few miles north of the city of Rajmahal itself. The *shamiana*, or tent, was probably also done by Zoffany and he probably completed much of the blocking in on the right-hand side of the composition. Other figures have either been added by an unknown Lucknow artist or finished over sketches by Zoffany. Inevitably, this reworking substantially altered the atmosphere of the painting. The Hastings version (cat. 86) of this famous composition marks the pinnacle of Zoffany's five years in India. It is the evocation of Asaf-ud-Daula's Lucknow itself – hot and humid, brilliantly colourful and vibrant – and captures the close relationship that then existed between Indians and Europeans. The painting is composed of intricately worked figures, and through a sophisticated method of painting Zoffany vividly conveyed the drama and the excitement of the occasion. Much of this energy is lost in the nawab's version, in which the finishing by the Lucknow artist is rather coarse. The composition

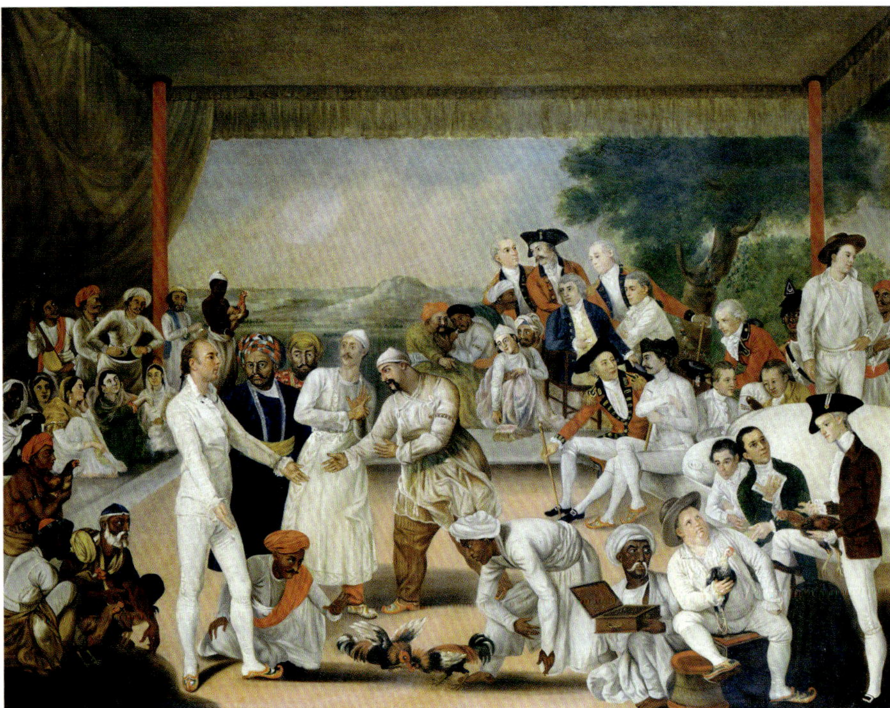

various versions of the *Cock Match* have been complicated by an intriguing piece of information that came to light recently, via a report in the *Public Advertiser* on 11 March 1791, where it was stated that Zoffany was engaged in painting a *Cock Match* from sketches he had made in India (see p. 41).[5] Just over a week later, perhaps coincidentally, Hastings recorded in his diary that he had paid a social call on Zoffany in London.[6] What, then, was the version alluded to in Zoffany's London studio? Intriguingly, an inscription on Hastings's version of the *Cock Match* (cat. 86) gives the date of the picture as 1790, which revives interest in the claim made in the 1820s that the original picture had gone down in a shipwreck.[7]

Zoffany is well known for making numerous versions of some of his paintings (there are up to four versions of some of the theatrical paintings) and he may have wished to paint another version of the *Cock Match* to coincide with the publication of the Earlom print. Future research into Hastings's *Cock Match*, and associated versions, may yield further clues.

CG

1. The painting has been called the 'Ashwick' version after the name of the Strachey family house.
2. Fanny Parkes, *Wanderings of a Pilgrim in Search of the Picturesque, during Four-and-Twenty Years in the East*, 2 vols., London, 1850, vol. 2, 181.
3. Royal Academy of Arts Archive, Ozias Humphry Papers 1753–1810, HU 14/24–25
4. On 9 June 2010 Auction Atrium sold a gouache copy of a portrait of Prince Jawan Bakht that was based on Claude Martin's lost version of the painting by Zoffany. Stylistically, it is quite possible that the artist of this was the same artist employed by the nawab to finish his *Cock Match*.
5. I am grateful to Martin Postle for drawing my attention to this hitherto unnoticed newspaper report.
6. Hastings called on Zoffany on 19 March 1791. See Webster 2011, 594.
7. *Somerset House Gazette and Literary Museum*, vol. XLVI, 1824, 315; Elmes 1825, vol. 1, 12. Conservation reports on cat. 86, made in 1994, following its acquisition by the Tate Gallery, neither confirm or disprove that the picture was made in India.

has been significantly altered with many fewer figures overall in comparison to Hasting's version, the crowded nature of which gives the scene much of its vigour. Many of the Indian painter's figures have the appearance of caricatures, and it is difficult to identify with certainty some of the Europeans.

On the bench Claude Martin is visible leaning forward and holding a cane. He is talking to a European in evening dress. He appears to be wearing a Mahratta headdress suggesting that he is Martin's friend Benoit de Boigne, then in the service of Mahadaji Scindia. Behind them is a group of Europeans. John Wombwell is seated in a corner armchair, and standing behind him, from left to right, are Colonel Harper (the Resident), Colonel Polier, an unidentified officer and probably William Palmer, dressed in a white shirt. (Palmer was Warren Hastings's military secretary.) To the right is Lieutenant Pigot and crouching behind the nawab's cushion throne, or *musnud*, is the artist, brushes in hand. His features bear little resemblance to Zoffany's. Marcus Sackville Taylor (top right) is shown in surprisingly casual dress with an attendant sepoy behind. In the right foreground Robert Gregory has been replaced by a young officer with a greyhound-like figure wearing a tricorne hat. Beside him James Orr has been given a swarthy complexion. On the left-hand side the grouping of the Indian figures closely resembles Lucknow miniature painting of the period and this passage shows almost nothing of Zoffany's hand.

This fusion of the two hands at work – Zoffany's and the unknown Indian's – is hardly surprising. On arrival in Lucknow Zoffany had high expectations of significant commissions from the nawab and his courtiers. Although these were forthcoming, he received painfully little in the way of payment from the much indebted nawab. This is confirmed in a letter from Martin to Ozias Humphry dated 11 March 1789: 'Our good and worthy friend … is not yet paid, tho' he was called by the Vizier and abandoned his own at Calcutta in the hope of doing better and to this day he has not received a farthing from the Vizier, Minister.'[3] Given this situation, it is inconceivable that Zoffany would have spent the necessary time to finish or even substantially advance the nawab's version of the *Cock Match*. After all, the Hastings version was worked on apparently over a number of years and the time involved in completing it was enormous. After Zoffany's departure the nawab, having in his possession a partly finished painting that he had not paid for, employed a local artist to finish his version of the *Cock Match*. This artist had evidently already made copies of Zoffany's work and was reasonably familiar with his style.[4]

In February 2005 a large oil painting of the *Cock Match* appeared at Sotheby's. It resembled the Hastings version. Obviously painted in Lucknow, it had been adapted from the Earlom print of the subject. Other copies of this type almost certainly existed. It now seems quite possible that what Fanny Parkes saw in 1831, and was presumed destroyed in the events of 1857, was one of these clever copies. When this particular painting appeared in 2005, it was considered by some to be at least in part Zoffany's own work. Fanny Parkes, seeing a damaged and probably dirty painting in India some 175 years earlier, may have been little wiser.

Evaluations of the history and status of the

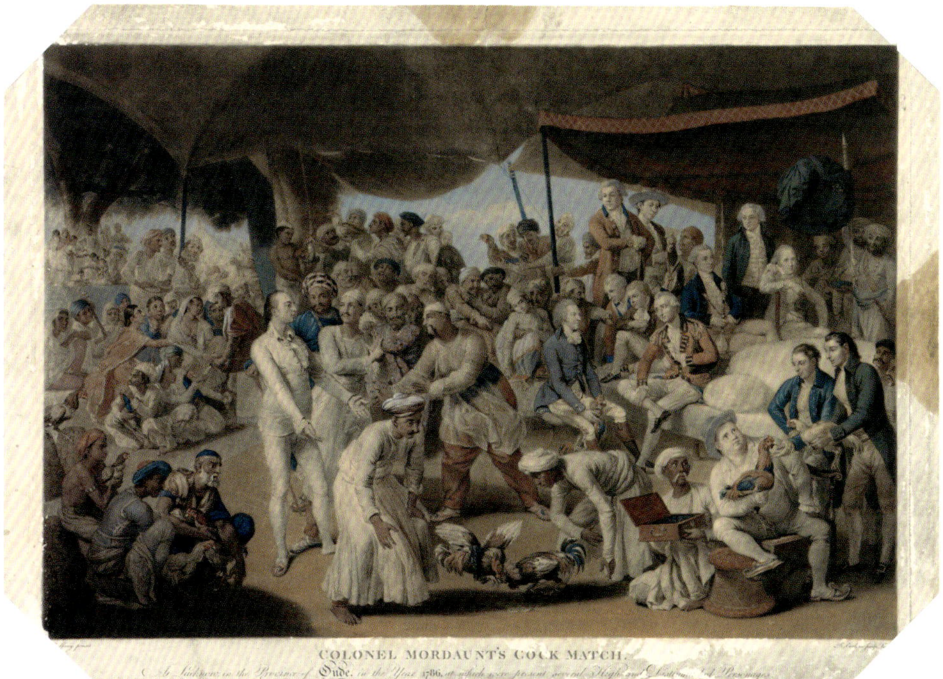

88

Richard Earlom after Johan Zoffany,
Colonel Mordaunt's Cock Match
1792

Mezzotint engraving, 53.3 × 73.3 cm (21 × 28⅞ in)
Inscribed under image with title in open letters and:
'J. Zoffany pinxit | R Earlom sculp Londini | At
Lucknow, in the Province of Oude in the year
1786 at which were present several High and
Distinguished Personages | For the Names see the
Index Plate | Published 1st. May 1792, by ROBERT
SAYER, Fleet Street, London.'
Yale Center for British Art, Paul Mellon Collection

Provenance: Purchased by Paul Mellon by whom
given, 1985

Selected references: Wessely 1886, 48, no. 120;
Chaloner Smith 1878–84, vol. 1, 253–4, no. 29

This mezzotint after Warren Hastings's painting
of a cock match at Lucknow (cat. 86) was made by
the high-profile engraver Richard Earlom and
published in 1792 by Robert Sayer, a close friend
of Zoffany's and his principal print publisher from
1770 onwards (see cat. 73).[1] The publication of the
engraving may have been intended to assist the
rehabilitation of Zoffany's career, which had stalled
after his return to India.

No subscription list is known, so it is impossible
to determine precisely the market for the
engraving, but there seems to have been demand
from collectors for prints after Zoffany and
presumably it would have been purchased by
members of Hastings's circle of friends and
supporters. There was also a market for British
prints in northern India, and impressions may have
been shipped there for distribution. Hastings's
ownership of the painting was not acknowledged
on the inscription. This may have been intentional,
since the engraving was published during a hiatus
in the impeachment trial, after the prosecution
side had closed their case and before Hastings's
legal team were to refute their accusations, and is
unlikely to have benefited his cause. Cock fighting
was widely deplored in Britain, particularly by
Nonconformists,[2] and the image might seem
to endorse the critiques of corruption and
extravagance levelled at him by his detractors.
Hastings lived in a succession of rented houses in
London after his return from Bengal and moved
in June 1791 to Daylesford, where the painting
hung in the library. The painting, which is inscribed
'Cockfight at Lucknow', may have acquired the
more specific title of *Colonel Mordaunt's Cock Match*
as a result of the inscription on the print. The
inscription also dates the cock fight to 1786,

though the inclusion of Richard Johnson, who held
a position with the Company in Calcutta at that
time, may indicate that, as with the *Tribuna*, the
painting may not have been intended as an accurate
reconstruction of a specific event.[3]

The index plate did not appear until two years
after the engraving and was published by Robert
Laurie and John Whittle, Robert Sayer's former
assistants who had taken over the management
of the business after Sayer's retirement due
to ill-health in 1792. One of the figures was
mistakenly described as Antoine Polier, and since
portraits of all the other figures are not known,
it is impossible to ascertain whether they were
correctly identified.

GF

1. Sayer had published a satirical print that seems to
   have been derived from Hogarth's engraving
   The Cockpit in 1776.
2. See Thomas 1983, 159–60.
3. For Johnson, see P.J. Marshall, 'Johnson, Richard
   (1753–1807)', *ODNB*, http://www.oxforddnb.com/
   view/article/63514 (accessed 12 March 2011).

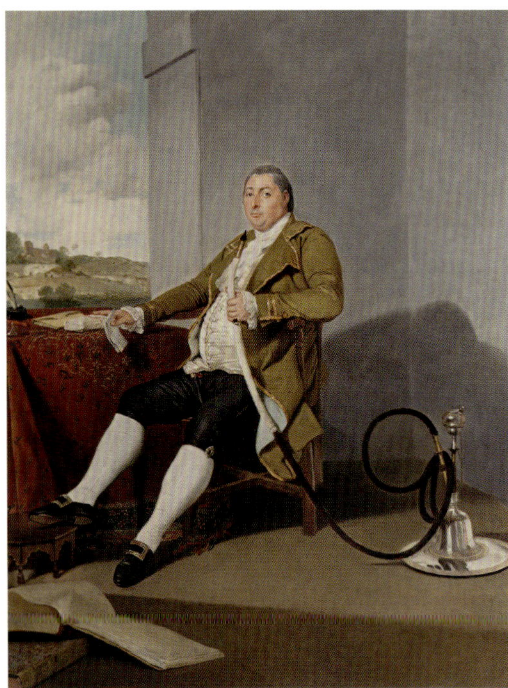

89

James Graham of Rickerby and Barrock Lodge
1786

Oil on canvas, 90.8 × 66 cm (35¾ × 26 in)
Tullie House Museum & Art Gallery, Carlisle

Provenance: By descent; Christie's (British Pictures), 10 April, 1992, lot 29 (unsold); gifted by a descendant of the sitter to Tullie House

Selected references: Webster 2011, 501, 505

William Hickey, the diarist, recorded in some detail frequent gargantuan dinners that he enjoyed with friends in Calcutta in the late 1770s and 1780s. No doubt these resulted in at least some of the many sudden deaths among Europeans in India in the eighteenth century. James Graham, on the other hand, seems to have thrived on such fare. Indeed, his chief claim to fame was his immense size. It is recorded that Zoffany intended to include him in the *Cock Match* seated in the foreground next to his cousin, Robert Gregory. Graham's huge girth would contrast with the elegant slim figure of his handsome cousin. Graham would have none of it and Zoffany was obliged to include another large European, Lieutenant Golding, in his place.[1]

Graham was descended from the Grahams of Kirklington in Cumbria. He seems to have decided to seek his fortune in India surprisingly late. Usually, young recruits to the East India Company travelled to India in their late teens, but Graham was only appointed as a Writer in the Bengal Civil Service on 1 August 1780 in his thirty-third year. His promotion was rapid and within three years he was appointed Deputy Paymaster to Sir John Cummings's Detachment. In 1786, the year of Zoffany's *Cock Match*, Ozias Humphry recorded him among the Europeans in Lucknow, and he was still there early in 1788 when Elizabeth Plowden spent a day in his company at Claude Martin's house.[2] It would appear that Graham returned to England in about 1790 and a year later he built Barrock Lodge in the Eden Vale. An insufficient fortune probably forced him to sell his new house a couple of years later, and he returned to India where he was appointed Collector of Rungpore. Thereafter he held senior posts in Purnea, Mirzapore and finally Dacca, before returning to Cumbria in 1804 to found the Carlisle New Bank. Within three years he inherited the estate of Rickerby, close to the city of Carlisle, from his kinsman William Richardson and with his replenished Indian fortune he significantly enlarged the estate.

This small full length is one of just four known surviving single portraits of Europeans that Zoffany completed in Lucknow. Until very recently none of these was accepted by scholars as Zoffany's work. The technical brilliance, rich colouring and singular composition of each, however, excludes the possibility of their being by the hand of any other European artist working in that city at that time. And there are other clues. Here Zoffany has used the same thick twill canvas that he used for Prince Jawan Bakht (cat. 85) and both are standard 'kit-kat' size (measuring approximately 36 × 28 in/91 × 71 cm). An indication of the picture's date can be gauged by the colouring. Up country, Zoffany appears to have used some local pigments for the first time. Graham is shown seated in a teak corner chair and wearing a buff coat with a dandyish, vibrant blue lining. This ultramarine blue, derived from Afghan lapis,

would have been exceedingly expensive. Zoffany painted Mrs Blair's sumptuous dress in this rich blue as a foil to her husband's scarlet tunic (cat. 92). The remnant he had over seems to have been used sparingly for the coat lining here. Similarly, the rich greenish buff of Graham's coat is repeated in the Indian girl's pyjamas in the Blair picture. All this points to 1786 when we know from Humphry that Graham was in Lucknow. The artist emphasized Graham's prosperity by showing him holding the snake of a fine Lucknow silver hookah in his left hand, and his podgy small finger boasts a jewelled ring. Graham sits at a table covered in rich scarlet brocade and his right leg is raised up on a carved Mughal footstool. Beyond, the rolling countryside recalls the landscape seen through the window in the Hasan Reza Khan portrait (cat. 84).

CG

1. Vere R.T. Gregory, *The House of Gregory: The Gregory Family in Ireland*, Dublin, 1943, 43.
2. Ozias Humphry's diary, Osborn Collection, Beinecke Rare Book and Manuscript Library, Yale University, f. 26. Elizabeth Plowden's diary, included among her husband's papers in the India Office Library, British Library: Papers of Richard Chicheley Plowden, MSS Eur C149 misc.

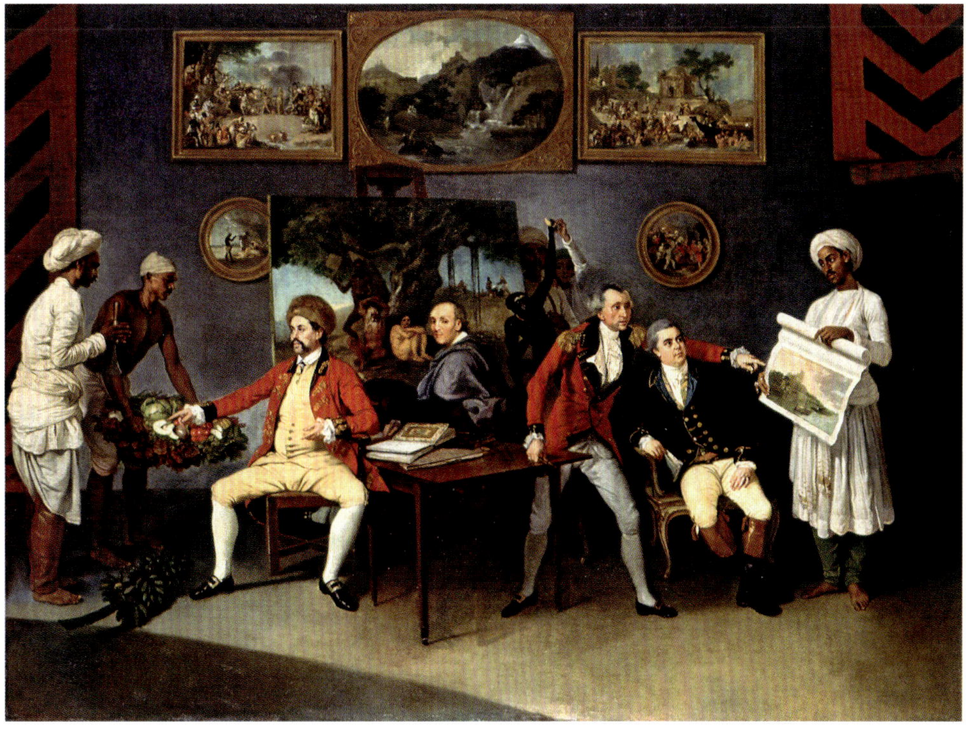

90

Colonel Polier and his Friends

1786–7

Oil on canvas, 137 × 183.5 cm (53⅞ × 72¼ in)
Victoria Memorial Hall, Calcutta

Exhibited at Yale Center for British Art only

Provenance: probably Edward Strachey; given by
his son Captain Henry Strachey, _c._1850, to Robert
Henry Clive in payment of debt; by descent to his
nephew Viscount Bridgeman, sale, Christie's, 28
June 1929, lot 75

Selected exhibitions: National Portrait Gallery 1977,
no. 105; National Portrait Gallery 1990–91, no. 138

Selected references: Manners & Williamson 1920;
Webster 1976, 79–80; Archer 1979, 154–6;
Llewellyn-Jones 1992, 123–4; Jasanoff 2005, 65–7;
Treadwell 2009, 362–4; Webster 2011, 518–23

Asaf-ud-Daula's Lucknow was a cosmopolitan
city, providing rich opportunities for those in search
of material, cultural and intellectual enrichment,
as well as a space in which the conventions of
European polite society could be set aside. Zoffany,
unsurprisingly, seems to have found Lucknow
particularly congenial, and his time there must
have been greatly enriched by his friendships with
Claude Martin (1735–1800) and Antoine Polier
(1741–95). The careers, private lives and collecting
interests of these two remarkable men, 'border
crossers' to use Maya Jasanoff's suggestive term,
have been exhaustively researched by Rosie
Llewellyn- Jones and Jasanoff, who have produced
compelling accounts of highly talented and
opportunistic individuals who found the political
and cultural climate of Lucknow highly conducive
to their drive both to enrich themselves and
explore their eclectic intellectual concerns.[1]

Born in Lyon, Martin fought with the French
army in India but defected to the British side in
1760. An accomplished surveyor, Martin arrived
in Lucknow in 1776 to take up the position of
superintendent of Asaf-ud-Daula's arsenal, and
remained there until his death. The Swiss-born
Polier entered the Company's army at the age
of sixteen. He became a military engineer of
considerable talent, but his career was stymied in
1766 when the Company passed a decree that no
foreign solder could rise above the rank of major.[2]
In 1773 Polier left Calcutta for Awadh to work for
Asaf-ud-Daula, a move that was to prove highly
lucrative. He moved to France early in 1788 and
was brutally murdered by intruders at his house
in Avignon in 1795.

Both Antoine Polier and Claude Martin were
accomplished amateur scholars of oriental culture
and used the fortunes they had amassed from their
generous salaries from the nawab and their diverse
business interests to form collections of Indian
manuscripts and art. In this remarkable painting
Zoffany portrayed himself in the background with
(left to right) Polier, Martin and John Wombwell
(1748–1813), the cousin of the East India
Company's chairman who held the highly lucrative
office of the Company's Accountant and Paymaster
General at Lucknow and who, like Martin and
Polier, was an avid collector of Indian manuscripts.[3]
Zoffany used the genre of the conversation piece
to portray homosocial society, which, as Durba
Ghosh has noted, was a critical structural feature
of colonial life in India,[4] and a central theme of
Zoffany's _Colonel Mordaunt's Cock Match_ (cat. 86).

The circumstances of the painting's production
is undocumented, but Polier's assertive pose and
intent appraisal of the local produce indicates that
the setting would have been his house, Polierganj,
and that he may have commissioned the work.
Mildred Archer has suggested that Zoffany may
have painted it in 1787 as a leaving gift for Polier,[5]
though it is possible that it may have belonged to
Martin, whose inventory listed an oil painting,
which may be misdescribed, of 'Col. Polier, General
Martin and a Native Planter' as well as a 'Group by
Zoffany'.[6] Zoffany signals Polier's hybrid identity
and his significant, if ambiguous, political status
in Lucknow by portraying him wearing a fur hat,
referencing Indian portrayals of the nobility, a
device used by Tilly Kettle for his numerous
portraits of Shuja ud-Daula, Asaf's father, who
constantly invoked the attributes of Mughal
kingship to fashion his identity as ruler of Awadh.[7]

Polier had commissioned the Indian painter Mihr Chand to copy Kettle's portraits of Shuja and his court,[8] and his history of Shah Alam II demonstrates his keen interest in Mughal kingship.[9]

The presentation of a cornucopia was a common trope denoting ownership of the land, but Zoffany may have had a specific example in mind, Spiridone Roma's 1778 ceiling painting depicting *The East Offering its Riches to Britannia*, commissioned by the East India Company for their London headquarters.[10] An album of Mughal style paintings rests on the pembroke table; the image is not sufficiently clear to be identified, but as William Hauptman has noted, the border design is identical to that of other paintings in an album belonging to Polier that was subsequently acquired by William Beckford.[11]

Martin is showing Wombwell, who has laid aside a pamphlet or some papers, an oil sketch of Farhat Bakhsh, a house that he designed for himself on the banks of the Jumna, completed in 1781 and celebrated for its technical innovations. Mary Webster has suggested that the image refers to a sketch by Zoffany that was listed in Martin's inventory (see p. 160). Zoffany positioned himself in the background but at the centre, looking directly at the viewer. The picture also functions as a showcase for his own work and his fascination with Indian life and practices, though the six paintings represented have not been identified. The canvas on the easel shows two ascetics and a naked woman sitting beneath a banyan tree, and Mary Webster has suggested that it might represent a site at Chapra, recommended to travellers by Colonel Gilbert Ironside, who noted the large banyan tree and advised 'Remark the devotee fakers there'.[12] Penelope Treadwell has interpreted the figure of the woman as alluding to the Indian mistresses kept by Martin, Polier and Zoffany.[13] The five paintings on the wall are also scenes from Indian life, including, on the left, a *sati* scene. Zoffany, like many of his contemporaries, seems to have been fascinated by this practice, and a number of paintings on the theme in varying states of finish were included in his posthumous studio sale, including cat. 93.[14] The picture in the centre is a view of the spectacular falls of the Moti Jharna in the Sahibganj district in Bengal; the painting to its right is a scene of pilgrims, presumably at Mela, bathing in the Ganges. The roundel below on the left depicts a dying Hindu at the river, the subject of a later drawing by Zoffany (cat. 98), and that on the right, a skirmish between an Indian on a white horse and a troop of sepoys.[15] None of these paintings is now known, but it seems likely that Zoffany would have made a number of such works while in India that have not survived. The significance of the black monkey flanking Zoffany, which grasps a banana in its paw, is unclear, but it may allude to the established use of an ape as an emblematic image for the artist.[16] In

Cesare Ripa's *Iconologica* the ape denotes insolence, and its inclusion in this painting may be interpreted as hinting at Zoffany's predilection for inserting subversive subtexts into his portraits.

Although cat. 90 was presumably intended to commemorate the close friendships between the four men, the figures seem oddly disconnected from each other apart from the exchange between Martin and Wombwell, and the artist's assumption of his characteristic persona of dispassionate observer strikes a dissonant note. This lack of engagement between protagonists characterizes many of Zoffany's conversation pieces, but nonetheless it seems surprising in a work that presumably had some personal significance for the artist. Polier's and Martin's emphatic gesturing suggests that the picture is as much to do with material possessions as personal attachments. If Polier did commission or at least own the painting he evidently did not take it with him when he moved to France, as it was almost certainly acquired in Lucknow by Edward Strachey, who was second assistant to the Resident between 1797 and 1801.[17]

GF

1. Llewellyn-Jones 1985, 1992, 2003; Jasanoff 2005. For Polier, see Alam & Alavi 2001.
2. Jasanoff 2005, 46.
3. Jasanoff 2005, 108. Wombwell was described in 1785 as 'Accountant at Lucknow and Paymaster General beyond the Province' as well as 'Paymaster to the Nabob's Troops under British Officers' (Archer 1979, 449 n. 65).
4. Ghosh 2006, 79.
5. Archer 1979, 449 n.6.
6. For the paintings by Zoffany owned by Martin and listed in his inventory, see Archer 1979, 447–8, n. 60.
7. For example, Yale Center for British Art (B1976.7.48). See also Archer 1979, 76, fig. 28.
8. Alam & Alavi 2001, 54.
9. Alam & Alavi 2001, 67.
10. Bayly 1990, 27–8, figs 6, 7.
11. Hauptman 1996, 33–4, fig. 5. The album is now in the Museum für Islamische Kunst, Berlin.
12. Webster 2011, 520.
13. Treadwell 2009, 364–9. Wombwell may also have kept Indian bibis; a drawing made by Ozias Humphry, who stayed with Wombwell in Lucknow in 1786, records 'the zenana in Mr Wombwell's garden' (British Library, Add. MS 15,962.11). For a detailed account and analysis of the practice of cohabitation between British men and indigenous women in colonial India, see Ghosh 2006.
14. For the European preoccupation with sati, see entry for cat. 93 and Schürer 2008.
15. The identification of these subjects is taken from Webster 2011, 520–21.
16. For example, Goya's satire on portrait painting, *Ni mas ni menos*, repr. H.W. Janson, *Apes and Ape Lore in the Middle Ages and the Renaissance*, London, 1952, pl. LII.
17. The Swiss draughtsman and engraver Michel Vincent Brandoin visited Polier in Avignon in 1788, with a commission from William Beckford to inspect Polier's collections and to make a copy of a picture by Zoffany portraying the 'Rajah', as Brandoin referred to him, 'dans son serail avec 10 femmes' (Hauptman 1996, 34–5), presumably the lost painting attributed by Mildred Archer to Tilly Kettle, (see fig. 122); see Archer 1979, 84–5, fig. 39.

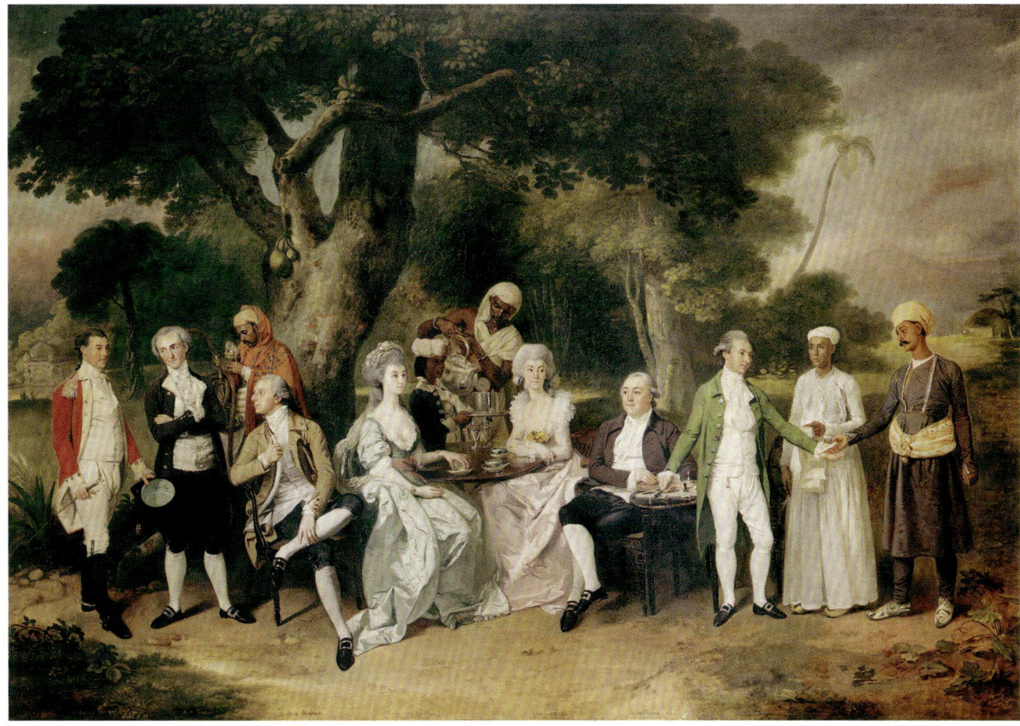

91

The Auriol and Dashwood Families
1783–7

Oil on canvas, 142 × 198 cm (55⅞ × 78 in)
Inscribed in a later hand with the names of
the sitters
From the Dashwood Family

Provenance: By descent

Selected exhibitions: Royal Academy 1881, no. 41;
Whitechapel 1908, no. 5; Park Lane 1930, no. 13;
National Portrait Gallery 1977, no. 100; National
Portrait Gallery 1990, no. 123

Selected references: Manners & Williamson, 110,
189–90; Archer 1979, 158–60; Ghosh 2006, 58–62;
Ray 2007, 211; Treadwell 2009, 343–6; Webster
2011, 460, 475–7

As Calcutta evolved in the later eighteenth century,
the British increasingly brought their wives and
children to live with them. The city also began to
attract single women, who typically married
Company officers, establishing families that often
maintained long-lasting connections with India.
Zoffany's complex conversation piece, known as
The Auriol and Dashwood Families, is a chronicle
of such a colonial dynasty in formation, as well
as a meticulous delineation of the structures of
Anglo-Indian domestic life.

James Peter Auriol, shown on the right in
green, went to India in 1770, rising through the
Company's ranks to become Secretary to the
governing Council of the Presidency of Bengal in
1782. His brothers Charles and John Lewis, shown
standing at the left (Charles in his red captain's
uniform), followed him to India, as did his sisters
Charlotte and Sophia, who are depicted seated at
the tea table. Charlotte subsequently married
Thomas Dashwood, who had come to Calcutta to
work for the Company in 1781, here seated at the
chess table between his sister-in-law, Sophia, and
James Auriol. Sophia was married to John Prinsep
(seated, to the left), who had defected from the
Company soon after his arrival in 1771 to work in
the indigo trade and founded a flourishing textile
business. The circumstances of the commissioning
of the portrait are unknown, but James Auriol's
resignation and subsequent departure for England
in December 1783 presumably was the impetus, and
he seems to be the chief protagonist, although the
portrait has been continuously in the Dashwood
family's possession since its completion.

Although tea consumption is now ubiquitous in
India, tea was a luxury item there in the 1780s and
was imported from China for European households.
The elaborate process of tea making using valuable
silver utensils and requiring the close attention of
two servants, whom Zoffany depicted in meticulous
detail, would have signified the wealth of the
families, as well as constituting an inscription
of British customs on an atmospheric Indian
landscape.

The setting presumably refers to the well-
stocked garden of James Auriol's large house at
Alipore, with the distant view on the right possibly
alluding to Prinsep's indigo plantation in Bengal.[1]
The practice of keeping enormous retinues of
servants was commonplace in British India, even
for those of modest incomes, and the object of
much derision and castigation in Britain. As
Lizzie Collingwood has noted, the British rigidly
interpreted what had been fluid Indian ideas of
caste to create complex and fixed hierarchies
in their households and workplaces, which were
cemented through visual representations and
textual descriptions.[2]

The five servants depicted in *The Auriol and
Dashwood Families* would have constituted a small
proportion of the sitters' household retinues,
but Zoffany provided an indication of the finely
calibrated hierarchy by precisely delineating the
status of the servants, who are, left to right, a
hookah-bearer; a household servant pouring
water from the kettle into the teapot; a page
wearing livery and a turban who may have been
the slave known to have been owned by James
Auriol;[3] a *banian,* or accountant, wearing white;
and a *hircarrah,* or courier, who is handing James
Auriol a letter. A teapot closely resembling the
one depicted in the painting, which was made
in England and hallmarked 1785, is still in the
possession of the family. As Mary Webster has
suggested, the teapot would not have reached
Calcutta until later that year, when Zoffany was
in Lucknow, and he may not have completed the
painting until he returned to Calcutta in 1787.

GF

1. For the importance of tea drinking in India,
   see Ray 2007, 211, and Lizzie Collingham,
   Curry: A Tale of Cooks and Conquerers, Oxford,
   2006, 188–208.
2. Collingham 2001, 18.
3. Webster 2011, 475–6.

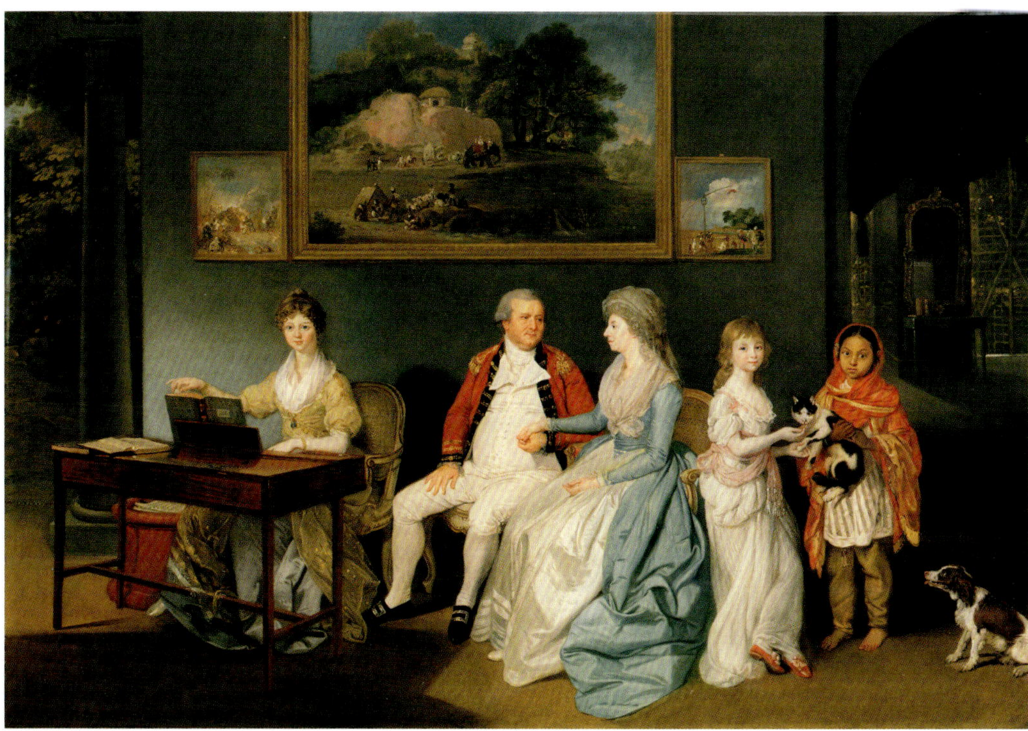

92

The Blair Family

1786–7

Oil on canvas, 96.5 × 134.6 cm (38 × 53 in)
Tate, London; bequeathed by Simon Sainsbury
2006, accessioned 2008

Provenance: By descent to J.P.F. Pepys; sold by
his executors, Sotheby's, 18 March 1981, lot 37,
bt Simon Sainsbury, by whom bequeathed to
Tate, 2006

*Selected exhibitions: Exhibition of Works by the Old
Masters and by Deceased Masters of the British School,*
Royal Academy of Arts, 1885, no. 29

Selected references: Manners & Williamson 1920,
226; Archer 1979, 157 (as untraced); Leppert &
McClary 1987, 97–102; Tobin 2004, 100, 102;
Treadwell 2009, 371; Webster 2011, 523–6

Colonel William Blair was a Bengal army officer,
who was promoted to Commandant of Chunar,
a garrison twenty miles up river from Benares.
Chunar had played an important role in Warren
Hastings's suppression of Chait Singh's rebellion
in 1781, for which the Company army had been
unprepared, and Blair was promoted for his support
of Hastings's troops to the rank of full colonel and
given the command of the Company's brigade at
Cawnpore. In 1786 Ozias Humphry recorded in his
diary that Blair, his wife Jane and their 'suite' were
among the Europeans staying in Lucknow; and
they may have commissioned Zoffany to paint
their portrait during their visit. Zoffany stopped
at Cawnpore during his expedition to Delhi with
John Wombwell in September of the same year.
The production of the painting is not documented,
but as Mary Webster has noted, Zoffany had
presumably finished the portrait by 1788 when
Blair resigned from the Company and returned
to Britain.[1]

Zoffany's painting probably shows the family
on the verandah at their home at Cawnpore, though
the relationship between the outside and inside
spaces is somewhat ambiguous. Blair and his wife
hold hands and gaze affectionately at each other,
flanked by their two daughters, Jane and Maria.
Jane is shown playing the pianoforte with a volume
of Handel's compositions displayed prominently
on the stand. As Raymond Head has noted, music
making was a popular leisure activity among
Europeans in India at the period.[2] Corelli, Haydn
and Handel were particularly favoured, and Handel
was revered above all, so Jane Blair's choice of
composer would have been an index of her

discerning taste. The first music shop was not
established in Calcutta until 1786, the date of this
picture, and pianofortes were still comparatively
rare,[3] so its inclusion in Zoffany's conversation
piece implies that the Blairs were both affluent
and particularly interested in music. Keyboard
instruments were specifically associated with
women. The elder daughter Jane was later to
introduce a note of disharmony into the household,
however, by eloping with her cousin, Captain
Thomas Blair, a match of which her parents
disapproved, though they evidently reconciled later,
since she was a beneficiary of her father's will.

Maria is shown stroking a cat held by a young
Indian girl, who typically has been described as an
ayah, but she seems too young for such a position,
and her relationship with Maria seems to be one
of friendship rather than of subservience. Zoffany
seems to have been careful to establish difference
between them, however: Maria is fashionably
attired in European clothes and shoes, whereas
the Indian girl wears indigenous garments and
is shoeless, and the contrast between their skin
tones is very pronounced.

The three paintings hanging on the wall,
all Indian subjects presumably referring to
compositions, either actual or imagined, by Zoffany,
seem by their exoticism to dramatize the issue
of difference articulated by the juxtaposition of
the two young girls. On the left is a *sati* scene,
similar to the one in the picture of *Colonel Polier
and his Friends* (cat. 90), and the painting in the
centre shows a European woman in a bullock-
drawn cart flanked by servants and elephants,
with an encampment in the foreground, which
Webster suggests may be Sacrigali (Sicri Gully;
see fig. 135), some 300 miles from Chunar. The
subject of the picture on the right is *charkpuja*, the
practice observed by devotees of Shiva who, in
order to appease the god, attached themselves by
wires threaded between their shoulder blades to
wooden structures symbolizing the god's wheel
(*charka*) and were suspended in the air for long
periods. Often termed 'hook-swinging', somewhat
misleadingly, this practice of self-mutilation,
like *sati*, was simultaneously the object of great
fascination and revulsion among Europeans and
must have been particularly compelling to Zoffany,
who from early in his career demonstrated a keen
interest in extremities of human suffering.

GF

1. Webster 2011, 523–4.
2. Head 1985. See also Leppart & McClary 1987,
   63–104, for a compelling analysis of the mediating role
   played by music and painting in 'racial estrangement'
   of the British and Indians in colonial India.
3. Head 1985, 550–51. Head has suggested that the
   pianoforte was probably made by either Johannes
   Pohlman or Johan Christophe Zumpe, who were both
   well-known German piano makers.

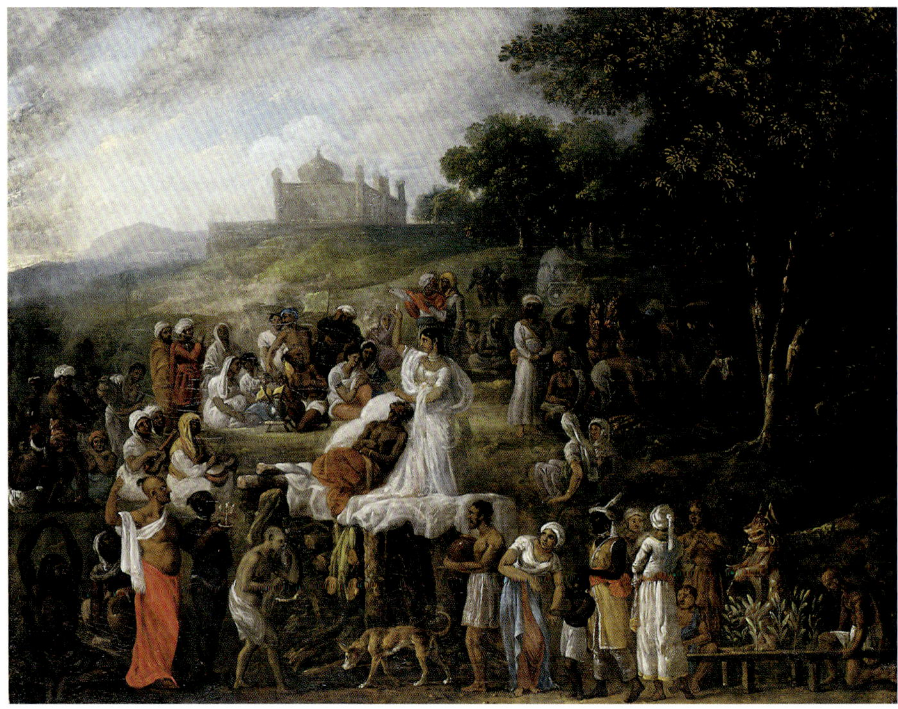

93

Sacrifice of a Hindoo Widow upon the Funeral Pyre of her Husband

*c.*1795

Oil on canvas, 101.6 × 127 cm (40 × 50 in)
Private collection

Provenance: Zoffany sale, Messrs Robins, 9 May
1811, probably lot 82; Sotheby's (British Paintings),
18 Oct. 1989, lot 302 (as Anglo-Indian School)

Selected exhibitions: National Portrait Gallery
1990–91, no. 278

Selected references: Treadwell 2009, 383; Webster
2011, 561–3

The Hindu deity Shiva, in all his aspects, was
perceived by many Europeans in the eighteenth
century to be a mirror of Hinduism itself. In
his benign form he was the creator, munificent,
possessed of enormous power and, as Lord of the
Dance, he trampled evil under foot. In his dark
form he was entirely destructive, hideous in feature,
his body covered in ash and snakes as adornments.
To even the most enlightened westerner this
conflict between the two sides of Hinduism was
difficult to fathom, and its darkest manifestation
was *sati*, or *suttee*, the self-immolation of a widow
on her husband's funeral pyre. Although an account
of the practice is recorded in the *Mahabharata*, the
practice is nowhere approved authoritatively in the
Hindu scriptures. The Mughals, like their European
successors, were appalled by the practice and tried
to ban it within their territories. It horrified and
fascinated European travellers in equal measure
and was frequently recorded in writings from
the seventeenth and eighteenth centuries.
An eyewitness account of a sati at Tanjore in 1783

by Donald Campbell of Barbreck relates in detail
the noble countenance and behaviour of the young
widow.[1] A succession of artists recorded the
practice of *sati.* Tilly Kettle perhaps never saw such
an event but made two paintings of a Hindu widow
preparing herself for *sati.*[2] William Hodges, on the
other hand, left a detailed eyewitness account of a
sati and made a drawing of the scene which is
reproduced in his memoirs.[3] It is uncertain whether
Zoffany actually observed a *sati*. It is probable that
Hodges related what he had seen in detail to his old
friend in the brief period that they were in Calcutta
together in 1783. Hodges's drawing of the scene
is now lost but Zoffany would almost certainly
have seen it.

In the eighteenth century *sati* was considered by
many Hindus to be an act of supreme heroism, and
this is certainly how Zoffany has shown the rite in
this painting – evidence of the depth of his interest
in 'Indian' India. The scene is a hilly landscape with
a Muslim tomb on the high ground. In the centre
of the composition the widow stands, fearless, on
top of the pyre beside her husband, her right hand
raised ready to give the sign for the pyre to be
lit. She is dressed in a long flowing white dress,
precisely as described by Hodges in his eyewitness
account of a *sati*. Beneath her stand three Brahmins,
one bearing a candelabra, another with an oil lamp
ready to light the pyre. To the right of the pyre
is a double row of figures resembling a classical
Gandhara frieze. At one end is a figure holding a
large jar for the oil to set the pyre ablaze and at the
other end a Brahmin supports a platform bearing
the Hindu deity Sarama, the messenger of Yama,
the Hindu god of death. To the left of the pyre are
three female musicians with drums and a veena
(stringed instrument), their music played to drown

out the cries of the widow. They are flanked by
numerous spectators and to their right are horses in
a grove of trees and *Doms* bearing more logs for the
pyre. In the holy city of Varanasi *Doms* still perform
the task of cremation on the ghats to this day.
Higher up the hill is the bullock cart that carried
the widow to the funeral.

Zoffany's studio sale in 1811 included three
such scenes all described as unfinished.[4] This is
probably lot 82 in the sale described as 'in a more
forward state'. The whereabouts of the other
two remains a mystery. Two of the artist's Indian
paintings, the Blair and Polier conversation pieces
(cats. 92 and 90), each include a painting of *sati*
in the background. They are rather different in
composition to this sole surviving painting: one
shows the widow ascending the pyre, the other with
her lying beside her dead husband. Whether these
paintings actually existed or were just included as
part of the composition of such conversation pieces
is contested among scholars. What is certain is that
none of the background paintings shown in these
conversation pieces have ever come to light.

CG

1. See Donald Campbell, *A Journey Overland to India*,
   London, 1795, 138–42.
2. Tilly Kettle was the first professional British portrait
   artist to visit India, arriving in June 1769 and
   departing in March 1776. Apart from numerous
   surviving portraits of both Europeans and Indian
   princes, he painted a number of scenes of Indian life
   including two versions of a south Indian woman
   preparing for *sati* (one in the Oriental Club, London,
   the other in a private collection). In the opinion of the
   present compiler Kettle's sati scenes, which are highly
   romanticised, are unlikely to have been based upon
   first-hand observation.
3. Hodges 1793, 79–84.
4. Robins 1811, lots 76, 81, 82 (9 May).

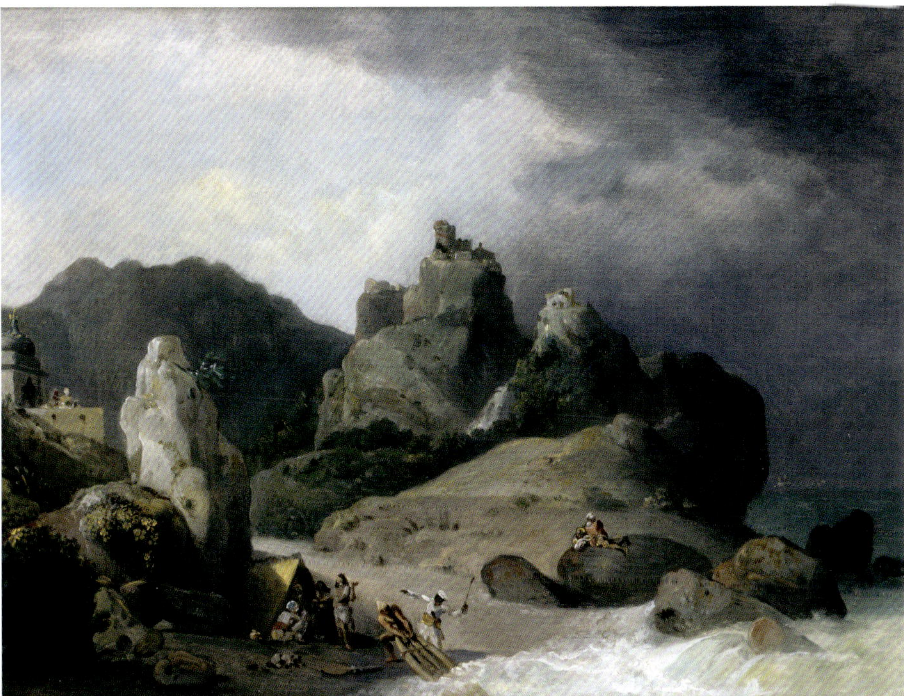

94

***A View on the Coromandel Coast,
Southern India***

*c.*1795

Oil on canvas, 66.1 × 83.8 cm (26 × 33 in)
Private collection

Exhibited at the Royal Academy of Arts only

Provenance: Probably Zoffany sale, Messrs Robins,
9 May 1811, probably lot 77, 'A Romantic View
on the Indian Coast'; Christie's, *Visions of India*,
5 June 1996, lot 131

Selected references: Treadwell 2009, 338;
Webster 2011, 454

Zoffany spent just five weeks in Madras between
22 July and 26 August 1783. The intense heat at
that time of year, monsoon rains and the dangerous
state of southern India following the war with the
French would have confined the artist to Fort St
George and its immediate environs. Yet, years later
back in England, he made a number of unfinished
sketches of the coast including 'A Goldmine on
the Coromandel Coast' and 'a Storm near Madras'.[1]
These must have been based on sketches that he
made on his journey north to Calcutta on board the
Lord Macartney. The log of Captain Hall suggests
that, initially at least, the vessel hugged the shore
line and dropped anchor from time to time to
communicate with the captain of the *Belmont*.[2]
This would have given Zoffany ample opportunity
to make sketches that he worked up back in his
studio in Kew.

   This vigorous oil sketch shows a rocky shoreline
beneath a dark and brooding sky just before the
onset of a monsoon storm. The surging waves
threaten a boatman wearing a typical south Indian
peaked hat of his caste. His bamboo boat is already
half submerged by the crashing waves. Behind him
his master, enraged at the possible loss of a valuable
boat, is brandishing a whip. A family, indifferent
to the approaching storm, has gathered in front
of a tent situated on the beach. High above on a
rocky outcrop is a fortified building recalling the
unsettled state of southern India throughout
this period.

   The present painting provides an insight into
Zoffany's mind during his highly productive
years of the early 1790s. For much of this period
he was preoccupied with creating grand historical
paintings like the embassy of Haider Beg (cats.
101, 102) and some now lost pictures including
Battlepiece against Hyder Ali (exhibited at the Royal
Academy in 1790) and the *Death of Ghulam Qadir*.
Alongside these is this intense landscape painted
for himself, perhaps to remind him of 'Indian'
India, where his *bibi* and son still lived. Zoffany
harboured romantic ideas of returning there again,
and in 1798 he once again applied to the East
India Company to go back to this country that so
captivated his mind. However, ill health prevented
him from doing so. In so many of Zoffany's
paintings from this late period violence and death
are never far away. It is as if Zoffany sensed his
own transience and approaching demise. Here it is
apparent in the approaching storm threatening to
engulf the shore dwellers and in the Muslim tomb
set high on a bluff.

   Zoffany never hesitated to re-use props and
images from previous works and this is apparent
in this landscape. The foreground is taken directly
from the view of Sicri Gully seen on the back wall
of the Blair conversation piece (cat. 92), the river
front of the Ganges here transposed to the rocky
Coromandel coast. It is these parallels in his Indian
work that may assist in the identification of the
numerous lost works by the artist, should any ever
reappear. Since it resurfaced, it has been presumed,
given the romantic nature of this landscape, that
it is the painting described in Zoffany's studio sale
catalogue as 'A Romantic View on the Indian Coast',
but there is an alternative possibility that it was
listed under sketches as 'A Storm near Madras'.[3]

CG

1. It is highly unlikely that Zoffany brought back from
   India to London any oil paintings in view of the high
   customs duties levied in England on oil paintings. His
   few surviving Indian paintings worked up in England
   are significantly more romanticized than those done in
   India itself, and for these works he reverted to using
   English colours, whereas in the subcontinent he had
   frequently used locally ground Indian pigments.
2. William Hall, appointed captain of the East Indiaman
   Lord Macartney on her maiden voyage, wrote his log of
   the voyage, 'Original Journal of own Hand Writing',
   Oct. 1782–27 Oct. 1783, National Maritime Museum,
   L/MAB/B/415A.
3. Robins 1811, lot 77, 'A Romantic View on the Indian
   Coast, ditto (unfinished)'; lot 67, 'A storm near
   Madras' (9 May).

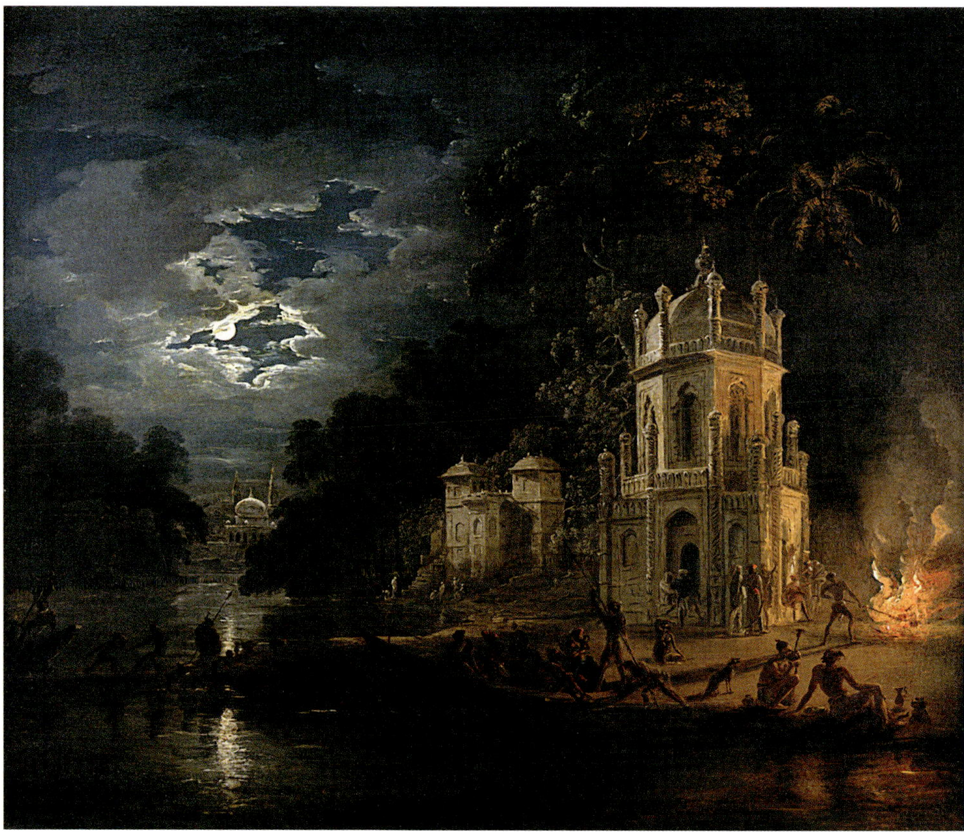

95

Nagaphon Ghut, Upper India

*c.*1786/7

Oil on canvas, 66 × 76.2 cm (26 × 30 in)
Private collection

Provenance: Almost certainly painted for Claude
Martin and included in the inventory of his
paintings sold in Calcutta in 1801 as 'Nagaphon
Ghut Zoffany'; Maharaja Bahadur Sir Prodyot
Coomar Tagore; P.N. Talukdar, 1956

Selected references: Treadwell 2009, 358–9;
Webster 2011, 527–8

In 1988 a disastrous fire swept through the
principal rooms of a West Country castle
destroying a large Indian landscape by Zoffany
of Claude Martin's estate at Najafghar.[1] At the
time it was the only identified Indian landscape by
the artist. Since then two further landscapes have
been recognized: a painting of the Coromandel
coast (cat. 94) and this enigmatic moonlight scene.
Known to scholars since the 1920s, it had up until
1998 been dismissed as a minor work by Thomas
Daniell.[2] But, as with all works by Zoffany, there
were numerous clues to its identity: a faint
pencil inscription on the reverse of the original
worm-eaten stretcher gave its title, which matched
one in the Martin inventory; a remarkably similar
boat and oarsman are shown in a print after Zoffany
of Martin's house, the Farhad Baksh, published in
the *European Magazine* for April 1790 (fig. 149);
and some of the figures are identical to those in
other Indian paintings by Zoffany.

The exact location of Nagaphon Ghat remains
uncertain. As with so many Mughal-style
buildings, those shown here have long since
disappeared. However, the architectural details
in the tomb or pavilion in the foreground suggest
that the location was in the Rohilla territory of
Faizullah Khan, through which Zoffany passed
with John Wombwell in the latter part of 1786 on
his journey back from Agra and Delhi. Zoffany
probably completed the painting back in Lucknow
before he left for Calcutta in December of that year
or alternatively after September 1787 when he was
once again in Lucknow. The ascetic with a long pole
shown in front of the fire is also present in front of
the tent in the background of Zoffany's full-length
portrait of General Macleod (fig. 156), which also
dates from 1787.

Nagaphon translates in Bengali as snake head.
Arranged around the fire are a group of itinerant
ascetics, probably Nagas or Snake Nagas, there to
perform the annual snake festival, which took place
at various times of the year in different parts of
India. This festival is associated with Shiva, with his
body and hair entwined in snakes as adornments.
His image is shown in front of one of the entrances
to the pavilion. The composition of the painting,
with the cold light of the moon providing a
spectacular contrast to the hot reds of the fire, was
commonly used by later eighteenth-century artists,
such as Joseph Wright of Derby for several of his
views of Vesuvius. The snake festival alone would
not have given the artist the scope for such a
composition. To achieve it, Zoffany seems to have

combined this festival with a cremation, a theme
linked with death that from the evidence of
surviving paintings and drawings, obsessed the
artist. The figures in the boats are arranged in a
flat plane reminiscent of a classical frieze, a
technique he used frequently to give the impression
of a large crowd of people. Here, their exaggerated
features and ghostly appearance lift the genre to
a mysterious realm.

Many unanswered questions remain about
Zoffany's years in India but one of the most
baffling is the disappearance of so much of Claude
Martin's collection after its sale in Calcutta in
1801.[3] A large view of Martin's house, the Farhad
Baksh, by Thomas Daniell appeared in the 1970s.[4]
This moonlight scene appears to be the only known
work by Zoffany from that sale to have survived.
More than sixty other works by the artist have
vanished without trace.

CG

1. C. Hussey, 'Ince Castle, Cornwall', *Country Life*,
   23 March 1967, 649–51.
2. According to Maurice Shellim, acquired, as by
   Thomas Daniell, by Maharaja Sir Prodyot Coomar
   Tagore in London in the 1930s.
3. Bengal Inventories, India Office Library, British
   Library, 1801, L/AG/34/27/24, no. 76, pp. 49, 60.
4. Christie's, 26 June 1981, no. 112.

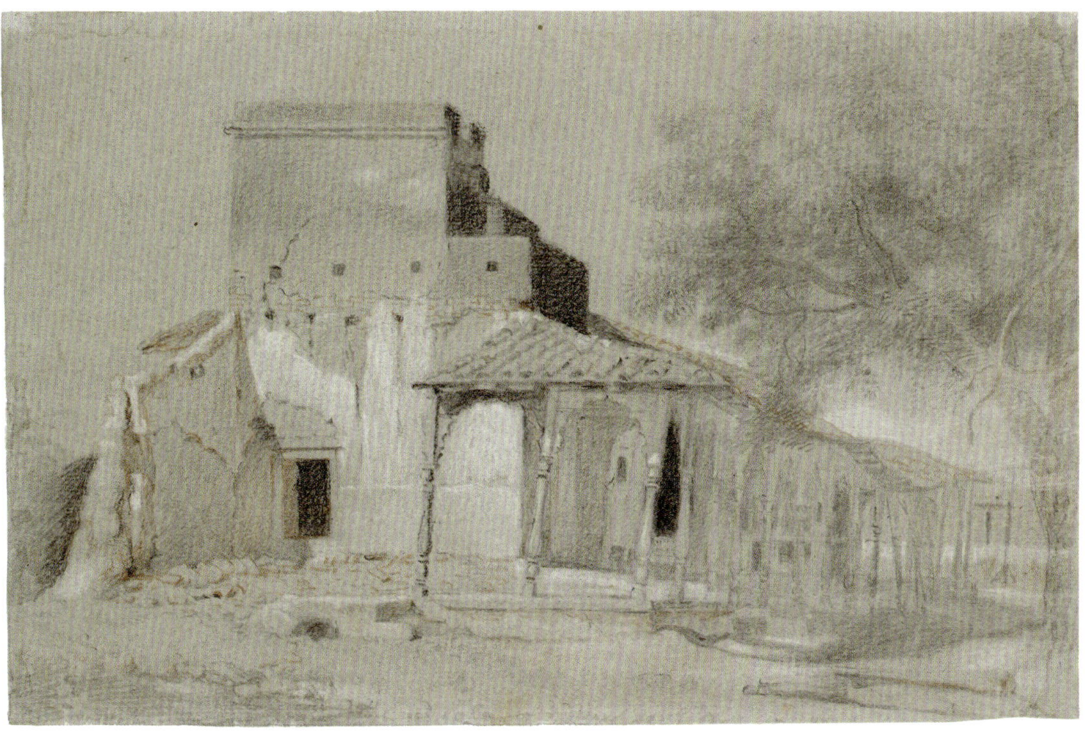

96

Resthouse or Caravanserai at Najafgarh
1788

Red, black and white chalk on grey paper,
23.3 × 34.6 cm (9⅛ × 13⅝ in)
Inscribed on verso in Zoffany's hand: 'Najef Gar
belonging to Collonel Martin | a Jagir Reigth |
to Haeng … or returns there to a curry … | …
Bibbee | Nov. 17. 88'
Ashmolean Museum, Oxford

Provenance: Brigadier Hutchinson; Major R.G.
Hutchinson; Sir Bruce Ingram; purchased by
the Ashmolean Museum, 1963

Selected exhibitions: National Portrait Gallery 1977,
no. 125

Selected references: Archer 1979, 164; Treadwell
2009, 381; Webster 2011, 517

Claude Martin was one of the most vibrant
European characters in eighteenth-century India
and by far the richest European in Awadh. Even
the Nawab of Awadh (cat. 83) was one of his many
debtors. Martin's vast fortune derived in part from
his position as superintendent of the nawab's
arsenal but to a much greater extent from trading,
money lending and property. Most of his property
purchases were in Lucknow itself, but in 1786 he
purchased his first property outside the city. He
acquired the estate of Najafgarh from his old friends
Colonel Antoine Polier (cat. 90) and Colonel
Hannay, the revenue collector. The estate lay a
few miles down the Ganges from Cawnpore and
included a fine house with zenana quarters for his
mistresses. Its extensive grounds produced both
indigo (for export to Europe) and roses (for the
production of attar for the Indian market). He later
acquired further properties including houses in
Calcutta, Benares, Ghazipur and in the French
settlement of Chandernagore. After his death the
estate of Najafgarh was given an estimated value
of 200,000 rupees, significantly more than any
other property that he owned and a huge figure
for the time.

Zoffany made three journeys up country from
Calcutta between June 1784 and November 1788,
which resulted in extended periods of residence in
Lucknow. During these periods he formed a close
friendship with Martin. Both were leading figures
of Enlightenment culture in India at the time.
Martin in particular was not just an officer in the
East India Company's army or a speculator, for
which he has too often been dismissed. He was
also a clever mathematician, architect, engineer,
cartographer and keen botanist and ornithologist.[1]
These qualities would have appealed to Zoffany,
but one other dynamic would have brought them
together. They were both foreigners and in the
closed and snobbish world of Anglo-India they
were always outsiders, forever on the fringe of
society that they both craved. Martin rewarded
Zoffany's friendship by becoming his most
important patron after Hastings. The inventory
of Martin's effects made after his death lists thirty
oil paintings and fifteen sketches by Zoffany.[2] There
were almost certainly others including the intimate
portrait of Martin's beautiful *bibi* Boulone with
his adopted son Zulfikar Khan (fig. 123). The
inventory lists one painting of Najafgarh, but
there is evidence that he did others. The Daniells
recorded seeing a slight sketch of the property,
and Martin's correspondence reveals that
Zoffany painted on canvas a plan for an orchard
on the estate.[3]

We can only surmise why Zoffany drew this
dilapidated building at Najafgarh just before he
bade farewell to his old friend for the last time.
But the inscription on the reverse of the drawing
in Zoffany's barely legible hand gives us a possible
clue. It may have been here that he shared a curry
with his Indian *bibi* and son before departing for
Calcutta and England, never to see them again.
His health was poor, and the poignancy of this
moment must have remained with him for the rest
of his life. This is the first in a sequence of drawings
that the artist made on his return journey and that
comprises almost all the known surviving drawings
of northern India by Zoffany. Many others that
were listed in his studio sale in 1811 are now lost.

CG

1. For a detailed analysis of Martin's career, see
   Llewellyn-Jones 1992.
2. The present drawing was not included in Martin's
   inventory.
3. William Daniell's diary, 27 July 1789, ' Un. (Thomas)
   finishing a slight Sketch near Nuguf Guss' (private
   collection on loan to India Office Library, British
   Library).
4. Llewellyn-Jones 2003, 165; letter no. 138 to Sahib
   Ram Pandit, 13 April 1788.

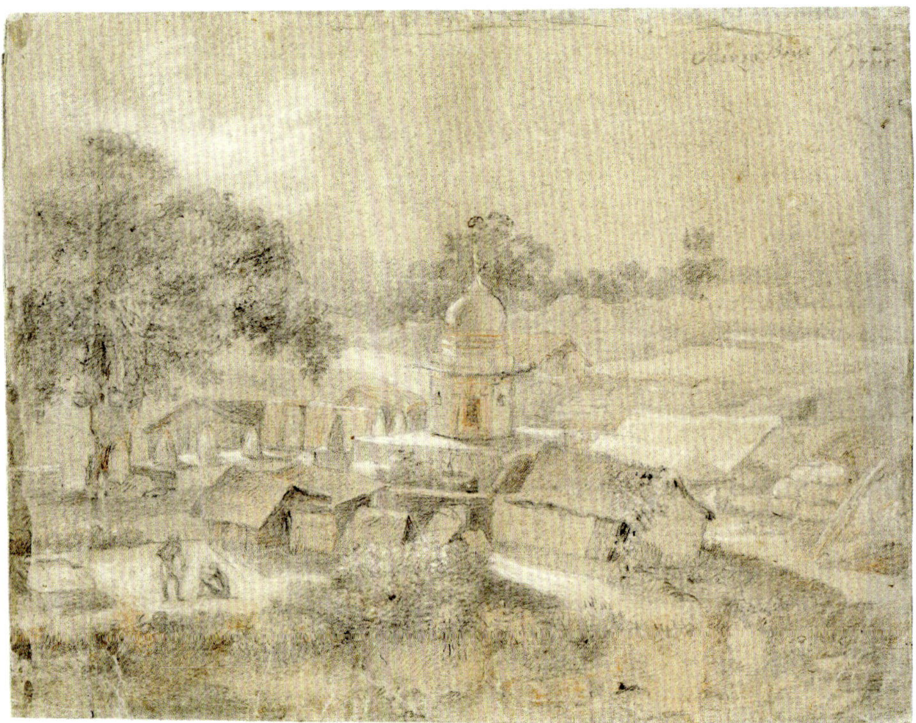

97

***A Group of Buildings Surrounding a
Suttee Memorial at Mirzapore, India***
1788

Red, black and white chalk on blue/grey paper,
28 × 35.3 cm (11 × 13⅞ in)
Inscribed by Zoffany: 'Mirza Bour Nov 27 1788 and
verso: to commemorate … have burnt themselves
… the Death of their Husband. Erected by the
nearest relation and consider it … and have
lamps burnt Every Night Nov. 27 88 J Zoffany'
British Museum, Department of Prints and
Drawings, 1955,0416.7

Provenance: Brigadier Hutchinson; Major R.G.
Hutchinson; purchased from Colnaghi, 1955

Selected exhibitions: National Portrait Gallery 1977,
no. 126

Selected references: Archer 1979, 164; Webster 2011,
540

Ten days after leaving Najafgarh, Zoffany
arrived in the large town of Mirzapore situated
on the south bank of the Ganges midway between
Allahabad and Benares. His slow progress
eastwards indicates that he was travelling by
palankeen at this stage of the journey. After
Mirzapore he proceeded much more rapidly and
it is feasible that it was here that he found a boat to
take him down the Ganges with the rapid flow of
the river in his favour. From early Mughal times
this ancient town had been famed for its carpets
and as a grand market for the trading of cotton,
but now such things were evidently of little interest
to Zoffany. Whereas in England and Italy he had
made detailed paintings of market traders and
artisans at work, now he left such scenes to his rival
Arthur William Devis. Claude Martin wrote to
Charles Townley on 8 January 1789 of his old
friend Zoffany: 'I will regret him, but he must quit
this country, he grows old!'[1] Zoffany's series of
highly personal drawings done on his last journey
back to Calcutta seem to centre on the theme of
old age and death: even the trees are gnarled and
ancient. With his health broken, Zoffany must have
wondered if he would ever get back to London.
His drawings suggest that he felt that death was
stalking him and they imply an almost morbid
fascination with the subject.

At Mirzapore he made two drawings of the town
both of which show *sati* memorials, an issue that
had captured his imagination from the time of his
arrival in India. The present drawing has at its
centre an elegant Mughal-style tomb, and at first
glance the viewer might presume that this is the
memorial erected by the family of the widow who

committed herself to her dead husband's funeral
pyre. But this is a Muslim tomb and the series of
stones visible nearby record not one but several
satis at this spot. For many Hindus at the time *sati*
was regarded as an act of supreme selflessness and
heroism and the erection of stones to record the
noble need was common in Upper India. That a
widow would be so honoured and remembered by
posterity was presumably an enticement for an
aspiring widow wishing to undertake *sati*.

CG

1. Llewellyn-Jones 2003, 171: letter 143, 8 Jan. 1789,
from Calcutta.

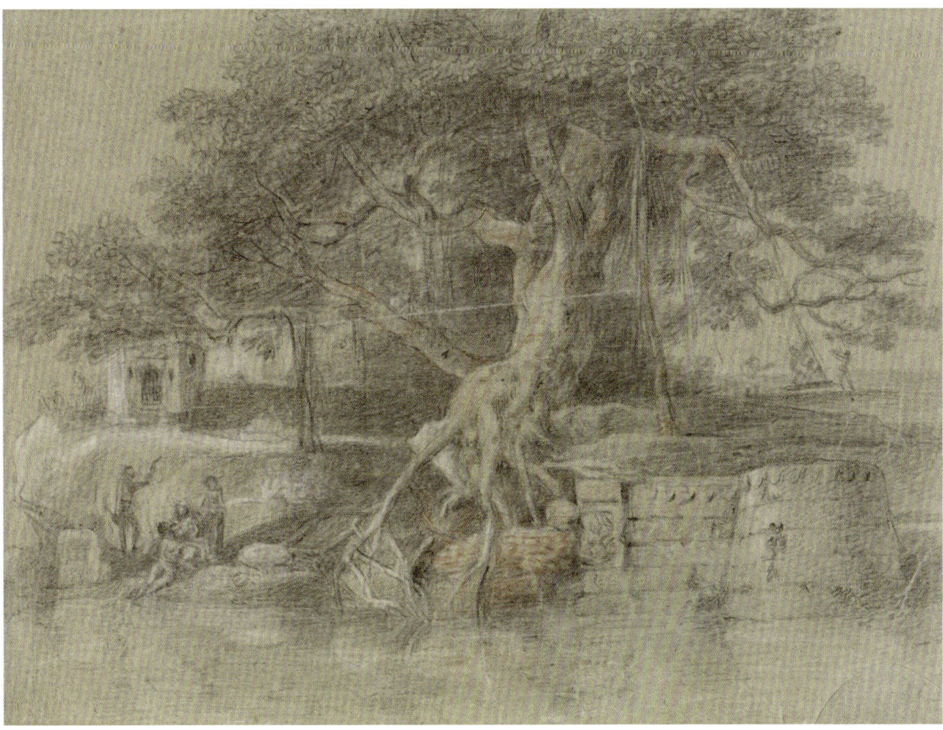

98
*A Hindu Brought to the Ganges
to Die at Ghazipur*
1788

Black, red and white chalk on blue paper,
27 × 34.6 cm (10⅝ × 13⅝ in)
Inscribed on verso in pencil: 'Gaysibour 28 Aug.
distance a Hindu brought to the Watter to die |
his Daughter officiating the Death [?] benevolent
Service doth [?she] give him So much Ganges
Watter till it Stops his Breath | being Given up by
their Doctors this Man deith very hard | [?death's]
to the River being weary Long I Saw him Die | Nov
29-88 in Seight of Bazar. Captain Hardaph | B.
Zoffany –'
Yale Center for British Art, Paul Mellon Collection

Provenance: Brigadier Hutchinson; Major R.G.
Hutchinson; A.R. Pilkington; Sotheby's, 20 March
1963, lot 6, bt Colnaghi

Selected exhibition: National Portrait Gallery 1977,
no. 127

Selected references: Archer 1979, 164; Treadwell
2009, 382–3; Webster 2011, 544

For Hindus the place and time of death are of
supreme importance in the cycle of life and rebirth.
It is considered most auspicious to die, and for the
body to be cremated, at the ghats (steps) in the
ancient city of Kashi (Benares or Varanasi). Hindus
believe that this ceremony will free their souls from
earthly existence and allow it to ascend directly to
the highest of the heavenly planes, Bramaloka (the
place of Bramha). For those unable to die at Kashi
the next best thing is to expire beside the holy
waters of *Mata Ganga* (Mother Ganges). This
great river is considered sacred from its source
above Gangotri in the Himalayas all the way to
the sea at the Bay of Bengal.

What Zoffany witnessed and recorded here
in this fine drawing, done on his last journey
from Lucknow to Calcutta, may seem strange to
westerners. Yet, for Hindus death was viewed as a
natural aspect of life, and many of the early texts
and epic tales describe death and give guidance on
the ultimate goal to transcend the need to return
to life on earth. The inscription on the reverse,
in Zoffany's hand, records the last hours of an
unnamed Hindu's earthly existence at the ghats in
Ghazipur, some 50 miles (80 km) down river from
Benares. Once his doctors had given up all hope
for his recovery, he had made the long and painful
journey to the banks of the Ganges to die,
accompanied by his daughter. The drawing vividly
records the scene of the old man lying close to the
river, while his daughter pours river water from a
lota (water vessel) into his mouth until he is at last
freed in death from the pain and illness that he had
suffered. In his last moments he would have taken
comfort in the belief that every droplet of Ganges
water would have helped erase the sins of his life.
Nearby, an ascetic, his arm raised, watches intently.
In sharp contrast, on the right side of the drawing
children play on a swing, entirely oblivious to the
unfolding event nearby. Zoffany emphasized the
theme of old age and death in the crumbling
masonry of the ghat and the ancient tree with its
roots reaching down in to the sacred river. The
scene can be pinpointed even today. It lies close to
the Chahal Situn – not far from the present burning
ghats – and there the stump of the masonry
buttress and the much worn carved-stone image
of Shiva, seen in the drawing, still survive on the
bank of the river. A little earlier, Zoffany painted a
comparable scene of a dying Hindu on the muddy
banks of the Ganges, in a roundel hung on the back
wall of the Polier conversation piece (cat. 90).

CG

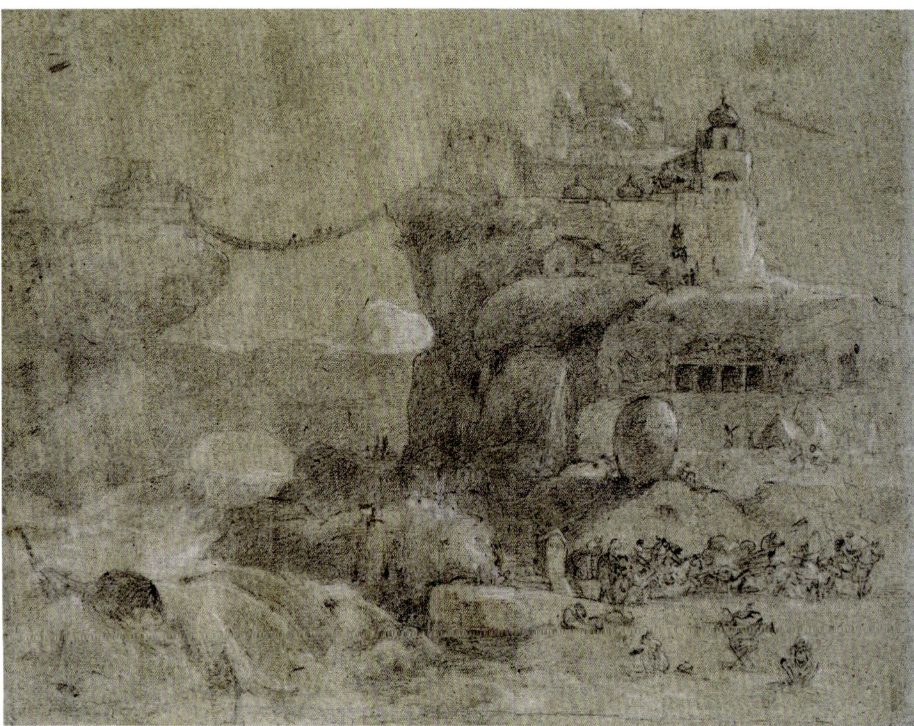

99

*Rocky Landscape with Waterfall and Temples,
Eastern India*

1788

Red, black and white chalk on faded blue paper;
27.1 × 34.1 cm (10⅝ × 13⅜ in)
Inscribed on verso in Zoffany's hand (mostly
illegible but including): '2 Fagal are trying to thro
a Eck of stone down the height … of the Deity …
taken of the Pagoda at the death of … in the solid
rock 300 yard deep … The Pagoda is wound? up
to a Rock 80 yard high … Pagoda D? 3 1788'
British Museum, Department of Prints and
Drawings, 1955,01416.9

Provenance: Brigadier Hutchinson; Major R.G.
Hutchinson; purchased from Colnaghi, 1955

Selected exhibitions: National Portrait Gallery 1977,
no. 128

Selected references: Archer 1979; Webster 2011, 545

The Chinese Buddhist monk and scholar Hiuen
Tsiang, travelling in Bihar in the seventh century
AD, recorded a visit to a marvellous cave system
with a beautiful underground garden. Scholars
have argued about the location of this fabulous
place and many have presumed it to have been the
Barari caves near Bhagalpur. A more likely location
is a cave at Champa a few miles away, which was the
site of the capital of the ancient kingdom of Anga.
Zoffany's lengthy inscription on the reverse of this
drawing alludes to such a cave, the entrance of
which is visible halfway up the hill in the drawing
itself. But sadly much of the inscription is now
impossible to read, in part a result of Zoffany's
poor handwriting and in part from the rubbing
of the artist's soft pencil over the passage of time.
In the past the drawing has been catalogued as
a 'mountainous landscape', but it is highly
unlikely that Zoffany ever went anywhere near
the Himalayas. Having left Ghazipur by boat on
29 November 1788, Zoffany would have reached
the vicinity of the old Mughal towns of Monghyr
and Bhagalpur by 3 December, which is probably
the date of this drawing. The exact location of the
landscape is still uncertain. There are other cave
systems in the hills south of the Ganges in this area.
At Khargpur a few miles south of Monghyr there
is the beautiful waterfall of the Five Princesses
(Panch Kumari) with a cave nearby. Further to the
east, near Colgong, there are several ancient cave
systems, the one at Patharghata being particularly
sacred to Hindus. A diligent search of this part
of Bihar may yet reveal the exact spot from which
Zoffany made this extraordinary drawing.

The strange scene that Zoffany witnessed here
and recorded in the drawing is of two fakirs or
ascetics rolling a giant egg-shaped stone down the
hill following the death of one of their sect. The
stone is probably a Shivite lingam, which may have
stood since ancient times in the cave system and
was now being rolled down the hill to stand in the
open and to provide a focus for worship. Below it
appears to be the funeral procession of the ascetic
accompanied by bullock carts and an elephant.
To the left a waterfall crashes over rocks through
a narrow ravine, while high above, a rope bridge
connects two temple complexes. This is the
penultimate surviving drawing in the sequence
of drawings done on Zoffany's final journey from
Upper India to Calcutta. Once again the central
themes are old age and death, represented here in
the ancient temples and Buddhist cave and in the
passing of a sage. It is probable that the artist
made a number of other drawings of scenes further
along the Ganges before he arrived in Calcutta a
fortnight or so later and these are now lost. Should
just one ever emerge from the shadows, it will give
us a further tantalizing insight into the artist's
final impression of rural India.

CG

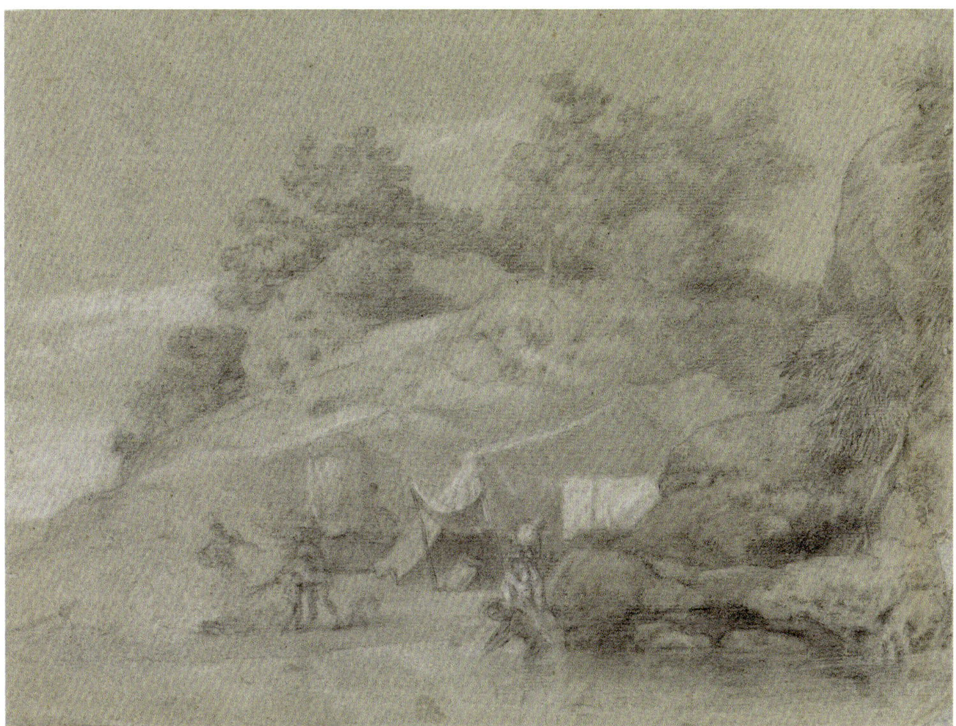

100

Indians Encamped on a Rocky River Bank
1788

Pencil and white chalk on blue paper,
26.8 × 34.9 cm (10½ × 13¾ in)
Yale Center for British Art, Paul Mellon Collection

Provenance: … Iolo Williams; … Colnaghi, from whom purchased by Paul Mellon, Aug. 1964

Selected references: Webster 2011, 540, 546

Almost all Zoffany's surviving dozen drawings of Indian scenes were done on his last journey from Lucknow to Calcutta. These private drawings were presumably done to remind him back in England of the intimate scenes of Indian life that he witnessed and possibly to work up later into oil paintings. Many are annotated on the reverse with a date, but not this one. As a result, identification of the specific location is to some extent guesswork. It shows a rocky river bank on which a group of Indians – presumably a family – have pitched a tent close to the river. A Brahmin, waist deep in water is doing puja (prayers), and behind him two women, one bearing a lota, are fetching water from the river. On the left two men and a child are bringing twigs to light a fire. Inside the tent a woman is crouched over a cooking pot.

At Colgong the Ganges is abruptly forced in a northerly direction by a series of small rocky outcrops of the Rajmahal range. The south bank of the river, all the way to Peer Pointy, closely resembles what is seen here in this drawing. Zoffany passed along this stretch of the river on his last journey at the beginning of December 1788. Even at that time of the year this part of the river is difficult to navigate, and his boat would have moored each evening well before dusk. Sailing in poor light risked being wrecked on the numerous submerged rocks in the river or being caught up in a hazardous eddy and swept onto the shore. He probably sketched this scene from the deck of his boat while he waited for his servants or perhaps the Indian family on the shore to cook his dinner. It has been asserted that Zoffany travelled to Calcutta on this occasion accompanied by Claude

Martin,[1] but there appears to be no evidence to support this, and it is much more likely that Zoffany was travelling alone with his servants, giving him ample time to make sketches along the river. This seems to be the last drawing done on that final journey.

CG

1. See Archer 1979, 164.

101

***Hyderbeg on his Mission to Lord Cornwallis,
with a View of the Granary erected by
Warren Hastings, Esq., at Patna***
*c.*1795–6

Oil on canvas, 101.6 × 127 cm (40 × 50 in)
Victoria Memorial Hall, Calcutta

Exhibited at the Yale Center for British Art only

Provenance: Zoffany sale, Messrs Robins, 9 May
1811, lot 96, as '*The March of a Native Indian Army*';
presented to the Victoria Memorial by Sir Rajendra
Nath Mukherji, KCIE AVCO, 1923

Exhibitions: Royal Academy of Arts, 1796, no. 125

Selected references: Manners & Williamson 1920, 95;
Archer 1979, 173–6; Treadwell 2009, 388–9;
Webster 2011, 558–61

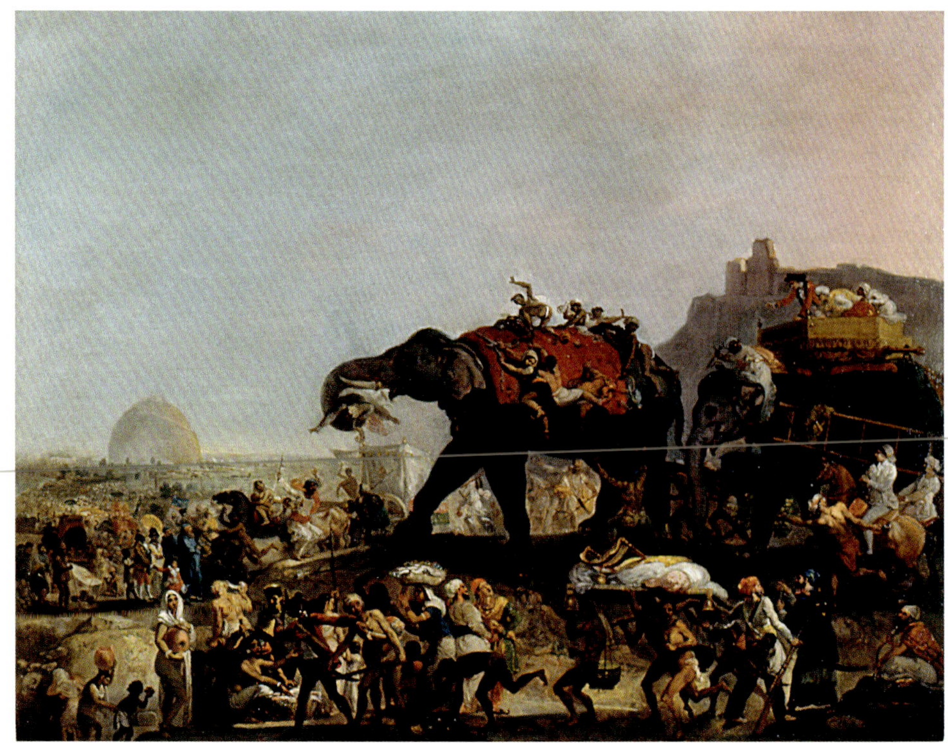

102

Richard Earlom after Johan Zoffany,
Embassy of Hyderbeck to Calcutta
1800

Mezzotint with stipple,
53.9 × 68.8 cm (21¼ × 27⅛ in)
Inscribed below image with title, artists' names and
further text: 'From the Vizier of Oude by the way of
Patna in the year 1788 to meet Lord Cornwallis |
For the names see the index plate' and 'Published
12ᵗʰ July, 1800, by Robert Laurie & James Whittle,
No. 53, Fleet Street, London'
British Museum, Department of Prints and
Drawings, 1872,0608.169: exhibited at the Yale
Center for British Art

Private collection: exhibited at the Royal Academy
of Arts

Selected references: Chaloner Smith 1878–84, vol. 1,
260, no. 49; Wessely 1886, 36, no. 98

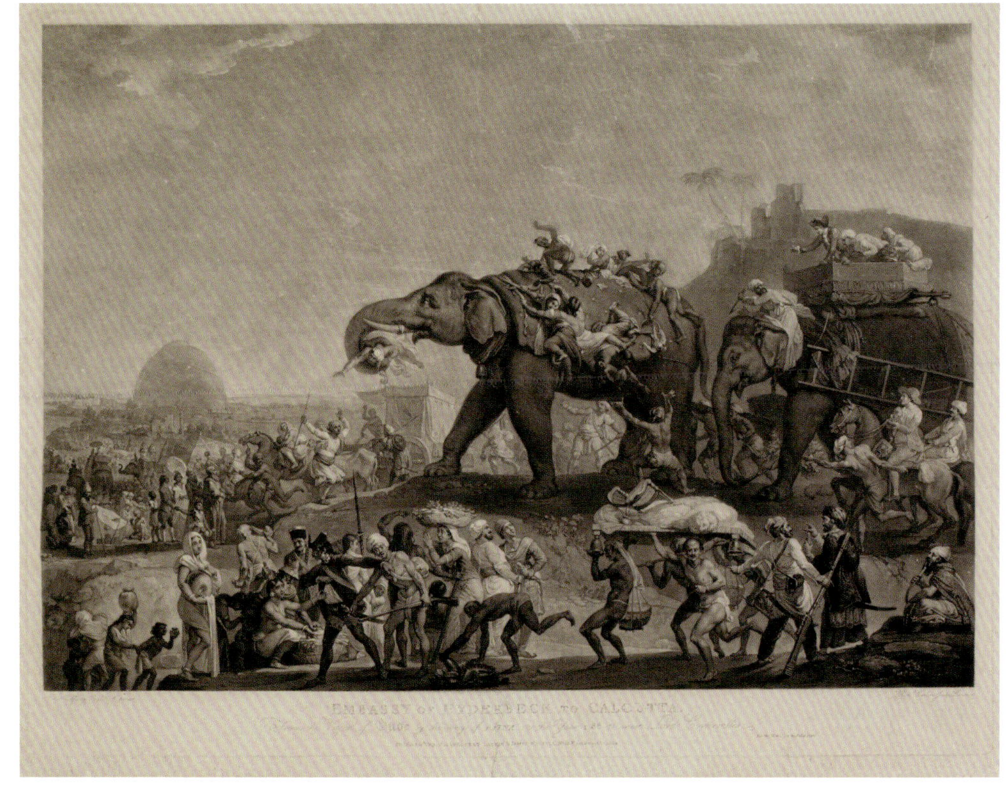

In 1796 Zoffany exhibited *Hyderbeg on his Mission to Lord Cornwallis* at the Royal Academy. The ostensible subject of the painting was the deputation of Asaf-ud-Daula's minister Haider Beg Khan to Calcutta to meet with the newly arrived Governor General, Lord Cornwallis, in 1786. The most significant political outcome of Hastings's sojourn in Lucknow in 1784 had been his drastic reduction of the revenues imposed on the nawab by the Company, but Cornwallis, whose highest priority on taking office was to scale back British control of Awadh, was resolved to reduce its financial burden further.[1] Cornwallis's arrival was an event of profound concern to Europeans with interests in Lucknow, and Claude Martin noted in a letter to Ozias Humphry of 19 October 1786 that he was planning to visit Calcutta the following month, adding: 'Zoffany intend [*sic*] setting off with Colonel Polier in the middle of November, Haider Beg Khan will set off in about 6 or 8 day.'[2] The title of Zoffany's painting implies that the artist caught up with Haider Beg Khan's delegation at Patna, though this event is undocumented.

As an ostensible representation of a historical event, Zoffany's painting is eccentric, however, since the figure of Haider Beg Khan is depicted in the distance on the left and is barely legible. The main focus, as was noted in a puff in the *Morning Post* for 5 March 1796, is the violent disturbance created by a huge elephant, which, evidently out of control, grasps a man in its trunk while other Indians desperately cling to its sides. The key to the mezzotint of the painting, which was engraved by Richard Earlom and published by Laurie and Whittle in 1800 as the *Embassy of Hyderbeck to Calcutta. From the Vizier of Oude by the way of Patna in the Year 1788* [sic] *to meet Lord Cornwallis* (fig. 196), provided a detailed account of this complex composition. First in the list is 'A Male Baggage Elephant, irritated by his Driver, who is taken from his Seat and destroy'd; and by the Violence of the Elephant's Actions are seen the Women and Children falling from his Back, this was the moment when Mr Zoffany took his Design for the Picture'. John Kennaway, the Company's translator in Awadh, who was appointed after the successful mission to Calcutta as Cornwallis's aide-de-campe, sits on a second elephant (identified as a female), gesturing, and Zoffany himself is depicted below, riding a horse.

Though relatively few of Zoffany's drawings and paintings representing Indian everyday life have survived, a large number were included in his studio sale. The enumeration of so many figures representing a wide range of religions, occupations and ethnicities in the *Embassy of Hyderbeck*, and their meticulous identification in the index to the print suggest that Zoffany was attempting to produce an encyclopaedic account of Indian society, on the lines of the proto-ethnographic publications of the costume-and-manners genre that were becoming popular in the late eighteenth century. The figures include women bringing water from

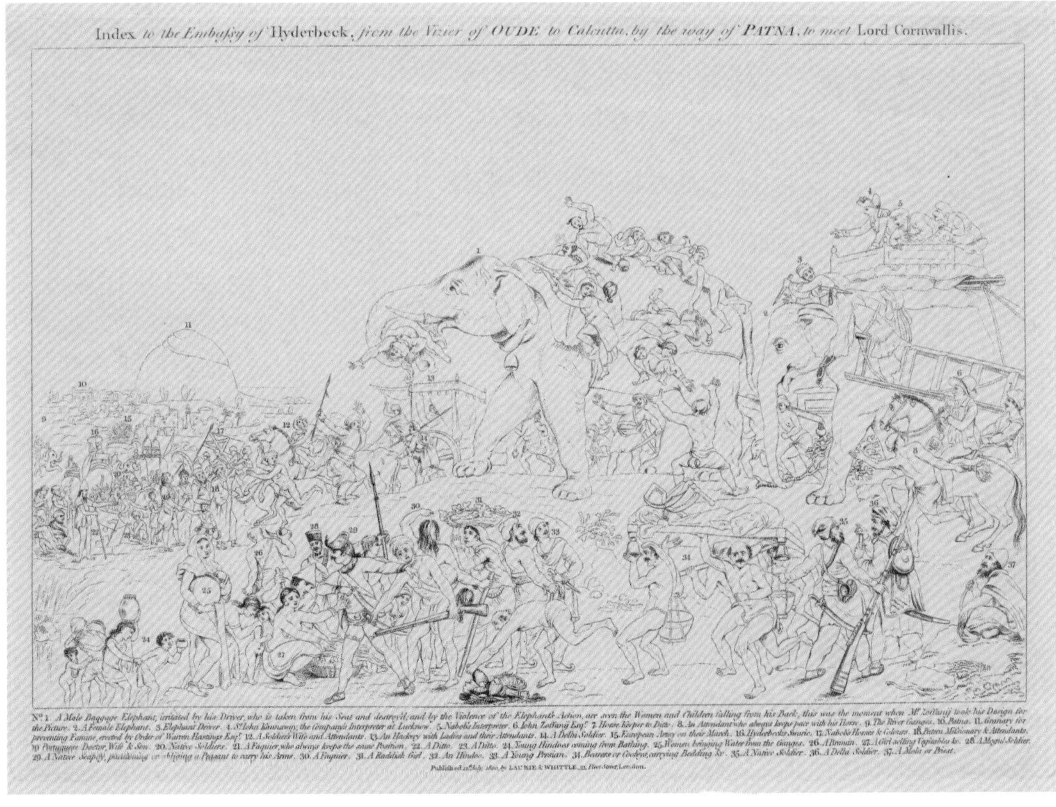

Figure 196
Unknown artist after Johan Zoffany, *Key to The Embassy of Hyderbeck to Calcutta*, 1800, etching, 26.2 × 36.3 cm (10¼ × 14¼ in). British Museum, Department of Prints and Drawings, 1863, 0725.462

the Ganges and selling vegetables, a 'Native Sepoy … obliging a Peasant to carry his arms', a 'Delhi soldier', a 'Mogul soldier', a Brahmin, various Hindus, a 'Young Persian', several 'faquirs', a Portuguese doctor, Catholic missionaries from Patna, and, at the extreme right, a mullah, smoking a hookah. The compiler of the catalogue for the posthumous sale of the artist's effects evidently regarded the picture as ethnographic in intention, describing it as '*The March of a Native Indian Army; completely illustrating the different Casts of the Inhabitants by their Dresses, Employments, &c.* and with which Mr. Zoffany was so completely acquainted by his long Residence in India and by his attentive observation'.[3] The true subject of Zoffany's painting, however, seems to have been the granary that was built at Patna at Warren Hastings's instigation in the aftermath of the disastrous famine in Awadh of 1783–4. The distinctive domed-top granary that is prominently placed in the background of Zoffany's composition was not completed until after Hastings's return to Britain (see p. 152 for an image of the granary and a further discussion).[4] Zoffany may have hoped that Hastings would purchase the painting for Daylesford, the estate that had formerly belonged to his family which he regained in 1788. Hastings refurbished the house at huge expense and moved there in 1791.

The change of title for the engraving, which was published after the conclusion of the protracted impeachment trial, might be interpreted as a sign that Zoffany had thought better of underscoring his association with Hastings. He also may have hoped for a commission from Cornwallis. In 1794 Claude Martin had written to Colonel Alexander Ross in London, asking if he could 'prevail on his Lordship to sit few hour for his portrait to my friend Zoffany',[5] but this initiative seems to have come to nothing.

Haider Beg Khan, deputy to Hasan Reza Khan (cat. 84), was among Asaf-ud-Daula's most able and influential ministers and was highly respected by the British, although, aside from his appearance in *Colonel Mordaunt's Cock Match*, Zoffany is not known to have painted his portrait. He did sit to Ozias Humphry and Robert Smith during their visit to Lucknow in 1786,[6] and a number of miniatures of him by Humphry are known (fig. 197).[7]

GF

1. Barnett 1980, 229–31.
2. Llewellyn-Jones 2003, 97.
3. Robins 1811, lot 96 (9 May); Webster 2011, 645.
4. Hastings's former secretary, George Nesbitt Thompson, wrote in a letter dated 30 December 1786: 'The granary is finished; I have applied for the commission to fill it' (*Bengal Past and Present*, vol. 17, series 33–4, July–Dec. 1981, 97).
5. *Bengal Past and Present*, vol. 17, series 33–4, July–Dec. 1981, 236.
6. Humphry diary, Osborn Collection, Beinecke Rare Book and Manuscript Library, Yale University, f. 26.
7. V&A, Alan Evans Bequest, repr. Katherine Coombs, *The Portrait Miniature in England*, London, 1998, 103; Christie's, King Street, 28 May 2002, lot 143.

Figure 197
Ozias Humphry, *Hyder Beg Khan, the Minister of Nawab of Wadh, Asaf-au-Daula*, 1786, watercolour on ivory, 8.9 × 7.5 cm (3½ × 3 in). Victoria and Albert Museum, London, Alan Evans Bequest, given by the National Gallery

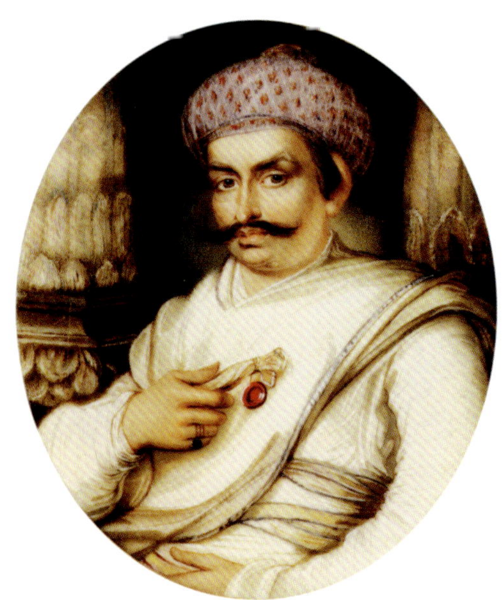

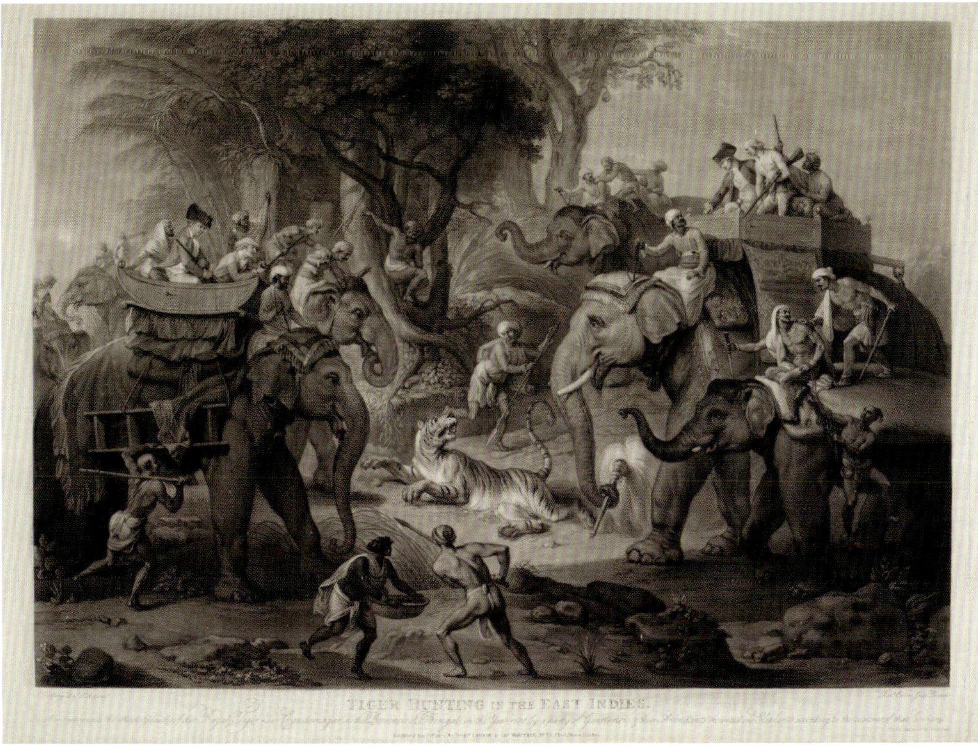

103

Richard Earlom after Johan Zoffany,
Tiger Hunting in the East Indies
1802

Mezzotint with etching and stipple,
53.8 × 68 cm (21⅛ × 26¾ in)
Inscribed below image with title, artists' names
and further text: 'This print represents the attack
& death of the Royal Tiger, near Chandermagur,
in the Province of Bengal, in the Year 1788, by a
party of Gentlemen & their Attendants mounted
on Elephants according to the custom of that
Country | For description see the index plate' and
'Published Decr. 2nd. 1802. by Robt. Laurie & Jas.
Whittle, No. 53, Fleet Street, London'
British Museum, Department of Prints and
Drawings, 1863,0725.459: exhibited at the Yale
Center for British Art

Private collection: exhibited at the Royal Academy
of Arts

Selected references: Manners & Williamson 1920,
94–6; Chaloner Smith 1878–84, vol. 1, 261, no. 50;
Wessely 1886, no.97; Archer 1979, 172–3;
Treadwell 2009, 386–8; Webster 2011, 472–4,
556–8

Hunting was a popular pastime in northern India
in the eighteenth century, both for Indians and
Europeans. Asaf-ud-Daula's twice yearly hunts,
which typically lasted for several weeks, were
legendary,[1] and when the British came to India,
they adapted their existing practices, exchanging
the pursuit of the fox for that of the tiger, often
on the prextext that they were protecting native
peasants from the ravages of the wild predators.[2]
Zoffany participated in at least one tiger hunt,
which was organized by Henry Ramus, the son of
George III's principal page, Nicholas Ramus, and
took place at Chinsura, near Calcutta, in April 1784.
Henry Ramus's sister Benedetta was married to
Sir John Day, the Advocate-General to the Supreme
Court in Calcutta. Ramus had moved to India when
his career at court had stalled, and held a series of
Company sinecures in Calcutta, including that of
Contractor for feeding Elephants and Camels,
which presumably allowed him abundant leisure
time. Sir John Day documented the epic tiger hunt
in detail in a letter to the judge Sir William Jones
and evidently commissioned Zoffany immediately
thereafter to commemorate the event, since the
Company official Joseph Fowke wrote to his
daughter Margaret: 'Sir John will have the pleasure
of seeing all his family immortalised by the
ingenious pencil of Zoffani who was present at
the chace [*sic*], devouring every object as fast as
the imagination could trace them.'[3]

The painting evidently was delayed by Zoffany's
visit to Lucknow, but on 2 May 1785 Benedetta
Day noted in a letter to Margaret Fowke:

Zoffany is making a delightful picture of it [the
tiger hunt], in which he has introduced Portraits
of the whole Party. I believe that there will be an
engraving of it by the first Hand at Home, I insist
on your purchasing the Print, you will then, upon
easy Terms, have a likeness of a far distant friend.[4]

The Days left India the following year, presumably
taking the finished painting, since it was mentioned
in Sir John Day's obituary in the *Gentleman's
Magazine*; however, it is now untraced.

A sketch described as 'Return from the Tyger
Chace' was listed in Zoffany's posthumous sale
catalogue,[5] and this may have been his original
sketch for the Days' picture. Zoffany evidently
decided to revisit the subject (see figs. 130, 198),
presumably around the time that he produced
A Battlepiece against Hider Ally and *Hyderbeg on
his Mission to Lord Cornwallis* (cat. 101), which he
exhibited at the Royal Academy in 1790 and 1796
respectively.[6] Zoffany did not exhibit the painting,
however, and it was unsold at his death, but cat. 103,
a mezzotint engraving of it by Richard Earlom, was
published by Robert Laurie and James Whittle in
1802. The tiger hunt and Haider Beg paintings are
identical in size, as are the engravings of the two
subjects, and Zoffany may have conceived them as
pendants.

Zoffany depicted the critical moment when
the defiant tiger was surrounded by the British on
their elephants flanked by Indians with spears on
the ground, and about to be slain. The subject of
the death of the royal tiger would have had a very
specific resonance for the public at the time the

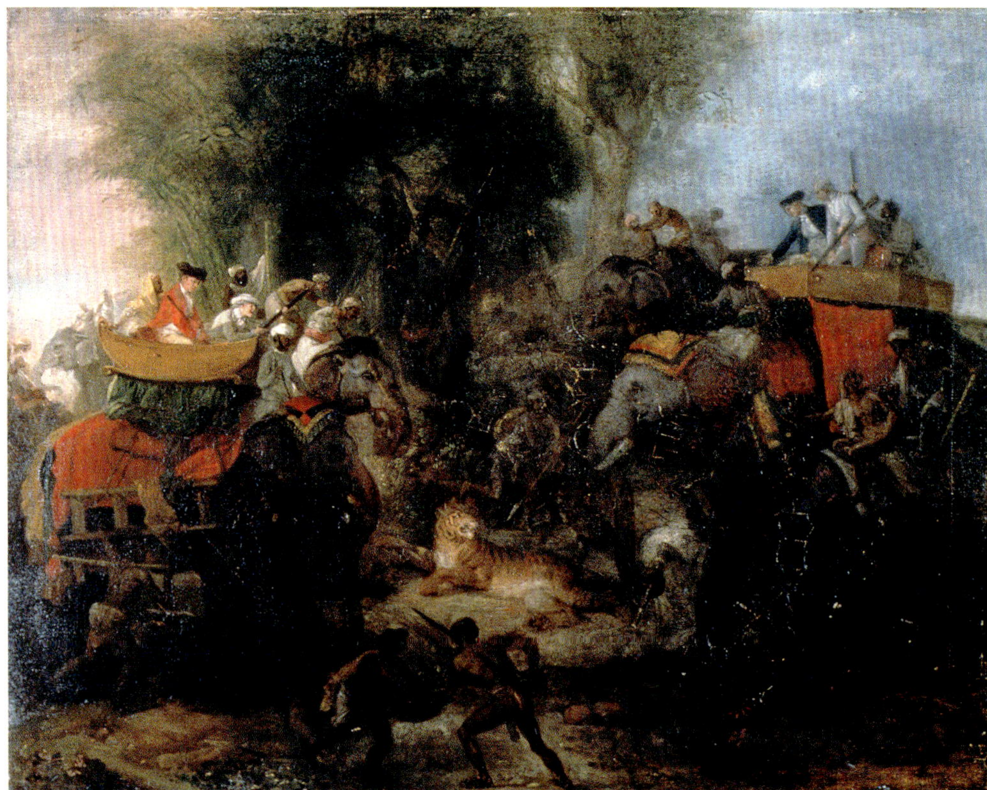

Figure 198
The Death of the Royal Tiger, c.1790,
oil on canvas, 102 × 127 cm (40⅛ × 50 in).
Victoria Memorial Hall, Calcutta

Figure 199
Unknown artist after Johan Zoffany, *Index to Tiger Hunting
in the East Indies*, 1802, etching, 26.4 × 35.8 cm (10⅜ × 14⅛ in).
British Museum, Department of Prints and Drawings, 1863, 0725.460

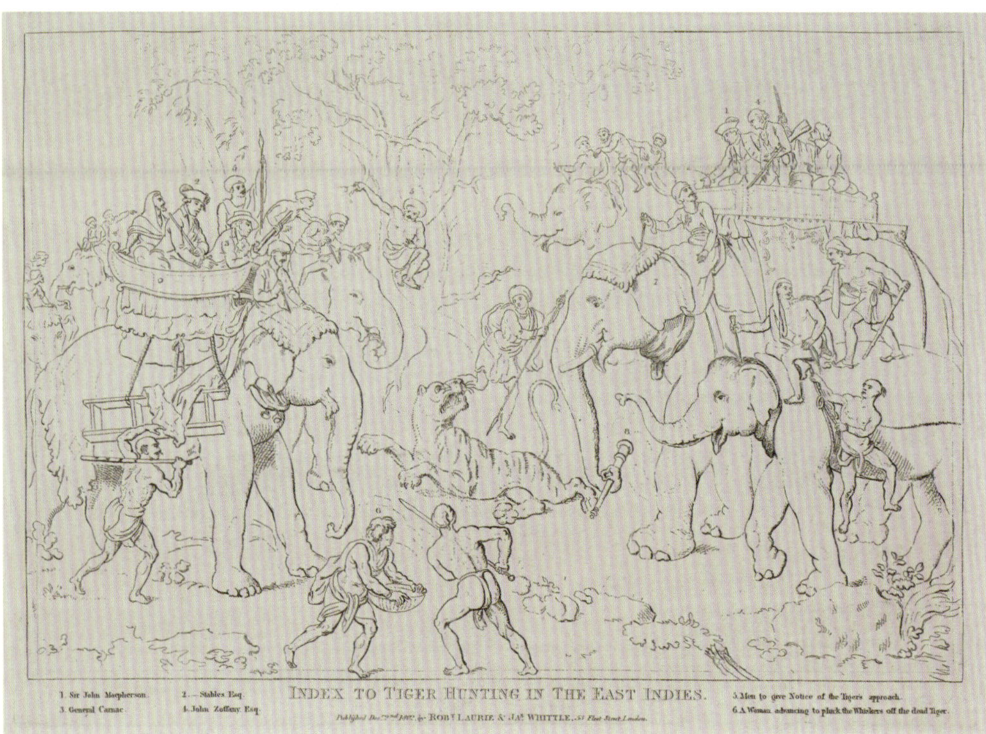

engraving was published since the long-term adversary of the British in India, Tipu Sultan, whose emblem was a tiger, had been defeated and killed at the Battle of Seringapatam in 1799. Tipu had acquired a cult status in Britain and France, and his death stimulated a proliferation of paintings and engravings, which typically focused on the dramatic moment of finding the sultan's body.[7] A painting of 'Finding the Body of Tippoo Sultaun' was included in Zoffany's posthumous sale, along with two related sketches, indicating that Zoffany, too, had decided to capitalize on Tipu mania, but the picture was never exhibited.[8]

GF

1. Barnett 1980, 217.
2. Collingham 2001, 30.
3. Quoted in Webster 2011, 473. This summary of the circumstances of the production of Zoffany's painting is indebted to Webster's account.
4. Webster 2011, 473.
5. Robins 1811, part of lot 59 (9 May); Webster 2011, 644.
6. Royal Academy of Arts, 1790, no. 157, untraced.
7. See Bayly 1990, 152–60, nos. 153–69, and Buddle 1999.
8. Robins 1811, lots 65, 66 and 78 (9 May); Webster 2011, 644.

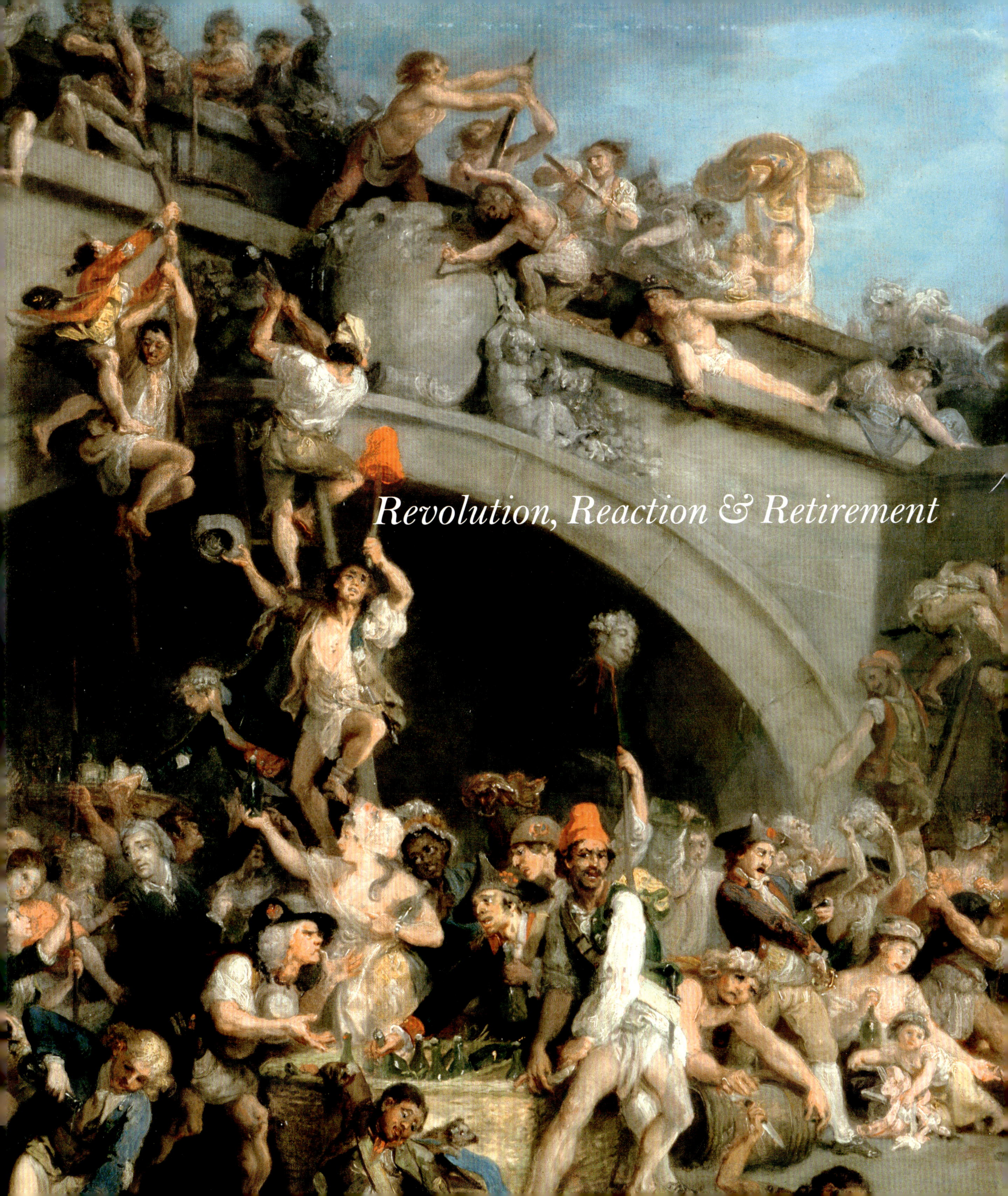
Revolution, Reaction & Retirement

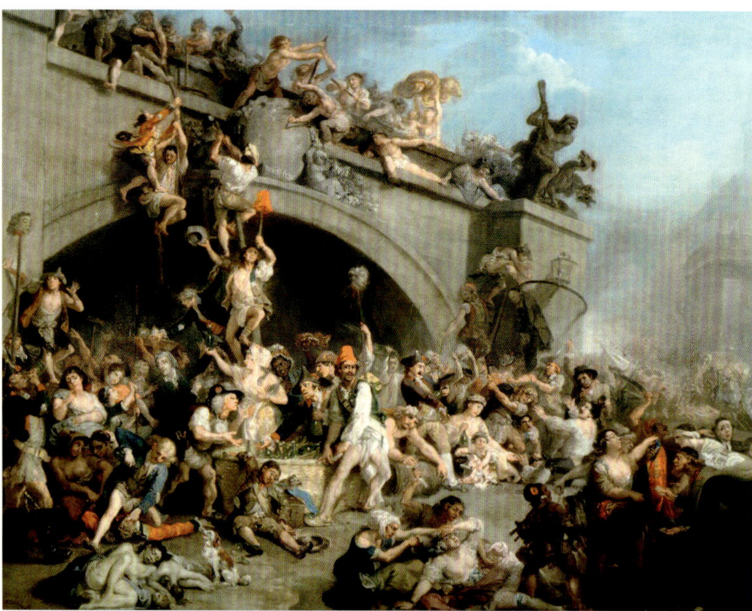

104

Plundering the King's Cellar at Paris
1794

Oil on canvas, 103 × 126.5 cm (40½ × 49¾ in)
Wadsworth Atheneum Museum of Art, Hartford,
CT. The Ella Gallup Sumner and Mary Catlin
Sumner Collection Fund

Provenance: Zoffany sale, Messrs Robins, 9 May
1811, lot 94, as 'THE 10TH OF AUGUST – at the
time of the Parisian Populace breaking open the
King's Wine Cellars; strongly characteristic of the
furor of the French Revolution, and the Outrages
then committed. This picture is engraved'; bt
Henry Phipps, first Earl of Mulgrave; … sold C.
Wolley, Christie's, 30 Nov., 1867, lot 88, bt Graves,
£20 9s 6d; … Earl of Rosebery by 1951; sold,
Sotheby's, London, Mentmore sale, 25 May 1977,
lot 2423; Noortman & Brod; Colnaghi, from whom
purchased 1984

Selected exhibitions: Royal Academy of Arts, 1795,
no. 18; Royal Academy 1951–2, no. 63; National
Portrait Gallery 1977, no. 108; Paris 1989, vol. 2,
no. 785

Selected references: Pasquin n.d., 35–6n; Manners
& Williamson 1920, 120–21; David Bindman,
'Sans-Culottes and the swinish multitude: the
British image of the revolutionary crowd', in
Christian Beutler, Peter-Klaus Schuster and Martin
Warnke, eds., _Kunst um 1800 und die Folgen: Werner
Hofmann zu Ehren_, Munich, 1988, 87–94, esp. 92–4;
Pressly 1999, _passim_; Treadwell 2009, 403–8, 415;
Webster 2011, 565–71, 576

Zoffany returned to London at a momentous time,
just weeks after the storming of the Bastille in
Paris. Given his pro-monarchical and increasingly
reactionary stance, Zoffany would have been
appalled by the events in France and presumably
was dismayed by the initial positive response
from British liberals. As the revolution gained
momentum and violence took hold, however,
euphoria and idealism in Britain gave way to
disillusion and fear, provoking intense debates
regarding the nature and desirability of democracy.

A landmark event in the trajectory of the
revolution occurred on 10 August 1792 and
effectively signalled the end of the rule of monarchy
in France. Tensions between the insurgents and
what they perceived as an intransigent Assembly
had escalated, and the revolutionaries marched on
the palace of the Tuileries, where the king and royal
family were confined. The palace was fortified by
around four thousand members of the Swiss Guard,
National Guard, police and nobility, who shot
down nearly four hundred insurgents. The question
of which side fired the first shot has never been
resolved, but when the king's troops laid down their
arms at Louis XVI's command, the revolutionaries
massacred the soldiers and looted the Tuileries.
The event provoked intense revulsion and outrage
in Britain, where the press reported accounts
of extraordinary brutality, singling out the
dismembering of the bodies of the Swiss Guard
in the gardens of the Tuileries in which women
allegedly played a dominant role. A catalogue of
atrocities followed: at least 1400 people were
killed in the 'September massacres', Louis XVI
was guillotined on 23 January 1794, precipitating
Britain's declaration of war on France on
1 February, and on 16 October of the same year
Marie-Antoinette was executed.

These events clearly resonated powerfully with
Zoffany, who exhibited a single painting entitled
Plundering the King's Cellar at Paris, August 10, 1793
[sic] at the Royal Academy in 1795. A companion
painting on the theme of the desecration of the
bodies of the Swiss guardsmen in the Tuileries was
included in his studio sale, but remained unfinished
and was never exhibited (cat. 106). Joseph Farington
noted in his diary for 1 August 1794 that Zoffany
was working on the latter painting, describing it as
'one of his Parisian subjects', and it seems likely that
the artist had already finished _Plundering the King's
Cellar_, since he published a mezzotint engraving
of it on 1 January 1795 (cat. 105).[1]

The historical background and critical reception
of _Plundering the King's Cellar_ and _Celebrating over
the Bodies of the Swiss Soldiers_ and Zoffany's
presumed motivations for producing the works
have been explored in meticulous detail by
William Pressly in his exemplary book-length
study, _The French Revolution as Blasphemy: John
Zoffany's Paintings of the Massacre at Paris, August
10. 1792_. As Pressly has noted, remarkably few
works overtly commemorating the events of the
French Revolution were exhibited or engraved
in Britain, and with the exception of a handful
of satirical prints, they tended to focus on the
sufferings of the royal family.[2] Zoffany's painting,
which depicted the revolutionary mob raiding the
palace's wine-cellars, intoxicated by alcohol and
bloodlust, was extremely unusual, in both choice
of subject and treatment. The chaotic composition
is a social and ethnographic _mélange_ comprising
aristocratic and plebeian revolutionaries, male and
female and a number half-naked; the dead bodies of
soldiers; clerics; blacks; and a solitary Jewish figure
bargaining for the jacket of one of the stripped
Swiss soldiers. At the centre of the composition is
a figure wearing a red cap of liberty, and staring
defiantly at the viewer, which William Pressly has
suggested may have been an allusion to Bernini's
sculpture of David.[3] The vividness of the scene
suggests reportage, but Zoffany's depiction of the
Tuileries bears no resemblance to the palace's
architecture .

Zoffany's painting made a strong impression on
its viewers, but they clearly found it repellent, and
it remained unpurchased at his death. The reviewer
of the _Morning Chronicle_ noted that 'the whole
scene, though well painted, is too horrid to be
contemplated'.[4] The following year John Williams,
writing under his pseudonym of Anthony Pasquin,
produced a searing critique of the painting in a
gratuitous footnote to his publication, _An Authentic
History of the Professors of Painting, Sculpture, &
Architecture, who have Practised in Ireland_, published
the year after it was exhibited:

> Of all the pieces I have seen from the pencil of
> Mr. Zofanii, this is the most unlike himself;
> he evidently labours to tread in the footsteps of
> Mr. Hogarth, but is truly unsuccessful. This savage
> assemblage of monsters are denied the possession
> of human lineaments by this indignant German.

Williams was notorious for his radicalism and
intemperate outbursts, but his remark nonetheless
suggests something of the raw power that Zoffany's
provocative image must have had for contemporary
viewers.[5]

The *Morning Chronicle* reviewer also noted affinities with Hogarth. As Pressly has argued, *Plundering the King's Cellar* seems to contain allusions to Hogarth's engravings, notably the figure of the half-naked aristocratic woman in the foreground about to be stabbed by a *sans-culotte*, which seems to have been derived from the reclining figure of the insane protagonist in the plate of Bedlam from the *Rake's Progress*. Zoffany owned a significant number of Hogarth's engravings, and his works frequently betray the influence of the earlier artist's satirical vision. Pressly reads Zoffany's allusions as a critique of Hogarth's sympathy towards the socially marginalized, but Hogarth's politics seem to have been more complex and ambivalent than his account suggests, as indeed was his avowed Francophobia.[6]

Pressly argues that Zoffany's primary motivation for producing his French Revolution paintings was to warn the British of the dangers of radicalism, and suggests that Edmund Burke was a key influence. Burke had responded swiftly and dramatically to the events of 1789, publishing his overwrought polemic *Reflections on the Revolution in France* in 1790, which was received with some bemusement by his contemporaries given his earlier fervent support for Irish independence, American liberty and religious toleration. Given Burke's leading role in the impeachment proceedings against Warren Hastings, Zoffany's former patron, this may seem surprising, but Zoffany's paintings arguably do constitute visual analogues for Burke's neurotic and vivid prose. The *Morning Herald* suggested that Zoffany might have been encouraged by a 'royal hint',[7] but though George III presumably would have approved of the political message underlying the picture, it seems unlikely that he would have been gratified by its final appearance.

Zoffany's political convictions do not completely explain the apparently racist, misogynistic and anti-Semitic aspects of the painting or the sense of disgust and relish for violence that threaten to overwhelm his composition, and Philippe Bordes has suggested that a psychoanalytical reading of the painting would be productive.[8] Bordes perceptively intuited 'a sense of tragedy' in Zoffany's revolutionary paintings, 'not the tragedy of the revolutionary violence he fantasises, but that of his artistic investment strained to excess, of a solitary enterprise which utterly baffled his contemporaries'.[9]

GF

1. Farington 1978–84, vol. 1, 223.
2. Pressly 1999, 43–7.
3. Pressly 1999, 111, 114–15.
4. *Morning Chronicle*, 6 May 1795, 3.
5. Pasquin n.d., 36.
6. See R. Simon 2007, *passim.*
7. Manners & Williamson 1920, 120.
8. Bordes 1999.
9. Bordes 1999, 628.

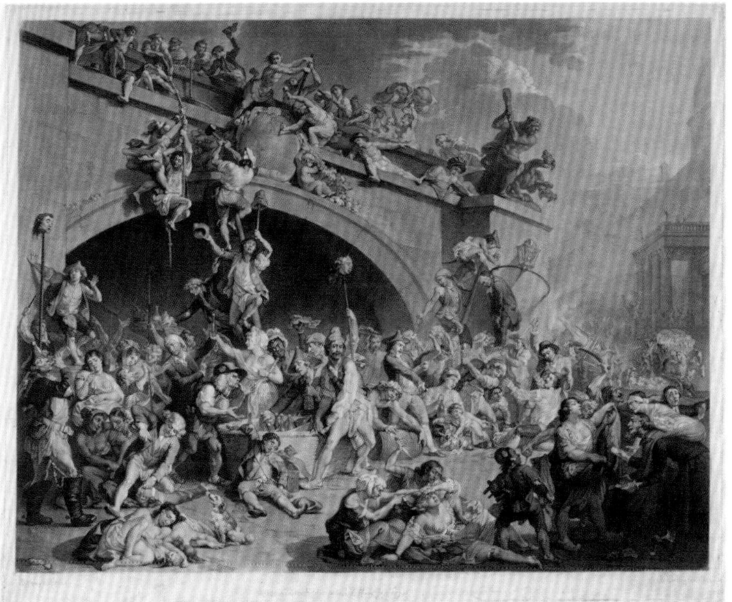

105

Richard Earlom after Johan Zoffany, *Invasion of the Cellars of the Louvre, 10 August 1792*
1795

Mezzotint with stipple, 57 × 68.3 cm (22½ × 26⅞ in)
Inscribed below image, scratched letters: 'J. Zoffany Esqr pinxt' (left), 'r Earlom Scupst' (right) and 'Publish'd as the Act directs J. Zoffany Jan 1, 1795' (centre)
British Museum, Department of Prints and Drawings, 1856,1011.106

Exhibited at the Yale Center for British Art only

Selected references: Wessely 1886, 39–40, no. 96; Bindman 1989, 105, no. 46; Pressly 1999, 156–7

On 1 January 1795 Zoffany published a mezzotint engraving by Richard Earlom after his painting of *Plundering the King's Cellar at Paris*, which he was to exhibit at the Royal Academy four months later (cat. 104). The painting clearly had great significance for the artist, since self-publishing such a high-quality engraving would necessitate considerable financial outlay and effort. Zoffany presumably hoped that the print would generate advance interest for his painting and, as William Pressly has suggested, he may also have been strongly motivated by a desire to disseminate his counter-revolutionary message to a wider audience. Lest any viewer should have been in doubt about the horrific nature of the event depicted, Zoffany also had two verses inscribed under the image, the source of which has not been identified:

> Say, where is sacred FREEDOM gone!
> From GALLIA's realm forever flown!
> Now DISCORD waves the flaming brand!
> Hark! RIOT pours the savage yell,
> And MURDER rushing from his hell,
> Plunges in streams of blood, his hand.

> Ah! Vainly from the fatal knife;
> The MOTHER begs her Infant's life.
> To earth they fall by many a wound.
> Lo, MERCY forc'd the scene to fly!
> The tear is dash'd from PITY's eye,
> And HORROR, HORROR, howls around.

It is uncertain why Zoffany opted to publish the engraving himself, a practice that he had abandoned as soon as he was sufficiently well established in London. The retirement in 1792 of his friend Robert Sayer, who had regularly published prints after his paintings since the 1770s, may have been significant. Although Zoffany collaborated with Sayer's successors, Robert Laurie and John Whittle, only a handful of engravings resulted, implying a diminished commitment on their part, and they may have felt that Zoffany's revolutionary subject was unmarketable. No prospectus is known to have existed, and Zoffany seems not to have solicited subscriptions. The original price for the engraving is also unknown, but given Earlom's high-profile reputation his fee was likely to have been substantial, and presumably Zoffany's price would have been commensurately high. In 1800 Laurie and Whittle sold proofs of Earlom's mezzotint of the *Embassy of Hyderbeck to Calcutta* (cat. 102), which was smaller than *The Tenth of August*, for four guineas, and ordinary prints for two guineas.[1] Few impressions of the engraving are held in public collections in Europe and the United States, and the scarcity of the print today relative to other engravings after Zoffany suggests that only a limited number may have been sold, and since the posthumous sale did not include any prints after his work, it is impossible to ascertain whether Zoffany still had stocks of unsold impressions at his death.

GF

1. *The Monthly Epitome and Catalogue of New Publications*, vol. 4 (Sept. 1800): 359.

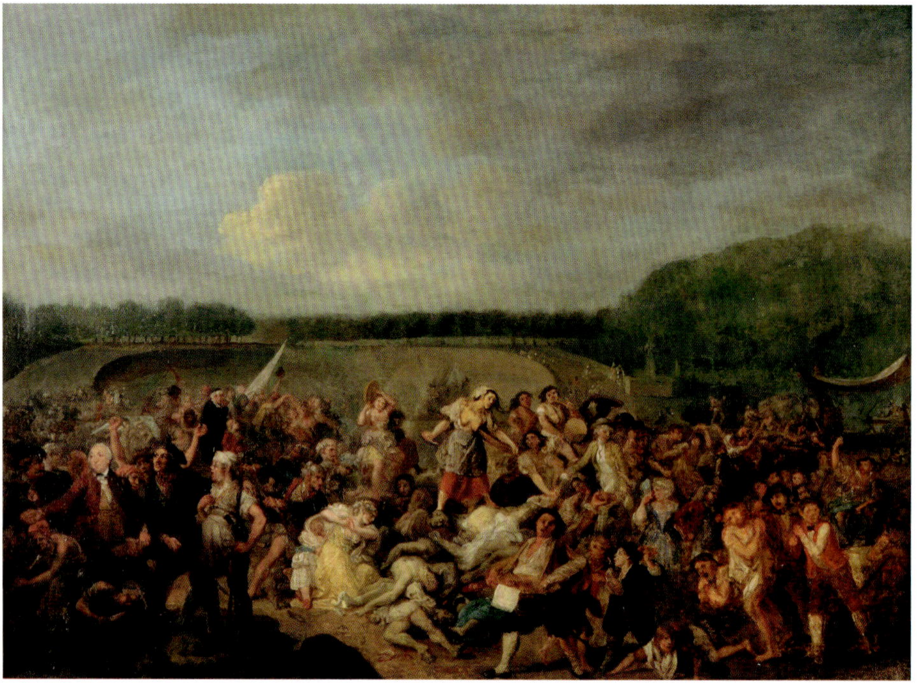

106

A Scene in the Champ de Mars, Celebrating over the Bodies of the Swiss Soldiers on the 12th August 1792, with a Portrait of the Duke of Orleans

*c.*1794

Oil on canvas, 92 × 125 cm (36¼ × 49¼ in)
Museen der Stadt, Regensburg

Provenance: Zoffany sale, Messrs Robins, 9 May 1811, lot 85 as 'A Scene in the Champ de Mars on the 12th of August, with a Portrait of the Duke of Orleans', 5 guineas; sold by Larkin, Edward Foster, London, 16 Dec. 1824, lot 47, as 'A sketch, The Day after the Memorable 10th of August, at Paris, with Portraits of the Duke of Orleans, and other remarkable Characters', bt Dyson, £5 15s; possibly sold Christie's, 30 Nov. 1867, lot 88; Sotheby's, London, the Property of a Gentleman, 18 March, 1981, lot 47, as 'A Scene in the Champ de Mars on August 12th, with the Duke of Orleans'; … purchased 1981

Selected exhibitions: Paris 1989, vol. 2, no. 607, as 'Le Massacre du Champs-Mars le 17 juillet 1791'

Selected references: Farington 1978–84, vol. 1, 223; Bindman 1989, 60; Phillipe Bordes, review of *La Révolution française et l'Europe, 1789–1799,* Galeries Nationales du Grand Palais, Paris, *Burlington Magazine,* vol. 131, no. 1035 (Jun. 1989), 441–3; Pressly 1999, *passim*; Treadwell 2009, 404–5; Webster 2011, 571–6

In his diary for 1 August 1794 Joseph Farington recorded: 'Called on Zoffany & I made a drawing of Kew Bridge from his window. – He was painting on one of his Parisian subjects. – the woemen [*sic*] & Sans Culottes, dancing &c over the dead bodies of the Swiss Soldiers.'[1] This painting, which Zoffany never exhibited, seems to have been conceived as a companion for *Plundering the King's Cellar at Paris* (cat. 104), which he showed controversially at the Royal Academy in 1795. The painting remained in Zoffany's studio and was sold as lot 85 in his posthumous sale, described in the catalogue as 'A Scene in the Champ de Mars on the 12th August, with a Portrait of the Duke of Orleans'. The painting retained this title until 1989, when David Bindman identified the subject as the desecration of the bodies of the Swiss Guards in the gardens of the Tuileries, which followed the execution of Louis XVI's troops by revolutionary insurgents on 10 August 1792.[2]

Eye-witness accounts of the chaotic aftermath of the massacre were often contradictory, and historians today remain uncertain exactly what had taken place, but reports in the British press capitalized on the horrific nature of the scenes in and around the Tuileries, stressing the dominant role played by women. On 21 August the *World* proclaimed:

> FATE itself seems to urge on the extirpation of the FRENCH! The WOMEN of PARIS have left behind them all the parallels that are delivered to us from history or memory. Such FIENDS, in *human shape,* the most savage nations have not exhibited. A SEX, whose nature should shrink from the narration of barbarous act – *that* Sex; stripping the dead soldier, pulling about his lifeless carcass, tearing open his wounds, and thrusting their hands into his mouth to open it, to make him drink – *the downfall of his King!*[3]

The coarseness and brutality of French women was already a well-established topos in the counter-revolutionary discourse. Edmund Burke's provocative account of the French royal family's forced return from Versailles to Paris, accompanied by the notorious *poissardes,* or fishwives, 'amidst the horrid yells, and shrilling screams, and frantic dances, and infamous contumelies, and all the unutterable abominations of the furies of hell, in the abused shape of the vilest of women', might well have been a vivid source of inspiration for an artist with Zoffany's imaginative resources. Zoffany, in any case, seems to have responded enthusiastically to this misogynistic strain of reportage, since the protagonists in his painting, including the central figure, standing triumphantly on the pile of bodies, are predominantly female. Zoffany also included the figure of the Duc d'Orléans, who had played a key role in the events of 10 August, appropriated from Joshua Reynolds's portrait, which he would have known from John Raphael Smith's engraving of 1786.[4]

Zoffany evidently abandoned the painting before it was finished, possibly in response to the unfavourable critical reception of *Plundering the King's Cellar,* which may have impressed on him that the graphic rendering of a highly freighted topic was unmarketable. He even may have intended to execute a trio of paintings on the theme of the French Revolution. An unfinished sketch, described as the 'Triumph of Reason' and now untraced, was included in his posthumous sale.[5] This composition was presumably related to the re-branding of Notre-Dame Cathedral as the 'Temple of Reason', as part of the revolutionary Festival of Liberty and Reason in November 1793, and may have been intended as a satirical reflection on the irrationality of the revolutionaries' project.

GF

1. Farington 1978–84, vol. 1, 223.
2. Bindman 1989, 60.
3. *World,* 21 Aug. 1792, 2, quoted in Pressly 1999, 81.
4. D'Oench 1999, 96 (repr.), 224, no. 273.
5. Robins 1811, lot 59 (9 May).

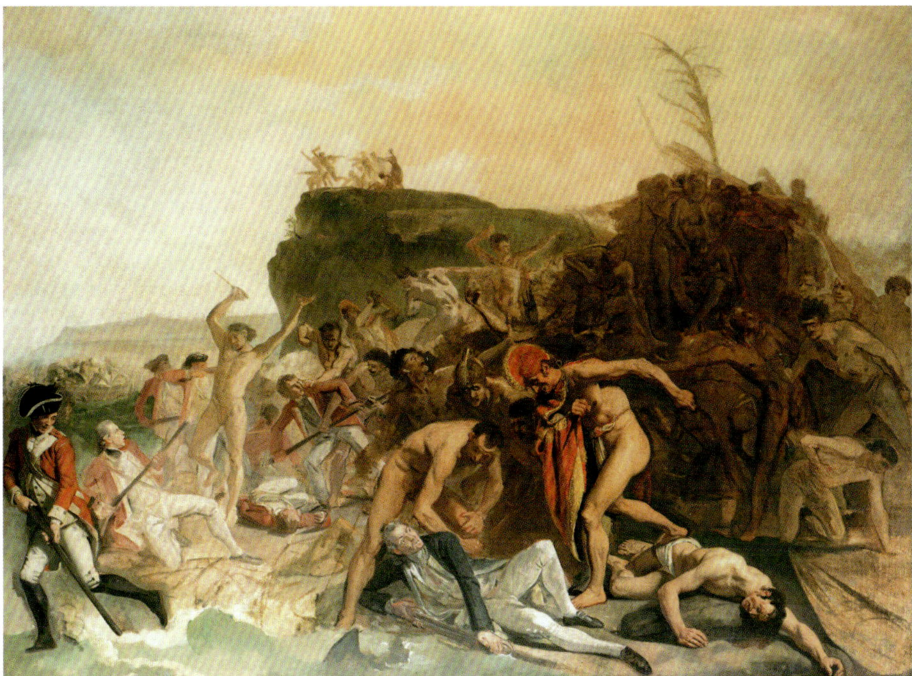

107

The Death of Captain Cook
_c._1798

Oil on canvas, 137.2 × 182.9 cm (54 × 72 in)
National Maritime Museum, Greenwich, London,
Greenwich Hospital Collection

Exhibited at the Yale Center for British Art only

Provenance: Probably Lieutenant-General Kyd, sale,
Christie's, 13 Sept. 1827, lot 94, bt Michael Peacock,
£10 10s; … given to Greenwich Hospital, 1835,
by J.K. Bennett, executor of James Cook's widow
Elizabeth Cook; transferred to National Maritime
Museum, 1936

Selected exhibitions: Royal Academy and V&A 1972,
no. 286; National Portrait Gallery 1977, no. 111

Selected references: Manners & Williamson 1920,
202–3; Mitchell 1944, 56–63; Smith 1985, 119–123;
Treadwell 2009, 406–7; Webster 2011, 587–9

On his return from India Zoffany renewed his
friendships with Joseph Banks and his circle of
natural historians. Zoffany had been Banks's
original choice as artist for Cook's second
circumnavigation of the world, but he withdrew
after a disagreement between Banks and the
Admiralty, and his friend William Hodges went as
his replacement on the voyage, which lasted from
1772 to 1775. As he was moving into retirement,
Zoffany must have speculated on how his career
would have evolved had he participated in the
expedition. Although Cook's violent death at
Kealakekua Bay in Hawaii had taken place on
14 February 1779, the event was still strong in the
public imagination when Zoffany returned from
India. It had been the subject of several paintings
and engravings, notably the painting made by John
Webber, the draughtsman on Cook's third fatal
expedition, which was widely circulated via the
engraving by Francesco Bartolozzi and William
Byrne.[1] Given his interest in the theatre, Zoffany
also may have been stimulated to embark on the
painting by the production of the _Death of Captain
Cook: A Grand Serious-Pantomimic-Ballet in Three
Parts_ that opened in London in 1789 and was in the
repertoire at the Covent Garden Theatre Royal
for more than a decade.[2]

As his French Revolution paintings demonstrate
(cats. 104–106), Zoffany, like Hodges, was eager to
take advantage of the vogue for contemporary
history painting that had been ignited by Benjamin
West's exhibition of his _Death of General Wolfe_ in
1771 at the Royal Academy. West had used the
traditional conventions of history and religious
painting, yet the topical subject matter and
depiction of the figures in contemporary dress
endowed his celebration of military heroism with
a highly modern sensibility, and Reynolds had
famously declared the picture 'a revolution in the
Art'. Zoffany may also have hoped to attract royal
patronage, since George III, having overcome his
initial reservations, had commissioned the first
of several replicas West made of the subject.

As Bernard Smith has noted, Zoffany, who had
maintained his friendship with Banks and his circle,
would presumably have been familiar with the
various textual accounts of Cook's death, and his
painting corresponds closely to the official account
by Captain William King in _A Voyage to the Pacific
Ocean … for Making Discoveries in the Northern
Hemisphere_, which was published by the Admiralty
in 1784.[3] Zoffany's recasting of the event in the
idiom of a grand manner historical picture was
innovative. Cook's prostrate figure is modelled on

the classical sculpture of the Dying Gaul, and that
of his killer, the chief Noo'an, on the Discobolus,
which had been discovered at Hadrian's Villa
in 1791, and acquired by Charles Townley the
following year. In 1798 Zoffany added the
Discobolus to his painting of Townley's Park
Street Library, which he subsequently gave to
Townley, and it seems likely that he also would
have been working on the Cook painting around
that time. The Hawaiian warriors wear helmets,
which contrived to suggest both classical and
authentic attire; the headgear of the south sea
islanders had been meticulously documented by
John Webber, and it is likely that Zoffany would
have seen the 'curiosities' that Cook had donated
to the British Museum.[4] The casting of Cook's
murderer in heroic guise may seem problematic,
but it does serve to elevate the somewhat
ignominious manner of Cook's death, 'with his
face into the water', as King noted. Zoffany may
have conceived of the picture as a companion to
his French Revolutionary subjects, contrasting
the nobility of the savage with the barbarity of
the allegedly civilized insurgents.

The early provenance of the painting, which
was not included Zoffany's posthumous sale, is
obscure. It was given to Greenwich Hospital by
the executor of Captain Cook's widow in 1835 but
may not have been acquired by her in Zoffany's
lifetime, since it may have been the work described
as 'The Death of Capt. Cook; a sketch', sold by
Lieutenant-General Kyd at Christie's in 1827.[5]
As Charles Mitchell noted, after the picture was
transferred to the National Maritime Museum,
conservation treatment revealed that the work
had been overpainted by another hand and was
unfinished.[6]

GF

1. Webber's painting is now in the collection of
   the State Library of New South Wales. For an
   iconography of images relating to Cook's death,
   see M.K. Beddie (ed.), _Bibliography of Captain
   James Cook R.N., F.R.S., Circumnavigator_, Sydney,
   1970, 380ff.
2. See Hogan 1968, Part 5, 2222, for details of
   performance on 21 October 1799.
3. Smith 1985, 120.
4. A 'Kamschatska Dress made of Fishes Bladders',
   which presumably was brought back from Cook's
   voyage, was included in the 1811 sale, lot 37. Zoffany
   was to have received 'a third share of the curiosities'
   from the third voyage (Manners & Williamson
   1920, 56).
5. Lot 94, purchased by Michael Peacock for £10 10s.
6. Mitchell 1944, 56.

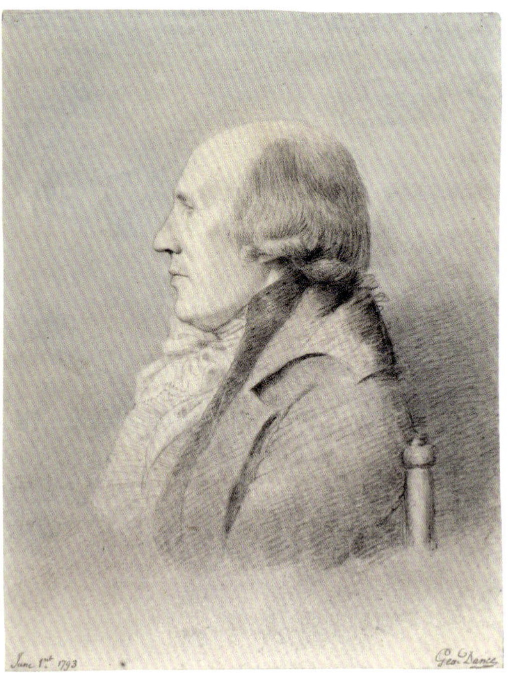

108
George Dance,
Portrait of Johan Zoffany, 1 June 1793

Pencil, black and pink chalks and blue wash on
cream wove paper, 25.2 × 18.8 cm (9⅞ × 7⅜ in)
Royal Academy of Arts, London; purchased from
George Dance, R.A., 1813

Provenance: Purchased from George Dance, R.A.,
1813

Selected exhibitions: Royal Academy 1907, no. 108

*Selected references: A Collection of Portraits sketched
from the Life since the Year 1793 by George Dance
Esqr. R.A. and engraved in imitation of the Original
Drawings by William Daniell, A.R.A.,* 2 vols., 1814;
Hugh Stokes, 'George Dance's Heads', *The Print
Collector's Quarterly,* vol. 16, no. 1, Jan. 1929, 8–32;
Ingamells 2004, 500; Webster 2011, 553–4

Engraving: By William Daniell, 1814

As the inscription on this drawing indicates,
Zoffany sat for his portrait to fellow Academician
George Dance, on 1 June 1793. Earlier that year
Dance, who was by profession an architect, had
begun to make profile portraits of members
of the Royal Academy; the profile portrait being
associated particularly with commemorative
images of celebrated personages found on coins
and medals. By the time Dance drew Zoffany, he had
in the preceding few months made similar profile
portraits of a number of Royal Academicians,
including Thomas Banks, Benjamin West, William
Hodges, James Northcote, William Chambers,
James Barry and Richard Cosway. In common with
the majority of Dance's other sitters, Zoffany's face
is devoid of expression, his features smoothed, and
his hair, which had been receding for some years,

neatly combed. As such, it forms a marked contrast
to the rather careworn image presented in Henry
Singleton's 1795 painting, *The Royal Academy in
General Assembly* (fig. 181) or Zoffany's own profile
self-portrait of around the same date (cat. 109). The
same simple wooden chair back, which appears here
and in a number of other drawings, indicates that
Dance made some of the drawings in his studio,
although at other times he is known to have visited
his sitters' homes. In 1793 he made at least thirty
separate portrait drawings, sometimes producing
more than one a day: Zoffany and the artist Edward
Edwards sat to Dance for their portraits on
Saturday, 1 June 1793, while Henry Fuseli sat the
next day. This was a particularly impressive work
rate since Dance, otherwise engaged in professional
activities, was generally limited to making
drawings at weekends. As well as artists, Dance
produced portraits of a wide range of individuals
in the public eye, including James Boswell, Horace
Walpole (the art patron), John Julius Angerstein
(abolitionist), Granville Sharp (see cat. 77), Joseph
Haydn and the celebrated soldier, diplomat, fencer
and transvestite, the Chevalier d'Éon, who sat to
Dance in a bonnet and woman's dress. Many of
Dance's drawings were reproduced as soft-ground
etchings by his fellow Royal Academician William
Daniell and published between 1802 and 1814.
A volume containing 146 proof plates of Daniell's
etchings, including Zoffany's portrait (no. 121),
is in the British Museum.[1]

MP

1. Collections of Dance's original portrait drawings are
   in the Royal Academy of Arts, the department of
   Prints and Drawings, British Museum, and the
   National Portrait Gallery, London. For Zoffany's
   portrait, see British Museum 1925,0511.26.1.

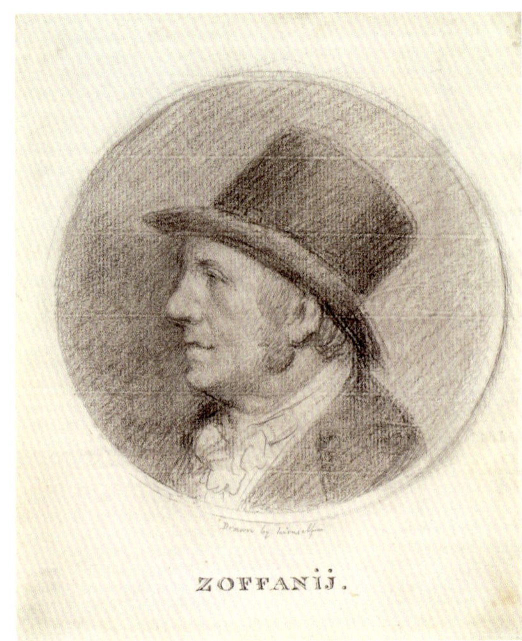

109
Self-Portrait
*c.*1795

Pencil and black crayon on paper,
22 × 17.8 cm (8⅝ × 7 in)
Inscribed: 'ZOFFANÌJ.'; and in a later hand:
'Drawn by himself'
National Portrait Gallery, London; given by
Iolo A. Williams, 1932

Selected exhibitions: National Portrait Gallery 1977,
no. 134; *Genial Company: The Theme of Genius in
Eighteenth-Century British Portraiture,* Nottingham
University Art Gallery and Scottish National
Portrait Gallery, 1987, no. 51

Selected literature: Ingamells 2004, 498–9, no. 2536;
Webster 2011, 553, fig. 421

Zoffany probably made this self-portrait sometime
during the mid-1790s, when he was in his early
sixties and living once more in London, following
his return from India. The format adopted, a
profiled head within a circular composition, is
designed to recall a commemorative medal or coin
and used conventionally to endow the individual
with the qualities found in antique images of
heroes, connoting an aura of timelessness and fame.
The profile portrait within a roundel was well
established by the eighteenth century, and by the
time Zoffany made the present drawing, it would
have been regarded as something of a cliché.
It is quite probable, as Desmond Shawe-Taylor
has suggested, that Zoffany's self-portrait was
conceived tongue-in-cheek, a proposal that accords
both with his penchant for satire and, visually, with
his decision to portray himself with prominent side
whiskers and a top hat pushed back on his head.[1]

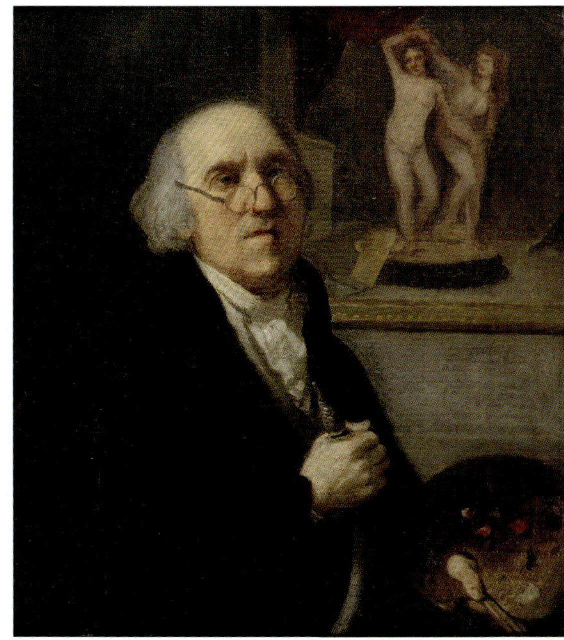

The top hat, then known as a beaver, was just coming into vogue in the 1790s, and Zoffany's determination to portray himself in resolutely modern fashionable headgear, quite at odds with his chosen pictorial format, was surely deliberate. Indeed, in contrast to his own earlier self-portraits, where he indicates his artistic profession, or the laurel-wreathed poets found in pictorial medallions, Zoffany's appearance appears rather to anticipate by a few years the earthy characters found in the sporting paintings of Benjamin Marshall, swapping banter on betting odds and horse flesh.

MP

1. Desmond Shawe-Taylor, *Genial Company: The Theme of Genius in Eighteenth-Century British Portraiture*, London, 1987, 57.

110

Self-Portrait with Hookah
*c.*1800–1803

Oil on canvas, 33 × 30.5 cm (13 × 12 in)
The British Library, India Office Library & Records, London

Provenance: Offered to the National Portrait Gallery, London, in 1868 (declined); Sotheby's, 13 July 1988 (189), withdrawn; purchased from Eyre and Greig 1989

Selected references: Ingamells 2004, 500; Treadwell 2009, 418; Webster 2011, 598–9

This is quite possibly Zoffany's final self-portrait. Although modest in size and deficient in execution, it demonstrates the same traits found in earlier self-portraits where wit is combined with a degree of self-critical introspection. Here Zoffany, now aged around seventy years old, peers over his spectacles at the viewer or, rather, at his own reflection in the mirror, since this is essentially a private portrait. He suffered from a squint and deteriorating eyesight and had probably worn spectacles to paint for some years, although it is only in the present portrait and the late portrait with his family (cat. 111) that he appears as such. In his left hand Zoffany holds a palette and brushes, and in his right the snake of his hookah, a reflection on his time in India. (Zoffany's posthumous sale in 1811 included several 'matchless Silver Hookers' [1]) Given Zoffany's penchant for rude jokes, the upwardly pointing hookah pipe also has a quite deliberate phallic presence, indicating that Zoffany, despite his old age, has retained his virility. He had, after all, fathered the youngest of his four daughters only a few years earlier at the age of sixty-three. The libidinous undertone of the portrait is continued from the space occupied by Zoffany to the oil painting behind him on the wall, which features a polychrome statue of two naked dancing female figures. Whether either the painting or the statue actually existed beyond the realm of Zoffany's imagination is not known.

The present portrait was almost certainly painted in Zoffany's house at Strand-on-the-Green near Kew. Based on Zoffany's physical appearance, it probably dates from the early 1800s. Zoffany was still at this time active as an artist and in the affairs of the Royal Academy, although by early 1807 his fellow Academician, Philippe Jacques de Loutherbourg, reported that he was deaf and confused over a piece of election business. Gradually, over the next few years, Zoffany's dementia intensified and by the spring of 1809, according to a niece of Benjamin West, he had 'become childish'.[2] He died on 11 November 1810.

MP

1. Robins 1811, lots 66–70 (10 May).
2. Farington 1978–84, vol. 8, 2943, and vol. 9, 3421.

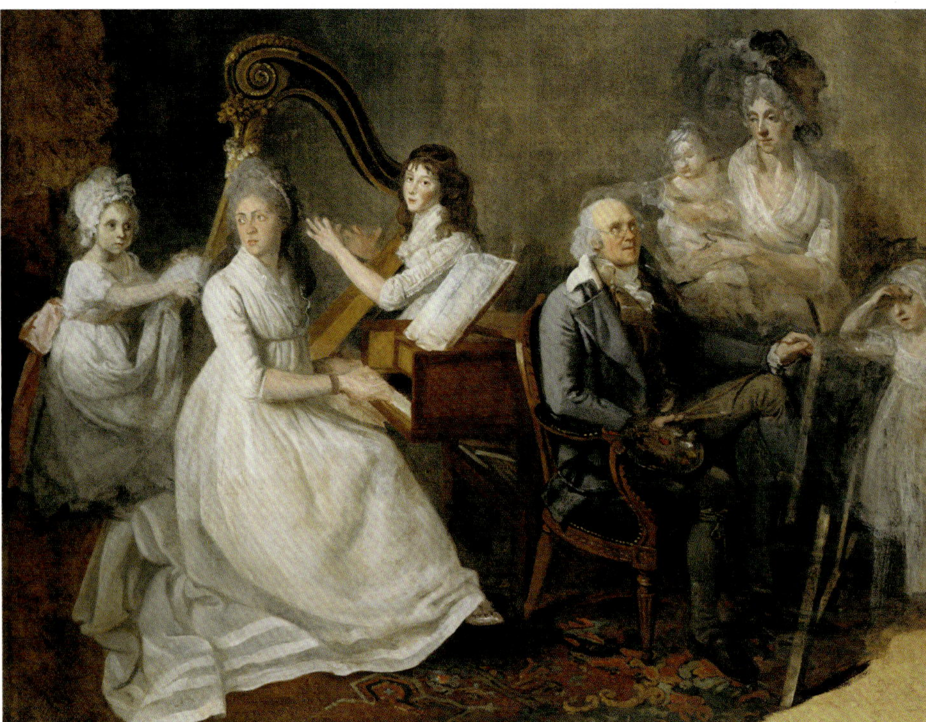

111

Self-Portrait with the Artist's Family
*c.*1802–3

Oil on canvas, 81.3 × 104.1 cm (32 × 41 in)
Private collection

Exhibited at the Yale Center for British Art only

Provenance: Claudina Sophia Beachcroft, the artist's
daughter; by descent to Mrs Kate Hesketh; her
sister, Mrs Frances Benwell; sold Christie's,
23 March 1934 (65) as 'The artist, with his wife,
four children, and a nurse, in an apartment',
purchased by F. Sabin; Christie's, 23 July 1954 (95)
[a pair]; Christie's, 15 July 1955 (129) [a pair];
Sotheby's, 23 Jan. 1957 (116) [a pair]; Christie's,
22 March 1974 (52) [a pair]; purchased by the
present owner and reunited successfully into
one composition

Selected exhibitions: Park Lane 1930; *Artists at Work,*
Nicholson Gallery, Leek, Staffordshire, 1943, no. 8;
on loan to the Fitzwilliam Museum, Cambridge,
1984–2005

Selected references: Manners & Williamson 1920,
132–3, 204–5; Williamson 1931, 8, pl. LI; Sitwell
1936, 98, pl. 51; Praz 1971, 267, pls. 345, 346, 348;
Ingamells 2004, 500; Treadwell 2009, 420–23;
Webster 2011, 596

By the early 1800s, around the time of the present
portrait, Zoffany was living in semi-retirement,
spending increasing amounts of time at his
attractive country residence at Strand-on-the-
Green situated on the north bank of the Thames
near Kew bridge, within a stone's throw of Kew
Palace. By now a wealthy man, Zoffany was able
to purchase adjoining properties in Strand-on-
the-Green, in one of which his mother-in-law was
lodged. In poor health following his return from
India in 1789, Zoffany suffered a second stroke in
the mid-1790s, although he continued to paint
fitfully until the early 1800s. Yet, despite his
disability, Zoffany continued to be active in the
affairs of the Royal Academy. This portrait is a
unique and valuable record of Zoffany's somewhat
hectic domestic circumstances at Strand-on-the-
Green towards the end of his career.

On his departure for India in 1783, Zoffany had
left his wife and two daughters Theresa and Cecilia
in London. The daughters were sent to boarding
school in order to obtain an education suitable for
young ladies. According to Mrs Zoffany's friend
Charlotte Papendiek, whose sister attended the
same boarding school, they 'appeared to be amiable,
but, poor dears, they preferred joining in all
the domestic arrangements, and cared little for
accomplishments'.[1] On Zoffany's return, the family
moved to 65 Strand-on-the Green, during which
time two more girls, Claudina and Laura, were
born. Zoffany may have been an errant husband,
but he was clearly fond of his family. For his
younger daughters he made a doll's house called
Lilliput Hall, for which he painted tiny portraits.
He could also be irascible, as for example when his
youngest daughter Laura crept into his studio and
dabbed some red paint on the face of one of his
portraits. As her daughter recalled, Zoffany 'was
so incensed by the child's action that Laura had to
be kept out of his sight for nearly a fortnight after
this exploit'.[2]

The portrait was probably painted, from
internal evidence, between 1802 and 1803.
Although there has been considerable confusion
over the sitters, the following identifications made
by Mary Webster would appear to be correct.
Seated at the harpsichord is Zoffany's eldest
daughter Maria Theresa Louisa (known as
Theresa), born in 1777 in Italy, who was apparently
also a talented guitar player and flower painter.
She glances back towards her youngest sister
Laura Eleanor Constantia (born 1796) in the pink
sash, who would have been around six years old.
As Webster has noted, at the time she was painted,
Theresa was still single, as she does not wear a
married woman's cap or hat. Behind Theresa,
playing the harp, is Zoffany's third daughter,
Claudina Sophia Anne, born in December 1791
and named presumably after Zoffany's great friend
in India, Claude Martin. Standing at the right of
the composition is Zoffany's second daughter
Cecilia Clementina Eliza, born in London in
November 1780.[3] Zoffany's only married daughter
at that time, Cecilia, cradles her infant son
John (born 1802), who reaches out towards his
grandfather's balding head. Standing at her side,
shading his eyes, is her elder son Thomas, born
1800, and then around three years old.

In time all four of Zoffany's daughters made
respectable marriages among the professional
classes. In 1802 Theresa married the surgeon John
Doratt, who had trained under Zoffany's friend
John Hunter. Claudina, in 1814, married Robert
Beachcroft, whose father had been Governor of
the Bank of England, while in 1817 Laura married
Lewis Bentley Oliver, a surgeon from Brentford.
The marriages appear to have prospered, apart
from that of Cecilia. In June 1799 she married
Thomas Horne, the son of a prominent local
schoolmaster and clergyman, whose portrait
Zoffany painted and who performed the ceremony
in Chiswick parish church.[4] As she was still a
minor, Cecilia had to ask Zoffany's consent, which,
although given, was evidently the cause of some
disagreement among the families. The couple went
on to have eight children, one of whom, a daughter,
married the son of her aunt Theresa. However,
it was not a happy marriage and they eventually
separated, custody of the children being given
to the father, who by that time was Rector of
St Catherine Coleman, Fenchurch Street. In
October 1825 Cecilia endured the shame of a
court appearance, charged with abducting her
ten-year-old daughter. As a result, she was found
guilty and sentenced to fifteen days' imprisonment.
She died in 1830.[5]

MP

1. Papendiek 1887, vol. 1, 302.
2. Manners & Williamson 1920, 129.
3. Treadwell 2009, 309.
4. For Zoffany's portrait of Dr Thomas Horne,
   see Webster 2011, 582, fig. 441.
5. Treadwell 2009, 424–5.

Bibliography

The following gives details of publication abbreviations – exhibition abbreviations are listed on p. 304.

Adorni *et al.* 1979
B. Adorni *et al.*, ed., *L'Arte a Parma dai Farnesi ai Borboni*, exh. cat., Palazzo della Pilotta, Parma, 1979

Alam & Alavi 2001
Muzaffar Alam and Seema Alavi, trans. and introd., *A European Experience of the Mughal Orient: The I'jaz-i Arsalani (Persian Letters 1773–79) of Antoine-Louis Henri Polier*, New Delhi, 2001

Angelo 1828–30
Henry Angelo, *Reminiscences of Henry Angelo, with memoirs of his late father, and friends, including numerous original anecdotes and curious traits of the most celebrated characters that have flourished during the past eighty years*, 2 vols., London, 1828–30

Anon. 1781
Anon., *The Ear-Wig; or, An Old Woman's Remarks on the Present Exhibition of Pictures of the Royal Academy*, London, 1781

Anon. 1808
Anon., 'Memoirs of the late Lieut. Col. Mordaunt', *Madras Government Gazette*, 15 Sept. 1808

Archer 1979
Mildred Archer, *India and British Portraiture, 1770–1825*, London, 1979

Archer 1986
Mildred Archer, *The India Office Collection of Paintings and Sculpture*, London, 1986

Ashton *et al.* 1997
Geoffrey Ashton, Kalman A. Burnim and Andrew Wilton, *Pictures in the Garrick Club: A Catalogue of the Paintings, Drawings, Watercolours and Sculpture*, London, 1997

Badinter 2008
Elizabeth Badinter, *L'Infant de Parme*, Paris, 2008

Barnett 1980
Richard B. Barnett, *North India Between Empires: Awadh, the Mughals, and the British, 1720–1801*, Berkeley, Calif., 1980

Bayly 1990
C.A. Bayly, ed., *The Raj: India and the British, 1600–1947*, exh. cat., National Portrait Gallery, London 1990

Beales 1987–2009
Derek Beales, *Joseph II*, 2 vols., Cambridge, 1987–2009

Bergounioux & de Boysson 1990
Pierre Bergounioux and Bernadette de Boysson, *Johan Zoffany: Venus sur les eaux*, Bordeaux, 1990

Bindman 1989
David Bindman, with contributions by Aileen Dawson and Mark Jones, *The Shadow of the Guillotine: Britain and the French Revolution*, London 1989

Black 2007
Peter Black, ed., *'My Highest Pleasures': William Hunter's Art Collection*, exh. cat., Hunterian Art Gallery, Glasgow, 2007

Bordes 1999
Philippe Bordes, review of Pressly 1999, *Burlington Magazine*, vol. 141, no. 1159, Oct. 1999, 627–8

Boyle 1885
M.L. Boyle, *Biographical Catalogue of the Portraits at Panshanger the Seat of Earl Cowper, KG*, London, 1885

Brewer 1976
John Brewer, *Party Ideology and Popular Politics at the Accession of George III*, Cambridge, 1976

Buddle 1999
Anne Buddle, *The Tiger and the Thistle: Tipu Sultan and the Scots in India 1760–1800*, Edinburgh, 1999

Campagnola 1978
Stanislao da Campagnola, 'Simon François Ravenet incisore a Parma', *Aurea Parma*, LXII, 1978

Campbell Orr 2002
Clarissa Campbell Orr, ed., *Queenship in Britain 1660–1837: Royal Patronage, Court Culture and Dynastic Politics*, Manchester, 2002

Campbell Orr 2004
Clarissa Campbell Orr, ed., *Queenship in Europe: The Role of the Consort 1660–1815*, Cambridge, 2004

Chaloner Smith 1878–84
John Chaloner Smith, *British Mezzotint Portraits: being a descriptive catalogue of these engravings from the introduction of the art to the early part of the present century*, 4 vols., London, 1878–84

Clifford 1985
Timothy Clifford, 'The Chelsea-Derby Royal Family Groups', *Burlington Magazine*, vol. 127, no. 990, September 1985, supplement, 'The Burlington House Fair. The Antique Dealers' Fair, Royal Academy, 11–22 September, 1985', 12–15

Collingham 2001
E.M. Collingham, *Imperial Bodies: The Physical Experience of the Raj, c.1800–1947*, Cambridge, 2001

Collins Baker 1937
C.H. Collins Baker, *Catalogue of the Principal Pictures in the Royal Collection at Windsor Castle*, London, 1937

Coltman 2006
Viccy Coltman, *Fabricating the Antique: Neoclassicism in Britain, 1760–1800*, Chicago, 2006

Coltman 2009
Viccy Coltman, *Classical Sculpture and the Culture of Collecting in Britain since 1760*, Oxford, 2009

Crosby 2001
Brian Crosby, 'Private Concerts on Land and Water: The Musical Activities of the Sharp Family, c.1750–c.1790', *Royal Musical Association Research Chronicle*, 34, 2001, 1–118

Cusatelli *et al.* 1997
Giorgio Cusatelli, Giuseppe Cirillo *et al.*, *Petitot, un artista del Settecento europeo a Parma* (Le mostre della fondazione, 6), exh. cat., Fondazione Cassa di risparmio di Parma, 1997

Davies 1959
Martin Davies, *National Gallery Catalogues: The British School*, London, 1959

Dircks 1997
Phyllis T. Dircks, 'David Garrick, George III and the Politics of Revision', *Philological Quarterly*, 76, Summer 1997, 289–312

D'Oench 1980
Ellen G. D'Oench, *The Conversation Piece: Arthur Devis and his Contemporaries*, exh. cat., Yale Center for British Art, New Haven, 1980

D'Oench 1999
Ellen D'Oench, *'Copper into Gold': Prints by John Raphael Smith, 1751–1812*, New Haven and London, 1999

Eaton 2004
Natasha Eaton, 'Between Mimesis and Alterity: Art, Gift, and Diplomacy in Colonial India, 1770–1800', *Comparative Studies in Society and History*, 46, 2004, 816–40

Egerton 1998
Judy Egerton, *The British School: National Gallery Catalogues*, London, 1998

Elmes 1825
James Elmes, *The Arts and Artists: or Anecdotes & Relics, of the Schools of Painting, Sculpture & Architecture*, 3 vols., London, 1825

Farington 1978–84
Joseph Farington, *The Diary of Joseph Farington*, ed. Kenneth Garlick, Angus Macintyre, and Kathryn Cave, 16 vols., New Haven and London, 1978–84

Foster 1924
William Foster, *A Descriptive Catalogue of the Paintings, Statues, &c, in the India Office*, 1924

Fox 1987
Celina Fox, *Londoners*, London, 1987

Fox 2010
Celina Fox, *The Arts of Industry in the Age of Enlightenment*, New Haven and London, 2010

Garrick 1963
David Garrick, *The Letters of David Garrick*, ed. D.M. Little and G.M. Kahrl, 3 vols., London, 1963

Ghosh 2006
Durba Ghosh, *Sex and the Family in Colonial India: The Making of Empire*, Cambridge, 2006

Graves 1905–6
Algernon Graves, *The Royal Academy of Arts: A Complete Dictionary of Contributors and their Work from its Foundation in 1769 to 1904*, 8 vols., London, 1905–6

Greenwood 1794
Greenwood (Auctioneers: Leicester-Square, London, England), *A Catalogue of the Magnificent Collection of Pictures of the Late Sir Lawrence Dundas, Bart …*, London, 1794

Hanson 2010
Craig Ashley Hanson, 'How to Portray a Trade? Identity and Interpretation in Johan Zoffany's "An Optician with His Attendant"', *Eighteenth-Century Fiction*, 23, no. 2, Winter 2010–11, 407–23

Hargraves 2005
Matthew Hargraves, *'Candidates for Fame': The Society of Artists of Great Britain, 1760–1791*, London, 2005

Harris 1967
John Harris, 'The Dundas Empire', *Apollo*, vol. 86, Sept. 1967, 170–79

Hauptman 1996
William Hauptman, 'Beckford, Brandoin, and the "Rajah": Aspects of an Eighteenth-Century Collection', *Apollo*, vol. 143, May 1996, 30–39

Hauptman 2011
William Hauptman, 'Before Somerset House: The Royal Academy in Pall Mall', *The British Art Journal*, vol. XIII, No. 1, Spring/Summer 2012

Hayes 2001
John Hayes, ed., *The Letters of Thomas Gainsborough*, New Haven and London, 2001

Head 1985
Raymond Head, 'Corelli in Calcutta: Colonial Music-making in India during the 17th and 18th centuries', *Early Music*, Nov. 1985, 548–53

Hibbert 1993
Christopher Hibbert, *Florence: The Biography of a City*, London, 1993

Hibbert 1999
Christopher Hibbert, *George III: A Personal History*, London, 1999

Hickey 1913–25
William Hickey, *Memoirs of William Hickey*, ed. Alfred Spencer, 4 vols., London, 1913–25

Highfill *et al.* 1973–93
Phillip H. Highfill, Kalman A. Burnim and Edward A. Langhans, *A Biographical Dictionary of Actors, Actresses, Musicians, Dancers, Managers and other Stage Personnel in London, 1660–1800*, 16 vols., Carbondale, Ill., 1973–93

Hilliard 2010
Kevin Hilliard, '"Ein Hogarthisches unsinniges Tollhauslächeln": The Portrait of La Mettrie and the Problem of the Laughing Philosopher in Eighteenth-Century Germany', *Publications of the English Goethe Society*, vol. 79, no. 3, Nov. 2010, 129–46

Hoare 1828
Prince Hoare, *Memoirs of Granville Sharp, Composed from his own Manuscripts*, 2nd ed., 2 vols., London, 1828

Hodges 1793
William Hodges, *Travels in India, During the Years 1780, 1781, 1782, & 1783*, London, 1793

Hogan 1968
Charles Beecher Hogan, ed., *The London Stage, 1660–1800: A Calendar of Plays, Entertainments & Afterpieces, Together with Casts, Box-Receipts and Contemporary Comments, Compiled from the Playbills, Newspapers and Theatrical Diaries of the Period*, part 5, 1776–1800, Carbondale, Ill., 1968

Holburne Museum 2003
Holburne Museum, *Every Look Speaks: Portraits of David Garrick*, exh. cat., Holburne Museum, Bath, 2003

Hone 1837
William Hone, *The Every-Day Book and Table Book*, 3 vols., London, 1837

Hoock 2003
Holger Hoock, *The King's Artists: The Royal Academy of Arts and the Politics of British Culture, 1760–1840*, Oxford, 2003

Hughes 1981
Clair Hughes, 'Zoffany's Trial Scene from The Merchant of Venice', *Burlington Magazine*, vol. 123, no. 938, May 1981, 290–94

Hyde 1977
Mary Hyde, *The Thrales of Streatham Park*, Cambridge, Mass., 1977

Ingamells 2004
John Ingamells, *National Portrait Gallery: Mid-Georgian Portraits, 1760–1790*, London, 2004

Jackson-Stops 1985
Gervase Jackson-Stops, ed., *The Treasure Houses of Britain: Five Hundred Years of Private Patronage and Art Collecting*, New Haven and London, 1985

Jasanoff 2005
Maya Jasanoff, *Edge of Empire: Lives, Culture, and Conquest in the East, 1750–1850*, London and New York, 2005

Kemp 1975
Martin Kemp, ed., *Dr. William Hunter at the Royal Academy of Arts*, Glasgow, 1975

Küster 2003
Ulf Küster, *Theatrum Mundi: Die Welt als Bühne*, Munich, 2003

Landon 1992
Theodore Luke Giffard London, 'The Landons: the first two hundred years (arrival, Spitalfields and onwards)', *Proceedings of the Huguenot Society*, vol. 25, no. 4, London, 1992, 331–2, 337–8

Lennox-Boyd 1994
Christopher Lennox-Boyd, *Theatre: The Age of Garrick: English Mezzotints from the Collection of the Hon. Christopher Lennox-Boyd*, London, 1994

Leppert 1988
Richard Leppert, *Music and Image: Domesticity, Ideology and Socio-Cultural Formation in Eighteenth-Century England*, Cambridge, 1988

Leppert & McClary 1987
Richard Leppert and Susan McClary, eds., *Music and Society: the Politics of Composition, Performance and Reception*, Cambridge, 1987

Lewis 1937–83
W.S. Lewis, ed., *Horace Walpole's Correspondence*, 48 vols., New Haven and London, 1937–83

Lichtenberg 1938
Georg Christoph Lichtenberg, *Lichtenberg's Visits to England as Described in his Letters and Diaries*, trans. and annot. Margaret L. Mare and W.H. Quarrell, Oxford, 1938

Llanover 1862
Lady Llanover, ed., *The Autobiography and Correspondence of Mary Granville, Mrs Delany: With Interesting Reminiscences of King George III and Queen Charlotte*, 2nd series, 3 vols., London, 1862

Llewellyn-Jones 1985
Rosie Llewellyn-Jones, *A Fatal Friendship: The Nawabs, the British and the City of Lucknow*, Delhi and Oxford, 1985

Llewellyn-Jones 1992
Rosie Llewellyn-Jones, *A Very Ingenious Man: Claude Martin in Early Colonial India*, Delhi and Oxford, 1992

Llewellyn-Jones 2003
Rosie Llewellyn-Jones, ed., *A Man of the Enlightenment in Eighteenth-Century India: The Letters of Claude Martin, 1766–1800*, New Delhi, 2003

Lloyd 2005
Christopher Lloyd, 'George III and his Painters', in Marsden 2005, 84–99

McIntyre 1999
Ian McIntyre, *David Garrick*, London, 1999

Mai & Repp-Eckert 1988
Ekkehard Mai and Anke Repp-Eckert, *Triumph und Tod des Helden: europäische Historienmalerei von Rubens bis Manet*, Milan and Zurich, 1988

Mander & Mitchenson 1955
Raymond Mander and Joe Mitchenson, *The Artist and the Theatre: The Story of the Paintings Collected and Presented to the National Theatre by W. Somerset Maugham*, London, 1955

Mander & Mitchenson 1980
Raymond Mander and Joe Mitchenson, *Guide to the Maugham Collection of Theatrical Paintings*, London, 1980

Manners & Williamson 1920
Lady Victoria Manners and G. C. Williamson, *John Zoffany, RA*, London, 1920

Mansel 2005
Philip Mansel, *Dressed to Rule: Royal and Court Costume from Louis XIV to Elizabeth II*, New Haven and London, 2005

Marsden 2005
Jonathan Marsden, ed., *The Wisdom of George III*, London, 2005

Millar 1966
Oliver Millar, *Zoffany and his Tribuna*, London, 1966

Millar 1969
Oliver Millar, *The Later Georgian Pictures in the Collection of Her Majesty the Queen*, 2 vols., London, 1969

Mitchell 1944
Charles Mitchell, 'Zoffany's Death of Captain Cook', *Burlington Magazine*, vol. 84, no. 492, March 1944, 56–62

Moore 1985
Andrew W. Moore, *Norfolk and the Grand Tour: Eighteenth-Century Travellers Abroad and their Souvenirs*, Fakenham, 1985

Namier & Brooke 1964
Lewis Bernstein Namier and John Brooke, eds., *History of Parliament: The House of Commons, 1754–1790*, 3 vols., London, 1964

Oppé 1950
A.P. Oppé, *English Drawings, Stuart and Georgian Periods, in the Collection of His Majesty the King at Windsor Castle*, London, 1950

ODNB
Oxford Dictionary of National Biography, ed. H.C.G. Matthew and Brian Harrison, Oxford, 2004 (www.oxforddnb.com)

ODNB George Nassau Clavering
Hugh Belsey, 'George Nassau Clavering, Third Earl Cowper (1738–1789)', *ODNB*, http://www.oxforddnb.com/view/article/61668 (accessed 30 April 2010)

ODNB Warren Hastings
P.J. Marshall, 'Hastings, Warren (1732–1818)', *ODNB*, http://www.oxforddnb.com/view/article/12587 (accessed 19 June 2011)

ODNB Mary Impey
J.P. Losty, 'Impey [née Reade], Mary, Lady Impey (1749–1818)', *ODNB*, http://www.oxforddnb.com/view/article/66116 (accessed 5 July 2011)

Papendiek 1887
Mrs Papendiek, *Court and Private Life in the Time of Queen Charlotte: Being the Journals of Mrs Papendiek, Assistant Keeper of the Wardrobe and Reader to Her Majesty*, ed. Mrs V. Delves Broughton, 2 vols., London, 1887

Pasquin n.d.
Anthony Pasquin, *An Authentic History of the Professors of Painting, Sculpture and Architecture in Ireland*, London, n.d. [1796]

Paulson 1975
Ronald Paulson, *Emblem and Expression: Meaning in English Art of the Eighteenth Century*, London, 1975

Piozzi 1789
Hester Lynch Piozzi, *Observations and Reflections Made in the Course of a Journey through France, Italy, and Germany*, 2 vols., London, 1789

Piozzi 1942
Hester Lynch Piozzi, *Thraliana: The Diary of Mrs Hester Lynch Thrale, Later Mrs Piozzi, 1776–1809*, ed. Katharine C. Balderston, 2 vols., Oxford, 1942

Pollock 2003
Grizelda Pollock, 'Cockfights and Other Parades', *Oxford Art Journal*, 36, no. 2, 2003, 141–65

Postle 1998
Martin Postle, *Angels and Urchins: The Fancy Picture in 18th-Century British Art*, London, 1998

Postle 2004
Martin Postle, 'Flayed for The art. The écorché figure in the English art academy', *British Art Journal*, vol. 5, no. 1, Spring/Summer 2004, 55–63

Poulet 2003
Anne L. Poulet, *Jean-Antoine Houdon: Sculptor of the Enlightenment*, exh. cat., National Gallery of Art, Washington DC, 2003

Praz 1971
Mario Praz, *Conversation Pieces: A Survey of the Informal Group Portrait in Europe and America*, London, 1971

Pressly 1987
William L. Pressly, 'Genius Unveiled: The Self-Portraits of Johan Zoffany', *Art Bulletin*, vol. 69, no. 1, March 1987, 88–101

Pressly 1995
William L. Pressly, 'Johan Zoffany as "David the Anointed One"', *Apollo*, vol. 141, 1995, 49–55

Pressly 1999
William L. Pressly, *The French Revolution as Blasphemy: Johan Zoffany's Paintings of the Massacre at Paris, August 10, 1792*, Berkeley, Calif., and London, 1999

A.G. Quintavalle 1955a
A. Ghidiglia Quintavalle, 'Il pittore Johann Zoffany alla corte di Don Ferdinando', *Aurea Parma*, XXXIX, 1955

A.G. Quintavalle 1955b
A. Ghidiglia Quintavalle, 'A proposito del Pittore Zoffany a Parma', *Aurea Parma*, XXXIX, III, July–Sept. 1955

A.O. Quintavalle 1939
A.O. Quintavalle, *La Regia Galleria di Parma*, Rome, 1939

Ray 2007
Romita Ray, 'Visualising Tea Consumption in the Empire', in Tim Barringer, Geoff Quilley and Douglas Fordham, eds., *Art and the British Empire*, Manchester, 2007, 205–22

Retford 2006
Kate Retford, *The Art of Domestic Life: Family Portraiture in Eighteenth-Century England*, New Haven and London, 2006

Reynolds 1997
Sir Joshua Reynolds, *Discourses on Art*, ed. Robert R. Wark, New Haven and London, 1997

Ribeiro 1984
Aileen Ribeiro, *The Dress Worn at Masquerades in England, 1730–1790, and its Relation to Fancy Dress in Portraiture*, New York and London, 1984

Ribeiro 1995
Aileen Ribeiro, *The Art of Dress: Fashion in England and France 1750 to 1820*, New Haven and London, 1995

Ribeiro 2000
Aileen Ribeiro, *The Gallery of Fashion*, London, 2000

Ricci 1896
Corrado Ricci, *La R. Galleria di Parma*, Parma, 1896

Roberts 2002
Jane Roberts, ed., *Royal Treasures: A Golden Jubilee Celebration*, London, 2002

Roberts 2004
Jane Roberts, ed., *George III and Queen Charlotte: Patronage, Collecting and Court Taste*, exh. cat., The Queen's Gallery, London, 2004

Robins 1811
Messrs Robins, *A catalogue of a most curious and unique assemblage of the valuable property of that distinguished artist Johan Zoffany …*, sale cat. Piazza, Covent Garden, London, 9–10 May 1811

Rosenthal 1999
Michael Rosenthal, *The Art of Thomas Gainsborough*, New Haven and London, 1999

Russell 2004
Francis Russell, *John, 3rd Earl of Bute: Patron and Collector*, London, 2004

Russell 2005
Francis Russell, *Pictures of Innocence: Portraits of Children from Hogarth to Lawrence*, Bath, 2005

Sainsbury 2006
John Sainsbury, *John Wilkes: The Lives of a Libertine*, Aldershot, 2006

Sanger 1991
Ernest Sanger, *Isabelle de Bourbon-Parme, Petite-fille de Louis XV*, Paris, 1991

Saumarez Smith 1993
Charles Saumarez Smith, *Eighteenth-Century Decoration: Design and the Domestic Interior in England*, London, 1993

Schianchi 2000
Lucia Fornari Schianchi, ed., *Galleria Nazionale di Parma: Catalogo delle opere: Il Settecento*, Parma, 2000

Schürer 2008
Norbert Schürer, 'The Impartial Spectator of Sati, 1757–1841', *Eighteenth-Century Studies*, vol. 42, no. 1, Fall 2008, 19–44

Shawe-Taylor 2009
Desmond Shawe-Taylor, *The Conversation Piece: Scenes of Fashionable Life*, exh. cat., The Queen's Gallery, London, 2009

Shefrin 2003
Jill Shefrin, *'Such Constant Affectionate Care': Lady Charlotte Finch Royal Governess & the Children of George III*, Los Angeles, 2003

Sitwell 1936
Sacheverell Sitwell, *Conversation Pieces: A Survey of English Domestic Portraits and their Painters, with Notes on the Illustrations by Michael Sevier*, London, 1936

J. Simon 1985
Jacob Simon, ed., *Handel: A Celebration of his Life and Times*, exh. cat., National Portrait Gallery, London, 1985

R. Simon 2007
Robin Simon, *Hogarth, France and British Art: The Rise of the Arts in Eighteenth-Century Britain*, London, 2007

Smith 1828–30
John Thomas Smith, *Nollekens and his Times: comprehending a life of that celebrated sculptor; and memoirs of several contemporary artists, from the time of Roubiliac, Hogarth, and Reynolds, to that of Fuseli, Flaxman, and Blake*, 2 vols., London, 1828–30

Smith 1985
Bernard Smith, *European Vision and the South Pacific*, 2nd ed., New Haven and London, 1985

Stuebe 1979
Isabel Combs Stuebe, *The Life and Works of William Hodges*, New York and London, 1979

Sutton 1956
Denys Sutton, 'Paintings at Firle Place: Home of Viscount and Viscountess Gage', *The Connoisseur*, vol. 137, June 1956, suppl., 78–84

Sutton 1967a
Denys Sutton, 'The Nabob of the North', *Apollo*, vol. 86, Sept. 1967, 168–9

Sutton 1967b
Denys Sutton, 'The Dundas Pictures', *Apollo*, vol. 86, Sept. 1967, 204–13

Taylor 1833
J. Taylor, *Records of my Life*, 2 vols., New York, 1833

Thomas 1983
Keith Thomas, *Man and the Natural World: Changing Attitudes in England 1500–1800*, London, 1983

Tobin 2004
Beth Fowkes Tobin, *Colonizing Nature: The Tropics in British Art and Letters 1760–1820*, Philadelphia, 2004

Treadwell 2009
Penelope Treadwell, *Johan Zoffany: Artist and Adventurer*, London, 2009

Tyak 1994
G. Tyack, *Warwickshire Country Houses*, Chichester, 1994

Vaughan 1996
Gerard Vaughan, 'Reflections on "Charles Townley and his friends"', *Apollo*, vol. 144, Nov. 1996, 32–5

Watson 1995
Michael Watson, 'Zoffany as punster and prankster: some comments on his David with the Head of Goliath', *Art Bulletin of Victoria*, no. 36, 1995, 7–14

Webster 1976
Mary Webster, *Johan Zoffany 1733–1810*, exh. cat., National Portrait Gallery, London, 1976

Webster 1990
Mary Webster, 'Horridly Like: Zoffany's portrait of Wilkes', *Sotheby's Preview*, Oct. 1990, 19

Webster 2011
Mary Webster, *Johan Zoffany*, New Haven and London, 2011

Wessely 1886
J.E. Wessely, *Richard Earlom: Verzeichniss seiner Radirungen und Schabkunstblätter*, Hamburg, 1886

Whitley 1928
William T. Whitley, *Artists and their Friends in England, 1700–1799*, 2 vols., London, 1928

Williamson 1931
G.C. Williamson, *English Conversation Pictures*, London, 1931

Wilmot-Sitwell 2009
Caddy Wilmot-Sitwell, 'The inventory of 19 Arlington Street, 12 May 1768', *Furniture History*, vol. XLV, 2009, 73–99

Wilton & Bignamini 1996
Andrew Wilton and Ilaria Bignamini, eds., *Grand Tour: The Lure of Italy in the Eighteenth Century*, exh. cat., Tate Gallery, London, 1996

Exhibition Abbreviations

Exhibitions cited more than once have been abbreviated in the form of town/city location (or just venue in the case of London galleries) plus date without any dividing comma, and full details have been given in the list of Exhibition Abbreviations. The location for unabbreviated exhibitions where none has been given is London.

Publication abbreviations in brackets refer to catalogues listed in the Bibliography.

Arts Council 1960–61
Johann Zoffany, Arts Council of Great Britain, London, 1960–61

Barnard Castle 1962
The Zetland Collection from Aske Hall, Bowes Museum, Barnard Castle, Co. Durham, 1962

Bath 2005
Pictures of Innocence: Portraits of Children from Hogarth to Lawrence, Holburne Museum, Bath, 2005

Bregenz and Vienna 1968
Angelika Kauffmann und ihre Zeitgenossen, Vorarlberger Landesmuseum, Bregenz, and Österreichisches Museum für Angewandte Kunst, Vienna, 1968

British Institution 1814
Pictures by the Late William Hogarth, Richard Wilson, Thomas Gainsborough and J. Zoffani, British Institution, London, 1814

Dulwich Picture Gallery 1997
Dramatic Art: Theatrical Paintings from the Garrick Club, Dulwich Picture Gallery, London, 1997

Guildhall Art Gallery 1964
Shakespeare and the Theatre, Guildhall Art Gallery, City of London, 1964

Hayward Gallery 1975
The Georgian Playhouse: Actors, Artists, Audiences and Architecture, 1730–1830, Hayward Gallery, London, 1975

Munich 2003
Theatrum Mundi; die Welt als Bühne, Haus der Kunst, Munich, 2003

National Portrait Gallery 1977
Johan Zoffany, 1733–1810 (Webster 1976), National Portrait Gallery, London, 1977

National Portrait Gallery 1990–91
The Raj: India and the British, 1600–1947 (Bayly 1990), National Portrait Gallery, London, 1990–91

Nottingham and Kenwood 1991
The Artist's Model: Its Role in British Art from Lely to Etty, University Art Gallery, Nottingham, and the Iveagh Bequest, Kenwood House, 1991

Nottingham and Kenwood 1998
Angels and Urchins: The Fancy Picture in 18th-Century British Art, University Art Gallery, Nottingham, and the Iveagh Bequest, Kenwood, 1998

Paris 1989
La Révolution française et l'Europe, 1789–1799 (exh. cat., 3 vols.), Galeries Nationales du Grand Palais, Paris, 1989

Park Lane 1930
Loan Exhibition of English Conversation Pieces in Aid of the Royal Northern Hospital at 25 Park Lane, March 4th to 30th (inclusive) 1930, London, 1930

Parma 1979
L'Arte a Parma dai Farnesi ai Borboni (Biennale d'Arte Antica X: L'Arte del Settecento), Palazzo della Pilotta, Parma, 1979

Queen's Bazaar 1833
Mr Mathews's Gallery of Theatrical Portraits, Queen's Bazaar, Oxford Street, London, 1833

Queen's Gallery 1974–5
George III: Collector and Patron, The Queen's Gallery, Buckingham Palace, London, 1974–5

Index

Note: Works by Zoffany are listed under his name; catalogue numbers appear after the page numbers and refer to the main catalogue entry and illustration; other illustrations of works by Zoffany and other artists which appear as figures are indicated by italicised page numbers. JZ = Johan Zoffany in index headings.

Photographic credits

© Aga Khan Trust for Culture, Geneva: figs 121, 122
Alice and Douglas Hyland: cat. 68
Amgueddfa Genedlaethol Cymru/National Museum of Wales: figs 90, 104, cat. 74
©Andreas Bestle, CTW Würzburg: fig. 9
© Antonio Martinelli, Paris: fig. 152
Ashmolean Museum, University of Oxford: figs 22, 63, cat. 78, 79, 96
Beinecke Rare Book and Manuscript Library, Yale University: figs 149, 150
Blair Castle: fig. 96
© Bonhams, London/The Bridgeman Art Library International: fig. 28
© BPK, Berlin/Museum Bildenden Künste, Leipzig: fig. 167
© The British Library Board: figs 68, 115, 117, 145, cats 83, 84, 110
From the Castle Howard Collection: figs 49, 50, cat. 22
Cecil Beaton Studio Archive at Sotheby's: fig. 48
Charles Greig: figs 126, 135, 136, 139, 140, 155
© Christie's Images Limited: figs 13, 93, 189, 194
From the Dashwood Family: cat. 91
Dunvegan Castle Collection: fig. 156
Erich Lessing/Art Resource, NY: fig. 113
By Permission of the Folger Shakespeare Library: fig. 54
© Foto Vasari Rome no Adf12/14072: fig. 186
Fürst Thurn und Taxis Museen: fig. 67
Galleria degli Uffizi, Florence/The Bridgeman Art Library International: cat. 59
Galleria Nazionale di Parma: figs 26, 29, 78, 79, 80, 187, cats 60, 61, 62
Garrick Club/AC Cooper: figs 44, 46, 56, cats 15, 27, 30
Garrick Club/Art Archive: fig. 42, cat. 31
Gerald Coke Handel Collection, Foundling Museum, London/The Bridgeman Art Library International: fig. 12
Photograph reproduced with the permission of the Herbert Art Gallery & Museum, Coventry: fig. 20, cat. 48
© The Holburne Museum, Bath: fig. 53
Courtesy of the Huntington Art Collections, San Marino, California: fig. 109
The J. Paul Getty Museum, Los Angeles: cat. 72
© 2011 Kunsthaus Zurich, All rights reserved: fig. 173
Kunsthistorisches Museum, Vienna: figs 66, 76, 77, 81, 87, cat. 39
© Manchester City Galleries: cat. 5
Martine LaRoche Photography: figs 2, 39, 193
© M.B.A. de Bordeaux/photographe Lysiane Gauthier: fig. 69, cat. 7
Mittelrhein Museum, Koblenz: cat. 4
Museen der Stadt Regensburg, Historisches Museum: figs 6, 89, cats 1, 2, 106
© Museo Thyssen-Bornemisza: fig. 118, cat. 81
Museum of Fine Arts, Budapest: fig. 165
National Gallery of Victoria, Melbourne: figs 8, 30, 184, cat. 3
© The National Gallery, London: figs 64, 110, cat. 66

© National Maritime Museum, Greenwich, London, Greenwich Hospital Collection: fig. 40, cat. 107
Courtesy National Museums Liverpool: figs 43, 95, 107, 112
By Courtesy of the National Portrait Gallery, London, and the Lloyd-Baker Trustees: fig. 103, cat. 77
© National Portrait Gallery, London: figs 71, 72, 179, cats 42, 76, 109
National Trust Photo Library: fig. 94
Noortman Master Paintings/The Bridgeman Art Library International: fig. 37, cat. 104
Norfolk Museums & Archaeology Service (Norwich Castle Museum & Art Gallery): fig. 99
Private Collection/©Tate Photography: figs 91, 92, 171
Private Collection/AC Cooper: fig. 128
Private Collection/Mark Fiennes/The Bridgeman Art Library International: cat. 75
Private collection/Martine LaRoche Photography: fig. 133
Private Collection/The Bridgeman Art Library International: fig. 18, cat. 50
Private collection: figs 11, 38, 41, 52, 102, 108, 129, 131, 146, cats 9, 18, 24, 26, 43, 70, 80, 85, 93, 94, 95, 111
Rheinisches Landesmuseum, Trier: fig. 10, cat. 8
Richard Caspole, Yale Center for British Art: figs 31, 51, 59, 61, 138, 142, 157a, 157b, 158, 159, 160, 161, 163, cats 10, 16, 17, 20, 21b, 23, 25, 29, 52, 56, 69, 88, 98, 100
© Royal Academy of Arts, London: figs 16, 178, 181, cats 41, 47, 108
Royal Bank of Scotland: fig. 162
Royal Collection © 2011 Her Majesty Queen Elizabeth II: figs 5, 17, 21, 36, 65, 73, 74, 83, 86, 88, 98, 105, 106, 176, cats 12, 32, 33, 35, 37, 38, 44, 51, 53, 82
© Royal College of Physicians: fig. 55, cat. 46
Scala/Art Resource, NY: figs 24, 182
Scala/Ministero per i Beni e le Attivita culturali/Art Resource, NY: fig. 23
Smith College Museum of Art, Northampton, Massachusetts: fig. 15
Somerset Maugham Theatre Collection, London/The Bridgeman Art Library International: fig. 45, cat. 19
Courtesy of Sotheby's Picture Library: figs 14, 35
Staatliche Graphische Sammlung München: fig. 7
Stadtmuseum Simeonstift Trier/Bernhard Matthias Lutz: fig. 70, cat. 6
© Tate, London, 2011: figs 1, 3, 4, 19, 27, 100, 101, 111, 125, 137, 190, cats 28, 45, 57, 64, 65, 67, 86, 92
Towneley Hall Art Gallery and Museum/The Bridgeman Art Library International: fig. 34, cat. 63
© The Trustees of the British Museum: Frontispiece, figs 60, 62, 116, 153, 154, 169, 170, 174, 177, 180, 183, 188, 191, 192, 196, 199, cats 11, 13, 14, 21a, 34, 49, 58, 97, 99, 102, 103, 105
Trustees of the Firle Estate Settlement: figs 75, 85, cats 54, 55

By kind permission of the Trustees of The Wallace Collection, London: figs 166, 175
Tullie House Museum & Art Gallery, Carlisle/Photograph by Richard Caspole (YCBA): cat. 89
University of Illinois at Urbana-Champaign: fig. 172
Vanni/Art Resource, NY: fig. 164
Photo © Victoria and Albert, Museum: figs 58, 197
© Victoria Art Gallery, Bath and North East Somerset Council/The Bridgeman Art Library International: fig. 32
Victoria Memorial Hall, Calcutta: figs 119, 120, 124, 127, 130, 132, 134, 141, 144, 147, 148, 198, cats 90, 101
White's Club: fig. 151, cat. 87
By courtesy of the Witt Library, The Courtauld Institute of Art, London: fig. 143
© Woolavington Collection, Cottesbrooke Hall & Gardens: cat. 73
The Zetland Collection/Jerry Hardman-Jones Photography: figs 84, 97, cats 36, 71